ATATURK

ATATURK

A Biography of Mustafa Kemal,
Father of Modern Turkey

▶ Lord Kinross

Quill
William Morrow
New York

► *To Christopher Sykes*

Grateful acknowledgment is made to Charles Scribner's Sons for permission to quote from *The Aftermath* by Winston Churchill.

First published in Great Britain in 1964

Library of Congress Cataloging-in-Publication Data

Kinross, Patrick Balfour, Baron, 1904-
    Ataturk : a biography of Mustafa Kamal, father of modern Turkey / Lord Kinross.
    p. cm.
    Originally published: New York : Morrow, c1964.
    Includes bibliographical references and index.
    ISBN 0-688-11283-8
    1. Ataturk, Kamal, 1881-1938. 2. Presidents—Turkey—Biography. I. Title.
DR592.K43 1992
956.1024092—dc20
[B]
                                                                    91-41211
                                                                        CIP

Printed in the United States of America

2 3 4 5 6 7 8 9 10

BOOK DESIGN BY ADRIANNE ONDERDONK

► *Acknowledgments*

My thanks are due in the first place to President Gürsel and the government of the Turkish Republic for granting me access to the Presidential Archives at Çankaya, Ankara, and for otherwise assisting my researches. They are due in particular to the Ministry of Tourism and Information for facilitating visits to Atatürk's battlefields and other parts of the country and for supplying me with photographs. I must also thank Professor Enver Ziya Karal, head of the Department of the History of the Revolution at Ankara University, for his assistance in supplying information and photographs and for his consistent encouragement.

In Britain my thanks are due to Sir Anthony Rumbold, Bt., C.B., C.M.G., for access to the papers of his father, the late Sir Horace Rumbold, High Commissioner and Ambassador at Constantinople 1920-24; Admiral Sir Bertram Thesiger, K.B.E., C.B., C.M.G., for the loan of his unpublished *Naval Memoirs;* Alan Moorehead for an unpublished translation of Atatürk's Gallipoli diaries; J. D. Latham, of the University of Manchester, for his unpublished translation of Ali Fuat Cebesoy's *Moscow Memories.*

Elsewhere I have to thank the Library of Congress, Washington, D.C., for access to the papers of Admiral Bristol; the Foreign Affairs Division of the National Archives, Washington, D.C., for access to certain official records; the Widener Library, Harvard University, for access to the papers of Ambassador Grew; the Hoover Library, Stanford University, California, for access to those of Louis E. Browne; S. Hassan, of the Pakistani Information Office, Istanbul, for papers concerning the relations between the Kemalist government and the Khilafat Committee, Bombay.

For oral information on the subject I am indebted to the following individuals:

In Turkey, President Ismet Inönü, the late Rauf Orbay (Hussein Rauf), General Ali Fuat Cebesoy (Ali Fuad), the late General Refet Bele (Refet Pasha), Tevfik Rüştü Aras, Bayan Fethi Okyar, Osman Okyar, the late Bayan Adnan Adivar (Halide Edib), Falih Rifki Atay, Kiliç Ali, Hassan Riza Soyak, Yakup Kadri Karaosmanoğlu, Bayan Ruşen Eşref Ünaydin, Dr. Afetinan (Afet), Bayan Sabiha Gökchen, Hamdullah Suphi Tanriöver, the late Hassan Ali Yücel, the late Behiç Erkin, the late Fuat Bulca, the late Tevfik Biyiklioğlu, Ismail Hakki, Kâzim Özalp, Fuat Köprulu, Şakir Zumre, Yusuf Kemal Tengirşenk, Dr. Hussein Pektaş, Ahmed Adnan Saygun, Uluğ Iğdemir, Cevat Dursunoğlu, Ahmet Emin Yalman, Şevket Süreyya Aydemir, Kadri Cenani, Ahmet and Abbas Celal, Behcet Cemal Cağlar, Dr. Akdes Nimet Kurat, Bayan Esma Nayman, Bayan Leyla Cambel, Bayan Şefika Urgan, and Bayan Süreyya Agaoğlu.

Elsewhere, H.R.H. the Duke of Windsor; the late Sir Percy Loraine and Sir Knox Helm, former British Ambassadors to Turkey; Monsieur Ponsot, former French Ambassador; General Hassan Arfa, former Persian Ambassador; and Monsieur Sokolnicki, former Polish Ambassador to Turkey; Lieutenant General Nicholas Rangabe and A. A. Pallis, of Athens; Madame Dayanova and Simeon Radev, of Sofia; Captain Webb Trammell, Edward Whittall, Sami Gunzberg, of Istanbul; Lady (Charles) Townshend, Mrs. Ethel McLeod Smith, the late Sir Clifford Heathcote-Smith, Colonel J. C. Petherick, J. G. Wilson-Heathcote, J. G. Bennett, and Mrs. S. F. Newcombe.

For other assistance I am indebted to Nejat Sönmez and Yussuf Mardin, now of the Turkish Embassy in London; L. T. Naslednikov and N. Todorov, of Sofia; B. T. Naslednikov, of Paris; Dr. Tayyip Gökbilgin, Kemal H. Karpat, Satvet Lütfi Tozan, Reşit Safet Atabinen, Özcan Ergüder, Captain and Mrs. Irfan Orga, the late Dr. Ernest Altounyan, Albert Hourani, Dr. Gotthard Jäschke, of Münster; Sir Hamilton Gibb, of Harvard University; Dr. L. V. Thomas, of Princeton University;

Dr. Dankwart A. Rustow and Dr. J. C. Hurewitz, of Columbia University, New York; Dr. Frederick P. Latimer, of the University of Salt Lake City; Dr. Walter F. Weiker, of Rutgers University; Lawrence Moore, of Ankara; Mrs. John Earl Davis, of New York; M. Gaston Bergery, former French Ambassador to Turkey; Sir James Bowker and Sir Bernard Burrows, former British Ambassadors to Turkey, Mr. and Mrs. Geoffrey Lewis, and John Hyde, of the British Consulate General in Istanbul.

With regard to the text, I have to thank Miss Adele Dogan, Robert Rhodes James, and Andrew Mango for constructive criticism of the completed work; W. E. D. Allen for advice at an earlier stage; and Mrs. Jasper Streater for helpful attention, on my behalf, to detail and general content.

Mrs. St. George Saunders has given me valuable assistance, by her work on English newspaper sources; Bayan Içten Erkin and Bilge Karasu, of Ankara, have helped me patiently in reading and translating from Turkish sources. Above all I must express profound gratitude to Dr. Mina Urgan, Professor of Literature at Istanbul University, for her devoted industry over a long period in research, reading, and translation on my behalf. Without her untiring and discerning collaboration, this book could not have taken the shape it has.

► *Note on spelling*

The transliteration of Turkish names into English presents problems in a book of this kind. Throughout most of the period which it covers the Arabic script prevailed in Turkey and was transliterated into European languages in various phonetic forms. It was only in 1928 that the Latin script was introduced. But the form of it chosen was not consistently phonetic. The *j* sound, for example, became *c,* the *ch* sound *ç,* the *sh* sound *ş*. Since these are misleading to the English general reader, I have preferred in principle to adhere to the earlier and more familiar transliteration, except in the case of place names where the new spelling coincides phonetically with the old, and of the proper names of Turks still living today (*e.g.,* Celal Bayar, Tevfik Rüştü). In the case of the Gallipoli place names I have preferred to adhere, for the convenience of readers, to the versions already familiar in English works on the campaign, even if they do not always exactly accord with the above principles. I owe apologies to Turkish readers for taking these various liberties, also for eliminating entirely the Turkish undotted *ı* from my text.

It was not until 1930 that foreigners were asked to use the Turkish versions of place names, instead of those current abroad—e.g. Ankara for Angora, Izmir for Smyrna, Bursa for Brusa, Antalya for Adalia, Edirne for Adrianople. For convenience, however, I have introduced these versions at an earlier stage in the text, from the inception of the Republic at the beginning of Part III onwards.

► List of Illustrations

(illustrations appear between pages 60-61)

► Contents

I The decline and fall of the Ottoman Empire

II The war of independence

III The rise of the Turkish Republic

► *Author's Note*

I have been especially careful about any passages of dialogue I quoted. Needless to say, none are invented. They are all "quotes" from Ataturk's own autobiographical passages, and from other writers (particularly Halide Edib) and from people I talked to. If there is any fiction it is theirs, not mine, but I doubt if in essence there is. I have only chosen passages which seemed to have the ring of authenticity, and have rejected countless others which did not. I don't see how (short of a tape recorder) one can authenticate dialogue more closely than this, and a biography without it makes pretty dull reading.

► *Prologue*

Mustafa Kemal, later Kemal Atatürk, was an outstanding soldier-statesman of the first half of the twentieth century. He differed from the dictators of his age in two significant respects: his foreign policy was based not on expansion but on retraction of frontiers; his home policy on the foundation of a political system which could survive his own time. It was in this realistic spirit that he regenerated his country, transforming the old sprawling Ottoman Empire into a compact new Turkish Republic.

Atatürk was no ordinary Turk. Fairer than most, with high cheekbones and broad-set steel-blue eyes, he was slight in build and deliberate in movement. His body radiated energy, even in repose; his cold eyes gleamed with it, all-seeing and alive with the light of his contradictory moods. Alternately outspoken and taciturn, the tension within him would now erupt into a harsh explosion of temper, now relax into an expression of urbane polished charm. Vain of his personal appearance, he dressed fastidiously, twirled up his eyebrows self-consciously, took a pride in his well-shaped hands and feet, which he liked to show off to his more intimate guests on the pretext of paddling in a pool he had made in his garden.

Vain of popular acclaim Atatürk was not. He needed it for the task he had imposed on himself, but often flouted it and was seldom deceived by it. Once, when a friend proposed a gesture to public opinion, he flashed back at him scornfully, "I don't act for public opinion. I act for the nation and for my own satisfaction." The two motives coincided. In so far as Atatürk was capable of love, he loved his country. His ambition, kindled by imagination, driven by a dominant nature and an inflexible will, was for power; but for power to give his people, in his own way, what he had determined, in his own mind, was best for them.

It was a restless mind, nurtured on those principles of Western civilization which had influenced Turkish liberal thought since the nineteenth century; continually refuelled by the ideas of others, which he adapted and adopted as his own; but always grounded in a common sense mistrustful of theory. In method he was pragmatic, restraining his natural impatience in order to progress "step by step towards the desired goal." The steps nonetheless were swift, liberal ends pursued often by illiberal means, with ruthless treatment of friends as of enemies.

Callous at times of human life, Atatürk was not personally inhuman. He knew and appreciated human beings, whether individually or in the mass, assessing their character and predicting their actions with shrewd intuition. Flexible in his methods of handling them, knowing just when to persuade, when to cajole, when to threaten, when to command, he was a master of political finesse. Convivial in his habits, he enjoyed human company, governing the country in effect from his dinner table. He loved, in a clear resonant voice which has been compared to that of "a masculine Sarah Bernhardt," to talk, always frankly, often long-windedly, sometimes pointedly, with a sardonic wit and an acute turn of phrase. Of Ismet Inönü, for many years his Prime Minister, he once said, "There are fifty foxes chasing around in his belly, but none of them ever catch each other's tails."

Atatürk enhanced the life around him. He relished and responded openly to the admiration of women. In the anticlimax which followed his death and succession by the more conventional Inönü, a feminine admirer remarked, "Turkey has lost her lover and must now settle down with her husband." It was a sentiment which many of his countrymen shared.

I

The decline and fall of the Ottoman Empire

1 ▶ *Birth of a Macedonian*

Macedonia, with its precipitous mountains and torrential rivers, was a land where the peoples of the Ottoman Empire met and merged and led their different lives. It was a projection in miniature of that loose but functioning organism by which the Turks had held together for five centuries a disparity of races of East and West. It lay at the centre of Turkey in Europe, the country which the Ottomans called Rumeli and which, to the Byzantine Greeks, had been "the land of the Romans." The Macedonians, whether Moslem or Christian or Jew, Turk, Greek, Slav, Vlach, or Albanian, were a vigorous people, hardened by the discipline of their landscape and of a climate which ran to extremes, yet tempered from within and without by the civilizing influences of the West. Compounded of these contrasting elements, they were a people of fiercely individual spirit.

Mustafa Kemal was a Macedonian. The place of his birth was Salonika, the cosmopolitan port where the province had its outlet to the sea; the date of it 1881, a time of unrest when Rumeli was disintegrating into its various component parts, Christian turning against Moslem, Greek and Slav against Turk and against each other. Inspired by nationalist feeling, they sought to break free of the Empire and carve up the country between them for the respective benefit of Greece, Bulgaria, and Serbia. The Great Powers, the rival expansionist empires of Austria-Hungary and Russia, intrigued from behind their adjoining frontiers, marking out spheres of influence, stirring up satellites, and preparing to move in when the moment was ripe. The British Empire strove to hold a balance of power, concerned not to grab territory but to secure communications with its own imperial possessions farther east. Thus at the time of Mustafa's birth the Ottoman Empire, the East succumbing to the West as the West had once succumbed to the East, was in decline and drifting towards its fall.

Hitherto the pressure against it had come from within its frontiers. But in 1877, four years before Mustafa's birth, it came from without. The Russians, pursuing Pan-Slav dreams of a drive to the Mediterranean, violated its frontiers and marched to the outskirts of Constantinople, where only the British fleet stopped them. Through the intervention of the powers a treaty was signed at San Stefano which in effect meant the dismemberment of Turkey in Europe, mainly to the advantage of an enlarged Bulgaria. But the powers had second thoughts: Britain and Austria grew alarmed at so substantial a Russian encroachment, and at the Congress of Berlin in 1878, thanks largely to the influence of Disraeli, these decisions were reversed in favour of concessions to Russia in the East. Hence Rumeli gained a last precarious lease on life, with smaller but more turbulent Bulgaria for a neighbour and a Macedonia still simmering explosively, but still within the Ottoman Empire.

Mustafa was thus born into a restless world, beset by internal upheavals and external threats from the foreigner. He was born an Ottoman Moslem, of lower middle-class family and ostensibly Turkish stock. Whether, like most Macedonians, he had about him a touch of the hybrid —perhaps of the Slav or Albanian—can only be a matter for surmise. But as he grew up a certain "apartness" in looks—in his colouring and the cast of his features—gave a hint of it. To the child of so mixed an environment it would seldom occur, wherever his racial loyalties lay, to enquire too exactly into his personal origins beyond that of his parentage.

Mustafa's parents were Ali Riza and his wife Zübeyde. Zübeyde was as fair as any Slav from beyond the Bulgarian frontier, with a fine white skin and eyes of a deep but clear light blue. Her family came from the lake district to the west of Salonika, in the direction of Albania, where the rough bare mountains sweep down into broad opaque stretches of water. It was a countryside in which, following the Turkish conquest of

Macedonia and Thessaly, groups of villages had been peopled by settlers from the heart of Anatolia. Thus she liked to think that she had in her veins some of the pure fair blood of the Yuruks, those nomadic descendants of the original Turkish tribes who still survive in isolation among the Taurus Mountains. Mustafa took after his mother in looks, inheriting her fair hair and blue eyes. She became his predominant influence, to which he was to react with alternate respect and a spirit of rebellion. A woman of the people, with no pretensions to be otherwise, she had a strong will and a robust peasant beauty. She was a woman of native intelligence but scant education, who barely learned to read and write.

Ali Riza was twenty years older and a more shadowy personality than she. But as the son of an elementary schoolteacher he had received some education, and this brought him a minor post as a clerk in a government office—the customs and the administration of Pious Foundations. He never rose high in his profession, and when he sought Zübeyde in marriage her family demanded a price which he could not afford. But her brother Hussein intervened in his favour and they were married in Salonika.

Afterwards they lived in a village on the slopes of Mount Olympus, where Ali Riza was stationed. In this richly wooded country Ali, confined by his meagre customs salary, saw that all around him fortunes were being made out of timber and decided, despite his total lack of commercial experience, to resign his post and go into the timber trade. He moved back to Salonika, where he formed a partnership with one Jafer Effendi, investing his savings in the business and, encouraged by an initial success, building a larger house for his family. It was a two-story house with spacious rooms, overlooking a cobbled street and an unkempt garden behind, its projecting barred bay windows shuttered against the fierce sun and the inquisitive neighbours.

But Ali Riza had chosen the wrong moment in history to embark on his enterprise. These mountains had for long been peopled by gangs of Greek brigands, many of them fugitives from the oppression of the Turkish beys and to some extent protectors of the local Christian peasantry. Now, following the defeat of the Turks by the Russians and the consequent weakening of provincial authority, they grew bolder in their depredations and more overtly rebellious in their aims.

Ali Riza soon fell a victim to their constant raids. They extorted money from him by threats to burn his timber. They burned it nonetheless. They blackmailed his labourers into deserting him. They made it impossible for him to transport his logs to the coast. He had fights with them in the forest. On the advice of the commander of the gendarmerie in Salonika, whose job was to clean up the brigands, he cut his losses and abandoned the business. Such was the measure of the decline of Turkish law and order in the Macedonian province.

Zübeyde bore her husband five children, of whom only one son, Mustafa, and a daughter, Makbule, were to grow to maturity. Ali Riza had given Mustafa his name, whispering it into his ear at birth according to custom. The child was called after a brother of Ali Riza's whom he had accidentally killed, spilling him out of his cradle in infancy. A Negro nurse, whose forebears had once been slaves, looked after him, crooning over his cradle the old Rumeli folk songs, compounded of Byzantine and Slav and Turkish melodies, which were to ring in his head throughout life.

Zübeyde was a pious woman, assiduous in her devotions, subscribing implicitly to the traditional beliefs of her Moslem forebears. She took pride in the fact that in her family and that of her husband there had been *Haji,* otherwise pilgrims to Mecca. She would have liked Mustafa to follow their example, to become a *hafiz* (a reciter of the Koran) or even a *hoja* (a teacher). In the meantime he must go to the clerical school, as the children of all good Moslems did, and receive an education based on the principles of the Koran.

This once Ali Riza was able to do his son a service. Anti-clerical by bias, liberal in outlook, with a respect for the new ideas which, in Macedonia especially, were seeping in from the West, he insisted that Mustafa should go to the private secular school of Shemsi Effendi, the first to be opened in Salonika with a modern curriculum. After some dispute an effective compromise was reached. Ali Riza appeared to give in to his wife and Mustafa was introduced with the usual religious ceremony into the school of Fatima Mollah Kadin.

On the morning of my admission [Mustafa later recalled with some irony], I was festively attired by my mother in a white dress and a gold-threaded scarf, wound turbanwise around my head; in my hand I carried a gilded bough. Then the teacher—a *hoja*—arrived before the green bedecked door of our house, accompanied by all his scholars. After a prayer had been offered, I made an obeisance to my mother, my father and the teacher, lifting my finger tips to my breast and forehead and kissing their hands. Then, amid the cheering of my new companions, I went in joyous procession through the streets of the city to the school, which adjoined the mosque. On our arrival there another prayer was repeated in chorus; then the teacher, taking me by the hand, led me into a bare, vaulted chamber, where the sacred word of the Koran was unfolded to me.

Thus Zübeyde's religious scruples were satisfied and she kept face in the eyes of the neighbours. Mustafa did not unduly object to the school. But already there was germinating in him an aversion to the old Moslem customs and practices which were still universal among the Turks and to which his mother subscribed with traditional fervour. He thus took a dislike to the calligraphy lessons in the Arabic script, and to the posture in which they were studied—the children sitting cross-legged on the floor to write on their knees. Foreign children, he observed, did not write or sit like this.

One day he got up, and was ordered by the teacher to sit down but refused, protesting that this position cramped him.

"You dare to disobey me?" exclaimed the teacher.

"Yes, I dare to disobey you," Mustafa replied.

At this the rest of the class rose and said, "We're all going to disobey you," and the teacher was forced into a compromise.

Shortly afterwards Ali Riza, without protest from Zübeyde, whose initial wishes had after all been met, took the boy away from the clerical school and sent him to that of Shemsi Effendi. Here his education proceeded satisfactorily enough.

In his looks Mustafa, with his fairer hair and his cleaner-cut features, stood out from the other boys. He developed grown-up ways, gravely watching them at their street games—dicing with knucklebones, gaming with fruit stones. But he never joined in. When they asked him to play leapfrog he refused indignantly to bend down, and challenged them to jump over him in an upright position. He was aloof and proud, with a superior air, quick to resent any hint of an affront.

The busy mercantile city of Salonika, with which he now grew familiar, was to have a formative influence on his childhood and adolescence and again on his youth. Clambering up its mountainside, sprawling along the waters of its broad sluggish gulf, Salonika had long since burst from its confining Roman and Byzantine and Turkish walls to throw out quays and boulevards on a modern Western scale. Given its geography and consequent history, it could hardly help being a cosmopolitan city. Above the ruins of its fortifications minarets and church-towers punctuated a confusion of rooftops. Its people lived as it were in layers. From the top, from the medieval battlements cresting the ridge, the quarter of the Moslems zigzagged downwards in a haphazard labyrinth of steep cobbled streets. At the foot of it around the harbour lived the Jews, nearly a half of the whole population, of whom an independent section, the Dönmehs, had been converted to Islam. In between, the

Greek quarter filled the centre of the city, while around it there spread, in various directions between the hillside and the sea, the quarters of the Bulgarians, the Armenians, the Vlachs (or gipsies), and above all the "Franks" of all nations—the prosperous merchants and powerful consuls of Britain, France, Germany, Austria, Italy, Portugal.

Mustafa, who lived near the foot of the hillside within earshot of the Greek church bells below, thus grew to manhood used to the ways of the foreigner, whom he learnt to appraise with alertness and caution. In his teens he was to see the railway come for the first time to Salonika, and to share in some of the excitement which the snorting steel monster created. "The century was drawing to a close," wrote a native of the city. "Stealthily the West was creeping in, trying to lure the East with her wonders. . . . She dangled before our dazzled eyes the witchery of her science and the miracle of her inventions. We caught a glimpse of her brilliance and timidly listened to the song of the siren. Like country folk at a banquet, we felt humble and awkward in our ways. But vaguely we sensed the coldness of her glitter and the price of her wooing." [1]

Meanwhile Mustafa was to leave Salonika for a while. Ali Riza lost the remainder of his capital in the salt trade. He applied for readmission to the civil service but was rejected. He took to drinking, developed tuberculosis of the bowels and, after an illness of three years, died. Zübeyde was left badly off, so she removed Mustafa from school and took him, with his sister Makbule, to the country, some twenty miles inland from Salonika, where her brother Hussein managed a farm near Langaza.

Here in the red earth of the plain, dry in summer and marshy in winter, mixed crops flourished and animals grazed on the stubble. Bullocks drew the plough, storks prancing behind them to pick at the upturned furrow, while creaking peasant carts took the produce to market. Breathing in the smell of green things, of the earth and the moisture and the mud and the dung, Mustafa developed for the first time some feeling for the soil and for nature. He enjoyed the open-air life and adapted himself easily to odd jobs on the farm. Makbule was his close companion, a plump, outspoken, self-willed girl of coarser grain than himself, with whom he frequently quarrelled. During the day the two children would be set to watch in the fields, sitting in a hut to scare the crows off the bean crop. In the winter evenings they would sit before the farmhouse fire, roasting chestnuts from a bag by the hearth.

Life on the farm was healthy, and Mustafa grew muscular and strong.

[1] Leon Sciaky, *Farewell to Salonika*. Op. cit. Bibliography.

The food was plentiful and his uncle Hussein was kind. But he soon grew restless. The peasant life was not for him. His mind was awakening. He wanted urgently to learn and his education was being neglected. Among local teachers there was little choice between the Greek priest and the Moslem *hoja,* and Mustafa was sent to each in turn. But he disliked the outlandish Greek tongue and the Christian boys cold-shouldered him, wounding his pride. After a brief spell under the *hoja* he protested, "I won't go to school in a mosque!" Zübeyde found him a tutor, but after three days Mustafa pronounced him ignorant and refused to be taught by him. A female neighbour then offered to teach him, but he would not take lessons from a woman.

Clearly, Zübeyde realized, the time had come for him to have some form of regular schooling. She sent him back to Salonika to lodge with her sister and to attend the civil school of Kaymak Hafiz, whose name meant Cream and who was known to the boys as "Slushy." Mustafa did not stay there for long. One day he became involved in a general scrap and the schoolmaster, singling him out as the ringleader, beat him roughly, leaving him covered with bruises. Mustafa resented this fiercely. He refused to remain in the school and his grandmother took his side and removed him.

By now, however, he had begun to know what he really wanted to do. Vain since childhood of his personal appearance, he took an interest in his clothes and liked always to look neat. Now he began to fret at the traditional Turkish costume, the wide trousers and the cummerbund which the schoolboy had to wear. It was a uniform that belonged to the past. Not so the uniform of the soldiers whom he watched with respect strutting through the streets, twirling their moustachios and rattling their swords on the cobblestones with a self-important air. He envied their panache, their authority, their assumption of superior status, their assured Turkishness in a city of foreigners.

He envied especially a neighbour's boy, named Ahmed, who attended the Military Secondary School and flaunted its uniform. Zübeyde had returned to Salonika, and he begged her to let him go there, but she refused. If he was not to follow in the steps of the Prophet, as she had so dearly wished, then she would prefer him to become a merchant as his father had failed to be. She had the mother's fear of war and death and the interminable exiles which an Ottoman soldier's life involved—more especially if he failed, as Mustafa might well fail, to obtain a commission.

But Mustafa was not to be crossed. He confided his ambition to the father of his young neighbour, a major in the army, and contrived with his help, and without telling his mother, to sit for the entrance exam to the Military Secondary School. He worked with intense concentration, passed it, and thus faced Zübeyde with a *fait accompli*. But her signed consent still had to be obtained before he could enter the school. Looking back to his early childhood, he shrewdly reminded his mother that his father had presented him with a sword at birth and had hung it on the wall above his cradle. That could only mean that he had wished him to be a soldier. "I was born as a soldier," he said, striking an attitude of heroism, "I shall die as a soldier."

Zübeyde began to weaken. But it was a timely dream that finally clinched her decision. In this she saw her son sitting on a golden tray on the top of a minaret. Running to the foot of the minaret, she heard a voice intoning, "If you allow your son to go to military school, he shall remain high up here. If you do not he shall be thrown down." Clearly she had been vouchsafed a vision of a brilliant military future for her son. She gave in and signed the necessary document. Mustafa kissed her respectfully and she gave him her blessing.

Mustafa was twelve years old when he entered the Military Secondary School in Salonika. After six years of educational vicissitudes at the hands of his family he had chosen his own vocation. He had chosen well, for the officer class was the elite of the country. Its academies, subsidized by the Sultan, were nurseries of instruction, giving their pupils a grounding not only in military matters but in history, economics, philosophy. They were democratic institutions, composed of all social classes, in which it was possible to rise by ability and merit alone. Their graduates moreover, on entering the army, had the opportunity, denied to the ordinary civilian, to travel, to see the world, and to learn of the ways of the remoter peoples of the far-flung Ottoman Empire.

Mustafa found his lessons easy and learned them quickly. His best and favourite subject was mathematics and he was already working on algebra problems before his companions had progressed beyond simple arithmetic. His teacher, another Mustafa, paid him the compliment of treating him as his mathematical equal. The young Mustafa thought up difficult questions for the old. One day, to distinguish between them, the teacher followed a common Turkish custom by bestowing a second name upon his pupil. He chose that of Kemal, a word meaning, in the broadest sense, perfection; and Kemal the boy became for life. Sometimes the teacher would challenge any boy who claimed proficiency to stand up for interrogation before the rest. Few dared to do so, but Mustafa, refusing to admit the superiority of any teacher to himself, would rise and vindicate himself as the best of his class.

Mustafa Kemal quickly reached the rank of sergeant, or monitor, and enjoyed the superior status of pupil-teacher, expounding lessons to his classmates in the master's absence, with the aid of a blackboard. Didactic by nature, he was at home in the teacher's role. This assumption of maturity set him apart from his schoolfellows. Here clearly was no child. He made few friends among them, seeking rather the company of senior boys. That unfamiliar fair complexion, that lone-wolf demeanour, the solemn, supercilious, even contemptuous look in those cold blue eyes seemed to classify him as a creature of a separate species. He instinctively rebelled against authority, and his teachers found him hard to handle.

At home his relations with Zübeyde were often stormy. The solitary male in a feminine household, he despised the ways of women and resented the fatherlessness which obliged him to live among them. Then Zübeyde married again. Her second husband was Ragib, a widower of some substance, with two sons and two daughters. Mustafa was as jealous as a lover of another man in his mother's life; he was humiliated at the financial necessity which had guided her choice. But he came to terms with his stepfather, seeing that he was a good husband to Zübeyde, and found a friend in his stepbrother, an officer in the army, who gave him sound advice. The young man preached to the boy of his honour and dignity. He must never allow another to beat him. He must never bear an insult. He must resist any attempt by another man on his sexual honour. He was given a knife to protect himself, but advised never to use it rashly. From now onwards Mustafa was much away from home, for at the age of fourteen he passed out of the Secondary School and entered the Military Training School of Monastir, as a boarder.

Monastir, placed high in a broadening plain between ranges of mountains, commanded at close quarters the frontiers of Greece and Albania and, farther off, those of Serbia and Bulgaria. It thus held an important strategic position. It was the principal military centre of Macedonia, aspiring in its provincial way to some of the cosmopolitan airs and graces of Salonika. The Military School, a stuccoed building of substantial dignity, lay on the fringe of it, looking up towards a graceful mountain peak, which the Greeks called *Pelister,* or the Pigeon, from the softness of its snowcap in winter.

Here Mustafa found himself for the first time right in the centre of strife. Turkish authority in Macedonia was continuing to disintegrate

at the hands of Greek and Slav guerrilla gangs. In this atmosphere passionate loyalties and rivalries flared up among the cadets. The school was
torn by conflicting views and had its own gang warfare of plots, intrigues, and fights, leading often to bloodshed. The strongest gang was
that of the cadets from Salonika, of which Mustafa Kemal was a leader,
shrewdly electing, however, to work in the background and keep clear
of the fights. A memory which still haunted him later in life was of
awaking one night in the dormitory to see a boy standing over the bed
of a comrade, one of his own gang, with a knife raised to stab. The
boy awoke just in time to snatch the knife from his assailant's hand.

Mustafa became for the first time aware of what was happening in
the larger world beyond the school. The boys had been fired by heroic
tales and songs and epics of the Ottoman conquest of Macedonia. Now
revolt and reconquest threatened. Throughout Rumeli, Greeks and Serbs
and Bulgarians were fighting to regain Turkish lands. In 1897 the
Greeks launched a war of liberation in Crete, and the Turks marched
against them in Rumeli. Monastir was fully mobilized. Crowds thronged
the streets; soldiers were recruited to the sounds of the drum and the
bagpipe. Students marched through the town, waving Turkish flags.
Turkish guerrillas fought to the death in the mountains around. One
night Mustafa and a comrade ran away in an attempt to volunteer for
the army. They were recognized and reluctantly returned to the college.
But there had been kindled in the young Kemal a flame of patriotism and
a fierce protective love for his country.

As volunteers poured in from all parts of the Empire Mustafa be-
moaned his inability to join them. He had made friends at Monastir
with a young poet named Ömer Naji. Together, while on vacation, they
used to go to the station at Salonika to see the troop trains leave for the
front. One evening they saw, among the crowd on the platform, a group
of sheikhs and dervishes in flowing robes and long pointed bonnets.
The dervishes seemed, as they clashed their cymbals and beat their
drums and piped on their flutes in a shrill pandemonium of sound, to
be in a state of fanatical ecstasy, while the people around them had
caught their infection and were shrieking and wailing and fainting
from hysteria. Mustafa looked on at the scene with a cold disgust. To
Ömer he confessed that it made him blush with shame. There was born
in him a horror of all religious fanaticism.

Mustafa grew strong under the spartan conditions of college life. He
did not, however, care for sports, apart from the routine gymnastic
exercises, preferring to concentrate on his work. Mathematics was still

his first concern. But his mind was opening to other interests. Ömer Naji liked to recite his poems, to which Mustafa would listen, responding to the lilt of the words as to that of the music of the Rumeli songs which he had learnt in his childhood. Ömer lent Mustafa books to read, making him realize the existence of "something called literature." He became interested in poetry and even tried his hand at some verses. But his mathematics master discouraged this fancy.

Through another friend there was born in Mustafa an awareness of "something called politics." This was Ali Fethi, a Macedonian like himself, from the neighbouring countryside, who combined an easy charm of manner with a lively and flexible mind. Fethi was proficient in French, a subject in which Mustafa was backward. Stung by the reproaches of his French master, he had begun to study the language independently on his first visit home, and now he redoubled his efforts. As his knowledge of the language improved, Fethi introduced him to the works of the French political philosophers—Rousseau and Voltaire, Auguste Comte, Desmoulins, Montesquieu. Soon the two cadets were eagerly discussing the ideas of these masters which were relevant to their own country's problems.

Back at home Mustafa, no longer a child, began to taste the pleasures of Salonika, where life was various and free. With a young friend related to his stepfather's family, Fuat Bulca, he took to frequenting the cafés at the crossroads down by the waterfront—the Olympos, the Kristal, the Yonyo—places run for the most part by Greeks. They preferred the Yonyo, where the price of a glass of beer entitled them also to a supply of *meze,* the local hors d'oeuvre, so ample that they did not have to put their hands in their pockets for a meal. At the others, where they sampled stronger drinks, they could afford to buy from the itinerant vendors only chestnuts, the cheapest fare available. This promped Ömer Naji to the sad poetic comment, "What is life but a dry chestnut?" But this was life *à la Franka,* preferable to life *à la Turka* in those cafés where Turkish music was played.

Seeking to see more of it, Mustafa and his friend were taken by their French teacher to a dancing class, frequented mainly by non-Moslems, where they made a show of learning the steps of the polka and the waltz—but only with other boys, since no girls attended the class. Girls, however, were available in the *cafés chantants* at the other end of the city. To these the elder brother of Mustafa's friend introduced them. Here there were orchestras to which the girls sang and danced. There were Neapolitan songs sung by stout Italian women. There were Arabian dances performed with cymbals and jingling anklets by Armenian girls. The girls came to sit and to drink at their tables—no Moslems among them, only Christians and Jews, unveiled and accessible. As they grew older the boys frequented the brothels. Here the unusually fair young Mustafa was so admired that women often allowed him their favours for nothing. Thus did the trend of his sexual life start to show—more sought after than seeking, but readily complying. Sentimentally he was more loved than loving, his vanity now gratified by the passionate attentions of a young girl of good family, whom he was tutoring on his vacations from Monastir.

From the bulk of his fellows he still remained aloof. When they tried to pierce his reserve and discover his aims he replied only, "I am going to be somebody." Ambition, still undirected, was already smouldering within him.

He passed his final examinations well, and on March 13, 1899, graduated to the infantry class of the War College at Harbiye, in Constantinople.

2 ► *The education of an officer*

Constantinople, at the turn of the century, was two distinct cities. To the north of the Golden Horn rose Pera, the city of the Christians; to the south of it Stambul, the city of the Moslems. To drive across the harbour by the Galata Bridge was to pass from one world, from one period of history, to another.

Stambul, with its ridge of domes and minarets and its array of palace buildings, jutting out above Seraglio Point, was a medieval city which had blossomed into an architectural Renaissance during the sixteenth century but was now tumbling into picturesque decay. It was a human hive where men still swarmed and multiplied and lived as they had done for centuries past. They busied themselves in the cavernous markets and labyrinthine streets; they sought relaxation in the spacious precincts of the mosques and sacred places. But the heyday was long over; the majesty had dwindled; the splendours were those of past history. Walls crumbled and fell, paint flaked off the houses, paving stones cracked in the courtyards, grass grew in the alleyways. The women were black-veiled phantoms, sidling along the pavements, scurrying to be home by dusk. The men sat mute on the ramshackle divans of the coffee shops, beneath the shade of the straggling vines and plane trees, stirring only at the call of the muezzin from the minarets, five times a day. At night Stambul, looming up above the Golden Horn, was a dead silhouette behind which the Turk lay rapt in an oriental hush.

Pera, with its bright lights, beckoned like a siren from across the water —the city of the present. From its congested quays, lined with taverns, the streets rose vertiginously through tall narrow canyons of buildings designed in an Italianate style. Here and there a handsome double doorway led into the courtyard of an embassy or a rich merchant's palace, more amply and gracefully built, with gardens that stepped down in terraces towards the shores of the Bosporus. Pera flaunted itself as the last word in modernity, combining what it took to be the airs and graces of the West with the garish vulgarity of the Levant. Its hotels were palaces, where ladies and gentlemen of fashion listened in palm courts to polite orchestral music. Its streets were thronged with smart carriages. Its shops purveyed the latest goods from Paris and Vienna. Entertainment abounded—theatres, music halls, cabarets, clubs with a Frenchified décor, where the "upper ten" played poker and retailed the gossip of the bazaar and the palace.

Pera was the city of the foreigner, and the wealth of the Empire was in the foreigner's hands. His strength lay in the Capitulations, extraterritorial privileges which exempted him from taxes and enabled him to trade freely, to practice his own religion, and to live by his own laws, regardless of the central Turkish authority. These privileges had been granted by earlier Sultans for their own advantage, at a time of Turkish expansion when foreign merchants were needed to open up Western markets. But as the West in its turn expanded and Turkey declined, they had rebounded to the advantage of the foreigner, confirming him in a freedom which the Turk no longer enjoyed, creating a series of powerful foreign states within the state, and so tightening the foreign hold over the Ottoman Empire as to make the Turk feel that the foreigner's word was law and that he was no longer master of his own affairs. Thus the modern city of Pera held the ancient city of Stambul in its power.

Mustafa Kemal, a lusty eighteen-year-old, with some of the rawness of the provincial still about him but with a zest for experience, plunged avidly into the life of the great capital, the old and especially the new. In the cosmopolitan atmosphere of Pera all pleasures were available, and Mustafa sampled them without inhibition—carousing in drinking shops, pacing the streets by night, gratifying his appetites in the brothels with women of all sorts and races. Sexually, his life fell into a pattern of promiscuity which it was never, for long, to forsake. Women, for Mustafa, were a means of satisfying masculine appetites, little more; nor, in his zest for experience, would he be inhibited from passing adventures with young boys, if the opportunity offered and the mood, in this bisexual *fin de siècle* Ottoman age, came upon him.

Quick in his perceptions, he soon summed up in his mind the true nature of this "harlot of the ages," Constantinople. To a fellow cadet, Ali Fuad, he expressed himself in no way surprised that only the early Sultans of the Ottoman dynasty had ruled honestly and well. For their capitals were successively the small homogeneous cities of Brusa and Adrianople. In this mixed seething city of Constantinople, with its ancient associations and its decadent influences, their ultimate decline was inevitable. It was a place made for the enjoyment of life, not for the business of government.

Ali Fuad was to fill a gap in Mustafa's life. At first the days and nights in Constantinople, for all their distractions, had been lonely. Mustafa found himself in a strange city without friends, relations, contacts of any kind. In Salonika he had at least had a background of his own, however modest and restricted in character. In the world of the metropolis which now engulfed him he became acutely aware of his provincial obscurity.

Then Ali Fuad became his friend. Fuad was younger than he but relatively old for his years. He had been brought up in Constantinople and had the poise and self-assurance of one who was at home in the world. He came of a good family, as Mustafa was quick to appreciate. It was one of those military families which, outside the aristocratic world of the palace with its prolific hereditary caste, fulfilled the role of an upper class and made Mustafa's own background seem humble and drab. Fuad's father, Ismail Fazil, had been a general of some standing, of whom Fuad spoke with affection and pride. Mustafa confessed, rather wistfully, that he had never known what it meant to have a father.

Fuad's family lived at Kuzgunjuk, on the Asiatic shores of the Bosporus, where the houses and gardens of the Ottoman gentry spread themselves along the water's edge. Here, one day, he brought his new friend Mustafa. Ismail at once sensed the qualities of this fair, wiry, alert young man, with the good manners natural to the people of Salonika, and encouraged him to treat Fuad's home as his own. Mustafa, for his part, began to see Fuad's father as in some sense a substitute for the father he had lost in childhood. He took to passing his weekends here with the family, among whom he soon felt at home.

He and Fuad spent much of their spare time together, exploring the widespread and infinitely various city, determined to discover all of it, and the more stimulated to do so by Ismail's suggestion that they should make a complete map of Constantinople. The two cadets would make excursions in caïques up the Bosporus and around the Sea of Marmara. One summer weekend they decided to go to Prinkipo, the largest of the Isles of the Princes, so called from the princes for whom they had been places of imprisonment and exile. The hotels were expensive, so they would camp in the pinewoods which ran down into sandy bays, giving to the islands a Mediterranean air. They would take food, cooking equipment, kindling wood for a fire—above all something to drink. Mustafa suggested a case of beer, his normal drink. Fuad protested that this would be too heavy to carry and proposed instead one bottle of raki, the raw Turkish spirit flavoured with aniseed with which Mustafa was still unfamiliar. He responded at once to its stimulus and thus contracted a habit in which thereafter he freely indulged.

It was a moonlight night. Warmed by the food and the raki, the two youths fell into a romantic mood. They sat enraptured by the natural beauties around them—the fragrant woods, the shimmering sea, the star-lit sky. Too exalted to sleep, they recited poems, they exchanged dreams of love. Mustafa said, "Fuad, you may be sure that, if I had given as much attention to poetry and painting as to mathematics, you wouldn't find me now locked within the four walls of Harbiye. I would run away from the school each moonlight night, I would come here, I would write poems. At dawn, as soon as it grew light enough, I would start to paint."

These were passing fantasies. Mustafa, after a first year at Harbiye in which his studies were often deflected by the dreams and distractions of youth, settled down in his second to serious study, developing his mind and striving to sort out the ideas which began to crowd in upon it. Military matters were still his main concern. But he was beginning to extend his range of knowledge. He was working to improve his French and was now able to read the French newspapers. At the same time he delved more deeply and with more comprehension into the works of the French writers to which Fethi had introduced him at Monastir. Such subversive books were banned to the cadets, and Mustafa read them covertly at night in his dormitory, together with the literature of Namik Kemal and other Turkish liberal poets, precursors of the Revolution to come, whose very names it was a mortal sin to mention.

Out of school, he and his fellow cadets held debates and practiced public speaking. On Kemal's initiative they organized contests in oratory. He would choose a subject on which each was to speak for a fixed number of minutes, while he kept time with a watch. He himself, in these orations, began to display a forcible capacity for convincing his audience. But politically he was still only on the threshold of experience. His mind wrestled with thoughts and emotions which he did not yet wholly understand. They were the growing pains of a young man's political consciousness. As it grew Kemal's personal ambition and love for his country coalesced into the realization that he himself might do something to save and redeem it.

Kemal had been born into an age in which tyrannical reaction had arrested a process of liberal advancement. Since the French Revolution, of which he now had some knowledge, the Ottoman Empire had been pursuing a chequered but continuous course from a medieval theocracy towards some form of modern constitutional state. Through the nineteenth century this trend assumed, at intervals, a concrete form, partly on the initiative of an enlightened young Sultan, Abdul Mejid, who, by the Tanzimat decrees of 1839 and ensuing reforms of a Western kind, confirmed the rights of the subject and the obligations of the sovereign; partly under pressure from the Western Powers who in 1876, concerned for the interests of their Christian minorities, induced a less progressive Sultan, Abdul Hamid II, to grant a parliamentary constitution.

Socially Abdul Hamid carried on, in certain directions, the progressive traditions of modernization and reform. But politically, fearful as he was, sometimes to the point of insanity, of the forces of disruption which seemed to threaten his Empire from every hand, he could not for long tolerate a democratic regime. Taking advantage of the war with Russia, he dissolved Parliament in 1877 and ruled for the next generation as a despot. He established a form of police state, effectively suppressing freedom of the individual, of speech, and of the press, employing a vast regiment of secret agents, and reigning no longer from the palace on Seraglio Point, as his forebears had done, but from within the security of the twenty-foot walls of the Yildiz Palace, at a safe distance outside the city.

Sooner or later indignation against such oppression and its accompanying corruption was bound to flare up into revolt. But at first the Turkish political reformers were driven either abroad or underground. In such cities as Paris and Geneva, traditional cradles of liberty, they formed committees, sought to win the West to their cause, published propagandist literature and infiltrated it into the Ottoman Empire through the foreign post offices and similar agencies. Reform was no longer enough for them; only revolution, the deposition of the Sultan himself, would achieve their purpose.

In Constantinople the reformers had to work secretly. They worked on the same revolutionary lines. Ironically, it was Abdul Hamid's own elite who were the first thus to plot for his overthrow, the young students of those very military schools which he had built up for the protection and reinforcement of his regime. The first secret revolutionary society in the Ottoman Empire was formed by students of the Imperial Military Medical School in 1889, the centenary year of the French Revolution. In 1896—while Mustafa Kemal was still a student at Monastir—they attempted a *coup d'état,* which failed. The ringleaders were rounded up, tried, and exiled to remote parts of the Empire. Abdul Hamid thus succeeded in postponing the revolutionary movement in Turkey for a further decade.

The political ideas of Mustafa himself rapidly assumed a more coherent shape when, in 1902, he graduated as a lieutenant to the Staff College. He began to devour history as he had previously devoured mathematics and poetry. He read all he could about the career of Napoleon, who became (with qualifications) one of his heroes. He read the works of John Stuart Mill. He caught the prevailing infection of the "popular" ideas. He and some friends of his year formed a secret committee and started a manuscript newspaper, most of which was written by Mustafa, with a view to exposing administrative and political evils.

The palace got wind of these activities. The director of the college was reprimanded and instructed to take action against the culprits. He entered a lecture room in the veterinary section, where Mustafa and his friends were in the act of preparing an issue of the newspaper. But, being a man of lenient disposition and, like many among even the older army officers, not wholly well disposed towards the Sultan, he chose to turn a blind eye, pretended not to have seen what the young men were doing, and imposed a mild punishment upon them—which was not even carried out—for neglecting their proper studies.

Mustafa, however, did not allow his new political interests to interfere with his military education. His mind soon had to grapple with those wider problems of strategy and tactics which a would-be staff officer must master. Far into the night he would lie wide awake in the dormitory, thoughts pounding away in his head while the other cadets slept. He would then fall asleep with the dawn, so that each morning, when the bugle blew for reveille, the officer in charge had to shake him until he awoke. He seemed to his comrades in a perpetual daydream, until suddenly in class he would prove himself twice as awake as the rest, raising some awkward question with the teacher which would force them to bestir themselves and rack their brains. He developed an intense interest in guerrilla warfare, and one day, with an uncanny prophetic sense, posed to the class the hypothetical problem of a revolt against the capital from the Asiatic shores of the Bosporus.

Mustafa finished his course at the Staff College in 1905, at the age of twenty-four, and was commissioned as a captain. He lodged in a house in the Bayazid quarter of Stambul, and with a few friends rented a room in the neighbouring house of an Armenian. Here they carried on with their political activities. These amounted in effect to little more than talk, the familiar outspoken criticism of the Sultan's regime, and the study of the "forbidden books," of which they had acquired a library. Among them was a cadet who had been expelled from the school and to whom, since he had nowhere to go, they had given a room in the house. He informed against them to the palace and, by a forged note, lured them to a neighbouring café, where they were arrested.

Mustafa, Ali Fuad, and two other newly gazetted captains were carried off to prison and interrogated singly. Mustafa was roughly handled. Ali Fuad, a man of the world conversant with protocol, protested that, as a wearer of the Sultan's uniform, he might not be struck by any officer below the Sultan's rank—a diplomatic evasion which afterwards evoked from Mustafa a wry smile at his own inexperience. Mustafa did not feel unduly concerned as to his possible fate, though his mother feared the worst. He whiled away the time in prison writing verses, reading books that were smuggled in to him, and planning what he would do when released.

The prisoners were kept in jail for some months while a judicial enquiry was held. The director of the college counselled lenient treatment for what he maintained was little more than a youthful misdemeanour, and his counsel prevailed. The officers were released, with a view to posting away from the capital. It was decided to send them to the Second and Third Armies, at Adrianople and Salonika respectively. If they could not agree among themselves they were instructed to draw lots to decide which should go to each. But, at a sign from Mustafa, they announced immediate agreement, and the swiftness of their decision aroused suspicions of a prearranged plot.

Thus several officers were exiled instead to "places from which they would not easily find a means of returning." Mustafa and Ali Fuad were posted to the Fifth Army at Damascus, in Syria. Mustafa was resigned. "All right," he jested, "let's go to this desert and found a new state there." They sailed forthwith, and some two months later landed at the port of Beirut.

3 ▶ *Service in the field*

Kemal thus embarked on the first stage of his career as a serving officer. As captain in a cavalry regiment his main duty was to instruct the other ranks, to pass on to them some of the military knowledge which he himself had acquired in the modern military schools and which not all his fellow officers shared. He took the task seriously and, with his taste and talent for teaching, performed it well.

Ali Fuad and he remained together until Fuad was sent on a mission to Ibn Saud, then a little-known tribal sheikh, under nominal Turkish suzerainty, in southern Arabia. He applied for permission to take Mustafa with him but this was refused. Thus history missed an opportunity. These two men, both destined to greatness in a similar field, were never to meet.

It was one of the tasks of the Fifth Army to control the Druses, those unruly people of cryptic ancestry, esoteric religion, and fiercely independent spirit who inhabited the black rocky country of the Hauran to the south of Damascus. They had for long resisted Turkish rule but some ten years earlier had been brought under control, agreeing to pay taxes in return for release from the obligation to serve in the Ottoman Army outside their own territory. Periodically it became necessary to send a force to the Hauran, to quell disorders, and these were frankly regarded by the Ottoman officers as an occasion for pillage.

Kemal first had an inkling of this when he learnt, to his surprise, that his regiment had been ordered to the Hauran and that he had not received orders to accompany it. He protested to his commanding officer that, as squadron commander, it was his duty to lead his troops. But the officer was evasive: Kemal was under training, his place was at headquarters. Kemal was angry. Clearly something was afoot which the old hands were trying to conceal from the young officers, fresh from the Staff College. With a brother officer named Müfit,[1] who had been similarly dropped from the expedition, he disregarded orders and went off to join his unit, which was encamped near a Circassian village. There were no tents for them and they slept in those of the soldiers.

Next day Kemal confronted the officer who had taken his place and who explained that he had been detailed for "special duty" on the operation on account of his previous experience. If, however, Kemal would promise to keep quiet about it afterwards, he would be allowed to take part. Kemal, anxious to learn the truth, gave the promise. What he learnt was that it was the practice of the troops, on the pretext of collecting arrears of taxation, to extort money from the inhabitants or, in default of it, to loot their homes and villages.

Kemal refused to be party to such methods. As a conscientious young officer he preferred to control the Druses by coming to terms with them. In one village he was able to persuade the inhabitants that he and a fellow officer had come not to rob but to help them. An understanding was immediately reached with the headman, who agreed to do what Kemal asked of him but declared that he would never obey this Ottoman government which sent troops to oppress and plunder his people. In another village he arrived in time to rescue a Turkish major from a menacing situation. He harangued the villagers, who trusted his good intentions and released his brother officer.

In such ways Kemal attracted attention to himself, earning the respect of the new school of officer and the mistrust of the old. The traditional Ottoman officer took the view that, provided he did what was expected of him by his master the Sultan, he was free to reap what personal advantage he could out of his military service, with no questions asked. The idea that soldiering might be a science, to be studied in a professional

[1] Later Müfit Özdeş, a member of Parliament in Ankara.

spirit and with a view to improvement in training, tactics, and modern techniques, seldom entered his head. For him, the new type of college-trained officer was an upstart, to be regarded with suspicion.

Kemal used to protest against the exaggerated operational reports which were concocted to impress headquarters in Constantinople. A certain engagement reported as a victory was not, he pointed out, a victory at all; the enemy had simply retired of his own free will. The commander mocked at his naïveté: "You are still ignorant," he said. "You do not understand what our Sultan wants."

"I may be ignorant," Mustafa replied, "but our Sultan should be a man clever enough to understand what types like you are really up to."

When the time came for the officers to divide up the spoils of their raids Kemal and Müfit were offered their share. As Müfit hesitated, Mustafa turned to him and asked, "Do you want to be a man of today or a man of tomorrow?"

"Of course, a man of tomorrow."

"Then you must refuse to take this money, as I have done."

Kemal's phrase was revealing. He had begun to see his own self in perspective, as one who belonged not to the past, like these dugouts around him, but to the future. The "Men of Today" stood for the incompetence and corruption of an Empire in decline. It was less the moralist than the realist in Kemal that was shocked by their attitude. It was not just morally wrong; it was worse; it no longer worked. The pacification of the Druses, the salvation of the Empire, could not today be attained by mere force and rapacity and bribery; it must be sought more scientifically, by skill and diplomacy and the use of intelligence.

In another respect Damascus was to leave a deep imprint on this Man of Tomorrow. For the first time he came to know a city which lived still in the darkness of the Middle Ages. The cities with which he was familiar—Salonika, Constantinople, and more recently Beirut—were cosmopolitan places, alive with the various amenities and pleasures of a modern civilization. But the holy Arab city of Damascus was a city of the dead. The narrow streets which he paced after dark were deserted and silent. Not a sound came from within the high shuttered walls of their houses. One night, to his surprise, he heard the sound of music floating out from a café. He looked in, to find it filled with Italians, workers on the Hejaz Railway, playing the mandolin, singing and dancing with their wives and their girls. As an officer in uniform, he might not enter. But on an impulse he went home, changed into rough clothes, and returned to join them in their gay and uninhibited Western pleasures.

Otherwise all was dark, smelling of bigotry, repression, and, beneath all, hypocrisy. Kemal began to see that the real enemy of his people was not simply the foreigner, from whom, despite his aggressive designs, they had after all something to learn. The enemy lay within their own ranks. It was the Moslem religion, which oppressed them and stunted their growth, shutting them off from the more advanced and enlightened ways of the Christian peoples. The Ottoman Empire, as he once put it, was a place where the joys of heaven were reserved for non-Moslems, while Moslems were condemned to endure the shades of hell.

Here in Damascus Kemal felt imprisoned. He longed to break his bars, to bring life to this moribund community. The remedy of course lay in political action. One day he was wandering in the market with two brother officers. Outside a shop they found a table and chairs and sat down. The shopkeeper greeted them—not in Arabic but in Turkish. Kemal became curious. He went into the shop, where he saw scattered on a table books in French on such subjects as philosophy, sociology, and medicine. He asked the shopkeeper, "What are you? A tradesman or a philosopher?"

"A tradesman," was the reply, "but I like to read books—the literature of liberty."

He then revealed that he had been a student in the Military Medical School in Constantinople, the cradle of the revolutionary movement, but had been thrown into jail for subversive activities and sent into exile. His name was Haji Mustafa. He invited Kemal and his friends to his house a night or so later.

Kemal went with Müfit and two other officers, all three sympathetic to his political ideas. The house was in a dark narrow street. Haji Mustafa opened the door cautiously, holding a petrol lamp above his head to make sure of their identity before he would admit them. Inside they began to talk freely. For some time their host had been trying to form a secret political society but had been unable to find trustworthy associates.

Kemal and two of his friends promised their support. The third said, "I am with you in sympathy. But I have a wife and children. You must not expect active help from me." At the others' request the married officer left them alone. They talked far into the night, the young officers growing romantic in their aspirations to "die for the Revolution."

Kemal, the realist, brought them down to earth. "Our aim is not to die," he protested sharply. "It is to carry out the Revolution, to make a reality of our ideas. We must live, to get them accepted by the people."

Thus, in the autumn of 1906, they formed a society known as *Vatan*, the Fatherland Society. Its importance lay in the fact that it was the forerunner of a number of revolutionary cells formed from then onwards among serving officers in field formations. It was in the field, no longer in Constantinople in the toils of the Sultan's security network, that revolution now had the best chance to develop.

Under cover of his military duties Kemal helped to found branches of the society in Jaffa, Jerusalem, and Beirut. But all this was too far from home. This country was a backwater, moreover an Arab country, where no Turkish revolutionary movement had a chance of popular support. It must remain confined to army officers alone. The obvious centre for it was Macedonia, which was closer to the outside world, hence more accessible to the new ideas, and where the ubiquitous presence of the foreigner not only intensified nationalist feeling but, paradoxically, made it easier for it to operate, owing to the greater freedom of movement and the consequent weakening of palace control. Three years earlier Austria and Russia, in their efforts to introduce reforms into the province, had imposed upon the Turks a gendarmerie under foreign officers, which made it harder for the Sultan's own secret police to operate in Salonika as effectively as in Constantinople.

Mustafa Kemal made up his mind that, somehow or other, he must get to Salonika. The commandant of Jaffa connived at his plans for departure, ostensibly on leave, and promised to warn him if there was any comment on his absence. He left for Egypt and Piraeus, where he boarded a Greek ship for Salonika. Dressed in civilian clothes, he was met by a friend and landed without undue interference. He went straight to his mother's house.

Zübeyde was overjoyed but disturbed to see him. How had he been so rash as to come here, contrary to the orders of our Lord the Sultan? Mustafa reassured her: "I had to come, so I came. I shall show you what your Lord the Sultan really is. But later." He stayed at home during the day, and in the evening went to the house of an artillery general, Shükrü Pasha, who held progressive political views and had encouraged him to come.

Shükrü was taken aback at his arrival. He explained that, in view of his position, he could give Kemal no active help. But he would do nothing to hinder him and would look with good will on anything he chose to do. He asked only that Kemal should not compromise him. Mustafa gave the necessary promise and went home to his mother's house. Put out by the pasha's attitude, he lay awake half the night, undecided what to do, where to go, how to begin.

In the morning he put on his uniform and went to headquarters. Here he saw a staff colonel whom he had known when a student in the Military School. Mustafa reminded him of his identity and, believing him to be a patriot, revealed his predicament. The colonel devised a means by which to help him. He told him to apply for sick leave, not in the name of his unit but simply as a captain on the General Staff. He would support the application. The subterfuge worked and Kemal was granted four months' sick leave. He was thus able to remain in Salonika and circulate freely.

Nonetheless he felt his way carefully, disconcerted by his initial rebuff and sensing currents in the atmosphere that were not always favourable to his designs, even among officers of his own political sympathies. But by the end of the four months he had succeeded in organizing a Macedonian branch of the *Vatan* society which he had helped to found in Damascus. Its name was expanded to *Vatan ve Hürriyet* (Fatherland and Freedom); its half dozen members included his old school friend Ömer Naji, the poet, and two officers of the staff of the Military School. Meetings were held in the house of one of them, an officer of musical accomplishments, who played the flute and received them in Japanese pajamas.

Here one evening they met to swear their first oath of allegiance to the revolutionary cause. After a number of speeches, suitably heroic in character, Kemal read out the three articles of the society, which he had jotted down on a card. After that a revolver was produced and laid on the table. The oath was to be sworn on this weapon, not on the Koran or on the honour of an officer as was the Ottoman practice. It symbolized their fidelity to the Revolution and their intention to resort to arms, if need be, to bring it about. One by one they kissed the revolver and swore. Afterwards Kemal remarked, "This revolver is now sacred. Keep it carefully, and one day you will give it to me."

It was known by now in Constantinople that Mustafa Kemal had left his post in Jaffa. Orders were sent to Salonika for his arrest. Warned by a friend, he left in secret and returned to Jaffa. The commandant, who had connived at his departure, met him on arrival and hurried him off to Beersheba, where a frontier force had been sent to protect Turkish claims in a dispute over the port of Akaba with the Anglo-Egyptian government. Following an enquiry into his movements, it was implied in a report to Constantinople that he had been at Beersheba for some months. The officer in Salonika was presumably another Mustafa. In the labyrinth of the Turkish bureaucracy, where records were haphazardly filed and the duplication of names caused convenient confusion, such a fiction was easy enough to sustain.

The Turks retained Akaba, and Mustafa Kemal returned to Damascus. There, bent on earning the remission of his "exile," he behaved circumspectly. In due course he obtained his promotion to adjutant major and a transfer to the General Staff at Damascus. In September 1907 he was posted, as he had hoped, to the Third Army in Macedonia, but on his arrival was transferred instead to the General Staff at Salonika itself.

4 ► *The Young Turk Revolution*

In Macedonia the sands were running out. No thinking Turk could fail
to sense that the Empire was on the brink of disintegration. "Macedonia
for the Macedonians" was the mounting cry. Russian and Austrian
agents abounded. The Bulgarians had a powerful underground organization, a state within a state with its own army of *komitajis*—"committee-
men" who were in fact terrorists—spreading panic and engineering continuous bomb outrages. Security on the frontiers had vanished, as bands
of Greeks, Bulgarians, Serbians, and Albanians scrapped with one another and with the Turkish authorities. The Great Powers closed in,
ready to dismember the body. They had lately been joined by a "latecomer at the feast of the vultures," the German Empire, bent on its
Drang nach Osten. Bismarck had taken advantage of the fall of Disraeli, and the advent to power of Gladstone with his Hellenophile
aversion to the "unspeakable Turk," to supply Abdul Hamid with a
German military mission under Marshal von der Goltz, and the Kaiser
had followed up this move with a much-advertised state visit to the
Sultan.

Abdul Hamid, making shift for a policy, played all against all, foreigner against foreigner and Turk against Turk. In Macedonia he reinforced a team of agents now reputed by the people of Salonika to number forty thousand. The Christian minorities at least had foreign governments to protect them. The Turks felt themselves to be a persecuted minority inside their own frontiers. They looked around them in search of salvation. Only the young Turkish officers seemed to offer it.

Thus the revolutionary movement gained in impetus and expanded with speed, founding branches in all parts of the Empire and training groups of propagandists whose duty it was to spread its ideas among all classes of the population. By the end of 1907 it had outgrown Mustafa Kemal, who on his return found himself faced with the bitter realization that his "exile" in Syria had effectively prevented him from becoming one of its leaders. His own limited Fatherland and Freedom Society had been outstripped by the growth of a wider organization, which was to be known as the Committee of Union and Progress, and whose members included such leaders in embryo as Talat, then a clerk in the post office, and Jemal, an army colonel, both men clearly destined for power. It contained few of his friends except Ali Fethi. On the initiative of Talat the Fatherland and Freedom Society was merged within this larger group and its name disappeared altogether.

The political atmosphere of Salonika had been conducive to secret societies ever since the early Christians of the city, converted by St. Paul, had gone underground to escape the persecutions of Nero. The Committee of Union and Progress made free use of both the premises and the techniques of the Freemasons, imposing a ritual of initiation by which the aspirant was blindfolded and led into the presence of three masked strangers in cloaks and was obliged to swear an oath, both on the sword and on the Koran, to redeem his country, to keep the secrets of the society, and to obey its orders, including the order to kill any person whom it might condemn to death. Such mumbo-jumbo went against the grain with Kemal. More especially, having initially sworn on the revolver alone, did he resent this Islamic symbolism of the new oath. For the moment, however, he had no alternative but to come to terms with the Unionists as best he could.

Instinctively they tended to dislike him, seeing him as opinionated, conceited, and brash. They found pretexts to push him out of the way, taking advantage of the fact that his staff duties involved inspection of the Macedonian railways and could thus be combined with propagandist activities outside Salonika. His beat became the valley of the Vardar, up as far as Üsküb, on the fringe of the Serbian plain. Gnawed by frustration, but more and more confident of his capacity to lead, he drew together with a small group of his friends and adherents, meeting and talking and planning with them far into the night in the cafés and in the house of Zübeyde, now widowed for the second time and living with her daughter Makbule. Both became resigned to his subversive activities and made coffee for the plotters at their nocturnal meetings.

The Revolution was ripening but not yet entirely ripe. The international situation helped to precipitate events. King Edward VII and the Tsar Nicholas II met on a yacht in the Baltic for a series of polite talks which were seen by the Committee as an ominous shift in British policy against Turkey. At home time was still needed to indoctrinate the officers in Thrace and Asia Minor. But speed became necessary, for Abdul Hamid began to wake up. Taking positive action, he sent commissions of enquiry to Salonika. The Committee shot at and wounded the leader of the first of them. The second resorted to conciliation and bribery.

A young major named Enver, a Committee member of no great seniority, was invited, together with others, to visit Constantinople on a promise of promotion and hints of other rewards. He ignored the invitation and took to the hills, where he began to organize a resistance movement. On July 4, 1908, another officer, Major Ahmed Niyazi, an experienced guerrilla warrior of Albanian origin, followed his example, taking followers from the garrison at Monastir. Ali Fuad, who chanced to be in the neighbourhood on Committee business, took a detachment of troops to Niyazi's aid and advised him to declare his intentions in public. Niyazi drafted a telegram to the Sultan proclaiming open revolt. The Committee came out into the open, demanding the restoration of the Constitution of 1876. The Sultan rushed reinforcements from Anatolia but their officers fraternized with the rebels.

Abdul Hamid realized that he was beaten. After two days of hesitation, during which he is said to have consulted his astrologer, he accepted an ultimatum from the Committee. This threatened, in default of his accession to its demands, to dethrone him in favour of his brother and to march on Constantinople. After an all-night sitting of his State Council the Sultan agreed to restore the Constitution, which he had violated a generation before. On July 24 the news was proclaimed to a rejoicing Empire.

Niyazi marched with his band of faithful followers into Monastir, beneath banners proclaiming "Liberty, Equality, Fraternity, Justice"; but, having little taste for politics, he soon retired to his native Albanian mountains. Enver, on the other hand, appeared, young and solemn and triumphant, on the balcony of the Olympos Palace Hotel in Salonika, where he was acclaimed by a vast crowd as the political hero of the hour. He announced to them ardently that arbitrary rule was at an end and that henceforward all citizens, of whatever race or creed, were brothers, glorying in being Ottomans together.

So indeed it seemed, for some days of delirious euphoria, when Moslem *hojas,* Orthodox priests, and Jewish rabbis embraced one another and walked arm in arm. Turkish women tore off their veils. The jails were thrown open and aged political prisoners emerged, blinking at the light and embracing their now unfamiliar relatives. Constantinople, according to Aubrey Herbert, was "glowing like a rose and tense with excitement." Continuous speeches were made to the crowds, proclaiming the principles of democracy. The magic but still meaningless word "Constitution" was on all lips, seeming to portend Utopia. Thus a new era began.

Mustafa Kemal played no part in these momentous events. On the balcony of the hotel in Salonika he was but a shadowy figure behind Enver. It was more or less by chance that Enver had been thrown up as the revolutionary hero. He was well enough cast for this popular role. Trim, polished, dapper in his uniform, with well-waxed moustaches and a stiff manner of saluting, he presented to the public the model image of the smart young Turkish officer. His courage was beyond reproach. He would stroll nonchalantly in front of his men under enemy fire. He was vain, basking in the plaudits of the crowd, glancing sidelong into a mirror whenever he passed one. But he was not bombastic. He was a good Moslem who rode into battle with the Koran at his breast. He neither smoked nor drank. His private life was impeccable, just such as to appeal to the bourgeois sentiments of a revolution aimed against palace corruption and decadence. But it was, at the same time, a romantic revolution, and Enver cut the dashing romantic figure it needed.

Kemal, his opposite in almost every respect, saw him as a marionette jumped up fortuitously into the hero's role. After the scene on the balcony he walked into the Kristal Casino, to find his fellow officers toasting the Revolution and glorifying Enver.

"What's this?" he exclaimed irritably. "You're praising Enver all the time. Nothing but Enver! Enver! It's not good that he should be praised so much."

An officer protested, "Don't be jealous of Enver. He took to the mountains for the sake of freedom. Of course I'm going to praise him."

"Naturally I'm jealous of him. I too come from a middle-class family. Don't you realize that all this praise and all these speeches will make Enver very proud, and so full of himself that in the end he will do harm to the country?" Jealous Kemal certainly was, but with a jealousy based on an irresistible belief in his own superior capacities. He was always quick to praise Enver's qualities as a soldier. But in the broader field he saw Enver from the start as a man inadequate to the tasks which he would be required to perform.

Difficulties indeed soon multiplied. The Young Turks, as they came to be called, were officers of unassailable patriotism, but without political experience and without, in effect, a policy. The sole aim of the Revolution was to force Abdul Hamid to his knees and to replace his despotism with the panacea which would inevitably cure all ills—a liberal Constitution. Otherwise theirs was an essentially conservative revolution. There was no ideology, no programme behind it, no understanding of the fundamental problems which confronted the Ottoman state. Imperialists in essence, blind to the new nationalist forces now at work in the modern world, the Young Turks aspired merely to conserve, if in a more liberal form, the Ottoman Empire of their forebears.

The present regime differed from previous ones in the important respect that it was now subject to constitutional safeguards, in which all had a share; that the inhabitants were promised union, in terms of equal rights and obligations for all races and creeds, progress, in terms of education and economic development, and the "Justice" that had been added to the French revolutionary slogan of "Liberty, Fraternity, Equality." But they were still to remain Ottomans. All that the Christian minorities were offered, in response to their yearnings for nationhood, was the privilege of becoming free citizens of a Turkish state with an alien religion.

Their reaction to this prospect was swift. The Revolution, far from arresting the disintegration of the Empire, as the Young Turks had hoped, at once accelerated it. The response was in effect a Balkan counterrevolution. Within a bare three months of the establishment of the Constitution, Bulgaria proclaimed her independence; within the same week Austria annexed the Turkish provinces of Bosnia and Herzegovina, and Crete voted for union with Greece. Austria's act, in defiance of the Treaty of Berlin, was a unilateral breach of international law to which Sir Edward Grey attributed the ensuing "era of European anarchy."

Mustafa Kemal saw all too clearly the muddled course which events were taking. His criticisms of the new administration were outspoken

Night after night he would sit talking and drinking with his officer friends in those Salonika cafés which he had known since boyhood. The Olympos and the Kristal, freed since the Revolution from all restrictions, had overflowed onto the pavements and into the streets, where their chairs and tables encroached even on the tram lines. A new open-air café, the White Tower, had appeared at the other end of the sea front beneath the round medieval tower which surveyed the whole sweep of the gulf and caught its evening breezes. Here the hubbub of conversation and of the street vendors' cries clashed with the vehement clap of the pieces on the domino and backgammon boards at the crowded marble-topped tables.

Kemal's trenchant voice rose above the noise, reverberating clearly and emphatically. Arguing vigorously, he overbore his interrupters. He criticized the Committee openly, indiscreetly. What need was there for a Committee at all, now that the Revolution had been accomplished and a proper constitutional authority established?

This Mustafa Kemal was a nuisance. He must be sent away from Salonika on some party mission—this time farther afield than Üsküb. An opportunity now offered. There had been trouble in Tripoli since the departure of the Committee representative. At a meeting in Kemal's absence it was agreed to send him to Tripoli to investigate conditions and to take any action on the Committee's behalf which might seem to be necessary. Confronted with the decision, he at once divined the motives behind it. He judged that Tripoli might well have been chosen by his enemies as his political, if not his actual, graveyard. But he thought it best to accept the challenge and, after drawing the necessary funds, embarked on a ship bound for the North African coast.

On the way the ship put in at a Sicilian port. He disembarked with a fellow passenger and went for a drive in a carriage. Children in the streets mocked at their fezzes and pelted them with lemon peel. Kemal's dignity as a Turk was not affronted, as it might well have been. On the contrary, there was born in him from that moment, not resentment at the insult, but a hatred for the fez, that outworn symbol of Ottoman prestige which could so arouse the mockery of street urchins.

In Tripoli, where the Committee had not yet succeeded in establishing its authority over the Arabs and the more reactionary Ottoman elements, Kemal found a hostile atmosphere. As its representative, he had first to win over the pasha who commanded the district. This, by a combination of threats and diplomacy over the coffee cup, he finally succeeded in doing. Learning that Arab rebels were planning to capture him, he went

boldly to the precincts of the mosque, where they had made their headquarters. After promising their leaders that his government would take
account of their grievances, he addressed the crowd in the courtyard.
Greeting them as his brothers in religion, he delivered them a long
patriotic harangue, emphasizing the power of the new regime but insisting that it would be used only for their protection. The crowd seemed
to be impressed.

But the Arab sheikh, a man with wiles of his own, sent for him and
demanded, "Who are you and what is your authority?" Kemal produced
from his pocket his references from the Committee. The sheikh laughed
openly and produced from his own pocket three identical papers, the
credentials of three of Kemal's predecessors who had been thrown into
prison on arrival.

Kemal changed his ground. "Take the paper," he said. "Tear it to pieces
if you like. I am a man who has no need for paper, a man who comes
to talk to you with no paper at all."

The sheikh replied: "Then I can talk with you." And the release of the
three other prisoners was finally agreed.

Before returning to Salonika, Kemal visited Benghazi. Here he found a
struggle for power between the Turkish authorities and a strong local
sheikh, Mansour, who had made puppets of the Turks, forcing them to
carry out his wishes. Kemal judged that this was a case for a tougher
line of action. When the sheikh called on them Kemal took the offensive,
rebuking him in menacing fashion. Then he asked the local commander
to gather all his troops in their barracks for an inspection.

When the other officers protested, suspecting him of an intention to examine and find fault with them, Kemal reassured them with congratula-
tory words. Then he suggested that he should lead them in a short infantry
exercise. To this they agreed, and Kemal briefed them: a regiment of infantry, facing Benghazi, marches to confront an enemy coming from the
left. While doing so it receives orders to turn about and confront a more
formidable enemy on the right.

The operation was carried out without arousing suspicion, and the
final objective proved to be the house of Sheikh Mansour, which was
immediately encircled. A man with a white banner came out, offering
surrender. Kemal agreed to raise the siege on condition that the sheikh
come to call upon him. At this interview he expounded the intentions of
the new regime and its policy of reform. The sheikh, producing a copy of
the Koran, said, "Can you swear on this Book that you will not do mischief to our Lord the Caliph?"

Kemal took the Koran, kissed it, and said, "I honour and bless this Book. I swear on this Book and on my word of honour that, in terms of the principles laid down in it, I will do no harm to the man who is called Caliph." Thus the sheikh, his face saved by the calming of his religious scruples, admitted political defeat. An agreement was reached by which government and army reaffirmed their authority and a reasonable balance of power was restored.

Mustafa Kemal left for Salonika satisfied with the results of his mission. If only on his own valuation, he had proved himself adroit in combining the functions of soldier and diplomat.

5 ▶ *The counterrevolution*

Mustafa Kemal returned home from North Africa to find an uneasy political situation. The inevitable reaction was at hand. The Committee of Union and Progress had suffered an initial setback from the swift opposition of the foreigner. It was now confronted with increasing opposition at home. Its enemy Abdul Hamid still sat upon his throne, largely because the revolutionaries had not felt strong enough to depose him. Time, he judged, might well be on his side. As long as he retained the Sultanate he was bound to become a focus for such reactionary forces as survived. He could still command the loyalty of the bulk of illiterate masses, who revered him as their religious chief, no less a personage in his capacity as Caliph than the shadow of God on earth.

The Revolution, moreover, had originated in Salonika; and Salonika was not the capital of the Empire. In Constantinople the Committee was less sure of its ground. From the outset the Young Turks had been divided into two conflicting groups. To the right was the Committee of Union and Progress itself, favouring Union in the form of a centralized government and tending to develop an authoritarian spirit. To the left, subdivided into several groups, were the liberals, favouring Progress in terms of a decentralized regime, on more democratic principles, and with autonomous rights for the minorities. In an open trial of strength the extremists prevailed, forcibly replacing a liberal Grand Vizier, Kiamil Pasha, with a nominee of their own. This not only angered the moderates but opened the door to the latent forces of reaction.

Tension mounted, and only an incident was needed to ignite the various elements of discontent. It was duly provided one night on the Galata Bridge by the murder—supposedly at the hands of the Committee —of the insignificant editor of a liberal newspaper and his subsequent well-staged public funeral as a martyr to the liberty of the press. The result was a counterrevolution in the name of the holy law of the *sheriat* and the over-all authority of Islam for which it stood.

During the night of April 12, 1909, several units of the First Army mutinied in their barracks, bound, imprisoned, or shot their officers, swarmed across the Galata Bridge, and from dawn onwards massed in the square of Santa Sophia, before the Chamber of Deputies. The procession was swelled, as it advanced, by other units, including even the Committee's own troops from Salonika, turning renegade, and by groups of theological students and white-turbaned *hojas* who harangued the men and inflamed their staccato cries of "We want the *sheriat!* We want the holy law!" Clamouring for the ejection of the president of the Chamber, the abolition of the Committee, the resignation of the government, and the appointment of a new one, the counterrevolutionaries swarmed into the Parliament building itself, from which the members of the Committee had fled into hiding. From the public galleries they listened, with some impatience and an occasional sarcastic interjection, to a rambling debate, the upshot of which was a decision to present their demands to the Sultan. It was not until the evening that Abdul Hamid finally made up his mind to appoint a new Grand Vizier. He chose Tevfik Pasha, a man of reasonably constitutional sympathies. At the news, given out by the new War Minister in a voice somewhat stifled by the fact that he had just suffered a slight stroke, the troops dispersed with joyous salvoes of rifle fire, happy to have held Constantinople in their power for a day.

This was not, however, to save Abdul Hamid's throne. The reaction from Salonika was sharp and swift. A meeting of the Committee decided on immediate military intervention and entrusted Mahmud Shevket, a competent general, with the command of a striking force for the purpose. Mustafa Kemal sat silent and morose at the meeting. His achievements in Tripoli had brought him little recognition from the

Committee, far less a promotion, and he was still only an adjutant major of insignificant status. Bitterly he foresaw another triumph for Enver, who had hurried back from his post as military attaché in Berlin to play his part in the operation.

For the first time, however, Kemal was given a chance to show his capacities as a staff officer. He was appointed chief of staff of a division —and at first in effect of the force itself—under Mahmud Shevket. He set to work with thoroughness and vigour to help plan the advance. It was partly on his suggestion that the force was named the Army of Liberation. Its staff work, discipline, morale, and rapidity of movement were a credit to the Young Turk officers and to the German mission which had helped to train them. Within a week the army had encircled Constantinople on the landward side, establishing its headquarters at San Stefano, just outside the walls of the city, while the circle was completed to seaward by a ring of warships whose crews had declared for the Committee. A deputation from Parliament, which came to assure Mahmud Shevket of the uselessness of his journey, met only with expressions of polite dissent.

The army had been joined by a number of prominent Committee members, including deputies who had been in hiding since the events of the previous week. Before entering the city they met with the officers in a "National Council" to decide what to do with the Sultan. All were in favour of his deposition; a band of hotheads called for his execution. The meeting decided on his deposition and replacement by his brother and heir apparent. The officers did not, however, show their hand publicly for fear of alarming the population of Constantinople and perhaps causing disaffection among their own troops.

Shevket issued a proclamation designed to tranquilize the city. It promised punishment to the mutineers and protection to the civil population. Kemal, one of whose tasks had been the drafting of Shevket's telegrams, had a hand in its composition. A naval officer named Hussein Rauf met him in the telegraph office, seeing him as a quiet young officer with a pale face and a tired expression. With a cloak over his shoulders, he was writing out orders to the dictation of Shevket, who sat in an armchair beside him. Jemal Pasha, the Minister of Marine, planning naval co-ordination, introduced them. It was a significant meeting, for Rauf was destined to become one of Kemal's closest friends and supporters.

During the night the liberating troops began to infiltrate silently into the city. After a morning of street fighting and a siege of the two principal barracks Constantinople was theirs. A number of ringleaders of the mutiny were publicly hanged on the Galata Bridge. But Shevket's promise was kept, and no civilians were intentionally molested, though *The Times* correspondent was shown a corpse in the gutter which he was assured by a Greek was that of *The Times* correspondent.[1]

The Committee had determined that the deposition of the Sultan should be carried out strictly in legal form, according to the principles of the *sheriat*. Parliament was summoned and a reluctant Sheikh of Islam induced to promulgate a religious decree which entitled it to depose him. Thus Abdul Hamid was deposed by a unanimous vote, and a deputation was sent to Yildiz to break the news to him. The Sultan replied, "This is kismet," then enquired whether his life would be spared. This was a question which the delegation had not the authority to answer. In a voice of fury he cried, "May the curse of God rest on those who have caused this calamity!" His small grandson then burst into tears and the deputation took its leave. In the evening officers came to escort him to the station, where a special train had been prepared for his departure. On learning that his place of exile was to be Salonika, the source of all his woes, Abdul Hamid fainted in the arms of his chief eunuch.

Meanwhile his younger brother, a timid delicate old man named Mehmed Reshad, was released from the palace where he had been imprisoned by Abdul Hamid for the past thirty years to ascend the throne. Proceeding by boat down the Bosporus to the ceremony of accession, the new Sultan turned white with fear at the sound of gunfire. He was informed that this was the start of the traditional salute of a hundred and one guns, fired in his honour. But the colour came back into his cheeks only as he landed to cries of "Long live the Sultan!" He was proclaimed Sultan and Caliph Mehmed V.

The counterrevolution had been broken. The Committee had survived. But clearly all was not well with its conduct of affairs. Externally it had failed to resist an intensified foreign pressure. Internally it had failed to establish a securely based political structure. Kemal and a small group of brother officers in Shevket's force were convinced of the reason why. It was the association of the army with politics. These were the views of Hussein Rauf, who now again met Kemal at Shevket's headquarters and discussed the situation with him at length. Rauf was a man with a profound respect for British democratic institutions, acquired while visiting Britain in the course of his naval duties. He contended with Kemal that the Unionist leaders, instead of basing their actions on

[1] Philip Graves, *Briton and Turk.*

the consent of a freely elected Parliament, had based them on force, on the support of the army. This was a policy disastrous not only to the constitutional regime, whose task was to regenerate the country, but to the army itself, whose task was to protect it. The official post-mortem confirmed these views. A court of enquiry, appointed to investigate the revolt, attributed it to the fact that a number of influential officers had neglected their military duties to engage in the insidious pursuit of politics.

The ideas of Kemal and Rauf were shared by another young officer, Kiazim Karabekir, who had been expressing them even before the Revolution of 1908. Also a supporter was Ismet (later Ismet İnönü), an officer of some education and a product likewise of the military schools, three years junior to Kemal, who had been impressed by Ismet's personality and had watched his career with respect. Ismet had been working for the Revolution with the Second Army in Adrianople, as Kemal had been working for it with the Third in Salonika. He had been in personal touch both with Fethi in Salonika and with one Dr. Nazim who had been working on the officers in Smyrna. He had the support of another officer at his headquarters named Refet, a lively young man who had been in charge of the rail transport for the striking force. Thus there now arose in the armed forces a small but active group of patriotic young officers—Kemal, Fethi, Rauf, Ismet, Kiazim Karabekir, Refet, Ali Fuad, Tevfik Rüştü, an army doctor and some others—who openly disapproved, not indeed of the regime, but of its methods, and who were to be regarded henceforward with growing suspicion by Enver and the Committee of Union and Progress.

Kemal had put forward their views to members of the Committee but they refused to listen to him. They suspected his motives—not without reason in view of his own clear ambition to play both the politician and the soldier. But in fact he was not wholly disingenuous. He knew well that, at this stage in the Revolution, only the support of the army could give it the necessary cohesion and force; for in effect no other organized parties yet existed. Thus the army need not be in practice—much as it might be in theory—harmful to politics. But politics could indubitably be harmful to the army, as the recent events had proved. As a soldier and a patriot, he sincerely felt this threat to its future and thus to the future of the country in its increasingly precarious position.

Three months after the "liberation" of Constantinople the party of Union and Progress held its annual congress in Salonika. Mustafa Kemal, sitting as its delegate for Tripoli, made his first public appearance in politics, acting as spokesman for his group of companions. He attracted the momentary attention of his fellow delegates by the unwelcome argument that, if Empire and Constitution were to be preserved, they needed not a military party but a strong army on the one hand and a strong party on the other. The officer, he argued, who tried to serve two masters became at once a bad soldier and a bad politician. He neglected his military duties—hence the counterrevolution. He remained out to touch with the population—hence political disorders and general discontent. The country was losing both ways. For this the remedy was obvious. Army officers must be called upon to decide whether to remain in the party and resign from the army, or to remain in the army and resign from the party. Then a law prohibiting officers from belonging to any political organization should be passed.

The logic of Kemal's thesis and his forceful exposition of it won him some supporters at the congress. All he achieved, however, was the despatch of two delegates to sound out the opinion of the Second Army in Adrianople. Despite emphatic confirmation of Kemal's views from Ismet, the resolution failed to obtain a majority. Agreeing with its terms, a few officers withdrew from the army while others withdrew from the party. But army and party had grown so close together that it was impossible effectively to break the connection. It obstinately prevailed at the higher levels in particular. In the previous year Enver had himself made the gesture of withdrawing from politics to become military attaché in Berlin. But he was hardly disposed to do so again just after a counterrevolution. Joint military and political power was needed to secure control of the masses, whom he now had cause to fear. Only time was to prove Kemal right and to justify his subsequent comment, "If my proposition had been followed, many later calamities would have been avoided."

Meanwhile the party bosses, for whom Kemal had hitherto been merely a nuisance, now saw him as a danger, and the *komitajis* were brought into action. A party member was detailed to dispose of him and called at his office for the ostensible purpose of discussing the question which he had raised at the congress. Kemal suspected the man's manner and, as he spoke casually, took a revolver from his drawer and laid it on the desk by his side. Then he dealt equably with the young officer's questions. The combination of Kemal's own forcible eloquence with that of the revolver drew from the man the confession that he had intended to kill Kemal but had now changed his mind. Kemal's boast, with regard to this and two subsequent attempts, was: "I am my own policeman."

His policeman on the second occasion was in fact his chosen assassin. This was one Yakub Jemil, who in the past had performed similar services for the party but who chanced to have a respect for Kemal. He not only refused the assignment but secretly warned Kemal, who then took extra measures for his protection while walking in the streets after dark. One night, realizing he was being followed, he retreated into a doorway with his back to the wall and waited, gun in hand, for his would-be assailant. But the man, whom he recognized as an uncle of Enver, passed by, pretending not to see him, and Kemal let him go.

6 ► *The maturing staff officer*

Kemal now suited his actions to his principles by withdrawing from politics and immersing himself in his military duties. The government was committed to army reforms and, with the enemy at the gates and within them, there was much to be done. Basically this was a matter of the education of other officers, most of whom had yet to learn the principles of commanding men and the techniques of modern warfare as taught in the military schools. Kemal was attached to the Training Command of the Third Army and he plunged with energy into his allotted task of instruction. He had criticized outspokenly the out-of-date system of training which still prevailed, and in doing so had annoyed some of the older officers. Now they sat back to see how this talkative and swollen-headed young man would fare at a practical task.[1] Thanks to his aptitude for teaching, his lectures soon won him the respect of his own

[1] He expressed to his friends his scorn for these seniors, maintaining that in this new army no officer above the rank of major was qualified to command. Jokingly, he added that if he had his way he would preserve only the register of officers up to that rank and destroy the earlier records, so that when the colonels and upwards came for their salaries at the beginning of the month they would be told, "Sir, your name is not on the books. We do not know you."

officers. He also surprised them by the fact that, however late he had been up talking and drinking the night before, he was usually the first to arrive at headquarters each morning.

As a patriot Kemal deeply resented the German officers whom Abdul Hamid had introduced to train the Turkish Army. As a professional soldier, however, he was ready to appreciate their worth, for he respected soldiery as a science whether it was practiced by his friends or by his enemies. He had indeed translated into Turkish a work by a former director of the Berlin Military Academy, General Litzman, dealing with platoon and company combat drill, and now published part of it as a supplement to a revised Turkish Infantry Training Manual, with the addition of a preface stressing the problems presented to troops through the sudden but necessary replacement of an old system of tactical instruction by a new one.

Army manoeuvres, discontinued by Abdul Hamid, were now revived, and in August 1909 Kemal was attached to the army chief of staff for the inspection of training exercises near Köprulu. It was a military gathering such as had not been seen for years—the muster for manoeuvres of a whole cavalry brigade, in the presence of the army commanders and chiefs of staff. To Kemal it was the real start of the long-desired soldier's life. One day he learned that the German Marshal von der Goltz, the respected head of the German military mission, was due to visit Salonika to command an exercise in the field. Kemal resolved to prepare a scheme for him in advance. The senior officers were shocked by such presumption.

"The marshal comes here to give us lessons," they protested, "not to take lessons from us."

Kemal agreed that it was important to profit from the knowledge of so great a master of the military art. But it was just as important for the Turkish General Staff to show the marshal that they had ideas of their own as to how their native land should be defended. Moreover, it would be courteous to save him trouble; and in any case he was perfectly free to reject the scheme and impose his own, if he wished.

In fact the marshal, on his arrival, was shown the scheme and decided to carry it out. The terrain chosen for the exercise was in an area unfamiliar to him but well known to Kemal from his journeys on the railway. The marshal kept the young officer at his side throughout the operation and sought his advice. After hearing Von der Goltz's final criticisms Kemal, glowing with self-confidence, became convinced that he was as good a soldier as the marshal himself. These manoeuvres in the open country became more and more frequent, and he now invariably took a lead in them. They gave him valuable experience and built up for him a military reputation out of proportion to his adjutant major's rank.

As a tactician he would act as though he himself were conducting a battle, making his own plan of campaign, writing down in advance the orders that he would give and comparing them with those that were actually given. As a strategist he would submit plans to General Rabe, a leading German expert, studying his answers with care, and with gratification when their two minds thought alike. As an instructor, summing up the results of an exercise, he was stimulating, lucid, ruthless in analysis. He was strict with his juniors, reprimanding them for inattention to detail—for reading maps incorrectly, for failing to consult their watches, for making those minor mistakes and omissions which can lead to major disasters in warfare. He gave them the will to excel, and they admired him accordingly.

But he continued to annoy senior officers—especially by his outspoken reports, written and otherwise, on staff work and military exercises. Regarding him as a theorist who might easily fail as a commander of troops in battle, they removed him from his staff post and put him in command of an infantry regiment. His rank was low for such a command, and they doubtless hoped that, given this rope, he would hang himself. But he proved just as able to command troops in the field as to instruct officers at headquarters.

As the process of disintegration in Rumeli continued, a revolt broke out in Albania, and here he saw active service. Mahmud Shevket took over the command and chose Kemal, whose service he had valued in the Liberation Army, as his chief of staff. It was in this campaign that Kemal first met Colonel Fevzi Bey, another picked officer who was to become one of his group of adherents. Kemal carefully weighed the position and drew up a tactical plan for the capture of a vital pass, which Shevket accepted and which proved so effective that it was taken, as Kemal afterwards boasted, without a single Turkish soldier "even bleeding at the nose." Thus the revolt was crushed and his reputation rose once more. But this merely intensified the jealousy of his rivals; it did not bring him promotion. Personal feuds riddled this close bureaucratic world of the Ottoman Army; and Kemal remained an adjutant major.

At a garrison dinner in Salonika, to celebrate the success of the operation, the German Colonel von Anderten raised his glass to the Ottoman Army, which had crushed the revolt. After the toast had been drunk

Kemal rose to his feet and subjected the company to a long display of rhetoric, ironically deflating their heroics. As a Turkish officer he could not drink to so small an event as the subjection of Albania, a place within the Turkish borders. But the time would come, he assured his audience, when the Turkish, not the Ottoman, Army would save the independence of the Turkish nation.

The Turkish Army, Kemal afterwards maintained to the German colonel, would accomplish its duty only when it saved the country not simply from the enemy but from fanaticism and tyranny of thought. The real problem of Turkey was its backwardness compared with the Western world, and the need to bring the Turks up to the level of contemporary civilization.

That autumn Kemal was made a member of the Turkish delegation which visited France for the manoeuvres of the French Army in Picardy. This was his first visit to western Europe. He prepared for it by fitting himself out, in Salonika, with a suit of what he took to be Western clothes, and a soft hat to wear when he had crossed the frontier. The officer with whom he was travelling kept on his fez, regarding it still as a symbol of Turkish prestige in those parts. But as he leaned out of the window at Belgrade a Serbian boy, selling fruit, shouted contemptuously, "*Tuh! Turkos!*" Kemal's Western costume, however, was not a success. On greeting him Fethi, now military attaché in Paris, burst out laughing. "What's this getup?" he enquired. The suit was dark green and the hat had a jaunty Tyrolean air to it. On Fethi's advice both were at once laid aside and clothes more in line with the Parisian style procured.

In uniform Kemal and the rest wore the kalpak, the cap shaped like a fez but made of fleece instead of felt, less cylindrical in aspect and moreover brown instead of red in colour, which was now regulation headgear for Turkish officers. This singled the Turkish delegation out from the others, giving them, in the eyes of the French officers, a faintly absurd *opéra bouffe* air. Kemal soon became aware that, at the conferences which accompanied the manoeuvres, he and his brother officers were not taken altogether seriously by the foreigners. Yet despite their stylishness he was able to discern certain flaws in their military science. He liked to consider himself inferior to no European, and it mortified him thus to be regarded askance, to be placed at a disadvantage not merely by his kalpak but by his halting French. Generally he was content to observe and absorb in a watchful, baleful silence, to form his own judgments as to the calibre of this modern Western army, the first he had seen. But at times he felt an urge to break his silence, to express ideas which he thought better than those of the rest.

One day he primed himself with cognac and, during a conference over a map on the next day's operational plan, broke out impertinently with a contradictory plan of his own, holding forth to the assembled staff officers on the need to change the agreed point of attack. They looked upon him with a certain disdain mingled with irritation at his patronizing, hectoring manner of speech. But next day he was proved right, as a high-ranking foreign officer admitted to him: "Your point of view was more correct than that of the others. But why," he added in jest, "do you wear that funny thing on your head? As long as you have it, you are never going to be given credit for your views."

At least Kemal made a good impression on the leader of his own delegation, who saw in him a clearheaded officer and listened with attention to his schemes. Back in Salonika, however, he fell into periodic moods of discouragement. There was still no talk of promotion. One evening he said to a friend who had come to fetch him from his office, "I have decided to resign from the army." As they walked together to the White Tower, Kemal reiterated angrily, "I can't continue with these people. I can't get on with them." But after an hour or so of drinking and talking he had changed his mind.

Politically he felt equally frustrated. For though he had withdrawn from active participation in the affairs of the Committee his ultimate ambition, as it had now crystallized, was for political power. At midnight sessions in the cafés he began to boast in his cups of the day when power would be his and to confer, right and left, government posts on the friends around him. Fethi would be his ambassador-at-large, Tevfik Rüştü his Minister of Foreign Affairs, Kiazim his Minister of War, a friend Nuri his Prime Minister. There were to be posts for all.

"But how about you yourself?"

"I shall be the man," he answered darkly, "who will be able to appoint you to all these posts." Fethi laughingly took to calling him Mustafa the drunken Sultan.

Kemal felt in himself that he would be great. Yet he had few illusions about greatness. One night, not long after the march on Constantinople, he went into the Kristal and, finding the main café full, moved to a smoke-filled room upstairs. Here he joined some friends who were drinking raki and beer and holding forth, with patriotic bombast, about the Revolution and the need for great men to carry it through with success. Kemal listened to their talk, knowing that each dreamed of himself as the great man his country was seeking. But what were the true qualities of greatness?

"I should like to be a man like Jemal," said one, naming the major who now dominated the party with Enver and Talat.

The others agreed. They turned to Kemal for his opinion, but he refused to be drawn, giving them a cold silent look which they took, not incorrectly, for a belief in his own superior qualities. Two views emerged from the discussion which followed. One was that a man must be born great if he was to save his country. The other was that only action could achieve greatness. A man must save his country first—and even when he had done so there should be no talk of greatness. The second view was Kemal's.

A few days later he chanced to leave his office with Jemal, to go in the tram to the Olympos Hotel. Jemal showed him an anonymous article from a Salonika newspaper which Kemal read and dismissed as mere journalistic scribbling. Jemal revealed that he had written it. This prompted Kemal to deliver a homily on the subject of greatness. It was a shortsighted policy to seek the applause of the populace. "Greatness consists," he said, "in deciding only what is necessary for the welfare of the country, and making straight for the goal. . . . In the belief that you are not great, but small and weak, and expecting no help to reach you from any quarter, you will in the end surmount all hindrances. And if any man, after that, calls you great, you will simply laugh in his face."

This was not the kind of lecture to which Jemal was accustomed. It reflected Kemal's genuine mistrust of heroics. He was a realist who thought in terms not of gestures but of action, thoughtfully conceived, scientifically planned, and systematically executed. Too many of those whom he saw around him, who were pretending to govern the country, were men of words, of undigested feelings and vague ideas. The oriental mind, that of the "men of the present," thrived on abstractions and their emotional impact. The Western mind, that of the "men of the future," rested on practical conceptions translated into action.

It was not merely the oriental mind but the oriental method that aroused his mistrust. The Committee of Union and Progress, as he saw it, was not a party in the Western sense of the word. It was simply a series of decentralized committees, scattered over the various provinces of the Empire, and but loosely linked together, without proper co-ordination or central control. It had no leader, only a changing series of leaders. Moreover, it was saturated with the oriental spirit of secrecy and intrigue.

It was still an underground organization, which took its decisions behind closed doors with all the abracadabra of the secret society, in which conspiracy flourished, rivalry was rife in the paying off of personal scores, and power was abused through the informer, the plotter, and the political assassin.

All this went thoroughly against the grain with Kemal. There was nothing he abominated more than "political murders at street corners." In mind and method he was a Westerner, neither born nor made but by deep-seated instinct. He realized that only in the West was there a constructive spirit capable of moulding the societies of the future. He detested the shifts and evasions of the oblique approach to oriental politics, the circumlocutions and imprecisions of its thought and speech. He liked to speak his mind directly, to call spades spades. His outspokenness indeed not only infuriated his enemies but, on occasion, embarrassed his friends.

Kemal differed from previous Turkish reformers in that his vision of change was, at this stage, essentially in terms not of law and administration—as that of the Tanzimat had been—but of politics. He wanted to change the political structure of the country, to rouse the people to a new conception of popular sovereignty, such as had been born with the French Revolution and was now growing to maturity in the various countries of western Europe. This would take time to achieve, and he understood the reason why. It lay in Islam. It was the forces of religion that would hold back democracy. Islam stood for authority, not discussion, for submission, not freedom of thought. The roundabout habits of mind and method which Kemal abhorred were habits inherent in the Moslem mentality. To him political reform meant, in the first place, religious reform.

Since childhood, in defiant reaction against his mother's beliefs and devotional practices, he had been developing subconsciously into an agnostic. Now his disbelief was conscious and militant. It was shared by Fethi, whose agnosticism was sealed by an association with the Freemasons. But by both it must remain unacknowledged, except to each other. In public Kemal still had to tread warily, conforming outwardly to the traditions of Islam, mentioning the unmentionable only in the company of his most intimate friends.

For he had not only the extremists, the illiterate masses, to contend with. The bulk of his own associates, the literate elite, were still religious conformists who had carried out their Revolution within the framework of Islam. The reactionaries might cry against their officers as godless. But they were in fact good Moslems, to whom Kemal was the godless one. He drank, he sought to shock, he was promiscuous with women, he scorned moral principles. He was a social *arriviste* who offended against the conventions of the decent middle-class Moslems which they smugly saw themselves to be. It was this, as much as his political views and military ambitions, that caused them to side against him.

Nonetheless some of the young men of the day had begun to turn away from Islam as a political, as distinct from a religious, force. In its place was arising a new concept of nationalism, which put race before religion and saw Turks, for the first time, as Turks. Hitherto the name of Turk had been used, even among Turks themselves, as a term of contempt applicable only to the more menial strata of the Anatolian peasantry. There was even a certain conscious irony in the coining by Kemal, years later, of the patriotic phrase, "Happy is the man who calls himself a Turk." But now the name was acquiring a new and more noble significance. Young Turks, in their search for fresh roots, began to reach back to a racial past in the Central Asian steppes. Here, where they were Turks before they were Ottomans and Moslems, they would surely find a common social and cultural heritage on which to build a common future.

A professor with such ideas had arisen to fulfil their need. He was Ziya Gökalp, who taught philosophy and the new science of sociology in a secondary school in Salonika. A prominent member of the Committee of Union and Progress, he had made his mark, more as an intellectual than as a practical force, in that same party congress of 1909 at which Kemal first attracted attention. His nationalist ideas first followed the path of Pan-Turanism, a movement which had grown up among the minorities in Russia as a retort to Pan-Slavism, and which aspired to unite all the Turks in the world, whether within the frontiers of Turkey or beyond them. Enver, a man of misty aspirations with a vague taste for universal brotherhood, religious or social, subscribed to this thesis. But as time went on it came to seem an impractical dream, and Ziya modified his ideas to a form of Pan-Turkism, embracing only the Turks within the Empire itself.

This strange-looking little scholar with the shy ways, the faraway eyes, and a scar on his forehead like the sign of the Cross (in his youth he had tried to shoot himself in a mood of despair), struck an incongruous note among the groups of stalwart young officers drinking and talking in the Salonika cafés. But they treated his ideas with respect and began, under his influence, to develop in themselves a new

sense of "Turkishness." There was nonetheless a certain difference of
intellectual outlook between Ziya, who favoured a return to the pre-
Moslem Turkish customs, and Kemal, who favoured those of the West.
In this respect Kemal was more in sympathy with the ideas of another
intellectual of the time, Tevfik Fikret, who sought to make the Turkish
reader familiar with the social and cultural life of Europe, and especially
of France; and later with those of Abdullah Jevdet, who held that "There
is no second civilization; civilization means European civilization, and it
must be imported with both its roses and its thorns."

Kemal could not keep clear of politics. His circle of friends had assumed the complexion of a political splinter group. Now he began to
hold regular meetings of his regimental officers for tactical discussions.
They too acquired, in the eyes of his seniors, a political significance. The
agents of the Committee reported on him to Constantinople. On the
instructions of Mahmud Shevket, now Minister of War, Kemal relinquished the command of his regiment and was posted to the capital,
where he was employed under close supervision in the offices of the
General Staff.

But he did not remain there for long. For in the summer of 1911 the
international situation took a new turn. Attention shifted from the imperialist activities of Austria and Russia in the Balkans to those of Germany, pursued hotfoot by Britain and France, on the African continent.
The "Panther's Spring" of the Germans to Agadir in Morocco, with its
threat of war, led to the conclusion of a Franco-German agreement, conceding Morocco to France and a small portion of the Congo to Germany.
This brought Italy onto the imperialist stage. If there was to be a scram-
ble for North Africa, she was not to be left out of it. She announced her
decision to take over the neglected Turkish provinces of Tripoli and
Cyrenaica, provoked a war with Turkey, and occupied Tripoli and Benghazi.

Here was a new chance for Enver to play the role of the chivalrous
hero that became him so well, this time in the guise of a crusader of Islam. Tripolitania could not be allowed to go by default, as so many of
the Balkan provinces and Crete had done. Too much face would thereby
be lost with the Moslem world. He left for North Africa, with a fervent
band of young officers, to form a defence force.

Mustafa Kemal had misgivings about the wisdom of the campaign. He
was acutely aware of the greater danger to come in the Balkans. His
comrades took things as they came, not seeming to grasp, as he did, that

the invasion of Tripolitania was simply one more step towards the ultimate liquidation of the Ottoman Empire, and that this process could
only be arrested nearer home. But he could hardly go against the tide of
public feeling; to win laurels in the field might help his position in the
party; and his movements were in any case hamstrung here in Constantinople under Mahmud Shevket's eye. Besides, he could not allow himself
to be left behind by Enver.

He thus sailed to join Enver, travelling with false papers in the civilian
guise of a newspaper reporter and taking with him his friend Ömer
Naji, the poet, who had now blossomed into a prize orator of the Union
and Progress party. Rather to Kemal's embarrassment, two other party
members joined them, one of them Yakub Jemil, who had been his destined assassin and whose company on such an enterprise he would not
himself have chosen.

Before leaving, he left his close friend and subsequent A.D.C., Salih
(Bozok), in charge of affairs at home, giving him money for Zübeyde but
instructing him not to tell her, meanwhile, where he had gone. From the
ship he wrote to Salih: "Give my best greetings to our friends in the regiment. The drill programme which we prepared together has produced excellent results. See that they don't get tired and give up. Nothing will ever
be done if they go on with their past laziness."

7 ▶ *The Tripolitanian War*

The North African front fell into two sectors—that of Tripolitania in the west, to which Fethi was hurrying from Paris; and that of Cyrenaica in the east, for which Kemal was bound. To reach it he had to pass through Egypt; and Egypt, being in the hands of Great Britain, was neutral. Turkish officers and troops were not permitted to traverse the country on their way to the war, so Enver and the rest had to move warily to avoid identification. One day a shopkeeper with a Salonika accent enquired of Enver: "You Enver Bey?" To this he replied coolly, "I wish I were," and completed his purchases without further questions.

Kemal cut a more conspicuous figure in the Cairo streets. Fair and striking, with an erect military carriage, it should have been easy enough to guess that he was a Turkish officer. He obtained an audience with the Khedive, Abbas Hilmi, who took a personal interest in his enterprise and promised him moral support. He requested extra funds and reinforcements of officers from Constantinople, and recruited locally some volunteers from among the Senusi Arabs, to send to Benghazi. He assumed the disguise of an Arab and left as soon as he could for the Western Desert, joined by two friends from Salonika who, posing as law students, had joined him at his request in Alexandria.

They reached the desert railhead in the company of three others, a Turkish gunner, an Arab interpreter, and an Egyptian guide. An Egyptian officer searched the train, divulging that he had instructions to arrest five Turkish officers on board it. Kemal, realizing that their Arab disguises would not deceive the officer, revealed their identity and harangued the Egyptian with an appeal to his religious sentiments. This was a holy war, he urged, against the infidel Christians. Surely the officer, as a good Moslem, would not stand in the way of the will of Allah, setting himself against the principles of the Prophet and the sacred Book.

Seduced by the eloquent flow of words, the officer agreed to a compromise. He allowed the three Turkish officers to proceed but insisted on holding their companions while he asked for instructions. One of them could probably be passed off to his superiors as Mustafa Kemal. Next day all but the Turkish gunner were released.

The party proceeded to a camp beyond the railhead, which the Egyptian "underground" had organized with notable efficiency. Pack camels were available for them, horses, stores, waterskins—all they were likely to need except a medicine chest, and this they had brought with them. One night, after riding for a week through the heart of the desert, they reached what they took to be the frontier and put damp cloths over the mouths of the camels to stifle their barks. They pitched camp, removed their Arab clothes, put on Turkish uniforms, and took out guns from their place of concealment. But a detachment of soldiers, with British and Egyptian officers, arrived and barred their progress.

Kemal again played the spokesman. This was Ottoman territory, he declared in a threatening manner. They had no business to be trespassing here. They replied that the frontier had lately been changed and that this was in fact Egyptian territory. Kemal maintained his truculent attitude and gave them an ultimatum to withdraw at once. Otherwise he and his party would fire. The British officers laughed at the discrepancy between their numbers but shrugged their shoulders and let them go. Two days later they reached the Turkish encampment on the outskirts of Tobruk.

The Italians had quickly occupied Tripoli, Benghazi, and the other Libyan ports. At Tobruk, with its surrounding heights, they had made a sound defensive position. The Turks were encamped to the west of the town. They had only a small garrison force of Turkish troops and depended on the support of the Senusi Arab tribesmen, of whose loyalty,

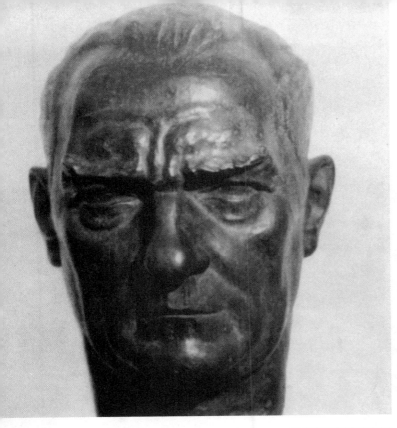

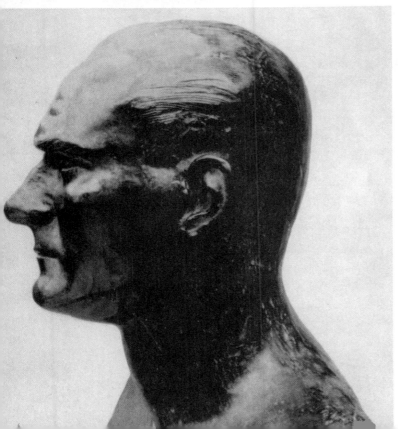

1. & 2. Bust of Kemal Ata-türk

3. Major Mustafa
Kemal, General Staff,
Salonika

4. His mother, Zübeyde

5. Mustafa Kemal at the Sivas Congress, 1919, with (left to right) Refet, Rauf and Bekir Sami

6. In Smyrna after his victory, 1922, with Fevzi

7. Mustafa Kemal as Commander-in-Chief, with Ismet, at a parade in Ankara before the final offensive, 1922

8. A pause on the Western front, 1921

9.–12. Mustafa Kemal in various roles: *(above left)* as an Arab Sheikh in Egypt, on the way to the Tripolitanian front, 1912; *(above right)* the man of the world; *(below left)* the countryman; *(below right)* as a Janissary at a masked ball in Sofia, 1913

13.–15. Mustafa Kemal: *(above)* receiving a petition in the train between Ankara and Istanbul, 1930; *(below left)* with Latife, his wife, on a journey in 1924; *(below right)* teaching the new alphabet in the park at Gülhane (Istanbul), 1928

16. Kemal Atatürk, President of the Turkish Republic

17. Mustafa Kemal, victor in the War of Independence

18. Kemal Atatürk in his last years at Florya, with his adopted daughter, Ulkü

despite the efforts of Enver, they were not entirely sure. He had been distributing gold to them, arraying himself in the robes of a sheikh and inviting their homage in a finely caparisoned tent. But they remained reluctant to fight.

Not to be outdone, Kemal donned a similar costume, which he found became him, and which he later enjoyed flaunting in the streets of Cairo. But his was a more down-to-earth military approach. Having reconnoitred the fortifications on horseback, he called a meeting of sheikhs and tribesmen. They proved a rough lot, armed for the most part with obsolete rifles and clubs. Summoning Sheikh Mebre, who controlled the rest, Kemal addressed him as a "brother in religion" and exhorted him to fight the holy war against the invading infidel. He proposed a night attack on a lightly defended position, east of Tobruk. But the sheikh was not to be roused so easily. How could his people fight, he protested, with only sticks for weapons? Kemal took out a notebook and pretended to consult it. Then he said, "Now I realize who you are, Sheikh Mebre. They told me about you in Egypt. You are a leading spy in the pay of the Italians. I came here to talk not to Italian spies but to Arabs ready to fight for their own land. Further talk is useless. I shall give my support to other tribes who are better armed and equipped."

The stratagem succeeded. Next day the sheikh declared that he would launch an attack with his own tribe alone, scorning the help of the rest. After some rifles had been distributed to the tribesmen and they had learnt how to use them, the attack took place at dawn and proved successful. Some seventy guns were destroyed or captured, and two hundred Italian prisoners were brought back to the Turkish camp, happy enough—as in subsequent desert campaigns—not to have to continue the fight. They were let loose in the desert to find their way home or across the Egyptian frontier as best they could.

It was, however, impossible to capture Tobruk, impossible indeed to do more than hold the Italians within its walls, as the other fortresses strung out along the coast. The value of such a minor engagement to the Turks lay only in the fact that it obliged the Italians to bring in reinforcements, an operation which was impossible to prevent since they came by sea. This campaign indeed taught Kemal a military lesson which was to serve him well later, in the Gallipoli campaign. He became aware of the importance of the command of the sea and of the impossibility of preventing the landing of enemy troops on a shore commanded by naval artillery. Turkish naval power had virtually ceased to exist. Abdul Hamid had deliberately allowed his fleet, permanently at anchor in the Golden Horn, to rot to pieces. Meanwhile Turkish arms and supplies had to be run into Tripoli in a variety of precarious ways. This was the task of Hussein Rauf.

Rauf had at his disposal the cruiser *Hamidiye,* the only Turkish warship now outside the Dardanelles. She had been procured from America and was under the effective command of an engaging American adventurer named Bucknam Pasha. A former captain of the United States mercantile marine, he had sailed her across the Atlantic, following the refusal of the American authorities to detail a naval officer for the task. He was now empowered to collect a convenient percentage on each shipment of arms for which he was able to return a receipt. The arms were to be shipped to Syria, then transferred in boats to the North African coast. His task was aggravated when in the spring of 1912 the Italians occupied Rhodes and the neighbouring Dodecanese Islands.

Kemal meanwhile had transferred himself to Turkish headquarters in Derna, alternating between there and Tobruk until the autumn of 1912. This was the first time he had served in the field at close quarters with Enver, thus his first opportunity to judge of his rival's military capacities. Kemal was quick to see Enver's limitations. He had always respected his bravery but he now found his powers of reasoning to be disconcertingly naïve. He was prone to wishful thinking, seeing only what he wanted to see, deluding himself with dreams which had little basis in tactical or strategical reality.

To Kemal, with his hardheaded military logic, it soon became clear that this campaign had a limited scope. The Turks could not dislodge the Italians from their positions on the coast. On the other hand the Italians could not advance into a waterless hinterland, held by Arabs whose support they had failed to obtain. The result was a stalemate. Any thinking staff officer could see that the maintenance of anything more than a holding force here was a drain on Turkish man power and resources sorely required elsewhere. But Enver saw—or rather felt—things differently. He dreamt of himself, in romantic terms, as a Sultan of the Tripolitanian Arabs, with a vast expanding domain. He thus convinced himself, and in his rose-coloured reports tried to convince Constantinople, that the Italians could be dislodged from Derna and the campaign brought to a glorious conclusion. In a series of costly engagements he tried in vain to recapture it, until the ravines of the Wadi Derna were filled with corpses. A section of his officers doubted the wisdom of these tactics but dared not express their doubts. They looked instead to Kemal, whom they saw to be a commander of superior calibre.

But Kemal was in a difficult position. He realized that a breach in so small a force would have disastrous repercussions both here and at home. Open disagreement between himself and Enver must thus, at all costs, be avoided. Hence he curbed his impatience and kept the peace, maintaining with Enver relations which were reserved but polite, and trying as far as possible to curb his more reckless projects. At last he had become a full major. His promotion came through in the course of the winter. His decision to volunteer for active service had, to this extent, been rewarded. Meanwhile there had been born, in those wadis around Derna, a band of patriotic young officers bent on injecting new blood into the Revolution; as time went on, they would tend increasingly to rally around Major Mustafa Kemal.

For all the tedium of the campaign, with its indecisive engagements, Kemal wrote of it in a heroic vein to his friend Salih in Constantinople:

I have no doubt that you are pleased by the fact that some of your brothers-in-arms have crossed the Mediterranean Sea, have covered distant deserts to confront an enemy based on his fleet, and, after embracing their fellow countrymen over here have managed to keep the enemy at bay at certain points on the coast. . . . You know that what I like best in the soldier's profession is its craftmanship. If we have here enough opportunity and enough time to carry out all the requirements of this craft, then we shall be able to perform services which will please the country. Oh, Salih, God is my witness that up to now my only aspiration in life is to be a useful element within the army! I have for long been convinced that, to safeguard the country and give happiness to the people, it is necessary first of all to prove once more to the world that our army is still the old Turkish Army.

But news soon reached the officers in the field that things were not well at home. The Committee of Union and Progress was drifting into difficulties, to which the long slow drain of the war against Italy contributed. Seeking to curb opposition, it dissolved Parliament and with a "big stick election" packed a new Chamber with a vast majority of its own supporters. Thus driven underground, the Opposition took military shape. History repeated itself in reverse as a group of young officers took to the Rumeli hills, rebelling in the name of democracy against the despotism of the Committee, much as, four years before, the officers of the Committee had rebelled against that of the Sultan. In concert with a group of "saviour officers" in Stambul, they demanded the removal of the new government and the restoration of a freely elected Parliament. They also demanded, as Mustafa Kemal had unsuccessfully done, the withdrawal of the army from politics. Following a revolt in Albania, they were able to bring down the government and replace it with another, of liberal complexion. An oath was at once imposed on all serving officers not to "enter any political society, secret or public, nor interfere in any way whatsoever in the internal or external affairs of the state." From Derna Kemal wrote bitterly of the Committee's debacle to an old Comrade-in-arms, Bfhich (Frkin), in Salonika, recalling his own unheeded prophecies and adding, "With time and the march of events all truths are shown and proved."

Soon, however, the internal upheaval was to be followed by an external crisis of catastrophic proportions. In the spring of 1912, for the first and last time in their history, the Balkan peoples, with the encouragement of Russia and to the diplomatic discomfiture of Austria, smothered their differences to unite against the Turks. Serbia and Bulgaria, the one aspiring to reach the Adriatic and the other to reach the Mediterranean, signed a treaty in March 1912 which embodied a military convention aimed at Turkey. Two months later Greece joined the alliance. The iron ring around Constantinople was at last complete.

The moment had come for the *coup de grâce* to the Ottoman Empire in Europe. The King of Montenegro, who was having a flutter on the Bourse in Vienna, jumped the gun by declaring war against Turkey on October 8, 1912. Serbia, Bulgaria, and Greece joined in a few days later. At the same time Turkey signed a peace with Italy and began to evacuate Tripolitania.

Mustafa Kemal left at once for home. This time he had no trouble at the Egyptian frontier. A British officer said to him, "I know you. You're Mustafa Kemal. You may go anywhere you like in this damned country." While in Cairo he heard of the fall of Monastir to the Serbs and of his native Salonika to the Greeks. He reached Constantinople after a roundabout journey through Italy, Austria, Hungary, and Rumania.

8 ▶ *The Balkan Wars*

When Kemal reached Constantinople the first Balkan War was as good as over. All Rumeli was lost. In a *Blitzkrieg* lasting barely a month the Turks had been routed on both fronts. Their collapse was due less to inferior numbers than to the virtual absence of any supply organization, and to the inability of both officers and troops to handle the modern equipment with which the Germans had furnished them.

Macedonia had gone. Mustafa Kemal's mother and sister had fled from Salonika, abandoning their home, borne away on the tide of fleeing Moslem refugees and wounded soldiers, many thousands of whom were never to reach Constantinople alive. The ex-Sultan Abdul Hamid had been hurriedly removed on a German warship, with his thirteen wives and suite, to end his days six years later in the Beylerbey Palace on the Asiatic side of the Bosporus—occupying a back room from which he could not be tormented by views of the city.

The Greek Army marched into Salonika behind a detachment of kilted Evzones, to be pelted with roses by delirious crowds shouting, *"Zeto! Zeto!"* The blue and white Greek flag waved from the roofs and the windows. The Star and Crescent vanished forever. Meanwhile, presaging a rift in the lute which was to cause a second Balkan War, the Bulgarians followed the Greeks in with a division, commandeering houses and churches and occupying a sector of the city.

Kemal was deeply affected by the loss of the place where he had spent most of his life. Meeting some brother officers in a café in Constantinople, he joined them silently and reluctantly, with hardly a greeting. Then he burst out: "How could you do this? How could you surrender that beautiful Salonika to the enemy? How could you sell it so cheaply?" He found thousands of its Moslem inhabitants massed together in the courtyards of the mosques, ragged and destitute and dying in the cruel winter weather. Eventually he found his mother and sister. Zübeyde sat rocking to and fro, suddenly aged and broken by the loss of her home. Fikriye, an adopted member of the family, was with them. She was a niece of Zübeyde's late husband, whom Kemal had known as a child but who was now blooming into adolescence, with a promise of ripeness to come. Kemal found them a house and turned to his duties on the General Staff, where he was detailed to look after the defence of the Gallipoli Peninsula.

Troops from Anatolia and officers from Tripoli had strengthened the defences of the Chatalja lines before Constantinople, and the Bulgarians could advance no farther. Adrianople still held out stubbornly, indifferent to hunger and bombardment. But it was the *Hamidiye* and her exploits that gave a real lift to the morale of the Turkish people. Holed in her side while bombarding Varna at the outset of the war, the "phantom" cruiser had limped home to the Golden Horn, navigated to safety by Rauf, but hardly expected to see service again. Then the news came that she had slipped out through the Dardanelles, running the gantlet of the Greek fleet, and was careering around the Aegean and up the Adriatic like some privateer of an earlier age, bombarding coastal towns and islands and sinking Greek transports, but in chivalrous style saving the lives of passengers and crew to put them ashore on some deserted coast. Rauf, in his gentlemanly modesty, sought no personal recognition for these exploits but insisted on giving the credit to his own sailors, who were thus collectively applauded as popular heroes.

Now the powers, having failed to prevent the war, devoted their efforts to peacemaking. The Grand Vizier, once more Kiamil Pasha, was ready enough to cede Adrianople, together with most of Thrace. This would have left Turkey in Europe reduced to Constantinople and a narrow strip of hinterland. At this moment, however, Enver returned from Africa and won over the Committee to strong action against the cession of Adrianople. As the Cabinet deliberated on the peace terms in the brocaded and gilded council chamber of the Sublime Porte, a crowd surged up to the building, with flags in their hands. Enver, at the head of it, ran up the marble steps, followed by Talat and others. He hurried across the vast hall to the door of the chamber. It was opened by Nazim Pasha, the Minister of War, who bore much of the responsibility for the Turkish defeat. He greeted the deputation casually, with a cigarette hanging out of his mouth. He was shot dead by one of them, crying as he fell, "The dogs have done for me!"

The Grand Vizier coolly remarked, "You want the imperial seal, I suppose." He handed it over and wrote out his letter of resignation. The Sultan acceded to the demand that Mahmud Shevket be appointed Grand Vizier. Shevket proceeded to the Sublime Porte and read his letter of appointment to the crowd. A *hoja* was forced to recite a prayer. The crowd dispersed, the ministers were released, and Enver was on the threshold of supreme power.

Mustafa Kemal deplored this *coup d'état* and especially the manner of its execution. Though not above judicial murder, as he was later to prove, he abhorred political assassination. As a realist he saw the necessity for peace on the best available terms. But he had urged on his friends in the Committee that the government should first be forced to resign by constitutional means. Only if they refused to do so and to grant free elections should a *coup* be considered. And then it should at all costs be carried out without bloodshed. Such was the farsighted and civilized way of dealing with crises of this sort. But only Fethi and Kemal's own group of friends heeded him.

Meanwhile the *coup* was generally popular. The country had been saved at the last moment from an ignominious surrender. The new regime hoped to save Adrianople, which the Bulgarians, now reinforced by the Serbs, were investing with a final burst of ferocity. The General Staff favoured a period of careful preparation before action was resumed. But Enver dreamed of a spectacular operation to relieve Adrianople by outflanking the Chatalja lines with an attack from the Marmara coast, thus encircling the Bulgarian Army. Though not himself in command, he became the moving spirit of a new offensive.

Kemal had been appointed director of operations with the army corps on the Gallipoli Peninsula of which Fethi was chief of staff. It was their duty to defend the Dardanelles, hence Constantinople, against a Bulgarian breakthrough. They were now to form the spearhead of this hazardous attack, though they were strongly opposed to so speculative an operation at this crucial stage; and indeed the offensive, after an initial success, failed disastrously. Thus Adrianople surrendered to the Bulgarian Army, its fall precipitated from within the walls by a fifth column of well-fed Greeks and Bulgars who undermined the defence of the starving Turkish garrison.

At a peace conference in London, Mahmud Shevket was forced to accept the very terms which he had previously rejected as degrading. To placate public opinion, it was explained that he had ceded the city after its fall, not, as his predecessors had tried to do, while it was still holding out. Less than a fortnight later he was driving in his car from the War Ministry to the Sublime Porte when another car drew alongside and its occupant fired at him. Shevket was hit on the cheek. He was carried unconscious into the Sublime Porte, where he died half an hour later. It was an act of reprisal for the murder of Nazim.

This deed gave Enver and the Committee of Union and Progress the pretext to force a military dictatorship on the country without further pretence at constitutional methods. They hanged the principal leaders of the Opposition and established a triumvirate, consisting of Enver, Jemal, and Talat, which ruled supreme henceforth. The Young Turk Revolution, designed to defeat an autocracy, was thus to end in a party oligarchy almost as despotic as the Sultan's rule had been.

External events at once sealed its prestige. The makeshift union of the Balkan states, formed for the purpose of the war, was too artificial to survive it for long. Inevitably there were quarrels over the division of the spoils. The result was a second Balkan War, in which Bulgaria turned on the rest. The Turks marched westwards, recovering Adrianople and a large part of eastern Thrace. As the main Turkish forces were about to enter the city in a planned operation, Enver, at the head of a detachment of cavalry, outdistanced them and entered it first, thus ensuring acclaim once more as a conquering hero.

His precipitate action angered a group of staff officers concerned with the plan of campaign, among them Fethi and Mustafa Kemal. The governor of Adrianople brought them together with Enver, in a local landowner's house, to compose their differences. A journalist present, Falih Rifki, thus records the scene: "A very blond young officer was sitting on a chair in front of the divan. He was handsome and very well dressed, he had keen eyes, and he was very proud. He attracted the attention of everybody, but he did not speak much. But it was obvious that in all this he was far more important than his rank suggested." It was his first impression of Mustafa Kemal, whom he was not to encounter again until the dark days of the First World War. He sensed that the young officer was of a different stamp to some of his fellows. He was not, he remarked, of the *komitaji* type.

Thus ended the second Balkan War. By a treaty signed at Bucharest, Greece and Serbia divided most of what Bulgaria had lost, while Turkey was confirmed in the possession of Adrianople. Enver emerged supreme: he became Minister of War, he became a pasha, he married an Ottoman princess and lived like a prince in a palace on the Bosporus. As the debonair "hero of freedom" grew into the all-powerful military dictator, it began to be said, "Enver Pasha has killed Enver Bey."

Jemal was the second figure of the triumvirate. Beneath a façade of elegant manners and a tigerish charm, there lay a hard and ruthless energy which combined with a cold intelligence to make of him a capable if often brutal administrator. Talat, the third figure, was the only civilian. A burly Thracian peasant, with a ruddy complexion and gipsy eyes, educated as the sole Gentile pupil in a Jewish school and afterwards entering the Post Office, he disarmed by a frankness of manner which masked a shrewd and supple mind. Only two other men played a significant part in the government. Its figurehead was Prince Saïd Halim, a rich Egyptian prince of gentlemanly manners and liberal sentiments whom, as an older man, it suited the triumvirate to co-opt meanwhile as Grand Vizier. Its *éminence grise* was Javid, a polite little Jew (a Dönmeh) from Salonika who looked like a cock sparrow and who had charm, the gift of the gab, and a quick financial brain.

When in 1913 the British general, Sir Henry Wilson, visited the scenes of the Balkan campaigns, he met Enver and Jemal in Constantinople. Neither of them impressed him by their military capacity. No more did the other officers he met. But he made one exception: "There is a man called Mustafa Kemal," he said, "a young staff colonel. Watch him. He may go far." [1] At the moment there was little sign of it. The men who ruled Turkey did not share the British general's vision.

Kemal, at the age of thirty-two—hardly younger than Enver—had made little headway in either his military or his political career. Events were passing him by. Impatient everywhere but on the battlefield itself, he had, under a regime based on personal power, scorned to conciliate those persons who could make him or mar him. He had still to learn self-control. No dissembler, no conciliator, he displayed his ambition to command, and forced on others his conviction that he was right and all of them were wrong. This angry young man thus spread around him a

[1] *The Times*, November 11, 1938.

mistrust and resentment which discounted his patriotism and barred both his military and political progress.

In politics he now saw an opening through the appointment of Fethi to succeed Talat as secretary-general of the party. For a while he moved into Fethi's house and they discussed at length what should be done. Their antagonism to Enver had come to a head in the recent campaign, and their accusations against him continued both openly and by means of anonymous pamphlets. Fethi felt strongly, as Kemal did, that the time had come to rid the party of the *komitajis,* its Balkan terrorist instruments, but went too far in proposing a cut in the budget, by which their salaries would be stopped. Kemal warned him that such tactics would provoke the *komitajis* to conspire with his enemies against him. He was proved right. Feeling against the new secretary-general grew.

One day when he was sitting at home with Kemal, Talat was announced. He took Fethi into another room and offered him the post of minister in Sofia. Fethi thought it wise to accept. Not long afterwards Kemal was summoned by Jemal, who invited him to go to Sofia too, as military attaché for all the Balkan countries. At first he protested. But, burn as he might with frustration, he knew that he had no choice but to accept the appointment. As in 1905, on his emergence from Harbiye, this was the punishment of exile for Kemal as for Fethi.

But it was an exile that may easily have saved his life. For the *komitajis* were out for his blood once more, as they had been after his first dispute with the party. And this time they might well have succeeded in their murderous assignment.

9 ▶ *A post in Sofia*

Life in Sofia was a new and formative experience for Mustafa Kemal. For the first time he found himself living in a Western society. His visit to Paris had been brief and, moreover, occupied with military duties. Now he was introduced for the first time to the refinements of social life in a European capital. Sofia was, it is true, a mere Balkan city of no great size or distinction. But it had about it in 1913 a strong Western veneer, reflecting, in Kemal's eyes at any rate, some of that atmosphere of *douceur de vivre* which stemmed from the larger capitals of Central Europe.

Its King was the ambitious and by European reputation "foxy" Ferdinand, a Coburg prince. In the eighties, under the auspices of his predecessor, the old Turkish city with its narrow tortuous streets had been razed to the ground and rebuilt in a European style, with long straight streets and spacious boulevards. Its wooded parks and gardens, laid out in the Romantic manner, suggested those of some small German capital. Its yellow stuccoed architecture, though provincial in scale, had about it an elegant rococo air. The ladies bought their clothes in Vienna and listened to Viennese music at the opera.

When Kemal arrived in Sofia, joining Fethi as his military attaché, there was a postwar feeling in the atmosphere. The Balkan Wars were being forgiven and forgotten in a round of entertainments—*thés dansants,* dinners, receptions, balls, weekly dances at the exclusive Officers' Club where the men, handsome in their Ruritanian uniforms, at once outshone and intrigued the ladies. The Bulgarians proved anxious to fraternize with the Turks, their recent enemies. Fethi, supple in his ways and charming in his attentions to all, they saw as the Europeanized type of Turk, and he was soon a popular figure in Bulgarian society.

Kemal was always at his side, and as bachelors they often came to be invited together. Soldierlike, striking in his slim taut way, with the clipped moustache which the Young Turks had substituted for the twirling moustachios of the Sultan's officers, the young military attaché dressed well and was correct enough in his manners. But it was easy to see that he was of a different sort from his polished sophisticated friend. He liked to drink freely; he had few airs and graces; he had about him a reserve and a dark taciturnity which stamped him, in Bulgarian eyes, as the "Turkish type of Turk." Impressed by the social world, Kemal was not yet at ease in it and felt his way carefully. His Bulgarian accent, picked up during his service in the Balkans, was still rough. But as he persisted in frequenting Bulgarian circles it began to improve. Light on his feet, with a sense of rhythm from the songs of his Rumeli childhood, he danced well and, after a lesson or two, was adept at the waltz and the tango. At the weekly dances of the exclusive Officers' Club, this brought him some success with the ladies, who responded to his interesting looks and sensed in him, behind a certain gaucherie and an absence of small talk, a hint of the mystery man.

One night he was taken by a friend, Shakir Zümere, a Bulgarian Turk, to a gala performance at the opera. It was a smart social occasion, and the glitter and elegance of the audience made a deep impression on Kemal. In the interval he was presented to King Ferdinand, who asked him for his impressions. He could only reply, "Wonderful!" Afterwards the two friends took a party to supper at the Grand Hotel de Bulgarie. When their guests had left, Kemal poured out his enthusiasm to Shakir. This was Western civilization. There was nothing like it in Turkey. Constantinople had barely a theatre, far less an opera house. One of these days his country must enjoy these amenities.[1] His people must be introduced to the graces and refinements of European social life. It was with difficulty

---

[1] The plans for a new Ankara, fifteen years later, allowed for a large modern opera house.

that Shakir, tired by the evening's entertainment, could persuade him to retire to bed.

Kemal, however, had not been an entire stranger to polite society before he arrived in Sofia. While in Constantinople he had formed a liaison with Corinne, the widow of a brother officer named Ömer Lütfü. A woman of Italian origin, with some musical talent, she kept a salon in Pera and gave soirées for a variety of people at which he became a frequent guest. She set herself to "groom" him for the *beau monde,* to give him a taste for European books and music, and especially to perfect his French. In his rather stilted and ill-spelt version of the language, and occasionally in Turkish with a European script, he now began to write to her of his doings in Sofia:

I received your last letter. It gives me great pleasure to know that you think about me every day, and I thank you for giving me the news as to what we have gained as a result of the war in Africa. . . . You know that I have left the Bulgaria Hotel, where I stayed on my arrival in Sofia. Now I am living at the Splendide Palace, which has just been built. It is a really comfortable hotel. It has bathrooms, and *femmes de chambres,* in short everything you could want, and the attractions at the hotel make it worth while to stay there. But no, no, Corinne—it isn't possible to see even one beautiful woman in Sofia. I am staying at the hotel because I can't find a proper house.

We are very friendly with Jevdet Bey. I never thought I should find him so charming and such a good friend. The night before last he took me to Madame Denigi, a Parisian lady whom he had known very well for a long time. There was a personage of importance at her house. Some ministers and other gentlemen were playing baccarat. As I do not play, we left them after a few polite greetings and some small talk. Let me tell you that I did not find this Parisian lady beautiful. I think it was she herself who asked Jevdet Bey to bring me to her house. As she said good-bye, she said to me, *"Mon Commandant,* you were not amused this evening at my house, but rest assured that I shall try to please you the next time." But I am not so sure.

Later we went to a café concert called Novia Amerika. There were a lot of female singers, German, French, etc., and these ladies walked by the boxes in the hope of being invited in by gentlemen. Jevdet Bey invited two Hungarian ladies. One of them spoke German. The other, who was smaller, could not speak anything but Hungarian. I don't know why, but I didn't enjoy myself. I was bored. And, leaving the ladies alone there in the box, we left the café. When I went to bed at the hotel, it was already past midnight. . . .

Give me your news always. I embrace you with all my heart.

Corinne's reply prompted her pupil to write: "You write that my last letter had fewer faults in spelling than you expected . . . that it must have come from the pen of another. I regard this little remark as a compliment."

Later he wrote to her in more self-revealing and high-flown terms:

How happy it makes me to think that, in spite of all your highly placed friends, you still continue to remember me, and that your continual relations with all those big hats—or, if you like, all those big vegetables—leave you a moment of respite to occupy yourself with me. . . .

I have ambitions, and even very great ones; however, they do not consist in material satisfactions like holding high places and gaining large sums of money. I seek the realization of these ambitions in the success of a great idea which, while profiting my country, will give me the keen satisfaction of a duty worthily accomplished. That has been the principle of my whole life. I acquired it while I was still quite young, and I shall continue to hold it until my dying breath.

After a while Kemal found himself a house, not far from the legation, which he shared with Shakir. When it was ready the two friends gave a house-warming dinner for the Bulgarian Minister of Justice, serving caviar, with the best brand of raki, procured from Turkey, and champagne to follow. The excellence of the meal and the success of the evening came to the ears of General Kovatchev, the Minister of War, who had fought against Kemal in the second Balkan War and who, with his Macedonian wife, had already entertained the young military attaché. He made it known that he would like to be invited, with his family, to Kemal's house, and another dinner was given. This started a close friendship with the Kovatchev family.

Kemal now often went to their house, where he and the general treated one another as comrades-in-arms, exchanging military reminiscences and engaging in long discussions on the art of war. He had not at first paid much attention to the general's daughter, an attractive and accomplished young girl named Dimitrina, with a slim figure and a head of dark curls. But now he slowly became aware of her, talked to her shyly and politely, and often asked her to dance when he met her at parties.

Kemal was soon invited everywhere. He was taken up by the leading hostess of Sofia, Sultane Rasha Petroff, the wife of a general. He achieved his social apotheosis at a masked fancy-dress ball at the palace. He had sent an orderly to Constantinople to procure for him from the museum a janissary's uniform, complete with turban and jewelled sword. Resplendent in this, he created a sensation, and when the guests unmasked at midnight King Ferdinand sent for him to congratulate him and presented him with a silver cigarette case. Many years later, when Ferdinand was in exile, Kemal returned the compliment by sending him a gold one as a token of his respect for his gifts as a statesman.

Life in Sofia seemed good. Kemal, as his cultural standards advanced, had come across the old French tag, which he quoted in a letter to a friend:

La vie est brève.
Un peu de rêve,
Un peu d'amour
Et puis bon jour.

La vie est vaine.
Un peu de peine,
Un peu d'espoir
Et puis bon soir.

But life in Sofia was not all social and amatory dalliance. Kemal took his duties seriously, and these, as he and Fethi saw them, were as much political as military. He made it his business to get to know the country, and especially to establish contact with its influential Turkish minority. With Shakir he toured around the Turkish districts and became impressed by the superior standard of living of his countrymen in this foreign land. In Bulgaria the Turks engaged freely and successfully in commerce, as in Turkey only foreigners were able to do. They ran their own industries, at Pleven and elsewhere. Many of them had made fortunes. Their women were more emancipated than those of the Fatherland, and many had discarded the veil. Everywhere there were schools such as had yet to be introduced into Turkey itself. Kemal began to form in his mind a concrete picture of the way of life to which his own people in his own land could and must be helped to rise.

In his tours he began also to appreciate the sturdy qualities of the peasant. One day in Sofia he was sitting in a fashionable café at the hour of the *thé dansant,* listening to the orchestra, when a Bulgarian wearing peasant clothes came in and sat down at the next table. He called several times for the waiter, who first disregarded him and then refused to serve him. Finally the proprietor told him to leave. The peasant refused, saying, "How dare you throw me out of this place? Bulgaria lives by my labour. Bulgaria is defended by my rifle." A policeman was called, who took his side, and the peasant was served with tea and cakes, for which he was well able to pay. Kemal, recounting the incident afterwards, added, "That's how I want the Turkish peasant to be. As long as the peasant is not master of the country there can be no real progress in Turkey." Thus germinated a Kemalist slogan of the future: "The peasant is the master of this country."

He now also acquired useful firsthand experience of the workings of a parliamentary regime. Shakir was a member of Parliament, one of the small group of seventeen Turkish deputies who had an influence out of proportion to their numbers in the confused deliberations of this multi-party assembly, holding a balance and sometimes turning the scale with their votes. Night after night Kemal would sit in the gallery, concentrating on the debates with deep attention, studying in detail, for his own future advantage, the political tactics of a Parliament, much as he would study the military tactics of the battlefield. Here, however, he had a more direct and immediate objective. It seemed possible, through the Turkish minority, so to manipulate the political machine as to influence it in favour of his country's policy.

First the mass of the Bulgarian Turks must be roused to a spirit of national consciousness. For this purpose he controlled through the legation two Turkish-language newspapers, which slanted news and comment in the required direction. He sent out agents to indoctrinate *hojas* and other influential members of the community, and distributed money judiciously from secret funds. In the course of these activities he found himself faced with a reactionary element which resented the fact that both he and Fethi were often seen in the streets of Sofia wearing hats instead of fezzes. Such behaviour on the part of a Turkish minister was found to be deeply shocking. This gave Kemal the chance to launch forth boldly into speeches and discussions on a pet subject—the respective merits of the two forms of headgear.

There was another element in the country which could be won over to the Turkish side. This was a group of Macedonians who had crossed the frontier to settle here after the second Balkan War. Kemal established close relations with the Macedonian Committee and helped it with funds. Madame Kovatcheva, the wife of his friend the Minister of War, was a Macedonian, and Kemal's growing association with her young daughter Dimitrina was assumed by the local gossips to have political undertones.

In fact it had a more romantic flavour. Kemal had never before come to know on close terms a young girl of good family and European refinement, and it was this that intrigued him in Dimitrina. His courtship came to a head at a masked ball, at which he danced with her for most of the evening. At first they talked of music, to which she was devoted. But soon his conversation shifted to politics. He began to pour out, with passionate earnestness, his plans for the Westernization of Turkey, and especially for the emancipation of its womenfolk. They must discard the veil and become free to dance and consort with men, as she herself and

the women in the ballroom around them were doing. They must be released from the bonds of slavery to which Moslem marriage condemned
them. Dimitrina found herself swept away on the irresistible flood of his
talk.

Kemal, for his part, saw her as the European wife of his desires. But he
would have to ask her father for her hand in marriage; and here he
risked a rebuff. Would the general, as a Christian, consent to her marrying a Moslem? He consulted with Fethi, who had himself taken a fancy
to another Bulgarian girl, the daughter of General Rasho Petroff. Tactful soundings were taken on behalf of them both, and the result was
discouraging. General Petroff's reaction was instantaneous. "I would
sooner cut off my head," he said, "then have my daughter marry a Turk."
General Kovatchev shared his view and politely refused for his family an
invitation to a ball at the Turkish Embassy. Thus Kemal and Dimitrina
did not see one another again.[2]

Meanwhile, as 1914 dawned, Enver and the triumvirate had embarked
on a career of swift and constructive reform. The Balkan Wars had at last
awakened the Turks to a sense of national identity, and they now had a
government competent, for all its arbitrary ways, to translate this into
some form of national unity.

Reforms went ahead more speedily in various home departments, but
above all in the armed forces. Enver applied himself to the radical reorganization of the army, Jemal to that of the navy. Working with energy
and a cold efficiency, Enver introduced a radical purge of the old type of
officer and promoted the new in his place.

He gained for himself a new reputation. He was no longer simply the
gallant young warrior; he was the clearheaded, competent young or-
ganizer. He won praise even from Kemal himself, who wrote from Sofia
to congratulate Enver on his work as Minister of War. To Tevfik
Rüştü he wrote in the same strain, but criticized the incompetence of
Enver's chief of the General Staff, and declared his own readiness to
serve under his rival in that position. It was an appointment hardly likely
to come his way.

There was, however, a price to be paid for this regeneration of the
Turkish Army: this was its increasing control by the Germans. The

[2] She did not forget him, for he remained in touch with her family. Four years later,
towards the end of the war, she was about to leave with her father for Constantinople, where she hoped to see him. But the collapse of the Bulgarian front prevented
their visit. She later married a Bulgarian deputy and still lives in Sofia, lately widowed.

army reforms were carried out under the auspices of the German military mission, which was now led by General Liman von Sanders, a reliable and intelligent commander, and which was invested with a high degree of executive authority over Turkish troops. German officers proliferated throughout the General Staff and the various army units, and their numbers swelled rapidly during 1914. Here was the culmination of that policy of "German aid" to Turkey which in the hands of Enver was to have catastrophic consequences for the Ottoman Empire.

For war was now imminent. On June 28, 1914, the Archduke Franz Ferdinand, the Austrian heir apparent, was assassinated in Sarajevo by a young student, armed and briefed by a secret Serbian terrorist organization. A month later the Austrians declared war on Serbia, the Kaiser supported them, and the First World War had begun. Two days before, with the knowledge of only four members of the Turkish Cabinet, a secret alliance, aimed against Russia, had been agreed between Turkey and Germany. It was signed on August 2.

Nevertheless it was still by no means certain that Turkey would enter the war. Talat had been driven to seek the alliance in his belief that Turkey needed the support of a Great Power and in his fear of isolation. For he had failed in his attempt to secure any positive guarantees from Britain and France against Russia, the hereditary enemy. Aware, however, that the Turkish Army, despite Enver's reforms, still needed time to recover and build up its strength, he favoured neutrality for as long as it could possibly be maintained.

In Sofia Kemal argued strongly against Turkey's entry into the war on the German side. If Germany won the war she would make a satellite of Turkey; if she lost it Turkey would lose everything. Kemal, unlike Enver, not merely disliked and mistrusted the Germans; he was unsure of their capacity to win. His visit to Paris had convinced him that the military situation held many imponderables. The German Army, it is true, was advancing swiftly on Paris. But the soldier in Kemal saw, and wrote to his friend Salih, that "under the influence of various factors it will have to advance in a zigzag manner, and this may have a harmful result for it. We declared mobilization without determining our aims. It will be harmful for us to maintain a large army for a long period. The outcome of this war will not be certain for us or our allies."

On the other hand he foresaw that if war spread Turkey could hardly stay neutral indefinitely. In this event he favoured her entry into it against Germany. In an official despatch to Enver, as Minister of War, on July 16, 1914, he had reported from his observations in Sofia that the Bulgarians were drawing together with the Austrians, hoping with Austrian aid to achieve their dreams of a great Bulgarian state. But this alone, Kemal argued, would not satisfy them. They would require also to expand eastwards, and this could only be at Turkey's expense. It would thus be dangerous for Turkey to remain inactive. The Bulgarians would doubtless try, in various ways, to win over the Turks. Being committed to no Western group, it should be the policy of Turkey at this stage to lie low, maintaining an appearance of friendship with Bulgaria. But if the war were to involve her in this way, as he predicted, then "the thing for us to do is to provoke a pretext and invade Bulgaria." Such a policy might also further Turkey's interests in Greece.[3]

Meanwhile he lobbied his friends in Constantinople insistently, writing views to them which showed a farsighted grasp of international realities. He even foresaw that, sooner or later, America might become involved in the struggle, and that it would in fact be the First World War. Clearly it was to the advantage of Turkey, for the present, to remain neutral and continue to build up her military strength, holding a balance between the powers and watching events until the moment arrived for a decision whether to intervene or not, and if so on which side. There was no need for hurry. For this would be a long war—of that he was convinced.

Enver, on the other hand, was convinced that it would be a short one, and that if Turkey was to reap her reward she must enter it at once. Two events helped to turn the scale in his direction. The first was the requisitioning by the British Admiralty of two cruisers built for the Turkish government by Armstrong Whitworth, which had been paid for and were ready for delivery. Though a clause in the contract had allowed for its cancellation in the event of war, this roused indignation against Britain, even among those who had favoured a pro-Allied policy.[4] The second event was the dramatic and opportune appearance in the Bosporus, with the connivance of Enver, of the *Goeben* and the *Breslau,* after running the gantlet of the British fleet through the Mediterranean. The ships, which should have been disarmed, were instead bought by the Turkish government and renamed *Yavuz* and *Midilli,* while the German officers and crews remained on board, gaining popular approval by exchanging their caps for fezzes.

Only an incident with the Russians was now needed to precipitate Turkey's entry into the war. Despite the opposition of the bulk of the

---

[3] *Presidential Archives, Çankaya.* Ankara.
[4] The women of Turkey had contributed their jewels and other valuables in a public subscription to help finance the purchase.

Cabinet, this was easy enough for Enver to aid and abet. The *Goeben* and the *Breslau* were sent frequently into the Black Sea "on manoeuvres," in the hope of provoking an attack. At the end of October the *Goeben* sailed up with the old *Hamidiye* and other ships, and proceeded, without warning or pretext, to bombard the Russian ports of Odessa, Sebastopol, and Novorossisk. The German admiral had in his pocket a secret order from Enver: "The Turkish fleet should gain mastery of the Black Sea by force. Seek out the Russian fleet and attack her wherever you find her, without declaration of war."[5] In the ensuing battle a number of Russian ships were sunk. It was an act of war.

Enver pretended not to have known of the attack. Talat learned of it only after it had happened. He remarked, "Would that I were dead! Would that the country had not been dead!" But he remained in office. Jemal received the news while playing cards in the Cercle d'Orient. He showed astonishment, turned pale, and swore on the head of his daughter that he knew nothing of the incident. He too remained in office.[6] Said Halim, the Grand Vizier, offered his resignation to the Sultan, who embraced him and begged not thus to be deprived of his sole source of comfort and left to the mercy of incompetent men. The prince agreed to remain. Tears were pouring down his cheeks when the British and French ambassadors came for their passports. Only Javid, together with three minor ministers, resigned. "It will be our ruin," he had said, "even if we win." Thus began the last phase in the decline and fall of the Ottoman Empire.

[5] Ernest Jäckh, *The Rising Crescent.*
[6] Later he argued that it was best thus to enter the war, "rather than fall miserably under the yoke of the Russians."

Mustafa Kemal had opposed the war. But now that it was a *fait accompli* he threw himself into it with energy and in a patriotic spirit. The Germans were his natural enemies. But now that they had become his military allies he was ready to make common cause with them so far as his patience allowed. His first task, in Sofia, was to help bring pressure on the Bulgarians to enter the war. Aiding Fethi, he worked to this end through all available channels, countering in the process a barrage of propaganda from the Russians.

At dinner one evening with Madame Petroff Kemal whom, as she afterwards recalled, "the wines had made talkative and generous," became free with his offers to General Petroff of all the territory Bulgaria had lost in the second Balkan War. She should have Adrianople; she should return to the Chatalja lines and stay there; all the hinterland of Constantinople should be hers. His imagination carried him further, to the prophetic conception of an Asiatic Turkey, with its capital in Anatolia, looking westwards in permanent alliance with a Bulgaria embracing Turkey in Europe, and co-operating in the joint defence against the Russians of a free Constantinople. He seemed about to offer the city itself to the general when a newly arrived Turkish attaché made naïve signs of alarm to Fethi, otherwise engaged in paying compliments to Mademoiselle Petroff, the lady of his choice, at the head of the table. Fethi burst out laughing at his military attaché's lavish cessions of territory and remarked to the general, "Well now, what are you going to give us in compensation?"

Another of Kemal's tasks was to obtain arms and supplies from the Bulgarians for the support of the Turkish armies. He secured a promise of a large load of flour against cash payment and sent Shakir Zümre to Constantinople to arrange the deal. He saw Talat, now Minister of Finance, but Talat passed him over to Javid who, though he had resigned from the post, still worked behind the scenes, giving influential advice on financial policy. Javid refused to recommend the payment. There was, he said, no money available for such a purpose. "You seem to think," he added, "that this war is going on for years."

Kemal met Shakir at the station on his return to Sofia, eager for news of his mission. When Shakir told him of Javid's refusal, Kemal exclaimed angrily—and, as it turned out, prophetically, "A man like that deserves to be hanged!" [1]

As the war proceeded Kemal began to fret with impatience. He was now a lieutenant colonel, and thus entitled to a divisional command. He wrote to Enver, asking for a post in accord with his rank. But Enver replied, "There will always be a post for you in the army, but as your retention at Sofia, as military attaché, seems especially indicated, we are leaving you there." To this Kemal retorted that a more sacred duty called him to the front, adding, "If you consider me unworthy to become an officer of the first rank, please tell me so openly." To this Enver did not reply.

Kemal was indeed sounded by an emissary from Constantinople about a project of Enver to send a force of three regiments through Persia into India, with the object of stirring up a Moslem revolt against the British. Would he accept the command of such a force? Kemal recognized the proposal as one of Enver's more fanciful dreams, a disquieting sign as to how his mind, at the outset of a war, was working. He treated it with cynicism, replying, "I am not such a hero." For such an operation, he added, three regiments would be superfluous. Only a single officer was needed, who would raise his troops on the way. The thing, of course, was impossible. "Had it been possible," he drily remarked afterwards, "I shouldn't have waited for orders. I should have gone by myself and found

[1] Javid was hanged in Ankara, following the treason trials of 1926.

my troops. I should have conquered India and become an emperor." Instead, he replied that he intended to fight at the front in his own country.

The first few months of the war had proved disastrous for Turkey. Had her leaders been wise, they would have devoted this period to a defensive strategy, conserving and building up such military strength as she had, completing the training of her forces and disposing them with forethought, waiting and watching to see from which quarter the Allied threat would come.

But Enver would have none of this. He preferred great and romantic adventures. He saw himself in the role of an Islamic Alexander the Great, moving against Britain in quest of a new Turkish Empire in Asia. This was a dream which coincided nicely with Germany's own plans for world conquest. For its realization he decreed two immediate offensives: the first northwards against Russia, the second southwards against Egypt. The first offensive, designed to encircle the Russian forces in the Caucasus, and executed against the advice of the German commander, General Liman von Sanders, ended in total disaster. In appalling winter conditions virtually a whole Turkish army was lost—a crucial force which should have been held in reserve for the defence of the east.

It was only after Enver had left on this catastrophic excursion that Kemal was given a command. He had decided to leave Sofia despite his orders, and even talked of enlisting as an ordinary soldier. But as he was on the point of departure he received a telegram from Enver's deputy at the Ministry of War appointing him commander of the 19th Division and instructing him to report at once to Constantinople.

Reporting at GHQ, he was shown in to Enver, who had just returned from the east, looking thin and pale.

"You are a little tired," Kemal said to him.

"Not particularly."

"What happened?"

"We were beaten. That's all."

"And the general situation, how is it?"

"Very good," replied Enver.

Not wishing to press him further, Kemal raised the question of his posting. "I must thank you for being good enough to appoint me to the command of the division which bears the number 19. Where is this division—in what army or army corps?"

Enver replied vaguely, "Oh yes. Perhaps you will be able to get more precise information from the General Staff."

Kemal then toured the various offices of the General Staff, in search of his division—but in vain. Finally someone advised him to try the army of Liman von Sanders, whose offices were in the Ministry of War. He was shown into the office of the chief of staff, who said, "We have no such division in our formation. But it is quite possible that the Third Army Corps, which is stationed at Gallipoli, may be planning to form the unit you mention. If you would care to give yourself the trouble of going there you will certainly be able to obtain all the necessary information."

Before he went Kemal was shown in to General von Sanders. They had not met before, but they were already known to one another through Kemal's outspoken anti-German sentiments. The German general received him with affable courtesy, asked him when he had returned from Sofia, and enquired, "Are the Bulgarians going to make up their minds to come into the war?"

Kemal replied that in his opinion they would not do so yet. They were waiting for one of two things to happen: either a striking German success or the extension of the war to their own territory. This remark provoked an irritable gesture from Von Sanders, who remarked with a sneer, "Then the Bulgarians don't believe in the success of the German Army?"

Kemal answered calmly, "No."

Von Sanders then asked him suspiciously, "And what is your opinion?"

Kemal hesitated. As a mere commander of a division which did not yet exist, how could he express an opinion? On the other hand he had for long been committing his views to paper and could hardly retract them now. Besides, for all that he might have said in public, he could not help privately sympathizing with the circumspect policy of the Bulgarians. He decided to be frank and said briefly, "I think the Bulgarians are right."

Liman von Sanders rose without a word and Kemal took his leave. He left for the Gallipoli Peninsula, where his division was in the process of formation.

Meanwhile Enver was proceeding—again against the advice of Von Sanders—with his second spectacular offensive. This was to be a swift descent upon the Suez Canal, with the object of ejecting the British from Egypt. The Turkish force, marching across the desert under the command of the German Colonel von Kress, took seven days to reach the canal. But it marched by night and surprised the British. A few of its troops succeeded in crossing the canal, but the west bank was strongly held and the defence was soon reinforced by British military and naval artillery. Thus the Turkish force had to retire. Its incursion acted as a warning to the British, who proceeded so to build up the defence of the canal zone as virtually to preclude any future attack on Egypt by the Turks.

Having failed in their own two offensives, the Turks were now faced with an offensive by the Allies. From the beginning of 1915 onwards it became evident, from intelligence reports of enemy naval and troop movements, that Allied forces were assembling on the islands before the Dardanelles, and that an Anglo-French attack on Constantinople, through the Narrows and across the Sea of Marmara, was imminent. The failure of the Caucasian and Egyptian campaigns had lowered morale, and the people of Constantinople began to talk despondently of the capture of the city as though it had already occurred. The Germans grew a trifle hysterical, fearing the arrival of the Russians, and began to talk of a separate peace. Turkish families began to leave for Anatolia. The Turkish government prepared two special trains on the Asiatic side, with steam up for departure at an hour's notice, one for the Sultan and his suite and the other for the diplomatic corps. Abdul Hamid, now in exile in the Beylerbey Palace, was invited to accompany the imperial family party but refused to move, saying shrewdly to his brother the Sultan, "If once you leave Constantinople you will never be able to return."

The government had made plans to move to Eskishehir, whither the archives of the Sublime Porte and the gold from the banks had already preceded them. Cans of petrol were stored in the police stations of Constantinople, ready to fire the city. Works of art were buried in the cellars of the museums, and plans made to dynamite a number of public buildings, including Santa Sophia. When the American ambassador protested that it should be spared, Talat replied that there were not six men in the Committee of Union and Progress who cared for anything old. "We all like new things," he explained.

Talat was a "picture of desolation and defeat." Thousands of Turks were secretly praying for an Allied victory, and the chief of police was sending gangs of unemployed out of the city for fear of revolution. When in February 1915 the British Army reduced by gunfire the forts at the entrance to the Dardanelles, the rumour spread that they had levelled two whole hills. Citizens began to listen for the sound of the guns and organized picnics on the islands in the Marmara to look out for the periscopes of enemy submarines.

Only Enver, who had kept out of the public eye since his defeat in the

Caucasus, remained cool and collected. This was a faculty for which he was remarkable, never seeming ruffled or excited, conveying a sense of calm whenever he entered a room. Now he expressed his absolute conviction that the British would never succeed in forcing the Dardanelles. All this, he declared, was a "silly panic." The fortifications of the Straits were impregnable. Even if they proved not to be, Constantinople would be defended to the last man and would never yield to the enemy. He was carried away by a new dream, that of going down in history as the man who had exploded the legend of the invincibility of the British Navy —a thing that neither Germany nor any other nation had succeeded in doing.

Enver, as events turned out, was proved right—for the wrong reasons. The British naval attack of March 18 failed to break through the Narrows. It was not followed up. The British, for a complexity of reasons, decided not to proceed with the campaign until they could support their fleet with a land advance—as indeed Liman von Sanders had prophesied that they would be obliged to do. Flags were put out by order in Constantinople. But few Turks seriously believed that this was a final victory. There was hard fighting still to be done.

Enver decided to form a separate army, the Fifth, for the defence of the Dardanelles, and appointed Liman von Sanders to command it. Liman asked for a new division, the 19th, and it was to the command of this that Lieutenant Colonel Mustafa Kemal had been posted, with his headquarters at Maidos. He had just two months in which to organize his troops before the Allies attacked.

11 ▶ The Gallipoli landings

Kemal knew the Gallipoli Peninsula from his operations against the Bulgarians in the Balkan War, when his headquarters as now was at Maidos. He had then formed strong opinions about its defence, which conflicted with those of his fellow staff officers. They maintained that any enemy could be prevented from landing on the peninsula by adequate barbed-wire defences on shore. Kemal argued, on the contrary, that any enemy could land under cover of naval fire and that it would be the task of the defence to tackle him after he had done so, from defensive positions inland.

Discussing these tactics with Rauf, who as a naval officer agreed with them, he had said at the time, putting himself in the place of the enemy, "You may have as many barbed-wire defences as you like, but I can easily break them to pieces and land; and if I don't find superior forces to stop my advance on land, I can very well occupy the peninsula." Kemal had learnt this lesson of military science during the Tripolitanian campaign, when the Italians landed their troops under the cover of naval fire, making shore defence by the Turks impossible. This had awakened him to the inherent tactical power of naval bombardment, of which the rest of the

Turkish staff, innocent of land-sea manoeuvres, was now for the first time to have harsh practical experience.

Under the German command it was, as Kemal had maintained that it should be, the principle of the Turkish defence to hold the ridges—the rugged vertebrae of the peninsula—and oblige the enemy to storm them when once he had landed. Liman von Sanders, finding his six divisions scattered into small units along the coast line, grouped them together into fewer and larger concentrations inland, leaving a minimum of covering detachments on shore. The question remained, where would the enemy land? Kemal was convinced, from his knowledge of the terrain, that he would do so at two main points—Cape Helles, at the southern tip of the peninsula, where he could command the land on every side with his naval guns; and Gaba Tepe, on the western coast, whence he could most easily cross to the Narrows on the eastern coast.

But the assessment of Liman von Sanders was different. In his opinion the two likeliest points for a landing were the Asiatic coast, where he sent two divisions to the region of the field of Troy; and the narrow northern isthmus of the peninsula at Bulair, for which he earmarked two more. Of his remaining two, one was sent to Cape Helles, while the last, the 19th, under his own direct control but under the effective command of Mustafa Kemal, was held as the main reserve of his army near Maidos, ready to move to any area, north, south, or west, where the main attack might fall. This role suited Kemal, who chose as his headquarters the village of Boghali, north of the Narrows and within reach of either coast. Here he sat down to watch for the landings and prepare for the subsequent defence of the heights.

Soon after dawn on April 25 the Allied troops landed in force, as he had foreseen, on these two groups of beaches—the British at Cape Helles, and the Australians and New Zealanders north of Gaba Tepe. There were besides two diversionary manoeuvres—a raid by the French on the Asiatic coast and a demonstration by the Royal Naval Division at Bulair. Von Sanders fell for this second diversion. The Allies, he judged, sought to cut the narrow neck of the peninsula and so isolate the whole of his army. He thus ordered a division northwards to Bulair, away, as it proved, from the battle, and rode there with his staff, later sending his corps commander, Essad Pasha, to look after the attack in the south, but leaving him, as the day wore on, without much-needed reinforcements.

Kemal on the other hand, awakened that morning at Boghali by the naval bombardment, found himself right at the centre of gravity. The sound of the guns came from beyond the Sari Bair range, a long and often precipitous ridge which ran parallel with the western coast, rising up to three prominent crests of a thousand feet, and breaking up near the sea into subsidiary ridges, scored with ravines. At once he sent a cavalry squadron up the eastern slope of the ridge to the northerly crest of Koja Chemen, to reconnoitre the position. Next he received a report that a "small enemy force" was advancing up its western slope to the southerly crest of Chunuk Bair, together with a request from the neighbouring division to send a battalion to check its advance.

Kemal saw at once what was happening. Here was no small enemy force; here was a major offensive. With his acute grasp of military essentials, he knew that the Sari Bair ridge, and especially the Chunuk Bair crest, was now the key to the entire Turkish defence. Its capture would enable the enemy to dominate all sides of the peninsula. A single battalion would be totally insufficient to hold it. The whole of his division would be needed. Acting on his own responsibility and exceeding his authority as a divisional commander, he thus ordered his best regiment, the 57th, with a mountain battery, to advance up the ridge to the crest of Koja Chemen. As it happened the regiment was already drawn up for a field exercise, planned for that day. Kemal reported what he had done to corps headquarters, then rode with an A.D.C. and his chief medical officer to regimental headquarters to hasten and lead the advance.

Kemal's decision was a bold one. He was committing the bulk of Von Sanders' reserve on the basis of no very clear information as to the strength of the enemy, but only on that of his own intuitive conviction that this was the crucial attack. Had his judgment been wrong, had the enemy planned another important landing elsewhere, there would have been only one Turkish regiment left to resist it. But he was right, and in his abounding self-confidence knew it.

The Australians and New Zealanders had indeed landed in force—not at Gaba Tepe, as they had planned and as the Turks had expected, but on a beach at Ariburnu, the "Cape of Bees," in more difficult country a mile to the north, to which an uncharted current had carried their boats. It was a place to be known as Anzac Cove. Here the Turks were unprepared, and despite the more formidable natural obstacles the Anzacs were able to advance, against only confused opposition, up the western slopes of the ridge.

On the eastern slopes the path of Kemal with his regimental officers and men, winding through strong scrubby undergrowth amid a confusion of dried-up watercourses strewn with boulders, was hard to find.

Two guides, sent on ahead, lost touch with the main body and it was Kemal himself, riding at the head of a company and consulting a map and compass, who finally led the way. From Koja Chemen he looked down on the shimmering sea and the ships of the enemy scattered across it, but his view of the advance, among the broken ridges beneath, was blocked. Seeing that his men were tired from their arduous climb, he ordered their officers to give them a ten-minute break. Then he moved on himself, with a few of his staff, towards Chunuk Bair. They started to ride but, finding the terrain too rough, dismounted and proceeded on foot. Near the crest they came upon a company of men streaming down over the ridge in full retreat. They were a unit of the outpost screen, spread out to watch for the landings, which for more than three hours had been the only force to oppose the enemy.

Kemal stopped them and asked, "What's up? Why are you running away?"

"They come, they come," was the reply.

"Who comes?"

"Sir, the enemy. *Ingiliz, Ingiliz.*"

"Where?" he asked. They pointed down the slope to a patch of scrub, from which a line of Australians was freely advancing. They were closer to Kemal than his own troops, whom he had left behind to rest. "Whether by logic or instinct" as he afterwards put it, he said to the retreating soldiers, "You cannot run away from the enemy."

They protested, "Our ammunition is finished."

"You have your bayonets," he said. He commanded them to fix bayonets and to lie down on the ground. He sent an officer back to instruct his own infantrymen to come up at the double, together with any available gunners from the mountain battery. Then, as he observed, "When our men lay down, the enemy lay down. This was the moment of time that we gained."

It was a moment of hesitation by the Anzacs which may well have decided the fate of the peninsula. While they hesitated the 57th Regiment began to come up, and Kemal sent it straight into action. He rode through the forward positions, driving the troops over the slope with unwavering energy. Placing his mountain battery on the ridge, he helped to wheel its guns into position. He directed operations from the skyline, with a complete disregard for his own safety. In an order of the day he wrote: "I don't order you to attack, I order you to die. In the time it takes us to die, other troops and commanders can come and take our places." By the end of the battle almost the whole of the 57th Regiment had died, charging continuously through a curtain of enemy rifle fire to win immortality in the annals of the Turkish Army.

But the Turkish fire was as deadly. Time after time it halted the Anzacs as they surged into view over a ridge, while the mountain battery poured shrapnel upon them in an awful baptism of shellfire, forcing them to scatter and take cover in the meagre scrub without means of retaliation. For their artillery was not yet in action, and even the naval batteries were silent, fearing to fire on their own forces on a front so confused. The confusion in this battle of sudden hand-to-hand encounters and shifting positions was indeed such that, with bullets raining from every direction, neither Turks nor Australians knew just who might prove to be an enemy and who a friend. Meanwhile Kemal, once again without authority, had ordered a second regiment—composed of Arab troops—into the line to reinforce the first. Then he rode back to corps headquarters at Maidos to report to Essad Pasha and urge upon him the necessity for an all-out attack with every man available. Essad agreed with his appreciation, approved of his actions, and handed over to him the remaining regiment of the 19th Division, thus putting him in command of the whole Sari Bair front.

As the afternoon wore on the Anzacs were slowly driven back, not indeed to the sea, as Kemal insistently urged, but to those coastal spurs and ridges which they had occupied early that morning. Night fell, lulling the storm of the main battle. But, in the words of the official historian, there was "no rest for anyone on those rugged hillsides that night. Worn out with fatigue, scattered and disorganized, it was impossible for either side to make further progress. But the noise of battle continued; and with only the flash of their assailants' rifles to guide them, invaders and invaded alike kept up a continuous fire."

Kemal himself spent the night without sleep, riding over the whole front, trying to obtain information, and giving orders for the following day. Reinforcements were being landed, under cover of darkness, as he rode. But the morale of the Anzacs was shaken—by the unfamiliar shrapnel fire, by the unforeseen rigours of the terrain, by the disruption of units, which drove leaderless men back to the beach in their hundreds.

Around midnight Sir Ian Hamilton, the British commander-in-chief, was awakened from his sleep aboard H.M.S. *Queen Elizabeth* by a message from General Birdwood, the Anzac commander. It was an admission of defeat and a proposal for an immediate evacuation. Hamilton wrote immediately to Birdwood that a supreme effort must be made to hold on. The southern force had established a bridgehead around Cape Helles and should advance the next day, diverting pressure from Ariburnu. He added a postscript: "You have got through the difficult business and you have only to dig, dig, dig until you are safe." Later he wrote in his diary: "Better to die like heroes on the enemy's ground than be butchered like sheep on the beaches like the runaway Persians at Marathon." Such were the fruits of Kemal's leadership of the Turks that crucial day.

The Australians pulled themselves together and dug. The clink of shovels was everywhere heard on the hillside. Next morning Kemal remained on the defensive. His losses in the initial battle had been heavy; moreover, he knew that the imminent danger was now in the south, at Cape Helles, where all available reserves would be needed. He resumed his attack only on receiving reinforcements from Bulair. Hamilton, from the deck of his warship, watched the operation, this time effectively countered by shellfire from land and sea. He recalled it in his *Gallipoli Diary:*

Under so many savage blows [he wrote], the labouring mountains brought forth Turks. Here and there advancing lines; dots moving over green patches; dots following one another across a broad red scar on the flank of Sari Bair; others following—and yet others—and others, closing in, disappearing, reappearing in close waves converging on the central and highest part of our position. The tic tac of the machine guns and the rattle of the rifles accompanied the roar of the big guns as hail, pouring down on a greenhouse, plays fast and loose amidst the peals of God's artillery. The fire slackened. The attack had ebbed away; our fellows were holding their ground. A few, very few little dots had run back over that green patch—the others had passed down into the world of darkness.

Kemal's surviving troops were exhausted and his new units were unused to the terrain. The naval bombardment had demoralized all. His force for the moment was spent. But he had driven the enemy back into a confined scrap of land along the seacoast. Its perimeter was hard to defend; it was supplied only by a beach, exposed not only to the varying winds but also to the enemy fire; it was dominated actually and psychologically by the Turks, looking down on it unseen. Kemal had held the heights, which he had seen to be the key to the peninsula. By his flair, his sense of urgency, the sureness of his decisions, and the insistence of his leadership he had, at the outset of an invasion on the lines he had predicted, saved the Turks from a defeat which might well have opened the road to Constantinople.

Like the Anzacs, the Turks now dug in. On both sides the initial impetus, with its element of surprise, had waned. But Kemal, following a minor attack on the enemy on April 30, was determined on a third counterattack before they could land further reinforcements. Aware of the necessity to keep up the morale of his men and the spirit of leadership in his officers, he called a group of them together at his headquarters, now known as Kemalieri—Kemal's Place. They sat cross-legged around him "à la Turk" on the floor of his tent, and wrote on pads in the palms of their hands as he briefed them. "I am convinced," he instructed, "that we must finally drive the enemy opposing us into the sea if it means the death of us all. Our position compared to the enemy's is not weak. His morale has been completely broken. He is ceaselessly digging to find himself a refuge. You saw how he ran away immediately when a few shells dropped near his trenches. . . . I am convinced that there is not one amongst the troops we command who would not rather die here than see a second chapter of our Balkan disgrace. If you feel there are such men, then let us shoot them with our own hands."

To the troops themselves he issued an order of the day:

Every soldier who fights here with me must realize that he is in honour bound not to retreat one step. Let me remind you all that if you want to rest, there may be no rest for our whole nation throughout eternity. I am sure that all our comrades agree on this, and that they will show no signs of fatigue until the enemy is finally hurled into the sea.

The section commanders were told to trust to only one thing—their soldiers' bayonets. The soldiers, advancing as they did to the sound of the bugles and drum, must not stop short of the enemy trenches. They must, when it grew dark, jump right into them.

On the eve of the attack the German Colonel Kannengiesser arrived at Kemal's headquarters to take over the command of another division— for the present inextricably confused with Kemal's own. He was impressed by this "clear-thinking active, quiet man, who knew what he wanted. He weighed and decided everything for himself, without looking elsewhere for support or agreement to his opinions. He spoke accordingly but little, and was always reserved and retiring without being unfriendly. He did not appear to be very strong bodily, although extremely wiry. His stubborn energy gave him apparently complete control, both of his troops and of himself."

The attack at first went well, against a single shore battery. But Kemal had miscalculated. Aware as he had been, as a strategist, of the impossibility of preventing an enemy invasion covered by naval fire, he had underrated its tactical power once the enemy had landed. The British

warships, strongly supported by the heavy artillery on shore, began to
shell Kemal's positions, protected only by out-of-date mountain guns, and
his onslaught immediately flagged. Attack after attack was smashed by
the overwhelming superiority of their gun power, and a number of Turkish battalions broke in panic and ran. Kemal threw in all his reserves in
the hope of a breakthrough by night. But he failed to penetrate the
enemy's positions. For once, he had suffered a major tactical defeat. "The
battle," he recorded, "which has lasted for twenty-four hours, had
caused great fatigue to our troops, and I gave an order for the attack to
stop."

Afterwards, to Rushen Eshref, who came to interview him for the
press, he recounted how at one point in the battle, faced by an attack
from the enemy lines a mere ten yards away, all the men in his first
trench fell. Those in the second, seeing them fall, at once took their
places, knowing that they too would die but remaining unshaken. Those
who could read died with a Koran in their hands. Those who could not
called upon Allah with a prayer. All were ready to go to heaven. Therein,
Kemal declared, lay the spiritual strength of the Turkish soldier, which
should make victory possible. But in down-to-earth terms the reckless
and profitless sacrifice involved in such frontal attacks was leading to
casualties which the Turkish Army could not easily afford. Essad, Kemal's
corps commander, realized that a conservation of forces was needed to
meet the Helles offensive. Thus Kemal received orders to desist from
further such operations.

On May 18, however, there was another major onslaught by the Turks
on the Anzac bridgehead. This time it was conceived by Von Sanders himself, but with a suggestion behind it of Enver's taste for a spectacular
enterprise. Kemal, as a mere divisional commander, played no part in its
conception. The plan, which displayed little tactical finesse, was to fling
an overwhelming force, reinforced from Helles and from the Asiatic side,
against Ariburnu, and thus either to annihilate the Anzacs or to drive
them once and for all into the sea. Since they had withdrawn troops from
the bridgehead to reinforce Helles, they were now in a minority of one
to three. But though the Turks were on top of the Anzacs, and sometimes only a few yards away from them, they were a vulnerable target,
obliged as they were to charge on prepared dug-in positions. The result
was a holocaust.

The losses were so great as to prompt a truce with the enemy, that
each side might bury its dead. Kemal was one of a party of officers who,
to negotiate the truce, was led blindfold into the Anzac bridgehead,

goose-stepped by the Australians over imaginary barbed-wire entangle-
ments to impress them with the extent of their defences, then conducted to a cave by the beach which was General Birdwood's dugout.
Here a cease-fire for nine hours was agreed. Pending agreement, Aubrey
Herbert was held as an honoured and contented hostage by his friends
in the Turkish lines.

In June Kemal was promoted to full colonel. Liman von Sanders,
though he found Kemal hard to handle, fully appreciated his qualities
as a divisional commander. Enver, however, still mistrusted him and
was forever seeking a pretext to find fault with his actions. He found
one on a whirlwind visit to the front at the end of the month, when the
friction between them flared up into a serious explosion. Kemal, reinforced by a crack Turkish regiment, had persuaded Essad to sanction
an attack on a crucial Australian position whose capture, he believed,
could force a withdrawal from the peninsula. Enver objected to it,
accusing Kemal, not without justification, of squandering lives. But Von
Sanders made peace between them and the attack took place. Partly
owing to a fierce thunderstorm which combined with an Australian
demonstration of star shells and flares to confuse the attackers, partly
owing to the death of the regimental commander before they attacked, it
failed.

Kemal blamed Enver's interference for the failure. Enver, while
praising Kemal's troops for their gallantry, threw aspersions on his leadership. Kemal resigned. But when Enver returned to Constantinople he
was pacified by Von Sanders and agreed to take over the command
of his division once more.

But he was not content. Though he had won for his country the first
round in the Gallipoli campaign, he still had no say in its general direction. There were continual disputes with corps headquarters as to the
extent of his command, the inadequacy of its forces, its exact delimitation
with the command adjoining, which was now given to a German officer,
Major Willmer. Kemal was convinced that Essad Pasha, the corps commander, did not attach enough importance to this Ariburnu area and
wrote to him of its defence problems in continual and laborious detail.
Fixed singly in his mind still was the Sari Bair ridge, with its peaks
Chunuk Bair and Koja Chemen. If and when the enemy reinforced his
troops and resumed the offensive, as he had openly shown his intention
of doing, it would once more be the major objective. Kemal had been
convinced of its importance before and had been proved right; he was
convinced of it still.

He tried in vain to convince Essad Pasha. A key to the defence of the heights was the ravine of Sazlidere, which led directly up to Chunuk Bair, offering valuable cover to an enemy advancing over the foothills towards it. It had at first been included in his command but was now, it seemed, to form the dividing line between the two commands. Who in fact was to control so important an area, he or the German major? It was essential that this should be clarified.

Essad Pasha came down to divisional headquarters with his chief of staff to see for himself. Kemal took them up onto the top of the ridge and gave them a lecturer's-eye view of the whole position, spread beneath and around them—the broken rocky country on either side of Sazlidere, the beach below it, the bay of Suvla and the Salt Lake beyond, the line of the ridge stretching northeastwards to the summit of Koja Chemen. Rising to meet the sky, it looked from where they stood like an unscalable slope.

The chief of staff remarked that only raiding parties could advance through such difficult country. Essad Pasha asked Kemal, "Where will the enemy come from?" Kemal waved his hand in the direction of Ariburnu and the line of the coast as far as Suvla: "From there."

"Very well," replied the pasha, "if he does come from there, then how will he advance?"

Kemal pointed again at Ariburnu and described a broad half circle towards Koja Chemen: "That's how he will advance."

The pasha smiled and patted him on the shoulder. "Don't worry, Bey Effendi. He can't do it."

Kemal saw that it was useless to continue the discussion. *"Insh'allah!"* he exclaimed. "Let's hope you are right."

Kemal recorded the interview in his diary. In the light of what afterwards happened he underlined the passage in red ink, adding to the entry a justified comment on those who had disagreed with him and whose inadequate measures had "greatly endangered the military position and the fate of the country." For the second time Kemal was right.

Meanwhile he wrote in French to Corinne Lütfü, with whom he had been in correspondence since the start of the campaign:

Here the view is not so calm. Every day and night shrapnel and other shells burst incessantly above our heads. The shells whistle and the noise of the bombs mingles with that of the cannons. In effect, we are living an infernal life. Happily our soldiers are very brave and much more resistant than the enemy. Besides, their easy comradeship greatly facilitates the execution of my orders, which often demand death. As it happens, this leads only to two celestial results: to become a victorious Gazi or a Chehad. Do you know what this last means? To go straight away to paradise, where the houris, God's most beautiful women, will come to receive them and remain permanently at their disposal. Supreme happiness!

He had a desire, he added, to read some novels to "help soften the hard character which present events have developed in me, and to make me capable of responding to some of the good and agreeable things in life." He asked Corinne to give a list of appropriate titles to a mutual friend in Constantinople who might procure the books for him. They could provide some slight substitute for that charming and intelligent conversation of Corinne's, with which it was her habit to seduce all the world.

12 ► *A Turkish victory*

For the second time in the campaign Kemal was right, while his superiors were wrong. On August 6 the enemy launched an offensive on the very lines he had foretold to Essad. This time it was indeed the intention of the British to shift the main weight of their offensive from the Helles to the Ariburnu front. Secretly landing and effectively concealing 25,000 more men in the Anzac bridgehead, they planned a frontal assault on the Sari Bair range. One column would advance directly up the Sazlidere ravine to the west of Chunuk Bair; another, by a more northerly and circuitous route, up the valleys and over the foothills to Koja Chemen and the crests between. This duel advance was to be supported by a fresh landing at Suvla Bay, north of Anzac, of some 20,000 troops, mostly of Kitchener's "New Army." They in turn would advance to the northern ridge of Anafarta, linking up in an enveloping movement with the Anzacs to march to the Narrows, cut the peninsula in two, and thus isolate the bulk of the Turkish forces.

As the thunder of the preliminary barrage rolled forth over the slopes, Kemal awaited the development of the attack as he had foreseen it, in the centre. Not so, once again, Liman von Sanders, who expected it to come either on his extreme right or on his immediate left—against Bulair, where he thus ordered increased vigilance; or against the southern spurs of the Sari Bair range, where indeed in the evening the Anzacs carried out an effective diversion, drawing off the bulk of Essad Pasha's reserves. This cleared the field for the main attack, which was to take place—against even Kemal's expectations—by night. It was planned to capture the summits by dawn.

The attack began well, with a successful ruse rehearsed for some days beforehand—the naval bombardment of a line of Turkish trenches. Punctually at the same hour after dark the shells had begun to fall while searchlights raked the hillsides. As punctually the Turks had left the trenches to take cover elsewhere. But this time, as they did so, the enemy moved in, their way lit by the searchlights, and the first Turkish position was captured. Fighting followed up the Sazlidere ravine, from which the Turks, owing to the inadequate defences which Kemal had criticized, were obliged to withdraw. Thus most of their outposts were occupied by the covering forces and the way lay open for the main assault on the crests. The outlook for the Anzacs seemed hopeful.

Though Kemal's own division was under continuous gunfire, it was not at first involved in this fighting, for the main line of the enemy's two-pronged advance was over the heights to the north of the Sazlidere ravine, which, together with the summits, came under the adjoining command. From his observation post on a spur which the British had named Battleship Hill, he was in telephonic contact all night with this sector and could hear continual infantry fire not only on his immediate right, beneath Chunuk Bair, but farther away to the north, from the Aghildere ravine. Sooner or later, perhaps towards dawn, he expected an attack on his own front. Thus he kept his units on the alert with a series of brief general orders. At 3:30 A.M. he signalled:

It is probable that the enemy will attack our front in the morning. The distance between us is very short. To be able to repel any sudden attacks, our troops must be wide awake and ready to use their weapons. I instruct officers to keep their men awake and to maintain the highest degree of readiness at all times, as the delicacy of the tactical situation demands.

An hour later, after the first streak of dawn, the attack came. It had been planned to coincide with the occupation of Chunuk Bair and thus to secure the right flank of the assailants against enfilade by Kemal's division. One force was to sweep down on Battleship Hill from the crest, while the other was to move up on it from the foothills.

But, though the enemy's night advance had begun well, it soon ran into trouble. The darkness had defeated the Anzacs. One section of the first column, misled by its guides, got lost, finding itself back, after a series of fruitless ascents and descents, at its starting point; the other reached a shoulder of the ridge but was unable to proceed farther without the first. The second column, in the Aghildere ravine to the north, had fared even worse. Similarly misled in the darkness, its men, after a long confused series of marches, now lay scattered over the slopes in a state of exhaustion, well below Koja Chemen and their other objectives. The Allies had missed their opportunity of capturing the Sari Bair ridge before dawn, while it was still thinly defended and the weapon of surprise was on their side.

Nevertheless, though no converging support was now available from above, and though Kemal's defensive positions below were known to be among the strongest in the Turkish lines, the dawn attack on them went ahead. It ended in disaster, wave after wave of heroic but inexperienced Australians perishing at the hands of Kemal's men, awake and prepared as they were, in a suicidal and fruitless assault.

Meanwhile to the north the men of the new British Army were landing on the beaches of Suvla Bay. Since the Turkish defences against them consisted of a mere three lightly armed battalions, under Major Willmer's command, they faced little effective resistance. But they seemed curiously reluctant to advance. Liman von Sanders, however, at last realized that here, in the centre, was the main attack. He summoned reinforcements to Suvla and Anzac from Bulair, from the Asiatic shore, and from Helles, where the secondary British attack had collapsed. But for the next twenty-four hours, until they arrived, the situation of the Turks and of the Sari Bair ridge would be critical.

Kemal was fully alive to the danger. A successful enemy advance from the northeast, with so little opposition, could easily outflank his own division and might lead to a general withdrawal from the whole Ariburnu front. He kept a continuous and anxious eye on Chunuk Bair, over which he had no control. Early in the morning, when he had won his own battle, he sent his divisional reserve to picket the spur beneath it. Later Colonel Kannengiesser arrived from the south with two regiments to hold the summit. This he succeeded in doing, at the cost of a serious wound in the chest, against a daylight attack from the Anzac right by troops physically weakened from three long months in the trenches.

Next day at dawn a fresh attack was launched, "the ferocity of which," in Kemal's words, "can hardly be described." But the Anzacs, expecting

casualties as heavy as those of the day before, were surprised to meet
with no fire from the dreaded ridge above them. On storming it, they
found only a Turkish machine-gun crew, asleep on the crest, from which
the infantry, for some unexplained reason, had gone. Thus Chunuk Bair
was captured.

But their foothold was precarious. Immediately, as the sun rose, they
were raked by a fierce fire from either flank—from Kemal's positions on
Battleship Hill to their right, and from those on the adjoining crests of
the ridge, where the assault had failed, to their left. The ground was too
hard for them to dig in effectively. Most of the men on the summit were
killed, and only the remnants, heroically led, held on. But when darkness
fell reinforcements arrived and they had a respite at least until morning.

Had they known it, the situation of the Turks was as precarious as theirs.
For Kemal it had been a day of nervous anxiety and frustration. From
an early hour he grasped that the Turkish defences to the right of him
were in a state of confusion which bordered on chaos. News coming into
his headquarters made it all too clear that no effective command existed.
A typical message from an officer ran:

An attack has been ordered on Chunuk Bair. To whom should I pass this
order? I am looking for the battalion commanders but cannot find them.
Everything is in a muddle. The situation is serious. At least a commander
should be appointed who knows the ground. We have no reports, no information. I am at a loss as to what I should do. . . .

All the units are mixed up. No officers are to be found. I am at a place where
the previous regimental commander was hit. I have been given no information
as to what is happening. All the officers are killed or wounded. I do not even
know the name of the place where I am. I can see nothing from my observation
post. I request in the name of the safety of the nation that an officer be appointed who knows the area well.

Another bewildered officer reported: "At dawn some troops withdrew
from Shahinsirt towards Chunuk Bair. They are digging in on Chunuk
Bair. But it is not known whether the troops are the enemy's or ours."

Kemal judged that they were the enemy's and sent his divisional
adjutant and his A.D.C. to reconnoitre and report. The A.D.C. was
killed. He sent the chief of the divisional staff, whose reports confirmed
his own observations. A regimental commander named Nuri (later to
become his A.D.C.) got through on the field telephone from group headquarters. He said that he had been ordered by the group commander to
advance on Chunuk Bair and to attack the enemy there. He had asked
for information about the units in the area and about the command. But

the commander, who was in a nervous state, and his chief of staff seemed reluctant or unable to give it to him. "Please enlighten me about the situation," he asked Kemal. "There is no commander anywhere."

Kemal ordered him to advance at once on Chunuk Bair, and added, "Events will appoint a commander."

In fact two commanders of the division now holding the ridge had been killed one after the other, and the command had been given in quick succession to two more. Now the commander was a lieutenant colonel with more experience of railway administration behind the lines than of action in the field, who had chanced to arrive from Constantinople and who was in the invidious position of giving orders to staff officers of superior rank. His only idea of dealing with the crisis was to pour as many troops as possible into Chunuk Bair, regardless of plan. Kemal criticized these tactics to group headquarters and urged that something be done. But he received only the reply that they were doing their best. He got the impression, over the telephone and from the orders he saw, that the staff had lost their heads and that officers were shifting responsibility onto others. This prompted, that evening, a solemn note in his diary: "The weight of responsibility is heavier than death."

The situation soon came to a head. The commander of the Anafarta Group, as it had now been named, was Colonel Feyzi, who had arrived from Bulair with the reinforcing divisions called up by Von Sanders. Kemal sent a message, begging him in the name of the country and its safety to attract Von Sanders' attention to the critical position on Chunuk Bair. Shortly afterwards the chief of staff called Kemal on the telephone, on Von Sanders' behalf, to ask for his views. He gave them forcibly. The offensive was general. The enemy, as a result of the landings, was greatly superior. Urgent action was essential if the whole ridge were not to be lost. "There is one moment left," he said. "If we lose that moment we are faced with a general catastrophe."

Asked what was the remedy, he replied, "A unified command." He went further: "The only remedy is to put all the available troops under my command."

The chief of staff asked ironically, "Won't that be too many?"

"It will be too few," Kemal replied.

Disaster threatened not merely the Sari Bair ridge but the Anafarta ridge to the north of it, on the Suvla front. Here Major Willmer's three battalions had been holding on for nearly forty-eight hours. Only British irresolution had saved them. Thanks to their corps commander, General Stopford, the British troops had spent the day bathing on the beaches instead of advancing to the hills. But this could not last. At any moment their attack might begin.

Feyzi had rashly promised Von Sanders that his troops, marching from Bulair, would be ready to go into action at dawn that day, August 8. But here too there was irresolution. By the afternoon they were still not ready, nor, Feyzi maintained, would they be in a fit state to attack until dawn the next day. Von Sanders angrily insisted that an evening attack was imperative. Feyzi replied that, in the opinion of his divisional commanders, this was impossible. The men were tired and hungry, the ground was unfamiliar, the artillery inadequate.

Von Sanders asked him, "You are the group commander. What do *you* say?"

Feyzi replied, "I am of the same opinion."

Liman von Sanders promptly relieved Feyzi of his command. "That evening," he wrote, "I gave command of all the troops in the Anafarta section to Colonel Mustafa Kemal Bey, commander of the 19th Division. . . . He was a leader who delighted in responsibility. . . . I had full confidence in his energy." Kemal, in a mood of self-congratulation, moralized in his diary: "What a fine mirror history is! Men, especially those races which are morally backward, cannot help expressing evil sentiments, even in the face of sacred causes. The actions and conduct of the participants in great historical events reveal their true moral characters."

At last Kemal was in control of the whole front. Calmly he handed over his divisional command, first making dispositions for the renewed attack on Chunuk Bair which would inevitably come in the morning. He issued a farewell message to the divsion, encouraging the troops and commending their self-sacrifice. Then shortly before midnight he rode off northward over the hills to the Anafarta ridge, where the more immediate danger now lay. Anafarta had not yet seen fighting, and Kemal wrote in his diary: "For the first time in four months I was breathing air which was more or less pure and clear, because in the Ariburnu district and its neighbourhood the air we breathed was polluted by the corruption of human corpses."

He took with him his divisional doctor, to look after him and to organize the hospital services on Anafarta where casualties were likely to be heavy. It was Kemal's third night without sleep, and he was weak, not only from exhaustion but from a severe bout of malaria, which he could not shake off and for which he needed constant treatment. Haggard and drawn, he had a preoccupied look in his sunken eyes. What worried him especially was the lack of information as to the strength of his own and the enemy's forces.

But beneath his outward tension there was an inward confidence. Responsibility acted on him like a tonic. No longer did he have to sit by and watch, in a growing frenzy of frustration, the errors and muddles of those whom he saw as his inferiors. He was free to act, and with his acute calculating grasp of the military position he knew, in the broad sense if not yet in detail, what action to take. He had no false optimism. He was taking over a battle already half lost by other commanders, at the expense of their lives or careers. He knew that he too might fail to save it. But with his will, his patriotism, his ambition, and his belief in his own powers, he was wholly determined on victory. In a heroic vein suitable for public consumption he said afterwards, "To assume such responsibility was no simple affair, but as I had decided not to survive the ruin of my country, I accepted the responsibility with all due pride."

Kemal soon found signs of confusion. He came upon a divisional commander and his staff sitting idle, at this moment "when the country was being stabbed," far away from the place where their troops were in action. He ordered them to move to the front. Reaching another headquarters, he found it in darkness. There was neither a light to be seen nor a sound to be heard. Everyone slept. Kemal and his party shouted. He described the scene in his diary: "A man came out of his tent in a nightgown and answered our calls. I asked him what the place was. He said it was Major Willmer's headquarters. But he didn't seem to know much about it. I asked him to take me to his commander. But this man, who didn't know who he was, was unwilling. He merely pointed somewhere in the darkness with his hand. I forced him to take us there. He took us to the hut where Willmer was in bed. Willmer was asleep. I talked to Haydar Bey, an officer on his staff. I asked where the headquarters of the Anafarta Group was. He answered, 'Today it was here. But later'—he pointed toward the north—'it was removed somewhere in that direction.' " He mentioned the name of a place unknown to Kemal.

Anxious to lose no time, he rode on in the darkness. At 1:30 A.M. he found group headquarters, where the chief of staff and his officers were awaiting him. He at once asked where the enemy was and what his strength was. Where were his own two divisions and what was their situation? What were the last orders given to them by group? But the chief of staff was vague in his answers. Where, Kemal then asked, was the ex-commander, Feyzi Bey? He was asleep in his tent. Kemal said that he must be awakened and confirm to him the last order he had given. The chief of staff showed him a note of an order, without signature.

"If Feyzi gave this order," Kemal insisted, "let him sign it."

The chief of staff went back and forth between Feyzi and Kemal. But Feyzi refused to sign. Kemal gave up, called a meeting of the staff officers, and asked them where were the divisions and what were their orders for the attack. They told him what they knew. One of them, a courier who had seen something of the front, was more explicit than the others. But the picture remained vague. Dawn was approaching and there was no time to probe further. Kemal issued an order, announcing that he had taken over the command, giving orders for a general attack along the whole line from one ridge to the other, and instructing his officers to inform him immediately of their positions and the measures they had taken. He sent copies of the order by the hand of two officers to the divisional commanders. He took measures for the organization of medical services and of food and other supplies, which he found to have been neglected. Then at 4:30 A.M. he rode with a few officers to an observation post beyond the crest of Great Anafarta. From here he was to survey and direct the battle soon due to begin.

Its fate was to depend on a preliminary race, between Turks and British, for the crest of the Anafarta ridge, and especially for the summit of Tekke Tepe. Both sides had wasted two days—the Turks with more reason than the British—and were hastening to make up for the lost time. While Liman von Sanders was ruthlessly changing his group commanders, Sir Ian Hamilton, less ruthless, was at least now himself on the spot before Suvla, insisting to his own reluctant divisional commanders on the occupation of Tekke Tepe by daybreak. Even a single battalion, forestalling the Turks on the crest, could provide invaluable support to the rest of the army when it advanced up to the ridge.

But the single battalion very soon got into difficulties. The commander took too long to assemble his men. They were dazed with fatigue, and there was a further delay before they were ready to start. One company went ahead, leaving word for the others to follow. Meanwhile the Turks were mounting the opposite slope. The going was hard through the scrub, and the British company split up into scattered groups. Dawn broke, and they met with a persistent fire from the Turks in front and on the flanks. Finally a handful of men reached the top of the ridge— only to be met by a detachment of Turks pouring over it from the opposite side. The Turks had won the race for Tekke Tepe by a mere half hour.

Kemal's men swarmed down the hillside, spreading slaughter and havoc among the enemy forces. Sir Ian Hamilton, watching through a telescope from the deck of his warship, described the scene:

> Very soon the shrapnel got on to those trenches of men on our left and there was something like a stampede from North to South. Looking closer we could see the enemy advancing behind their own bursting shrapnel and rolling up our line from the left on to the centre. . . . Our centre made a convulsive effort (so it seemed) to throw back the steadily advancing Turks. . . . Then about 6 A.M. the whole lot seemed suddenly to collapse:—including the right! Not only did they give ground but they came back—some of them—half way to the sea.

Over all the hillside the picture was similar. The men of Kitchener's army broke with the cry: "The Turks are on us!" The Turkish fire was so intense that the scrub caught alight, sending them scurrying helter-skelter for safety. By midday Kemal was satisfied that the Suvla battle was won. He ordered his men to dig in. With a single incomplete division he had routed a far stronger enemy. Later he attributed his victory to the element of surprise. The enemy, advancing in small groups, had expected only slight skirmishes. But in the aggregate his skirmishers, well co-ordinated by their leaders and superior in marksmanship, had by the momentum of their downhill charge broken the enemy's morale. Kemal expressed surprise at the hesitancy of Hamilton, unable, though present in person, to ensure the carrying out of his orders. He discerned among Hamilton's commanders an incapacity to make decisions at the right moment, "that fear of responsibility which leads to defeat." General Stopford, he sardonically observed, seemed out of politeness to have been postponing the start of the battle until he himself should arrive.

Anafarta was thus secure. The Suvla offensive had failed. But the enemy had yet to be dislodged from the Sari Bair range. Here the situation on Chunuk Bair was more acute than ever. During the night a further attack had helped the Anzacs, despite only partial success, to consolidate their hold on the crest. Kemal, for whom Chunuk Bair was still the pivot of the whole campaign, at once halted the advance across the Suvla plain and ordered his two most trustworthy regiments up to the ridge for a counterattack. They had been in action half the night and required some rest. Thus he instructed his two acting divisional commanders, "Tonight I am going to demand great sacrifices from the troops on Chunuk Bair. Meanwhile I ask you to find means of providing hot soup for the two infantry regiments which are proceeding to the area."

Then he went to confer on the plan of attack with Liman von Sanders. Liman favoured a flank assault on the enemy's left, in the Aghildere region below Koja Chemen; Kemal preferred a frontal assault on Chunuk Bair itself, the immediate source of danger. If this was recaptured the enemy in Aghildere would ultimately have to retreat. Liman gave him a free hand, saying, "You have accepted the responsibility for this action. I don't want to influence you in your plans. I only wanted to tell you, purely as an observation, what came into my mind."

Kemal planned to direct the battle from the front line in person. In the evening he rode with his staff along the crest of the ridge towards Chunuk Bair. An enemy aircraft swooped low over their heads; his officers dispersed, but he continued, with one of them, to ride down the middle of the track, and the aircraft, though it followed them, did not attack. On arrival at divisional headquarters, behind the summit, he rode through the trenches, talking to officers of the various units.

He instructed them to call their men together and encourage them to fight with renewed spirit. Their morale had been shaken by the breakdown of the command. To this they attributed all their troubles. The Turkish soldier, lacking initiative, primitive in training and education, was lost without leadership and it was now Kemal's task to restore it. He ordered the 8th Division to prepare for an attack at dawn, reinforced by the two regiments which were on their way. But a little later the divisional commander came to see him with a staff officer, named Galib, who asked permission to put forward the views of a group of his officers. For two days they had been attacking Chunuk Bair. They had suffered heavy losses and had achieved no success. They were in a state of deep discouragement and did not believe that a new attack could succeed, even with the support of two extra regiments, one of which had in any case not yet arrived. Without it an attack might end in disaster.

Kemal knew and respected this officer. He had seen his bravery under fire. Though he was at first annoyed at the insubordinate method of his approach, he had to admit to himself that the man's attitude was logical enough. But, as he recorded in his diary, "certain convictions are hard to explain in terms of logic and reason. Such are the convictions which arise from what we feel in the blood and the fiery moments of battle. What Galib had said described the situation very well. But his opinion could not make me change my mind. I had come to the conclusion that we could defeat the enemy by means of a sudden, surprise assault. To achieve this, we needed more than numbers, we needed a cool and courageous command."

He thus told the divisional commander that his decision was irrevocable and would be carried out whether the second regiment arrived or not. He spent the night at divisional headquarters, in personal control. It was his fourth night without sleep and he was feverish and in acute physical discomfort from the malaria. But rest was impossible. Besides preparing for the attack he had to direct the Anafarta front, from which information was scanty and unreliable; and he had to sort out the tangle among his forces on the spot, continually disturbed in his tent by officers seeking lost units or commanders.

As dawn approached Kemal stood in front of the tent and looked around to make sure that all was ready. In his observation trenches, which were a mere twenty yards from the enemy, he had placed one of his fighting regiments. Into another line thirty yards behind it, as quietly as possible and under cover of darkness, he had moved two more. If the last regiment arrived in time, it would be thrown into the battle as the situation demanded. The initial attack was to be totally silent. Strict orders were given that there was to be neither artillery nor rifle fire. No weapon but the bayonet must be used. Both lines would move swiftly forward on the enemy in the dark, without making a sound. The fate of the battle would depend on the surprise of those first few minutes. The next phase of it would be decided by events.

Kemal looked at his watch and saw that it was almost four-thirty. In a few minutes it would be light, and his men, massed close together, would be visible to the enemy. If he saw them and fired the attack would fail. Kemal ran forward. His divisional commander joined him. Together with other officers they stood before the troops. Kemal passed down the line and in a low voice instructed them, "Soldiers, there is no doubt at all that we are going to defeat the enemy in front of you. But do not hurry. Let me go ahead first. As soon as you see me raise my whip, then you will all leap forward." He told the other officers to give their men the same signal. Then he took a few steps forward and raised his whip. Instantly the soldiers, with fixed bayonets, and the officers, with drawn swords, leapt into the darkness, as he afterwards put it, "like lions. A moment later, the only sound which came from the enemy trenches was the heavenly cry of 'Allah! Allah!'"

The British soldiers had no time even to raise their rifles. They were overwhelmed in their trenches by sheer weight of numbers, while those in the open were swiftly annihilated. Hamilton's front line was broken.

"The ponderous mass of the enemy," as he described it, swept over the crest and down the slopes, turning his right flank and piercing his lines below, so that his troops were driven "clean down the hill." It was a series of struggles "in which generals fought in the ranks, and men dropped their scientific weapons and caught one another by the throat. . . . The Turks came on again and again, fighting magnificently, calling upon the name of God. Our men stood to it, and maintained, by many a deed of daring, the old traditions of their race. There was no flinching. They died in the ranks as they stood."

But with their artillery they gave the Turks back as good as they got. From daylight onwards they poured shells onto Chunuk Bair, turning it, as Kemal wrote, "into a kind of hell. From the sky came a downpour of shrapnel and iron. The heavy naval shells sank into the ground, then burst, opening huge cavities all about us. The whole of Chunuk Bair was enveloped in thick smoke and fire. Everyone waited resignedly for what fate would bring." Few of the heroes of that first charge survived. The dead lay all over the hillside, fingers still gripping their rifles as though awaiting the order to charge. Asked by Kemal where his troops were, a commander replied, "Here are my troops. Those who lie dead."

Kemal stood recklessly in the line of fire, giving orders and encouraging his men. At one moment a piece of shrapnel struck him in the breast. In consternation an A.D.C. exclaimed, "Sir, you have been hit!" Kemal put his hand over the officer's mouth, lest others hear, and said, "Nothing of the sort." The shrapnel had hit his breast pocket, shattering the watch inside it and leaving only a superficial flesh wound. Later he took out the watch, which he had used since his days at the military school, and philosophized, "Here is a watch that is worth a life." When the battle was over, at Liman von Sanders' request, Kemal gave it to him as a souvenir, receiving in return a handsome chronometer engraved with the Von Sanders family arms.[1]

The artillery bombardment, devastating as it was to the Turks, could not save the Sari Bair ridge for the Anzacs. By 10 A.M., though scattered units fought doggedly on until the evening, the bulk of their force had been driven off it into the foothills and back to the beachhead below. On the right superior enemy forces, stranded with their flank in the air by the central attacks, had been forced to withdraw, thus justifying Kemal's argument with Von Sanders for a frontal in preference to an outflanking attack. Sir Ian Hamilton was still sanguine enough to write, "Well,

---

[1] Later when the Turkish authorities tried to recover the watch from Germany to place it in a museum, they were informed that it had been stolen.

we had Chunuk Bair in our hands the best part of two days and two nights. So far the Turks have never retaken trenches once we had fairly taken hold. Have they done so now? I hope not. . . . The Turks were well commanded: that I admit. Their Generals knew they were done unless they could quickly knock us off our Chunuk Bair. So they have done it. Never mind; never say die."

Nonetheless there was only one more slender hope. Chunuk Bair was lost beyond recovery, but there was still a chance of retrieving the situation at Suvla. Another attempt to capture Tekke Tepe failed. But the Turks were in a weak position at Kirech Tepe, at the north of the Anafarta line, and Liman von Sanders was seriously afraid that an attack here, before he could consolidate, might turn his right flank and envelop his army. Thus for the next ten days there was no disposition among the Turks to regard victory as certain. Kemal, strung up as he himself was, continued to keep up the pressure on his overtaxed troops, leading them still from the front line in person. Supremely confident now that he could never be hit, he led a charmed life under enemy fire such as invested him, in the eyes of his men, with the magic quality of a hero of legend. This leader of theirs had skill. He had courage. But above all he had luck.

It was told of him how once in the battle an enemy field battery opened fire on a trench where he was sitting. They had the range exactly, dropping one shell in front of the trench, then two more, each twenty yards nearer. It became mathematically certain that the fourth shell would fall just where he sat, on the edge of the trench. Urged by an officer to take cover, he replied, "It's too late now. I can't set my men a bad example." He continued to smoke, but his face grew perceptibly paler. The men in the trench looked paralyzed with fear as they waited for the next shell to fall. But nothing happened. No fourth shell was fired.

Now, in the battle of Kirech Tepe, he rode to the rear for reinforcements, which could only be brought up along the shore, between the ridge and the sea, under fire from the enemy's fleet. Here the column of troops had stopped. He was told, "The enemy spreads death. Not even a bird can pass." Kemal swiftly retorted, "You can pass this way." He ran forward himself, with his chief of staff and A.D.C., ordering the others to follow. They did so, running after him in single file, and despite many casualties retrieved the position.

His own evident readiness to die made others ready to die at his orders. This also became part of his legend. During a battle a few days later for two spurs of the Anafarta ridge, it became necessary to gain time for the infantry reserves to move up. Remembering the report of a *chevaler-esque* charge which the French had made on the Asiatic shore, riding to almost certain death to cover the advance of their infantry, Kemal decided in a ruthless spirit to repeat the operation and ordered his cavalry commander to charge. The commander assented, then hesitated. Kemal called him back: "Did you understand what I said?"

"Yes, sir. . . . You ordered us to die."

Many of them died, but their charge delayed the enemy advance and thus helped to save the vital hilltop.

These last fierce battles of Anafarta were in fact the ebb tide of the Gallipoli campaign. Already, a week after the loss of Chunuk Bair, Sir Ian Hamilton had cabled to Kitchener announcing its failure. Not only were the Turks now superior in numbers and in reserves, but they had gained for the moment a moral ascendancy over some of his new troops. As surprise would now be absent, he would need close on another 100,-000 men to resume the offensive. "We are up against the main Turkish army," he concluded, "which is fighting bravely and is well commanded."

The weapon of surprise had indeed twice failed the British, offset as it was by an exacting terrain, faulty planning, and indecisive leadership. Instead the Turks, whom they at first underrated, had turned the weapon against them. The first surprise was the emergence, at the crucial time and place, of a Turkish commander equal if not superior in military skill to their own. The second surprise was the Turkish soldier himself. Besides a sure grasp of tactical essentials, Kemal had shown a shrewd understanding of his men. He knew the psychology of the Turk, and the dogged fanatical fighting spirit of which he was capable, once he had faith in his leaders and his blood was roused; and he knew how to rouse it. Thus between them Kemal and the Turkish soldier saved the Gallipoli Peninsula. "Seldom in history," wrote the British official historian, "can the exertions of a single divisional commander have exercised, on three separate occasions, so profound an influence not only on the course of a battle, but perhaps on the fate of a campaign and even the destiny of a nation."

Kemal afterwards declared that the battles for Chunuk Bair and Ana-farta ranked among the closest in history. Nor was there any false sentiment in a remark which he made years later, on revisiting the battle-fields. Asked by a companion why no great monument marked them, he replied, "The greatest monument is Mehmedjik himself.[2] It is thanks to him that these lands have remained within the Turkish frontiers."

[2] The Turkish "Tommy Atkins."

Kemal could now rest and try to recover his health. He made himself tolerably comfortable, as he had the gift of doing even in battle, moving from his tent into a hut like a snug log cabin. Members of a delegation from Constantinople were impressed by its neatness, by its atmosphere of a place built "not for fighting but for watching the sea in peace," by the four-course meal which he served to them.

A German friend [3] found him still weak with malaria and was shocked by his ravaged appearance. But his mind was as active as ever and he plunged into a strategical discourse. He had no illusions as to the permanence of his victory. He knew, as he had known from the start, the vital importance of sea power. "We are landlocked," he said, "just like the Russians. They are bound to collapse because I have locked them into the Black Sea by blockading the Dardanelles and the Bosporus. I have thus cut them off from their allies. But we too are bound to break down, and for the very same reason. True, we sit on the fringes of the Mediterranean, the Red Sea, the Indian Ocean, but we are unable to venture out on any ocean. As a land power without sea power, we will never be able to defend our peninsula against sea powers which can bring up their land forces unchallenged."

The months went by and the campaign grew static, relapsing into trench warfare. Kemal became convinced that the enemy was preparing to evacuate the peninsula. This was the moment, he argued, for one last Turkish attack, to destroy him before he could do so. But he could not convince his superiors. Permission for the attack was refused on the grounds that "We have no forces, not even a single soldier, to waste." He then asked to be relieved of his command in the peninsula, and Von Sanders agreed to post him elsewhere. His health was in any case worse, and he was in no fit state to remain. Nor was there anything left for him to do.

His friend of the Salonika days, Tevfik Rüştü, arrived on a visit in his capacity as a doctor. On impulse, Kemal said to him, "I'll come back with you now to Constantinople." He had accumulated arrears of back pay and they would spend it together. Thus he left the Gallipoli Peninsula.

Ten days after his arrival in the capital he heard the news that the Allied forces had withdrawn from the peninsula, without detection or loss. Up to the end he had been right.

[3] Ernest Jäckh.

13 ▶ *The eastern fronts*

The British failure at the Dardanelles gave a momentary psychological lift to the Turkish people. For the first time within living memory they had won a victory against a European power. Few Turks perhaps nourished the illusion that the tide of foreign pressure had been turned, that the Empire could look forward to a period of resurrection and recovery. But at least there had been a flicker of light and hope to illuminate the dark defeatist horizon. There was life in the old Turk yet. The national qualities of tenacity and courage and pride had vindicated themselves once again, as in the glorious past, here on the ridges of the Gallipoli Peninsula.

The Turks are a race who seek heroes; and a new hero had arisen to save them. No triumphal welcome, it is true, awaited Mustafa Kemal on his return to Constantinople. The exploits of this hitherto unknown young colonel were played down in the press. His name was barely mentioned. Hardly a photograph of him appeared. An interview which he gave on the campaign was suppressed by Enver.

But through that word of mouth that creates myths his name and his deeds became known to the people. The legend spread of this young

Turkish warrior who knew no fear, whose life was so charmed that no bullet could kill him, who could advance immune to all hurt through a hail of fire, the naval shells of the British sailing over his head like birds. To the elite of the young generation in particular, disillusioned now by their Young Turk rulers, he was a symbol to be quietly cherished. Could this Mustafa Kemal be the national hero they craved?

Admittedly Enver, who appreciated Kemal's qualities as a soldier, had been known to refer to him as his only possible successor. But he saw no reason to precipitate the succession. He knew very well that high military rank and the title of pasha that went with it meant prestige and authority, not only in the army itself but outside it; and Kemal knew it too. He had been promoted to full colonel in the peninsula, and a colonel, so Enver determined, he should for the present remain.

Thus Kemal, back in Constantinople, was frustrated and restless. While recovering his health he lodged with his mother and sister in the house which he had found for them on their evacuation from Salonika, at Beshiktash, on the Bosporus. But he chafed at the pervasive atmosphere of feminine fuss, though it was mitigated a little by the maturing charms of Zübeyde's adopted niece, Fikriye. The time had come all the same for him to live by himself. Meanwhile, for relaxation in a maturer and more worldly atmosphere, he sought again the company of Corinne Lütfü, with whom he had corresponded throughout the Gallipoli campaign and who encouraged him by her belief in his star.

At a musical party one evening, while she was at the piano, he had to take his leave and tiptoed silently out of the room. Corinne, noticing his departure, stopped short in the middle of the piece she was playing. One of the guests, a Turkish poet, went up to her anxiously, thinking she was ill. But she turned to the company, saying, "Do you know who that officer is who has retired on tiptoe? He is Mustafa Kemal, someone who will become a great man and will be renowned, not merely in Turkey, but in the whole world."

Few of those with whom Kemal had to deal seemed to think so. He had become a nuisance again, with his outspoken opinions and his blunt disconcerting ways. Seething inwardly, he sought out his friends and acquaintances, hammering his convictions into the heads of any who had the patience to listen to him. The successful defence of Gallipoli had in no way blinded him to the fatal course of the war in Turkey and its increasing misdirection by the German military mission. He wrote detailed reports to the Grand Vizier, backing up his contentions with documents. Troops and supplies were being wasted. Wrong decisions were being made. He poured out his criticisms to his friend Rauf, in the Ministry of Marine. All was the fault of Enver, who was a toy in the hands of the Germans.

The Germans, for the sake of their own interests in the West, were dragging Turkey to ruin in a war they could not win—all with Enver's acquiescence and approval. Some of the best Turkish troops, armed with equipment much needed at home, were indeed about to be sent to fight the German battles in eastern Europe. Such units as remained, apart from mere paper organizations, consisted very largely of raw recruits, conscripted as young as sixteen, whom the officers spent most of their time in training, at the expense of all other military exercises. Arms were short; one unit, eight thousand strong, had a mere thousand rifles. Yet German officers were deceiving their own high command into thinking that Turkey's resources were inexhaustible and that its military situation had never been better.

To give the government the benefit of his views and forebodings, Kemal secured an appointment with the Minister of Foreign Affairs. The minister spoke with rosy optimism of the general position. Kemal disagreed with him and, speaking as one who had seen the war at close quarters, expressed his misgivings. The minister, growing irritable, suggested that Kemal enlighten himself as to the true situation from the General Staff. Arrogantly Kemal retorted that, as one who had devoted his life to a military career, he knew the Turkish Army and its value better than most—and certainly, he implied, better than the minister himself. He added that the only General Staff that existed was that of the German military mission, who had tried to have him expelled from the army as a rebel.

To escape from the atmosphere of Constantinople, he went for a while to Sofia, where he relaxed in the company of his old friends. He left instructions with his A.D.C. to accept, on his behalf, any reasonable posting that was offered him, and he presently received news of an appointment which was to amount once more to an exile. It was to the command of the Sixteenth Army Corps, then resting at Adrianople on withdrawal from Gallipoli, but destined for transfer farther afield. He rode into Adrianople at the head of an infantry division which had just arrived from the Gallipoli front, and his newly gained reputation won him cheers from the crowd. Still with the idea in his mind of hastening Bulgaria's entry into the war—for King Ferdinand was shrinking from the inevitable plunge—he took the opportunity to invite a party of Bulgarian Turkish deputies to Adrianople for a tour of inspection. He remained there for a bare six weeks. The Second Army, with his Sixteenth Army Corps, was then sent to the Russian front to help retrieve some of the debris of Enver's disastrous initial campaign. It was to reinforce the Third Army, which had been driven back in the subsequent Russian offensive, and to join with it in a counteroffensive in the summer of 1916.

Though this was a responsible command, Kemal had still not received his promotion from colonel to general. This was partly due to the influence of Dr. Nazim, an early evangelist of the Committee of Union and Progress, who had always mistrusted Kemal's ambitions and after the Gallipoli campaign had seen fit to warn him not to "play Napoleon." "A man like that," Kemal exclaimed to Shakir Zümre—as he had previously exclaimed of Javid—"deserves to be hanged." [1] Nazim advised Enver to promote Kemal only after his safe but reluctant departure for the Caucasus. He had been there some weeks before his promotion to general, and thus at last pasha, came through.

Soon after reaching his headquarters at Silvan, near Diyarbekir, he wrote to Corinne:

After travelling for two months over a long and tiring road which stretches from the West to the East, one is entitled to hope for a moment of rest, don't you think? But alas! It seems that that will only come after death. All the same, to achieve this imaginary rest, I shan't agree too easily to go to your *Bon Dieu's* Paradise.

To show her, no doubt, that he was keeping up with his reading, he quoted a passage from a work of French military history and ended with an aphorism from Chateaubriand: "I should like not to be born rather than be forever forgotten."

On arrival Kemal found chaotic conditions. The troops on the spot were the mere remnants of an army, exhausted and demoralized, rotting with disease, exploited by unscrupulous officers in league with corrupt contractors, and reduced to bedrock in arms and ammunition. He telegraphed Constantinople for arms, reinforcements, medical supplies, but was hardly surprised when he received no answer. He must use his own efforts to turn the army corps into some sort of fighting shape. In this he was fortunate to have the assistance of a steady, industrious second-in-command, Kiazim Karabekir, who had been one of his supporters in his attempt, at Salonika, to separate the army from politics.

Earlier in the year the Russians, taking tardy advantage of Enver's debacle, had advanced into Anatolia to capture the important fortress of Erzurum, then to occupy Trebizond, the principal Turkish Black

[1] Nazim, like Javid, was hanged following the Ankara Treason Trials in 1926.

Sea port. The Turks planned their counteroffensive for the recapture of Erzurum in July. But the Second Army was not yet ready, nor had it yet established proper liaison with the Third Army. Thus the Russians forestalled the Turks by attacking once more in force along the whole of the front, and they were obliged, after violent fighting, to withdraw still farther.

Kemal, fighting with his army corps on the right flank of the Second Army, was in the thick of the battle. At one moment he and his men were involved in a hand-to-hand fight with a large force of Russian infantry amid a "forest of bayonets" which almost surrounded them. Only by a cool head and a ruthless use of his own bayonet did he extricate himself from the fray and thus from probable capture or death. Then, on his own responsibility, he ordered a general retreat, gambling on the belief that the Russians would not follow it up. They did not and, since he was acting without orders, may thus have been responsible for saving his military career.

In the course of the retreat a Turkish soldier grumbled, "What cowardly commanders are these? I was killing Russians all the way. Why do they drag us back?"

Kemal replied, "Very good. But the battle will not be decided just by your killing Russians. This is a big army, and there may be reasons for the retreat that you don't understand."

"And who may you be?"

"I am your commanding officer."

The soldier looked surprised and conceded, "Oh well, that's different." He believed that his officers had run away first, as they all too often did.

The Turks regrouped their forces. Kemal's army commander was Izzet Pasha, to whom he acted as second-in-command. A general of the old school but of liberal political ideas, Izzet had found himself in opposition successively to Abdul Hamid and (after a spell as their Minister of War) to the Committee of Union and Progress. Like Kemal, he had overtly protested against Turkey's entry into the war and from 1914 onwards had prophesied a German defeat on the grounds that the Kaiser had not the stuff in him to rule a country and command an army at the same time. Izzet was a man of amiable countenance, bulky proportions, and an irresolute disposition.

Early in August the Second Army began its counteroffensive. Kemal had so strengthened the morale of his force, following its defeat, that within five days his two divisions captured not only Bitlis but the equally important town of Mush, greatly disturbing the calculations of the Russian command. Izzet, with the rest of the Second Army, failed to match these successes on other parts of the front and the offensive petered out. Mustafa Kemal, however, could claim the only Turkish victory in a round of defeats. He was rewarded for his efforts with the medal of the Golden Sword. To Corinne Lütfü he wrote, from Diyarbekir: "What pleasure it is to face fire and death among those one esteems." The letter ended, as was becoming his custom, with a French quotation. With time now on his hands he kept up with his reading. "Continuing," he recorded in his diary, "to read the book, *Est-il possible de renier le Dieu?*"

The troops settled down to a winter which was to be hard and bitter. Izzet's force, at the mercy of long and badly planned lines of communication, was deficient not merely in guns but in foodstuffs. Nor could an army any longer subsist here on the country, for the ironical reason that in the earlier stages of the campaign the Armenians had been massacred or deported *en masse,* leaving the land a virtual desert, without peasants to grow food or artisans to provide service. One division was reduced to a third of a ration per man, and there was almost no fodder for the draft animals. Many of the troops had only their summer uniforms, with foot rags for boots, and, following blizzards, whole detachments were found in caves, dead from hunger and cold.

It was to the command of this decimated army that Kemal was promoted in the course of the winter, succeeding Izzet, who was now put in over-all command of both the Second and Third Armies. As it happened they did not have to fight a spring campaign. For in March 1917 a political event of world importance supervened—the Russian Revolution. The Caucasian front remained more or less static while the Russian armies fell slowly to pieces and finally withdrew towards Tiflis, disorganized by soldiers' committees which gave orders to the staff and deprived officers of their badges of rank.

Meanwhile this, Kemal's first army command, was notable chiefly for the fact that it brought him for the first time into intimate contact with one who was to become the closest of all his associates. He was Colonel Ismet, his chief of staff who, like Kiazim Karabekir, had backed him in his dispute with the party in Salonika. Ismet was a small silent man, slightly deaf, with a twinkle in his mild eyes, a sound slow brain, and a conscientious disposition. The education and subsequent careers of the two officers had followed roughly parallel lines. While Kemal was fighting the Italians in Tripoli, Ismet was dealing with an Arab revolt in the Yemen, deploring, as Kemal did, the Pan-Islamic policy which tied down troops in these remote Arab regions at a time when the Balkans were threatened. Fretting here, he was able to console himself only with games of chess, with Izzet Pasha, his commanding officer, and bridge, a game which the pasha had introduced into the officers' mess.[2] Now on Izzet's staff once again, he had followed Kemal to the Caucasian front, stopping for two days on the way to marry, at his father's insistence, a neighbour's daughter whom he had not before seen and whom indeed he was barely to see after the ceremony was over. Thanks to the demands of the soldier's career, it was not for another six years that he was able seriously to embark on a long, happy, and respectable married life.

Ismet was a man with a scholarly mind, better read than Kemal. The two shared the same radical ideas and found many opinions in common. Both saw clearly the fatal course of the war—the trench warfare in the west which was wearing the Germans down; the need, if Turkey were to be saved, for an early peace; the disastrous policy of sending Turkish troops to Europe; the deplorable state of the Turkish armies in Asia. Ismet, as a practical modern officer, was especially concerned with those problems of supply which had bedevilled the Second Army. As a "man of the future," he realized the vital importance of railways. The Russians were ahead of the Turks in this respect. On capturing Erzurum, they had immediately built a narrow-gauge line to the city and beyond, linking it up with their internal supply lines. The Turks on the other hand were hamstrung, in terms of supply, by the absence of any railway line east of the Taurus.

Though Kemal and Ismet had similar views and aims, they were so opposite in temperament as to complement one another. The mind of Kemal moved swiftly and flexibly, with a grasp of broad issues, unorthodox reactions, and a capacity for making bold judgments; Ismet's mind worked within a narrower, more literal compass, slowly and deliberately, with a laborious attention to detail. Kemal was adventurous in spirit, independent in character, decisive in action; Ismet was cautious, dependent on the views of another, lacking in initiative and hesitant in making decisions. Kemal had an intuitive understanding of human behaviour and character; Ismet was an unsure judge of people, whom he treated with reserve and a certain suspicion. Where Kemal was restless, quick-tempered, temperamental, hard-drinking, and promiscuous with women, Ismet was calm, stolid, patient, sober, and a model family man. He was the

---

[2] What gave him more solace was a pile of gramophone records, left behind by some British officers. These bred in him a lifelong devotion to classical music.

antithesis of Kemal, hence just the assistant Kemal needed. Ismet was in fact the born chief of staff, painstaking and loyal, to whom Kemal could dictate his plans, confident that he would interpret them correctly and carry them out with efficiency. He became Kemal's indispensable "shadow."

In the army commander's mess, in this wild remote outpost of the Empire, Kemal insisted on keeping up civilized appearances. Officers had fallen into the habit of wandering into meals at all hours, loosening their tunics and keeping their kalpaks on their heads as they ate. Kemal put a stop to such unceremonious habits. Always fastidious in matters of uniform, he ordered that officers should be properly dressed and observe correct behaviour. They should eat bareheaded, as European officers did. The mess, especially at times when there was a lull in the fighting, was to maintain a certain style, like the messes of Western armies. And so it did, with Kemal himself sitting at the head of the table, drinking and holding forth and drawing his officers into provocative discussions at which he liked to shine. Once, when a new wireless operator arrived at headquarters, Kemal asked him what was happening in Constantinople.

"Sad scenes, sir," was the report. "The old traditions are being forgotten. Everywhere our women are starting to discard the veil."

Such scenes, Kemal decided defiantly, should be repeated here in the East. He at once organized a dance in the Officers' Club, at which a few surviving Armenian ladies were provided as partners for the Turkish officers.

But Kemal, during this lull in the fighting, had other matters to preoccupy him besides reading and dancing. Back in Constantinople Yakub Jemil, who had been briefed as a *komitaji* to kill Kemal in Salonika six years earlier, but who had since become one of his staunchest disciples, was arrested for plotting to overthrow the government and assassinate its leaders. The war, he argued, was lost; the country had reached the end of its resources. A new government should be installed, and Kemal should be appointed Minister of War and deputy commander-in-chief in Enver's place, to negotiate a separate peace—a course of action of which he knew that Kemal was in favour.

In the course of Jemil's trial there were hints of Kemal's complicity. It was recounted that he had sent a circular telegram from Diyarbekir to other army commanders, criticizing the management of the war and the indecision of the government, and proposing a meeting to discuss what steps should be taken. This was reported to Enver by a general, who was one of Kemal's enemies, and Kemal's cipher correspondence was thereafter tapped. Yakub Jemil was sentenced and executed, while his confederates were imprisoned. To Rauf, Kemal later denied the story of the telegrams, attributing it to a personal grudge on the part of an enemy. As for the plot, he admitted that if it had succeeded and he had been invited to take Enver's place he might indeed have accepted. But his first action would have been to hang this Yakub Jemil.

Meanwhile neither he nor Ismet was to remain much longer on the crumbling Russian front. There were more urgent tasks to be tackled elsewhere, notably on the Syrian front, to the south. Ismet was the first to be transferred to Syria, in command of an army corps. Kemal soon joined him, first as commander of the Second Army, then as commander of the important Seventh Army, now forming in Aleppo.

The British forces were pressing, both in Syria and in Mesopotamia. In March 1917, to release troops for these fronts, Enver was persuaded by the Germans to evacuate the army corps which garrisoned Medina, in the Hejaz, now a beleaguered enclave at the end of a long, highly vulnerable railway. The holy city of Mecca had already been lost to the Arabs, through the revolt of its chief, the Emir Feisal; and now the British, through Colonel T. E. Lawrence and other officers, were giving Feisal effective support.

Enver picked on Mustafa Kemal as commander of an expedition to carry out the evacuation. It was a task which, the holy status of Medina being second only to that of Mecca, could hardly fail to bring national odium on any officer who succeeded in carrying it out. As an operation, moreover, it involved a grave military risk and, in face of Arab pressure, might well have led to the destruction or capture of the whole Turkish force. Kemal firmly refused the assignment; and, indeed, Fahri, the devout commander of its garrison, refused as firmly to abandon the city. Thus the plan, through which Kemal might well have ended his career at the hands of Lawrence, was dropped. Medina remained in possession of the Turks, "sitting in trenches," as Lawrence put it, "destroying their own power of movement by eating the transport they could no longer feed." [3]

---

[3] In *Seven Pillars of Wisdom*. Fahri continued obstinately to defend the grave of the Prophet until some time after the armistice. Finally, in response to repeated orders from Constantinople, and to a meeting of his own staff officers, he reluctantly surrendered the city, offering his sword to the Supreme Master at the foot of the Holy of Holies and afterwards fainting away. He thus won the acclaim of all good Turkish Moslems, save those who resented the fact that he had cut down the palm trees shading the sacred tomb.

Now Medina was thrown into the shade by a major disaster—the loss of Baghdad to the British and Indian forces. It caused widespread dismay throughout the Empire and started for the first time some popular clamour against Enver, who made immediate plans to retrieve the position. The remedy was to be another of his grandiose strategical schemes, this time under the virtual command of the Germans. An army group was formed for offensive purposes, with the dramatic designation of Yildirim, otherwise "Lightning." [4] Its objective was to be nothing less than a spectacular march across the desert and the recapture of Baghdad from the British. And beyond Baghdad lay Persia and India, tempting attractions to Von Ludendorff, who was becoming convinced that only big acquisitions of territory in the East could now save the German Empire.

There was to be an end to all pretence that the Germans were merely instructing and advising the Turkish Army. This was a German army group, with a German staff and a German commander, General von Falkenhayn, who had been replaced by Von Hindenburg as chief of the German General Staff, following his failure to reduce Verdun in the previous year, and who now sought to redeem his reputation in a glorious Eastern campaign. The nucleus of Yildirim was to be the Turkish Seventh Army, and of this Mustafa Kemal, of all people, had been placed in command. When his A.D.C. brought him the relevant telegram he was asleep in bed. He sat up, read the message, and in reply to the enquiry of the A.D.C. said, "Yes. Of course I shall accept. But not for the reasons you think." He made a rude gesture. "I shall accept only to prevent this German commander from making a bloody offensive against Baghdad."

Kemal knew that the recapture of Baghdad was impossible, for the same reasons that its capture had been inevitable—bad desert communications, gaps in the railway line and lack of fuel for the trains, the absence of barges on the Euphrates.[5] Von Falkenhayn knew nothing of the country, its conditions, its climate, its people. Nor did he consult those of his countrymen who did—the German officers of the military mission. He was stubborn, overbearing, tactless in his dealings with others, and had soon antagonized all around him, with the exception of Enver himself.

The general had an idea that all Turks could be bought and injudiciously tried to bribe Kemal. Through one of his officers he offered Kemal a present of several "elegant little boxes," which proved to contain

---

[4] It was a name which had been applied by the Turks to Napoleon's campaign in Egypt.

[5] The trains were being fired on cottonseed, licorice, olive branches, vines and even camel dung.

gold. Kemal, enjoying the comedy of the proceedings, chose to assume that the gold was intended for the expenses of his army and suggested that it be sent to the paymaster's department. The German officer explained in some embarrassment that this was not the intention. Kemal then asked him to count the money and gave him a receipt for it, which the officer took with reluctance. Kemal lodged it with the paymaster in return for another receipt.

From the outset Kemal criticized Von Falkenhayn freely. In his presence, before other German officers, he poured scorn on the general's plans, fixing him sardonically with a cold stare. In his attitude Kemal had the strong support of Jemal Pasha, who reigned over Syria with all the trappings of a monarch and whose word until now had been law. As commander on the Palestine front Jemal vehemently opposed the Baghdad project, on the same grounds as Kemal. He wanted to concentrate the available force between Aleppo and Damascus, ready to move wherever the situation might demand its support. To this Enver, at a conference in Aleppo of army commanders who included Kemal, merely replied that the campaign was decided upon, with the best German general available. "Please don't waste time," he added, "in trying to make me change my mind."

But thanks largely to the sage advice of one of his principal staff officers, Major Franz von Papen, the general began to change his own mind. After a tour of the Palestine front with Von Papen he saw the danger that if the British attacked they might break through the Turkish positions, overrun Palestine and Syria, and cut all lines of communication with Baghdad. He thus decided to sacrifice prestige to prudence and to postpone, for the moment, the Baghdad offensive.

As a face-saver Enver revived his pet dream of ejecting the British from Egypt. An offensive would be launched through Sinai, to drive them back to the Suez Canal before they themselves could attack. The plan went ahead, despite strong opposition from Jemal, who now found himself superseded in his over-all command by Von Falkenhayn. Kemal himself opposed the plan as strongly. Von Papen met him on his way south to Nablus with his army, "in a fearful temper with Von Falkenhayn over the measures to be adopted . . . a most regrettable situation." [6]

At that moment Kemal was in fact on the point of resigning his command. Before doing so he wrote a long and considered report to Talat and Enver, on the situation of the Ottoman Empire as he saw it in September 1917. He was helped in drafting the document by Ismet, who had

[6] Franz von Papen, *Memoirs*.

arrived in Aleppo after a visit to Constantinople to take up a new army group command, and whose energy had been renewed by a week's delayed honeymoon on the salubrious slopes of Mount Olympus. Kemal argued first that the Turkish people were tired of the war:

There are no bonds left between the present Turkish government and the people. Our "people" are now nearly all women, disabled men, and children. For all alike, the government is the power which insistently drives them to hunger and death. The administrative machine is devoid of authority. Public life is full of anarchy. Each new step taken by the government increases the general hatred against it. All officials accept bribes and are capable of all sorts of corruption and abuse. The machinery of justice has entirely broken down. The police forces do not function. Economic life is collapsing at a formidable speed. Neither the people nor the government employees have any confidence in the future. The urge to keep alive rids even the best and most honest people of every sort of sacred feeling. If the war lasts much longer, the whole structure of the government and the dynasty, decrepit in all its parts, may suddenly fall to pieces.

He then went into some detail to show the weakness of the Turkish Army. Most formations were at one fifth of their proper strength. One of the divisions of the Seventh Army, sent at full strength from Constantinople, consisted of men so weak that fifty per cent of them could not stand on their feet. The best-organized divisions were losing half their numbers through desertion and sickness before they reached the front.

Kemal propounded the military strategy needed to meet this situation:

It must be wholly defensive, aimed at saving the life of every soldier possible. We should not hand over a single man for foreign governments' purposes. No Germans should be employed in the service of Turkey. What is left of the Turkish Army must not be senselessly endangered for the personal ambitions of a Von Falkenhayn. The Germans should not be given the opportunity to prolong this war to the point of reducing Turkey to the position of a colony in disguise.

Kemal's objective was the restoration of the command to Jemal. All Turkish forces should be recalled from Europe to help defend Syria against the forthcoming British offensive. The whole front should then be placed under the orders of "an Ottoman Moslem commander," to whom Von Falkenhayn, if it were necessary to use him, should be subordinate. He himself would be prepared to serve in such a chain of command, though it meant loss of rank. Unless this were agreed, he begged to be relieved of his command of the Seventh Army.

Both Enver and Von Falkenhayn tried to persuade Kemal to change his mind. But he remained adamant and Enver had little alternative but to accept his resignation. This was awkward, for Kemal was unlikely to keep quiet and might well cause trouble at home. Von Falkenhayn talked of disciplinary action. To save appearances Kemal was posted back to command of the Second Army in Diyarbekir but he refused the posting. The General Staff finally compromised by granting him a month's leave.

Having fought and lost Jemal's battle for him, Kemal considered that Jemal too ought to resign. He replied that he was thinking of doing so but preferred to await Enver's imminent arrival in Damascus. When Enver arrived Jemal submitted to his persuasive entreaties and to those of his own provincial officials and decided to remain at his post. Before relinquishing his command Kemal remembered the boxes of gold with which the general had tried to buy his compliance. He handed them over to his successor in exchange for a receipt, then insisted on exchanging this for the original receipt which he had sent to Von Falkenhayn. He sent his two A.D.C.s to the general with the message: "Your money is lodged here, but the signature of Mustafa Kemal, which is infinitely more valuable, cannot remain in your possession." Von Falkenhayn at first denied all knowledge of the money and declared that the receipt was not in his files. But when Kemal persisted, with veiled threats to expose the transaction, the receipt was handed over.

Kemal now found that he had not the money for his train fare back to Constantinople. He told his A.D.C. to sell his dozen horses. There were no offers in the market, for fear that the horses would be requisitioned by the army. But Jemal, aware that they were good horses, bought them, and Kemal was able to take the train for Constantinople. Nonetheless he remained angry with Jemal for his refusal to resign with him. It was Rauf who finally reconciled them, on Jemal's arrival in the city, over a dinner at the Pera Palace Hotel. Kemal was further mollified when Jemal sent him a message saying that he had resold the horses for more than twice what he had paid for them, and asking him where he should send the balance. It was a payment which, as the outright purchaser of the horses, he was under no obligation to make. Kemal expressed gratification at the gesture; the money would be useful to him in Constantinople now that he was without a command and supposedly in disgrace.

He left his mother's house, as he had for some time wanted to do, and moved to the Pera Palace Hotel, where he would be freer. He seethed with impatience and a burning conviction as to what should be done. At all costs he must persuade the more influential of his countrymen that the war was lost and must be brought to a conclusion by a separate peace. In this view he had the strong support of Fethi, who was a leader of the

Opposition, such as it was, and a few other friends. One of these was Rauf, who kept a watchful eye over Kemal, trying to steer him clear of political intrigue which might land him in trouble. He was forever giving Kemal brotherly lectures on the need for discretion, patience, and self-control.

In the general atmosphere of discontent there was indeed scope for intrigue. Kemal and Fethi found some willing listeners in high quarters who wanted, as they did, to end the war. A friend of Kemal in the War Office sounded him as to whether, if a new military Cabinet were formed to make peace, he would be willing to serve in it. This friend divulged the information that Enver, without the knowledge of his colleagues, had recruited a secret military force to forestall or resist any such move. Kemal and Fethi passed on this information confidentially to Talat, who was not himself happy about the course of events. He extracted an admission from Enver that such a force existed but an assurance that it would not be used against any Cabinet of which he, Talat, was a member.

Enver, meanwhile, continued to look upon Kemal with suspicion. Hoping to allay this, Rauf, once again the peacemaker, brought the two men together over a luncheon at the Pera Palace Hotel. Kemal behaved well throughout the meal, as Enver admitted to Rauf at the end of it. He added only, echoing with unconscious irony Kemal's own protests of seven years earlier: "But I won't have him bringing politics into the army!" One day Enver summoned Kemal and invited him—repaying him in his own coin—to withdraw from the army and enter Parliament. Kemal retorted that he had no desire to become a deputy and no intention of withdrawing from the army. He knew very well that the deputy of that day was a mere civil servant and that the army was the only source of power.

Meanwhile events in Syria soon gave support to Kemal's main argument. To his secret satisfaction, since he had forecast its failure, the famous "Lightning" operation failed to materialize. Forestalling it, Allenby's forces attacked on the Sinai front. Von Falkenhayn, far from being able to launch an offensive, was inadequately prepared even to meet this thrust. The line was soon broken by an attack, not against Gaza on the coast, as the Turks had expected, but on the Beersheba front inland. They had been deceived by the successful ruse of a British staff officer on "reconnaissance" who, pursued from a Turkish outpost, dropped a haversack with papers ingeniously contrived to suggest that the Beersheba attack was no more than a feint. Driven back by a ferocious artillery bombardment, the Turks failed to bring up their reserves in time to form an effective second line of defence.

Lloyd George had asked Allenby to capture Jerusalem as a Christmas present for the British nation. He did so and thus dealt the morale of the Turks one last grievous blow. After the loss of Mecca and Baghdad, Jerusalem was the third great holy city to fall to the enemy. Nineteen seventeen had been a year of catastrophe for the Ottoman Empire.

14 ► *A visit to Germany*

As events turned out, Kemal was now to have the chance of seeing for himself how the situation in Germany stood. In December 1917 the Kaiser invited the Sultan to pay him a visit at German Imperial Headquarters. Since the Ottoman ruler was clearly incapable of making the journey it was decided that his younger brother and heir apparent, Prince Vahided-Din, should go in his place. Enver, seeing a good opportunity to get rid of Kemal for a spell, invited him to accompany the Prince as a member of his suite. Kemal accepted the invitation.

Mustafa Kemal, the republican, the rebel, had always poured scorn on the palace and all that it stood for, but if it could be made to serve his own purposes, so much the better. A contact of this kind with the future Sultan might well be of value. The journey besides would give him a good opportunity to spy out the nakedness of the German land. Enver doubtless calculated that it might have the reverse effect.

Before leaving he was received by the Prince. The audience took place in a drawing room, filled with men in morning coats. Presently another man in a morning coat came in and sat down at the end of the sofa. He was, it turned out, the Prince—a lean man in his fifties, with drooping shoulders, a long bony face, and a prominent nose.

Kemal took in the subsequent proceedings with an observant and cynical eye. "This man," he afterwards recounted, "first of all shut his eyes, appearing to be absorbed in a deep meditation. Some time afterwards he raised his eyelids and deigned to pronounce these words: 'I am flattered and pleased to make your acquaintance.' He then shut his eyes again. I was preparing to answer these courteous words when I saw that this man was again lost in reverie. I hesitated whether to answer or not, but decided to wait until he had recovered his powers of speech. After a while he opened his eyes again and said: 'We are going to travel, are we not?'" Kemal replied that this was indeed so. In the carriage driving away from the palace, he exchanged bitter reflections with his companion on the lot of a country which was doomed to have such a being as its sovereign.

Kemal suggested to a member of the palace staff that, since this was a military visit, the Prince should wear uniform. Arriving at the station, he observed that Vahid-ed-Din was wearing civilian clothes. He had taken offence because his rank had been reduced from that of divisional general to brigadier and he preferred to travel as a civilian. "In reality," Kemal subsequently remarked, "he was worthy of no military rank whatsoever." At the station the Prince walked past the guard of honour, raising his hands inappropriately to his forehead in an oriental gesture of salute. Before the train left Kemal suggested that he should greet the crowd from the window. Was this really necessary? the Prince enquired. On being advised that it was, he obeyed.

As the train proceeded across the plains of Thrace Vahid-ed-Din invited Kemal to his own compartment. This time he received with his eyes open. He made a little speech, excusing himself for the fact that he had only just learnt of Kemal's identity and adding that he knew Kemal well by repute for his successful campaigns in Gallipoli and was pleased and honoured to have him as a travelling companion. "I am one of your greatest admirers," he said. Kemal immediately decided that the Prince was after all a man of intelligence. His strange behaviour in the palace could no doubt be ascribed to its inhibiting influences; now that he was free of them his real qualities would emerge. Here, Kemal began to imagine, was a man who might be stimulated to action in his interests and those of the country. During subsequent talks on the journey he worked assiduously to indoctrinate the Prince on his own view of the course of events.

The party arrived at the small town where the Kaiser had established his general headquarters. The Kaiser, standing on a dais at the end of an imposing hall, was there to welcome the Prince, flanked by Von Hindenburg, Von Ludendorff, and all the General Staff. Wilhelm and Vahid-ed-Din embraced each other and exchanged a few polite words. The Prince then presented his suite. When Kemal's turn came the Kaiser, one hand lodged in a Napoleonic pose between the buttons of his tunic, stretched out the other with a loud exclamation: "Sixteenth Army Corps! Anafarta!" The company turned towards Kemal, who remained momentarily silent. The Kaiser repeated, in German, "Are you not the Mustafa Kemal who commanded the Sixteenth Army Corps and held Anafarta?" Kemal, in his best French, replied that this was so.

Comfortably installed in the hotel which served as imperial headquarters, the Prince, accompanied by Kemal, paid official calls on Von Hindenburg and Von Ludendorff. In Von Hindenburg's office, contrary to protocol in so formal an interview, the marshal delivered to the Prince, and through him to the Turkish people, an optimistic assessment of the war situation. The Prince expressed thanks for this consoling pronouncement. Kemal, whose own ideas on the war situation were less sanguine, preferred to assume that the marshal's words were dictated merely by courtesy.

Von Ludendorff was equally affable and reassuring. He explained his reasons for confidence and remarked especially on the brilliant offensive just launched against the Allied armies on the western front. At this Kemal could not keep silent. Knowing something of the offensive and well aware that Von Ludendorff was exploiting it as a means of raising the morale of the German people and impressing their allies, he asked bluntly, "What eventual line is the offensive likely to reach?"

Taken aback by so direct a question, Von Ludendorff reflected a moment, then looked at Kemal and replied evasively, "As far as we are concerned, we are carrying out our offensive. We shall see how events develop."

Kemal retorted, "To assess the effects of this offensive, I don't consider it necessary to await events or a final result. Because, in fact, the new offensive is only a partial offensive." Von Ludendorff looked at him narrowly but gave no answer.

By now Kemal had established a frank relationship with Vahid-ed-Din, who listened to his discourses with apparent attention and seemed to respond to his views. Never favourably disposed to the Committee of Union and Progress, the Prince confessed his antipathy to Talat and Enver and his belief that they were harming the country. Talking to him in his hotel room one day, Kemal tried to persuade him that it was useless to put about among the Turkish people, as the high command was doing, the idea that, thanks to the support of the German armies, their sacrifices would be rewarded with ultimate victory. Had not Von Ludendorff implied that the fate of the war was being left in the hands of the Almighty? Kemal spoke forcibly and his words seemed to meet with the Prince's approval.

At that moment they heard a clamour throughout the hotel, with shouts of "The Kaiser! The Kaiser!" The Emperor had come to pay his respects to the Sultan's heir apparent. Very much the gentleman, the Kaiser spoke warmly of the faithful and devoted Ottoman state and its value to Germany as an ally. He stressed that Enver Pasha was accomplishing his task with a sense of the high importance of the alliance, and added that the German high command and General Staff had unlimited confidence in this eminent officer. To this discourse the Prince, using the circumlocutions which he considered proper to this occasion, replied through his interpreter:

"The words which Your Majesty has just pronounced on the subject of the fidelity and loyalty of Turkey towards Germany, and on your hope that the allies of the Empire will soon see the realization of their desires, have produced in me, whose duty it is to think of the future of my country, a feeling of joy and consolation. But, setting aside reflections that may be inspired by an examination of the general situation, I feel the need for enlightenment on a particular point: the blows which are being struck at the very heart of Turkey do not slacken; they are falling more strongly all the time. If this goes on for much longer, Turkey will be annihilated. I have not been fortunate enough to notice among your declarations any assurances which permit me to hope that these blows will be counteracted: perhaps you will be kind enough to throw some light on this point, which may reassure me a little."

The Kaiser rose stiffly to his feet. He realized, he said, that certain people were trying to sow trouble in the Prince's mind. "But now that I, the Emperor of Germany, have spoken to you of the future and of our coming success, do you still—can you still—have any doubts?" The Prince replied that his anxieties were not entirely at rest. The Kaiser remained standing, making it clear that he wished to leave.

At a dinner given by the Kaiser, Kemal found himself seated on the right of Von Ludendorff. He was bursting to talk and argue with these imposing German commanders about the course of the war, the subject which filled his thoughts. But Von Ludendorff refused to be drawn. After dinner Von Hindenburg was more talkative, remarking that the situation in Syria had been restored; that during the last few days a new cavalry division had been sent to the front there. Kemal knew that he was simply repeating the reports of the local German commanders. The division in question was one for which he himself had asked many months before, for the reinforcement of Yildirim. It proved to be in so weak a state that its horses had to be put out to grass and fed before they were fit for service. Some time later he asked whether the division was ready and was told to expect nothing from it. After giving these details to Von Hindenburg, he continued:

"I fear that what I say does not agree with the reports that you are receiving, but I can assure you that they are the truth. The situation has not been restored in Syria, believe me." Emboldened by the lavish potions of champagne which he had drunk at dinner, Kemal added: "Apart from this, Marshal, you are launching at the moment an important offensive. But I do not think that you have much belief in it. Will you tell me, for my ear alone, just what aim and objective you feel sure of achieving by it?"

Kemal hardly expected an answer to his question. He summed up Von Hindenburg afterwards as "a man whose eyes seemed to see to the heart of things and whose tongue knew the value of silence." The marshal rose and said merely, "Excellency, may I offer you a cigarette?"

The heir apparent and his party were conducted to various sectors of the western front, chosen with a view to impressing them and inspiring their confidence. Thanks to personal reconnaissance by Kemal, disregarding the prescribed programme and interrogating officers in the field, the trips were unsuccessful. After a visit to Krupp's they proceeded to Berlin, where they were the guests of the Kaiser at the Adlon Hotel. After so long a period of tension at his royal master's side, Kemal sought relaxation in the night life of the city, drinking and dancing and seeking women in its cabarets and *Nachtlokals*. Drinking too freely one evening at the embassy with the Turkish ambassador, he let his tongue run loose with denunciations of Talat and Enver, of all the Germans in Turkey, of the scenes of prostitution in the streets of Berlin at this critical time in the war. He walked out into the street, straight into the arms of a prostitute, from whom the ambassador, with some trouble, detached him, taking him back to his hotel and seeing him safely to bed.

One day in the Adlon, when they were alone together, the Prince turned to Kemal and asked, "What ought I to do?"

Kemal replied, "We know our Ottoman history. It embodies many vicissitudes such as inspire you, and with good reason, with fear and anxiety. I am going to propose to you something with the promise that, if you accept it, I shall link my life to yours. Will you allow me?"

"Speak."

"You are not yet Sultan. But you have been able to see that in Germany the Emperor, the Crown Prince, and other Princes all have a job to do. Why do you stand aside from public affairs?"

"What can I do?"

"Ask for the command of an army as soon as you get back to Constantinople. I shall be your chief of staff."

"The command of which army?"

"The Fifth." This was the army whose task it was to defend the Straits. Vahid-ed-Din objected: "They will not give it to me."

"Ask for it all the same."

"We shall think about it when we get back to Constantinople," was the Prince's guarded reply.

Passing through Sofia on the return journey, Kemal was met at the station by Shakir Zümre and other friends. He told them, "Germany has lost the war." Back in Constantinople he continued, with redoubled urgency, his campaign for a separate peace but he was frustrated by again falling ill. The kidney trouble which had dogged him for a number of years, and which may have been aggravated by an early bout of venereal disease, was now giving him considerable pain.[1] His doctors sent him to Vienna to consult a specialist, who treated him for a month in a cottage hospital outside the city. Then they sent him to Carlsbad to recuperate. Shakir, who had joined his train at Sofia, kept him company.

This enforced rest gave him the opportunity to resume his reading and to sort out his ideas as to the possible future of his country. He kept a daily diary, in French, in which he clarified his political views. He enjoyed a flirtation with an Austrian girl who fell in love with him—or so he afterwards boasted to his friends—and seemed to have marital designs on him. To discourage these he told her that he had a fiancée at home. She appeared upset and asked who she was. He answered lightly, "My country." When she looked puzzled he explained in a heroic vein, "I

[1] In his youth Kemal had contracted gonorrhea, which was inadequately treated and caused complications later. Despite rumours put about by his enemies, he never suffered from syphilis.

am a soldier. I am obliged to love my country and to live with her until the end of my life."

One day early in July 1918 a friend came to see him with the news that the Sultan had died and that Vahid-ed-Din had succeeded to the throne. Kemal's immediate reaction was a feeling of annoyance that he was not in Constantinople. All he could do was to send a telegram of congratulation to the new Sultan, which was duly acknowledged.

Vahid-ed-Din mounted the throne with misgiving. To the Sheikh of Islam he confessed that he was not prepared for the post. "I am at a loss," he said. "Pray for me." Driving to his enthronement with Enver, he complained of rheumatism. On arrival he asked for his stick but it had been left behind. "What a catastrophe!" he lamented. They were his first words on entering his palace—words ominous for the future of his reign.

In Carlsbad Kemal was encouraged by the news that Izzet Pasha, with whom he had served on the eastern front, had been given the high post of adjutant general, in effect military adviser and chief of staff, to the new Sultan. Since Izzet had no love for the Committee of Union and Progress, his appointment might be said to encroach, in an encouraging fashion, on Enver's domain. In response to telegrams from his A.D.C., recommending his immediate return to Constantinople, Kemal left Carlsbad at the end of the month but was delayed en route at Vienna by a severe attack of that Spanish influenza which was already beginning to decimate Europe. When he arrived Izzet came to see him at the Pera Palace and suggested that he renew his contact with Vahid-ed-Din, now Sultan Mehmed VI. They discussed the prospects of orientating the Sultan towards their ideas on the grave state of the war. With Izzet's agreement Kemal applied for an audience, which was granted.

The new Sultan received him amicably and seemed to treat him as he had done before. With permission, Kemal reiterated his previous views, now suggesting that the Sultan should personally assume the supreme command of the army and appoint Kemal his chief of staff.

But Mehmed reverted to the demeanour he had shown at their first meeting. He closed his eyes. After a while he opened them and asked: "Are there other military leaders who share your ideas?"

"There are."

"We shall think about it." The audience was ended.

A few days later Kemal was summoned to another audience, together with Izzet, but this time the Sultan was even more circumspect. Only generalities were discussed. Undeterred, Kemal applied for a third audience at which Mehmed forestalled him.

"Pasha," the Sultan said, "I am under the obligation, above all things, to feed the population of Constantinople. This population is hungry. Until we can find a remedy for this state of affairs all other measures will be vain."

Kemal replied: "Your reflections are proper. But the steps required to feed the population of Constantinople need not prevent Your Majesty from taking those firm and urgent measures which the safety of the country demands. Any effort to ensure public security involves the proper functioning of the whole machine. If the whole does not function, one cannot expect even partial results from its mechanism. I am convinced that what I say is true. Perhaps Your Majesty will not approve of my attitude, but I feel compelled to state that the first act of the new Sultan should be to assert his power. As long as that power—the power which safeguards the country, the nation, and all the allies—remains in the hands of others, you will be Sultan only in name."

Kemal realized that he had spoken too freely. The Sultan, in his reply, used the phrase, "I have discussed with Their Excellencies Talat and Enver Pasha what requires to be done." He closed his eyes once more and gave his hand to Kemal in silence.

The Sultan had been won over by Kemal's enemies. Nonetheless, in his capacity as an army commander, Kemal continued to put in a formal appearance at the weekly ceremony of the *selamlik* in the Yildiz Palace. One Friday he found himself in the anteroom with Enver, Izzet, and a number of "old school" generals from the Balkan Wars. After the prayer he was told that the Sultan wanted to see him in his private drawing room.

"Is he alone?" Kemal asked.

"No. There are one or two German generals with him."

Mehmed presented Kemal to the generals, saying, "This is a commander whom I much appreciate and in whom I have great confidence."

When they had sat down he continued: "I have appointed you army commander in Syria. The operations there have assumed great importance. It is necessary for you to go there. And I must ask you this: do not let these regions fall into the hands of the enemy. I have no doubt that you will acquit yourself brilliantly in the task I confide in you. You must take up your post at once." Signing the order, he turned to the German generals and said, "This man will be able to do what I say."

Ostensibly a mark of great favour had been conferred on Kemal but he did not see it as such. He felt like saying to the Sultan, "Your Majesty, you are giving me a duty which other generals, already on the spot, have been charged to carry to a conclusion. You consider putting me over their heads as commander? If so, I submit willingly to this order, which honours me greatly. But have you understood the nature of the problem? You are sending me to command an army whose command I resigned some time ago and, to tell the truth, an army which has since been defeated, like all the others on this front. How in these circumstances is it possible for me to carry out the task which you assign to me?" But he knew he could say nothing.

Taking his leave, he returned to the anteroom where Enver came towards him with a smile on his lips. Kemal exclaimed, "Bravo! I congratulate you. You have won the day." Then, in more earnest tones, he added, "My friend, I want at least to talk to you of certain essential questions. As far as I know and understand it, our army, our strength, our position in Syria exists only in name. In sending me there you have taken a fine revenge. You have also done something quite contrary to the proper practice. You have made the Sultan give me a personal order."

Enver and the Turkish general beside him laughed. The rest of the company looked indifferent. In a corner of the room a group of veterans from the Balkan Wars were engaged in an animated discussion. One of them was saying, "There is nothing to be done with these Turkish soldiers. They are cattle who only know how to run away. I don't envy anyone who has to command such a senseless herd."

Overhearing the conversation, Kemal intervened angrily: "Pasha, I am a soldier too. I also have had a command in this army. The Turkish soldier does not run away. He does not know what flight means. If you happen to have seen him turning tail, it is certainly because his commander has fled himself. It is unjust of you to make the Turkish soldier bear the shame of your own flight."

The pasha, not knowing Kemal—or pretending not to—was silent for a moment, then turned to his companions and asked, "Who is this man?" There was a whispered reply, and Kemal took his leave in silence.

Rauf saw him off from Haydar Pasha station. Kemal told him of the audience, then, just before the train left, he whispered in Rauf's ear, "Keep in touch with Fethi. Follow the situation closely."

Rauf delivered a final rebuke: "As long as I keep my military post, I have absolutely decided not to get mixed up in political matters. I have known Fethi since the Constitution but do not find it right to join him politically."

The train drew out of the station en route for the southeast.

15 ► The Turkish defeat

Mustafa Kemal arrived in Palestine to resume his command of the Seventh Army a month before the final offensive, planned to eliminate Turkey once and for all from the war. Von Falkenhayn had gone and Liman von Sanders had succeeded him as commander of the army group. Kemal found his own army in an even more depleted and exhausted state than he had feared. Enver had given him not merely unwarranted predictions but incorrect figures. Three Turkish armies held a line from west to east, two (the Eighth and Seventh) between the coast and the river Jordan, and the third (the Fourth) to the east of it. But they were mere skeletons of armies, with no reserves to supply them. Before leaving Constantinople Kemal had urged that what remained of these units be combined into a single compact force under a unified command. But the proposal was cynically discounted as a move to further his own personal ambitions. Now after a long and thorough tour of inspection of the central sector of the front, from his headquarters at Nablus, he reached the conclusion that the battle was lost in advance.

Many troops had been in the line for six months without relief. The traditional Turkish fighting spirit had been undermined for want of a bare minimum of rations. Reinforcements had been arriving depleted by large-scale desertions en route. And now there would be no more reinforcements, for a second front had been opened. Enver and the Germans had chosen this moment of acute national peril to launch a new force into the Caucasus, in pursuit of the disintegrating Russian armies and of the old Pan-Islamic, Pan-Germanic dream of an Asiatic empire. A regiment destined for one of Kemal's divisions arrived minus its commander and staff, who had been transferred to the Caucasian front without warning or replacement. One of its two battalions deserted in a body, in response to propaganda by Arab agents of the British which described the situation of the Turkish armies as hopeless.

Early in September Kemal wrote to a doctor friend:

> Syria deserves pity. There is no governor, no commander. There is a lot of British propaganda. The British secret service is active everywhere. The population hates the government and looks forward to the arrival of the British. The enemy is strong in men and transport. We are like a thread of cotton before them. The British now think that they will defeat us by their propaganda, rather than by fighting. Every day from their aircraft they throw more leaflets than bombs, always referring to "Enver and his gang. . . ."

This was part of the softening-up process, in preparation for the "strategical masterpiece" which General Allenby, with an over-all two-to-one superiority and an overwhelming advantage in cavalry and air support, was about to inflict upon the remains of the Turkish Army. His plan was bold and simple. He would break through the Turkish front line with his infantry, then strike with his cavalry to the rear of it at the three points from which the three armies drew their main supplies. If all went swiftly and without mishap, he had hopes not merely of defeating these armies but of destroying them altogether. The initial breakthrough was to be along the coast, against the Eighth Army, but the Turks were to be deceived into expecting it inland, against the Seventh—an exact reversal of the tactics which he had employed in the previous campaign.

The deception was so elaborately planned as to include the taking over and preparation of a hotel in Jerusalem as a false GHQ, the throwing of new bridges over the Jordan, the pitching of new camps in its valley and the manning of them with fifteen thousand dummy horses, made of canvas, for which mule-drawn sleighs raised clouds of dust at intervals to suggest that they were trotting down to drink in the Jordan. Meanwhile the real attacking force was moved by night from the hills to the coastal plain and concealed without tents in the olive woods and orange groves, doubling itself without even the local inhabitants becoming aware of any change in its numbers.

The deception succeeded. The day before the offensive the Turks still had no inkling of the enemy's coastal concentrations and were concentrating their own forces to meet an attack up the Jordan Valley, where Kemal was in command. On the previous day an Indian deserter from the British forces had divulged to the Turks the date, hour, and direction of the attack. But only Kemal seems to have paid any serious attention to his report. On receiving it, he immediately got up from his bed, where he was lying in pain from a recurrence of his kidney complaint. He called a meeting of his staff, then dictated an order based on the assumption that the enemy would attack in the early morning of September 19. Taking no chances as to the intended direction, he detailed the measures to be taken by his various units. Liman von Sanders, to whom a copy of the order was sent for information, discounted Kemal's prediction of the date but replied that there was no harm in taking precautions.

On the night of September 18 Kemal telephoned to his two army corps commanders—his two friends, Ismet and Ali Fuad—to ensure that they had taken the necessary steps. They had barely answered him when he heard the first roar of the British artillery bombardment—fifteen minutes of sudden and intense fire by every available gun, followed by a barrage which moved as fast as a hundred yards a minute.

It soon became clear that, after a preliminary skirmish on his own front, the main blow was falling not here in the centre but away on the right, as the deserter had foretold. It fell on the Eighth Army, which was too stunned and surprised to resist it. Soon the Turks were swarming northwards in hopeless confusion, across the plain of Megiddo where, as Allenby well knew, decisive battles had been fought since the beginning of history. His infantry pursued them, his cavalry wheeled eastwards to cut off their main line of retreat. Their communications were disrupted by effective bombing. Thus Liman von Sanders knew nothing of the extent of the rout until twenty-four hours later, when enemy cavalry, after a night ride, surprised his headquarters at Nazareth, while he still lay in bed, and almost succeeded in capturing him together with his whole General Staff.

The swift encircling movements of Allenby's cavalry were soon effectively closing the net around the Turkish armies. What he had done was, as Wavell described it, to push open by the handle "a wide and heavy door of which the hinges were in the foothills and the handle by the coast." Kemal's Seventh Army was on the hinge. Its right wing was cut to pieces or captured. Holding the remainder together, he stood firm for as long as he could, to prevent the infection of the defeat on the right from spreading. He realized that it was vital to prevent the enemy from passing east of the Jordan, where the Fourth Army was already being harassed by the Arab legions of Feisal and Lawrence in an endeavour to cut the only remaining Turkish line of retreat. With its aid the enemy was momentarily contained, and Kemal ordered the retreat in the direction of the Jordan, keeping in touch as far as possible with the remnants of the army on his right and with that on his left.

Passing through Nablus, their former headquarters, his troops found an indifferent, silent population. Elsewhere the Arab villagers had dressed themselves in festive clothes, ready to welcome the enemy. The Turks retreated step by step and in good enough order, checking the attacks of the British here and there, despite inferior numbers, compelling them to halt and make fresh dispositions. Given adequate reserves, they might have held the position; but no reserves existed.

There were heavy losses from air attack, which had a paralyzing effect on the morale of the Turkish forces. But Kemal, by ruthless and determined leadership, still contrived to keep a portion of his army in being and, after a week of hazards and hardships, had transported it across the Jordan, free of the enemy's net. Ismet, bringing up the rear with his army corps, found that the attacks were now coming from the north, not the south. The British were fast moving southwards to prevent his troops from crossing the Jordan. Already the valley was strewn with the shattered remnants of Yildirim and its equipment. Ismet, destroying his transport, setting his horses to swim, trying to keep his divisions in some sort of order, waded across with his men in a strong current under enemy fire, with the water above their waists. The German colonel accompanying him was worried because a photograph of his wife and daughter had become wet. But Ismet consoled him with the thought that this was an augury of happiness, since they were now baptized in Jordan water.

At Ajlun—beneath the walls of the Transjordan fortress from which the more redoubtable Saladin had persistently prevented the Latin Crusaders from crossing the Jordan—Ismet found Kemal, sick and in pain. Neither man could tell just what was happening or was likely to happen. Already the Fourth Army was retreating across tracts of waterless desert towards Damascus. Would Von Sanders make a stand before the city? From here it was impossible to know. They moved on next day across the mountains to Der'a, harried by Arab villagers, who nevertheless dispersed when they turned and fought back. Here they received orders to retreat towards Damascus and Kemal ordered the Seventh Army to assemble to the south of the city at Kiswe.

He entered Damascus alone, with a small personal escort, leaving his troops to catch up with him and rest. Familiar as he was with it from his earlier soldiering days, he was quick to sense among the inhabitants a cold hostility to the Turks. Feisal's Sherifian flag hung from the windows. Armed Arab bands were roaming the streets, drunk with excitement, diverting themselves with equestrian fantasias and firing salvoes of cartridges into the air. The city was evidently doomed. Returning to Kiswe, Kemal found orders from Von Sanders to hand over his troops to the commander of the Fourth Army and to proceed to Rayak, there to rally and command a mixed group of units salvaged from various parts of the front.

Von Sanders had indeed planned to defend Damascus, but the general confusion and exhaustion of the troops, the lack of liaison, and the unforeseen speed of the advance forced him to abandon the plan. It was at Homs, farther north, that he now hoped to regroup his fugitive forces, under the protection of a line running from the valley of the Barada across the plain of Rayak, which might also serve to protect Beirut. Thus the Emir Feisal triumphantly entered Damascus, preceded a day or so earlier by Colonel Lawrence, for whom the women of the city tore off their veils and leaned screaming with laughter through their lattices, splashing him with bath dippers of scent as he drove through the streets in his open Rolls-Royce.

As the Arab troops marched into Damascus, Kemal was on his way to Rayak. He met Liman von Sanders at the headquarters of the German Asia Korps. The German colonel in command offered each of them a glass of cold beer. While they drank he proceeded to illustrate over a map, for the benefit of his new commander, the excellent situation, in spite of everything, of his excellent force.

When he had finished Kemal asked Von Sanders: "Is this officer under my orders?"

"Yes."

"In that case, Colonel, would you be kind enough to tell me where your troops are, what is their strength, and their position?"

The colonel, taken aback, said, "I can't yet give you a definite answer. The movements of the troops make the situation a little confused."

Kemal replied, "Colonel, my country is at stake. Those whose task it is to defend it can't be content with approximations. I have at this moment to take decisions. Can you tell me what I may count on from you?"

After reflecting for a moment the colonel told the truth: "I must admit, sir, that I have no force on which we can count."

"Which means that I have before me a colonel with his staff, and nothing else?"

"That is so."

"Then let us go to our headquarters."

Kemal's headquarters was at Rayak and Von Sanders' at Baalbek. As far as Kemal could see, the only troops left in the neighbourhood were scattered bands which had lost their units and were quite demoralized. He instructed the officers he could trust to assemble the men and organize them into units. He was informed that certain senior officers had passed northwards on horseback; the general who had been ordered to defend Damascus had left the city; the commander of one army corps had surrendered and bolted to Beirut.

That evening Kemal realized that there no longer existed any authority on any front or in any unit. The time had come for him to take the situation into his own hands. Exceeding his powers, he issued an order that all his forces were to make for the north—those in the area of Damascus, under Ismet, and those in the area of Baalbek, under Ali Fuad. This order, which he communicated, for information, to Liman von Sanders, now at Homs, laid him open to serious censure, for it envisaged a drastic burning of boats and a further retreat on a major scale. But Kemal trusted his own judgment, confident that he would be able to justify his action.

Von Sanders had already ordered the evacuation of Rayak, no longer tenable since the British were now on the road north of Damascus. Kemal fired the railway station, amid shots from the populace, and demolished its installations and waterworks. When his last troops were gathered in he proceeded to Baalbek. Here he confirmed his order to Ali Fuad. At night he went on to Homs by train. Here he confronted Von Sanders and put it to him forcibly that his decision was, in the circumstances, the only one possible. Von Sanders agreed with him.

"What you say," he admitted, "is true. But I, after all, am only a foreigner. I cannot take such a decision. Only the masters of the country can do so." The German realized that this involved the abandonment to the enemy, without resistance, of almost the whole of the treasured Turkish province of Syria.

In his most masterful manner Kemal replied, "In that case the orders will be executed."

Together they went to see the Turkish chief of staff, who was ill. He too agreed with Kemal. Their decision was to move all surviving forces to Aleppo, a hundred and twenty miles north, in the extreme corner of Syria, and there to reorganize pending a further decision. It was Von Sanders who issued the final order but it was in effect Mustafa Kemal who from now on commanded. Ironically, the unified command of the three armies, for which he had pressed at the outset, had materialized now that they had virtually ceased to exist. But at least by his efforts some sort of a Turkish force could now be kept in being.

Thus Allenby's war of movement, a "lightning" operation if ever there was one, came to a temporary halt. He boldly decided to press forward with a small force which could not yet be supported by the rest of his army. But Kemal, with a safe distance between them, had won a respite to collect his scattered forces and prepare a defence of Turkish territory. Torrid heat paralyzed the city of Aleppo, and the military traffic threw up thick yellow clouds of dust which choked the streets. Kemal formed committees of reorganization under his two corps commanders, Ali Fuad and Ismet. Two new divisions were gradually assembled, one of them at Katina, commanding the mountain roads to the north and west, leading down to the port of Alexandretta. Von Sanders transferred the greater part of his staff beyond the port to Adana and presently followed himself, thus virtually retiring from the scene of battle.

Soon after his arrival in Aleppo Kemal went down once more with the kidney complaint which had troubled him throughout the retreat. He lay under treatment in the Armenian hospital, using the nurses' sitting room for conferences with the generals and the local authorities, and impressing the doctors with the stamina which had enabled him to fight the disease. Meanwhile an advanced detachment of British armoured cars, after an engagement with a Turkish rear guard, had drawn near to the city and called upon the Turks to surrender. They refused to do so. Two days were then spent by the British forces reconnoitring the defences until their supporting troops arrived. For a while Arabs occupied the citadel and government building. Kemal, in bed and in pain, heard firing in the street outside the Baron Hotel where he was now staying. He went to the balcony to see what was happening. There was a confused uproar. A crowd of Arabs was trying to break into the hotel, past a group of panic-stricken Turkish soldiers, in search of the pasha and his staff. Kemal went down and, wielding his riding crop, drove a group of them out of the lobby. The commander of the garrison then handed him a report which he was too paralyzed with fear to read. Kemal looked through it calmly. It stated that the city was under attack.

The crowd then saw him emerge onto the terrace of the hotel, a slim blue-eyed assured figure, in impeccable uniform, with a cigarette between his lips. Quietly and without fuss he gave certain orders. Then he strolled down the street. Sardonically he observed that certain inhabitants of Aleppo, whom he aspired to defend, were throwing grenades at him from the rooftops. Soon his men, stationed nearby, moved swiftly down the streets and dispersed the Arabs with a rain of machine-gun fire, leaving corpses strewn over the pavements. They quickly restored order throughout the city.

But the time had come to evacuate Aleppo. Apart from Allenby's imminent advance, there was danger of a landing in the rear at Alexandretta. Calling for his car, Kemal drove around the city, giving the necessary orders to those concerned. Then he drove back to the hotel. That evening the rear guard was withdrawn from the south of the city, to create the impression of a complete retreat. In fact the main force was withdrawn only to the city's northwestern outskirts.

An English nurse, one of two who had been marooned throughout the war in the hospital which Kemal had recently left, described the "day of excitement" which followed:

At 6 A.M. firing was going on all over the city, it seemed to rain bullets, and quite impossible to put one's head outside a door or go on the balcony: the Arabs were stationed in the streets letting off their guns at random. Many houses were looted of everything the Arabs could carry off, even to cooking and washing utensils; we watched them break into a house on the opposite side to us and load up their horses with bedding, pillows, and all kinds of articles obtainable. At 8 A.M. the Hedjazi Arab troops forerunning our own army entered the city, shouting, singing, galloping their horses, swaying in the saddles, wielding their swords and guns in the air and carrying their banner; we knew that the English were not far from us, and at 9 A.M. we had the great joy of seeing our helmeted men gliding through the city on armoured cars. Our feelings of thankfulness knew no bounds, we hoisted our Union Jack, to the cheers of outsiders, and away over the hills facing our hospital was to be seen a moving black streak getting nearer and nearer, until our cavalry were also in the city; after half-an-hour's halt they passed out to the north side of the city to take position, but unfortunately the Turks were in wait, and an attack took place, where some of our men lost their lives and many were wounded.[1]

[1] Sister Ethel Curry (Mrs. E. McLeod Smith), "A Prisoner in Aleppo," *Nurses' League Journal*, VII, December 1919.

This was the first of a series of rear-guard actions in which Kemal's army, repeatedly attacked but never defeated, withdrew to a line on the heights behind the city, obliging the British to call up reinforcements from Damascus. For the first time it was defending not Arab territory but the soil of Turkey itself, of which this was the natural frontier.

The end, however, was not far off, as Kemal well knew. The Ottoman Empire was an empire no longer. The Balkan Wars had deprived it of Turkey in Europe; now the World War had deprived it of all its Arab provinces. Kemal, though he smarted at the thought of defeat, did not regret this; in a sense he had always foreseen it. It brought nearer his vision of a new Turkish nation, surgically freed from the canker of its outlying limbs to regenerate itself as a compact healthy body rooted in the good earth of its forebears. Syria, the land of the foreigner, had gone. But Anatolia, the heartland of the Turk, still survived and must continue to survive. It was there, behind this range of mountains, that both the past and the future of his country lay.

16 ► *The armistice*

This vision, however, had yet to be realized. The danger meanwhile was acute. Throughout the retreat from Homs and during the subsequent days in Aleppo, Kemal had been turning over and over in his mind the political implications of the defeat which he knew to be imminent. Had Turkey made peace independently of Germany in the previous year, as he had repeatedly urged, she might have earned such treatment from the Allies as to ensure at least an honourable survival. But now he saw that her very existence would be threatened. How was this threat to be confronted?

The Cabinet was expected to resign at any moment. It was imperative to sue for peace but impossible for Talat, exhausted and now discredited, to do so. There must be a new government, and in Kemal's view the person to lead it was Izzet Pasha. He had opposed the war; he was a man of moderate but patriotic political views; he had consistently worked against the Committee of Union and Progress and was favourably inclined to the Nationalists.

Kemal telegraphed accordingly to the Sultan, through his principal A.D.C. "The situation," he urged, "is extremely serious. Our troops are becoming more and more demoralized. . . . Not only is our army threatened but the future of our state is at stake. I therefore urge that . . . peace be brought about at any cost." The A.D.C. was invited to put this view before the Sultan and to urge him to entrust Izzet with the formation of a Cabinet. Its members, he frankly proposed, should include Fethi, Rauf, and himself, Mustafa Kemal, as Minister of War, hence deputy commander-in-chief. "This Cabinet," he concluded, "should immediately get in touch with the Allies and sign an armistice which will cease military operations."

In Constantinople events were already moving in this direction. Talat had returned from a visit to Germany. On the station platform at Sofia he was greeted with the news that the Bulgarian front had broken and that King Ferdinand was suing for an armistice preparatory to his own abdication. Turkey was thus menaced from the west as from the east. Constantinople itself now lay wide open to attack from Allied forces based as near home as Salonika. The bazaars began to buzz with rumours of the imminent entry into the city of the hated French General Franchet d'Espérey, a man bent, it was believed, on turning it into a French capital and enslaving its Turkish inhabitants.

Talat offered his resignation to the Sultan, who after an initial refusal accepted it. Soon afterwards, with Enver and Jemal, he fled across the Black Sea in a German warship. Talat proceeded to Germany, where he was to be shot dead by a vindictive Armenian three years later. Enver and Jemal found an eventual refuge in Russia, where no less violent deaths awaited them. In due course the Union and Progress party held a last convention, at which it admitted its guilt and decided on its own dissolution.

After the aged Tevfik Pasha, a perennial stopgap, had failed to form a Cabinet, the post was offered to Izzet Pasha who, as urged by Kemal and his friends, agreed to accept in the spirit of a soldier obeying an order from his commander-in-chief. It would be his policy, he declared, to seek peace on the Wilson principles.

Rauf pressed Izzet to make Kemal either Minister of War or chief of the General Staff, but Izzet preferred for the moment to keep both posts in his own hands. Kemal, he argued, was still needed in the field; he could take over the War Ministry later, when peace was achieved. Meanwhile he made Ismet Under-Secretary of War, while Rauf became Minister of Marine and Fethi Minister of the Interior. Despite Kemal's absence it was the first Cabinet with effective Nationalist representation. Its immediate task was to seek an armistice.

Unofficial British overtures had previously been made to Talat through Colonel S. F. Newcombe, one of Lawrence's officers, who had been taken prisoner in Palestine and brought by the Turks to Brusa, escaping thence to Constantinople with the aid of a girl (destined to become his wife) who was a native of the city. As a British staff officer he was able to give the Turks some idea as to the terms which his countrymen might accept, and offered them his services as an intermediary. He repeated the offer to Izzet's government but now suggested a more senior officer for the role—General Sir Charles Townshend, the British commander of the abortive defence of Kut, in the Baghdad campaign, who was now a respected prisoner of the Turks on the island of Prinkipo. The general, through Rauf, then proposed to Izzet his own intervention with the British authorities for peace talks. Izzet had no choice but to sue for an armistice, and this was as good a channel as any.

He thus sent for the general and granted him his liberty. After speaking of his admiration and feeling of friendship for Britain, Izzet deplored as a crime his country's entry into the current war on the opposing side. If England would cease operations immediately, he continued, Turkey would be prepared to give autonomy to all the Arab provinces now in Allied possession, provided her political independence was respected in the other occupied territories and in the rest of the country. Rauf followed up this interview by a visit to the general on Prinkipo. He expressed a hope that the terms would respect Turkey's military honour. "We are not," he said, "Bulgarians. . . . Let England do things quietly and trust Turkey as a gentleman." General Townshend was conveyed to the island of Tenedos, whence he crossed in a Turkish naval tug to Mytilene. Here he was met by a British naval officer in a launch. The following dialogue took place between them:

"Who are you?"

"General Townshend."

"Good God! I am glad to see you, sir."

"I am once more under the British flag." [1]

On October 24, 1918, Izzet was informed that the British government was ready to negotiate for an armistice and had delegated Admiral Calthorpe for the purpose. It was suggested privately by Townshend that Rauf should be a member of the Turkish delegation. Izzet called a Cabinet meeting, then went to report to the Sultan. The Sultan congratulated

[1] Major General Sir Charles Townshend, *My Mesopotamian Campaign.*

his government but went on to declare that he wished his brother-in-law, Damad Ferid, to head the delegation.

Izzet was taken aback by this extraordinary proposal, delivered as it was in tones of imperial authority. He received it at first in silence, then he exclaimed, "But he is mad!" Damad Ferid was a personage of no account but for the fact that he was married to the Sultan's sister, Princess Mediha. The marriage had been contracted on the death of her first husband, in response to an order by Sultan Abdul Hamid that a husband should be found for her between the ages of thirty and forty, who was of good family and had never seen the face of a woman. Fulfilling these requirements, Ferid had been brought back from London, where he was an obscure First Secretary in the Turkish Embassy, and the union was solemnized. Later he sent his wife to Abdul Hamid to beg from him the post of ambassador in London. But the Sultan replied, "Sister, London is not a school. It is a most important embassy. Only those who have real political capacities and experience can be appointed." Ferid, thus snubbed, returned to his house, from which he had not been seen to emerge for thirty years.

This was the man whom Abdul Hamid's brother now proposed as negotiator of an armistice for his country.[2] Izzet replied that he must consult his Cabinet. The Sultan agreed but insisted that Damad Ferid must accompany Izzet to the Sublime Porte to receive the Cabinet's instructions.

Izzet left Damad Ferid in an anteroom and went into the Cabinet room to report to his colleagues. At first nobody spoke. Then an explosion from Rauf broke the silence. As he saw the move, the Sultan feared that he might be forced by the Allies to abdicate. The choice of his own brother-in-law as delegate, a man known and by repute well liked in Britain, might dissuade them from such a course. Rauf conceded that this was a natural impulse on the part of a man who sought only to save his own throne. But did the Sultan seriously believe, at this crucial moment in his country's history, that his government was less capable of defending its rights than a half-wit? Izzet and the rest of the Cabinet supported Rauf and a message was sent out to Damad Ferid that he need wait no longer. The Sultan was obliged to accept the decision. Rauf himself was chosen as delegate in Damad Ferid's place. He proceeded with his delegation to

[2] Later Admiral of the Fleet Sir Somerset Gough-Calthorpe, G.C.B., G.C.M.G. If necessary, he is said to have promised, he would go to England, see King George V, whose father King Edward VII he had known during his service in London, and ask him as a favour to restore to Turkey all the Ottoman territories lost since 1914.

the island of Lemnos, where H.M.S. *Agamemnon,* the temporary flagship
of Admiral Calthorpe, was anchored off Mudros.

The negotiations were conducted on board in a gentlemanly atmosphere. They lasted for thirty-six hours and covered only military and
naval clauses. Rauf loyally contested them point by point. Admiral Calthorpe, as one sailor to another, was conciliatory. Within twenty-four
hours initial agreement had been reached, subject to confirmation from
Constantinople. The main provisions demanded by the British were the
opening of the Dardanelles and the Bosporus; the Allied occupation of
all important strategic points; the demobilization of the Turkish Army
apart from troops neeeded to police frontiers and keep internal order; the
surrender of all Turkish garrisons in the occupied territories—but not, in
specific terms, the surrender of their arms. The Turks proved sensitive to
any suggestion of interference with their internal affairs and were especially concerned lest these terms involve the occupation of Constantinople. But they were assured that there was no question of this unless they
themselves failed to maintain order and it became necessary for the Allies
to protect their own subjects.

In the middle of the conference there came a sharp request from the
French that they be represented, through Admiral Amet, their man on the
spot. This was refused on the grounds that the Turks were accredited
to the British delegation only. Lately the French had concluded an armistice with the Bulgarians without consulting the British. The main reason,
however, for now excluding them was the fear of delay through their
insistence on reference to Paris. This was obviated by a high-level approach to Clemenceau, who agreed in advance to the British terms and
to the proposal that a British admiral should command in the Bosporus.

Thus the armistice was signed on October 30, with compliments all
round, and an accompanying unofficial letter from Admiral Calthorpe,
interpreting and amplifying some of its terms. Calthorpe remarked after
signature, "By signing this armistice I hope we shall put an end to this
bloodshed which has been going on for so many years." He shook Rauf
by the hand and confirmed his "ardent desire" for friendly Anglo-
Turkish relations, assuring him that Britain was always loyal to her signature. He turned to his staff, who confirmed the assurance. Every clause
would be carefully and meticulously respected. Rauf, in replying, expressed a hope that Britain would now send to Turkey a representative
of the highest attainments, since he was anxious that Great Britain
should occupy an "unrivalled position" in the country.

Kemal, when he received the news of the armistice and the order to cease fire, was still resisting with his forces in the hills behind Aleppo. "In the fighting of the last few days," wrote Liman von Sanders, "the army held high the honour of its arms." Thus, after four long disastrous years of war, Kemal emerged from the general carnage as the only Turkish commander without a defeat to his name.

The armistice, for Kemal, was not an end. It was a beginning. Undefeated in battle, he was more than ever undefeated in spirit. There would now be peace of a kind. But he knew that a just peace would have to be fought for and that the struggle would be hard and long. He began to envisage himself as a leader in this struggle.

Just how this would come about he could not yet foresee. For the moment he was devoured by frustration. Deeply resenting Izzet's refusal to appoint him Minister of War, he was not mollified by a promise that they would work together "after the peace." A critical interim period must elapse during which, he felt, he would be capable of rendering valuable services to his country. As for the period that would follow, there would be others better suited than he to become Minister of War. He continued to agitate for the post, sending an emissary to Rauf to beg him to press Kemal's claims further. But Rauf had to reply that there was nothing to be done for the moment. Kemal bombarded Izzet with insubordinate telegrams and when Izzet appointed a new chief of the General Staff he protested that he would refuse to obey him.

Meanwhile, Kemal had received orders to take over the command of the army group from Liman von Sanders and he hurried to its headquarters at Adana. The German general received him with his usual punctilious reserve but there was a note of sincere regret in his voice as he said his farewells.

"Your Excellency," Von Sanders said, "I have known you at close quarters when you were commanding at the front, at Ariburnu and the Anafartas. To tell the truth, there have been certain vicissitudes and incidents between us; but when all is said and done they have only helped us to know one another better. I think we have become sincere friends. Today, at the moment when I am obliged to leave Turkey, I confide the armies under my orders to an officer whom I have been in a position to appreciate ever since my arrival in this country. In this general catastrophe, how can one help feeling a great weight of sorrow? Only one thing consoles me: the thought that I am leaving the command with you. From this moment onwards, it is you who are the master: I am your guest."

Moved by these words, Kemal said simply, "Let us sit down." They lit cigarettes. At Kemal's request Von Sanders ordered two cups of coffee. They sat and drank in silence, facing each other and reflecting on the past and the future.

That night the sky over Adana was lit by flames from the dumps of material which the Germans had fired. At a farewell party of German and Turkish officers, a German general paid a tribute to their mutual companionship-in-arms, concluding, "We are defeated. All is over for us now." Kemal, in his own speech of farewell, concluded: "The war may be over for our allies. But the war which concerns us, for our own independence, begins from this moment."

Despite his rebuff from Izzet, it was with a certain elation that Kemal thus took over the post of commander of all the troops in southern Turkey. Now that the war was over, such a command might not seem to offer him serious scope. Demobilization, under the armistice terms, was imminent. On the other hand it gave him a political advantage: it put him for the first time in direct official touch with the Constantinople government. Since it was a government favourably disposed to him in principle, he should now at least be able to make himself heard and perhaps influence policy. His enemies were gone; his friends were in power. At long last he saw a prospect of achieving those political ambitions which had eluded him throughout the past decade.

In the military field too there was something to be done. For the time being at least he had two armies directly under him, the Second and the Seventh, whose ostensible task under the armistice was to patrol the frontier. Handing over meanwhile to Ali Fuad, he set to work at once to ensure that this should be no mere local token army but an effective national defence force. He reassembled and regrouped his units, dispersing forces to stations in the interior, transferring arms, ammunition, and stores to places of safety, and giving the necessary directions to the commanders concerned. These he sorted out and selected with care, removing a number of officers who did not share his militant views. He established a close liaison with the neighbouring Sixth Army at Mosul, on whose support he hoped to be able to count for an unbroken defence line. Whatever might happen in the immediate future, he could at least preserve the nucleus of a self-contained force which at a later stage might contribute to the defence not merely of the southern frontier of Turkey but of Turkey as a whole.

Of what was germinating in his mind there were already some signs.

Before the armistice, he had chanced to meet one Ali Jenani on his way from the capital to Aintab to see to his family. Already, Ali told him, the town was being plundered, and when the army retired to Adana its inhabitants would be at the enemy's mercy. He planned to evacuate his family to some safer place. Kemal asked him, "Are there no men left in the country? You should find some way of defending yourselves."

"But how? With what?"

"Organize yourselves. Recruit a national force. I will give you the necessary arms."

His loyal officers were enjoined to "get ready, in groups, for guerrilla fighting." Irregular bands must be formed to resist enemy encroachment on the territory of Turkey itself. With an eye on the future he doled out arms to various possible centres of resistance in the interior, such as Aintab and Marash, to be stored in secret until the time came to make use of them.

For the moment his task was to fight, without quarter, the terms of the armistice itself. He saw it as an unconditional surrender, and worse. Here were Turks promising to help the enemy to take over their own country. Kemal determined to convince the Cabinet that, in giving in to all the demands of the powers, they would see Turkey occupied from one end to the other, until the moment arrived at which the enemy would be forming the Cabinet itself. "One did not need to be a sorcerer to see that," he said later.

Kemal thus embarked on an impatient interchange of telegrams with Izzet, in which a number of pertinent queries were raised. He was especially concerned about the clause demanding the withdrawal of all Turkish garrisons from Syria. Where, by this definition, was the frontier of Syria? Did it follow the line of the mountains behind Aleppo, the long-accepted northern boundary of the Ottoman province of Syria? Or was it to be prolonged down into Cilicia, to include the port of Alexandretta? The enemy were now claiming that its garrison, the Seventh Army, was stationed in Syria, hence liable to surrender.

It was clear to Kemal that here was an ambiguity which the British were deliberately exploiting. "It is my sincere and frank opinion," he wrote, "that if we demobilize our troops and give in to everything the British want, without taking steps to end misunderstandings and false interpretations of the armistice, it will be impossible for us to put any sort of brake on Britain's covetous designs."

Izzet replied that the armistice did not give the British the right to occupy Alexandretta. However, since the railways to the south, with their bridges, had been destroyed during the Turkish retreat, there was a verbal gentleman's agreement that the British should be allowed to use the port and the road to Aleppo for the transport of their wounded and supplies to their forces. But the port and city of Alexandretta were to remain under Turkish control. Kemal was requested to inform the British commander accordingly.

In an urgent reply marked "Penalty of death for delay," Kemal persisted in his objections, arguing that the British armies had access to ample food supplies in Aleppo itself and in the surrounding districts, and that their real purpose was to occupy Alexandretta and thus cut the retreat of the Seventh Army and force it to surrender. He confessed that he did not hold with all this gentlemanly procedure. He was therefore not prepared to pass on Izzet's communication to the English commander. He went further. "I have," he wrote, "given orders that any British attempt to land troops, on any pretext, at Alexandretta shall be opposed by force." Since, he added, he felt unable to suit his actions to the official views of the high command, he begged to be relieved of his command as soon as possible.

Izzet replied sharply that this order of his was totally contrary to the policy and interests of the state and instructed him to cancel it forthwith. Certainly there had been mistakes in the interpretation and execution of the armistice terms, "but if, in spite of all this," Izzet continued, "we have accepted these unfavourable demands it is not from lack of foresight but as a result of our total defeat. The state is taking diplomatic steps to deal with the present situation and hopes that they will be crowned with success. I sincerely believe that, at this difficult time, I can confidently rely on your handling of these measures and negotiations, which are of the highest importance to the future of the state. Since, however, the situation is too critical to admit of argument or delay, the instructions we give to our armies must be carried out to the letter." He added that Kemal's army group was now to be dissolved as such and to be reduced to the Seventh Army alone.

Having made his gesture of defiance and protest, Kemal drafted a conciliatory reply. He expressed the hope that the Almighty would smile upon Izzet's political efforts and gave assurances of his loyalty to Izzet and to the country. His misgivings, however, were wholly justified by events. Izzet was being sorely pressed by the British. Rauf, mindful of their undertakings to honour their signature, was protesting about this to Calthorpe, and Calthorpe, mindful of them too, was protesting to London. The gentlemanly atmosphere which the two old sailors had achieved on the decks of H.M.S. *Agamemnon* was dissipating all too quickly in Whitehall. The old sailors and the old politicians, for once but not for long in concord, had a more ruthless approach to the armistice. They were determined to read into it and take out of it just what suited them. Alexandretta was one strategic point they wanted; another was Mosul, as indeed Kemal had been quick to observe in one of his telegrams.

When the armistice was signed the British troops, pursuing the Turks up the Tigris, were still forty miles south of Mosul. On the instructions of the War Cabinet, they pushed on and entered it three days later. The commanding general demanded the surrender of the city and the Sixth Army which garrisoned it. Rauf protested that the occupation was contrary to the terms of the armistice as interpreted to him by Calthorpe. "The Turkish government," he added, "are sure the commander-in-chief will keep his word."

The admiral hoped he could be as sure. He telegraphed to London, upholding Rauf's point of view as reflecting his own. But the War Office was adamant, pointing out that on the Turkish General Staff map Mosul figured in Mesopotamia, not Turkey. Calthorpe had to yield. Thus the evacuation of Mosul and the surrender of its arms was ordered. Izzet, in his acknowledgment of the order, hastened, a shade obsequiously, to assure the admiral that he had received his telegram at 8 P.M. and had passed on his own orders to Mosul "at nearly the same hour."

With Alexandretta the story was similar. Calthorpe was overruled by London, as Kemal was overruled by Izzet. The British government demanded the cession of Alexandretta, within a stated time, to General Allenby, who would otherwise resort to force. Izzet again gave in, and the Seventh Army was forced to withdraw. For this drastic move by the British he implied that the blame lay with the stiff and discourteous attitude of the Turkish commander towards their requests. "In the higher interests of the country," he instructed, "it is essential that we remember how weak we are, and that we be circumspect in our words and actions, without, nonetheless, demeaning ourselves too far."

Kemal hotly contested Izzet's implication and insisted: "I know very well just how weak and powerless we are. That does not alter my conviction that we must decide upon a limit to the sacrifices which the state is obliged to accept. Otherwise if we ourselves, completely defeated in a war fought to a finish at Germany's side, help the British to secure the advantages which they are already preparing to get without us, we shall be adding a very sombre page to the history of the Ottomans in general and of the present government in particular."

The Seventh Army was nonetheless abolished, and Kemal was left with a single army corps on which to build his hopes for a national defence force.

17 ► *The Sultan dissolves Parliament*

Constantinople, under Allied "protection," was listless, defeatist, fraught with a sense of doom. "They'll do to us whatever they want," was the general foreboding. It was to be a cold dark winter. There was no coal to be had. The trams were not running, the Bosporus steamers were few and far between. The main streets were lit dimly, the side streets not at all, so that criminals prospered and no citizen would stir out at night without a pistol in his pocket.[1] The police were scarce, besides being corrupt and universally mistrusted. Profiteering was shameless, the currency valueless, the prices of foodstuffs exorbitantly high. Turks shut themselves up in their houses, emerging, shadows of themselves, only to buy bread, perhaps at half a crown a loaf. Some even pretended they were not Turks at all, shed their fezzes, and tried to get jobs with the Allied forces which had moved into the city.

Greeks, on the other hand, swaggered through the streets, jostling the Turks to the wall. They flaunted the blue and white flag from their

[1] "If you see me in the dark never greet me," was a typical counsel from one friend to another. "Something might happen."

headquarters and expected the Turks to salute it, driving them to slink down side streets to avoid the disgrace. One day a panic rumour spread through Stambul: "They are putting the bells into Santa Sophia." A Moslem crowd surged in hysterical waves up to the mosque, to breathe again when they found the Turkish troops still guarding the courtyard.

Towards the middle of November the Allies moved in. With formal pomp and ceremony Admiral Calthorpe led a sixteen-mile convoy of British and other Allied warships through the Dardanelles and into the Bosporus. Here they anchored off the Golden Horn, so closely congested that the water could scarcely be seen between their decks. It was another black day for the Turks when General Franchet d'Espérey made a triumphal entry into the city at the head of his troops, riding without reins on a white horse, aspiring thus to lay the spectre of Fihat, the Moslem conqueror of Byzantium, who had done the same. Soon the French were established in Stambul, the British across the water in Pera, the Italians up the Bosporus. Technically they did not "occupy" the city since the Turks retained, at least in theory, political and administrative control. But to the average Turk it was an occupation in all but name.

The political situation was intricate. The flight of the members of the triumvirate had caused a crisis in Parliament. The deputies of the party of Union and Progress, seeking to save their own skins and conveniently forgetting their collective responsibility for Turkey's entry into the war, now turned on the former ministers and demanded their trial. Three of Izzet's own ministers, formerly involved with the party, were attacked with them: Javid, his Minister of Finance, who had in fact resigned from the Cabinet over the declaration of war; the Sheikh of Islam, who had approved it; and Fethi, who had been Secretary-General of the party in 1913.

This situation was now exploited by the Sultan as a means of establishing his own personal power. He sent Ahmed Riza, the President of the Senate, to Izzet, requesting the resignation of the three ministers or, alternatively, that of the Cabinet and the formation of a new one in which they would not be included. Izzet refused, putting forward, with the backing of Fethi and Rauf, the constitutional argument that the Sultan had the right only to give opinions, not to make demands, that he had no personal responsibility but could only respect the collective responsibility of his ministers.

In his frank way Rauf took the opportunity to give the Sultan a warning, when summoned to report to him on the armistice terms and on Calthorpe's accompanying unofficial letter. Calthorpe, Rauf explained, had promised that there would be no full occupation of Constantinople unless law and order broke down and the lives of Allied subjects were endangered. Just such disorders might now arise from the fact that Damad Ferid, a man known only as a relative of the Sultan, was making mischief against his government, accusing it of plotting massacres of Greeks, and thus creating disunity and conflict. Rauf went on to refer with telling emphasis to the unrest in Bulgaria and Austria since the armistice, which had brought only misfortune to their rulers.

At this the Sultan grew excited. His hands began to tremble and his cigarette fell from its holder, to be picked up by his chamberlain and placed in an ashtray. He disclaimed any sympathy with his relative's opinions. Then he stood up, indicating that the audience was over. He looked at Rauf with a glance full of meaning and said with some harshness: "Sir, we have a nation here that is a herd of sheep. It has to have a shepherd. I am that shepherd."

Rauf said nothing but lifted his right hand in a reluctant salute and departed. It was all too evident that the Sultan, in the role of shepherd, meant to herd his sheep together and lead them into the fold of the Allies. Next day Rauf reported to the Cabinet. Izzet was sick. Moreover, a fighter by profession on the battlefield, he was a fighter only up to a certain point in the political arena. Least of all was he equipped by either temperament or tradition for a fight against his legitimate sovereign. At this moment, with the Allied fleets on the Bosporus, he considered it important to preserve unity and avoid any political crisis. Even if the Sultan gave in on this issue there would be further such conflicts in the future. His only course, as he saw it, was to resign with his Cabinet, on the grounds of the Sultan's unconstitutional attitude. His other ministers had little choice but to agree.

The Sultan accepted their resignation. Taking leave of Izzet, he remarked, "I am ill. I can't look out of the window. I hate to see them." He nodded towards the ships in the Bosporus. Thus was to end, after little more than a month in office, the last Ottoman government which genuinely sought to establish, in the country's real interest, a democratic and liberal regime.

One last bid was made to retrieve the position. It was animated largely by Mustafa Kemal who, in a fighting spirit, at once took the train from Adana to Constantinople. His arrival in the city coincided with that of the British fleet. The spectacle angered him but prompted the philosophic reflection, "As they have come, so they shall go."

With Rauf he went directly to see Izzet and set to work to argue him out of his decision. The Sultan had replaced Izzet with the reluctant Tevfik Pasha, overriding his complaint that he was forever being called in as Grand Vizier, to clear up the mess made by others. But the appointment had still to be confirmed by Parliament. Kemal therefore persuaded Izzet to accept nomination again and to form a new Cabinet of a stronger and more nationalist complexion. Rauf, after some hesitation, supported him. Together they drafted a ministerial list in which Kemal's own name was at last prominent. They then mobilized all their resources to achieve, by assiduous lobbying of deputies, the defeat in Parliament of the vote of confidence in Tevfik.

This was Kemal's first direct experience of Parliament and its ways. In civilian clothes he circulated actively in the lobbies and committee rooms. Many members, he found, were hostile to Tevfik but preferred to vote for him rather than risk a dissolution of Parliament. They would thus at least gain time. Kemal, with his more realistic sense, argued that a dissolution was inevitable whichever way they voted, and could be used to gain time for Izzet. Through Fethi, he was enabled to address a meeting of members at which he put forward his views with eloquence and force, urging the members to vote their lack of confidence in Tevfik, whatever might follow. They listened with interest and apparent sympathy to this young victorious general, with the compelling eyes and the confident voice, so neat in his civilian clothes, so emphatic and frank in his speech. Some gave him definite promises and, when the time came to vote, expressed hopes of a successful outcome.

Kemal found a place in the gallery and watched the proceedings. The vote was taken, the ballot was counted, the President announced the result. It showed a large majority for Tevfik Pasha's Cabinet. Kemal confessed himself taken aback. An appreciable number of members had seemed to accept his proposal. As a soldier and thus a stranger to parliamentary life, he confessed his surprise at the fickle nature of their opinions. Unsure of their position and mistrustful of the military element, they had preferred the line of least resistance.

Kemal interpreted the vote as the defeat of the national will. Only the will of the Sultan now reigned. Here he saw his one remaining chance. He applied for an immediate audience, for the purpose, as he put it, of explaining frankly to the Sultan what measures the situation demanded. After a delay of some days he was bidden to the *selamlik*.

Vahid-ed-Din took the initiative. "I am convinced," he said, "that the commanders and other officers of the army respect you greatly. Can you give me a guarantee that they will take no action against me?"

This point-blank question took Kemal by surprise. After reflection he said, "Has Your Majesty specific knowledge of any army movement directed against the throne?"

The Sultan shut his eyes. Then he repeated his question.

Kemal replied: "I must explain that I have only been in Constantinople for a few days and I am not very familiar with the situation, but I do not consider that there can be any motive for the commanders and officers of the army to set themselves against Your Majesty. Accordingly I can assure you that you have nothing to fear."

The Sultan put on a solemn expression and said: "I am not speaking only of today but of tomorrow as well."

The Sultan, Kemal judged, had decided on a policy which might displease the army and was sounding him as to his reactions towards it. This being so, he could hardly press his own proposals without compromising himself and his cause. Vahid-ed-Din had effectively muzzled him. Kemal thus kept silent, and the Sultan, reopening his eyes, concluded: "You are an intelligent officer, and I am sure you will know how to enlighten and calm your comrades."

The audience, though little enough had emerged from it, had lasted an hour. On reappearing in the anteroom, Kemal received significant and questioning looks. Ironically, it was generally believed that he had promised the Sultan the support of the army for a dissolution of Parliament, as a prelude to a regime in which he and his military friends would predominate. He could have hoped for nothing better. But the Sultan's decision was otherwise. He did indeed plan to dissolve Parliament. His motive in doing so, however, was to please not the army but the Allies. The Sultan had elected to throw in his lot with the occupying powers.

Kemal, since it no longer suited his purposes, now came out in strong opposition to the dissolution of Parliament. He had a platform in Fethi's newspaper *Mimber* and, posing as a champion of constitutional practice, he warned his countrymen of the dangers that threatened them. A dissolution would leave the government free to do what it wanted; and what it wanted was co-operation with the enemy:

Let us remember that the symbol of the Constitution of the Ottoman nation today is Parliament. The constituencies of its present members are still in a state of emergency, which rules out new elections. This alone should show us the madness of dissolving Parliament. It is essential that the present government, which will decide on the peace terms, should have the support of the deputies.

But the Sultan was determined to rid himself of "this cursed Parliament." In consultation with Tevfik and his legal advisers, he found a pretext for doing so among the various contradictory articles of the Constitution. The dissolution, by right of Article 7, was proclaimed in a *firman* read out in the Chamber by the Minister of the Interior. It caused considerable hubbub. Members cried out in protest, started to speak all at once and in shrill contradiction of each other. Many protested against the Sultan's action. But since most of them had backed the vote of confidence in Tevfik they were not on strong ground. Thus the *firman* was executed and the deputies dispersed.

The Sultan, true in his own pale fashion to the tradition of his brother Abdul Hamid, had for the moment vanquished the forces of democracy.

18 ▶ The partition of Turkey?

What, under the auspices of its Sultan, was now to become of the relics of the Ottoman Empire? The Peace Conference, assembling in Paris in January 1919, aspired to decide its destiny. In applying for an armistice the Turks had notified President Wilson that they were ready to treat for peace on the basis of his Fourteen Points—namely the principle of consent. Lord Curzon, the British Foreign Secretary, now produced, in a memorandum to the British Cabinet, a solution based, as he saw it, on this principle. It allowed the right of self-determination not merely to the Arabs and Armenians—the subject races of the Empire—but to the Turks themselves. Besides an independent Arabia and Armenia, there should be an independent Turkish state, confined, as it had been in the past, within the boundaries of Asia Minor, and with its capital at Angora or Brusa. Only thus, Lord Curzon foresaw, could the aspirations of the Turks be satisfied in such a way as to forestall a nationalist outbreak.

On the other hand, Curzon wanted to remove the Turks altogether from Europe, where they had been for centuries "a source of distraction, intrigue and corruption . . . of unmitigated evil to everybody concerned." Thus they should be deprived of Constantinople and the Straits, which should be entrusted to the League of Nations. Such a solution, at this psychological moment, might well have been accepted by a weak Turkish government.

It was not, however, accepted by the British government. For Lloyd George, with whom Curzon was in perennial conflict, had different ideas. These arose from the need to maintain harmony with the other Allies, France and Italy, on other more vital problems. Ignorant of the Middle East and indifferent to its problems, he saw Turkey not as a living organism with a past and a present and aspirations for a future, but simply as a space on the map, a convenient repository from which other powers might be compensated and other concessions obtained in return.

The British government was already committed to four secret agreements, contracted during the war as bribes or rewards to her Allies for entering it. Under these the Entente Powers now planned, in effect, to carve up Turkey in Asia just as the Central Powers and their satellites had carved up Turkey in Europe during the Balkan Wars. The first allowed Constantinople, eastern Thrace, and the Straits to the Russians, in return for a British sphere of influence in Persia. This agreement was no longer in force since the Soviet government had renounced all such tsarist claims. The second—the Sykes-Picot agreement—partitioned the greater part of the Arab world between France and Britain, allowing Mesopotamia to the British and Syria and Cilicia to the French. The third and fourth allowed the Italians a still larger portion of Asia Minor, namely the province of Adalia, to the west of Cilicia, the Dodecanese Islands, and the port of Smyrna, with much of its hinterland. This would have left almost the whole length of the Mediterranean and Aegean coasts of Asia Minor, together with a substantial share of the interior, in the hands of France and Italy. It would have reduced the Turkish state to a few provinces in Anatolia, with access to the Black Sea coast but only a single outlet to the Aegean.

But the crucial—and, it turned out, fatal—element in this scheme for dismemberment was the mounting ambition of the Greeks. As an inducement to come into the war, Sir Edward Grey had, early in 1915, offered Greece "large concessions on the coast of Asia Minor." These were in principle accepted by Venizelos, her Premier, who began to play with the traditional "Grand Idea" of "a really big Greece, to include practically all the regions in which the influence of Hellenism has been paramount throughout the ages." But a neutralist policy prevailed, Venizelos resigned, and it was not until 1917, when he returned to power on the expulsion of King Constantine by the Allies, that Greece in fact came into the war.

As soon as it was over he approached Lloyd George with a Greek claim to the whole Aegean coast of Asia Minor and much of its hinterland—a territory already promised to the Italians. Venizelos based this largely on the ethnic argument that the Greek population formed a majority in the area. Similar arguments applied to the Greeks of "Pontus," in the mountains along the Black Sea. Venizelos thus invoked those principles of self-determination on which the peace was to be based. Two months later, in fluent French and with an "engaging appearance of frankness," he put his case before the Supreme Council of the Peace Conference in Paris.

To Lloyd George, who considered Venizelos "the greatest statesman Greece had thrown up since the days of Pericles," such a demand seemed both fair and expedient. The Greeks could serve Britain's interests by replacing the Turks as the protectors of her imperial communications with India. Thus, despite Lord Curzon and the Foreign Office, who preferred to compensate the Greeks in Thrace; despite doubts from the generals as to the military feasibility of Greek penetration inland; despite the claims of the Italians, which he brushed aside; despite the opposition, on the very grounds of self-determination which Venizelos had invoked, of President Wilson—despite all these powerful factors, Lloyd George resolved to give his wholehearted support to the claims of the Greeks in Asia Minor.

Such was the trend of the peace terms which the Allies were planning to impose on the Turks and which the Sultan was prepared to facilitate; such were the prospects that confronted Kemal as he settled down in Constantinople on his return from Cilicia—a general out of a job. Irked by the restrictions of his mother's household, he rented a tall roomy house for himself in the district of Shishli. Here he was able to enjoy visits from his "cousin" Fikriye, now divorced from an Egyptian husband to whom the family had married her off. His interest in her had been aroused largely by her own evident feelings towards him, her hero-worship turning to love. Now, free in his own house from the disapproving presence of Zübeyde, she shed all inhibitions and a close intimacy developed between them.

After the dissolution of Parliament a sense of defeat weighed on Kemal and his friends. Pessimism infected them; frustration confined them. Rauf became pained and disillusioned at the ungentlemanly actions of his friends the British, and hardened against them. Fethi, in his Opposition newspaper, launched a campaign against Tevfik, whose Cabinet, at this moment when a strong government was needed, he denounced as nothing but a silent spectator of the country's catastrophe. Kemal invested some of his savings in the paper and worked with Fethi in its offices, hoping to influence opinion by his anonymous pen.

In the large room on the first floor of the house in Shishli the three friends talked and plotted to find a way out for their country. They formed in effect a secret revolutionary committee whose aim was to force the resignation of the government, to form a new one, if necessary to dethrone the Sultan. But one at least of their confederates found Kemal too extreme. He feared the risks involved and the committee was disbanded. Maybe, after all, revolution was not the answer, for any attempt at it would immediately be suppressed by the Allies.

Perhaps, it occurred to Kemal, something could be achieved through the Allies themselves. With his compelling presence and his immaculate uniform, emblazoned with medals and with the insignia of an A.D.C. to the Sultan, he was already a conspicuous figure in the Pera Palace Hotel, its mock-oriental marble halls now teeming with officers in the occupying forces and in the Inter-Allied High Commission. He attracted their curiosity as soon as it became known that he was the hero of the Dardanelles. At first he had chosen to keep his distance.

But now he began to see that some contact with the Allies might serve his designs. They were, after all, in virtual control of the country. The French had landed in Alexandretta and were pressing forward into Cilicia. The Italians were about to land at Adalia, thence likewise to penetrate inland. The British had control officers scattered over Turkey from Thrace to the Caucasus, supervising demobilization and disarmament. The Sultan was in power and unlikely to give Kemal a post of any consequence in the dwindling Turkish Army. For what he sought—and this was just such a national resurgence as Curzon feared—any position of authority was better than none. Might he not obtain some post from the Allies themselves—preferably the British, who had no ultimate territorial designs on the country? Power obtained under their auspices, now that they had come, might well be turned into other and more patriotic channels once they had gone.

Deciding to sound them out indirectly, he chose as intermediary a British correspondent of repute, G. Ward Price, of the *Daily Mail*. Through the manager of the Pera Palace Hotel he sent the correspondent an invitation to take coffee with him. After consulting the responsible colonel in the intelligence branch of the General Staff, Mr. Ward Price accepted. He found Kemal not in uniform but in a frock coat and fez, and accompanied by his friend Refet. The hero of the Dardanelles struck him as handsome and virile, restrained in gestures, quiet and deliberate in voice.

Kemal confessed that his country had joined the wrong side in the war. The Turks should never have quarrelled with the British. They had done so as a result of Enver's pressure. They had lost—and now they must pay heavily. Anatolia was to be divided. Kemal was anxious that the French should be kept out of the country. A British administration would be less unpopular.

"If the British," he said, "are going to assume the responsibility for Anatolia, they will need the co-operation of experienced Turkish governors to work under them. What I want to know is the proper quarter to which I can offer my services in that capacity."

Ward Price gave the staff colonel an account of the interview, which he dismissed as unimportant, remarking, "There will be a lot of these Turkish generals looking for jobs before long."

The Italians, on the other hand, took the initiative with direct overtures towards Kemal. Count Sforza, the Italian High Commissioner, was implacably opposed to Lloyd George's support of the Greeks. While committed to a united front on the policy of partitioning Turkey, he was crafty enough to reinsure, in the event of probable failure, with the Nationalist movement, whose leaders impressed him as "sincerely conscious of a force of their own."

One of his emissaries sounded Kemal and Fethi on the prospects of their forming a Nationalist government. Two others—Turkish journalists favourable to the Italian cause—dangled an offer of armed support for a military resistance against the Greeks behind Smyrna, under Kemal's command. When the ground had been prepared, Kemal was invited to meet Count Sforza himself. The count made it clear to him that, whatever he did, he could rely on Italian support. "You may be sure," he said, "that if you are in trouble this embassy is at your disposal." Kemal was reserved in his reply but he was astute enough to see that Italian support might be of use to him if and when his schemes matured.

Meanwhile Allenby had paid a whirlwind visit to Constantinople from Palestine. Certain Turkish generals were showing reluctance to disband their forces according to his interpretation of the armistice terms. Allenby summoned the Ministers of War and of Foreign Affairs and, without giving them the chance to negotiate, read them out a list of demands, which included the removal of the chief offender, the commander of the Sixth Army on the Mosul front. Having achieved his objective within five minutes, Allenby returned at once to Palestine and the offending army commander, on his return to Constantinople, was arrested by the British authorities.

Soon after Allenby's visit—and, he judged, as a result of it—Kemal was notified by the War Ministry of a reduction in his status as an army commander. He was deprived of his privileges as an A.D.C. to the Sultan. His official car was withdrawn from him and his salary reduced. He was offered no less a command than that of the Sixth Army, which was to be disbanded following its commander's recall. Kemal instantly refused it and was thus farther back than ever on the shelf.

At the end of February 1919 the Sultan changed his government. He judged that the moment had come for the scheme which he had planned from the start. He released Tevfik, who had tried several times to resign, and made his own despised brother-in-law, Damad Ferid, Grand Vizier. It was Ferid's first official post since that in the foreign service thirty years before. To the patriotic Turk he was a nonentity, a man devoid of capacity. But to the British Ferid, with his reassuring Western appearance, his drooping moustaches, his veneer of European culture, and his polite pompous manners, was "a typical Turkish gentleman." He was just the puppet they needed.

Determined to wipe out opposition, his first action was to launch a new wave of arrests. He did so with the backing of the British authorities, who had begun to deport political and military suspects to Malta. Already Tevfik, in response to foreign demands, had imprisoned the remaining members of the Unionist government. Now Ferid's Ministry of the Interior embarked on a further purge, using summary methods of trial by court-martial. Fethi was singled out as one of his victims. A prewar Secretary-General of the party, he had been unjustly blamed by his enemies, as a postwar Minister of the Interior, for allowing the escape of Enver, Talat, and Jemal. Kemal got wind of the fact that he was likely to be arrested and urged him not to return home but Fethi, in his casual way, made light of the warning. Ferid, he said, had assured him that he was in no danger. But he was arrested that night when he returned to his house.

Kemal contrived to pay him a visit in the War Ministry prison, feeling like a prisoner himself in its grim surroundings, taking the precaution to shake hands with the gendarmes he met on the staircase. For they might well, as he drily observed, be of use to him if he himself were arrested.

He found his friends on the top floor, in cells facing each other along a dark narrow passage. Here were ministers, politicians, journalists, public men of importance—all treated as war criminals. As he opened the doors of the cells they gathered around him, eager to talk. Among them was Prince Said Halim, the Grand Vizier of the early war years. With Fethi, Kemal went up onto the roof, where they walked and talked. But Kemal felt they were being spied upon and thought it prudent not to stay too long.

He began to fear for his own security, starting a little at each ring at the doorbell, late at night. A newspaper enquired why, with the Unionists under arrest, Mustafa Kemal and Rauf were still "walking about freely in Pera, swinging their arms." Kemal cultivated his Italian contacts, suspecting that if he were known to be under Count Sforza's protection the British might hesitate to order his arrest.

Indignation at the arrests helped to stir national feelings, and a number of vague political groups, of a liberal complexion, gathered together in a house in the old quarter of Stambul, with the aspiration of uniting in some kind of "National Congress." They did little, however, but talk. Kemal and Rauf, with their more positive views and plans, trod circumspectly among them. They found good will enough, but few, even among their own supporters, proved capable of translating it into concrete ideas, far less into plans of action, while many, demoralized by the irksome conditions of the Allied occupation, were preoccupied mainly with their personal interests and rivalries.

The solution clearly lay elsewhere. A possible way to it was shown by Ali Fuad, who returned on sick leave from Cilicia, following the demobilization of the Seventh Army. On arrival he went straight to see Kemal at the house in Shishli and spent the night there, as he was to spend many nights during the next few weeks. Kemal appeared in a dressing gown, for he had been lying ill in bed, this time with ear trouble. Taking Fuad into his bedroom, where piles of newspapers lay by the bedside, he put his friend into an armchair and himself sat on the bed. They talked, then dined, then talked again, for half the night.

Fuad gave Kemal gloomy accounts of the general insecurity and administrative paralysis throughout Anatolia. The local administration was inert and inefficient. There was no unity among the local political parties. Kemal frowned and said, "Not good at all." To both it was clear that the Allies were bent on occupying most of the country and that the government lacked both the capacity and the will to resist them. The Allies were hastening demobilization and the collection of arms. Efficient men were being dismissed from the administration and from the army on the grounds that they were Union and Progress supporters, and were being replaced by yes-men, ready to submit to the Allies. The only solution was a movement of national resistance, for which they drew up a programme.

It could be realized only in one of two ways—from without, by forcing the government to resign, or from within, by introducing into the Ministry of War and the Ministry of the Interior partisans of the resistance. The first having proved impossible, it was now time to try the second. Kemal himself, of course, should be Minister of War. A suitable candidate for the Ministry of Interior would be Mehmed Ali, a friend of Fuad and his family and an influential figure in Damad Ferid's coalition. Through such as he they might be able to achieve their designs by a process not of revolution but of infiltration.

Fuad spoke of Kemal to Mehmed Ali, who already knew of him by repute as an intelligent, energetic, and patriotic young officer. On being reassured that he was not a Union and Progress man, Mehmed Ali said that it would be an honour to meet him, and a dinner was arranged at Ali Fuad's home on the Asiatic shores of the Bosporus. Mehmed Ali explained that he was out for a government in which his own group, which was gaining in influence, predominated. He feared, however, that the key portfolios of the Ministry of War and of the Interior would be given to men personally trusted by Damad Ferid. Thus the process of bringing new nationalist blood into the regime had its difficulties.

Kemal discreetly cultivated contacts among the Cabinet ministers. Some, knowing him to have been an opponent of Talat and Enver, showed signs of wanting to win him over. One of them was Avni Pasha, the Minister of Marine, who showed however no disposition to overthrow the government. Another was Ahmed Riza, the President of the Senate, who was exploiting his influence with the Sultan in the hope of succeeding Damad Ferid. At a secret rendezvous with Kemal he discussed the idea of forming some kind of a national bloc. But Kemal remained cautious and noncommittal; and indeed nothing came of Ahmed Riza's intrigues. Damad Ferid remained firmly in power.

Clearly it was not going to be easy to undermine the government from within. The key to the situation lay in Anatolia itself; the problem was how to get there. Ali Fuad's period of leave was now over, and the time came for him to rejoin his army corps, the only remaining unit of Kemal's former army. With Kemal, whom he still regarded as his commander, he agreed to transfer his headquarters northwards to Angora, a central position suited to become the pivot of any resistance. At the moment it was difficult to do so, since the Italians controlled the railway. But if necessary he would march his troops there. He urged Kemal to join him.

With Rauf, they had a last dinner together in Shishli. They spoke of the resistance as though it were a hard fact rather than a vague aspiration. It would not be easy for Rauf, as a naval officer, to get to Anatolia. But he was prepared to resign his commission to do so. As for Kemal, he would do all he could to secure a post for himself in Anatolia with sufficient authority. If nothing materialized, he would go there of his own accord.

Rauf applied to the Minister of Marine for his release from the navy. He was summoned by Damad Ferid, whom he visited wearing civilian clothes. Ferid asked him to change his decision. Rauf spoke openly. If the government continued on its present track, he declared, the army would rebel against it. He dwelt on the plight of the demobilized troops. The government had contracted to send them home but did not do so. They were left stranded without shelter or food. They were to be seen begging from foreigners in the streets of the city. These men, who had fought for their country through fire and bloodshed, were now condemned to a state of misery worse than death. All this would lead to rebellion.

Unused to such glimpses of reality, Ferid muttered, "How's that? What's this?"

Rauf continued: "I only tell you what I have seen with my own eyes. I have seen all the revolutions which have taken place in this country, before the Constitution and since. . . . As a man who knows these things I tell you that there is bound to be a rebellion. I don't want to take part in that rebellion as a member of the forces. . . . I want to get rid of all official titles and privileges and be free to act on my own responsibility."

Ferid looked at him in blank amazement. He could only say, "Very well, sir." Rauf's resignation from the navy took effect.

Kemal invited Ismet to the house in Shishli, where they greeted one another as old friends. Ismet was working in the War Ministry, in an under-secretary's post, preparing material for the Peace Conference and hoping to be sent to Paris as a member of the Turkish delegation. He greeted Kemal with a twinkle, saying, "What's the news? What are you up to?"

In reply Kemal brought out a map of Turkey. Ismet, the trained staff officer, instinctively brought out a pair of compasses. Kemal asked his advice as to the best way to reach Anatolia. What would be the appropriate district to choose, from which to organize some kind of resistance?

Ismet looked at him with an air of gay anticipation. "Then you have made up your mind?"

"We won't talk about that yet," said Kemal.

Ismet sat over the map in thoughtful silence. He then got up and said cautiously, "There are many ways of getting there, many districts." He added, smiling, "When are you going to tell me what you are going to do?"

"When the right time comes," was the reply.

Kemal was not a man to make a decision of this kind in a hurry. The gamble was a big one; much was at stake. The situation must be coolly examined from all angles. Time was still needed to lay his plans, to convince his associates, to stiffen their resolve, to clarify in his and their minds the ideological basis on which any resistance must be based. Many people still clung to hopes of a solution through the Sultan's government, the Allies, the Almighty, or some alternative source. Opinion must evolve and events develop to the point at which it became clear that there was no other way out but resistance.

Then Kiazim Karabekir Pasha arrived from Thrace, where he had been commanding the remnants of an army corps. Heavy and staunch and slow, militarily a fighter of the old Turkish stamp, but politically a convinced and obstinate democrat, Kiazim had been second in command to Kemal in the Caucasian campaign. He now visited Kemal in Shishli before returning to the east to take over command of the Fifteenth Army Corps, which was all that remained of the demobilized army on the Caucasian front. He urged upon Kemal his belief that the salvation of Turkey lay there, in the eastern provinces.

He himself was trusted and liked in those regions, where he had seen so much of his war service. His army was strong, and the people were behind it. All that was needed was positive and vigorous leadership. Kemal must at all costs secure for himself a command in Anatolia. Other patriotic young officers must follow him, officially or otherwise. Once there, Kemal must come to the east. Having laid the foundations of a national government there, he could return to rally the west, leaving Kiazim in charge in Erzurum. If Kemal could not contrive to come, then Kiazim proposed that he should act on his own. Kemal agreed with these ideas and promised that he would try to reach Kiazim at Erzurum. Kiazim promised that he would prepare the ground for his arrival.

For a revolutionary the outlook in Anatolia was beginning to look hopeful. The spirit of resistance, it became evident, was far more positive here in the interior than in Constantinople. There had been, since December 1918, a spontaneous germination of local nationalist groups, describing themselves as Defence of Rights Associations or Anti-Annexation Societies. These were at their strongest in those parts of the country where the foreign threat was most direct. They were strong in Thrace and in Smyrna, in opposition to the Greeks; in Cilicia, where the French had recruited an Armenian legion to help them occupy the country; above all in the east, where the Allies were projecting an artificial Armenian state and where, moreover, the inhabitants were a fighting race, imbued with a lively spirit of independence. It was Kiazim's plan, which Kemal approved, to draw these various eastern groups together as a basis for a national government.

Kiazim's visit had been encouraging, even decisive. Kemal was now sure of the support of two Anatolian armies, one in the centre and now one in the east. But one question still remained unanswered. How was he to reach Anatolia? The answer was to be provided, unexpectedly, by the Allies themselves.

19 ► *Plans for resistance*

As seen by the Allies, the unoccupied parts of Anatolia were drifting perilously close to anarchy. In many districts law and order had in effect ceased to exist. Gangs of brigands held the country to ransom, as they had done in Macedonia before the Balkan Wars. They terrorized the population, ambushed and robbed peaceable travellers, committed murders and barbarous atrocities.

To meet this situation the Allies, short of occupying the whole country as, despite Turkish fears, they had neither the desire nor the means to do, had to rely on the co-operation of the Turkish authorities. They realized that they might well lose this co-operation when the peace terms, inevitably unfavourable to Turkey, were announced. Haunted by memories of a Balkan past, they feared massacres, on a large scale, of the Anatolian Christians.

The situation around Smyrna, where the Italians were setting the Turks against the Greeks in pursuit of their own territorial claims, was to some extent covered by the admonitory presence in the harbour of two British warships. The situation behind the port of Samsun, on the Black Sea, where the Greeks had pretensions to establish an independent state of Pontus, was assessed in a report from the local British commander. It was despatched by the High Commission to Damad Ferid, with a demand that his government take instant steps to curb the outrageous Turkish attacks on Greek villages and to re-establish law and order. This was, they urged, an imperative duty to humanity. They implied that if the government failed to perform it the Allied forces would be obliged to intervene themselves. Damad Ferid took immediate alarm and sent for his Acting Minister of the Interior. This, as it now happily chanced, was Mehmed Ali, with whom Kemal and Ali Fuad had lately conferred and had since kept in touch, seeking ways to further Kemal's interests. Here now was his chance.

Damad Ferid asked for Mehmed Ali's advice as to what should be done. The reply was that clearly, from the British report, the situation could no longer be controlled from Constantinople; nor was the local administration equipped to cope with it. The solution, Mehmed Ali suggested, was to send an energetic young officer, whom the government could trust, to Samsun. His task would be to combine the civil and military elements into an organization strong enough to restore law and order, and thus reassure the British authorities. Damad Ferid asked for the name of a suitable officer. Mehmed Ali suggested Mustafa Kemal.

Damad Ferid hesitated. He had grounds for suspicion about Kemal. On the other hand this might prove a good opportunity to get him safely out of the way. Before deciding, he said, he would like to investigate Kemal's record and see for himself what kind of a man he was. Mehmed Ali brought the two men together over dinner at the Cercle d'Orient and Kemal took care to make a good impression.

Shortly afterwards he was summoned by the Minister of War, Shakir Pasha, who said that the Grand Vizier thought him a suitable person to go to Anatolia and report on the situation between Turks and Greeks. Kemal replied without hesitation, "I shall be pleased to go. But is that to be my only duty?"

"Yes, that is what we have decided."

"Good. But you will allow me to suggest that my appointment should be given proper form. I don't want to trouble you with this. Shall I discuss it with the chief of the General Staff?"

"Certainly," the minister replied. "Do it that way."

The chief of the General Staff at this time was Kemal's old friend Fevzi, who had succeeded him, and whom he had later succeeded, in command of the Seventh Army in Syria. But Fevzi was sick, so Kemal went instead to the deputy chief of the General Staff. Here luck was with him, for this officer, Diyarbekirli Kiazim, was also a friend, and a neighbour in Shishli, to whom Kemal had often confided his ideas.

Kiazim knew nothing of this appointment until Kemal walked into his office. Reading the expression in his eyes, he enquired with a laugh, "What's up?" Kemal replied that Kiazim's superiors had invented a job for him, as a pretext to get him out of the way. This suited his purposes nicely. Let Kiazim now confirm with the minister just what was required of him. Then together they would work out the details.

Kiazim returned with a directive instructing Kemal not merely to punish the Turks who were attacking the Greeks around Samsun but also to disband the various Nationalist organizations in the neighbourhood. Kemal exclaimed: "Splendid! Now take pen and paper."

Together they concocted such terms of reference as would give him the maximum scope. Kemal's post was to be that of an inspector. The main point at issue was the extent of his authority. He must be in a position to give orders throughout Anatolia. Let two articles be inserted, giving him the command of all troops east of Samsun and the right to issue instructions to provincial governors.

Kiazim raised his eyebrows, then laughed again, and said, "It is our duty. We shall do our best." He drew up a draft, which they read over together next day, making corrections and additions.

Then Kiazim said doubtfully, "Don't you think these powers are too far-reaching, Pasha? I'm afraid the minister won't accept them."

"Well, if he won't sign the paper, persuade him to seal it."

Kiazim took the document to the minister, who was not feeling well. He said, "Read it aloud. I shall listen."

Kiazim began to read and presently the minister said, "You have not created an inspectorate of the Ninth Army but an inspectorate which will extend over the whole of Anatolia. What does this mean?"

Kiazim explained that this was normal procedure. Part of the task of an inspector was to maintain contact with the civil administration in districts beyond his own. If the title Inspector-General of Anatolia were used, it would be nothing new. The minister was clearly reluctant to sign. Finally he looked up at Kiazim with a smile, took his seal, and threw it across to him, saying, "My signature is unnecessary. Take this and seal it yourself."

On hearing this, Kemal insisted on making some additions to the document. These Kiazim inserted—with a mock protest that they were not in the instructions read out to the minister. Two clean copies were then made, and Kiazim sealed them with the minister's seal, giving one to Kemal with the jest, "Pasha, are you trying to get me put in a sack?"

The instructions covered the restoration of law and order and an enquiry into the causes of the present disturbances; the confiscation and storage of all arms and ammunition; disbandment of all groups under unofficial army protection; and the prohibition of further recruitment and distribution of arms. For these purposes Kemal was given command of two army corps, with direct authority over five provinces and indirect authority over five others which were instructed to "take his demands into careful consideration." Two other provinces were added later, by a verbal understanding with the Ministers of War and the Interior.

As he left the War Ministry with this brief safely in his pocket, Kemal found himself biting his lips with excitement at his "indescribable luck." The men he had thought to be his enemies had played, in all apparent innocence, into his hands. "I felt," he said afterwards, "as if a cage had been opened, and as if I were a bird ready to open my wings and fly through the sky."

With Rauf he hastened to see Fethi, who was still in prison, and tell him the news. The director of the prison, an officer who owed a debt of gratitude to Kemal, received him with a great show of respect. He said, "Pasha, we've got the news. It is said you are going to Anatolia. The moment you order it, I will let out all the prisoners you wish and join you there, with them."

This time Kemal was able to see Fethi in private. Speaking more freely than before, he confided to his friend the plans which had been revolving in his head and which now at last he had the chance to carry out. He would form and lead a national revolutionary army. He would establish a Parliament in Anatolia, based on the will of the people. He would not return to Constantinople until he had achieved his objectives.[1]

The terms of his mission still required Cabinet approval. There was a danger that some minister might question the extent of his powers. Mehmed Ali found a means of circumventing this. Catching Damad Ferid in a relaxed mood over the card table at the Cercle d'Orient, he secured a signature to the document. When the other ministers saw this, he calculated, they would not dare protest. Among them there was indeed only one dubious voice, that of the Sheikh of Islam. "I can see in that man's eyes," he is reputed to have said, "that he means to abolish

[1] Fethi was later deported to Malta.

the Caliphate and all religion." The appointment, nonetheless, received
the approval of the Cabinet and the seal of the Sultan on the last day of
April 1919.

Damad Ferid, his eyes drooping behind gold-rimmed glasses, received
Kemal and confirmed that he had been given full authority, adding,
"You may communicate all your wishes to me directly. You may be sure
that they will be carried out without delay." Kemal was taken to see
Mehmed Ali, who turned to congratulate the Minister of War on his
choice. He too gave Kemal authority to communicate with him direct.
The chain of communication was thus complete.

Kemal now began to select his staff, which was to consist of some
twenty officers. He invited Ismet to command one of his two army
corps—the Third—at Sivas, acting as opposite number to Ali Fuad,
in command of the Twentieth, destined for Angora. But it was too soon
for Ismet to take such a plunge. The exact course of Kemal's venture,
as he saw it, was still problematical. Even Kemal could not foresee, until
he reached Anatolia, just how it would develop. Ismet, patriot though
he was, lacked the temperament and the capacities for so speculative
an enterprise. He was cautious by nature, moreover essentially a military man, used to cut-and-dried situations. Kemal's initial problems
would be largely political; he would be dealing with a fluid situation.
For the moment Ismet, or so he himself argued, might be of more use
as a listening post here in Constantinople, where he was well ensconced
in the War Ministry and had friends at court. It was still possible too
that he might be sent as a delegate to the Peace Conference, where he
could hold a watching brief for the Nationalists, diagnose the attitude
of the Allies, and learn a few tricks of the diplomatic trade. He could
join Kemal later.

Kemal then selected Colonel Refet as his army corps commander. Refet
was as old an associate as his five other stalwarts, Ismet, Rauf, Fethi,
Ali Fuad, and Kiazim Karabekir. Kemal had known him since the
earliest revolutionary days in Salonika. More recently he had been commander of the gendarmerie in Constantinople, and Kemal had talked to
him of his plans for overthrowing the regime, here at the source. Small
in stature and dandyish in costume, Refet was alive in his movements
and quick in his mind, with a French culture and an impish irreverent
humour. His panache as a cavalry officer was matched by a carefree gallantry of manner, with which he charmed his way through many an
awkward situation.

Finally there was Rauf, the loyal sailor and unquestioning patriot, staunchly devoted to the liberal principles of the Western world and, ironically enough, to the institutions and traditions of Britain, the present enemy. It was decided that he should travel as a civilian through western Anatolia, starting in the country around Smyrna, to study the situation and collect information about the various Nationalist groups. He would thus proceed to Ali Fuad's headquarters in Angora and get in touch with Kemal from there.

While Kemal was laying his plans for Samsun, in the north, Lloyd George and Venizelos were planning their own course of action for Smyrna and this western region. Lord Curzon, now deputizing for Mr. Balfour at the Foreign Office, watched the situation in Turkey with growing concern. Towards the end of March he voiced his apprehensions in a memorandum to the Cabinet, warning them of the dangers of a revival of Turkish resistance, owing to the delays at the Peace Conference and the apparent decline in the Allied will to victory. It was upon a picture of Allied indecision and disillusion that "the Old Turk, who still hopes to re-establish the former regime, and the Young Turk, who means to cheat us, if he can, of the spoils of victory, look out from the crumbling watch-towers of Stambul."

Only a group of his adherents in the Foreign Office heeded him. And now the Supreme Council was proposing to cede Smyrna and its hinterland to Greece. Curzon launched another memorandum. How could the Greeks, "who cannot keep order five miles outside the gates of Salonika," be trusted to administer so important a part of Asia Minor? When it was realized, he argued, "that the fugitives are to be kicked from pillar to post and that there is to be practically no Turkish Empire and probably no Caliphate at all," Moslem passions might easily "burst into savage frenzy" throughout the Eastern world.

None of this had any effect on Lloyd George, who, when the Italians walked out of the Supreme Council on the issue of Fiume, seized the chance of clinching his Greek designs. He won over President Wilson to the side of Greece, against the advice of his own Turkish experts; Clemenceau was otherwise preoccupied and raised no objections; and early in May the three decided that the Greeks should be permitted to occupy Smyrna. The Italians, on their return to the Council, registered a formal if reluctant acceptance. Venizelos could thus plead that he was acting under a mandate from the four Great Powers. But he went, as Winston Churchill remarked, "as readily as a duck would swim." [2]

[2] *The World Crisis: The Aftermath.*

On May 15, despite all warnings and protests, twenty thousand Greek troops began to land at Smyrna, advanced inland up the railway and, in Churchill's words, "set up their standards of invasion and conquest in Asia Minor." By a slip in co-ordination the Allied High Commission in Constantinople had not yet received official news of the landings. The report, brought to them in session, caused as much consternation as though it had been a *coup d'état*. Count Sforza could not trust himself to speak, but rushed from the room, banging the door behind him. The Italians retaliated at once by landing troops, without consulting the Allies, in the zone to the south, which was theirs by secret treaty.

The governor of Smyrna had received notice of the landings from the Allied naval authorities. He proposed to resist, with the few Turkish troops which still remained under arms, and telegraphed accordingly to Constantinople. Fevzi, the chief of the General Staff, had previously urged that any such incursion should be met by force. Now, however, his Minister, without consulting him, gave orders against resistance, on the grounds that the landings accorded with the terms of the armistice. At this Fevzi resigned.

The Greeks thus entered Smyrna as though on parade, shouting, "Long live Venizelos!" They stacked their arms, and some danced around the stacks in celebration. The Greek civilian population swept along the streets, crying curses on the Moslems. A stray shot was fired, which led to intermittent firing and bloodshed. The Turkish troops hoisted the white flag and, with their officers, were marched down to the waterfront to a troopship, with their hands above their heads, while a mob of civilians jeered at them, struck at them with clubs, and tore at their fezzes. A Turkish colonel, who refused to take off his fez and stamp on it, was shot and killed. The governor was arrested and similarly marched off to the quay, at bayonet point, together with other Turkish notables who had been dragged from their houses.

The Greek troops then got out of hand and some hundreds of Turks were killed. Their bodies were thrown over the sea wall into the harbour. Admiral Calthorpe had to intervene, virtually ordering the Greek admiral to take charge on shore. A group of Turkish Nationalist officers held a meeting of protest, in favour of the Wilson principles and thus against any form of annexation, in the Jewish cemetery in the centre of the city. They received no support from the Turkish authorities and dispersed for the most part into the interior, to organize centres of resistance. The Greek forces meanwhile advanced inland up the two broad river valleys of the Gediz and the Menderes—the classical Hermus and Meander—towards the cities of Manisa and Aydin.

Constantinople was dismayed at the news, but it was a dismay stiffened by deep indignation, which gave sudden reality to the Nationalist movement. Occupation by the Great Powers could be accepted as an inevitable evil; but occupation by the Greeks, insolent and disloyal subjects for a century past, was an affront which no patriotic Turk could endure. Here was just the spark that was needed to inflame the fighting spirit of the Turks once more. Fifty thousand people gathered in the great square before the mosque of Sultan Ahmed. Many of them carried black flags, while a black drapery was lowered behind the speakers, symbolically enshrouding the red and white flags of the star and the crescent. A woman in black, her face unveiled, delivered a passionate oration, addressing the crowd with the words, "Brothers, sisters, countrymen, Moslems: when the night is darkest and seems eternal, the light of dawn is nearest."

She was Halide Edib, one of the few Turkish women in politics, who was destined to become an active force in the new revolution. Her feelings at this moment reflected those of countless others. "After I learned about the details of the Smyrna occupation," she wrote afterwards, ". . . I hardly opened my mouth on any subject except when it concerned the sacred struggle which was to be. Turkey was to be cleared of murderers, the so-called civilizing Greek Armies. . . . I suddenly ceased to exist as an individual. I worked, wrote and lived as a unit of that magnificent national madness." Lord Curzon was proved to have been right.

The news of the landings reduced the Sultan to tears. Leaning on the arm of his cousin Abdul Mejid as he left a meeting of his council, he said, "Look, I am weeping like a woman." Kemal heard it at the Sublime Porte, where, on the eve of his departure, he chanced to be conferring with Mehmed Ali and a group of ministers.

"By God, what an impertinence!" Mehmed Ali exclaimed. "Have you heard? The Greeks are landing in Smyrna."

"Has that happened too?" Kemal asked. He was stirred but not altogether surprised. The press had been foreshadowing such a move for some days. He looked around at the fussed, astonished faces of the ministers and coolly enquired, "What do you mean to do?"

"We are going to protest," was the helpless answer.

"All right. But do you think your protest will make the Greeks or the British retire?"

The ministers shrugged their shoulders. "What else can we do?"

"There are perhaps more definite measures that might be taken."

"What, for example?"

He did not express his thoughts but suggested, "You can come and join me." He turned to the Minister of Marine and asked, "Is my boat ready to leave for Anatolia?"

"It has been ready for some days," was the reply. "The *Bandirma*—at your orders."

He would leave next day. His A.D.C. drafted an order to the captain, which the minister signed. Kemal left the ministers to their dazed deliberations.

On the previous evening, before the news of the landings arrived, Kemal had dined with Damad Ferid and Jevad, who had succeeded Fevzi as chief of the General Staff. Ferid seemed worried. He had reason to be, for the British, through Ryan,[3] their first dragoman, had expressed doubts regarding the wisdom of the inspectorate scheme, though Kemal's own name still meant little to them. Ferid had reassured them, but he now asked Kemal, "Can you show me on the map the exact extent of your command?"

With a gesture of studied vagueness Kemal put his hand over a province or two on the map and said, "I'm not quite sure. Perhaps a small area like this." He exchanged glances with Jevad, who supported him, and strolled away with an air of indifference. The Grand Vizier seemed relieved.

As they left the dinner Jevad asked, "Are you going to do something, Kemal?"

"Yes, Pasha, I am going to do something," was the reply.

Next day he proceeded to the Yildiz Palace, where the Sultan received him in audience. "My Pasha," he said, "so far you have done great services to the state. All this is past history. Forget it. The services you will now render are more important than all the rest. Pasha, you can save the country."

Kemal concluded that the Sultan meant to say, "We are powerless. The only way we can save the country is to submit ourselves to the will of those who rule Constantinople."

He said to the Sultan, "Have no fear. I have understood Your Majesty's point of view. . . . I shall not for a moment forget your orders."

---

[3] Later Sir Andrew Ryan, K.B.E., C.M.G.

The Sultan wished him success and he was presented with a gold watch engraved with the imperial cipher.

For Kemal all was now in order. Back at the War Ministry, Fevzi was handing over his duties to Jevad, confident that he would carry them on in the same spirit. Bending over a map on the table, Fevzi pointed at Constantinople and thundered, "I don't understand. We are surrendering the whole country in order to be comfortable in this one spot. This is madness."

Jevad seemed to agree. Kemal said to Fevzi, "You are right. I am going to Anatolia in order to prove that you are right. I see no need for us to talk at great length. I expect only one thing from you. You must help me."

"Of course I will. You may be sure of it."

Kemal turned to Jevad. "And you too, especially. For yours is now the responsible post. Shall we be able to work together?"

"Of course."

Kemal then asked him, "Will you at once order the Twentieth Army Corps, now at Ulukishla, to march to Angora? Don't let them be transported by train."

"I shall give the necessary orders." Jevad also gave Kemal his secret cipher, with which to communicate with him in person.[4]

Only some last-minute action by the British could now prevent Kemal's departure. The granting of visas for himself and his large staff had indeed been queried a week before by a junior British liaison officer in the War Ministry, Captain J. G. Bennett. Reading through the list, he was struck by its high-powered military calibre. In the absence of his superior officer, he took it across to GHQ to ask for instructions, suggesting to the staff officer on duty that this looked more like a war-making than a peacemaking mission. He was told to wait while the British High Commission was consulted. After about an hour he was called in and instructed to grant the visas. "Mustafa Kemal Pasha," he was told, "has the complete confidence of the Sultan." The visa, signed by the British authorities, was thus now safely in Kemal's possession.[5]

---

[4] Certain protagonists of the Sultan claim that at this time he was pursuing an ambivalent policy, openly supporting Damad Ferid on the one hand but secretly reinsuring with the Nationalists on the other. He used to discuss such matters with his dentist, Dr. Sami Gunzberg (whom he nicknamed Dish Pasha, otherwise Tooth Pasha). To him, after Kemal's success, he put forward, in the presence of Ali Riza, a later Grand Vizier, the dubious pretension that he had sent Kemal to Anatolia when all else had failed, hoping to save at least the heart of his country.

[5] J. G. Bennett, *Witness.*

He paid a last visit to Fethi in prison. After they had said good-bye, Fethi's fellow prisoners realized that something was up. He was nervous, preoccupied, replying to their questions with polite evasions. He preferred not to talk, and lay down on his bed with his face to the wall, as though to sleep.

But finally he confided to his neighbour, Yunus Nadi, that Kemal was leaving the next day and that for the following three days, waiting for the news of a safe arrival, he would not sleep. The British, it was true, seemed unaware of the real situation. But one or two of their officers were intelligent and might try to prevent him from landing or pursue him once they found he was gone.

"These are our birth pangs," said Fethi. "But we must not attract the attention of the others. We must not discuss them even here."

Kemal spent his last evening in Constantinople with his mother and sister at his mother's house in Beshiktash. They squatted on cushions around a Turkish tray by the mother's bedside, while he told them of his imminent departure on an "important mission"; he could not tell them where. It would be some days before they had news of him. To achieve his object he must be easy in his mind, he must not feel that they were worrying about him or had worries of their own. He had money in the bank, on which they might draw freely, whether with his own seal or theirs.

Zübeyde grew faint at the news, then prayed for his safety and success. Makbule expressed bewilderment. In the past he had gone off to the wars and they knew he was fighting. But this time it was hard to grasp where he was going and why. Kemal could only tell her not to worry. Next day Zübeyde came to Shishli to bid him good-bye. When he had gone she consoled Makbule with the proud injunction that, as the sister of a soldier, she must never weep for her brother, must never show sorrow to a stranger. Then they settled down to wait, perhaps for many days, for the ring of the telephone which would tell them of his safe arrival at his new destination.

The *Bandirma* lay at the quayside, a small British-built cargo boat bought from a Greek. Rauf accompanied Kemal there, then left him, so that Mehmed Ali, who was coming to see him off, should not see them together. Rauf himself was to leave secretly, with four friends, a week later.

Refet, recruited at short notice, had no visa from the Allies but this did not disconcert so resourceful an officer. He came down to the quay without badges of rank, ostensibly to embark a dozen horses which his brother had bought for him. He saw them on board and remained there, hiding among the horses, until the ship was safely out of the Bosporus.

She sailed on the evening of May 16. Kemal was nervous that the British might try to sink the ship or arrest him en route. Rauf had thought it unlikely. Had they any such intention they would have prevented his departure. Refet too scorned his fears. But Kemal was taking no chances. The ship looked unseaworthy, her compass was inaccurate, her captain seemed inexperienced. Kemal ordered him to alter his course and sail close inshore, where it would be possible to disembark in a hurry if an Allied ship threatened.

The British authorities meanwhile had awakened, belatedly, to the imminence of Kemal's departure and its possible implications. Wyndham Deedes, military attaché to the High Commission, was hurriedly sent down to the Sublime Porte at midnight to warn the Grand Vizier. But Ferid leant back in his chair, put the tips of his fingers together, and said slowly, "You are too late, Excellency; the bird has flown." [6]

However, no steps were taken to intercept the ship, which anchored off Samsun in rough weather on May 19, 1919.[7] Boats came out from the beach to row the new inspector general and his staff officers ashore. They landed on one of the rickety wooden jetties, striking out through the shallow water, which were the small port's apology for a quay. Kemal was received by three officers, with a small detachment of troops, and by two local notables. They took him to a house, the property of a Greek, which he requisitioned as his headquarters. A few hundred yards down the dusty street, one French and two British control officers were installed in the local bank.

Thus, four days after the Greeks had set up their standard of conquest on the shores of the Aegean, Kemal set up his standard of liberation on the shores of the Black Sea. The battle for Anatolia was about to begin. A new chapter had been opened in the history of the Turkish people.

[6] Later Brigadier General Sir Wyndham Deedes, C.M.G., D.S.O. Quoted by John Presland, *Deedes Bay*.
[7] When Kemal, in later years, was asked the date of his birth, he liked to reply, "May 19, 1919."

II

The war of independence

The Mustafa Kemal who now embarked on the crucial phase of his own and his country's career was a seasoned and self-confident campaigner, two years short of forty, who had proved himself as a soldier in fourteen years of hard service. He had now to prove himself also as a politician and statesman. The challenge which he had sought, through those smouldering years of frustration, at last confronted him, bold and exacting and clear.

Kemal had lately grown stronger in build, his face had filled out and showed traces of lines, his hair and moustache had dulled in colour. But his skin was as clear, his gaze as alert, his responses as swift as those of a younger man. With his erect bearing and clean-cut features, Mustafa Kemal had the lines of the soldier. But latent within him was the hint of an extra dimension, of a singularity of tempo and rhythm and scale which outranged the companions around him. Strangely, for all his slightness of frame, he seemed bigger, for all his slowness of stride he seemed quicker than they. Already the pale complexion and the broad high cheekbones, the long feminine hands with their spatulate fingers and quick-changing movements, set him apart from the rest.

But it was above all through those eyes, pale and stern and unblinking, that this other element in Kemal was reflected. Wide-set beneath the broad brow and the eyebrows that curled upwards like whiskers, they gleamed with a cold steady challenging light, forever fixing, observing, reflecting, appraising, and uncannily capable of swivelling two ways at once so that they seemed to see both upwards and downwards, before and behind. With these eyes, with his massive head and his lithe assured limbs, he had the look of a restless tiger. In a more military idiom, he combined in his person the hardness and coldness but also the flexibility of steel, suggesting, with his high-strung nervous tension, a coil flexed and ready to spring.

It was this "extra dimension" in Kemal that his friends needed and valued at the initial stage of the national struggle which they all had at heart. In mind he was always one leap ahead of them, in action one degree more decisive. He had just those qualities of leadership which they severally lacked. Rauf was a man of principle but deficient in imagination; Kiazim Karabekir was loyal but inflexible; Refet was brave but impulsive; Ali Fuad was adroit but lacked intellect. All were patriots, practical soldiers, men of common sense and intelligence. But among them only Kemal had the necessary over-all grasp of both internal and external affairs, that peculiar compound of intuition and reason, resilience, energy, and above all will power, required to carry such a hazardous enterprise to a successful conclusion.

With a lucidity of vision amounting almost to clairvoyance, he saw his ultimate objective and the intermediate steps that must be taken to reach it. With his insight into the personal psychology of both enemy and friend, he sensed the obstacles, political and military, which would stand in his way and for which tactics would have to be devised. The realist in him knew that the struggle would be long and must be planned in patient stages, to be revealed not in advance but by a careful process of timing in relation to circumstances and to the current climate of feeling. The intellectual side of him knew that it was to be won by the force not merely of guns but of an idea, which must be sown and cultivated in the minds of the people. The achievement of all this would demand an intense concentration, a superhuman effort of will, the kind of elemental driving force which Kemal alone possessed.

The spirit which fired it was a passionate ambition overriding all else. But it was the ambition of a patriot, bound up with what he saw to be his country's interests. Power for its own sake, for the sake of glory, did not interest Kemal. He sought it solely for the purpose of realizing his own radical and constructive ideas for the future of Turkey. In human terms, Kemal was a man without love in his nature. He understood people but he did not love them. He had little time for women, except as distractions. He enjoyed the comradeship of his men friends and remained loyal to those who did not aspire to compete with him—old brothers in arms, young A.D.C.s.

But with equals and would-be equals there was always a wariness behind his approach. With his present associates this was sharpened by the feeling that they too had an extra dimension, which he himself lacked, less definable than his own. This derived from their several social backgrounds. Rauf came of good Caucasian stock; Ali Fuad of a military family respected for some generations; Refet's forebears had been independent landowning beys, in the Danube Valley. All, in an English idiom, ranked as "gentlemen," armed with the assurance of an inherited prestige, an easy integrity, and a natural habit of leadership.

Kemal, for all those refinements which smoothed his rough edges, came of an insignificant middle-class family and knew it. Far from pretending otherwise, he exploited his more plebeian origins to shock and defy, to assert his personality and flaunt his power, to override the conventions of his social superiors.

They, for their part, regarded him more with respect than with love. Rauf, the idealist, saw him as the man for the moment but not necessarily for the future; Ali Fuad, tougher and less concerned with political principles, took him for granted as one man of action and one old comrade takes another; Refet, appreciating his gifts but suspecting his motives, treated him with less respect than the others. All, however, had one quality in common: they had a deep and genuine love for their country.

In Kemal this derived from a pride in its destiny, nourished in boyhood; from a sense of shame at its visible decline at the hands of the foreigner and of its own decadent rulers. This feeling was rooted in a certain earthiness of spirit and love of the soil—the mountains and valleys of Rumeli, the wide-open spaces of Anatolia—for which he had fought and was about to fight again. It was animated above all by a knowledge of the men who had fought with him. Kemal saw the Turkish people without illusion. He knew that they were dour, conservative, fatalistic, slow in mind and initiative. But he knew also that they were stubborn, patient, capable of endurance; a race of fighters ruthless in battle, responsive to leadership and ready to die on order.

The peasantry of Anatolia had been neglected and despised by their Ottoman rulers. Yet it was they who gave the Empire its backbone; and it was through them that Kemal and his friends now aspired to save what remained of it. Instinct told him that the spark in them might still be rekindled for the defence of that soil to which inheritance and possession gave a half-sacred quality, and for the rescue of that nation which, after six centuries of empire, still inspired them with pride and an obstinate sense of freedom. War-weary and demoralized as they were, it was being said that even God himself could not move them to fight again. Could a Mustafa Kemal hope to succeed in a task thus surpassing the powers of the Almighty?

He started with one great advantage. The Allied occupation of Smyrna was an unhoped-for asset, to exploit to the full. But the people of Anatolia must first be roused to an awareness of its facts and implications. At Samsun he found that they were scantily informed about the landings. Thus one of his first actions, making use of the excellent telegraph network which Abdul Hamid had installed to perfect his espionage system, was to send out instructions to the various civil and military authorities within his jurisdiction, to stage mass meetings of protest and to bombard the Sublime Porte and the foreign representatives with telegrams appealing for national justice. In Samsun itself he arranged for meetings to be addressed in the principal mosque, to rouse the people to a spirit of resistance. In the military field Kemal established rapid liaison with all the Turkish Army units surviving in Anatolia and Thrace; in the political field he began to form links between the various Defence of Rights groups and, far from disbanding them, as he had been ordered, to form new ones.

Meanwhile, in a series of telegrams to the War Ministry, he kept up, as he had done from Adana at the time of the armistice, a running fire of complaint against the British. They had reinforced their troops in the area without notifying the Turkish authorities; they were planning to move more units into the interior, in defiance of the armistice terms; they were aiding and abetting the Greek partisans, who sought further Allied occupation and the creation of a Greek state of Pontus.

Back in Constantinople, the British now became alarmed. Having awakened to the danger too late to prevent Kemal's departure, the commander in chief, Sir George Milne,[1] now firmly requested the War Ministry to recall him. The War Minister at first replied that Kemal's presence in Anatolia would be a calming rather than a disturbing influence. The Cabinet met, however, to discuss a compromise proposal for the

[1] Later Field Marshal Lord Milne of Salonika, G.C.B., G.C.M.G., D.S.O.

limitation of his authority, for in fact they shared some of Milne's mis-givings. They were increasingly concerned at the disdainful and disre-spectful tone of Kemal's telegrams, which seemed to imply their igno-rance of the Anatolian situation and his determination to handle it in his own way, not consulting them in advance but merely informing them afterwards. When they were read out to the ministers, the Unionist sym-pathizers smiled in a knowing way, while all looked at Damad Ferid. "The inspector," he remarked, "almost seems to be scolding us. He writes as though to say, 'We know what we are doing, and you may mind your own business.'" The Cabinet thus decided on his recall and informed Milne accordingly.

The inspector meanwhile—and the people of Samsun knew him only as such, for he had not yet chosen to advertise his identity as the hero of Gallipoli—felt restricted in his actions here on the coast. The British control officers were too close for his comfort. Already Refet had shown alarm at the indiscretion of his pronouncements and propagandist ac-tivities. Wishing to act freely, Kemal, after a week in Samsun, moved his headquarters fifty miles inland to Havza. He did so on the pretext that he wished to take advantage of its thermal springs, since he had been ill in Samsun with a recurrence of his kidney disease.

Thus his small band of officers set off up the road which climbed by rough and serpentine stages to the great Anatolian plateau. Four thou-sand feet above the sea, it spread for a thousand miles from Mount Ara-rat and the frontiers of Persia and Russia in the east to Eskishehir and the mountains of the Marmara and the Aegean in the west. The Yeshi-lirmak (the Green River) curled away beneath them, down towards the shore, as they drove up into a landscape of ripening maize and wheat-fields and patches of deciduous forest. They passed through villages of sagging mud-brick houses, those of the Turks punctuated with a min-aret, those of the Greeks with a dome. Kemal's antiquated open car broke down several times during the journey. Finally, with two compan-ions, he left it and walked up the road. Here in the hills there was fresh air to breathe and the fruitful earth to smell, and as the officers responded to the freedom of their surroundings they found themselves humming a romantic Swedish song of misty hilltops and trees and birds and silver flowing rivers:

"Let us march, friends!
Let our voice be heard by the earth, by the sky,
    by the water,

Let the hard ground moan from the harsh tramp
of our feet."

It was to become a song of the Revolution, to be sung by a growing band
of companions right across Anatolia, and eventually—its foreign origin
forgotten—to be enshrined as a "theme song" of the youth of the Turkish Republic.

Havza was in the thick of the Greek guerrilla warfare. During the
war the Greek villagers had made trouble, causing the government to
deport groups of them to the east. Afterwards they had remained quiet
until the armistice. But now a political organization, formed to press for
the state of Pontus, was stirring them to rebellion once more, largely under the leadership of a Greek bishop. Kemal was told how gangs of black-
clad bandits, their belts bristling with cartridges, were terrorizing the
Turkish population, robbing and killing them on the roads, burning
their villages, kidnapping their prominent citizens, lying in wait to ambush their soldiers—much as they had done in Macedonia in the days
of his youth. Against this the Turks could do little since the British,
much as they might complain to the Sublime Porte of the lack of law
and order, were confiscating their arms under the terms of the armistice,
while allowing the Greeks to keep theirs.

Havza and the surrounding villages thus provided a fruitful field for
the start of a resistance movement. Receiving the local notables at his
headquarters, Kemal, whose identity as the hero of Gallipoli had now become known, declaimed to them against the invading foreigners. "They
do not seek to kill us. They seek to bury us alive in our graves. Now we
are on the edge of the pit. But if we stir ourselves to a final effort, we may
still be saved." He then left them to confer among themselves. In his
methodical military fashion he drew up a long questionnaire for the
mayor, requesting a comprehensive report on such matters as the relative population in the area of Moslems and Christians and their respective political attitudes; the nature of the conflict between them and the
steps taken to deal with it. He demanded a dossier concerning the identity of the leading Turkish inhabitants and their behaviour and character.
Did the people owe taxes, and if so, how much? What were the stocks
of the army? How much transport was available? It was by such thorough and practical attention to detail, wherever he went, that Kemal
now informed himself, for his revolutionary purposes, of the state of the
country.

Meanwhile, at two successive meetings from which he chose to remain absent, the leading citizens decided of their own accord on a policy of resistance, forming as its foundation a branch of the Defence of Rights Association. Following a crowded service in the mosque, with prayers for success, a mass meeting was held in the small square of the town. Careful still not to seem directly involved, Kemal watched it from a window at his headquarters, sending his officers into the crowd to test the popular reaction. The speakers insisted that the country was in danger; thus all Moslems must be armed, lest they die beneath the feet of the enemy. An oath was sworn to this effect, in religious terms. Kemal had established the first active cell of resistance, the prototype of others that were to proliferate during the next few months in different parts of the country.

In the region of Smyrna resistance had been swift, inspired largely by individual officers. The Turks had established a loose front linking together the various resistance groups, until forced to retire to a line laid down by the Allies—the Milne Line—through the War Ministry in Constantinople. But the other groups continued to wage guerrilla warfare in the mountains. When Rauf arrived in the neighbourhood from Constantinople he found his countrymen thoroughly roused. The bandit chiefs came to him, lawless men known by the local designation of Efe, whose bands had been fighting the Ottoman government since pre-war days. They now rejoiced at the chance to go into battle once more, this time against their rivals, the Greeks. One of them, Demirji Mehmed Efe, assured Rauf that his followers were rallying to him "as innocently as lambs," asking for orders and declaring, "It is for today that our mothers gave birth to us."

For Kemal, the time had now come to move on from Havza. British troops were stationed a mere twenty miles up the road at Merzifon, and reports of the open-air meeting in Havza had reached them. Moreover its people had made them look foolish by capturing a consignment of some tens of thousands of rifle bolts, confiscated from the Turkish forces in the east and despatched all across Anatolia by a convoy of baggage animals to the port of Samsun. A band of Turkish patriots surprised the convoy, hid the rifle bolts in a local warehouse, and sold the animals to raise funds for the resistance. Foreseeing a stiffer British attitude, Kemal moved on to the remoter and more important city of Amasya, whose inhabitants had sent him a deputation declaring their loyalty.

He thus said good-bye to the people of Havza, dressed now in civilian clothes as a symbol of the fact that this was not merely a military but a civil resistance, and with a procession of them walked to the bridge outside the city, where his car awaited him. As he was giving last instructions to the mayor, two cars drew up, carrying Americans from the college at Merzifon. The mayor lowered his voice and advised Kemal to do the same. But with defiant indiscretion he talked even louder. "We have nothing to hide," he declared. "Let them all hear. We have gone too far in this to draw back."

Kemal had a mind, as he had an eye, which could see in several directions at once. While he looked inwards on Anatolia, he had at the same time been looking outwards on the world. Since the armistice, Turkey's only hope had seemed to rest on President Wilson and his Fourteen Points. A Wilsonian League, composed of intellectuals, had drafted a proposal for a period of American aid and a guaranteed peace to assist Turkish recovery. Now, as a counter to the threat of partition, an alternative idea, born in Paris, was gaining ground in Constantinople—that of a mandate over Turkey or a part of it by America, Britain, or some other power.

On May 14, at that meeting of the Supreme Council which had ordered the occupation of Smyrna, President Wilson agreed to consider the acceptance of a mandate over Armenia, Constantinople, and the Straits. On May 26, Damad Ferid announced his decision "to put Turkey under the protective assistance of one of the Great Powers." This provoked an immediate protest from Kemal. Early in June, Ferid was given the opportunity to state his country's case at the Peace Conference, and a government delegation—from which Ismet, to his disappointment, was excluded—left in a French cruiser for Marseilles and Paris. Kemal reacted at once to the news of his forthcoming departure. He sent out to his group of commanders and governors a strongly worded circular, stressing the national rights. Insisting on complete independence and the safeguarding of the interests of the Turkish majority on Turkish soil, he attacked especially the acceptance by Damad Ferid of the principle of Armenian autonomy and the proposal for a British protectorate elsewhere.

Two days later he received an instruction from the War Ministry to return to Constantinople. He disobeyed this and all such subsequent orders. The time had come to muster his friends and proceed to serious action. A telegram arrived from Ali Fuad, who had reached Angora with the Twentieth Army Corps. He announced that Rauf—whom he described mysteriously as "a certain person whom you know"—had arrived there after his tour of the southwest and suggested a rendezvous at some point between their two headquarters. Kemal replied that he could not himself move from the Havza region, owing to shortage of petrol. Instead he asked them to find their way to Havza, suggesting that they should travel in disguise and not divulge their names. The party thus set out in horse-drawn carriages on a six-day journey over primitive roads, seldom stopping and doing their best to look inconspicuous. They followed Kemal to Amasya.

This was a place well fitted to become the cradle of a Nationalist Revolution. Throughout a long and distinguished history it had shown a consistent spirit of independence. Saved from the Mongol occupation, it had been for a while the Ottoman capital and after the capture of Constantinople the tradition persisted that the heir to the Sultanate should receive his education in Amasya and serve as its governor. Thus Amasya preserved a high status and felt that it had something to teach Constantinople.

As Kemal approached it the mountains rose up abruptly before him. Ahead, as he passed through its orchards, green and warm and fertile as those of Damascus, their ridges closed in on the narrowing valley of the Yeshilirmak. Bold and rugged, pitted with the tombs of the Pontus kings and crowned with an ancient fortress, they formed a precipitous gorge in which to clamp the city to the banks of the green-flowing river. It was a place isolated in its atmosphere from the outside world, but the centre of a world of its own; a Moslem city as holy in its aspect as Brusa, with its wealth of mosques and tombs and religious buildings, but free in its remoteness and its pure Islamic traditions from the domination of the Sultanate and its crippling reactionary influence. It was a city, as Kemal had suspected and soon confirmed, which looked to the future, not to the past.

Already, in its mountains, a stalwart Moslem dignitary had recruited a force of Turkish volunteers to fight against the Greek partisans, under their Orthodox bishop. He at once came out openly for Kemal and preached for his cause in the mosque. Kemal himself delivered a speech to the citizens, announcing the start of a national resistance on three separate fronts—in the west against the Greeks behind Smyrna; in the south against the French and their Armenian collaborators from Adana; in the east against the Armenians from Erzurum. "Citizens of Amasya," he declared, "what are you waiting for? . . . If the enemy tries to land in Samsun, we must pull on our peasant shoes, we must withdraw to the mountains, we must defend the country to the last rock. If it is the will of God that we be defeated, we must set fire to all our homes, to all our property; we must lay the country in ruins and leave it an empty desert. Citizens of Amasya, let us all together swear an oath that we shall do this." The citizens declared that they awaited his orders.

It was the holy men who proved to be his strongest adherents. For the first time he was to receive public and official support from a powerful religious authority. Among the civil population he had support from a more questionable source—the local adherents of the party of Union and Progress. During the resistance he was to be wary of encouraging the co-operation of the Unionists, of whom he had a chronic mistrust. But often he had little choice, since in many districts it was they who had formed an original nucleus of resistance and since there were, after all, genuine patriots among them.

So the Kemalist Revolution was born. The four friends who had planned it in Constantinople now met together, here in Amasya, to draft its "Declaration of Independence." Ali Fuad and Rauf were the first to arrive. Refet was to join them next day. Kiazim Karabekir was informed of their arrival by telegram. Kemal now disclosed his intentions.

The ground had been prepared, so he explained to his friends, by a close-knit liaison with the various civil and military authorities and with the Defence of Rights organizations. There was an encouraging response; the idea of a resistance was growing. The time had now come to give it a corporate identity. He had thus decided to convene immediately a Nationalist Congress at Sivas. Situated high on the rim of the plateau, some hundred and fifty miles to the east and a similar distance from the sea, it was "by all odds the safest place in Anatolia." He had drafted a circular, calling upon delegates from each province to proceed there at once and, if necessary, incognito. His friends approved the circular. Meanwhile, he told them, a preliminary Congress of delegates from the eastern provinces would meet at Erzurum, a further two hundred and eighty miles to the east. This had in fact been summoned by Kiazim Karabekir, before his own arrival in Anatolia.

Next day he submitted a declaration for approval and signature by Rauf, Ali Fuad, and Refet. The independence of the country, it asserted, was in danger. The capital was under Allied occupation and the government subject to foreign control, hence incapable of governing. The nation must save itself by its own will power. Its resolve to resist foreign domination had been proved by the rise of the numerous defence organizations. These must now be co-ordinated into a central national body, capable of judging the nation's needs and voicing its demands, free from outside influence and control. Hence the Nationalist Congress at Sivas. The place and date of it would be kept secret meanwhile.

It was clear to all that the declaration went further than the mere organization of the defence of the country. It envisaged the possible formation, by the Sivas Congress, of a national government, independent of Constantinople. Ali Fuad accepted this without hesitation and signed. Rauf, after a moment's reflection, signed also. Refet, whose late arrival had caused him to miss their earlier discussions, seemed reluctant at first to commit himself so far. But Ali Fuad overcame his doubts, and he added his own swift flourish of a signature. The band of four friends thus made history with a "Sacred Alliance" which sealed the first concerted plan in the Turkish struggle for independence.

When they had signed it they telegraphed its contents to Kiazim Karabekir and to Mersinli Jemal, the army commander in Konya. Both gave it their approval, thus extending its range from the east and south. Following the signature, a call to arms was declaimed after the Friday prayer in the mosque.

From Constantinople, the new Minister of the Interior, Ali Kemal—who had unfortunately replaced Kemal's ally, Mehmed Ali—now issued a circular of his own. Following Mustafa Kemal's refusal to return to the city, he directed, no one must in future have official correspondence with him and his orders must not be obeyed. Thus from now onwards Kemal must clearly expect attempts by the Sublime Porte to apprehend or dispose of him.

He received warnings of probable trouble at Sivas, where he intended to stop on his way to the Erzurum Congress. He left secretly one morning at daybreak, accompanied only by Rauf and his aides, but instructing a detachment of troops to follow and to try to keep in touch with him. Emerging from the Amasya gorge, he drove up the broadening valley of the Yeshilirmak, where the peasants were gathering in the harvest, to Tokat, a town similarly crowned by a rock-bound fortress. Here he took over the telegraph office and ensured that his arrival was not announced to Sivas. He called together a group of local notables to whom he made a rousing speech. "If we have no weapons to fight with," he declaimed to them, "we shall fight with our teeth and our nails." Before leaving for

Sivas, six hours' journey away, he drafted a telegram to its governor, announcing his arrival but ordering it to be sent only six hours after his departure.

He hoped thus to take the governor by surprise. For a plot was afoot, at the instigation of the Sultan's government, to arrest Kemal in Sivas, prevent the Congress, and thus nip the national movement in the bud. For this purpose a certain Ali Galib, a retired staff colonel, had been sent to Sivas from Constantinople, ostensibly proceeding as governor to the neighbouring province of Erzinjan. He had bills posted on the walls, proclaiming Kemal "a dangerous man, a mutineer, a traitor," and urged the governor, Reshid Pasha, to arrest him in terms of the order of the Ministry of the Interior. The governor was hesitant; so were his associates. They were still debating as Kemal drew near to the city.

His road wound up successively over two mountain barriers until it reached the plateau itself. At the top of the second pass—the Pass of the Pines—Kemal stopped at a spring to drink some water. A driver at his side started to fill a cup for him. But Kemal restrained him, saying, "*Dur, Baba* [Stop, Father]. I prefer to use my hands." The driver was to pass into Anatolian folklore with the sanctified nickname of Dur Baba.

Beyond the last ridge Kemal at last breathed the high dry air of the plateau. The sea and its marginal barrier of mountains were behind him. Before and around him a wide tawny prairie, broken only by hazy insubstantial hills, spread away to remote horizons. Here was his battleground. On this roof of the world, to which the Turks had trekked centuries earlier from the Central Asian steppes, was their new destiny now to be decided. Driving along the banks of another broad river, this time the Kizilirmak, or Red River, he reached the outskirts of Sivas.

The governor hurried out to greet him and tried to delay his entry. But Kemal politely manoeuvred him into his open car in place of Rauf and made him sit by his side, for all to see as they drove towards the city. By this time the news of Kemal's arrival had spread, and they were greeted at the gates by a detachment of troops under arms and by an interested crowd lining both sides of the road. Their welcome effectively forestalled any attempt to arrest Kemal and ensured Reshid's subsequent if qualified loyalty.

Instead Kemal turned the tables by arresting Ali Galib, who appeared before him to be upbraided and then treated to a long harangue, elucidating the principles of the resistance and branding him as a traitor to his country. That night Ali Galib thought it prudent to revisit Kemal and declare his good intentions. As Kemal recorded, he "tried by all kinds of sophistries to convince me that I ought not to judge from appearances that were so deceptive." He pretended that he had stopped at Sivas to meet Kemal and place himself under his orders. "I must admit," Kemal said drily, "that he managed to keep me busy till the morning."

That morning Kemal left for the east in his antiquated motorcar, on the long weary week's journey across the plateau, with many stops for information and instruction on the way, towards Erzurum.

21 ► *The Erzurum Congress*

Erzurum was the "capital" of eastern Turkey. A rough grey city of the Anatolian plateau, placed where its mountain barriers converge in the direction of the Persian and Trans-Caucasian frontiers, it had been an early citadel, on their incursion into the country, of the Seljuk Turks, and was thus embellished with buildings combining martial strength with civilized grace. Always a military stronghold, it had served in more recent centuries as a bastion of Turkish defence against a series of Russian invasions.

Here Kiazim Karabekir, the fifth of the founders of the Revolution, had salvaged from the remnants of Enver's last Caucasian Army a force which was stronger than any surviving in other parts of the country. Kiazim had become the "father figure" of this eastern region, ruling it benevolently and nurturing its independent spirit, which had been roused by the threat to incorporate it in a greater Armenia. It was a region depopulated and devastated, beyond all others, by the war, by the ebb and flow in the fighting which had accompanied the Russian advance and retreat, by the consequent expulsions of Turks by Armenians and Armenians by Turks, by the scorched-earth policy which had destroyed the crops and reduced the herds to a fraction of their former strength. The population was down to a mere ten per cent of its prewar numbers. Disease had been rife, food was still scarce, except for eggs and black bread. For want of glasses the people were drinking their tea out of sawn-off bottles.

Kiazim, with his paternal and charitable instincts, had personally adopted more than a thousand orphan boys, between the ages of four and fourteen, whom he dressed in a paramilitary uniform and to whom his officers gave a form of military training. He established schools to give them an elementary education and to teach them useful trades. Since his own hobby was music and he liked in his leisure hours to play the violin, he gave them also musical instruction, together with training in arts and crafts. The children knew him as "Pasha Baba [Father Pasha]" and so trusted and revered him that he was able to control them with a minimum of punishment and to encourage them to develop as free individuals.

Colonel A. Rawlinson, who had arrived in Erzurum on an official mission to investigate the prospects of creating an independent Armenia and to organize the surrender of arms, was so impressed by these educational activities that he wrote, "If this is going on throughout the whole country, the Turk of the future, with his natural gifts of courage and endurance, will become a power in the East, if not in the West also, that will presently have to be reckoned with in a very different spirit from that adopted by the European Powers at their post-war conferences hitherto." He admired the pasha's intelligence, his conscientiousness, his mastery of every branch of his profession. He was "the most genuine example of a first-class Turkish officer that it has ever been my good fortune to meet."

The colonel, with the ostensible co-operation of Kiazim, was as conscientious in his efforts to inspect armaments, military stores, arsenals, fortifications, and army muster rolls and pay sheets, with a view to completing demobilization and reducing arms to the level allowed by the armistice. His main task was to confiscate breechblocks of guns and breech bolts of rifles, and to send them across the frontier by the railway into Trans-Caucasia, where two English divisions were stationed.

But his progress was slow, owing to "a suspiciously large number of accidents on the railway." These were engineered by Kiazim's men, who had the additional habit of holding up trains and unloading their cargoes onto mules and into horse wagons to carry them away. When the railway was out of action—once for months at a time—Rawlinson had to organize camel caravans across the mountains to the port of Trebizond. One day his men found a hidden artillery park with forty modern guns and their ammunition which, the Turks explained, had been "overlooked." There were many other such caches which they failed to find, including stores buried by loyal Russians just before the Revolution.

Colonel Rawlinson soon realized that Kiazim had no intention of surrendering his arms. Kiazim replied to all his enquiries with polite evasions and ambiguities. The two soldiers fenced amicably enough with one another. Once Rawlinson asked Kiazim with a menacing air, "Do you know how many dreadnoughts the British have?" Kiazim replied, "The Turk never fears." This was the title of a spirited march of which the pasha had composed the words and music, and which was later to become a theme song of the War of Independence. "Every Turk," he continued, "is a dreadnought in himself. How can millions of dreadnoughts be taken under a mandate?" Rawlinson said, "Your coffee is excellent. May I have another cup?"

On hearing the news of the occupation of Smyrna, Kiazim, who had a talent not merely for music but for drama, at once wrote a play on the subject, a patriotic tragedy which was performed in public by a cast of officers and teachers. He also set to work to organize a Congress at Erzurum of the various Defence of Rights groups, aimed against the parallel Allied threat to this region.

Kiazim had a specific object in planning this Congress. As an officer of the traditional stamp, he had a rigid sense of duty and a deeply ingrained respect for superior authority. When sounded by the leading local Nationalist leaders as to what he would do if ordered to evacuate Erzurum, he had replied that it was his duty as a soldier to obey orders. But "above the order of the government," he added, "there is the superior will which is that of the nation. If there is a national desire, expressed by its representatives, I will obey it and resist the invasion." The Congress would thus equip him with the legal pretext to act as he had resolved to do.

Kiazim accorded Kemal a ceremonious welcome, designed to give him a much-needed confidence in the loyalty of this eastern province. For Kemal felt far from sure of his position. During the past few days he had been bombarded, at each place en route, with telegrams from Constantinople, from the palace and the War Ministry, repeatedly pressing him to resign his command and return. For in fact, despite the circular of the Minister of the Interior, he had not yet been officially dismissed. The British, he was told, were concerned as to his activities. Let him accept an exchange posting until the situation was clarified and peace agreed. To these injunctions he replied in the negative.

At Erzurum the bombardment came to a head with a series of "conversations" over the telegraph with the Sultan's chamberlain, in which commands gave place to entreaties. In pleading tones the chamberlain declared that he himself was jealous of Kemal because of the Sultan's great love for him. If he came to Constantinople his life and future would be guaranteed. If he did not care to do so, then let him remain in Anatolia on leave. Such was the wish of the Sultan. Kemal answered courteously, stressed his loyalty and devotion to His Majesty, but persisted in his refusal to relinquish his post.

It became clear nevertheless that his dismissal was imminent. Rauf and Kiazim both urged that he should forestall this by resigning of his own accord, not merely from his post but from the army. This would create a better impression on public opinion. Refet, from Sivas, had expressed the same view, on the grounds that resignation from the army would preclude his recall to the capital. Kiazim assured Kemal that he personally would respect him more as an ordinary individual than as an army inspector.

But Kemal hesitated. For what he planned to do, he realized, the prestige of an official position was important. "It is a fool's belief," he once said, "that people like their leaders only with ideals. They want them dressed in the pomp of power and invested with the insignia of their office." His military rank had meant everything to him since he first contrived, as a boy, to enter the Military School in Salonika. It had given him a sense of security and purpose which, with his family background, he had previously lacked. Now he became nervous, depressed, uneasy as to the extent of his power and support if he lost it. His inner self-confidence seemed suddenly to waver.

But finally he agreed with his friends that resignation was inevitable. He sent a telegram to the Minister of War and another to the Sultan, resigning both his post and his commission in the army. They were crossed by another, from Constantinople, which dismissed him from both. In announcing his resignation to the people of the Erzurum province, he declared that henceforward he would fight as an individual "for the achievement of our sacred national purpose." Rauf declared, more specifically, that he would fight at his side "until the safety of the Sultanate and Caliphate are definitely secured."

Next day, after they had gone through the official telegrams together and Kemal had ordered coffee, his chief of staff, Colonel Kiazim Dirik, got up and said quietly to him, "Pasha, you have resigned from the army. Henceforward I cannot keep my post with you. With your permission, I shall ask Kiazim Karabekir Pasha to assign me to a military duty. To whom shall I deliver these documents?"

Kemal turned pale. He was so shaken by the colonel's words that he could only say, "Is that so, sir? All right, sir. You can hand over these documents to Hüsrev Bey." He gave the officer leave to go.

Kiazim Dirik strode out of the room with an air of bravado. Kemal sank into an armchair, in deep dejection. Presently he said to Rauf, "Do you see, Rauf? Wasn't I right? Do you see how important it is to have an official post and rank? The attitude of this man, who has worked with me so earnestly, shows that my point of view was correct. . . . I have known him for a long time, very intimately, and I have never seen him so disturbed."

Rauf tried to reassure him. His resignation from the army would not diminish his prestige and influence. "It is better," he said, "that we should get rid of these weaker elements before our struggle begins."

Kemal replied, "You may be right in your feelings, but in practical terms you are wrong. Let us hope that this is not the first of other such actions." He added with an air of unaccustomed pessimism, "There is only one thing for you and me to do. We shall have to retire to some safe place where we shan't be ground underfoot."

Rauf disagreed. Kemal's prestige would, on the contrary, be enhanced by his resignation. Kiazim Karabekir had fastened on him as the only man capable of leading them, and his affection and respect had increased rather than otherwise.

But Kemal had fallen into the depths of despondency. "Let us hope so," he said. Then he burst out, "God curse this American mandate, or whatever it is! Let them accept it as soon as possible, so that the country may get free of this chaos!"

The A.D.C. came into the room and said that Kiazim Karabekir Pasha wanted to see him. There was a lost look in Kemal's eyes. He knew that the Ministry of War had offered his post to Kiazim. He feared that after all Kiazim might now accept it. Smiling bitterly, he said to Rauf, "You see, I was right." He told the A.D.C. to admit the pasha.

Kiazim entered the room with the air of an officer who confronts his superior. Greeting Kemal with official respect, standing at attention and saluting, he said, "I have brought you the respects of my officers and men. You are still our honoured commander, as you were in the past. I have brought your official carriage and cavalry escort. We are, all of us, at your orders, Pasha."

Kemal swayed a little, overcome with emotion. He rubbed his eyes, as though awaking from a dream. Then he walked up to Kiazim and hugged him, kissing him on both cheeks, thanking him many times over. Rauf had not seen his friend thus moved since, after the battle of Anafarta, he had said, "Thank heaven, we have saved Stambul." Kemal's position was now assured, his confidence restored. He had the army of the east securely behind him. He began, with redoubled energy, to telegraph orders throughout the country, signed for form's sake by Kiazim Karabekir.

A few days later he was able to joke when another officer, seeing him no longer in uniform but in breeches and a hacking jacket, showed reluctance to obey him. Kemal firmly rebuked him, saying, "It was not the uniform with the epaulettes and the stars that gave you the orders. It was Mustafa Kemal who gave you the orders, and he is still here in front of you. So take down this order and carry it out at once." The officer did so. Telling the story later, Kemal said, "I thought to myself, 'Suppose he presses a bell now, calls in two soldiers, and has me arrested, what then?' "

As soon as his resignation was known Kemal was elected chairman of the executive committee of the Erzurum branch of the Defence of Rights Association, with Rauf as vice-chairman. But as to his participation in the forthcoming Congress there were obstacles still to be overcome. Its delegates were a mixed cross section of merchants, farmers, lawyers, journalists, *hojas,* Kurdish sheikhs, and Laz chieftains from the various eastern provinces. They regarded it as largely a local affair, designed to strengthen the hand of the civil and military administration, to organize the secret storage of arms and their recovery from the British control officers, and to discuss the protection of their homes and property against the threat from Armenia. It was true that this general from the west had expressed himself publicly against the creation of an Armenian state. All the same, he was not one of them. They knew only his reputation; and this aroused misgivings.

Some were members of the former Union and Progress party, and thus looked upon him as an enemy. Others saw in him despotic ambitions, noting that even after his dismissal from the army he had been seen still wearing full uniform and the cordon of the Sultan's A.D.C.—a choice of costume not wholly due, as his protagonists claimed, to the limitations of his travelling wardrobe. Others again suspected him of designs on the Sultanate. They had, moreover, heard tales of his drinking habits.

Eventually, however, the prestige and influence of Kiazim turned the scale. He was able to convince the doubters that Kemal, having sacrificed everything to the Nationalist cause, had earned their trust and must now have their support. He should be not merely admitted as a delegate but elected president of the Congress.

Two delegates thus gave up their seats to Kemal and to Rauf. The Congress opened a fortnight late, on the eleventh anniversary of the 1908 Constitution, with a large picnic, given by Kiazim, at which his officers and orphan children gave moving theatrical performances. Coincident with its opening Damad Ferid issued an order throughout the country to prevent all such assemblies, "held under the pretence that they are parliamentary sittings."

The Congress was held in an Armenian schoolhouse and lasted a fortnight. At its first session, despite some opposition, the delegates elected Mustafa Kemal as their president. He had an official position once more, but as a civilian, a status he now symbolized by donning a frock coat borrowed from the governor of Erzurum. When asked, years later, what he would have done if the delegates had failed to elect him, Kemal boasted without hesitation, "I should have called a new Congress."

From Havza and Amasya, Kemal had launched a military resistance; from Erzurum he was now to launch its political counterpart. In his opening speech to the Congress he laid down the twin principles which were to become the foundations of the revolutionary programme. One was the rights of the nation; the other was the will of the people. The one was to be achieved by the formation of a government based on the other. He spoke of the "dark and tragic dangers" that surrounded them, of "the undaunted spirit that inspires the national movement and which, like an electric flash, penetrates even to the remotest parts of our country." The resolution of the Turkish nation to be master of its own destiny could spring only from Anatolia. Moreover it could spring only from the people's will.

Kemal's was to be no mere military movement, imposed from the top by the rule of the few, as that of the Young Turks had become. It was to be the rule of the many, such as neither Turkey nor any other Eastern country had known in its history, a movement arising organically from the heart of the nation itself. Turkey was to have a regime chosen and backed by the whole community of Turks, a government deriving its authority and strength from the desires and decisions of a majority of its people. A man might act no more as an individual, he must act only in the name of all. Such, from Erzurum onwards, was to be Mustafa Kemal's message, reiterated without respite across Anatolia. It was the message of a man brought up at close quarters with the Western subjects of the Empire, who had studied something of its principles of Western democracy and who sensed that, in the long run, these ideals must provide the only political foundation on which his country could survive in the modern world.

To a trusted friend who enquired privately of Kemal at the Congress, "Are we going towards the Republic?" he replied, "Is there any doubt of it?" But this could not yet be divulged. He was careful at this stage to make it clear that the movement was not aimed against the monarchy and the Caliphate but was united behind them against the threats of the foreigner. Its purpose was, on the contrary, to preserve their rights. He was also scrupulous to ensure that his movement remained ostensibly within the law, that its acts were duly recorded with the offices of the various provincial governments, in compliance with statutory Ottoman practice.

Within this framework the main fruit of the Congress was the draft version of a declaration which was later to be known as the National Pact.[1] This document asserted by implication the principles of self-determination to which the Peace Conference pretended. It insisted on the preservation of Turkey's existing frontiers—in effect, those that contained a Turkish-speaking majority; resistance against any attempt to alter them; the establishment of an elected provisional government; the denial of privileges to non-Turkish minorities. It was made clear by the Congress that if a provisional government were formed it should follow the established laws of the central government and should, after realizing the National Pact, cease to exist.

The Pact was circulated in the form of a manifesto throughout the country and to the representatives of foreign powers. It was with some justification that Kemal told the assembly that it had "passed serious resolutions and had proved in the face of the whole world the existence and the unity of the nation." History, he added, would characterize the work of the Congress as "a wonderful performance that has seldom been equalled."

---

[1] For full terms, as finally agreed, see Appendix.

As the Congress ended a telegram from the Minister of War arrived at army headquarters:

As the Sublime Porte has decided to arrest Mustafa Kemal Pasha and Rauf Bey immediately, on the charge that they are disobeying the orders issued by the government, and send them both to Constantinople; and as the necessary orders have already been given to the local authorities, your army corps is commanded to execute this order without delay and to report that this has been done.

Kemal records laconically, "The officer commanding the army corps sent an appropriate reply." In the course of it Kiazim protested that these two "enlightened and worthy citizens" were furthering the interests of the country. In a further report to the government on the work of the Congress, he insisted on its national character: "By attributing the movement to two people only you diminish its whole scope." It arose out of the feelings and aspirations of the people, on whom the government's circulars had made a deplorable impression.

The Congress had so strengthened the hand of Kiazim that he was now able deliberately to flout the British control officers and the terms of the armistice—to say nothing of the instructions of his own government —regarding the surrender of arms. The people themselves, he now insisted, had taken matters into their own hands and would no longer allow any arms to leave the country. Shortly afterwards Colonel Rawlinson received orders from London to move all his men out of the country and to watch the situation from Sarikamish and Kars, in Armenia. The British had begun to reduce their military commitments in Anatolia, and the evacuation of Batum was in prospect.

A copy of the Pact was now sent to Colonel Rawlinson, who had been favourably impressed by Kemal in a long interview before the Congress opened. He now left for London, where he tried in vain—as Admiral Calthorpe had also done—to awaken the British government to the future potentialities of the Nationalist Movement. Only Lord Curzon displayed some interest. He wanted to know what peace terms Kemal really expected and would be prepared to accept—short of those of the National Pact, which he dismissed as out of the question. He sent Colonel Rawlinson back to Turkey to sound Kemal out on these lines, but when Rawlinson reached Erzurum the winter had set in, Kemal had moved westwards, and the subsequent march of events precluded any such meeting between them.

··

Meanwhile Damad Ferid's mission to the Peace Conference had ended in failure. On behalf of his country he recited a long plea compounded of self-abasement, self-justification, and extravagant demands. He admitted that Turkey, during the war, had committed crimes such as "to make the conscience of mankind shudder with horror forever." But "it would be fairer to judge the Ottoman nation by its long history as a whole rather than by a single period which shows it in the most disadvantageous light." All these crimes were the fault of the Committee of Union and Progress, whose leaders had now been tried and found guilty, thus rehabilitating Turkey in the eyes of the civilized world. Henceforward she could devote herself to "an intensive economic and intellectual culture." In view of these mitigating factors Damad Ferid proposed the maintenance, on the basis of the *status quo ante bellum,* of the integrity of the Ottoman Empire, which during the last forty years had been reduced to its least possible limits. In support of this claim, which went far beyond the Wilson principles agreed at the armistice, he invoked the Pan-Islamic argument. The Empire, he pretended, formed a compact block whose disintegration would be "detrimental to the peace and tranquillity of the East."

The Council were not impressed by the Grand Vizier's apologia. After a few days they sent an acid reply which agreed with his estimate of the Turkish government's crimes. Turkey, however, could not escape the consequences simply because her affairs, "at a critical moment in her history, had fallen into the hands of men who, utterly devoid of principle or pity, could not even command success." However excellent the qualities of the Turkish people, the Council "cannot admit that among these qualities is to be counted capacity to rule over alien races." As to their aspirations to economic and intellectual culture, "No change could be more startling or impressive, none could be more beneficial!" The Turkish delegation was then given permission to leave. These problems, it was explained by Mr. Balfour, touched other interests besides those of Turkey, and their immediate solution was impossible. Negotiations must be suspended until the United States was in a position to say whether it could accept any form of mandate. A few days later President Wilson had a paralytic stroke, a misfortune which was to delay them for many more months.

Thus Damad Ferid returned to Constantinople with no consolation to offer his people. Abdul Mejid, the Sultan's first cousin and heir apparent, chose this opportune moment to write for him an official memorandum on the state of the nation—a statesmanlike document which Kemal himself could hardly have bettered. The government, he urged, was dividing the country. The Sultanate should rise above party politics and hold a neutral balance. He called for immediate elections and the formation of an all-party Cabinet, with Nationalist representation. No attention, however, was paid to this enlightened proposal by either the Sultan or his Grand Vizier.

Kemal meanwhile took advantage of Damad Ferid's humiliation in Paris to send him a telegram of condolence, laced with threats. From the point of view of the national dignity, he wrote, it was unfortunate

to be compelled to admit that the different Cabinets that have succeeded one another during the last nine months have all shown gradually increasing weakness, until, unhappily, they have now shown complete incompetence. . . . As an answer to the candour and seriousness which characterize the ideals of the nation in its struggle for life and independence, the government prefer to maintain a passive attitude. This is most deplorable, and is liable to drive the people to take regrettable action against the government. Permit me to insist in all sincerity that the nation is capable of enforcing its will in every way. No power can hold it back. . . . If the government will abandon its resistance to the national movement, which is quite legitimate, and leans for support on the nation . . . it must guarantee as quickly as possible that it will convene a Parliament that shall represent the well-being of the nation and carry out its will.

It was in this mood that Kemal left, at the end of August, for Sivas, having ascertained that delegates were already on the way there from various parts of the country. Thus began the next and most crucial stage in the foundation of the Turkish resistance movement.

22 ▶ *The Sivas Congress*

Loaded with follies, stained with crimes, rotted with misgovernment, shattered by battle, worn down by long disastrous wars, his Empire falling to pieces around him, the Turk was still alive. In his breast was beating the heart of a race that had challenged the world and for centuries had contended victoriously against all comers. In his hands was once again the equipment of a modern Army, and at his head a Captain who, with all that is learned of him, ranks with the four or five outstanding figures of the cataclysm. In the tapestried and gilded chambers of Paris were assembled the law-givers of the world. In Constantinople, under the guns of the Allied Fleets there functioned a puppet Government of Turkey. But among the stern hills and valleys of "the Turkish Homelands" in Anatolia, there dwelt that company of poor men . . . who would not see it settled so; and at their bivouac fires at this moment sat in the rags of a refugee the august Spirit of Fair Play.

So wrote Winston Churchill of Mustafa Kemal.[1]

At the moment these operations of his were still on the threshold of what has been aptly called "a twilight zone between diplomacy, planned popular rising, guerrilla and open warfare."[2] He was not yet sure of all

[1] In *The World Crisis: The Aftermath.*
[2] Dankwart A. Rustow, "The Army and the Founding of the Turkish Republic," in *Foreign Policy in World Politics.*

his company, nor indeed of his modern army and its equipment. Asked by a pessimistic friend at Erzurum of what use the Nationalist troops, many of them irregulars, would be against the regular armies of the Allies, he answered, "The Nationalist troops are like the revolver beneath an honest man's pillow. When all hope of his saving his honour is lost utterly, he can at least commit suicide with his revolver."

At Erzurum Kemal, apart from his political tasks, had been contending with the problems of the assembly and organization of these Nationalist forces. First he had to bring together his various loyal commanders with each other and with the civil authorities; secondly he had to sift and uproot those who seemed less loyal than the rest. In this task he was helped by certain friends in the War Ministry, notably Jevad Pasha, who was still chief of the General Staff. But he was also hindered there by enemies trying to plant in Anatolia commanders inclining to the Sultan's cause.

Of the united and unqualified support of two army corps he was now sure—that of Kiazim Karabekir here in the east, and that of Ali Fuad in the west. At Angora, supplementing his regular troops, Fuad had created the nucleus of a sound irregular defence force. Moreover, on returning there from Amasya, he had seized the telegraph offices of central Anatolia and assumed control over the civil and administrative machine.

Elsewhere the position of the Nationalists was less secure. Since the Amasya conference there had been continuous pressure on commanders to leave their posts and return to Constantinople. Mersinli Jemal, the army commander at Konya and a supporter of the Amasya Declaration, was one of those who now yielded to this pressure. Kemal thus sent out to all commanding officers a circular urging that, if obliged to vacate their posts, they should at least remain in the neighbourhood and that in any event they should disobey any orders to disband their units. No officer, in any circumstances, should return to Constantinople.

Refet, as commander of Kemal's Third Army Corps at Samsun, now found himself in a hazardous position. He had taken a truculent line with the British, who asked for his recall and, with Damad Ferid's consent, sent a destroyer to fetch him. On board was his replacement from the War Ministry, Colonel Selah-ed-Din, with a British staff major. Refet refused to embark, explaining playfully that he suffered from seasickness and could not stand the voyage. When the major rebuked him for so frivolous an excuse, Refet replied, "The truth is, I'm afraid you'll take me on to Malta." To return in a British warship would be an affront to his dignity. But he undertook to return of his own accord in a few days' time. He thus relinquished his army corps to Selah-ed-Din, a man whom he hoped to win over to the Nationalist cause. Then he sent in his resignation to the Ministry of War and prepared to leave for the Congress at Sivas, to which delegates were already on their way from various parts of the country.

The Sivas Congress was to raise the Nationalist counsels from the local to the national plane. It did not, in terms of the number and provenance of its delegates, strictly fulfil this role. Though some two hundred had been invited, only thirty-nine came, and of these more than a dozen were members of Kemal's own immediate staff and entourage. None came, despite prior warning, from the plains of Thrace, where the Greeks were threatening; only a few from the valleys and mountains behind Smyrna, where they were pressing inland; none from the plateau of the salt lakes around Konya and the coastlands of Adalia beneath them, from the hot rich plains of Cilicia, beyond the Taurus, or from the arid deserts and foothills of Mesopotamia and Kurdistan, where the Italians, the French, and the British were in respective possession; none, more surprisingly, from the Black Sea coast and its mountains, from which the British were now preparing to withdraw. Constantinople, the reactionary stronghold of the Sultan and citadel of the Allies, had only one representative, though a young student claimed to represent the Sultan's Medical School.[3]

Thus Kemal had to start from small beginnings. In terms of population he seemed to have with him less than a quarter of the country. But in terms of territory he had more. He had the greater part of the plateau of Anatolia within its mountain walls, from Erzurum westwards. He had what he had initially sought, the Turkish heartland. Here at least was the nucleus from which a new country could grow.

The Congress opened on September 4, 1919, in a cream-washed secondary school built in the classical manner. In the garden before it stood a single protective field gun, manned by the men of Selah-ed-Din, the new army corps commander. Around it rose the graceful monuments of the thirteenth-century Seljuk Turks. For Sivas had been one of their strongholds, its people imbibing throughout the centuries a certain Turkish purity of tradition and a respect for freedom which, as at Amasya, persisted still. The place was now a cattle-ranching centre, with a peasantry of sturdy Anatolian stock.

The deliberations were held in a classroom, a long rectangular chamber

[3] A delegate who described himself as representing the Hakkiari, the wild, mountainous frontier land of the Kurds, came in fact from Erzurum.

decorated in a provincial rococo style. Carpets had been brought by the inhabitants to cover the floors and adorn the walls. A rostrum had been contrived at one end, the carpentry of its bare planks disguised under a prayer mat. The delegates sat in half a dozen rows on benches, at rough school desks with holes for inkpots. There was a special table for Kemal, and a rug on the wall above it inscribed, "Long live our Sultan." But Kemal preferred to sit on this, removing it to cover the seat of his faded plush armchair. Often, however, he sat at a desk with the rest. The adjoining room had been furnished for him as a bedroom, with a large iron bedstead, ormolu lamps, and a set of chairs on which his companions could sit when in private conference. On the bed was a silk coverlet, finely embroidered with lovers' knots and floral emblems, an item from the trousseau of a young girl who had brought it to him as a personal gift.

The delegates lived largely on school commons of pilav and beans, and lodged in various houses throughout the town. In the evenings they played dominoes in the cafés or strolled through the streets, wandering down to a bridge across the Red River. Here the inhabitants would converse with them, gathering news of the Congress. Rauf they found accessible and ready to talk. Kemal himself kept his distance, remaining behind in the Congress building, where he conferred only with the delegates and the more influential local citizens, talking incessantly to convince, to instruct, to manipulate, to reconcile, to unite. His arrival had attracted much public attention, a leading *hoja* remarking on his handsome looks and exclaiming, *"Ma'shallah'*. God save him from the evil eye." Behind those commanding eyes was a leader to fear and revere. Lesser men hesitated to approach him, sensing that here was a man who would sum them up at a glance, divining and respecting the truth and at once stripping them of shams and pretensions.

With an eye to the need still for acting in the name of the Caliphate, the oath taken by the delegates was sworn with a hand on the Koran. It had been drafted as follows:

I shall follow no personal interest or ambition but the salvation and peace of my Fatherland and nation. I shall not try to revive the Union and Progress party. I shall not serve the interests of any political party. This I swear in the name of Allah.

This time it was Rauf himself who at first opposed Kemal's election as chairman. Imbued with a sense of democratic proprieties, concerned to emphasize the national and popular character of the movement, he feared that Kemal's chairmanship might give it from the outset too personal and autocratic a stamp. Kemal was, however, elected chairman with only three dissenting votes. The Congress then proceeded to business. More aware than the delegates themselves of the precarious situation that threatened them, Kemal set to work with a sense of urgency and so managed affairs that it was over in a week.

The Congress agreed at once to the resolutions passed by the Erzurum Congress, together with amendments which strengthened the draft National Pact. To enforce its decisions, a Representative Committee was formed. Here there was no conflict. Where it arose was over the future status of the country itself. Among these delegates at Sivas there were probably few who, for all their patriotism, sincerely believed that complete independence was likely in fact to be achieved. This involved an act of faith and of will of which only Kemal himself and a handful of others were capable. The rest were inclined to snatch at the straw which now seemed to be offered to them—the American mandate. In Constantinople this new and dignified word—the "gilded pill of the moment," as Ismet, one of its tentative supporters, defined it—was on all lips, replacing the dirty word "annexation." Even patriots began to see in it a possible formula for peace without dishonour, worthy to be explored if only as the lesser of misfortunes.

At the Erzurum Congress Kemal, sounding out opinion, had raised the question of aid from some Great Power without territorial designs on the country. He was astute enough, however, to avoid mentioning the name of America. For in the East it was a name bracketed in the popular mind with the hated project of an independent Armenia. But here at Sivas it was different. To these delegates from other parts of the country the name of America carried no such sinister undertones. Thus the question of the American mandate loomed larger at the Congress than that of the National Pact, which was already agreed.

A lucid protagonist of the mandate, in relation to the international position as seen from Constantinople, was Halide Edib. A woman of intelligence, with an international political outlook, she was in close touch with Mr. Charles R. Crane, whose King-Crane Commission, appointed by the Big Four in Paris to study the mandate question in special relation to the Arab provinces, had reported also in favour of three mandates for Turkey itself—one over Armenia, one over Constantinople, and one over the rest of Anatolia.[4]

In a long letter to Kemal she summarized the designs of the Allies on Turkey and referred to the feeling in Constantinople that an Ameri-

[4] The report was in effect to be stillborn, since the State Department suppressed it.

can mandate might be "the least harmful solution." It would strengthen Turkey against the pretensions of the foreign minorities; it would ensure the transformation of the Turkish peasantry into a modern nation, a task for which Turkey herself lacked the experience and the financial resources; it would secure her defence against European imperialism. She referred to the achievements of the United States in the Philippines and declared that only America had the "political efficiency . . . that could create a new Turkey within the space of twenty years."

At her suggestion an American journalist, Mr. Louis E. Browne, was sent to the Congress, ostensibly as the correspondent of the Chicago *Daily News,* but in fact rather as Mr. Crane's personal emissary. The only non-Moslem to attend it, he was well received by Kemal. In a series of talks with him Kemal used the term "American aid" rather than "mandate" as being more acceptable to Turkish pride. It should have a social and economic as opposed to a political character. Asked whether the Congress would pass a resolution inviting America to take over such a mandate, Kemal replied, "Yes," but added the crucial reservation: "Provided you can assure me that America will accept it, if offered." Browne expressed doubts as to whether his country would do so. Kemal said that without some such assurance he could not risk an official admission that Turkey required foreign help.

Two long and confused sessions of the Congress were devoted to the discussion of the mandate. Kemal took a guarded line. Finally, with Rauf, he found a compromise which the Congress accepted. The Congress of the United States should be invited to send over a delegation to study the country and report upon its real situation. A telegram signed by Kemal, Rauf, and others was sent to the American Senate, reporting on the Congress of Sivas and conveying this request.

The despatch of this document conciliated those who favoured the mandate, without committing Kemal and his associates; it brought the standing of the Nationalist movement to the notice of the world; it might steal from the movement some local credit with the American mission of General J. G. Harbord, which Kemal knew to be on its way to Armenia, on the authority of President Wilson, to examine the question of mandates in the American interest. It was a tactical move in Kemal's diplomatic offensive, which could do little harm and might do some good.

A week or so after the end of the Congress, General Harbord and his mission arrived in Sivas. Harbord found Kemal to be "a young man of force and keen intelligence," whom he judged, from his light brown hair and high cheekbones, to have "Circassian or other blond blood in his ancestry." Kemal was suffering from malaria and seemed under strain. But in the course of an interview which lasted for two and a half hours he talked easily and fluently, marshalling his facts in an orderly logical fashion. He seemed to envisage a "big brother" relationship with America, based on such advice and assistance and "slight exercise of authority" as would not interfere with his country's internal affairs. Harbord, referring to the past record of the Turks, replied that no self-respecting nation would accept a mandatory responsibility without complete authority. He referred to the Armenian massacres. Kemal assured him that his own movement stood for just treatment of all races and religions and that he was prepared to allay Christian fears with a declaration to this effect.

"What do you expect to do now?" Harbord asked.

Kemal as he talked had been playing with a string of prayer beads, drawing them through his fine-drawn hands. Now with a gesture of nervous tension he pulled the string apart and the beads were scattered all over the floor. Picking them up one by one, he remarked that here was the answer to the general's question. He meant to draw the pieces of his country together, to save it from its various enemies, to make of it an independent and civilized state. Harbord suggested that such a hope was against logic, against military facts. "We know that individuals, now and then, commit suicide. Are we now going to see the suicide of a nation?"

Kemal replied, "What you say, General, is true. What we want to do, in our situation, is explainable neither in military nor in any other terms. But in spite of everything we are going to do it, to save our country, to establish a free and civilized Turkish state, to live like human beings." Kemal put his hand on the table, palm upwards. "If we can't succeed," he continued, "rather than fall into the palm of the enemy like a bird, and be condemned to a gradual, ignoble death"—he closed his fingers little by little as he talked—"we prefer, being the sons of our forefathers, to die fighting." His fist lay clenched before him.

Harbord was impressed by his resolution, his spirit. "I had taken everything into account," he said. "But not that. Had we been in your place, we should have done the same thing."

But to a Turkish member of Harbord's staff Kemal, indicating the people around him, said, "Pray for me, back in Constantinople."

23 ▶ *Fall of the Sultan's government*

The Sivas Congress meanwhile neared its end. Kemal had good reason to speed up the deliberations. He had rightly discounted the danger of which Refet had warned him, of an attempt by the British to march on Sivas and prevent the Congress, and a more specific threat by the French to occupy the area. Neither power, he judged, was likely to commit itself to so costly a military enterprise. But Kemal now knew, from a series of intercepted telegrams, that the Sultan and his government were trying to break it up and to arrest himself and the delegates. This was the task of Ali Galib, now governor of Erzinjan, who was instructed to proceed secretly to Sivas for the purpose, with an escort of Kurdish cavalry. Concerned chiefly with the bad impression created abroad by the Erzurum Congress, Constantinople telegraphed: "The government is well aware that nothing of real importance can result from a meeting that comprises only five, or even ten, persons in this town; but it is impossible to make Europe understand this."

Kemal acted quickly. He at once ordered troops to Malatya, where Ali Galib was assembling his Kurdish force. With him was a British officer, Major E. W. C. Noel, who, after the capture of Mosul, had been sent to

Sulimaniye to help organize the Kurds of northern Iraq into a series of semi-autonomous provinces. He had now been sent across the frontier to Malatya by the British authorities, with the approval and backing of the Sultan's government, to enquire into the situation of the Kurdish tribes in Turkish territory. Noel, a political officer whose unorthodox activities and contacts were sometimes a source not merely of suspicion to the Turks but of embarrassment to his own colleagues in the Allenby administration, was accompanied on his mission by two members of the Kurdish feudal Bedkhan family, which had formerly dominated the region.

Kemal gave orders that both Ali Galib and Noel should be arrested. Ali Galib, despite the urgency of his instructions, delayed his departure for Sivas while he bargained for a final settlement on the expenses involved in the enterprise. He delayed too long and had to flee ignominiously into the mountains from Malatya to avoid capture by the Nationalist troops. He left behind him incriminating documents and a large sum of money, with a receipt showing that its purpose was "the suppression of Mustafa Kemal and his followers."

The tribes dispersed, and Major Noel was escorted in the direction of the frontier. Meanwhile he had, a shade innocently, telegraphed in clear to the High Commission in Constantinople, complaining of his own treatment by the Nationalists. Thus, as Ryan commented in a minute on the telegram, the fat was in the fire. Kemal had been presented with evidence to incriminate not merely Damad Ferid but the British in an infamous conspiracy against him. He was to exploit this evidence to the full.

From all points of view the Ali Galib operation was a notable success for Kemal. He had spent long hours at the telegraph, ordering and cajoling into action various commanders who were reluctant to act against an official of the Sultan, and in any case sparingly equipped with troops; and he had finally achieved his ends. He owed much to a group of telegraphists loyal to the Nationalist cause, who copied and relayed to him the government's messages. Fully informed as he now was, he could not resist sending an abusive telegram to Adil, the Minister of the Interior, accusing him of cowardice and treason against the nation. It was a telegram whose tone shocked Kiazim Karabekir, as unbecoming to the president of the Congress and "a man of his social position."

The end of the Ali Galib conspiracy coincided with that of the Congress itself. Kemal, not wishing unduly to alarm the delegates, had told them little of its course. But now he proposed to draw from it, and from the complicity of the government which the documents concerning it revealed, the maximum public and political advantage. When the final resolution, concerning the National Pact and other matters, had been agreed, he took it across to the telegraph office, a room over a shop which became his headquarters for the next few days. There he launched, amid mounting curiosity outside, into a battle of the telegraph which was to lead to the rupture of relations with the Constantinople government.

First he called upon the Minister of the Interior in Constantinople to come to the instrument, and transmitted the resolution to him with the request that it be taken to the Sultan. The minister refused. Thereupon, in the words of Louis Browne, who was present throughout, "for many minutes the telegraph wire sizzled with Turkish expletives. He [the minister] called Mustafa and Rauf traitors and criminals and other things besides and they responded with the accusation that Adil was nothing but a cheap skate who had sold out to the British for a pittance."

Kemal was in his element, planning each move as though he were conducting a battle in the field, swiftly drafting telegrams, drily commenting on the replies, pacing up and down, smoking and talking and consulting with Rauf and the others, while the crowd waited outside for some announcement as to what was afoot.

They decided that it would be good tactics at this stage to avoid a frontal attack on the Sultan: "It was wiser to concentrate our endeavours on a single point, and not scatter our forces. Therefore, we chose Ferid Pasha's Cabinet alone as our target and pretended that we knew nothing about the complicity of the Padishah. Our theory was that the sovereign had been deceived by the Cabinet and that he himself was in total ignorance of what was really going on."

A telegram was thus addressed to the Sultan which, "after the usual rigmarole of expressions of our devotion, as was customary at that time," declared that his government had "conspired to shed the blood of Moslems in a fratricidal war, by planning a sudden attack on the Congress," and had spent public funds in an attempt "to dismember our territory by raising Kurdistan into revolt." It continued: "The nation demands that immediate steps shall be taken for the pursuit of this gang of traitors; that they shall be severely punished, and that a new government shall be formed that will be composed of men of honour."

Kemal was soon in touch with the rest of Anatolia. Browne, in a despatch to the Chicago *Daily News,* wrote: "I have never heard of more efficient communications than I witnessed that night. Within half an hour

Erzurum, Erzinjan, Mosul, Diyarbekir, Samsun, Trebizond, Angora, Malatya, Kharput, Konya, and Brusa were all in communication. Mustafa Kemal sat at one end of the wire leading to all these places, and at the other end sat the military commanders and civil authorities of the respective cities and villages. The whole situation was explained and, with one exception, Anatolia ordered Mustafa Kemal to use his own judgment and go to the limit. Konya responded that owing to the presence of Italian troops in the city it had to be neutral." During that day and the night that followed, telegraph offices throughout the country were occupied by the corps commanders.

"But the Grand Vizier," Kemal recalled, "seemed to have disappeared. He did not reply." The answer finally came that the message had been relayed to him by telephone. He had replied that such communications should be passed to him only through the proper channels. This provoked an ultimatum, signed in the name of the Congress:

"The nation has no confidence left in any of you other than the Sultan, to whose person alone therefore it must submit its reports and petitions. Your Cabinet . . . is coming between the nation and the sovereign. If you persist in this obstinacy for one hour longer, the nation will consider itself free to take whatever action it thinks fit, and will break off all relations between your illegal Cabinet and the whole country. This is our last warning. . . ." The telegraph office at Constantinople refused to accept this message and was warned that, unless it did so within an hour, all telegraph lines between Anatolia and the capital would be cut.

As the battle proceeded, wild reports of it were spreading around Sivas. "Let us execute Damad Ferid," cried the people. "We shall drive the Greeks into the sea. If the British support them, we shall smash them too." The crowds became jubilant at a rumour that war was about to be declared against Britain and Greece. Demonstrators paraded through the streets and surged down the alleyways, carrying torches made from oil-soaked rags, to mass before the telegraph office. Kemal appeared on the balcony amid frantic cheers. Then in dead silence the town crier read aloud the resolutions of the Congress. The crowd remained silent for a moment, then yelled its approval.

Throughout the night Kemal and his counsellors kept vigil in the telegraph office, while at other instruments throughout the country his loyal officers did the same. At five o'clock in the morning of September 12, since Constantinople persisted in its refusal to open communication with the palace, a circular was sent out from all districts, breaking off all official relations and all telegraphic and postal communication with the government "until it is succeeded by a legal government." Ali Fuad was ordered to station troops across the railway at Eskishehir to prevent reinforcement of British or government forces, and to apprehend officials of the Sultan's government attempting to reach the interior.

The next move was to force the resignation of the Cabinet. For this purpose the General Assembly of the Sivas Congress declared that its Representative Committee would serve as a provisional government, pledged to conduct the affairs of a nation according to the laws and in the name of the Sultan until a national government, possessing the confidence of the people, should be formed. It guaranteed the maintenance of law and order throughout the country. It effectively confirmed the executive power of Kemal and the Nationalists over a great part of Anatolia, on what they could pretend to be a legal and constitutional basis. In effect the committee became the first revolutionary "government." But since it never in fact met as a committee, it was Kemal himself who ruled, signing documents with its seal to preserve the fiction that he did so on its behalf. Under its auspices, the legitimate government was subjected to a barrage of thousands of telegrams from all parts of Anatolia, demanding its resignation.

Meanwhile Kemal was sifting out his enemies from his friends, persuading and threatening those districts which still held back from joining the cause, hectoring into submission or driving out officers of whose support he was doubtful. The time had come to force, throughout the country, a choice between the Sultan and the Nationalist movement. But in the process of forcing it he was still careful not to offend religious susceptibilities or to attack the Sultan in his capacity as Caliph.

He carried on an eight-hour "conversation" over the telegraph, in flowery Islamic language, with one Abdul Kerim Pasha, a staff officer of the old school and an intimate friend from his Salonika days, who, at Damad Ferid's instigation, tried to persuade him to agree to a joint meeting between the Sultan's representatives and his own. In the course of their exchanges of telegrams, which contained continual invocations of the Almighty and texts from the Koran, Kemal addressed him by the Islamic title of Most Exalted Excellency, while Abdul Kerim for his part referred to Kemal as "Pole of Poles," a designation "by which he intended to confer on me the attribute of the spiritual representative of God on earth."

Kemal regretfully informed his "highly honoured brother with a pure heart" that he could not accept Damad Ferid's conciliatory move: "The questions I am urging you to answer with 'yes' or 'no' have unfortunately remained unanswered. Undoubtedly, my most venerable Pasha, 'the hand of God is over all others,' but it is nonetheless a fact that those who try to find a way to solve this question . . . must have a fixed aim." The old man grew tired, and telegraphed, "Only two more words, my Soul . . ." But Kemal insisted on having the last one, which affirmed the national strength and suggested that it was time for the Sultan to "deign to come to a decision and settle this question."

It became clear that Damad Ferid could not last much longer, however confidently the British High Commission might count on his "wonderful faculty of hanging on." At first the Nationalist movement had been underrated in Constantinople. What was it but a few undisciplined gangs, led by a man who had been dismissed from the army, hence had no regular forces under his command and little authority over the irregulars? But the rebel seizure of telecommunications finally awakened the Allied Powers and Damad Ferid's Cabinet to the true danger which faced them. They recognized it as a "declaration of war" against the central government. Kemal had prepared his ground well and it was evident that the Sivas Representative Committee was a power, backed by a formidable array of army commanders and civil authorities, which must now be seriously reckoned with.

Damad Ferid, having failed in conciliation, fell back on the idea of a show of force and begged the Allies for help against the rebels. He proposed to send a large Turkish force to confront the Nationalists at Eskishehir. But the Allies refused to sanction this; nor would they provide him with Allied troops for the purpose. The threat from the Nationalists had placed them in a quandary. Only the withdrawal of the Greeks and the Italians from the region of Smyrna could appease them; and this was impossible. Resistance to them on the other hand would mean the end of the armistice and a resumption of war—this time a civil war, of unpredictable outcome.

The British thus decided to withdraw their remaining forces from the danger points in Anatolia. First they withdrew from the Samsun area, a departure celebrated in Sivas with torchlight processions and shouts of "Down with the occupation!" Two days later Ali Fuad started operations against the important junction of Eskishehir, where they had a force protecting the railway. But they were forestalled by a British withdrawal. The western rim of the Anatolian plateau was now securely in the hands of Kemal and his Nationalist forces.

At the instance of the Sultan, Damad Ferid now resigned. His bid to remain in the Cabinet as Minister of Foreign Affairs, and thus continue to enjoy the amenities of the official residence that went with his office, was firmly rejected. In his place Ali Riza Pasha, a former staff officer who had served in Tevfik Pasha's Cabinet, was invited to form a "Ministry of Conciliation." He was instructed to hold early elections for a new Parliament, thus appearing to meet the Nationalists' demand. He established some popular confidence. The censorship was at once relaxed. The press became free, not only to attack Damad Ferid but to publish for the first time the statements of Mustafa Kemal and full news of the Nationalist movement.

Kemal had good reason to declare in an interview to his friend Rushen Eshref, "Now the first phase is at an end." Within a little over four months of his landing in Samsun he had brought down the government which had dismissed him from the army and the Grand Vizier whom the Allies were using. Thanks to astute and single-minded leadership, to an efficient and expanding organization, and to a simple and clearly defined programme, he had indicated to the Allies that they might have to deal no longer with a supine puppet government but with a positive new national force, conscious of its rights and firm in its demands, which was struggling to rise from the ashes of the Ottoman Empire.

24 ▶ *Move to Angora*

Ali Riza suspected Kemal's motives. To Izzet, whom he brought into the Cabinet as one of his ministers, he exclaimed, "You will proclaim a Republic—a Republic!" Nevertheless he had little choice but to come to terms with the Nationalists. In the exchange of telegrams which followed his accession to power, he returned the soft answer to the uncompromising demands on which Kemal thought it politic to insist. Behind his truculent façade Kemal too took a conciliatory line, announcing to his people "the glad news that complete unity had been arrived at between the new Cabinet and the national organizations." But he firmly refused to dissolve the Sivas Representative Committee until the promised elections had been held.

One of Ali Riza's first actions was to send emissaries to Anatolia, to report on the situation in the various areas. To Amasya he sent Salih Pasha, the Minister of Marine, for discussions with the Representative Committee. Kemal received him there in person amid the plaudits of those citizens who had assisted at the birth of the movement, with such imponderable prospects, only a few months before. Now they were to see it officially recognized by the Constantinople government. On its behalf

Salih and his delegation approved in effect the resolutions of the Sivas Congress. Their discussions led to agreement on all points—the principle that the new government would send to the Peace Conference only delegates who had the confidence of the Nationalists.

The important question then arose as to where the new Parliament, due to be elected, should meet—in Constantinople or in Anatolia? Kemal nourished a deep and intuitive distrust of Constantinople and its ways. He had for long aspired to shift the centre of political gravity to Anatolia and hoped that the moment for this might have arrived. He thus urged that Constantinople, "being under foreign occupation, was not a very favourable spot for the deputies to carry on their legislative duties unmolested." He quoted the precedents of the French sitting at Bordeaux in 1870, and of the Germans lately at Weimar, as an argument that the new Assembly should sit in Anatolia until peace was signed. He succeeded in arguing Salih Pasha into personal agreement with him. He could not bind his own Cabinet but promised to do all he could to convert them to a similar view. But they were not to be converted. Nor indeed did Kemal get support from his own organizations in Constantinople, who insisted that the Parliament could very well meet there without danger—though some took the view that it would be imprudent at present for the Nationalist deputies to take their seats.

Kemal then called a conference of his army corps commanders at Sivas to discuss the question. Here he argued that Anatolia must retain its initiative as the centre of affairs, lest the national movement lose its momentum and the people relapse into inertia. He thus urged that Parliament should meet either in Angora or Eskishehir, and that the Representative Committee should become, in effect, its Cabinet.

Kiazim, with his orthodox constitutional outlook, was cautious. Rauf was at first undecided but eventually agreed with Ali Fuad that the Sultan and the Allies would probably suppress Parliament in any case and that this would provide ample justification for a new Assembly in Anatolia. To put the Allies in the wrong would enhance the moral position of the Nationalists in other foreign eyes.

Kemal saw that he would have to give in; the moment was not yet ripe for an Anatolian Parliament, and thus he agreed that Parliament should meet in Constantinople. But the deputies were to meet the Representative Committee beforehand to decide on means of protection in the city and to agree on a united policy. Kemal then set to work to secure the election as deputies of those friends—not forgetting his A.D.C.s —who would best serve his cause.

While they were conferring an element of some discord arrived in the shape of Fevzi Pasha, with a mission of investigation from Ali Riza. Fevzi was a friend of the Nationalists, who had resigned from the War Ministry on the Smyrna issue and had supported Kemal on his departure for Anatolia. But his attitude now, and that of his colleagues, was dubious. He sought to convert the Nationalists to a moderate line, counselling them not to take too firm a stand against the government in Constantinople.

He had hoped for co-operation from Kiazim Karabekir, whom he now found in Sivas and to whom he even confided an idea of arresting Kemal and Ali Fuad. Kiazim, crusty and punctilious, had periods of friction with Kemal, who was apt to be offhand, failing to keep Kiazim informed as to his actions and often bypassing him with orders and appointments of his own. Kiazim had misgivings, moreover, that, in Kemal's hands, the Nationalist movement was assuming too personal a trend and he shared some of the suspicions of those around him in the east who mistrusted Kemal's ambitions and resented his arbitrary ways. In reply to Fevzi, however, Kiazim adhered loyally and sensibly to the view that for the present it was essential to support Kemal, since he was the only leader capable of accomplishing the national aims and provided the only alternative to submission to a government controlled by the Allies. Fevzi after a while came round to this view, and Kemal, who had himself at first talked of arresting Fevzi, bade him a polite if reserved farewell on his return to Constantinople.

With his Representative Committee, Kemal spent four months in Sivas. But, with the elections approaching, the time had come to move westwards—despite the misgivings of Kiazim, who feared that the east would thus be left in isolation and a prey to disorders. Kemal decided on Angora as his headquarters, a central place linked to Constantinople by rail and in touch besides with the western and southern fronts, where irregular bands, whether independently or under Nationalist orders, were engaged in guerrilla warfare against the occupying troops of the Greeks, French, and Italians. Thus the Nationalist deputies were invited to assemble at Angora for indoctrination before proceeding to take their seats in Constantinople.

Kemal and his companions left Sivas for Kayseri, en route for Angora, on December 18, 1919. Well received everywhere, he proceeded to Kirshehir, whose inhabitants greeted him with especial enthusiasm. He conversed with the leading citizens, made a speech to the Youth Association, and at a torchlight procession launched into poetry, quoting and adapting Namik Kemal: "A Kemal who came from the midst of this nation said:

> "The foe thrusts his knife into the heart of the land.
> There was none to save our ill-fated mother.

"Again a Kemal coming from the heart of this nation says:

> "The foe thrusts his knife into the heart of the land.
> But yes, one is found to save our ill-fated mother."

Next day he left for Angora, which he was to see for the first time. He had chosen Angora as the seat of his movement because of the exceptional loyalty of its people and those of the surrounding villages to the Nationalist cause. The place had shown a similar spirit of patriotism at the time of the Young Turk Revolution—a spirit not shared by the people of Konya, with their fanatical Moslem spirit, or those of Eskishehir (his first choice), who were closer to Constantinople and to European influences in general. In terms of its population, Angora was one of the securest centres in Anatolia.

Kemal's choice was amply vindicated by the tumultuous welcome which the people of Angora gave him. The town crier strode through the streets, proclaiming, "Mustafa Kemal and his Green Army are coming." Outlaws from the Sultan's regime, turned bandit, came out from their mountain hideouts to greet him; crowds swarmed out of the city to intercept him on the road from Kirshehir; dervishes stood by the roadside ready to chant prayers to him.

Kemal appeared in a decrepit Benz touring car whose worn-out tires he used to declare were stuffed with rags. Walking down with his friends into the city, he was welcomed by an army of irregulars—thousands of horsemen and infantrymen, swaggering by in their picturesque kilted costumes, bristling with antiquated weapons of formidable size, waving flags and breaking out of the procession to leap around in their national dances, while the beat of the drum and the clash of the cymbal and the reedy melody of the flute rang through the steep narrow streets of the citadel. A more sedate procession of the various trade guilds brought up the rear.

Never before within the memory of its inhabitants had Angora seen such a gathering. The few foreigners looked on in some astonishment— the British at the station, which they had occupied a few days before, and whither the procession made a detour to demonstrate the fervour of the national feeling; the French, with their Tunisian soldiers perched on the walls around the future Parliament building, where at present the tricolor flew. Kemal took the precaution of paying a brief visit to the Haji Bayram Mosque, with its sacred tomb. Then from the balcony of the government building he made a speech of thanks to the people massed below. That evening he sent out a circular telegram, announcing the arrival in Angora of the Representative Committee, which had been "the object of sincerely patriotic and enthusiastically cordial demonstrations on the part of our great nation, not in Angora alone but along the whole of their journey."

Not long after his arrival Kemal was joined at long last by Ismet. In Constantinople Ismet had been working in the War Ministry with Fevzi. His late arrival in the field, and only on an exploratory visit, won him a guarded reception. Kemal treated him at first with less than his accustomed warmth, while Ali Fuad and the rest, who had unquestioningly risked all for the sake of the resistance, regarded him with definite coldness. Among Kemal's adherents it was the beginning of a conflict between the founders of the Revolution and its late-comers which was to increase in intensity as time went on, and was indeed never wholly to be resolved.

The deputies now began to arrive, singly and in small groups. Day after day Kemal set himself patiently to talk to them, working to clarify their ideas and convince them of the need for cohesion. To unite Turkish opinion in Parliament, however, was no easy task. These deputies represented a diversity of interests. Each man was to some extent for himself. The habit of combining for a disinterested national purpose had yet to mature among them. There were many who mistrusted Kemal, many more who were irresolute. Others considered that he had served his purpose, now that their period of outlawry was over and they were free to return to Constantinople in the honourable guise of legislators. Many disregarded this summons. Among those who obeyed it were others whom he afterwards had cause to lash with his tongue for their lack of faith in the movement, their timidity in avowing support of it and pressing its views, their poor fighting spirit, their inability to see that this was a moment in history when the nation must act or perish.

As he had feared, their resolution was soon undermined by the various influences of Constantinople, and the united party for which he had urged the necessity was not to materialize. Nor, when Parliament met, did the deputies support his own candidature for the presidency of the Chamber, a position he had sought in his zeal for constitutional practice. His titular presidency would strengthen his position if the Parliament were dissolved, as was sure to happen, and the time came for him to summon a new one. But the deputies voted against it, preferring him to remain "the power behind the Chamber."

Ismet meanwhile returned temporarily to Constantinople, to discuss resistance measures with Fevzi and other friends in the War Ministry. Momentarily nothing remained for Kemal but to consolidate his position in Angora and await what he saw to be the inevitable events in Constantinople. He did not have long to wait.

25 ▶ *The Allies raid Parliament*

The Ottoman Parliament met in Constantinople on January 16, 1920. The first with a Kemalist majority, it survived for a bare three months. For the Allies at once showed their hand. They demanded the resignation of Jemal Pasha, the War Minister, and his chief of the General Staff, Jevad Pasha, on the grounds that they had been aiding the Nationalist forces. To this Ali Riza agreed, rather than resign with his Cabinet and so permit the Allies to appoint one of their own, perhaps once again under Damad Ferid. This highhanded action at least precipitated the acceptance by the Chamber of Kemal's final draft of the National Pact, which thus acquired the stamp of official recognition.[1]

The key to the situation now lay largely in London and Paris. The illness of President Wilson, with his hopes for American intervention, had delayed the discussions of the Turkish peace treaty for a further six months—just the time needed by Kemal to build up that effective national resistance which Lord Curzon had always predicted. Within a few months the President was to disappear altogether from the American scene, "a broken and baffled prophet," as Lloyd George put it, "unable

[1] Mersinli Jemal, a supporter of the Amasya Declaration.

to put up any further fight for his faith." Nothing more was to be heard
of American commitments in Middle Eastern affairs.

Lord Curzon thus judged that the moment had come to prepare a
draft Turkish peace treaty. He remained faithful to his plan for an independent Turkey in Asia but still sought to eject the Turks "bag and
baggage" from Europe. In this, if in little else, he had the support of Lloyd
George. Both, however, were strongly opposed by Mr. Edwin Montagu,
the Secretary of State for India, who maintained that the expulsion of
the Caliph from Constantinople would gravely offend the Moslem world
and thus threaten the British position in India. His view, supported
for different reasons by the War Office, ultimately prevailed in the Cabinet, which decided by a large majority that the Turks should remain
in Constantinople, subject to international arrangements for the free
passage of the Straits.

With French concurrence the decision was conveyed to the Turkish
government. Kemal, in Angora, was not impressed by such a "gilded
promise," especially as it was accompanied by a demand that all operations against Allied troops, including those of Greece, should cease
forthwith. This, he judged, was an Allied threat to occupy Constantinople on the pretext that the government could not control the national
forces.

It coincided, on the other hand, with a more conciliatory policy towards the Nationalist movement on the part of the French. At Sivas Kemal had received a visit from Monsieur Georges Picot, the French High
Commissioner in Syria. Though in fact his journey had the official blessing neither of Beirut nor of Constantinople, he announced himself at
Sivas as "the representative of the French government." Kemal received
him as such, and they discussed at some length their joint desire for
Franco-Turkish friendship. Picot was concerned primarily with the disturbed situation in Cilicia, where he asked Kemal to help keep the peace.
But Kemal, for whom Picot's visit implied, for the first time, recognition
of the Nationalist movement by an Allied power, felt himself to be in a
strong position. Building it up for the benefit of the Frenchman, he
talked grandiloquently of his "national armies"—to the surprise of Rauf
and the rest who knew them to consist only of a few irregular bands.
Unless the French could show that they had no designs against the
Turks in Cilicia, they would fight there to defend their independence.
Picot was impressed by this positive attitude, comparing it favourably
with that of the government in Constantinople. Not long afterwards the
Paris press began to reflect certain Nationalist sympathies.

From such signs Kemal judged that the moment had come to force the hand of the French in Cilicia. In view of "the friendship which we have felt towards France for centuries," he protested, in the name of the Representative Committee, against the occupation of Urfa, Aintab, and Marash, as contrary to the terms of the armistice, and called upon the population to act against it.

The objective of his first attack was Marash, a place thinly held by the French, which they were thus forced to evacuate. His guerrilla bands poured over the mountains to reinforce the Turkish gendarmerie and set fire to the Armenian quarter. They were well enough armed, drawing on the caches which Kemal had had the foresight to form at the time of the armistice. The Turkish population fired on the Armenians from their windows and the rooftops as they fled from their own burning houses to take refuge in schools and churches. These were fired in their turn, burning hundreds, including women and children, alive. Meanwhile fanatical Moslems were slaughtering and committing atrocities against the Christians in the villages around.

It was only after nearly three weeks of bloodshed that the French could muster a column strong enough to attempt the relief of Marash. But as it approached the city orders were given to its troops, from an unexplained source and to the bewilderment and panic of the Christian inhabitants now confident of rescue, to retreat. They struggled back southwards over the mountains towards the Syrian frontier, in weather of arctic severity, followed by thousands of Armenian fugitives, falling in the snow by the wayside. Two hundred French soldiers lost limbs, some all four, from frostbite alone. In the whole operation some seven or eight thousand Armenians lost their lives, a massacre which, accompanied by others in the neighbouring areas, caused consternation in the capitals of Europe.

The retreat from Marash was the first move in a reversal of French policy which was to lead to the ultimate evacuation of all Cilicia. The city of Urfa was besieged, and surrendered when its supplies were exhausted. Other places fell to irregulars, better armed than the French and raising forced levies from the villagers. Aintab was to hold out for some time longer. But the Turks had gained control of the mountain regions and were soon carrying out murderous sorties down into the wide Cilician plain to threaten the important centres of Adana, Tarsus, and Mersin. Thus at the end of May 1920 the French were finally driven to seek an armistice, and sent a delegation to Angora for the purpose. Though the armistice was later broken, it enabled Kemal to regroup his southern forces. More important, he had raised his prestige and won recognition for his regime by a victory against one of the Great Powers.

In the eyes of the British, Kemal's success simply made more urgent the execution of the policy towards which they were moving already— the suppression of the Nationalist movement. The illicit traffic of arms to Anatolia was beginning to cause them serious concern. This was well run by underground organizations, staffed largely by demobilized Turkish officers. Their task was not hard, since the guards on most of the depots were Turks and there were plenty of willing porters, boatmen, and drivers to run the stolen arms into Anatolia through the gantlet of British patrols and Greek guerrillas. The arms were concealed in peasant carts, beneath loads of hay or sacks of coal, transported only by night, then buried before dawn and reloaded at dusk for the next long slow stage of the journey. In the War Ministry itself there had been, since the armistice, a systematic evasion of its disarmament terms with the connivance of such patriotic generals as Fevzi, who was once more Minister of War.

The French now began to connive at the theft of arms. From a depot under their protection in the Gallipoli Peninsula the Nationalists secured a large haul, the French merely giving the excuse that their guard had been outnumbered by the raiders. The Italians, in their antagonism to the Greeks, had from the start sympathized with the Nationalists and were now, as they prepared to withdraw their own troops, selling arms to them and helping the gun runners to avoid the Allied control points. As for the British, they had from the start been casual over the confiscation and storage of arms. A British staff officer was heard to express the opinion in GHQ that it was unfair to disarm the Turks without also disarming the Greeks.[2] Thus the arming of the Nationalist forces continued.

With the news of the French defeat in Cilicia and of the massacre of Armenians that went with it, a sense of the Nationalist threat had at last percolated through to the delegates in Paris. Regarding Kemal,

[2] An element of comedy attended the continuous raids on a large Allied depot by the shores of the Golden Horn. Each evening seals of wax were placed on the doors; each morning they were found to be broken. But all the guards protested innocence. When finally a British officer sat up one night to watch the building, he observed that a flock of goats had been let into its grassy compound. It was these bearded creatures who, in the intervals between mouthfuls of grass, approached the doors as he watched and nibbled off each of the seals. Harold Armstrong, *Turkey in Travail.*

Lloyd George admitted that "our military intelligence had never been more thoroughly unintelligent." Even now there seemed to be some doubt as to whether he was acting on his own or under orders from the Sultan's government. Lord Curzon himself confessed to the Conference that he had not been aware "that the connection between the two was as close as now appeared," and disclosed that, according to his latest information, Mustafa Kemal had recently been made "governor of Erzurum"—a city included in the proposed state of Armenia. Whatever his official position, it became obvious that no treaty should be framed without looking into the prospects of its enforcement.

Consulted on this point, the High Commissioner, Admiral de Robeck,[3] considered that if the treaty were to be drastic resistance to its terms should be forestalled by a strengthening of the Allied position in Constantinople. A plan thus arose in the Supreme Council for a show of force to teach the Turks a disciplinary lesson. It was to take the form, as Kemal had anticipated, of a more complete and stringent occupation of Constantinople, where the Allied forces in theory had hitherto only been "present." This would involve control of the War Ministry but not of the civil administration, and the establishment of a military censorship. The Supreme Council proposed also, not very realistically, the "dismissal of Mustafa Kemal from Erzurum [sic]." The occupation was to continue until the execution of the peace terms.

Kemal heard of the impending occupation from the French. He passed on the news to Rauf, urging that the Nationalist leaders should prepare to leave the city. Let the Chamber, by all means, continue to defy the Allied decision and carry out its duties. But it was important that Nationalist supporters should come to Anatolia in sufficient numbers and of such a calibre as to form an alternative government. He telegraphed money to the Ottoman Bank to assist their escape.

Under cover of darkness in the early morning of March 16, 1920, British warships drew in to the Galata Bridge, British armoured cars rolled through the streets of Stambul and Pera, British troops occupied police stations, military posts, and the main public buildings. The news came through to Angora in a series of messages from a telegraphist loyal to the Nationalist cause: "The English have made a surprise attack this morning on a government building at Shehzade Bashi and have had a skirmish with the soldiers. At the present moment they are beginning to occupy Constantinople. . . . We have just this moment heard that the Military School has been occupied. English soldiers are on guard out-

[3] Later Admiral of the Fleet Sir John de Robeck, Bt., G.C.B., G.C.M.G., G.C.V.

side the telegraph office at Pera, but it is not yet known whether they intend to occupy it or not."

Kemal sat in the telegraph office in Angora, receiving the telegrams,
instructing his secretaries to summarize and pass them on to all commanding officers. From the Ministry of War came a message: "At this
moment the English are patrolling the town. They are now entering the
ministry. They have occupied it. They have reached the Nizami Gate.
Interrupt the connection. The English are here."

Confirmation came from the Central Telegraph Office: "Your Excellency, English sailors have occupied the telegraph office at the Ministry
of War and have cut the wires. They have occupied Tophane, and troops
are being landed from their men-of-war. The situation is getting worse.
Early this morning while our soldiers were still sleeping, English sailors
occupied the Post Office; our men, being suddenly aroused, were still half
asleep when the fighting began which resulted in six of our men being
killed and fifteen wounded. . . . The Telegraph Office at Pera does not
reply any more. Probably it is also occupied. God grant that they will
not occupy this office. . . . The director and officials of the Telegraph
Office at Pera are just arriving here; they have been turned out of their
office. . . . Your Excellency, I have just heard this moment that this
office will be occupied within an hour."

Kemal asked: "Have you heard anything about the Chamber of Deputies? Is the telegraph office there in working order?"

"Yes," the reply came, "it is." But from this moment the connection
ceased. The Allies had occupied the office.[4]

French and Italian troops did not at first take part in the operation
but joined in later to claim their share when the city seemed securely in
the hands of the British. The casualties were relatively few, but some
bitterness was caused among the Turks by the killing of several musicians of a military band who had been mistaken for active soldiers. On
the morning of the occupation the entire Turkish staff of the War Ministry including Fevzi, the minister, was seen standing in the square outside while British officers searched the building. All over the city they
searched houses and dug up tombs in the graveyards where arms might
be hidden.

Entering the newspaper offices, they ordered editors what to print and
introduced a strict censorship. The communiqué, explaining the occupa-

[4] Later Kemal paid a public tribute to the telegraphist, one Hamid Effendi of Monastir, who had kept him informed, and brought him to Angora to take charge of the
main telegraph office there.

tion and blaming the Turks for it, must be printed word for word—an injunction which pleased one subeditor, who noticed, as every reader was bound to do, that the word for battle was wrongly spelt, in the Armenian style, clearly not by a Turkish translator. Signed by "The Army of Occupation," the communiqué reiterated the crimes of the Committee of Union and Progress and denounced the new crimes of their partisans of the "National Organization." While the Allies sought peace they had embarked on a new period of war. Thus the city was to be provisionally occupied; the Turks were still not to be deprived of Constantinople, but in case of general troubles or massacres this decision would probably be modified. One newspaper ingeniously responded to the censorship by refusing to comment on the occupation at all, confining itself to daily editorials about the old public fountains in Constantinople and thus implying to the public mind disapproval of all that was happening.

In the course of the occupation some eighty-five deputies were arrested. Those who kept away from their homes at first escaped. One of these was Rauf. Carrying out the decision he had reached at Sivas, he deliberately courted arrest in Parliament itself, thus hoping to put the foreigners in the wrong. Some others shared his view, among them Dr. Adnan, the husband of Halide Edib, who confided his intention to her on returning home that evening.

"Haven't you yourself been urging," he said to his wife, "that the peoples are our friends and governments our enemies? Let the peoples —let the English people—see to it that their government, the oldest parliamentary government in existence, does not do injustice to a representative institution."

Halide Edib, with her down-to-earth feminine realism, "suddenly had a vision of old Roman senators sitting tight in their seats while Rome was taken by strangers." The more who could get clear away to Anatolia the better. Knowing Rauf's "chivalrous and impossibly heroic nature," she could understand his point of view. But Halide "realized with sensible clearness how painfully and irrevocably there existed in Europe two separate standards of humanity." [5] Thus, in common with many others, she went with her husband into hiding and prepared to leave for Anatolia with the aid of the underground organization.

In the Parliament building Rauf's friends tried in vain to persuade him to escape. They produced two Turkish private soldiers' uniforms, begging him and Kara Vasif, another prominent supporter of Kemal, to

[5] *The Turkish Ordeal.*

disguise themselves for the purpose. But both refused. Rauf put up a show of gaiety, saying, "Let the scoundrels come. Here we are." Parliament, he urged, must on no account disperse of its own accord. It must be dispersed by the Allies.

The Sultan summoned a delegation from Parliament with Rauf at its head. They drove to the Yildiz Palace through streets lined with British soldiers, their bayonets fixed. The Sultan referred to the power of the foreigner and warned them to take care what they said in Parliament. "These people," he said, "are capable of anything, they will not stop at what they have done so far." Several deputies spoke up in patriotic protest. One pointed out of the window at the Allied fleets in the Bosporus and said, "Your Majesty, these waters are as far as these infidels can go. They cannot go beyond. Anatolia is made of steel. It will succeed in its struggle." The Sultan repeated his warnings to be careful. "If they wish," he insisted, "they can be in Angora tomorrow."

Rauf then spoke. "As stated in the National Pact," he said, "our problem is how to save the Sultanate, the Caliphate, and the country. If we may interpret the nation's feelings, may we ask of you that you do not sign any international treaty without Parliament's consent?" The Sultan showed his irritation by rising to his feet. This was the signal for the rest to rise. He bade them a cold farewell.

The delegation returned to Parliament and the debate began. A detachment of British troops marched into the lobby, demanding that the Parliamentary Guard surrender Rauf and Kara Vasif. There was pandemonium in the Chamber; Rauf urged that the Guard should resist this attack on the Assembly. But the president of the Chamber instructed its commander that arms must not be used. Thus the two Nationalist leaders were arrested and led away to a British warship, where they were herded together with some hundred and fifty others, including deputies and prisoners of various and dubious kinds, to be shipped off to exile in Malta. As a reprisal for the deportations Kemal immediately ordered the arrest of all remaining British officers in Anatolia, including Colonel Rawlinson in Erzurum.

Two days later Parliament met again. A majority decided that, in view of the aggression of the foreign troops and the arrest of members by force, they could no longer perform their duty in freedom. It was thus agreed to prorogue Parliament indefinitely. Salih Pasha, who had succeeded Ali Riza as Grand Vizier, refused, in response to a note from the Allies, to disavow Kemal and the Nationalist leaders, and resigned. The post of Grand Vizier was offered once again to Tevfik. He refused it

—to his subsequent regret and that of many of his compatriots. For his refusal enabled the Sultan to bring back Damad Ferid, who proceeded, in the words of Winston Churchill, "to brew the thinnest government he had yet attempted." Its first action was to dissolve Parliament—the last in the history of the Ottoman Empire. It then proceeded to launch what proved to be a civil war against the Nationalist forces.

The British High Commission rated the occupation as a success. Admiral de Robeck reported to Lord Curzon, in *couleur de rose,* that without being a knockout blow it had been a severe blow for the Nationalist movement. Sir Henry Wilson, the chief of the General Staff, thought the reverse. "The Frocks," he wrote in his diary, "are completely out of touch with realities. They seem to think that their writ runs in Turkey in Asia. We have never, even after the armistice, attempted to go into the background parts." (Here indeed their occupation had been limited to a few strategic points, now evacuated.) In fact, thanks to these two successive acts of aggression—the despatch of the Greeks to Asia Minor and now, ten months later, the occupation of Constantinople—the Allies ensured that the writ to run in Turkey in Asia, as eventually in Turkey in Europe, would be that of Mustafa Kemal.

26 ▶ *The trek to Anatolia*

The British had presented Kemal, for the second time, with a major political advantage. He lost no time in exploiting it. The occupation of Constantinople, as he saw it, and as he declared in an immediate proclamation, had "destroyed the seven-centuries-old existence and sovereignty of the Ottoman Empire." Throughout the consequent fight for the survival of the Turkish nation he took care as usual to invoke Islam. "God," he assured his people, "is with us in the Holy War which we have entered upon for the independence of our country."

Kemal, good staff officer and shrewd politician as he was, forgot nothing. He remembered the rest of the Islamic world, to which he sent a similar proclamation. He remembered the foreign powers, appealing not merely to the governments but to "the conscience of the scholars, intellectuals and civilized men of Europe and America" to take notice of action "inconsistent with the honour and good name of the nations concerned." By "a criminal attempt hitherto unrecorded in history" an armistice based on the Wilson principles had "resulted in a trick by which the nation has been deprived of its means of defence."

He remembered the Christian minorities, sending out to his various local authorities a circular to stress that, as contact had been temporarily broken between Turkey and the outside world, the minorities would no longer enjoy foreign protection, hence to insist on a humane attitude towards them as "conclusive evidence of the civilizing factors existing in the character of our race." All these steps were taken within an hour or so of the occupation.

Kemal then went ahead as swiftly with his major task—that of summoning a new Parliament to meet, under his own auspices, at Angora. For two days he sat at the telegraph, communicating and exchanging views on this problem with all his commanding officers. Then he issued a communiqué, convening an "assembly with Extraordinary Powers"—in effect a Constitutional Assembly with powers to alter the system of government. It was to be attended by all available members of the previous Chamber, and by new members to be elected on a specified date by the various constituencies.

Meanwhile it became the duty of every serious patriot, every able-bodied soldier, to make his way through the Allied cordon from Constantinople into Anatolia. The British authorities plastered the city with posters, in English and Turkish, signed by the commander-in-chief and threatening DEATH, in large letters, to anyone harbouring a Nationalist. But since, in making their arrests on the eve of the occupation, they had chosen to employ uniformed troops instead of plain-clothes agents who might have known where to find them, large numbers got away, often in disguise, across the Bosporus and thence, by a number of "underground" routes, inland.

Halide Edib disguised her husband, Dr. Adnan, and herself respectively as a *hoja* and his aged wife. Crossing the Bosporus by night, "brilliantly illuminated by the lights of the warships," their guns glistening and their sailors pacing the decks, they reached the *tekke* at Scutari where they knew that the dervishes would give them sanctuary. There they found four other deputies, also escaping. Halide judged one of them to be wise for his remark: "What we want is a really good map and a guide"; another to be foolish for his boast, "I have five bombs and three revolvers in my bag. Have no fear."

Her journey to Angora with Dr. Adnan was typical of innumerable others, and her description of it reflects the conditions in Anatolia at this time. The roads from Scutari eastwards down to the Izmit Peninsula, which was occupied by the Allies, were well guarded by British infantry and cavalry. The mountain paths were constantly raided by bands of Greeks whom the Allies were arming. A few Turkish bands struggled to keep them at bay and to help the Nationalist refugees to get through. They were helped too, all along the line, by an efficient system of communications run by loyal telegraphists, who passed news secretly from one post to another of the arrival and departure of each Nationalist group, and of such movements of the Allied forces as were likely to impede them.

At the start of the journey Halide travelled by carriage, while the men of the party, who were more easily identified, walked by circuitous routes. She describes her arrival one evening at a village where she ran into a detachment of English soldiers: "Suddenly a pair of very blue and very tired eyes peered into the carriage. . . . But the soldier simply turned his head and walked on, certain that there was nothing to worry about." After dark she reached the agreed destination. At once the news of her arrival was telephoned to the central post: "This is Samandra. . . . Is that Guebze? Yes, she is safe, she has escaped without accident. . . . Yes, the others are walking through the fields." Late at night they arrived safely, but all had to leave again almost immediately, driving through the darkness on an oxcart by side tracks, since the British had heard of their arrival and were lighting up the fields with their searchlights so the guerrillas could see them.

On the way Halide Edib had the chance to study the different types of fighting men who were forming the raw material of the resistance. There were the Macedonian gendarmes, with "the wildness, the enthusiasms, the emotions, the rebellious instincts under tyranny, the dominating cruel instincts when in power, common to their race. Hero-worship, desire for change, desire for some vague thing called a New Turkey prompted them." They had fought in the mountains with Enver who, according to rumour, was now fighting with the British at the Khyber Pass. He was the brave man; the Sultan the traitor. It was surely the Sultan who was selling them to the enemy—"shame on him—a Padishah from the House of Osman!" Their commander led the conversation away from Enver and back to Mustafa Kemal—a great soldier too, who would beat the Greeks back to Athens.

Of a different stamp, quiet in his manner and more down to earth in his attitude, was a tall Anatolian with a gentle face and a round black beard. "In him," she writes, "I saw the humour—quiet, sardonic, buried deep down; in him I saw this intensely practical nature. One felt with this man that he was not going to believe easily in the possibility of Mustafa Kemal Pasha's marching to Athens or Enver Pasha's fighting with the English in the Khyber Pass. However deeply he had felt injured by the Padishah's treachery, probably nothing would have induced him to swear at the Sultan. Yet for all that he would not work one particle less stoically for what he considered to be almost a lost cause."

As they went on every possible road seemed to be held by the British cavalry, and they had to take to the mountains, escorted over the rough paths by a local band of irregulars. To Halide, "they seemed such boy-ish creatures with their personal ideas of right and wrong, mingled hu-manity and cruelty, all subservient to a very definite sense of the inviola-bility of the given word. They had an invincible resentment against the government, considering all governments promise-breakers and capable of performing any dirty trick in the name of the law, and were very well aware that the Nationalist government, to whom they happened to be useful at the moment, would as likely as not have them all killed if it suited them to do so. Yet they would always consider themselves the faithful children of Turkey."

Then a party of regular staff officers arrived, on their way to Angora. "It was strange to contrast these officers, perfect in their bearing and their exquisite Old World manners, with the tiger types!" Between the two types—the regulars and the irregulars—there now arose in microcosm those elements of discord which, as the war developed, were to grow into a source of conflict on a major scale. Which was to command? The romantic bandit chief, for all his intrepidity and panache, lacked the powers of planning and organization required to confront serious risks. A regular staff officer was needed, and the choice fell on the senior of the newcomers, Colonel Kiazim. "Oh, these wretched irregulars!" was the impatient thought in his mind. But he tactfully shook the chief by the hand and renounced any command over him and his men. Halide's own corporal and henchman, Mehmed Chavoush, was relieved. "He never could stand these irregulars giving orders to soldiers of the Turk-ish Army—the pride of caste."

Thus the cavalcade, after many vicissitudes and detours, reached the last peak from which the Sea of Marmara and the waters of the Gulf of Izmit could still be seen: "All the horses stopped and all eyes were turned toward the patch of enchanting blue-green liquid. No one looked at his neighbour; every eye was turned toward that part of his life which he was abandoning—perhaps forever. Each and every one of us seemed entirely apart from the rest. I wrenched myself round first, and turned my horse's head downhill, down the other side of the range. The sea was shut out." Only the wide-open waterless spaces of Anatolia lay ahead of them.

Thus slowly and arduously they moved from one world to another, from the orbit of Constantinople into the orbit of Angora. A telegram came from Mustafa Kemal himself. It brought good news. Now that Ali Fuad had forced the British to retire from Eskishehir the railway was open, and they should proceed to the nearest railhead for the last stage of their journey. Here they were joined by Yunus Nadi, a well-known journalist who had come from Constantinople by a different route. From Eskishehir the train passed on to Angora. As they approached it towards evening Yunus Nadi came up to Halide in some agitation, saying, "Oh, Halide Hanum, the station is full of a tremendous crowd. There will be speeches. You will speak for us, won't you?"

"Don't worry," she said, "I will do it."

The crowd on the platform looked sombre in the twilight. A slender grey figure emerged from it and "moved quickly towards the train, pulling his gloves off. His face, with its large-cornered kalpak, had become indistinct and colourless in the dusk. . . . The door of our compartment opened suddenly, and Mustafa Kemal's hand reached up to help me down the step. . . . It is a narrow and faultlessly shaped hand, with very slender fingers and a skin which nothing darkens or wrinkles. Its swift and sudden movements reminded me of Mehmed Chavoush and of that new revolutionary type of whose existence I had become aware in Samandra. It seemed to me that the merciless hunting of the human tiger in Turkey had its answer in this hand. It differed from the large broad hand of the fighting Turk in its highly strung nervous tension, its readiness to spring and grip its oppressor by the throat."

"Welcome, Hanum Effendi," he said in a low voice.

This was Angora. This, she thought to herself, was to be the Kaaba—the Mecca—of the Nationalist movement.

Angora at this time was little more than a pair of twin hills rising like nipples from the bosom of the Anatolian plateau. Crowning one of them were the half-ruined walls of a citadel which had seen and survived notable Turkish conflicts. Clambering up to it and around it and within it was a human warren of mud-brick houses and ruins of houses, huddled lattice to lattice and roof above roof amid dunghills and winding precipitous lanes. Rough with stones and, at this season when rain was frequent, awash with mud, they provided a hard climb for the horses and the ramshackle carriages which, apart from the long peasant bullock carts with their spokeless wailing wheels, were Angora's only means of transport.

To a Turkish war correspondent[1] who saw it for the first time after a weary journey across the mountains from Inebolu, the Nationalist port on the Black Sea, the place seemed a "horrible hole." The innkeepers greeted him with a cynical smile. The congestion in the town was such that accommodation was measured by the square yard and he would be lucky to get a numbered step of a staircase on which to sleep. As it was, he slept in a cupboard.

Angora was in fact hardly more than a large village, its population reduced to a mere 20,000 by a disastrous fire which had wiped out a section of it during the war, leaving blackened remains which still scarred the lower slopes of the hillside. The citadel looked out to all points of the compass over the naked treeless plain, snowbound in winter, sun-baked in summer, waterless but for the rainfall and a few scattered wells.

From a distance a low ridge of undulating hills, rough and colourless, half embraced the site. And "site" it still was. The city—still to become a city—had begun to spill itself down onto the plateau but had yet to spread far across it, obstructed largely by a stretch of wasteland which in the winter became a marsh. Here stood the railway station and a few public buildings which the Young Turks, remedying Ottoman neglect, had erected. Here was also a small and unkempt municipal garden.

This "Mecca of the Nationalist movement" had little to offer in terms of distinction, far less of amenity. But there was, in its immeasurable skies and its clean translucent air, in the asceticism of its landscape and the contrasting softness of the violet and amber lights which bathed and transfigured it at dawn and again at dusk, a rarefied atmosphere which set it apart from other places. Even its inhabitants were a people apart, with their own individual brand of strong silent cussedness and earthy self-respect; with, moreover, an outlandish pronunciation of Turkish, which the men from Constantinople did not easily understand.

This sense of "apartness," of isolation in the midst of a converging hostile world, generated in the small and still intimate band of patriots who had thrown in their lot with Kemal that strange spirit of elation and comradeship which animates men in a desert. Here was a desert indeed, to which life must be given, on which order must be imposed, whose hidden scattered elements must be drawn together into a unity and an effective positive force for the regeneration of the heart of Turkey in Asia. Such was the challenge to be faced against odds which seemed, at this moment, overwhelming.

[1] Alaeddine Haidar, *A Angora auprès de Mustapha Kemal.*

27 ► *Parliament in Angora*

The War of Independence, launched as a resistance movement against the foreigner, now developed besides into a civil war—and at that a holy war —between Turk and Turk. The Sultan declared open hostilities against the Nationalists. The Sheikh of Islam, in a *fetva*—a legal ruling—entitled "Insurrection against the Sultan," proclaimed them to be rebels. It ended with the words: "Is it permissible to kill these rebels? Answer: It is a duty to do so." It was distributed throughout the country, and in places dropped by Allied aircraft. Damad Ferid as Grand Vizier further denounced the Nationalists as "the false representatives of the nation," a corrupt group of men, ready to sacrifice the country for their own personal ambitions.

Religious leaders were sent into Anatolia to preach war against them in the name of the Sultan-Caliph. The soldiers in the Nationalist forces were incited to rebel against their officers or to desert and return to their villages. An Army of the Caliphate was formed to fight the Nationalists, recruited at a good rate of pay from among men who included the unemployed riffraff of Constantinople. Officers were hurriedly commissioned to command them and march them to a headquarters at Izmit.

Very soon this army and its affiliated bands of irregulars had gained a wide measure of control over northwestern Anatolia.

With such a campaign on his hands, and the consequent need to organize his army, Kemal yet realized that the organization of a Parliament must be his first concern. Only thus could his resistance have the necessary popular backing. In a talk with Yunus Nadi he said, "In the age in which we are living, everything has to be legitimate and legal. All actions must be based on the decisions given by the people and must interpret the general wishes of the people." Military action must thus be based on the sanction of a legally elected Assembly.

In creating it Kemal must reply in kind to the Islamic manifestoes of Constantinople. Thus he still acted outwardly in the name of the Caliphate, whose abolition was his ultimate objective. With every appearance of deference, he mobilized the *ulema,* the religious authority of Angora, which now issued a counterblast to Constantinople in the form of a *fetva* of its own. It declared that a *fetva* issued under foreign duress was invalid and called upon Moslems to "liberate their Caliph from captivity." The fiction must be preserved that he was not a traitor, as he was later to be branded, but a prisoner of the enemy.

Kemal knew that the feeling among many of his supporters was hesitant. Though proscribed as rebels, they shrank from the semblance of overt rebellion, clinging to their religious scruples and to the desire to preserve traditional forms. To reassure them and to encourage such deputies as might be reluctant to come to the newly elected Assembly, he thus circulated throughout the country his own proclamation which outdid the Sultan-Caliph himself in its Islamic invocations. The opening of the Assembly, it announced, was to take place on a Friday. It was to be initiated by a solemn prayer in the Haji Bayram Mosque. "All the honourable deputies," it instructed, "will take part in this prayer, in the course of which the light of the Koran and the call to prayer will be poured forth over all the believers." In order to emphasize the sacred character of this day, the whole of the Koran and the Buchari, a screed concerned with the traditions of the Prophet, were to be recited everywhere for two whole days beforehand, together with prayers for the liberation from the foreigner of the "Sublime Person" of the Sultan-Caliph. Sermons were to be delivered on the sacred nature of the Nationalist movement. There would be prayers for the deliverance and salvation of the Caliphate, followed everywhere by a ceremony of congratulation to the Assembly, and the recital of the *Mevlud,* the hymn in verse which honoured the birthday of Mohammed.

Adhering strictly to this sacred ritual, the first Nationalist Parliament opened its doors on Friday, April 23, 1920, some five weeks after the British occupation of Constantinople, while Kemal's soldiers kept watch from the neighbouring hilltops for a possible incursion by the Sultan's irregulars. From dawn onwards the population of Angora and the surrounding countryside, flaunting such glad rags as it possessed, swarmed into the streets. By noon, the hour of the inaugural service, the congestion inside the Haji Bayram Mosque was so great that all the deputies could scarcely gain entrance.

With Kemal and the rest they processed, jostled by the crowds, to the converted Parliament house, a solid structure with a mock-oriental façade, which had formerly served as the premises of the Committee of Union and Progress. The procession was led by three imams, bearing the green flag of the Prophet. The red flag of the Turkish state flew from the roof of the building; the green flag was draped inside, beneath a text from the Koran. After a pair of wethers had been sacrificed in the garden, Kemal advanced to cut a ribbon across the door of the Chamber, and a hundred and fifteen deputies filed in to take the oath, swearing to safeguard the independence of Sultanate, Caliphate, country, and people. When all had finally taken their seats, their numbers amounted to three hundred and sixty-nine.[1]

The Chamber was a long rectangular room, with balconies at either end, equipped with varnished school desks and a makeshift tribune for President and speaker. It was observed that, in the headgear of the deputies, the fez and the turban, both symbols of reaction, outnumbered the now more progressive kalpak by sixty-five to fifty. An adjoining room had been set aside as a small mosque, furnished with lecterns and prayer rugs oriented towards Mecca. In the absence of electricity the members began their deliberations by the light of a single petrol lamp borrowed from a café. Within a few days notices had appeared on the walls prohibiting any indulgence on the premises in backgammon or other games of chance, while the consumption of alcoholic liquors was strictly forbidden. Only in the seclusion of a dark back room, behind a neighbouring tobacconist's shop, could the more emancipated members refresh themselves with a drink.

··

[1] The sittings of this Assembly, to which members rode on horseback, tethering their horses to a trellis outside the building, have been compared to the early meetings of the North American farmers, after the Declaration of Independence. Dagobert von Mikusch, *Mustapha Kemal.*

This Grand National Assembly, as it was to be named, was the product of days and nights of exhaustive discussion between Kemal and his closer associates. With a selection of them he had taken up his headquarters four miles outside the city, in the serviceable stone building of the Agricultural School, which the Unionists had erected. It stood on a hilltop, in the midst of a model farm, an "oasis" in the arid treeless plateau, where the acacias were now springing into bloom and the fields were lightly flushed with green. Here among others lived Dr. Adnan and Halide Edib, who with Yunus Nadi had taken in hand the organization of a new Anatolian News Agency. Ismet had returned to Angora shortly after them with a party of deputies and others, inconspicuous in his soldier's uniform until Kemal singled him out at the station, smoking quietly at the fringe of the welcoming crowd, to give him, this time, a warm and cordial embrace.

There was much work to be done. Yunus Nadi describes the scene. Rising in the morning, Kemal calls his secretary, Hayati: "Come, child, what is there in that file? Read it to us."

There is a report from Aintab, where operations against the French still continue.

"Anything new?"

"The French in the American School were repulsed, but the enemy counterattacked and fired on the city, causing damage."

"Write this down," Kemal orders. "The only way to solve this situation is by direct contact between Aintab and Urfa. . . ."

Another file is opened: "The Nationalist troops in Suruch have repulsed the French. But they complain they have no weapons or ammunition. They say there is some in and near Mardin. They want it."

"Tell Mardin to give it them."

"The siege of Urfa continues."

"The garrison must be strengthened. Tell them to do that, and report to me."

"The Nationalist troops based on Adana fired on a French destroyer, near the shore."

"That is the best way of fighting. Molest the enemy all the time. They did well to fire on the ship."

"Demirji Mehmed Efe sends you greetings."

"Does he still call me his brother Mustafa Kemal Pasha?"

"Yes."

"Good for him."

Life at headquarters was austere. "We lived," wrote Halide Edib, "like members of a newly founded religious order in all the exaggerated puritanism of its inception. Mustafa Kemal Pasha shared our life, and while among us was as strictly pure as a sincere Catholic priest. But some evenings he disappeared. . . ."

Lunch at headquarters was a hurried affair. But in the evenings all relaxed for dinner around an enormous horseshoe table. Here was the atmosphere that suited Kemal. He liked, as he had done in his army mess, to preserve certain standards of ceremony, as though all were partaking not of sparse and simple rations but of a civilized Western repast. He dominated the table with his talk, sometimes amusing, sometimes boring, always astringent as he reminisced with the others of past experiences, always pointed in his anecdotes, ironic and outspoken in his assessment of enemies and friends alike. Ismet, with his gentle manners and his large thoughtful eyes, proved a contrast to Kemal. Leaning a little forward in his deafness to catch what was said, he spoke more slowly, commented less harshly, inserted his innuendoes with more caution.

In the discussion of ideas Kemal swept away pretences in a way which disconcerted and often shocked his more conservative listeners. But the next moment he might be setting up other pretences, more in line with his own purposes, to take their place. To Halide Edib he seemed "to have no convictions whatever and he adopted now one thing and now another with the same vehemence and energy, no matter how contradictory they were, so long as he thought they would benefit him and the cause in some way."

Kemal was no lofty idealist. He had few moral principles, only a determination to attain his ends. But, cynic though he was, these ends were nonetheless the country's. His was no negative cynicism but that of the realist who seeks practicable solutions. Opportunist he might be in his means of achieving them but, once achieved, they must prove inherently sound, they must work. Turkey under his aegis must not merely be saved from the foreigner; she must be rebuilt on an enduring foundation.

After dinner at headquarters came the serious business of the evening. The party would move out into the big central hall, there to talk and to work, sometimes until five o'clock in the morning, on the numerous problems which confronted them. Foremost among these was the nature of the government which was now to be set up.

Kemal himself, and a handful of his friends, saw this as a turning point in Turkish history. It was "a matter of admitting that the Ottoman Sultanate and the Caliphate were finished, and of establishing a new state based on new foundations." But here as at Erzurum and Sivas this ultimate goal could not then be openly specified. When in the course of their discussions Yunus Nadi tried out the suggestion that they were, in fact, being called upon to form a new Turkish state in Anatolia, the general reaction was one of dismay, and Kemal quickly silenced him. The opinion of the company, he stressed, was required only on the nature of the new Turkish Parliament.

The debates on this subject were long, now hidebound by academic pedantries, now wandering off into misty speculations. The deputies from the dissolved Ottoman Parliament in Constantinople had come with the idea that the new government was merely temporary and should thus be a replica of the old. They envisaged no break with the principles inherent in the Sultan's regime. Jelal-ed-Din Arif, as President of the old Parliament, saw himself as thereby President of the new. Dozing a little through the nocturnal discussions, he would awake to reiterate the word, "Continuity, continuity." As a professor of constitutional history, with a rigidly legalistic mind, he expounded his idea of the new government as that of a constitutional monarchy of a liberal Western kind, equipped with legislative and executive, but temporarily deprived of the monarch, who should be represented by a regent in the shape of a neutral President of the National Assembly.

Kemal and his intimates were working for something quite different. Scrupulous as he was to preserve legal forms and appearances, the last thing Kemal in fact sought was political continuity. Anatolia must break away altogether from Constantinople, its institutions, its traditions. It must be animated by a new spirit, hence by a new system of government. Adroitly—and, in view of his ultimate republican intentions, disingenuously—he turned Arif's argument against him by declaring, "What you want sounds like a republic; but the republic is a form which will frighten the people. And why should we adopt an old form already known? We can create something for ourselves that will suit us." What he proposed to create was something derived more literally from those theories of Jean-Jacques Rousseau which he had devoured in his student days. It should be based on the principle that power—whether legislative or executive—is indivisible and belongs unconditionally to the people.

Kemal's mind was a compound of intuitive ideas with a smattering of such ready-made theories. Halide Edib saw it as "two-sided, like a light-house lantern. Sometimes it flashes and shows you what it wants you to see with almost blinding clearness; sometimes it wanders and gets itself lost in the dark." Some such confusion of thought lay behind the form of government which he now forcibly put forward as original, but which seemed to Halide and others "merely an adapted convention," somewhat clumsy and loose, with affinities to the Soviet form in its political—as distinct from its social and economic—sense. It allowed for a National Assembly which should exercise both legislative and executive powers, to the extent even of electing each member of the Cabinet. Ministers should be commissaries of the people, with no collective responsibility to the Cabinet as such, but only an individual responsibility to carry out the decisions of the Assembly. Nor was the President of the Assembly himself to be endowed with personal responsibility.

As, night after night, Kemal poured forth these ideas, reducing his listeners to exhaustion, some of them ventured to argue, on practical grounds, that in a country so little used to the ways of democracy the Cabinet should be appointed not by the Assembly but by the President. But Kemal had his motives in propounding the other system. Firstly he saw the vital necessity for an idea, as fuel to keep the Revolution aflame. Only this could unite the disparate elements and give positive substance to the patriotic impulse—an ultimate war aim, conceived in those more abstract terms to which the oriental mind responds. What better than the slogan "The Sovereignty of the People"? The autocracy of the Sultan and the oligarchy of the Young Turks was to give place in the new Assembly to a form of popular democracy in which the people enjoyed full power, even to the extent of appointing the Cabinet.

Kemal's second consideration was tactical. He must at all costs control this Assembly. But he knew very well that its members would not be easy to handle. Professionally and socially they were a mixed crowd, many of them with a deep distrust of Kemal and his dictatorial ambitions. The need to disarm them prompted his rejection of the orthodox view that the President should appoint his own ministers. The only way to control such an Assembly was to encourage it to think it was controlling itself.

Thus Kemal assiduously lobbied not only his friends but the deputies, visiting them in the dormitories of the Teachers' Training School where they were lodged in barracklike conditions, living on a diet of free beans and rice, armed with revolvers beneath their pillows and called to prayer five times a day from the top of the stairs.[2] He sat on their beds to answer their questions and to deliver them long and patient expositions. For the

[2] Later, whenever there was money in the exchequer, the deputies were paid a salary of a hundred Turkish pounds (£20) a month, and contributed to its funds by paying for their board and lodging.

most part plain Anatolians, with little comprehension of theories of government, they were persuaded without too much trouble of the merits of his proposals. Finally Arif and his friends gave in and agreed to accept them. Arif also agreed, with some reluctance, to concede the presidency of the Assembly to Kemal and to step down himself into the role of Vice-President or Speaker.

Kemal's opening speech to the Assembly took the form of a motion, but in view of the scruples and doubts of so many members, "a motion of which the intention remained concealed." He proposed a government which should not be defined as provisional, nor should its head be a regent. No power should stand above its Grand National Assembly. This should combine the legislative and executive functions and should elect a council to conduct its affairs, under the President of the Assembly. A note, in brackets, was added to this: "As soon as the Sultan-Caliph is delivered of all pressure and coercion he will take his place within the frame of the legislative principles which will be determined by the Assembly." Kemal had succeeded in relegating this sole reference to the Sultanate and Caliphate to an ambiguous footnote.

The Assembly greeted these resolutions with enthusiasm and accepted them after a short debate. Kemal issued in its name a proclamation confirming them. It elected him as its President, then elected a Cabinet whose seven ministers had been previously chosen in effect by Kemal and his inner circle, and the choice afterwards canvassed among the deputies. Prompted by Kemal, they co-opted Ismet, chief of the General Staff, as an additional member. The ministers began to work in the bare rooms of the government building, with hardly enough chairs and tables to accommodate them.

What the Grand National Assembly had done in effect was to accept, without knowing it, the prototype of a future republic. A parliamentary committee was appointed to draft a Constitution Act, giving legal form to the Assembly and government. Nine months were to elapse before it succeeded in doing so, thrashing out with some heat the contradictions inherent in a system by which national sovereignty lay on the one hand with the people, hence with the Assembly, and on the other with the monarchy which the Assembly was pledged not to destroy but to liberate. But Kemal finally succeeded in pushing it through the Assembly, firmly sidetracking discussions on the future of the monarchy and Caliphate to pass an act which confirmed the unconditional sovereignty of the people and must thus eventually prove incompatible with the continuance of the Sultanate.

Meanwhile, announcing the opening of the Assembly in a personal message to the Sultan, Kemal reminded him in eloquent terms of a dream of his forebear, Sultan Osman, the founder of the dynasty, which had passed into oral tradition. The sacred tree, he dreamt, which cast a shadow over three continents and sheltered a hundred million Moslems, had been deprived of its branches, and only its bare trunk remained. "The trunk of that sacred tree," Kemal assured the monarch, "is in our hearts." Loyalty to Caliph and Sultan was the first and last word of this Assembly. Printed and judiciously circulated, such sentiments had notable propaganda value in the more backward parts of Anatolia.

One evening at this time a retired officer, who smuggled arms and brought news from Constantinople, arrived at the Agricultural School with the news that seven of the Nationalist leaders had been condemned to death by a special tribunal convened in the name of the Sultan. They included Kemal himself, Ismet, Ali Fuad, Dr. Adnan and Halide Edib— the first woman in Turkish history, as the officer remarked, kissing her hand, to be so honoured. The sentence was confirmed by a *fatva* of the Sheikh of Islam, by which it became the religious duty of any Moslem to kill them on sight, with the certainty of a reward in heaven if they succeeded in doing so.

When the news came Kemal and Dr. Adnan were sitting in the dusk near the window of the central hall, while Ismet leant against the table. Anxious to know their reactions, Halide Edib asked her husband, in a jesting tone, what he thought of the honour.

He turned towards Kemal and said, "I feel very much upset, myself—I hate to be condemned to death. How do you feel about it?"

"I also mind it very much," Kemal said frankly.

Halide herself argued that the sentences showed a lack of any sense of political values. "Nothing," she said, "could make us more popular than this."

Ismet, more cautious and practical, considered that, while this might apply in the occupied regions of Constantinople and Smyrna, it would operate otherwise among the large populations which had not yet decided whether to support the Sultan or the Nationalists. In the civil war areas it could win undecided minds to the other side. It was therefore necessary to keep the Constantinople newspapers out of Anatolia and to prevent the news from spreading.

A few days later the Assembly retaliated by condemning to death Damad Ferid and the others responsible for the judgments, a sentence confirmed by the local religious authorities in a series of *fetvas* distributed throughout Anatolia. Thus the Angora government returned blow for blow against that of the Sultan. The Grand National Assembly then embarked on its task of governing, at least in theory, a divided country and of waging war against enemies, both from within and from without, whose numbers mounted day by day.

28 ► The Civil War

Kemal was now free to concentrate all his energies on the planning of the crucial campaigns which confronted the Nationalists. First, he needed to organize his staff. In Ismet, Ali Fuad, Kiazim Karabekir, and Refet he had four loyal and seasoned commanders. An important but still doubtful quantity was Fevzi Pasha, whose somewhat equivocal attitude had been exploited to discredit the cause in the rebellious districts.

But now he arrived unexpectedly at Ali Fuad's headquarters, after an arduous journey by the "underground" route. To Fuad he remarked, "Mountains cannot join each other, but people can join each other." He sat down and added frankly, "We have joined each other, but I think it's a bit late."

Fuad announced his arrival by telegram to Kemal but received the reply, "Return Fevzi Pasha to the place he has come from." After a further exchange, however, he telegraphed, "Send Fevzi Pasha immediately by train to Angora, under custody but without his being aware of it."

Kemal in fact fully appreciated the value of a man of Fevzi's calibre. He was the conservative type of Turkish officer, who had won a sound military reputation during long campaigns in the Balkans and later in the

First World War. Afterwards his successive positions in the War Ministry had brought him political prestige. His character, steady and slow and industrious, his strict habits of life and his middle-class virtues were such as to earn him popular respect. He was above all a man of deep religious beliefs, the devoutest of Moslems, who never touched alcohol and recited the Koran to his troops in the heat of the battle. He was thus an especial asset to the cause at this moment.

Much was made of his arrival in Angora, where he delivered a stirring address to the Grand National Assembly. He became Minister of Defence and head of the Cabinet—thus in effect Prime Minister. His weight helped Kemal to hold the balance between the rival commanders. Kemal had made Ismet chief of his General Staff. A born staff officer, familiar with the workings of his master's mind, he was the obvious choice for the task, which at this stage was one primarily of organization, of planning a new army from its foundations upwards. But both Ali Fuad and Refet were hostile to Ismet, from whom they differed profoundly in temperament. They strongly opposed his appointment on the grounds that he was a latecomer, while they themselves were pioneers who had been with Kemal in Anatolia from the start. Kemal nonetheless confirmed the appointment, and Ali Fuad and Refet retained their commands in the field, for which, as men of action and resource, they were more suited at this difficult time. Ali Fuad, however, remained bitter against Ismet and once, at a party given in his honour in Angora, became so angry at a guest's praise of him that he banged violently on the lid of the piano and almost broke it.

Refet had lately brought off a coup, in the settlement of an awkward situation at Konya. He had been organizing the irregulars on the Smyrna front, living with the guerrilla war lords and building up for himself a legend, under the pseudonym of Aydin Efe, as a dashing and elusive figure who made madcap visits, at great risk, to Constantinople, to maintain contact with the revolutionary groups in the city. When he arrived in Angora in April, Halide Edib met him for the first time. He seemed to her "to be made of nothing but nerves and muscles of steel, without an atom of flesh on them anywhere. His face was as thin and strong as his slim, wiry and rather elegant military figure. . . . Energy of an unusual quality sparkled from his face, his eyes, his movements; his head, hair, and hands all talked together with dramatic gestures. His clothes were faultlessly cut, his spurs and buttons flashed, his boots were of the shiniest patent leather, his whole attire just glowed with fastidiousness."

The holy city of Konya, some hundred and fifty miles across the bare salt plateau which stretched away southwards from Angora to the rim of the Taurus Mountains, was showing signs of unrest. Instructed to hold elections, its commander, backed by the leading citizens, had begun to waver in his allegiance. How could elections be held, he asked, without the authorization of Constantinople?

This was a key city, of considerable standing throughout Anatolia, whose loss would be a damaging blow to the Nationalist cause. Urgent action was necessary, and Refet was sent to Konya to report on the situation. From a station on the railway nearby he sent a polite request to the commander and other notables to meet him for a conference. Then he sent a number of telegrams to non-existent units in the area, instructing them to march on the city. The bluff succeeded. Early next morning the delegates arrived at the station. Refet at once coupled their train to his own and set off with them to Angora.

Here, after a patriotic harangue from Kemal, the kidnapped citizens were left to make up their minds whether or not to collaborate with the Nationalists. Finally the commander agreed to break with Constantinople and bring Konya into the Nationalist camp. This led to the withdrawal by the Italians of the detachment of troops which had moved up there from the Adalia region.

Thus Konya—though it was to rebel twice more—was for the time being quiet. But from all other directions Angora was beset by enemies. During these months of spring and early summer Kemal had to contend not merely with the threat from the foreigner but with internal upheavals, successive and often simultaneous, in no fewer than thirty-four different districts. "The flaming fire of rebellion," as he put it, "raged and reduced the whole country to ashes." It raged to the east as well as to the north and west of the city, thus obliging Kemal, while still holding the Greek front, to keep his scanty forces constantly on the move from one point of the compass to the other. Active encouragement was supplied by the British with the provision of arms for the rebels.

Typical of the leaders of this Caliph's Army was an aged and illiterate Circassian bandit named Anzavur, operating in the region north of Smyrna. A fanatical Moslem, who fought under the flag of the Prophet with a Koran round his neck and hanged his enemies, likewise Moslems, on fig trees, he enjoyed the active favour of the Constantinople government. Kemal pitted against him another of his kind, a younger, cooler-headed, and not wholly illiterate Circassian named Ethem, who proved more than his match, and whom indeed the Nationalists themselves had to watch lest he gain too much personal power. Thus the southwestern area was for the moment cleared of insurgents.

Now the Nationalists were faced with a more serious insurrection led also by Circassians in the northwestern area, around Bolu. From their relatively isolated mountain strongholds, the revolt spread down to the plains around Angora and, gathering supporters, reached a village no more than seventeen miles from the city. When Kemal sent two deputies to parley with the villagers they were arrested and all but executed.

To control such local situations the Nationalists set up a series of emergency tribunals, somewhat on the lines of those established during the French Revolutionary "Terror," which would administer justice of a swift and summary kind on the spot. Given the name of Independence Tribunals, they were responsible not to local authorities but to the Assembly itself, thus affirming the supremacy of Parliament. Later these courts were to be used and abused for political purposes. But at this stage they were rather a military instrument, a necessary agent of rough justice for the condemnation and immediate public hanging of rebel leaders as a warning to others.

The revolt spread "like a prairie fire," by spontaneous combustion, sparks blowing across the countryside to set alight districts far apart from one another. This could not be quenched by regular forces, tired as they were from the war and reluctant to fight their own countrymen. Kemal had to rely largely on undisciplined irregular bands whose leaders were hard to control. Ethem the Circassian was able to occupy the important centre of Bolu. On doing so, he insisted on the execution of a number of rebel leaders who had been promised their lives by Angora in return for sparing those of the two deputies previously sent to the district. The death sentences were referred to Kemal, creating tense feeling among his associates at the Agricultural School when it became clear that he was determined to sign them.

As was his habit, even when he had made up his mind in advance, he asked for the opinion of each one before announcing his decision, and it was clear that all were against the executions. Halide Edib in particular spoke with passion against what she saw as an act of deep treachery, tainting the high principles of the Nationalist movement. But she spoke in vain: "I soon saw that Mustafa Kemal was obdurate. Occasionally his eyes flashed, then again went cold and pale; the lines of his face deepened, his eyebrows stood out, and altogether he looked extremely dangerous. He openly avowed that in our condition there was no place for mercy, pity and sentimental morality; that scruples about breaking a promise were a sign of weakness; that any who indulged in such considerations were bound never to succeed."

The ruthless cynicism of this view shocked his hearers. But only Ismet, listening thoughtfully as Kemal spoke, rose to answer him, walking across with a light springy step to the desk where Kemal sat, and leaning over it to engage him in earnest argument. Speaking in the simplest terms, Ismet contended that their government, if it was to have any claims to decency, must keep its word, that there must at all costs be mutual trust between government and people. Their discussion grew intense and continued until the pearl-white Angora dawn began to light up the window behind Kemal's back.

Finally Kemal rose, angrily rang the bell on his desk, and sent for his secretary. Then, as Halide describes it, "he leaned over, wrote a few lines, and signed. I see again Colonel Ismet's eyes hurriedly scanning the lines, then lifting his head with a smile of joy like a small boy. Mustafa Kemal Pasha had asked Ethem not to kill Sefer and those of his men who had been given a promise of pardon." But the reprieve came too late. By the time it had arrived Ethem, without waiting for Kemal's signature, had executed the prisoners, as Kemal may well have known that he would do.

This was a time of tense and continuous anxiety in the offices of the Agricultural School. The Nationalist fortunes fell to a low ebb. Kemal himself, drinking endless cups of coffee, gazing silently out of the window at the bare colour-lit Angora landscape, "looked harassed and at moments almost hopeless." Nevertheless, "he continued with the utmost subtlety and energy trying to keep in touch with and direct the dispersed units which were struggling for the cause."

His secretary would come in with copies of telegrams: "Is that Angora? This is the town of X. I am the governor. The anti-Nationalist Caliphate Army is approaching. I can hear the uproar in the town. I believe the townspeople will join them. Can you give me instructions before they cut the wires?" Then the secretary would add, with a military salute: "The wires show earth," meaning "The wires are cut."

Again: "Is that Angora? I am the telegraph operator of the town Y. The wires are cut but I have managed to place an instrument at two hours' distance from the town and can communicate at night. I have been listening to the conversation of the governor of Z with the anti-revolutionaries. He has come to an understanding with them. I will now repeat the conversation. . . . He is a traitor."

Every night they found themselves cut off from more centres and shrank more into themselves, weary and haggard, working until the yellow oil lamps went pale with the light of the approaching dawn, then sleeping briefly and fitfully for fear of an attack by the enemy. Morale was low in the Assembly itself, where groups of deputies were grumbling against Kemal and his apparent inability to check the rebellion. In the Assembly building one morning Kemal, himself in a nervous mood, called a friend, Kiliç Ali, who was a cavalry commander, took him to a window, and showed him what appeared to be a crowd moving down towards the city from the hills. He ordered Ali to take out a group of his men and reconnoitre, taking care to do so unobtrusively, without alarming the deputies. Then they looked again and saw that the "crowd" was a herd of cattle.

Finally, after a night when nearly all the wires were cut and firing was heard quite near, the point was reached at which an emergency plan was drawn up to leave Angora for Sivas if need be, and large numbers of horses were mobilized for the evacuation. As the time ticked by it seemed more and more likely that the plan would be executed. Dr. Adnan supplied himself with a phial of poison, for use in an emergency. Kemal himself began to say that the moment to leave had arrived.

When Refet reached Angora from the southwest he found an atmosphere of despondency, if not of defeatism. With his resilient optimism he laughed off all the talk about withdrawing to Sivas. He himself, for one, had every intention of staying, and if Kemal insisted on going—well then, he joked, he would shoot him. Did he not remember the vows they had taken at the outset of the campaign—either to succeed or to die? The road to Sivas was in any case threatened by hostile forces. There was, he concluded darkly, another obstacle to their journey. He had hidden the saddles of the horses. Let them instead sit down and discuss means of relieving the military position. They had still some resources available. There was, for example, his own company of faithful irregulars, his three hundred Zeybeks, whom he would summon from the mountains of Smyrna.

These wild men were soon swaggering around Angora, picturesquely caparisoned and bristling with weapons, disconcerting the citizens with their outlandish undisciplined ways. The women of the village, in the plain below their quarters, complained that they came too often near the river, staring at them and frightening them as they spread out their laundry to dry on its banks. One evening the secretary came into the central hall and announced to Kemal that the wires were cut. At that moment firing was heard outside—sometimes solitary shots, sometimes a continuous volley. "At once," records Halide, "everyone was excited; Mustafa Kemal Pasha walked about and gave orders, gesticulating, his eyes gleaming, and everyone else was on foot and moving about too. Perhaps everybody thought we were living our last minutes."

Faced with this moment of apparent danger, the two men, as she observed, reacted differently. Refet, with his natural insouciance and strong nerve born of implicit moral reserves, sat calm and apparently indifferent, continuing to smoke "in the same peaceful and slightly sleepy way." But Kemal, with his more highly strung temperament and more animal responses, was nervous and showed it. Outstandingly brave in battle, capable as he had proved in Gallipoli of standing up alone before his men under the fiercest fire without thought for his personal safety, he was the man of action who lacked the more restrained moral courage needed to face a mob. Here was a passive situation quite new to him, and he reacted to it "like a powerful tiger caught in a trap, angry and afraid." Then the telephone rang and, as Refet may well have guessed, it proved only to be his own wild mountaineers who had caused the alarm.

Refet left with them next day. Without consulting Kemal he backed his luck—and perhaps his skill in irregular diplomacy—and took the calculated risk of going out at night to parley with the rebels. Kemal rebuked him severely by telegram, but he returned and announced, "The business is settled." In fact the pressure of the rebels on this front was slackening. The immediate crisis was over. Angora could breathe once more. For the moment at least there was no more talk of withdrawing to Sivas.

Meanwhile, in May 1920, while the Nationalists thus struggled with the Sultan's forces, the Allies had settled on the peace terms which they intended to impose on the Ottoman Empire, embodying them in the aforementioned Treaty of Sèvres. "Like fresh fuel thrown on the smouldering fire of hatred which the Western world had provoked by its conduct in Turkey," as Churchill wrote, it was destined wholly to vindicate the Nationalist cause. From now onwards Kemal was to have the support not merely of a small band of patriots but of the bulk of the Turkish people.

29 ▶ *The Greek invasion*

The Treaty of Sèvres was an early product of that "circus" of Allied conferences which, with continuous rounds of entertainment, followed the signature of the Treaty of Versailles. The final draft of the Turkish peace terms was agreed by the Supreme Council at San Remo in a sumptuous villa named after that Hindu paradise where souls pass several centuries of delicious inaction between two incarnations, which provoked Lloyd George to say, "Here we are all three in paradise. Who is going to be the serpent?" [1]

On this issue the French and Italians, disliking the Greeks and disinclined to underrate the Turks, were not in easy accord with him. Nor was Lord Curzon, consistent to the end in his opposition to any Greek encroachment on Asia Minor. He had circulated to the Cabinet, before San Remo, a despatch from Admiral de Robeck, whose advisers saw the occupation of Smyrna and its proposed perpetuation as a "canker for many years to come, a constant irritation which would lead to bloodshed in Asia Minor for generations." Did the British people realize, the admiral enquired, that the proposal to dismember the Ottoman provinces of Tur-

[1] From *Le Matin*. Quoted in *The Times*, April 20, 1920.

key in the interest of Greece would drive the remaining Turks into the arms of the Bolsheviks?

These views were expounded in vain. At the end of the conference Lloyd George said to Vansittart, a young Foreign Office official, "We've got all we wanted." "You have, sir," Vansittart replied—a distinction which seemed to escape his Prime Minister.[2] What he wanted, and got, was a peace treaty described by Keynes as Carthaginian. It amounted, as Kemal had long foreseen, to the end of the Ottoman Empire and its breakup into a series of small states and foreign spheres of interest. All that was to remain of Turkey was a rump of an inland state, with most of its outlets to the sea under foreign control and its sovereignty reduced to a shadow.

She was to lose all her Arab possessions—a loss to which she was already resigned. But she was also to lose, to the despised and hated Greeks, the whole of Thrace, leaving Constantinople with a mere enclave of European territory a few miles wide; and she was to lose, for all practical purposes, Smyrna and its hinterland. The Greeks would also get eight Turkish islands in the Aegean, while the Dodecanese Islands would go to Italy. In the east there was to be an independent Armenia and an autonomous Kurdistan. By an additional Tripartite Agreement, much of the rest of Anatolia was partitioned into French and Italian zones on the lines of the original secret treaties.

Nearer home, the Straits were to be placed under international control. Turkey's finances would be wholly directed by the Allies. The hated Capitulations would be maintained and even extended. The Turkish Army would be reduced to a token force under Allied supervision, while a limited Turkish gendarmerie would be officered by foreigners. Though the Turkish delegation in Paris was given a month in which to reply to the terms, it was clear that they were those of a dictated peace.

Venizelos, on his own account, at once made them public in Athens. This premature disclosure played into the hands of Kemal by the shock which it gave to an unprepared Turkish public opinion. The Constantinople press was unanimous in its condemnation of the treaty, which amounted in effect to the end of the country's very existence. The mass of the people began at last to awaken to these realities and to the meaning of the national idea which Kemal had been preaching for a year past. The flow of recruits to Anatolia soon swelled from a trickle to a slow steady stream.

[2] *The Mist Procession.*

Kemal took advantage of the situation, at this moment when the Bolu revolt was under control, to despatch a force which drove the Caliphate troops out of Izmit and advanced to the last outpost before Constantinople, which was held by a British battalion. It was a critical moment. The British Army blew up depots of stores, in preparation for a retreat. Under naval fire from the Sea of Marmara, the Turks wavered and retired out of range. But Kemal had once more shown his defiance of the Allies. As Winston Churchill observed, "We were once again, this time with scanty forces, in the presence of the enemy."

Plans for a possible evacuation of Constantinople were hurriedly drawn up. General Milne called for reinforcements. He had insufficient forces to defend Constantinople and the Izmit Peninsula against a serious Nationalist attack. Here was Venizelos' chance. He was summoned by Lloyd George to the Cabinet and, in Churchill's words, "presented himself as the good fairy. Two divisions of the five already in Smyrna would march northward, and would fall upon the Turks menacing the Izmit Peninsula and drive them away." Another Greek division could also be sent from eastern Thrace.

The pundits met in international conclave once more, this time informally in the elegant Italianate villa of Sir Philip Sassoon at Lympne. Here Venizelos, calm, optimistic, and plausible, repeated his offer. It was strongly opposed on military grounds by Marshal Foch, who was supported by General Weygand. Even if the Nationalists were at first defeated in the field it would still be necessary, they insisted, to liquidate the irregular bands and to protect lines of communication with the coast by the subjugation of all western Anatolia. For such a campaign the Greek forces, of which half were required to defend Smyrna, would not be adequate. The British General Staff supported the French.

But Lloyd George, still persuaded that the Greeks were the coming power in the eastern Mediterranean, and Venizelos, convinced that the views of these experts were animated by anti-Greek prejudice, were bent on the adventure. As Harold Nicolson put it: "In the Attic sunlight of his serenity the Allied statesmen surrendered to optimism." The party thus moved across the Channel, and at a more formal conference in the agreeable Villa Belle at Boulogne, with tea parties at the Pré Catalan and a fête at the Casino, the Supreme Council authorized a Greek advance from Smyrna. It began on June 22 with the crossing at four points of the Milne Line, which had been laid down in Paris as the limit of demarcation between Greeks and Turks. It was a further violation of the armistice which Kemal compared to the German invasion of Belgium.

The Greeks, with their superiority in numbers and modern equipment, had hoped for an early battle in which they were confident of breaking up Ali Fuad's sparse and ill-equipped forces, "mere skeletons," as Kemal described them, "without ammunition and incapable of being reinforced." They met with little resistance. Kemal was too shrewd a strategist to give them such a chance. "The Greek columns," as Churchill described the offensive, "trailed along the country roads passing safely through many ugly defiles, and at their approach the Turks, under strong and sagacious leadership, vanished into the recesses of Anatolia." For here the plateau, the natural frontier of Anatolia, rises behind tiers of mountain walls, beyond the head of two long river valleys and up over a rugged escarpment—a march of some two hundred and fifty arduous miles from the sea.

The Turks retreated in orderly fashion on Brusa, the holy city on the slopes of Mount Olympus. Every man who could hold a rifle was mobilized for its defence. But it could not be saved. Its capture led to a link-up by the Greeks with a force which had advanced along the shores of the Sea of Marmara to recapture Izmit. The main Turkish forces retired eastwards, followed by a swarm of Moslem refugees, up to Eskishehir, where Kemal at once began to regroup and reorganize them for the onslaught on Afyon Karahissar which must inevitably follow. Concurrently another Greek force overran eastern Thrace and captured Adrianople.

These "remarkable and unexpected manifestations of Greek power," wrote Churchill, "were hailed by the Ally statesmen; the Ally generals rubbed their eyes; Mr. Lloyd George became enthusiastic. He was right again, it seemed, and the military men wrong."

"They are beaten," Lloyd George boasted, in full conference (this time at Spa), "and fleeing with their forces towards Mecca."

"Angora," corrected Curzon acidly.

"Lord Curzon is good enough to admonish me on a triviality," the Prime Minister replied. "Nevertheless . . ."

It was in this atmosphere that Damad Ferid, with a new "ministry of marionettes" (in Churchill's phrase) formed for the purpose, signed the Treaty of Sèvres, a document "obsolete before it was ready. . . . At last peace with Turkey: and to ratify it, war with Turkey! However, as far as the Great Allies were concerned, the war was to be fought by proxy. Wars when fought thus by great nations are often very dangerous for the proxy."

··

For the moment it was the Nationalists who seemed to be in danger. The Grand National Assembly was dismayed at the spectacle of Brusa, a symbol, both religious and historical, of the Turkish spirit, under Greek occupation. How could it have fallen to the enemy so easily?

During the past two months Kemal had devoted much time and effort to the tactical handling of this motley fraternity. "Before reorganizing Anatolia," he said once, "I had to conquer its people." He had to conquer, first, the obstinate and querulous spirit of their elected representatives. The Assembly was manifesting all the fussiness and self-importance common to newly formed public bodies. He could count on the unquestioning support of no more than a minority of its members—his own immediate entourage, the few intellectuals, most of the army officers and civilian officials. But the majority still viewed him in a critical spirit, forever watching his actions with an eye to catching him out in a blunder or in an attempt to enhance his personal power. For the most part they were Anatolian notables tasting power for the first time on something more than a local scale, and bent on exercising it to the full. They included also a group of clericals, reactionary in spirit, who could swing the vote one way or another.

Thus daily Kemal would go down to the Assembly. Youthful-looking, ironical, a trifle distant, handsome in his morning coat and kalpak, he would move with his quick step into the Chamber, sitting down in his place, taking notes, then tapping with his pencil to indicate that he wished to speak. He would fix them with his cold stare, address them with a frankness and clarity that took them aback. Determined to show no undue respect, taking advantage of that familiarity which Islam allowed, they would interrupt and heckle him. With complete self-possession and a few brief words he would silence their murmurs. In that clear resounding voice which combined the accents of persuasion and authority, he would continue to expound his arguments, his ideas, his demands. The charm would begin to work, their voices to acclaim him, their hands to rise in an affirmative vote.

Often however, lacking the habit of communal deliberation or indeed of democratic procedure, they behaved in an unruly fashion. Each man, occupied with his own impulses and ambitions, would rush to the rostrum, jostling his fellows aside to pour forth on the Assembly streams of fluent but often irrelevant rhetoric. The din of conversation was continual, and the Speaker's hand bell did little to quell it. Fights often took place, and the more responsible members would intervene to prevent revolvers being brandished, faces slapped, and insults exchanged. On important occasions the deputies would be subdued by the spectacle of Kemal's own henchmen and drinking companions, glaring around the Chamber with ugly looks and hands straying towards holsters. Years later, when the Grand National Assembly had become a more seemly institution, an American senator, after a sight-seeing tour of Angora, expressed to Kemal his disappointment that he had not seen it at work. Kemal turned to the senator's guide and said, "What? Did you not show him our zoo?"

Kemal now returned from the front to face a parliamentary crisis. The deputies had draped the rostrum in black as a sign of mourning for the Brusa disaster, vowing that the draperies should remain there until the achievement of final victory. Their lamentations flowed freely. The call to prayer would no longer be heard from the minaret of the Green Mosque. The sacred city had been trodden underfoot by "our worst enemies." But the Sultan's government and his Sheikh of Islam came in for a healthy share of curses. "Do they think they can establish our religion with the help of Greek bayonets?"

One deputy rose to speak but burst into tears and was obliged to sit down. Another protested that this was no time for tears. "Gentlemen, I pray you, put back your handkerchiefs in your pockets; don't weep. Weeping is only fit for women. If you are men, instead of weeping roar like lions in the face of such a tragedy. Show by your actions the sublimity of Islam." To save the Caliphate fiery speeches were not enough: "We must unite and work together night and day. Let us leave aside the wearing of elegant clothes, drinking, pleasure, and love-making." More practically, a secret session was called to discuss measures of defence.

Here the deputies demanded on the one hand the court-martial of the officers responsible for the loss of the city, on the other an operation for its immediate recapture, whatever the cost. The chief of the General Staff promised to furnish a report and was thus able to stall for some weeks. But the deputies were not satisfied. Kemal waited for their indignation to cool, then himself took the black-shrouded rostrum. Patiently, lucidly, and in factual terms he set himself to enlighten the deputies, so unversed in military affairs, as to the real situation. They were demanding the concentration of all available troops for the recapture of Brusa. He granted them that such an operation might indeed be possible. But its ultimate outcome would be dubious. The city would be hard to hold for any length of time. The enemy, having command of the sea, could land more troops at Mudanya and so outflank it; he could endanger the Turkish line of retreat; he could, moreover, advance from the south to the vital railway line between Eskishehir and Afyon, which the Turks would thus have no troops left to defend. What mattered was not the recapture of Brusa but the defence of Anatolia itself. For this vital purpose it was essential to think realistically, act cautiously, curb the emotions, await developments, and prepare coolly to meet the next stroke of the enemy, from whichever direction it might come.

Kemal turned to the question of the internal unrest in the country. To deal with this it had been necessary to withdraw four important detachments of troops from Brusa, thus doubtless facilitating the advance of the Greeks. The prime necessity was national unity. Thus it was surely more important, for the present, to suppress the revolts than to resist the Greek offensive. He tried to bring home to the deputies the scantiness of the Nationalist forces, which was the fault not of a Cabinet two months old but of the Sultan's government in Constantinople:

"It is not reasonable to make a great fuss and to say that the catastrophe would not have happened if our troops had taken up a position on this or that river or in this or that village, or if the officers commanding them had stopped the enemy in his advance. . . . Fronts can be broken through, but it is necessary to fill up the gaps in the line as soon as possible. This is only possible if reserves drawn up in echelon can be held in the rear of the forces in the front line. But were our national forces facing the Greek Army in such a position, and had they such reserves behind them?"

The answer was no. Driving into the obstinate heads of the deputies the conception that "facts, bitter as they might be, must never be lost sight of," he concluded on a note of optimism, trusting that the situation would soon improve and that means could be found to give the nation hope and confidence. Meanwhile there was to be a call to arms by the Cabinet of men in various categories. Thus the Assembly, for the moment, calmed down.

But there was little calm for Kemal. The need to exercise patience with this rabble of mediocrities, as they often seemed to him, tired his nerves, already tense from the anxieties of confronting a war on all fronts with inadequate resources. Through the hot summer months of 1920 his growing but still inadequate staff, at close quarters within the hermitlike bounds of the Agricultural School, found him irritable and explosive. To Halide, seeing him in part through the eyes of a disillusioned romantic:

He was by turns cynical, suspicious, unscrupulous and satanically shrewd. He bullied, he indulged in cheap street-corner heroics. Possessing considerable though undistinguished histrionic ability, one moment he would pass as the perfect demagogue—a second George Washington—and the next moment fall into some Napoleonic attitude. Sometimes he would appear weak and an abject coward, sometimes exhibit strength and daring of the highest order. He would argue with all the intricacies of the old-fashioned scholastic till he had become utterly incomprehensible, and then illumine some obscure problem with a flash of inspired clarity. . . . Of course, one knew all the time that there were men around him who were greatly his superior in intellect, and far above him in culture and education. But though he excelled them in neither refinement nor originality, not one of them could possibly cope with his vitality. Whatever their qualities, they were made on a more or less normal scale. In terms of vitality he wasn't. And it was this alone that made him the dominant figure.

At this critical period Kemal needed to persuade, to consult, to seek co-operation. But at moments the mask fell, revealing a deep-seated desire only to dominate. One evening he was engaging anyone at hand in an obscure and pointless dialectical argument. He called upon Halide for her opinion. She replied that she did not grasp his point. Suddenly his tone changed and he became brutally clear and frank.

"What I mean is this: I want everyone to do as I wish and command."

She replied, "Have they not done so already in everything that is fundamental and for the good of the Turkish cause?"

Sweeping aside her question, he continued, "I don't want any consideration, criticism, or advice. I will have only my own way. All shall do as I command."

"Me too, Pasha'm?"

"You too."

"I will obey you and do as you wish as long as I believe that you are serving the cause."

"You shall obey me and do as I wish," was his reply.

"Is that a threat, Pasha'm?" she asked quietly but firmly.

At once his mood changed. The mask went up once again over his innermost feelings. He was eagerly apologetic.

"I am sorry," he said. "I would not threaten you."

Later in the summer, while all was momentarily quiet on the Greek front, Kemal was faced with another major internal revolt. Based on Yozgat, across the plateau to the east of Angora, where the powerful feudal family of Chapanoğlu had presumed to set up an independent government in support of the Sultan, its objective was the capture of the rich city of Kayseri. Unless checked, it could lead to the loss of a large part of central Anatolia and to the separation of the Nationalists in Angora from their forces in the east. To help deal with it Kemal summoned, from the Greek front at Eskishehir, the most arrogant of his war lords, Cherkess Ethem.

The Circassian swaggered into headquarters in a truculent mood. This revolt, he declared, was no business of his. Let Kemal and his generals deal with it themselves. He did not disguise his contempt for them all. But Kemal, short of troops, had to humour him. At his invitation, Ethem paid a formal visit to the Grand National Assembly, where the deputies rose solemnly to greet him. Such attentions helped to appease his vanity and he finally agreed with an air of condescension to help Angora out of its difficulties. A special train was sent to bring his "army" from Eskishehir.

Angora, as the heterogeneous Nationalist forces assembled from the various districts with their unorthodox equipment and their variety of ragged or picturesque uniforms, acquired the aspect of an armed camp. And indeed it was a substantial enough force which advanced to attack Yozgat, leaving Angora for a while virtually undefended. Before dawn they reached the town. All day they besieged it and after dark they swept in "like a black cloud."

The fighting, street by street and house by house, was venomous and brutal. The Chapanoğlu defended themselves ferociously, pouring volleys of fire from the rooftops on the invaders, who bombarded and set fire to the houses until much of the town was ablaze. With the thundering of gunfire, the roaring of flames, and the shrieking of victims, it was a "night in hell." The carnage continued until dawn. By now the Nationalists were in control of the town. Those caught were tried and hanged on the spot. Those who escaped tried to fight back but they too were defeated.

Thus ended the bloodiest, the last, and in a sense the most crucial of the anti-Nationalist rebellions. Kemal had been fortunate. Had the Caliphate forces proved capable of synchronizing their operations he might well have been defeated. As it was their three main revolts occurred singly, one after the other, giving the Nationalists just enough time in between to regroup and transfer their meagre forces. Hence by the narrowest of margins Kemal was able to contain the rebellion.

He was just in time. For the autumn offensive of the Greeks was now imminent. All hinged on the ability of the Turks to hold the railway line running from north to south between Eskishehir and Afyon, thence eastwards to the vital strategic points of Angora and Konya respectively. Were they to lose it, all central and much of southern Anatolia would be open to the enemy. The Greeks held the advantage, with their regular army. The Turks had to rely largely on their irregulars. Kemal's policy was still the strategic retreat—that of the Parthians against the Roman invasion—widening the enemy's front and lengthening its lines of communication.

Forecasting the offensive, Kemal remarked to a foreign correspondent, Alaeddine Haidar: "Tomorrow, if Venizelos, obeying the orders of his dictator, Lloyd George, wants to sacrifice an army of half a million, he will perhaps succeed with difficulty in occupying Angora and even Konya. If we retire to Sivas, our guerrilla campaign will redouble and our army will be able more easily to pierce their front, which will by then be six hundred miles long. Monsieur Venizelos has got himself into a scrape in Anatolia, and the Greek Army will end by having to quit—after burying thousands of corpses—this country which does not belong to it."

The Greek offensive was launched in the direction of the railway. The Nationalists suffered an initial defeat all along the line. "The Turks," Lloyd George exulted in the House of Commons, "are broken beyond repair." But the French and the Italians took alarm. The imminent prospect of a Greek conquest of Anatolia did not appeal to them. They insisted that the Greeks had already achieved their objective, by freeing the Marmara coast and the zone of the Straits from the Turks. The moment had come to restrain them. This time they were able to swing the Supreme Council round to their point of view, against that of Lloyd George and Venizelos. The Council telegraphed instructions to the Greeks to advance no farther.

They were obliged to halt and dig in at the points they had reached, halfway to the railway and the main rim of the plateau, in rough mountainous country, with a front tripled in length and inadequate railways and roads to supply their forces. Their new front was scattered in pockets over a dangerously wide area, less easy to hold than the continuous line in the lowlands which the Supreme Council had encouraged them to abandon, or than that which they might have reached had it allowed them to advance. The French and the Italians rejoiced—and Kemal won a new lease of life in which to build up regular forces sufficient to drive the Greeks back to the coast.

In the pursuit of this aim, as De Robeck had warned Curzon and Curzon had in vain warned the Cabinet, Kemal had already turned, with serious diplomatic attention, towards Russia.

"Until you have crossed the bridge," runs a Turkish proverb, "you should call the bear your uncle." Since the days of Peter the Great, with his expansionist designs, each generation had seen a Russo-Turkish war. Now both the Kemalists and the Bolsheviks, attacked from the west, had bridges to cross, hence at this moment in their history turned, with tentative steps, towards one another. From the moment of his landing in Anatolia Kemal had begun to think circumspectly of an understanding with the Soviet Union, if only for use as a threat against the Allies.

The immediate reaction of the Russians to the Turkish Revolution was favourable. Publicly it was interpreted as a counterpart and extension into the Moslem world of their own. *Izvestia* heralded it as "the first Soviet revolution in Asia." Strategically Turkey was important to the Bolsheviks, who were at this moment threatened with civil war by the armies successively of Denikin and Wrangel, and with Allied intervention. Revolutionary Turkey could protect their exposed flank in Trans-Caucasia, where Turks and Russians had spheres of interest and where the Allies had stationed troops as a bulwark between them.

From Sivas, after the Congress, Kemal had sponsored the journey of an unofficial emissary to the Soviet Union, to explore the possibilities of securing money and arms from the Soviets. He was Halil Pasha, a former Unionist and an uncle of Enver, and it was due partly to his efforts that limited supplies began to trickle into Anatolia in the early days of 1920.

But it was the aggressive action of the British, in the spring of 1920, that precipitated and indeed made officially possible the first serious overtures by Kemal to the Soviets. Their occupation of Constantinople, the publication of the terms of the Treaty of Sèvres, and the consequent war made Russian supplies urgently necessary. The despatch of Kiazim Karabekir and a military delegation to Baku, in Azerbaijan, had produced negative results. The formation of the Grand National Assembly enabled Kemal to take the more positive step of sending an official diplomatic mission to Moscow, led by his Circassian Foreign Minister Bekir Sami, the son of a Russian general who had fallen out with the tsarist regime and had emigrated to Turkey. He followed this up with a note to Lenin, asking for the establishment of diplomatic relations and appealing for aid to revolutionary Turkey in its struggle against imperialism.

In due course he received a letter from Chicherin, recognizing the National Pact, acknowledging the decision of the Grand National Assembly to "co-ordinate our activities and your military operations against the imperialist governments," and proposing the immediate establishment of diplomatic and consular relations. With regard to their mutual territorial interests, Chicherin favoured a referendum in the various Turco-Russian areas and proposed Soviet mediation in the settlement of Turco-Armenian and Turco-Persian frontier problems. Agreeing to this proposal in principle, Kemal offered a deal by which he accepted Russian claims to Azerbaijan in return for a free hand to invade Armenia. In conclusion he asked for "money and arms in order to organize our forces for the common struggle."

These exchanges made it necessary to postpone meanwhile the operations against Armenia for which Kiazim Karabekir had been impatiently pressing and which Kemal had authorized for the end of June. Kiazim was thus obliged to put up with a further spell of inaction, growing increasingly irritable and consoling himself only with his Children's Army, which now amounted to seventeen regiments. To keep up the morale of his soldiers, thus thwarted of action, he organized competitions in floral arrangement, encouraging them to adorn their mess tables with bouquets of flowers in harmonious shades. "Making bouquets," he considered, "has a very good influence on the souls of people, especially people of nervous, harsh temperaments."

Kiazim grew testy in his isolation, sending countless telegrams which criticized Kemal's conduct of affairs. In fact, as he failed to realize, time was working for Kemal. While he sat fretting in Erzurum at the inaction of his forces, the Supreme Council sat wrangling in Paris as to whether or not to give the city, and most of the surrounding province, to the Armenians as a "free and independent state." It became clear, however, that the Council was unprepared to reinforce the grant by any form of military action. Nor was any country prepared to undertake the necessary mandate. When President Wilson, invited to arbitrate on its frontiers, finally announced his award, it had ceased to bear any relation to realities. Together the Kemalists and the Bolsheviks were ensuring, on the spot, once and for all, that no independent state of Armenia should ever appear on the map of Asia.

The Turkish diplomatic mission had reached Moscow in July after a tortuous seventy-day journey from the Black Sea, over a Russian railway system disrupted by war and revolution. Smarting a little from its rigours and frustrations, they raised at once the urgency of opening up the route through the "independent" republics of Armenia and Georgia to allow the passage of arms to Anatolia. They added that they had come to seek not only aid but an alliance. The Russians hedged and prevaricated. Chicherin admitted that they were pledged to defend Turkey but stressed the dangers that now threatened them from Wrangel's army and from the Allies in Poland—dangers that might delay any concrete arrangement. It soon became clear that the Russians were manoeuvring to trade aid to Turkey for the cession of Turkish territory to Armenia, which they would later appropriate for themselves.

After some weeks of delay the delegation was received by Lenin, who showed a more conciliatory spirit over the opening of the supply route for arms and support for the Turkish cause in general. But he made little secret of impending Russian designs on Armenia and Georgia. Here, the Turks judged, was the old tsarist policy all over again; but to be exercised by peaceful penetration rather than war. Reporting on the interview to Angora, Bekir Sami expressed his conviction that the Russians might at any time overthrow the Armenian government. There should thus be no delay in military action from the Anatolian side.

On receipt of it, Kemal drew up for the Assembly his own cool analysis of the position. Russia's policy, as he assessed it, was governed by the present need to reassure the Moslem world as to her intentions and to discourage the spread of Turkish influence within it; by the desire to emerge, in the eyes of the Western world, as the power behind the Turkish Revolution; by the ultimate determination to establish Communism in Turkey and tie her, as a satellite, to Moscow.

On the other hand, threatened as they were by the West and by the anti-Bolshevik feeling among the Moslem peoples, the Russians could not yet do without Turkey. Thus they were probably ready to conclude an alliance. The Turks, Kemal wrote, must make a start with a piastre and a cartridge, and transportation via the Black Sea must begin. There is no doubt that even if munitions were in short supply, they nevertheless had gold to offer. Above all, "decisive action must be taken against Armenia, independently of Moscow's concurrence or otherwise."

The Russians meanwhile had convoked in the month of September a Congress of Eastern Peoples in Baku, designed at once to flatter and to menace their Moslem neighbours. To this Kemal sent a large delegation. The Russians were playing, as Enver had done, with the idea of a Pan-Islamic dominion extending to the frontiers of India, and indeed Enver in person aspired to assist their purpose. For both he and Jemal had reached Moscow from Germany, Enver attracting attention in the streets and in the government offices by a high black tarbush which concealed his small stature. At Baku he was a delegate among the Moslem leaders, most of them suspicious of Russia but ready to see what they could get from her.

Already Enver had embarked on a correspondence with Kemal, assuring him that he had come to work "for the establishment of an organized Islamic world and the delivery of our country." Making free use of the first person singular, he went to some pains to impress on Kemal that he personally stood well with the Soviet leaders. He might be in a position, he indicated, to provide not merely arms but military support for Kemal. "I have heard," he wrote, "from colleagues reaching here that you are in difficulties. This I had already supposed." He was not hopeful, however, that the Russian assistance would amount to much. "I therefore think," he advised in tones of patronage, "that you should take measures to diminish dissension in the country."

Kemal replied politely enough to these various missives. Enver might have his uses. Acting as he still was in the name of the Caliphate, Kemal was ready enough to exploit Islamic influence in defeating the British and balancing the power of Turkey against that of the Soviet Union. He thus approved of Enver's basic aspiration to unify the various Eastern national movements. On the other hand he strongly discouraged any Pan-Islamic adventures, which could only arouse Russian mistrust.

Kemal replied to a letter from Jemal in similar if more informal terms. To both he expressed confidence that an agreement with Moscow would not be long delayed. And indeed a treaty of friendship was soon initialled in Moscow and entrusted to a Turkish delegate, Yusuf Kemal, who travelled back with it to Turkey. As he was leaving Moscow, his train took on a million gold roubles (destined largely for the payment of the civil servants in Angora), together with a token instalment, designed to be shipped across the Black Sea by motorboat, of the arms, ammunition, and supplies which the Turks had requested.

But a few days afterwards Chicherin raised with Bekir Sami the question of frontiers and insisted on the cession to Armenia of territory in the Turkish provinces of Van and Bitlis. Aid to Turkey, he declared, must depend on the acceptance of this principle. On learning of this Kemal saw that the moment had come to strike. He firmly rejected Chicherin's proposal and ordered the Army of the East to march against Armenia.

Thus, at last, Kiazim Karabekir's long and impatient vigil was at an end. The objective of his offensive was the recovery of those "Armenian" districts of Turkey, including Kars, Ardahan, and Batum, which had been lost to the Russians in the war of 1877, regained from them by Enver in 1918, but lost once more to the dictation of the Allies at the armistice.

On September 28 Kiazam's troops advanced and captured Sarikamish. After a pause Kiazim continued his advance to Kars, which fell without resistance. The Russian-Armenian commander was in bed at the time, and his A.D.C. did not dare to wake him until the enemy had marched into the city, capturing his headquarters and many thousands of prisoners. The Armenian Army was no match for Kiazim's and retired in disorder towards the Arpa Chai, followed in a panic by droves of civilians dreading, not wholly without reason, rape, robbery, and massacre at the hands of the Turks.

The news of the fall of Kars caused rejoicing in Angora. Kemal had now removed his headquarters to a building at the railway station, and the large hall at the Agricultural School had been divided into separate compartments to accommodate the expanding staff. When Halide Edib entered it she was greeted with the news by the chief of Kemal's military cabinet, who then stood in the corridor and called out to the officers in their boxlike offices, "The Department of the East will have sweet dishes tonight. But the Department of the West will have only leeks boiled in water." As he spoke "thirteen doors flew open and some twenty staff officers assembled in the narrow corridor and talked at once with suppressed emotion. This . . . was the first incident to give us confidence; and it rewarded us in some measure for those long and hopeless months." Ismet came in overjoyed, patting her kindly on the shoulder, and together they drafted their congratulations to Kiazim Karabekir.

The Armenians, having appealed in vain to Chicherin and received empty assurances from President Wilson of mediation and "adjustment of differences," sued for an armistice. Early in December, at Alexandropol, Turks and Russians signed the Treaty of Gümrü (its Turkish name). The first international agreement to be contracted by the Nationalist government, it restored to Turkey her traditional eastern frontier along the banks of the Aras and the Arpa Chai.

The Russians meanwhile had defeated Wrangel's army, thus loosing onto Constantinople a flood of refugees to enrich the merchants of the bazaars with treasures exchanged for bread, to enliven the cabarets and, in the eyes of Sir Horace Rumbold, the new High Commissioner, further to debauch "this already debauched capital." The Russians were thus now free to annex the rest of Armenia. Their cavalry entered Erivan, their horses treading softly through the snow without a shot fired or a sound from the crowds. From the balcony of the Parliament building there were speeches with fervent quotations from Lenin and Marx, cries of "Long live Soviet Armenia! Long live Soviet Azerbaijan! Long live Soviet Russia! Georgia will soon be a Soviet too. Turkey will follow. Our Red Armies will sweep across Europe. . . . Long live the Third International!" The crowds in the street remained silent. An Armenian murmured, *"Quelle blague!"* His country thus became the Armenian Sovietic Federative Socialist Republic.[1]

During the months that followed the Turks and the Russians disposed, between them, of the rest of Trans-Caucasia. The Russians marched into Georgia, which became another Soviet republic. The Turks occupied Ardahan and Artvin. There was a race for Batum, which was won by the Red Army. These military gains were now to be sealed in a political form.

Kemal sent a new treaty delegation to Moscow under Yusuf Kemal. This time the delegates were able to travel by the direct route through Georgia—and incidentally to fortify themselves en route through the purchase of the cellar of an exiled Georgian nobleman. Their reception was friendly and they negotiated no longer with Chicherin the diplomat but

[1] Oliver Baldwin, *Six Prisons and Two Revolutions.*

with Stalin the realist, who proved more amenable. In response to Yusuf Kemal's gesture of gratification at this, Stalin lifted up two fingers and remarked laconically of Chicherin, "Diplo!"

On March 16, 1921, the Treaty of Moscow was signed between the Kemalist government and that of the Soviet Union. It followed the lines of the initialled treaty with certain additions. Each party, taking note of "the points in common between the movement of the Eastern peoples for national emancipation and the struggle of the workers of Russia for a new social order," recognized "the right of these peoples to freedom and independence" and a free choice of government. Each undertook to refrain from subversive activities in the territories of the other.

It was thus that those two notable realists, Kemal and Stalin, settled between them by negotiation and action, not indeed all their mutual problems, but their mutual frontiers, drawing a line across the map which survives today without dispute as the boundary between these hereditary enemies, Turkey and Russia.

31 ▶ End of the irregulars

While the Turkish delegation negotiated in Moscow, Kemal and his associates had been striving to guide into safe channels the consequent currents of opinion at home. Kemal himself, committed from his earliest youth to the ideas of the West, was no Bolshevik. His opposition to Communism was categoric. "For our nation," he said while his mission was negotiating, "there is no such problem as that of becoming Bolshevik. . . . We as a nation have principles and habits of our own to which we are faithful. . . . The Soviets have means and resources and are the enemies of our enemy. But there can be no such thing as abandoning our aim and becoming slaves of the Soviets."

For the moment, however, political expediency made it necessary to become their friends. Kemal's task was to conciliate the Bear and yet to keep free of his greedier embraces. This involved him in intricate problems, not merely in Moscow itself but at home. Here he had to manipulate with care and adroitness the conflicting trends of Nationalist opinion, to mobilize on the one hand its pro-Russian elements while ensuring on the other that they did not go too far.

Ever since the Young Turk Revolution there had been two main schools of thought as to the direction which Turkey should take in the future, and these now crystallized sharply. Ranged to the right were the adherents of the Western ideal; ranged to the left were those of the Eastern ideal. The Western ideal envisaged a government shaped on Western lines and with Western social and economic institutions, such as the liberals of the Ottoman Empire had sought since the nineteenth century. It was, however, a bold man who would advocate in Angora the ideals and institutions of a Europe now hated as the enemy. The "Westerners" were thus driven into the same camp as the "Easterners," remaining firm, however, in their condemnation of the internal Soviet system, to which tradition and impulse opposed them.

The Eastern ideal was less easily definable. It arose from a vague and confused search for a new system, derived from the feeling that Western civilization had outlived its time. It was born from among those idealists of the party of Union and Progress who sought a solution for humanity in terms of an idea rather than in relation to facts. The fact of the Russian Revolution gave it an immediate and powerful impetus.

Its chief protagonist was Kemal's Finance Minister, Hakki Behich, who had studied Marxist philosophy and had in fact drafted the plan for the new government which the Assembly had accepted in a modified form. Other adherents of the Eastern ideal were to be found in the Grand National Assembly, where the nature of Communism was now freely discussed if not well understood. Paradoxically, some sympathizers were to be found among the religious classes, where some interpreted the Eastern ideal as (in Halide Edib's words) "a revival of the first democratic age of Mohammed."

As paradoxically, there was a strong trend towards Communism among the irregular chiefs, who chose to exploit it as a means of consolidating their power over their illiterate bands. For this purpose they made increasing use of an institution named the Green Army.[1] A secret organization of which Hakki Behich was the secretary-general, it had been formed with Kemal's approval at the time of the internal rebellions. Here was a regular force sufficiently imbued with the Nationalist ideals to counteract defections among the troops and to inject new life into the national forces in general.

Kemal had approved the Green Army to meet an immediate situation but soon it began to develop two disturbing trends. It built up the irregular bands at the expense of the regular army on which, in the

---

[1] Its name was derived from that used in prerevolutionary Russia by Communist rebel organizations in Moslem provinces.

long run, the Nationalist movement would have to rely; and it became an instrument, conscious and otherwise, of the Communists and in particular of Cherkess Ethem, whose arrogance, puffed up by success, took the form of an increasingly overt defiance of Kemal. The Green Army began to see itself as a Turkish counterpart of the Russian Red Army and to spread its influence through a subversive newspaper named *Yeni Dunya (New World)*, springing originally from Moscow and Baku and now published in Eskishehir. Its ranks became fertile ground for Russian agents, exploiting the discontents of the Turkish peasantry and indoctrinating the irregular soldiers.

During the Greek invasion signs multiplied that the Green Army might well be used to stab Kemal in the back. The time came when he could no longer infiltrate into its ranks his own trusted supporters. Appointments were made to it without his sanction, and its activities began to pass beyond his control. When he discovered that its leaders, without consulting him, had enrolled one of his own A.D.C.s in the army, he decided that the moment had come to suppress it.

He called a conference of its leaders and commanding officers at Angora where, at a sitting which lasted far into the night, he was able to achieve this object. The meeting provided a characteristic example of his faculty for imposing his will on others, while leaving them with the impression that they had got their own way. At the end of it a list of resolutions was drafted and agreed by all. After it had broken up, Kemal turned to his henchman Tevfik Rüştü and said, "Look in that flower pot." Tevfik did so and found a paper.

"Read it out," said Kemal.

Tevfik read it and found that it comprised exactly those resolutions to which the meeting had just agreed as its own. They had been drafted by Kemal, with his chief of staff, that morning.

The result was the dissolution of the Green Army and the trial and sentence by the Independence Tribunals of a number of those, including deputies, who had been involved with it. This was a setback which the Russians, who had set some store by the army, were to attribute to its "lack of proletarian leadership."

Concerned at this episode, and at the general growth of underground Communist activities, Kemal now came out into the open and replaced the Green Army with a Communist party of his own. By this astute move he hoped to canalize and control such elements. The editorial offices of the *New World* were removed from Eskishehir to Angora, where they could be effectively supervised, while action was taken to liquidate the more dangerous Soviet agents.

At the head of the party he placed Hakki Behich, who accordingly circularized as "Dear Comrade" the principal Nationalist authorities. The party, he explained, was based on the principles of the Third International and directly attached to it. It had the approval of the Ministry of the Interior. Its programme would be put before the next General Congress of the Communist party. The secret Green Army would be merged with it, and all other Communist organizations engaged on Communist propaganda would henceforward be invalid. To Ali Fuad, as to the other army commanders, Hakki Behich wrote, "We are proud to have you, our Commander Comrade, included in the military sections and rely on your valuable opinions and military spirit." Ali Fuad was taken aback by this move, which he felt could only weaken the Nationalist cause. But Hakki's circular was followed by a covering telegram from Kemal himself, which reassured Fuad as to its motives.

Kemal intended the formation of the party as a measure of expediency to tide over the present crisis. If the Nationalist movement succeeded it could very quickly be disbanded. If, on the other hand, it collapsed, at the hands of the Greeks or otherwise, Anatolia, with its capital withdrawn to Sivas or east of it, would inevitably fall into the orbit of the Russians. In this event, Anatolia's own Communist party might have to serve as its instrument of government and, as an established national institution, would be better equipped to uphold against the Soviets some degree of Turkish independence. Meanwhile, with the party behind him, he felt strong enough to liquidate the most dangerous of the Soviet agents in Turkey, a Turkish Socialist named Mustafa Subhi. With sixteen of his confederates he was arrested, placed on board a boat at Trebizond—and disposed of. Chicherin's enquiries as to his whereabouts merely produced the polite answer that the party must have met with an accident in the Black Sea.

In the autumn of 1920 the Russians had sent a large embassy to Angora. The need thus arose for Kemal to send a reciprocal embassy, of a permanent kind, to Moscow. He took advantage of this to help resolve a conflict which had developed within his own ranks at home. Its focus was the commander of the western front, Ali Fuad; its essence the latent cleavage between the respective protagonists of irregular and regular forces, which the affair of the Green Army had brought out into the open. The Greek advance had made it obvious that no effective resistance was possible without a regular army to match that of the enemy. But, pending the organization of such a force, it had not proved possible to dispense with the irregulars, whose power had in consequence grown.

Kemal suspected Ali Fuad of a prejudice in favour of the irregulars. He had earned a black mark in connection with an unsuccessful attack on the Greeks before their main offensive, which was carried out in response to pressure from Ethem and against the judgment of the General Staff. Its failure was followed by demands from Ali Fuad for reinforcements and equipment for his troops, which Kemal chose to criticize, causing a meeting of the Cabinet to record that, though they would be met, they were considered "quite unreasonable." This incident was symptomatic of growing friction between Ali Fuad and the Angora government, which he claimed was manufacturing difficulties for him.

Angora's quarrel with Fuad was in fact a matter of personalities as much as of principle. His enmity against Ismet had increased since the newcomer had contrived to establish himself more firmly in Kemal's favour than those who had been with him from the start. It was an enmity reciprocated by Ismet. The two men differed in outlook and temperament, and now they had become rivals for power. Kemal started an insidious campaign of propaganda against Ali Fuad's capacities. On the one hand he saw Ismet, safely under his own control, as the indispensable key to the new phase of regular warfare which was about to begin. On the other hand he saw that Ali Fuad, in close relations with an ambitious war lord and thus with an irregular army under his virtual control, might become too independent and powerful a figure in the Nationalist hierarchy.

The time had thus come to remove him. The Russian situation provided Kemal with the pretext he sought. Ali Fuad received a summons to Angora. Observing that his reception at the station was more ceremonious than usual, he sensed from the atmosphere that something untoward was afoot. He stepped forward from the circle of ministers and the guard of honour, to be greeted by Kemal and led back into his compartment for a private talk. Kemal spoke of the necessity to send an embassy to Moscow, with a leader of high calibre. Using the intimate second person singular, he begged his old friend to accept the post of ambassador to the Soviet Union.

Ali Fuad realized that his military career was at stake and tried to play for time. But it was clear that Kemal wanted an immediate decision. Ali Fuad promised to call upon him and give him a positive answer. Kemal's expression brightened and with a warm handshake he left.

Sitting back in his compartment, Ali Fuad speculated as to the motives for his removal. At the front he had heard disquieting rumours of the changing trend in Angora. Kemal, it was said, was moving perceptibly towards personal rule. He had gathered around him adherents, notably Ismet, who subscribed to this trend. Gone were the days when five loyal comrades in arms launched the Revolution together in a spirit of mutual trust. Rauf was in exile, Kiazim, Refet, and Ali Fuad were in the field, Kemal ruled Angora with an Assembly to bend to his will, and Fevzi and Ismet to serve as his intermediaries. Ali Fuad was no longer close to Kemal. But by quarrelling with him he would create a breach in the movement. He thus had no choice but to accept the Moscow embassy. Soon afterwards he left, with a large staff, for Russia.

With Ali Fuad safely out of the way, it was time to come to grips with Ethem, the recalcitrant war lord. In the mountains around Kütahya he had set up what was little less than an independent feudal principality. Here he levied his own taxes, dispensed his own system of arbitrary justice, and recruited his own forces, paying his soldiers three times as much as those of the regular army and indeed encouraging them to desert from its ranks. Ismet stood in the garden of the Assembly one day while a detachment of Ethem's troops marched past. As he looked at them he remarked sadly: "The horses are mine, the weapons, the soldiers. Only the command is not mine."

Kemal and Ismet now decreed that this force, together with all the surviving irregular bands, should be incorporated into the regular army. The decree led to a straight trial of strength between Kemal and Ethem, with Ethem's two brothers, one a deputy, behind him.

Ismet announced that Ethem's forces would now become a division, subject to regular inspection and discipline. Ethem's brother Tevfik defied him, contending, "It is impossible to put officers or paymasters in charge of these vagabonds or induce them to agree to such a thing. At the sight of officers they will go mad as though they had seen the Angel of Death." Already in Angora they were saying, "Mustafa Kemal will make us all button up our tunics. And we won't. We will wear Ethem's uniform." Tevfik spread around the report that he was about to launch an attack on Ismet's army, in the direction of Eskishehir.

In Angora it became clear that Ethem, with his other brother Reshid and their friends in the Assembly, was planning a revolt against the government. Kemal was equal to this. The two adversaries, so alike, despite their disparity of build, in the steeliness and pallor of their looks, watched and weighed one another warily, animal craftiness pitted against human guile. One day when Kemal was lying ill in bed the Circassian burst without ceremony into his room. Kemal calmly put his hand under the pillow, making it clear that it clasped a revolver. Ethem had a hand on his own revolver, finely embossed and notched for each kill. His bodyguard, bristling with arms, filled the landing and staircase. An A.D.C. went to warn Ismail Hakki, the commander of a detachment of troops outside, to surround the building and shoot Ethem's men if necessary. Ethem demanded the removal of Ismet and Kemal quietly refused. Ethem heard, through the window, the sound of rifles being loaded. He muttered to one of his guards in a Circassian dialect, "The situation is dangerous. Let's give it up." On the pretence that he had been paying a mere courtesy call, he quietly took leave of Kemal.

Afterwards Kemal overheard the A.D.C.s discussing the incident, laughing wrily at the fact that they had only a single revolver between them, and suggesting that he himself should have a personal bodyguard. He immediately called Ismail Hakki and ordered him to recruit one. This was done from among the Lazes around Giresun, the Georgian warriors of the Black Sea mountains. With their ferocious demeanour and their all-black uniforms and turbans, they soon became a familiar and picturesque spectacle in Angora, escorting Kemal and patrolling before the Parliament building as the "President's Guard."

Realizing the power of Ethem, Kemal made last patient efforts to bring his men under control. He invited the Circassian to proceed with him to Eskishehir, there to thrash out their differences with Ismet. But when the train reached the station Ethem disappeared.

Back in Angora his brother Reshid was called to a meeting of ministers and Kemal put before him once more the need for a disciplined army with which to defend the country. After pouring contempt on the regulars, who would "run like hares at the first noise," Reshid exclaimed, "What does this word 'country' mean? I could live anywhere just as happily. I could live with Venizelos." Kemal reproved him with polite scorn for his foolishness, then despatched a parliamentary delegation to Kütahya to make a last appeal to Ethem's common sense. Its members were virtually placed under arrest, to be treated as hostages. But they escaped from the hospitality of Kütahya and returned to Angora.

Ethem now sent a telegram to the Assembly, in which he questioned its legality. Declaring that the country was too tired to fight, he insisted on negotiations for peace with the enemy. He signed his telegram, "The Commander-in-Chief of all the National Forces." Playing for the support of Constantinople, he sent a copy of it to the Grand Vizier, implying in a covering message that he meant to attack the Assembly's forces and had reached an understanding with the Greeks for the purpose.

The deputies met in indignant secret session. In a subsequent open debate Kemal, exposing the intrigues of Ethem and his brothers both with the Russians and with the Greeks, still chose to refer to them with studious politeness by the title of bey. The deputies shouted, "God damn them!" and one of them exclaimed angrily, "Your Excellency, don't call them bey. These men are traitors!" Kemal proposed Reshid's expulsion from the Assembly, at which the deputies cheered and raised their hands in assent.

Kemal's troops marched on Kütahya and occupied it without resistance. They pursued Ethem southwestwards. His men showed little fight against the regular army, seeking only to save their own skins. Soon, in Kemal's words, "Ethem Bey and his brothers with their force occupied the most suitable position for them, namely in the ranks of the enemy!" [2]

---

[2] The Greeks in fact made little use of Ethem's forces, preferring, ironically, to incorporate them into their own regular army.

32 ▶ *The first battle of Inönü*

In the West and in Constantinople the political climate was changing. First Venizelos, then Damad Ferid disappeared from the scene. The change in Greece was fortuitous. Early in October 1920 the young King Alexander, while watching the antics of a pair of pet monkeys in the garden of his palace, was bitten by one of them and died. "It is perhaps no exaggeration," commented Churchill, "to remark that a quarter of a million persons died of this monkey's bite."

Venizelos, overestimating, after an almost unbroken absence of two years in Paris and London, his own prestige as a popular hero and his countrymen's capacity for political gratitude, declared a general election. In this he gave the royalists freedom to vote if they chose for the restoration to the throne of King Constantine, discredited and exiled in 1917 for complicity with the Germans. They promptly did so, defeating Venizelos and his party by a handsome majority. Lloyd George, when he received this shocking news, pulled himself together and remarked with a grin, "Now I am the only one left." To Venizelos he wrote: "It almost makes one despair of democracy." Venizelos replied with more realism that his defeat was due rather to the war-weariness of the Greeks and to the discontent which arose from their continued mobilization.

The French, war-weary too, seized upon the change, at the Supreme Council in Paris, as an excuse to liquidate their commitments to the Greeks. The Italians followed the French example. Here was a chance for the British too to withdraw, with reasonable honour, from a policy which was proving unprofitable. But Lloyd George remained true to his dreams, announcing that the King's return would make no difference to Anglo-Greek friendship, which "is vital to us in that part of the world." Even he, however, realized that the full implementation of the Treaty of Sèvres and its policy were doomed.

In Constantinople the Sultan could no longer maintain Damad Ferid in power. He had been discredited both by the popular rejection of the treaty and by the failure of his civil war policy. The public now saw him as a nonentity, a weakling, a figure of fun in a tragic situation. He was reputed to fall asleep at Cabinet meetings and he had difficulty in finding ministers to serve under him.[1] His own party turned against him, and the Sultan at last intimated that his services were no longer required. Thus Damad Ferid resigned and retired to Carlsbad, to take a long cure. His place was again taken by Tevfik, who at once brought into his Cabinet two ministers friendly to the Nationalists—Izzet Pasha as Minister of the Interior and Salih Pasha as Minister of Marine.

This "new broom" chanced to coincide with changes in personnel by the British. General Milne was replaced by General Sir Charles Harington and Admiral de Robeck by a professional diplomat, Sir Horace Rumbold. There was a general feeling among the Turks in Constantinople that these changes might lead to a shift in British policy. The Allies must surely realize that the Treaty of Sèvres was no longer enforceable. The French had recognized that this was the moment to come to terms with the stronger Turkey which was arising. Would the British do the same?

Izzet, in the hope that they might, decided to re-establish contact with Angora. If officially the two governments must still appear to differ, at least unofficially they might agree to work together for peace. With the approval of the Cabinet he sent an emissary to Kemal to propose a visit of himself and Salih Pasha (both former Grand Viziers) to Angora, to dis-

[1] It was related of him that, in Cabinet-making, he called a bunch of elderly pashas out of retirement, stood them in a row, and appointed them according to the personal apearance of each—the erect and martial pasha as Minister of War, the lean and intellectual as Minister of Justice, the bearded and devout-looking as Minister of Pious Foundations, the stout and plebeian as Minister of Commerce.

cuss the prospect, of which he reported signs, that the British might now be prepared to consider some sort of settlement.

Kemal's attitude to the proposed visit was cautious. He was sceptical as to the prospect of any such peace offer as the Nationalists could afford to accept. In war-weary Angora, on the other hand, there was a strong feeling in favour of peace. In this atmosphere there was a danger that any public revelation of overtures from Constantinople might undermine the spirit of resistance and the growth of the army. The new friendly government might thus prove a greater threat to the cause than the last, which could be denounced as an enemy. Kemal could not but agree to the proposal but he insisted that the meeting should be secret and should take place not in Angora itself but in the seclusion of Bilejik, a station on the line between Eskishehir and Constantinople.

It took place in the station waiting room. Izzet, in his political innocence and ignorance of the true position in Anatolia, had expected a series of informal man-to-man chats between two former companions-in-arms. What happened was different. Kemal at once created an official atmosphere by presenting himself stiffly as the President of the Grand National Assembly. To whom had he the honour of speaking? Salih explained that he was Minister of Marine, while Izzet was Minister of the Interior in the Constantinople government. Kemal replied, politely but firmly, that in his view no such government existed, that he could not therefore receive them as its ministers but only unofficially as private individuals.

On this basis they talked for some hours. Izzet tried to persuade Kemal that an out-and-out Nationalist resistance could achieve no positive results and that the moment had come to seek a reasonable peace. What he evidently had in mind, as Kemal saw it, was a submission by Angora to Constantinople, followed by a joint approach to the Allies. This was out of the question; Kemal knew that if once he compromised he was lost. But to reject Izzet's proposals outright would be impolitic. Kemal thus decided to give him a taste of the Nationalist atmosphere. He closed the discussion and conducted the members of the delegation to the train. At once, to their surprise and apparent concern, it started to move towards Angora. With a glint in his eye, Kemal explained that he could not permit them to return to Constantinople. They would continue their talks on the train and again, more seriously, in Angora itself. "You shall be the guest of us Anatolians for a while," he said.

Having thus disarmed the two pashas, he published the news of their arrival throughout Anatolia but omitted to reveal that they had come to discuss peace. To exploit their visit as a means of raising rather than lowering the spirit of resistance, he issued a shrewdly phrased communiqué, indicating that they had come of their own accord to meet the government of the Grand National Assembly and work for the country's cause.

Izzet was dismayed at this act of sharp practice. Known always as a man given to straightforward dealings, he was now placed in a position which could only be seen by his government as dishonourable. A trifle ingenuously, he had seen the Nationalist movement simply as a struggle against the foreigner, designed to save the seat of the Sultanate and Caliphate from Western domination. He only now realized that it was a struggle against the government of the Sultanate and Caliphate itself. To this he could not subscribe.

For all his opposition to Abdul Hamid and Vahid-ed-Din, Izzet remained a legitimist in principle. It was his genuine belief that the best solution for his country still lay in the continuation of the Sultan's regime in collaboration with the Nationalists. Kemal on the other hand saw that the country's only hope lay with the government of the Grand National Assembly and that there could be no question of peace negotiations unless it were recognized. In his view it was Izzet's duty as a patriot to forsake Constantinople and remain at Angora.

Meanwhile the two pashas, as "honoured but unwilling guests," were given the best available house, furnished with such rudimentary comforts as the town possessed. On the day after their arrival they called on Halide Edib, who later recalled:

I have a vivid recollection of Salih Pasha, twice Premier and several times Cabinet Minister of the Empire, over six feet in height and beautifully dressed, nearly doubling himself in half to get through my tiny door, and then walking up the rickety stairs of what must have seemed to him to be a mere mud hut. Izzet Pasha and the rest followed in dignified but significant silence till both the pashas involuntarily exclaimed, "Poor Hanum Effendi! Oh, poor Hanum Effendi!" The tone of pity in their voices actually hurt me and made me feel rebellious almost to the point of wanting to be rude. . . . But they did look so fine as they came in and brought back my old world to me in my little hut with such genuine affection that I only said in a laughing tone, "Please don't pity me; it is my choice."

After some five or six weeks the pashas were allowed to return to Constantinople on the understanding that they would resign from their posts in the government. This they did, though they accepted other posts later. But Izzet, still seeking co-operation, worked honourably for the

Nationalist cause, supplying arms for Kemal's forces for the next phase
of the fight with the Greeks.

The natural outcome of Venizelos' defeat would have been the reversal
of his policy. But the supporters of the King chose to become, in this respect, more Venizelist than Venizelos. They carried out, it is true, a drastic
purge of Venizelist officers from the army. But then they proceeded—in
"a mad outbreak of regal vanity," as Lloyd George, wise many years after
the event, described it—with plans for a renewal of the offensive against
Angora. Bereft now of Allied support, hence freed from the hampering
limits which the Allies had placed on the Venizelist advance, they
sought to readjust their military position.

Their present awkward line was composed of three fronts, isolated one
from the other and based on inadequate communications with Smyrna.
Parts of it were disturbingly vulnerable and exposed the Greek troops to
unnecessary hardships in winter. Hence the strategy of the royalists
was to advance to the railway and seize its key points, Eskishehir and
Afyon Karahisar, thus uniting their forces, cutting the communications
of the Turks, and driving them back upon Angora and Konya respectively. A major advance must be delayed until the spring, when the
weather was favourable. But now on January 6, 1921, they embarked on
an interim action which was in effect a reconnaissance in force.

Kemal broke the news of it to the Assembly and prayers were read for
the success of the army. The situation was thought by all to be grave.
Day after day deputies and others, their faces grey with worry, besieged
Kemal's room in the Assembly, which became a bureau of information.
Here, with the aid of a map, he retailed to them the daily reports from
the front. He had an appearance of confidence, even of gaiety. Playing
with a string of beads, he dealt with their questions, avoiding definite replies, expounding tactics, counselling patience, calming their anger at the
news of the retreat of the Turkish advance guard.

The offensive was aimed at four points between the northern and
southern sectors of the front, the weight of it falling in the north, where
Kemal had concentrated the bulk of his forces. The main thrust came
from Brusa. Aimed upwards over layers of steep but broken ridges in the
direction of Eskishehir, it came within sight of the plateau before it. Ismet met the Greeks in a valley at Inönü, a position which had been par-
tially fortified to cover the city.

His troops put up a resistance which surprised and disconcerted the
Greeks. In the light of the earlier campaign, they had expected an easy

walkover against undisciplined and ill-equipped men. Instead they found themselves, for the first time, faced with a resolute and disciplined force, greatly inferior in numbers and equipment, but not in leadership and fighting spirit, to their own regular divisions, whose troops were in any case now commanded by unfamiliar and often inexperienced royalist officers. Knee-deep in mud and snow, the Turks stubbornly defended their own territory. After an all-day battle they counterattacked with success. Next day the Greeks, fearing that they had fallen into a trap, accepted failure and retired, as speedily as they had come, towards Brusa, there to prepare, with the new lessons thus learnt, for a major campaign in the spring.

The Nationalists chose to play up this first battle of Inönü for the benefit both of local morale and of Russian opinion, as their first major victory against the foreigner, and it was celebrated in Angora with unbounded rejoicing. In the Assembly thanks were expressed to the army. Kemal flattered the deputies by praising their own behaviour in the face of the threat. Their serenity had given the soldiers a feeling of confidence.

After the battle Halide Edib was sent to Eskishehir to visit the wounded in hospital. She was struck, as she travelled down the railway, with the change in the atmosphere:

Gone were the good-humored, "swanky" irregulars who used to fire from the train windows to display their marksmanship. The station no longer echoed with the din of their wild songs and their live, lively repartee. All seemed under an iron discipline, and if the regulars who were there instead were priding themselves on their recent achievements, they certainly repressed any expression of it under their quiet manners. . . . Everybody moved as though by machinery; there was an occasional chink of spurs, a single voice here and there commanding—nothing more.

Such was the spirit of the new army with which the Greeks, as they now began to realize, would have to contend.

33 ► *The London Conference*

As the Nationalist organization grew, so did the atmosphere of Angora change. Much of its intimacy disappeared. The small "band of brothers" had grown into a large general staff, divided and subdivided into various departments. Kemal, moreover, was more aloof than before. No longer did he sit around at headquarters of an evening, working and talking and sharing problems with the rest. First he had moved his own office to a building near the station where he could be near the telegraph office, for this was a war of wires, and Kemal, with his modern outlook, realized the paramount importance of communications.

Then he had changed his place of residence. He had moved to a large stone villa on a hillside at Chankaya, some five miles away. Built by a Levantine merchant, it flaunted pinnacles and a pentagonal turret, while its interior was heavily ornate. But the rooms were spacious and light, such as appealed to Kemal, with many windows looking down over the plain to the twin hills of the city beyond it. Here he now lived what might well be described as a marital life.

The strain of the previous autumn had told on Kemal's health, and Dr. Adnan felt that he needed feminine care. At this moment, as though in answer to the need, Fikriye announced her impending arrival from Constantinople. She had contrived, against the strong disapproval of Kemal's mother and sister, to follow him to Anatolia. She travelled alone on one of the rough tramp steamers which plied along the Black Sea coast, carrying discreet and anonymous male passengers who, on arrival at the small port of Inebolu, would put on Kemalist kalpaks and reveal themselves as officers and others come to serve the Nationalist cause. A small boat took her ashore from the roadstead, to be warmly greeted by the local director of posts and telegraphs, all too unused to seeing a young and attractive girl disembark with the rest.

The pretext of her journey was to nurse the wounded, but she indiscreetly confided to him that she had come to marry Mustafa Kemal. She was sent on her way by carriage over the rough mountain road which at this time was almost the only supply line for the national forces, conveyed like the rest in one of the "covered wagons" of Anatolia, where she was able at will either to squat cross-legged or to lie, not too uncomfortably despite the jolts of the road, at full length. On arrival in Angora she settled into the house at Chankaya.

Kemal was a man wedded to his career and his country and the society of other men, to whom women meant little save as a source of distraction, an outlet for his appetites, and a stimulus to his masculine vanity. For all his refinements, he was in this respect still the rough soldier. Asked once what qualities he admired most in a woman, he replied: "Availability." Fikriye fulfilled this specification and gave him something more. Restless and sporadic in his sexual appetites, he had had to be content through years of campaigning with such *femmes faciles* or other promiscuous companions as garrison cities provided. Fikriye's arrival provided him with a regular outlet in which affection and intimacy played their part. He was fond of her and flattered by her love; he enjoyed her feminine ways; she was a woman who, at this stage of his life, suited him well.

Dark and slender, Fikriye was receptive and gentle in manner. She had a natural intelligence, with just enough education to make a show of responding to Kemal's ideas. She was tactful, never seeking to interfere with his work, but holding her own by her charms at his table. She put his friends at their ease, she spoke their language, and they came to appreciate the domestic atmosphere which she had brought to the house. They could drink in her presence, but she would always know when to leave them alone with Kemal for more serious drinking. To Kemal Fikriye gave, without family ties, that sense of familiarity and ease which marriage afforded. But he did not contemplate marrying her. Were he ever to marry he would seek a wife who could take her place beside him, as a Western wife should do. The place of Fikriye, still the oriental woman, would always be behind him.

The unveiled young Fikriye became familiar to the people of Angora as she drove through the streets in Kemal's open carriage or rode over the hills above the city. No hothouse plant, she liked open-air pursuits and could not only ride but shoot. It was on horseback that Halide Edib first saw her, "someone with a very pretty face, though she looked very tired and very cold—the tip of her nose was almost blue and the lips had no colour. Framed in black, the delicate lines in the oval face were at their most effective. Her eyes were grave and dark, and with long brown and curling lashes. . . . She looked at me with something of a smile on her wan face, and when she had passed I was haunted by the ineffable sadness of her look." It was the look, Dr. Adnan revealed to his wife, of the incipient consumptive. The sadness was due in part to the intuitive feeling that Kemal would not marry her. She must live for the moment— and this was a moment at which she could provide him with an environment in which to relax and calm his nerves.

His other method of seeking to calm them was through alcohol. Kemal had been drinking freely all his life. In his early youth, less sure of himself than he liked to appear, he had drunk to gain confidence, to impose himself the better on others. As his brain developed, he drank to relax it. At night his thoughts denied him peace; in the daytime they drove him like a dynamo. In the evening—but seldom before sundown— he would drink to release nervous tension.[1] Kemal drank not from weakness but deliberately, because he enjoyed alcohol and needed it. He made no secret of the practice, preferring to flaunt it without hypocrisy.

When foreigners wrote of his drinking habits, he expressed his approval. "If those things are not written," he argued, "people can't understand me." When the governor of Smyrna once ordered the curtains in the restaurant where he was at table to be drawn, that the people in the street should not see him drinking, he protested, "If you do that they'll think we're going to make women dance on the table. At least let them see that we're only drinking!" A French journalist wrote that Turkey was governed by one drunkard, one deaf man (Ismet), and three hundred deaf mutes (the deputies). At this Kemal commented, "This man is mistaken. Turkey is governed by one drunkard."

[1] The release was not only mental but physical, for he was chronically constipated, and maintained that the alcohol loosened his bowels.

Kemal seldom drank when in action, when a situation was serious. At Erzurum during the Congress he had drunk only black coffee. In the Agricultural School, when the Sultan's armies threatened, he had remained—thanks perhaps to the influence of such fellow workers as Dr. Adnan and Halide Edib—relatively abstemious. But the present period was one of inaction, of improvisation, of suspense. So he drank once more.

It was a habit which did not endear him to his more strict Moslem deputies. One of the Assembly's first actions had been the passage of a bill against the import and general sale of spirituous liquors. The consumption of alcohol, contrary to the laws of Islam, was alleged to be paralyzing the armed forces, ravaging the population with illness, dragging the country to the edge of an abyss. It was now punishable by heavy fines, flogging, or imprisonment. When, however, an emissary was sent to Kemal in his office, begging him to abstain from the practice, he was laughed out of the door.

The drinking table had always been Kemal's natural orbit: the café tables of Salonika, with the torrents of talk which he could never translate into action; the mess tables of his various headquarters, where the talk ran on war. And now in the dining room of Chankaya he returned to it, surrounding himself night after night, over bottles of raki, with colleagues and cronies for whom his words could at last become deeds.

Often the sessions were rough and convivial, leading to a casual game of poker which might last until dawn. But as time went on they came to play a more constructive role. "The table" was to become something of a national institution. Around it, as much as in Parliament or at Cabinet meetings, was policy formed. It became Kemal's indirect instrument of government, as well as a school in which he trained and modelled in his own image a new ruling class for a country whose government was indeed to be for but not by the people. State secrets, it is true, were not bandied about. The discussion—usually one-way—was at this time on the general principles, political, social, and economic, on which the state was to be based.

Few men in Angora could afford to be excluded from the table, though some shunned it—and begged the secretary to strike them off the list—on account of the long drinking hours it entailed, while others, like Ismet, with his sober domestic habits, graced it as seldom as possible. On the other hand many yearned to be invited and became unabashed sycophants when their yearnings were realized. The "regulars" were the henchmen, the ex-brother officers and aides (become deputies), and now a young "court" of journalist-intellectuals to whom, though they held their own in conversation, Kemal always remained a hero. As Falih Rifki wrote later in a starry-eyed mood, "All the things that died within us all the dreary lifelong day, by degrees and one by one came alive again. It was there . . . that we understood, more vividly than ever again, how the will of a believer can become the creator of miracles."

But the miracles had yet to be performed. For the next Greek offensive was looming. Before it could open, the Allied powers joined in a move towards peace. The Supreme Council invited delegates of the Turkish and Greek governments to attend a conference in London in February 1921, under the presidency of Lloyd George, to consider a new solution of the Eastern question—in other words, a revision of the Treaty of Sèvres. The Council insisted, moreover, that delegates from the Angora government should form part of the Turkish delegation. This invitation was relayed by Tevfik, the Grand Vizier, to Kemal over the district tele-graph line between Constantinople and Angora which, after a lapse of nine months, was reconnected for the purpose.

Kemal was quick to exploit this *de facto* recognition of his government. Manoeuvring tactically with a view to strengthening his ultimate stra-tegic position, he replied that the invitation was a matter not for himself but for the Grand National Assembly, "the only lawful and independent sovereign power," which had lately been given constitutional form. The Angora government should thus be officially recognized, not merely by the Allied powers but by the Sultan himself. Tevfik replied that this was a constitutional, hence a domestic matter, appropriate for settlement after an agreement had been reached with the Allies; insistence upon it at this stage could lead to a refusal of all Turkish representation at the con-ference.

Having made his point against the Sultan, Kemal called upon the Assembly to pass a resolution for despatch to Tevfik. In this, after a lengthy preamble in which appropriate feelings were vented against the Sultan's government—"nothing but a discarded authority no longer wielding any power in the country"—the Assembly declared its refusal to be involved in any delegation formed in Constantinople. Instead it would send a separate and independent delegation of its own, which alone represented the Turkish people, independently of Tevfik's. Bekir Sami, who had resumed his duties as Foreign Secretary on returning from Russia, was appointed its leader. The delegation left for London, not via Constantinople, but via Adalia and Rome, where it was greeted by

Count Sforza, the Foreign Minister and chief Italian delegate to the conference.

The two delegations stayed at the Savoy Hotel. They occupied separate floors and at first preserved an official aloofness. Bekir Sami seemed, to *The Times,* unwilling to ask to see Tevfik. As the representative of a "bandit government," the reporter found him disappointing. "He might have been tailored in Bond Street. Well groomed, dressed in a morning coat and smart striped trousers, he does not even wear a fez." Tevfik, who looked unwell and sat with a rug over his knees, set all divergences at rest from the outset by deferring to the Angora delegation as the legal representatives of the Turkish nation. Bekir Sami was thus left to present the Turkish case and act as spokesman throughout the conference, continually irritating Lloyd George by his failure to make clear what he really wanted.

"The conference," observed Aubrey Herbert in *The Times,* "need not necessarily break the crockery of the Treaty of Sèvres; with a different glaze it may become tolerable porcelain." No such metamorphosis occurred. The Turks opened with a demand for the restoration, in Europe, of Turkey's 1913 frontiers, a proposition which the Allied statesmen received with smiles and, from one quarter, a murmured, *"C'est ridicule."* Otherwise they demanded the evacuation of Smyrna, full Turkish control of the Straits, and the withdrawal of foreign troops from Constantinople—demands "so extravagant," remarked *The Times,* "that to grant a tittle of them would be tantamount to tearing up the Treaty of Sèvres." The Greeks, who refused to sit down with the Angora delegation, were heard separately. They were content to reiterate the claims already made at other conferences by Venizelos, amplifying them with a well-selected flow of population statistics.

After hearing these statements the Allies proposed the appointment of an international commission, to investigate on the spot the distribution of the population in eastern Thrace and the province of Smyrna. They laid down the prior condition that both Greeks and Turks should accept the results of such arbitration. The Turks, confident that it would produce statistics in their favour, accepted the proposal on certain conditions. The Greeks, for the same reason, rejected it. The two delegations then had tea together "in apparent amity."

Thinking again, the Allies proposed a series of modifications of the Treaty of Sèvres, allowing concessions to the Turks on the Straits, Constantinople, and Kurdistan, with a League of Nations commission to

examine the now academic question of Armenia. Over Thrace there was
no further mention of a count of populations. Over Smyrna there was to
be an "equitable compromise." This amounted to a form of Greek autonomy which, as the Turks knew only too well from past experience,
was likely in the long run to lead to the severance of the province from
Turkey. Far from ensuring peace, Bekir Sami insisted, it would become a
"source of permanent conflict." Expressing, nonetheless, qualified approval
of the other proposals, he left for Angora to consult his government. The
Greeks likewise left for Athens.

The Greeks took with them the impression that Lloyd George, whatever the attitude of the French and Italians, was still on their side. Not
wholly satisfied, however, with his modification of their original claims,
they weighed in the balance against acceptance the more tempting solution of a renewed military offensive, whose success might well strengthen
their bargaining position. Whatever the official attitude of his government,
Mr. Lloyd George, they felt confident, would not disapprove of such a
step. They thought, "The great man is with us, and in his own way and
in his own time and by his own wizardry he will bring us the vital aid
we need."

Their psychology was not far wrong. "The Prime Minister," Lord
Curzon wrote to his wife, "is as convinced a Venizelist and phil-Hellene
as ever, and uses all the advantage of his position as Chairman in that
direction." Mr. Churchill, his adversary and Minister of War, urged upon
him in a memorandum the need for a peace with Turkey. "The alternative of the renewal of war," he wrote, "causes me the deepest misgivings.
I dare say the Greeks may scatter the Turkish Nationalists on their immediate front, and may penetrate some distance into Turkey; but the
more country they hold, and the longer they remain in it, the more
costly to them. . . ." After outlining the unfavourable effects of such an
action, he added, "In these circumstances it seems to me a fearful responsibility to let loose the Greeks and to re-open the war."

But Lloyd George was in no mood to heed such warnings. On March
23 the Greeks launched an offensive from Brusa and Ushak. At a Cabinet meeting Lloyd George explained that there was "a great concentration" of Turkish troops in front of them and that it was impossible to
prevent the Greeks from attacking in self-defence. According to War
Office information, there was, wrote Sir Henry Wilson, "no concentration of Turks on that railway, and therefore this coming attack is
entirely uncalled for and wholly unprovoked. And Lloyd George knows
this. The whole thing is a ramp, and a disgusting ramp. Because the

Turks are at this moment considering the terms offered to them a fortnight ago here in London, the Greeks, with the full knowledge of Lloyd
George, attack the Turks."

The London negotiations had at least given the Turks time to complete
the grouping of their forces, to bring up more arms, and to strengthen
the defences of Eskishehir. The two-pronged attack of the Greeks was
aimed against Eskishehir in the north and against Afyon Karahisar in
the south. The Greek forces captured Afyon without too much difficulty,
then established themselves to the east of it on the road towards Konya,
obliging Kemal to withdraw forces from the north to hold them. This
attack he later criticized as a strategical error. They should rather have
moved northwards to support and ensure the success of the attack on
Eskishehir.

As it was, following the same line of advance as before, they now met
with a stout resistance from the Turks, well entrenched and well supplied
with artillery on the escarpment before Eskishehir. It was only after
several days of fighting that they broke through the Turkish positions
at Inönü to look down once more over the plain before the city. But the
Turks brought up reinforcements, of which the Greeks had none, and in
a counterattack drove them back once more from the escarpment.

An American correspondent with the Greeks named Ernest Hemingway proceeded to "where they had made the attack with the newly arrived Constantine officers that did not know a god-damned thing, and
the artillery had fired into troops and the British observer had cried
like a child." It was the first time he had seen "dead men wearing white
ballet skirts and upturned shoes with pompoms on them." The Turks
had come steadily and lumpily, and running there themselves, and he
and the British observer had run too until his lungs ached and his mouth
was full of the taste of pennies and they stopped behind some rocks and
"there were the Turks coming as lumpily as ever." [1] This necessitated a
retreat of the Greek southern force from Afyon, the strategy of whose
advance Kemal had justly criticized.

The Greek losses were heavy but their forces had escaped destruction.
Professor A. J. Toynbee, retreating with one of their divisions towards
Brusa—"an interminable procession of troops, mules, ox-carts and lorries
crawling along a foundered road"—was puzzled that no enemy attacked
them from the mountains commanding their southern flank. [2] In fact the

---

[1] *The Snows of Kilimanjaro.*
[2] *The Western Question in Greece and Turkey.*

Turks had despatched all their available forces to cut the railway and the line of retreat of the southern force. But this they failed to do.

It was a failure blamed by Kemal on the faulty tactics and judgment of Refet whom, after an enquiry on the spot with Fevzi, he moved to Angora, offering him the post of Minister of Defence and placing both the armies on the western front under Ismet's command. Refet irked Kemal by an insouciant disrespect for his authority and a free-lance spirit in the field which amounted on occasion to irresponsibility. In Angora he could be kept under Kemal's vigilant eye, while Ismet could be trusted to carry out Kemal's intentions at the front.

Such was the second battle of Inönü, a place from which Ismet was later to take his name. Kemal telegraphed to him in the name of the Assembly: "The greed of the enemy has foundered and broken up on the rugged rocks of your resolution and zeal." Congratulating him on this great "holy war" and victory, Kemal declared that few commanders in the history of the world had been entrusted with a task so difficult as these two battles.

The victory was far from being final, but it was, as Kemal recognized, a turning point in the Nationalist fortunes. Still inferior in numbers and equipment, the Nationalists had shown themselves superior in staff work and strategy to the Greeks. It was hard for the Greeks to admit this. Taken by surprise, despite their preliminary reconnaissance, by the transformation of irregulars into regulars, they sought, in their disrespect for the Turk, to explain it, as Professor Toynbee recalls, by the myth of the hidden hand: "The Turkish artillery must have been served by Russian or German gunners to make such good shooting, Italian sappers must be traced in the trenches, French officers have kept the infantry steady. I convinced myself to my own satisfaction that this was a hallucination."

The old military spirit of the Turk had revived. A new army had been created, and it was led by young officers well trained in the art of modern warfare. From now onwards Kemal could see ahead of him, however remotely and faintly, the prospect of possible victory.

34 ► *Fall of Eskishehir*

The Allies, following the breakdown of the London Conference, declared their neutrality in the Greco-Turkish conflict. Neither this nor the Greek defeat at Inönü had any effect on King Constantine, who preferred to believe that Lloyd George, if not his government, would still give him backing. He might yet reign, as his namesake had done, in Byzantium.

Early in June 1921 he proclaimed himself supreme commander of the Greek forces in Asia and left for Smyrna—the first Christian king to set foot on Anatolian soil since the Crusades. Symbolically he stayed in the seaside suburb across the gulf, where Richard Coeur de Lion was supposed to have landed. In an interview with *The Times* he spoke of his forthcoming offensive and of his confidence that the Greek troops would finally break the Kemalist power. Then he left to inspect the front and to decide on the date of the offensive.

It was, as Churchill wrote, "the worst of all possible situations. The Greeks deserved at least either to be backed up through thick and thin with the moral, diplomatic and financial support of a united British Government, or to be chilled to the bone with repeated douches of cold water." Lord Curzon made yet another attempt at a settlement. Obtaining agreement from Briand in Paris, he repeated the former proposal for the autonomy of Smyrna, but with the withdrawal of Greek troops. If the Greeks would agree to this, the Allies would approach the Turks for a suspension of hostilities. The Greeks refused on the grounds that only military considerations now counted.

Thus the Greek Army, in Churchill's words, was soon "marching steadily forward through harsh and difficult country to engage in the greatest campaign undertaken by Greece since Classic times." It had a slight superiority in arms, aircraft, and supplies. The initial objective once more was the railway. This time, however, the main attack came in the south instead of the north, and was aimed at Afyon Karahisar and Kütahya instead of Eskishehir. It was planned to take Eskishehir, the key to western Anatolia, not by a frontal attack but by a turning movement from the south.

The plan was successful. From Brusa the Greeks sent one column eastwards to hold the Turkish northern forces and another southeastwards, by a march through the mountains, to attack Kütahya; from Ushak, which had the advantage of a direct railway link with Smyrna, they sent a third and stronger column to attack Afyon Karahisar. They captured it, then moved northwards up the railway to converge with the second force and capture Kütahya. Eskishehir and its communications with Angora were immediately threatened with encirclement.

Ismet, from his headquarters in a village on the outskirts of the city, was faced with the responsibility of deciding on its evacuation. He was anxious, discouraged, indecisive. Halide Edib, retreating with a party of wounded, found him seated in a bare low-ceilinged Anatolian room. He wore, as he always did during a campaign, the khaki uniform of a private soldier. Behind his cordial manner "his face was haggard and his eyes feverish, and the lines about his mouth and eyes had multiplied." Here, for the first time in his career, was a crisis which might well prove a catastrophe. He was called upon to order a retreat whose results for his country would be incalculable and which would inevitably be criticized as a major national failure.

Halide tried to tell him that the heroic efforts of his army outweighed any failure. "But he did not agree with me. He told me with bitterness that it was only success that mattered. The world never considered sacrifice, however sublime and great it might be, if it was not crowned with success." But later, as they dined together off grilled tomatoes in the open air of the hot summer night, Ismet told her with an air of relief, "Pasha is coming." The decision would be his.

Halide proceeded on her journey. At the station in Eskishehir

the lamps glared like so many wicked eyes. Women sat on the open trucks, near their goods, nursing their babies. Women swarmed over the station, trailing their household goods and holding the hands of their bewildered children. . . . Women looked up at the sky, frightened; the station lights were brilliant; the aeroplanes might come. Mustafa Kemal Pasha stood on the platform and talked with the high officers. His face was greyer than his kalpak, a kind of rigid mask which hid the man behind. They all looked unconcerned, while the women squatted in rows with their kitchen utensils scattered around them. They stared at the group with infinite bitterness, but with the inexhaustible patience which belongs only to Anatolians.

Beneath the grey mask Kemal was resolute. None of this was wholly unexpected. Had he not himself criticized the strategy of the Greeks three months before, in storming Eskishehir by a frontal attack from the west instead of a flank attack from the south? This time, as though answering his criticism, they had done just that. They had reached the city, whose loss thus became inevitable. Unlike Ismet, Kemal, as his military career had shown, had no fear of making ruthless or unpopular decisions. As soon as he reached Ismet's headquarters he surveyed maps and telegrams, summed up the position, and without hesitation, on his responsibility as head of the government, ordered a general retreat. Rear-guard actions must be fought to cover the withdrawal and to allow time for the dismantlement and removal of the munition works, arsenals, and training camps which had been assembled in the city. But its fortifications, strong and laboriously constructed as they were, would have to be scrapped. Having arrived at this drastic and courageous conclusion, Kemal returned by train to Angora.

Here, from his headquarters, he followed the retreat. Halide Edib found him "discomposed and sullen." Ismet, with his rear guard, was still fighting before Eskishehir. Kemal invited her to stay to hear the result. As they sat over cups of coffee he incessantly nagged at his staff for news.

As his aide-de-camp came in to tell him the whereabouts of this or that regiment, he grew restive, and his language became more and more realistic; the men in command at that unfortunate battle would have been aghast at the names he called them. Again the morning came, the lamp paled out, and he said with a tone which was almost a groan, "Ismet has lost the battle for Eskishehir. Let us have another cup of coffee." Then he leaned against the desk, his face greyer and more discomposed as he smoked. Dr. Adnan came in, with a smile on his face. He had been with Fevzi, who he declared to be "the most hopeful sight in the universe; he believes that all this is tending to the final defeat of the Greeks." Pasha laughed and called Fevzi Pasha a name which is not usually complimentary, though one saw that he was well pleased at Fevzi Pasha's optimism. He was always most superstitious at the critical moments.

Halide and his intimates saw him with the mask down. For others whose morale needed boosting he put on another mask and assumed another mood. To his journalist friend Falih Rifki he proclaimed with defiance as though to the world, "Whatever happens, we are going to remain in this country. We are going to defend every hill of our sacred Fatherland. We are going to die under our flag in the furthermost frontiers." Together they sat looking out into the moonlit August night and down over the plateau which spread nakedly away to the west. Now the enemy had reached its outer rim, and the future, to many at headquarters, seemed ominous. But Kemal spoke as coolly as though he were expounding a routine manoeuvre.

A map lay before them, and with his fine long-fingered hands, surely created, as it seemed to Falih Rifki, "only for handling the most delicate works of art," he traced the position. Drawing a line with his finger tips, he said: "Here we are now. Our forces are retiring in a half circle from the north and south of Eskishehir. The night is bright, and suitable for marching. But after the exhaustion and heat of the day this weather may lead to sleep. I have seen soldiers asleep while marching and especially while riding on horseback. I have a friend, a cavalry officer, who told me he only slept comfortably on horseback. When he got to bed he could not sleep."

The moonlight poured in through the curtainless window, merging with the harsh glow of the single petrol lamp to give Kemal's face the colourless aspect of death. But as he mused and joked he seemed to Falih Rifki to radiate vitality and power.

"They say drink is a touchstone among men," he continued, "but I say the real touchstone is a field of battle. At this moment, when I close my eyes, I can see just how all my friends are behaving. For instance, I know that the commander of this division has reached this village"—he pointed to the map—"that he has got himself the most comfortable house in the village and that he must be in a deep sleep of oblivion on his camp bed. Would you like me to prove this to you?"

He rang the bell for the duty officer and instructed him, "My child, get me at once the commander of the X Division." Falih Rifki could hear the telegraphist tapping away downstairs as Kemal continued, "By to-morrow we must have put a distance of at least a hundred miles between ourselves and the enemy. The most suitable place to stand is here, north of the Sakarya River. We shall fight a big battle only after we have reached it. The Greek Army, of course, will follow us. They will cross the plain here and advance towards here. This means . . ."

He was interrupted by the duty officer, who saluted and said, "Sir. The divisional commander has reached the village and is resting. Shall we wake him up?"

Kemal chuckled at his own psychological perception. "Didn't I tell you so? Now let's look at this man. Find me," he ordered, "the commander of the Y Division." He turned to Falih Rifki and winked. "He is not going to find him, because this man is marching very quickly to reach his appointed place as quickly as possible." The telegraphist returned to report that he had been unable to contact the divisional commander.

Kemal changed his tone. "The really important thing is to know what the enemy is going to do and how he is going to do it. Is he going to follow us now, while we are withdrawing in this systematic way?" Continuing to talk, he gave a feeling of confidence. Kemal knew in the calmer recesses of his mind that there was reason for optimism, as Fevzi had said. He knew that the enemy was superior in arms. His own army was still an incomplete fighting force. Lack of transport hampered its mobility; arms still came only slowly from Russia. There could be no question yet of risking the reserves—behind Angora, in Cilicia, around Amasya—which gave him on paper a numerical superiority over the Greeks. Confronted by this major offensive, Kemal, with these various factors in mind, judged that the moment had not yet come to risk a stand. Territory must still be sacrificed in the interests of time. His plan of campaign remained as he had laid it down in a general directive after his visit to Ismet's headquarters:

After the army has been concentrated north and south of Eskishehir, we must establish a large area between it and the enemy's forces, so that we shall be able to carry on our reconstitution, reorganization, and reinforcement. For this purpose we should be able to retire even to the north of the Sakarya. If the enemy should pursue us without coming to a halt, he would be getting farther away from his base of operations and would be obliged to take up new positions. In any case, he would find that there were many difficulties in front of him which he would have to provide for. Taking this into account, our army will be able to rally and meet the enemy under more favourable conditions. The disadvantage of such tactics would be the moral shock which might be produced in public opinion by the fact that a wide territory and places so important as Eskishehir would be abandoned to the enemy. But these disadvantages will automatically disappear in a short time as a result of the successes which we shall achieve.

As Churchill summed up the position: "The Greeks had gained a strategic and tactical success; they had gained possession of the railway for the further advance; but they had not destroyed the Turkish Army or any part of it." That army had soon vanished from sight. It was trekking across the long weary wastes of the plateau towards Angora and the heart of the Anatolian homeland. Soon, essentially intact after casualties no greater than those of the Greeks, it had reached a point within fifty miles of Angora, behind the great bend in the Sakarya River on which Kemal had decided to stand.

All this had to be convincingly explained to the Turkish people. Their "moral shock," which Kemal had predicted, now fell upon him with full force. The Assembly was aghast at the catastrophe. The deputies bayed, first for the blood of Ismet, then for the appointment of Kemal himself as supreme commander-in-chief. Some sought by this to discredit him finally, to shift onto his personal shoulders the responsibility for what they took to be the irretrievable defeat of the army and the collapse of the Nationalist cause. Others, more loyal and less pessimistic, sought it from confidence that he could still save the situation. Others again opposed the appointment on the grounds that his personal implication in a further retreat would damage the cause irremediably. He should be held in reserve, they argued, only as a last resource, for which the moment had not yet arrived.

But by an ironical chance Kemal in this crisis had for the first time the support of the bulk of the Assembly—from his friends for the right reasons, from his enemies for the wrong ones. He would thus obtain the supreme command. But he must obtain it on his own terms. While the storm raged within and without the Assembly, he kept a wary silence, showing no disposition to accept the command, and thus turning into a positive conviction the general fear that disaster was inevitable. As soon as he judged that feeling had reached this point he called a secret session and mounted the rostrum. He agreed to accept the supreme command provided he was given the full powers of the Assembly. Only thus could he prepare the army with sufficient speed for the next round in the struggle. But, in view of his respect for the principle of national sovereignty, he requested that these powers be granted him only for a period of three months.

At this his opponents came out into the open. Some objected to his investment with such comprehensive powers. Others objected to the title of commander-in-chief, as being one inherent in the Assembly itself. Kemal insisted that they were passing through extraordinary conditions which called for extraordinary actions and decisions. He must be able to act energetically and swiftly, freed from the delays which would result from an appeal to the Cabinet or to the Assembly's authority. He must be able to give orders unconditionally, and this could be done only with full powers. Finally he overcame their objections and put before them an act conferring on him the functions of commander-in-chief. "In order to develop the forces of the army materially and morally to the fullest extent, so as to secure and consolidate the leadership and administration of these forces, the commander-in-chief will be authorized to exercise full powers in the name of the Assembly in these matters." The act was passed and Kemal undertook "to prove myself worthy in a short time of the confidence that you have reposed in me."

For the next three months Kemal was thus military dictator. He made immediate use of his powers by a drastic series of requisitions throughout the country, to obtain equipment for the forces. He commandeered, against ultimate compensation, forty per cent of all stocks of cloth, leather, foodstuffs, oil, and a variety of specified articles. The public were ordered to hand in all arms and ammunition suitable for military purposes. Ten per cent of their ox- and horse-carts were confiscated, and twenty per cent of their riding and draught animals. A census was made of all smithies and workshops. To bring home to all the gravity of the threat to their homes, Kemal demanded from each household a contribution for the forces of a parcel of linen, a pair of socks, and a pair of shoes.

This, as Kemal saw it ahead of his time, was total war. It was not "two armies fighting against one another but two nations who are both risking their existence and who summon for the fight all their resources, all their possessions, and all their material and moral forces. For this reason I had to interest the Turkish nation in the war in all their actions, their sentiments, and their conceptions, in the same way as the army at the front. Every single individual in the village, in his home, in the fields, had to consider himself in the same way as those fighting at the front." He added prophetically: "In future wars also the decisive element of victory will be found in this conception."

Churchill, who was to find it so many years later, describes how Kemal now "called upon the wives and daughters of his soldiers to do the work of the camels and oxen which he lacked." This mobilization of the women played a key part in Kemal's plan to rouse national sentiment, to point the need for a total effort, from civilians and soldiers alike. The arms and supplies, brought from centres as scattered as Erzurum and Diyarbekir, Sivas and Trebizond, were loaded onto the long peasant oxcarts beneath loads of hay for the oxen. The women, jacketed and pantalooned, with their feet in rope-bound woollens, drove the carts over mountain and plateau, covering hundreds of miles to the front at a mere three miles per hour, the solid wooden wheels creaking and sighing over the tracks as they had done since Sumerian times. Many of the women carried babies, lashed securely to their backs, as they loaded and unloaded the artillery shells and the rope-handled boxes of ammunition, carrying a shell on each shoulder and carefully covering it with a shawl, often at the expense of the baby, to protect the delicate fuses from dust or rain. When the carts broke down they hoisted the loads onto their backs and carried them thus for miles. To those who stayed at home fell the task of plough-ing and sowing and gathering in the harvest, despite the requisitioning of animals and implements, to produce foodstuffs for the fighting forces.

Refet was now an energetic and resourceful Minister of War. He speeded up the oxcart convoys by a system of relays, no longer changing the carts at each village as the peasants had preferred, but changing the oxen instead at fixed staging points, to draw them right through to the battlefield. He had carpets cut up to make tunics for the soldiers, and petrol tins converted into medicine canteens. In the absence of flour he instructed the peasants to boil up their raw grain or to grind it with pestle and mortar, until a single disused flour mill could be put back into commission. In the absence of timber, on this plateau denuded of trees, wooden houses were demolished to fire the trains.

Ploughshares were almost literally beaten into swords. The railway workshops in Angora were turned over to the forging of daggers and bayonets. Everywhere maintenance workshops were improvised, so that no weapon might go unrepaired. Refet was searching for recruits for the army from the remotest corners of the country. Recruiting appeals were broadcast from the tops of the minarets. Those who responded might have to travel on foot for hundreds of miles, often through country harassed by bandits. They might find, when they arrived, that there were no arms to equip them. On leaving for the front they would be instructed to pick up those of the dead and wounded—and those of the enemy. Meanwhile deserters were rounded up and rigorously punished, new classes were called up, and reinforcements drafted from Cilicia, the eastern provinces, the Black Sea coast, and other outlying parts of Anatolia.

The Turks had a respite of a bare three weeks in which to complete these preparations for the crucial battle. In Angora they were anxious weeks. Civilian morale fell to a low ebb. Many of the richer beys and merchants left the city with their families and possessions for the security of Kayseri. Others, even men in responsible positions, prepared to do so. Infected by their example, the peasant classes began to waver. The city was full of stragglers and deserters from the army; the Greeks were said to be near; nothing seemed safe. The women sat patiently waiting, veiled and dressed for the journey. Should they too abandon their lands and go?

Kemal himself left for the front with Fevzi, now his chief of the General Staff, on August 12, and took up his headquarters at Polatli, on the railway some fifty miles to the southwest of Angora. On arrival he rode to the top of a commanding hill, Kara Dağ, and dismounted to survey the probable line of the enemy advance. As he was remounting he lit a cigarette. Taking fright at the flash of the match, the horse reared away and threw him violently onto his side. A rib was broken, pressing on his lung and momentarily affecting his breathing and speech. A doctor warned him, "You will die if you go on."

"I shall be all right when the battle is over," he answered.

He returned to Angora for treatment but was back at the front after twenty-four hours. The injury continued to trouble him; he walked with difficulty and had often to rest, leaning against a table. Rumour exaggerated the accident: it was a bad omen that the commander-in-chief should be put out of action before the battle had begun. But even such an incident as this could be turned to propagandist advantage. Among the soldiers he was quoted as saying, "It is a sign from Allah. On the spot where one of my bones has been broken the resistance of the enemy will also be broken."

35 ► The battle of the Sakarya

The Greeks resumed their advance on August 13, 1921. Constantine's battle cry was, "To Angora!" and the British liaison officers were invited, in anticipation, to a victory dinner in the city of Kemal. The Anthens press drew a parallel with the noble conquests of Alexander the Great. The Greek armies were to cut once again the "Gordian Knot" as he had done, and thus to found an empire in Asia. For Gordion was on the direct line of advance. They forgot, as Professor Toynbee observed, that Alexander had not after all outwitted the oracle, since he had cut, not untied, the knot, thus failing permanently to annex western Anatolia to his kingdom, as Constantine now aspired to do.

In fact he did not intend permanently to occupy Angora itself. The object of the advance was predominantly political: to drive the Nationalist government out of the city to Kayseri or Sivas, and so fatally to undermine its authority and precipitate its fall, with the aid of risings in Konya and other disaffected areas. The campaign was in fact the product of divided counsels, for there were two general staffs, those of the King and of General Papoulas. There were officers on the general's staff who preferred, thinking in military terms, to dig in at Eskishehir, thus ultimately luring the Turks into a hazardous counteroffensive.

But the King's will prevailed, and now the Greek troops moved forward across the stern unending steppe, marching and halting and marching again for ten long days before they could see their enemy, getting farther and farther away from the gentler valleys and coasts they knew. The drought and the heat of the sun were more merciless than the blizzards and frosts of the earlier campaign. They carried no tanks for the storage of water, hence suffered from thirst. Their modern lorry transport broke down on the rough tracks and they had to depend on oxcarts, camels, and the normal regimental pack transport for supplies. Often they had little to eat but fried maize. When taken prisoner in the subsequent battle, they would beg bread from their Turkish captives. The dust choked them and the malignant malaria of the plateau thinned their ranks as they marched towards the valley of the Sakarya River— a ribbon of green in the tawny threadbare landscape.

Here the Sakarya, one of the three great rivers which carve their way across the Anatolian plateau into the Black Sea, throws out a loop before Angora. Flowing from the west, it coils suddenly northwards over a fifty-mile reach, then as suddenly turns back on its tracks to the west. It was beyond this reach, in a bare primitive region of plains patched with stubble and of hills rearing up from them, broken by outcrops of rock, that Kemal and his army awaited the Greeks. Their front was flanked north and south by two tributaries of the Sakarya, completing as it were a loop in reverse, while the main channel of the river protected its centre. Narrow, and at this season shallow, the stream ran through a series of gorges with precipitous banks and was bridged at only two places, north and south. Altogether the Turks had a good defensive position, with the advantage of an accessible railway and a well enough watered country to the rear of them.

Kemal's headquarters were at first on the railway, at Polatli, then on the hill of Alagöz which surveyed all the region, in a half-built mud-walled house with cobwebs festooned from the beams. Around him at all times was his black-clad Black Sea bodyguard, who had increased sufficiently in strength to fight in the battle as a separate unit. He wore the uniform of an ordinary soldier, without badges of rank, for the Assembly had given him no official military status and he had had none since his dismissal from the Ottoman Army. With his injured rib still in bandages, he directed the battle from a seat brought from the train, unable—perhaps

fortunately—to hurry on horseback from one sector of the front to another, and thus always on the spot to conduct its general course.

With him as he welcomed Halide Edib—now an acting corporal—was
Colonel Arif, a boon companion of his drinking and wenching life,
whom he had known from his cadet days, who had been at his side
since the start of the Revolution, and whom, in his recent dismissal from
a divisional staff post, on account of his drinking habits, Kemal had
attached to his military Cabinet. Arif resembled him closely, with "the
same stern elegant figure, the same lines of the head, the same cynical
curve on the thin-lipped and tightly closed mouth. . . . The same blue
eyes, but they protruded slightly and were not so pale." Arif was his most
intimate confidant at this time.

To Halide there was something about Kemal, here at the Sakarya,
"which he never had before or after. He was less cynical; he was not quite
sure that this would lead to victory, and he saw that he had to die with
the rest if the disaster took place. He was feeling almost as a condemned
man would feel towards his comrades who will die with him." Leaning
painfully over a map on the table, he treated her to a lucid survey of the
military position.[1]

There, as she saw it, "was the Sakarya traced out 'like a magic coil' on
the paper." To her feminine imagination "the Greek Army was a long
black dragon coiling towards Angora to devour it. The Turkish Army was
another long coil stretching out in a parallel line on the east of the
Sakarya in order to reach Angora first and prevent the black dragon
from swallowing it." What would happen, she asked, if the Greek dragon,
"so much thicker and so much bigger than ours," reached Angora first
and left the Turks behind? Kemal "chuckled in his dangerous, tiger-like
way" and replied: "I will say *'Bon voyage, messieurs!'* And I will attack
them behind and they will perish in the wilds."

This was, in fact, the first Greek plan of attack. Their intention was to
turn the enemy's left flank and so open the road to Angora from the
south. They made an exhausting detour through the desert to do so, their
long marches hampered by shortage of water and lengthened by the
use of inaccurate maps. On August 23 they engaged a division on the
Turkish left, south of the stream, and forced its withdrawal after an all-
night battle from the hilltop of Mangal Dağ. This initial setback brought
a ruthless order from Kemal, dismissing the divisional commander for
retiring without orders and stressing that any such failure in future
would be as drastically punished. For it was the task of the army to pre-

[1] See maps following page 587.

vent any Greek soldier from setting foot in the centre of Turkey. On hearing afterwards that the commander had in fact been acting under superior orders, Kemal reinstated him. But the order had served as an example to the rest, putting them on their mettle for the battle to come.

Then suddenly General Papoulas changed his tactics. An error in air reconnaissance contributed to the change. This showed substantial Turkish concentrations on the left flank and suggested that the Turks were shifting their forces in that direction. The outflanking movement thus seemed to him too hazardous, extending too far a line of communication already harassed by the Turkish cavalry. Thus he switched his main force northwards to make a frontal attack nearer the centre, where in fact the Turks were more strongly entrenched. For the purpose the general threw bridges across the river.

The ensuing battle lasted for twenty-two days and nights. Kemal afterwards claimed that it was, by one day, the longest pitched battle in history. The fighting was fierce and murderous. The Turkish positions were centred on a series of heights, and the Greeks had to storm and occupy them, one after the other, against the stubborn infantry defence at which the Turkish soldier excelled. The Turks held certain hilltops and lost others, while some were lost and recaptured several times over, in assaults which wiped out unit after unit. Yet they had to conserve men, for the Greeks held the numerical advantage. Thus circumstances taught Kemal a new tactical lesson: this was no longer the Gallipoli Peninsula, where he had thousands of fully armed reserves to throw recklessly into the battle. He talked once or twice of possible failure and withdrawal to Sivas. But Arif twitted him ironically: "You will always find enough men in this country to send to death with or without reason. No one ever asks questions about the waste of human life." [2]

Kemal kept in his head every detail of the forces at his disposal—the strength of each unit, its disposition in the field, the qualities of its commanding officer. Perusing each evening the order of battle, he would pounce on any error, however minute. Arif, who had been trained by the Germans, complemented him with his knowledge of the lie of the land and of the other officers and men. As Halide describes them:

He leaned over the pasha's shoulder, his face looking like that of a twin brother and saying in his low voice, "The village X lies ten kilometres to the north; there are two mounds on the left." "Excellent—the commander of the regiment?" "Like wood—stupid—but what a soldier!—and then men are veter-

[2] Arif was executed following the Smyrna trials, in 1926.

ans. No fear of artillery panic in that quarter: when they exhaust their ammunition they will fight with bayonets, commander and all."

Sometimes at these sessions Kemal reminded her of a novelist working out a plot, as she herself might have done. The battle was the theme, the pins in the map were the characters. The characteristics of each must be considered in fitting together the general pattern and prompting the story's development. Kemal studied the forces of the enemy as minutely as his own. At one crucial moment during the battle his intelligence reported that the position was lost, because the Greek concentrations were too strong for the Turkish defences. Kemal instructed, "Bring me all last week's reports on the placing of the Greek units." He studied them, then said, "The intelligence branch is mistaken. We have the enemy beaten."

The front which Kemal had to control was some sixty miles long. His tactics were defined in an order to his officers, issued at a critical stage in the battle: "You will no longer have a line of defence, but a surface of defence. Retiring groups will halt when they can, but the whole line will not retire to form a new front. All of Turkey shall be our surface of defence, upon which our units will resist everywhere and all the time." Not an inch of the country should be abandoned until it was "drenched with the blood of the citizens. Every unit, dislodged from its position, but every unit, large or small, re-establishes itself in face of the enemy at the first spot where it can hold its ground, and goes on fighting. Units which observe the neighbouring ones forced to retire must not link their own fate to theirs; they must hold their positions to the end."

Section after section of his front was pierced by the Greeks, but the gap was filled by reinforcements for as long as they lasted, in as short a time as possible. Thus, though the Greeks advanced, their progress was slow. In ten days' dogged fighting they gained ten miles. In attack, Papoulas could not apply the same principle as Kemal in defence. Units which had broken through would have to halt until their neighbours caught up with them, thus giving the enemy time to reinforce and recover.

The Turkish situation, nonetheless, was acute. Though the attack had come virtually in the centre, it shifted round once more to the left. The outflanking of the Turkish armies and the advance on Angora was still the main Greek objective. Here gradual progress was made, and the Turks had to abandon several positions. Their line had swivelled round until its axis was rather from east to west than north to south, and at the eastern end of it the Greeks were now nearer to Angora than the Turks themselves at the western.

The central key to the defence—and thus to the salvation of Angora—was a long broad broken ridge named Chal Dağ, rising a thousand feet from the plain between the two principal Turkish positions, to command the railway to Angora and the whole battlefield. Flatly scored with a pattern of vertebrae like the hide of a reptile, it offered little cover and was hard to defend. "Until they occupy the Mount of Chal," Kemal would say, "there is nothing serious to worry about; but if they do that, we had better look out—they could easily occupy Haymana, and after that they have us in a trap." The people of Angora might console themselves with the heroic thought that there were still several more hills between Chal Dağ and the city and, as one of them put it, "if we leave so many dead on the summit of each one of them, the enemy, on arriving here, will be reduced to about fifty. And those we shall beat to death with sticks." But at the front the position was known to be critical.

One evening the news came that Chal Dağ had fallen and that the Greeks were advancing towards Haymana. Halide recounted the scene at headquarters:

There was grim silence everywhere, and the ugliest sort of fate seemed to hang over everyone in the headquarters. Mustafa Kemal Pasha was most affected. He fumed, swore, walked up and down, talked loudly, summed up the situation with the rare lucidity of a delirium, and tormented himself with indecision as to whether he should order the retreat or not. And I sat opposite him feeling as if the iron curtain of doom, something like the fire curtain of a theatre, was coming down, ever so slowly but surely.

The fight for Chal Dağ had raged for four days. First the Greeks, exploiting a gap in the Turkish line, drove back the cavalry unit which held it, but were that night driven back in a counterattack by the infantry. They maintained their pressure, at the same time now reinforcing it with an attack on Haymana, which the Turks resisted with the loss of as many as eighty-two officers and nine hundred men, until lieutenants were commanding battalions and a division of artillery was reduced to seventeen shells. Next day the Greeks captured the mountain in an engagement so confused that at one moment two soldiers, drinking from a spring beneath it, looked up at one another and ran off in different directions—for one was a Turk and the other a Greek. Having taken it, the Greeks advanced towards the village beyond.

But in Kemal's headquarters, at two o'clock in the morning, the telephone rang. Fevzi Pasha was on the line. He had been in the field throughout the battle, coming little to headquarters. He still maintained the serenity and certainty of success which had sustained him and those around him. He had a strange light in his eyes and "the air of a man who has a great secret conviction." This came in part from his religious faith. At the front he moved from trench to trench, reciting passages from the Koran to strengthen the morale of his men. On one occasion, when Kemal sent for him urgently, he could not be found. Finally an officer came upon him behind a large rock, out of sight of headquarters. He was tranquilly performing his devotions.

Now, at this critical moment, Kemal's voice is heard speaking to him over the telephone: "Mustafa Kemal speaking. Is that you, Pasha Hazret-leri? What? Did you say that the day is in our favour? Did I understand right? Haymana is nearly occupied—do you say that the Greeks are at the end of their strength? What? A coming retreat of the Greeks?"

As he returns to the group, "there is a strange chuckle in his throat, half amused, half pleased. Will the division he is sending to close the gap be there before the Greeks make another move? He calculates, writes, the red and blue flags are moved hither and thither. There are enormous blue circles around his eyes, he looks like a face in Dante's inferno, tortured beyond words."

"Hadn't you better rest, Pasha?" Halide says.

"No, I cannot," he says hoarsely. "Let us have another coffee. Is that rascal Ali asleep?"

This was the turning point of the battle. The two armies had momentarily fought themselves to a standstill. Each was ready to retreat. But it was the Turks who held on the longest. The Greeks were too exhausted to follow up their attack on Haymana, and the Turks brought up reserves to close the gap in their line. It looked as though the force of the Greeks was spent. Their shortage of food and water had begun to tell. Their artillery had so squandered its ammunition in the early days of the battle that few shells remained. Their casualties were such that, according to prisoners in Turkish hands, their companies were reduced from a hundred and fifty to thirty men.

The Turks were now in a position to strike back. But there was more hard fighting to be done. Kemal had checked the Greeks on his left and had so saved Angora. But he still had to drive them out of central Anatolia. He switched troops to the right and the centre for a counter-offensive. Here they confronted Greek units which outnumbered and out-gunned them. For three days they fought stubbornly. More effective, however, in defence than in attack, the Turks were repulsed on three fronts, with heavy losses on both sides. They too were expending their last reserves of ammunition. A group commander warned Kemal that only one counterattack would be possible. Kemal decided on the point at which to make it and called up reinforcements. He insisted on commanding one of the artillery units in person. When the engagement was over Kemal saluted and reported to him, "Commander, the position is taken. We have no more ammunition."

Units were clamouring for it everywhere. Kemal-ed-Din Sami, an army group commander, demanded shells from the general inspector of artillery, and on his refusal raged and threatened him with death, receiving only a smile in return. In the middle of the night he telephoned to plead with Kemal personally, but with no more success. The officers at headquarters talked in awed tones of the group's grave losses. But Kemal, who knew his commanders, merely grinned and remarked, "It is not as bad as he says."

Despite Fevzi's insistence, it could not yet be certain that the Greeks would retreat. In a brief reversion to positional warfare they were digging in at points east of the Sakarya. Then the fighting was resumed. Halide Edib watched the scene from a hill overlooking the wide Sakarya Valley, where clouds of earth and smoke rose into the air. Kemal's sergeant, Ali, came to her. "Your left spur is put on the wrong side. Pasha sent me to put it right," he said with a grin. And over his shoulder she saw Kemal's face peering from a trench and laughing at her. He called her into the trench, saying, "We are fighting," with the delighted voice of a boy who is at his favourite game.

"We are attacking Dua Tepe," Kemal explained, "the highest hill on the left." The hills surrounding the valley below were "lively with the lugubrious intonation of artillery and the nervous *tic-tac* of machine guns. Through the field glass . . . I could see men coming nearer and nearer and even the fall of the men in the front line, leaving it indented and broken, and the final onslaught with bayonets. Thus the ants take their exercises around the small yellow mounds of their nests."

Then Kemal said to her, "Do you see that black pyramid, very pointed? It is called Kara Dağ. Look there through the opening and you will see the Greek retreat."

She looked and saw "a mighty cloud of dust rising from the ground to the sunlit sky, and a dark mass flowing ceaselessly like a flood."

Kemal went on: "The Greeks are fighting gallantly, their artillery is doing its utmost, and sacrificing itself to cover the retreat of the main forces."

Kara Dağ, the summit on which Kemal had broken his rib and which had been the centre of some of the fiercest fighting, was recaptured, at

the cost of half a division. On September 9 Kemal moved his headquarters forward. Corporal Halide was with them. They established
temporary offices on a train near Polatli, loading the horses onto trucks.[3]

Would the retreat become general? Would the Greeks face the hazards
of a last defensive battle with the Sakarya River at their backs? The
Turkish cavalry was continuing to harass their supply lines beyond the
river. Farther still to their rear the Turkish guerrillas came to life once
more, sweeping down from the mountains to harry the Greek transport,
raid stations, destroy stretches of railway. The Greek troops, many of
them Turkish subjects who, if captured, stood to be court-martialled
and shot for treason, were growing discouraged. A young prisoner had
said, "They tell us that Angora is behind every mountain we attack; but
sixteen days have passed and no Angora. They tell us that if we fall into
the hands of the Turks we'll be killed, and they drive us on with machine
guns." Now the Turkish net threatened to close around the Greeks as,
a few days earlier, the Greek net had threatened to close around the
Turks.

Then the order for a final retreat came from Athens. By September 12
no Greek unit remained east of the Sakarya. The Greeks were trailing
back to their starting point on the rim of the plateau, scorching the earth
as they went, evading the pursuit of the Turks, who were too exhausted to
press it home but for a spectacular cavalry sweep on the town of Sivrihisar. King Constantine had attempted, for political motives, a task beyond
his military powers. Geography had defeated him. The Gordion of
Alexander, with its bridge across the Sakarya River, had been abandoned,
the knot still untied. As Professor Toynbee enquired: "Would a Greek
army ever penetrate that distance into Anatolia again?"

Kemal, in praising his troops, ascribed their salvation of "our sacred
country" to the grace of God, but later credited it to their sense of a new
ideal, that of national independence. After the battle he changed into
civilian clothes, with a pair of smart white suede gloves, and returned
unannounced, in his decrepit staff car, to Angora. Walking into the
Assembly, he received an ovation, which the people of Angora, who had
lived for three weeks with the sound of the guns, then had heard it
recede, carried on through the night amid a blaze of torches. With the

[3] Here Halide met Captain Fazil, the hero of the Turkish Air Force and a man of
French education, who with a single reconnaissance aircraft claimed to have
achieved more important results than the Greeks with a squadron. When she had
asked his liaison officer what she could do to help Fazil, he replied: "Please send *Le
Temps.* Fazil wants only that." And thenceforward he got it.

aid of maps Kemal gave the deputies a precise review of the battle and the lessons to be drawn from it. Jesting to a friend, he remarked, "I think that what I do best is my job as a *soldier*."

Simultaneously *Te Deums* of thanksgiving were being sung in the churches of Athens. The battle had been, in a sense, a drawn one, since both armies remained in being to fight another day. But as Churchill summed it up: "The Greeks had involved themselves in a politico-strategic situation where anything short of decisive victory was defeat: and the Turks were in a position where anything short of overwhelming defeat was victory. No aspect of this was hidden from the warrior-chief who led the Turks." He was now promoted by the Assembly, on the motion of Fevzi and Ismet, to the rank of marshal and endowed with the honorific Moslem title of Gazi, meaning "Conqueror," or traditionally "Destroyer of Christians."

Years later Kemal was presented by an artist with a large picture of the Battle of the Sakarya, in the foreground of which he was shown prancing across the battlefield on a magnificent charger. The painter, awaiting his congratulations, was taken aback when Kemal ordered sternly, "That picture must never be exhibited." There was an embarrassed silence. "All those who took part in the battle," Kemal explained, "know very well that our horses were all skin and bone and that we were hardly any better ourselves. Skeletons all of us. In painting those fine warriors and sleek horses, you dishonour Sakarya, my friend."

36 ► *The Turco-French treaty*

The repulse of the Greeks at the Sakarya was swiftly followed by a strengthening of Kemal's international position. Secret negotiations with the French, which had been dragging on throughout the hot Angora summer, now reached their conclusion with the signature of a Franco-Turkish agreement. The intense indignation of the British was thereby aroused.

It clinched a policy which the French had been pursuing for some time past—that of opposition to the Greek offensive and support for Kemal. This was based on three main considerations—economic, political, and military. Firstly the French enjoyed comfortable financial and cultural assets in Turkey, with which the extension of Greek rule into Asia Minor might well interfere. Secondly they were jealous of British political power in the Middle East and saw Lloyd George's support of the Greeks as a design to perpetuate it. Finally the French, looking more realistically than the British at the Anatolian scene, soon saw that the Allies would not be able to enforce drastic peace terms on a Turkey which was prepared to resist them, and that the Greeks would not be able to enforce them without a degree of aid which the Allies were not prepared to give. Their own military experts had declared that the Greek invasion of Anatolia was not a practicable operation; and this was a view which the Battle of the Sakarya now seemed to have vindicated.

At the London Conference the French had come to a separate agreement with Bekir Sami by which hostilities in Cilicia, which had continued sporadically since the breakdown of the local armistice, would end. The French would evacuate the territory north of the agreed Syrian frontier and receive in return economic concessions, covering mines, railways, and other development projects on a fifty-fifty Franco-Turkish basis. The Italians had reached a parallel agreement by which Italy would support Turkey's territorial claims in return for similar economic privileges over a wide area of southern and western Anatolia.

On Bekir Sami's return to Angora, both these agreements were repudiated by Kemal without even consulting the Assembly, on the grounds that they simply acknowledged the division of Anatolia into Allied spheres of interest. He wanted peace in Cilicia, if only to release troops much needed for his western front. But he wanted it, and with the evident deepening of the rift between France and Britain now knew that he was likely to get it, on his own terms. He had not long to wait. In June 1921 the French sent a semi-official emissary to Angora in the corpulent form of Monsieur Franklin-Bouillon, an ambitious ex-deputy of jovial demeanour and unorthodox outlook, whose mission could be explained away in terms of his journalistic and business interests.

Franklin-Bouillon was soon on close terms with Kemal, presenting him with a consignment of French brandy which lent a convivial air to their initial conversations. They talked freely and at length, with much frank disagreement on either side. One night, when deadlock seemed to have been reached, Kemal's Foreign Ministry adviser turned to him and whispered, "It's no good. Let's stop for tonight." "No," Kemal replied firmly. "They'll stop"—and after another round or so of brandy the French delegates proposed an adjournment until the morning. Kemal had talked and drunk them to a standstill.

The two sides started from opposite poles, Kemal insisting on the National Pact, Franklin-Bouillon on the Treaty of Sèvres. But the gap was gradually narrowed and in due course Franklin-Bouillon was able to return home with an optimistic report for the French government. Kemal's concrete proof of power at the Sakarya, soon afterwards, resolved any doubts in Paris as to his capacity to win. It was swiftly followed by

Franklin-Bouillon's reappearance in Angora. Here, on October 20, he signed an agreement with Kemal which amounted to little less than a separate peace between France and Turkey.

It gave the Turks all they needed. It allowed for the evacuation of Cilicia, an adjustment of frontiers to Turkey's advantage between Cilicia and Syria, and the establishment of a special regime in Alexandretta to safeguard the interests of the Turkish population. In return the French obtained the concession they sought covering rights over certain stretches of the Baghdad Railway. But no other economic concessions were incorporated in the treaty.

On the French side the agreement represented a realistic move to reduce unpopular military commitments and to strengthen their position in Syria, where their true Middle Eastern interests lay. They now handed over to the Nationalists large stocks of arms, including Creusot guns, munitions, and other war materials, with the implication that more might well be available. This went far to redress the military balance between Turks and Greeks.

The Angora agreement, following and seeming to confirm his victory at the Sakarya, secured Kemal's prestige in the eyes of the world at large. For the first time, thanks to his determined and patient diplomacy, Nationalist Turkey had won official recognition from a Western power. She had won it, moreover, on terms wholly favourable to her national interests.

In London the agreement inspired Lord Curzon with feelings of "astonishment and almost of dismay." Here was an end to all mediation. Rumbold wrote to him from Constantinople that the "dishonourable" action of the French had compromised the whole Allied position: "The Nationalists are more uppish now than they have been for a long time past." Curzon, after a series of interviews in London with Monsieur Gounaris, the Greek Prime Minister, sought to retrieve the position by arranging a meeting of the Allied Foreign Ministers, to agree upon new peace terms, and subsequently a meeting of the Supreme Council in Constantinople, to place them before the belligerents. But early in January 1922, following a meeting of the Supreme Council at Cannes, Briand fell from power. He was succeeded as Premier by Poincaré, who refused to agree to any such conference. He had his way, and received support from the fact that the Italian government too had fallen. Thus the Anatolian winter wore on, the campaigning season approached—and the Allies did nothing.

··

It was not only the French who made peace overtures to Mustafa Kemal in the course of 1921. The British War Office—though not the Foreign Office—was thinking on similar if more tentative lines. Ever since the Allied entry into the city the British authorities in Constantinople had been inclined to divide into two camps, one supporting the Greeks and the other the Turks.

The diplomats were generally pro-Greek, imbued as they were with Hellenophile ideals and the Gladstonian conception of the "unspeakable Turk"; they were unfamiliar with the interior of the country and indeed with any Turks beyond a limited circle in Constantinople. The soldiers were generally pro-Turk, respecting "Johnny Turk" for his fighting qualities; regarding him, despite certain appearances, as a "gentleman." The military were in closer personal touch with the Turks in the course of their duties and were more aware of the strategical realities which underlay the position of Kemal and his forces. As the resistance proved more and more effective, the rift deepened and there were now in effect two policies in Constantinople: that of GHQ, which thought one thing, and of the British Embassy, which thought another.

Presiding over GHQ was Lieutenant General Sir Charles Harington, general officer commanding the Allied Forces of Occupation in Turkey. Summoned to London after the failure of the London Conference, Harington addressed a meeting of the Cabinet at which Churchill urged some arrangement with Kemal. The Cabinet was as divided as ever, and no decision was reached. But the idea gained ground among the soldiers in Constantinople of a direct personal approach to Angora.

A convenient pretext arose in the form of a specific need—that of negotiating for the return of British prisoners still in Nationalist hands, in return for Turkish prisoners in Malta, which had been agreed in principle at the London Conference. The general now sent an emissary to Anatolia to expedite the exchange and at the same time to sound out the Nationalist political attitude. The officers he chose for the mission were Major J. Douglas Henry, who had business interests in Turkey, and Major Stourton.

They arrived early in June and were received at Inebolu, the Black Sea port, by Refet. Kemal had arranged for a car to convey them to Angora, but the state of the road, owing to recent storms, made the journey impossible. He thus authorized Refet to speak for him, and through Refet expressed his readiness to release all the prisoners.

Major Henry gathered from Refet that Kemal wished to make contact with General Harington, to discuss broader issues. Refet claimed to reflect Kemal's general views—his antagonism to the French but not to the British; his mistrust of the Bolsheviks; his readiness for a plebiscite in Smyrna and Thrace. These remarks were interpreted by the major, and in due course by the general, back at GHQ, as a move towards peace talks. A meeting with Kemal was suggested, either at the general's villa on the Bosporus or at Inebolu. The British government, still hoping at this stage that the Greeks would agree to mediation, opposed any definite negotiations with Angora but favoured an unofficial preliminary contact to exchange views with Kemal. With the prior agreement of the French and Italians, Harington was thus authorized to proceed with his plan.

Major Henry was sent back to Anatolia, this time with a representative from the British Embassy, bearing a letter from General Harington to Kemal. He had been informed, he wrote, by Major Henry that Kemal wished to put certain views before him as one soldier to another. If this were so, he was authorized by the British government to proceed on board the battleship *Ajax* either to Inebolu or Izmit to discuss the situation openly and frankly. He was empowered to listen to any views which Kemal might express and to report them to his government, but not to negotiate or to speak on its behalf. He proposed that the interview should take place on board the British warship and assured Kemal that he would be appropriately received and would enjoy full freedom until he landed.

Harington's letter implied that it was Kemal who had asked for the interview. Kemal, in a polite but uncompromising reply, made it clear that it was Harington, through Major Henry, who had asked for it. Kemal was prepared to negotiate on the basis of those complete national demands with which the general was familiar. If this were recognized in advance he was ready for a meeting on land at Inebolu, where "the most agreeable reception" would be prepared for the general. But if he merely wanted to exchange views Kemal would send one of his colleagues instead.

Harington made no reply to this intransigent note. Talks on such a basis were out of the question. It was clear that Major Henry had exceeded his instructions, giving Refet the false impression that it was the British themselves who sought peace talks. Clearly, in the present confused state of British policy, no such man-to-man approach as the general envisaged was feasible. Kemal had thus negotiated instead with Franklin-Bouillon, on the basis that he had suggested to Harington. Hence the Angora agreement.

But the soldiers in the War Office and in Constantinople were obstinate. The fact that the French had stolen a march on them rankled. They were determined to have one more try. A few months later General Harington sent Major Henry to Inebolu again, but this time without Foreign Office approval. Sir Horace Rumbold knew nothing of the mission until the day after the major's departure from Constantinople. As before, its ostensible pretext was the exchange of the British prisoners.

In fact Major Henry had a week of talks with Refet, as one officer to another, on quite other matters. In the course of them he stressed the dangers to the British Empire from Soviet Russia. Refet did the same. He referred to the prewar threat of Pan-Slav expansion from imperial Russia which had prompted Britain to uphold Turkey's integrity, and the even more dangerous threat of it from Soviet Russia today, which called for a similar policy. To meet this, Britain should withdraw the Greeks from Asia Minor and Thrace and let the Turks defend the Straits on her behalf. Refet impressed Major Henry with the idea that Turkey was an altogether new nation, with which the British should negotiate. He remarked that in this respect he would sooner deal with Harington than with the embassy. Major Henry returned home to the War Office with a document in his pocket recording the talks.

Kemal, in the hope of driving a wedge for his own purposes between the two British departments of state, had briefed Refet astutely enough. But the wedge was not to be driven. The Foreign Office did not share the confidence of the War Office in Kemal's reliability, and moreover deplored such "escapades of amateur diplomatists." The military were thus firmly requested to keep out of politics. Rumbold was glad to hear from the head of his department that Henry had been given a "flea in the ear"; but the affair, as he confessed to Sir Horace, had been "the very devil."

The ostensible purpose of Major Henry's missions—the release of British prisoners—had now been achieved. Arrangements were concluded for the final exchange. The most important of the prisoners was Colonel Rawlinson, who had for eighteen months been imprisoned in Erzurum, growing sick and weak and near to starvation as time went by. The colonel and his men were now escorted to the coast. The exchange took place in the open roadstead of Inebolu, where a British cruiser awaited them with Rauf and other Turks from Malta on board. Here, as Rawlinson recalled, the British sailors, observing their pitiful condition, "came forward to assist us with the utmost gentleness and care to climb on board the launch."

On arrival in Constantinople Rawlinson was embarrassed to learn that there had been indignant questions in Parliament and reports in the press about his treatment in Turkish hands. Still, despite his experiences, a staunch believer in Anglo-Turkish friendship, he resented their exploitation for anti-Turk propaganda: "I considered our treatment to be due to the ignorance and neglect of duty of subordinate officers, and under these circumstances it appeared to me that a much larger view should be taken of the whole question."

Thus Rawlinson returned to London and Rauf to Angora. Fethi was there already. With the exception of Ali Fuad, still in Moscow, Kemal was surrounded by his old colleagues once more. They were to find many changes.

37 ▶ *Support from the east*

During the eighteen months that Rauf and Fethi had spent in exile, the face of their country had been transformed. Mustafa Kemal had set up a Parliament in Angora; he had laid down a Constitution; he had established, for all practical purposes, a new Turkish state. He had reduced the government of Constantinople to impotence; he had broken the unity and weakened the resolve of the Allies; he had all but defeated the Greeks. All this had followed directly on the actions of the Allies themselves—the occupation of Smyrna and of Constantinople, the Treaty of Sèvres, the civil war, the Greek invasion. But none of it could have been achieved without the blinding conviction and driving will power of Kemal. The Allies had furnished the spark for the smouldering national pride of the Turks but no other living Turk could so have lit and enflamed it as to confound altogether the Allied designs.

On the other hand he could hardly have done so without the initial help of his friends. From the start it had been in essence a joint and concerted effort by Kemal, Rauf, Ali Fuad, Refet, and Kiazim Karabekir, the five who, from Amasya, had issued the Declaration of Independence. Kemal was their leader, but it was the rest in a sense who had chosen him as such. His actions were based on their support and common counsel. He had needed at this stage their ideas, their co-operation, their encouragement, the free expression of their views. He needed Kiazim for the backing of his army, Rauf for his sage advice, Ali Fuad and Refet for their competence and influence in the field. Thanks to the four, he had progessed step by step from Amasya to Erzurum, to Sivas, to Angora. Thanks to the foundations which they had enabled him to lay, he was now the commander of a strong army and the head of a united state which was becoming recognized by the world at large. He was the Gazi.

But Kemal was not born for co-operation, except in so far as necessity demanded it. He was born to dominate. Aware of this, the early founders of the Revolution, while following him loyally, had watched him warily. They accepted his leadership but remained on their guard against the personal ambition that conditioned his patriotism. This was growing with every step in the country's resurgence. Had he not exclaimed unguardedly to Halide Edib, "I want everyone to do as I wish"? Was the original "band of brothers" to be supplanted by one Big Brother?

Already Ali Fuad, a possible military rival, had been moved out of the way, to Moscow. Kiazim Karabekir, petulantly voicing complaints and suspicions and criticisms, was conveniently out of the way on an eastern front where the battle had already been won. The position of Refet, outspoken, irreverent, fully aware of Kemal's failings, was productive of continual friction. The pattern had changed. Kemal's inner circle now consisted of Ismet and Fevzi, latecomers to the Revolution, men, for all their qualities, to be commanded rather than consulted, men who would "do as he wished." And on the periphery were yes-men of a lesser order —unscrupulous henchmen, unquestioning younger officers, admiring intellectuals and journalists.

It was into this atmosphere that Rauf, preceded by Fethi, returned at the end of 1921. In Angora Rauf was given an ovation by the Assembly and offered the Ministry of Public Works. There were insufficient votes to secure his election to the post: after all, despite his high reputation, he was personally unknown to most of the deputies. His opponents withdrew and he reluctantly accepted the post but resigned some weeks later on the pretext of ill-health. He had by now had time to study the parliamentary situation and judged that he could play a more useful role in opposition.

Of all Kemal's early associates Rauf, though there was at this time no quarrel between them, was the most opposed to him in outlook and character. Rauf was not a man to be commanded, as in his frank sailorly way he would tell Kemal; he was one to be consulted, to share, to discuss. Rauf was a democrat by conviction and temperament; Kemal was a democrat by conviction but an autocrat by temperament.

Rauf believed profoundly in the liberal principles of government by consent and lived up to them with the democratic virtues of tolerance, moderation, a sense of political balance and compromise. His experiences in Malta had done nothing to shake his deep respect for the British parliamentary system and for its constitutional monarchy—no more than Colonel Rawlinson's experiences as a prisoner in Turkey had shaken his belief in Anglo-Turkish friendship.

Kemal believed in these ideas less from theoretical principle than from a sense of their practical necessity for the conversion of his country from an Eastern empire into a Western state. Outwardly he lived up to them. He was assiduous in his respect for constitutional practice and in his observance of democratic forms. He made a habit of open discussion, seeming to consult his friends, seeking their opinions and using them, claiming to act with their agreement. But in fact, as a rule, he bore down their resistance by the weight of his words. It was his own rather than the general will that prevailed—though it might well be to the general advantage.

Within himself he was an amalgam of East and West. Western he was in his respect for the power of reason as opposed to that of emotion. Oriental he was still in his habit of overriding the principle of consent by the practice of authority. By contrast with Rauf, his were the autocratic vices of ruthlessness, intrigue, jealousy of rivals, and a demeanour towards his associates in which good fellowship alternated with suspicion and barely disguised contempt. For at the root of his attitude lay a profound belief, not altogether unjustified, in the superiority of his own ideas and capacities. Who but he could prescribe the national aims and achieve them?

Rauf, looking at the Assembly through Western eyes, saw that if it was to function as a healthy body it needed an organized opposition. This balancing factor was all the more essential at this time when Kemal held full powers, as commander-in-chief and President of the Assembly in one. Granted originally for three months, they were now renewed, despite some grumbling from the deputies, at three-monthly intervals, on the grounds that the military situation still called for a strong centralized control. Kemal had already strengthened his ascendancy over the Assembly through the formation of a Defence of Rights group—a party in embryo, with himself as chairman. Now, under the commander-in-chief law, it was redoubled through his personal control over the Cabinet itself.

When Rauf resigned from his Cabinet post Refet resigned from the Ministry of Defence, objecting ostensibly to the separation of its functions from those of Fevzi as chief of the General Staff, but actually to the Gazi's increasing arrogation of power to himself. Refet, according to his periodic habit with Kemal, temporarily withdrew from the scene. But Rauf, with Kara Vasif, a fellow exile from Malta, became the nucleus of an organized Second Group in the Assembly, designed to draw together the various elements of opposition and thus balance Kemal's First Group. He chose to work for it largely in the background, maintaining his good relations with Kemal and thus serving as a go-between, endeavouring to act among the rest as a calming and conciliatory influence.

To all these manoeuvres Kemal acceded with a good enough grace. He approved of an Opposition in theory—was not this the Western way? Moreover its leaders now were his friends and thus open to his influence. But in practice he mistrusted it. As he commanded in the battlefield of war, so he must command in the battlefield of politics. The ends of both were after all the same, the salvation and regeneration of the country, and to his military mind the means too should be similar. But this battle with his Opposition was not yet to be joined. Latent it was, but latent it must for the present remain. Rauf hoped, by the encouragement of a moderate and responsible Opposition, to hold the balance against the Gazi's extremists, and the Gazi did not openly discourage him.

This was a further period of waiting, of outward satisfaction fraught with inward tension. Many months must elapse before the fight with the Greeks could be resumed; and they were months to be devoted to the strengthening and arming of the Nationalist forces, this time up to the hilt. But now that the sound of the guns was momentarily stilled, Angora, for all its sense of discipline and dedication to the labours of the cause, permitted itself a mood of relaxation and even of gaiety, which was their natural complement.

The Gazi, well guarded by his turbaned Black Sea bodyguard, surveyed and dominated the expanding city from his house on the hillside at Chankaya, which had grown in size and where he was now able to live in reasonable comfort. A community of satellite chalets and villas was springing up among the vineyards around it, and his staff officers, now joined by wives unveiled in the Nationalist fashion and by families, were moving in to be at hand when required. During his walks he would drop in to call on them, impressing them by his informality. From midmorning onwards there was a continual coming and going of visitors toiling up the hillside on horseback or in carriages from the city below, to whom he was always accessible.

Kemal had furnished the rooms of the house in a comfortable if ponderous style. Leather armchairs were disposed among pieces of furniture of a noticeably Germanic origin. Turkish carpets covered the floors and a collection of arms, including a jewelled sword from the Grand Senusi, hung on the walls. The two principal rooms were greatly enlarged by a wide pentagonal alcove with high double windows around it. One of these was Kemal's office, the large modernistic desk so placed that he sat with his back to the windows, his eyes fixing a visitor already dazed by the light, whichever way he turned his head, and thus placing him at some disadvantage. The dining room, where each day visitors remained to meals, resembled an interior courtyard, reflecting Ottoman taste with its pots of flowers, marble fountain, and table of blue Kütahya faïence.

Kemal liked to walk in the gardens, starting to grow green with the shrubs and the trees he had planted, thrusting his hands in his pockets as he strode up the paths through the vineyards, smelling the freshness around him and watching the cloudscapes which played over the infinite expanses of the plateau. Over the crest of the hill a long track of dust betokened the ox-drawn convoys, winding towards the horizon, with the peasant women still in command as they bore arms to the front and returned for more.

At the end of the garden was a pink-washed kiosk which Kemal used as a guesthouse and where for some months Madame Berthe Georges-Gaulis stayed. A Frenchwoman and a journalist, he could talk with her, as he could not with Turkish women, of international affairs and of his plans for the country, while she could play a useful part in making the cause of the Nationalists known and understood among his new French allies.

One evening, suddenly relaxing after a heated diatribe against his British enemies—which Madame Georges-Gaulis, who had fiery political prejudices, was only too ready to echo—he called for music. The officers in the neighbouring houses were invited in with their wives, who came in evening dresses, their heads—but not their faces—covered with veils of the same material. Each of them carried a lute, which they played at his request and to which they soon began, in low voices at first, to sing traditional Turkish songs, tales of love and death and military glory. This was music which Kemal had loved from his childhood, and as they sang he took pleasure in translating and explaining the songs to his guests, humming in time with the solemn and often melancholy rhythm.

"Then," Madame recorded later, "forgetting for a moment the bitterness of conflict, he relaxed for the first time; his past came back to his mind. He described his first childhood; his mother who loved him passionately, his youth, his first troubles, his first successes, and he relived all this with the intensity, the fullness of impressions which he brought to everything. He became once more the man of the early days, the young officer surprised himself by the abundance of his gifts."

Zübeyde had now come to live at Chankaya. Sick and aging, bent with rheumatism, she had never recovered from the loss of her native Salonika. Anatolia meant nothing to her, but she fretted and pined to see Mustafa and finally, sensing that she had not very long to live, he fetched her to Angora. Presenting her to his friends, he made a move to kiss her hand, as he had always done, but she stopped him. He might be her son, but he was also now effectively head of the state, so it was for her to kiss his hand instead, and this she did. At Chankaya she had a house of her own, furnished in the old Turkish style to which she was accustomed. Here she would sit cross-legged on the floor before a brazier of charcoal. Her son treated her with the ceremony and respect due from a Turk to his mother. Each day he visited her formally, always sending to ask permission to do so, and thus giving her time to prepare for him. This, even if she were sick, she did with care. She grew harassed by the restless life of Chankaya and liked to pay visits to a tree-shaded spring near the Agricultural School, named Nectar of Willows, where Kemal arranged for her a one-room cottage, mud-walled and roughly timbered in the old peasant style.

She was like Mustafa in looks but, as Halide Edib recalls, "without the sinister expression of the face and the tiger-like agility of his slim body. She was built on a majestic scale. Although she was seventy, her big round face was hardly lined at all, and it still retained its milk-white and pink complexion. The eyes were of a darker blue, warm and affectionate, and the mouth was benevolent, although she had a temper equal to his in her own way."

She disliked Fikriye, largely from feminine jealousy, partly from a feeling that she was not good enough for her son. When Fikriye came into the room she "would bristle all over with resentment and boom out hints at young people in general which were meant to be for Fikriye Hanum in particular. The young woman sat opposite her, respectful but cool, and very conscious of the old lady's animosity."

Zübeyde scolded Kemal and spoke of him as though he were still a schoolboy, calling him "little Mustafa." Once at a circumcision party the Azerbaijan minister asked to meet her. Kemal had her fetched from the women's tent and made her sit down beside them. After they had talked for some minutes Zübeyde turned to Kemal and said with a frown, "Listen to what he is saying. He says you should be Sultan, that would be suitable for you." She added, "You must not be Sultan."

Kemal reassured her. "Don't worry. I'm not going to be Sultan, but I'm certainly going to be the head of this country. That's what the ambassador meant."

The social life of Angora at this time had more of an Eastern than a Western flavour. This followed inevitably from the close relations now established with the Soviet Union and its satellite republics. The Treaty of Moscow, preceded by a treaty with Afghanistan, had been followed by the Treaty of Kars, which confirmed the Moscow treaty in respect of relations with Armenia, Azerbaijan, and Georgia. This was followed in its turn by an economic and military agreement with the Ukraine and the arrival of a Ukrainian mission. A Turkish mission was sent to Tiflis, in Georgia, while diplomatic feelers had come from Bokhara, in Turkestan.

These small Turco-Slav countries, precariously placed as they were, saw Nationalist Turkey, with its aspirations so akin to their own and its independence now so evidently assured, as a potential bulwark against Russian domination. They thus sent to Angora embassies so large as to cause embarrassment in a city still short of accommodation. Their influx brought a convivial spirit to the austere city of the plateau. They entertained lavishly, with vodka and caviar, providing Kemal with an outlet for those festive proclivities which had been starved in him since his departure from Constantinople. They furnished him also with feminine company of a free and unconventional kind, soon giving rise in the strait-laced Moslem circles of Angora to lurid rumours of his carousals among the loose-living Slavs.

The Azerbaijanis were the most hospitable. At one of their dinners, when Ukrainians and Soviet Russians sat grouped around the table, the Soviet ambassador, Aralov, rose to his feet and, speaking for the benefit of Madame Georges-Gaulis in French, launched a strong attack on France as the Oppressor of the Oppressed in her policy towards the Russian Revolution. The Gazi, speaking in Turkish, dexterously retorted with a counterblast on the theme that "there are neither oppressors nor oppressed. There are only those who allow themselves to be oppressed. The Turks are not among these. The Turks can look after themselves; let others do the same."

One night at the Soviet Embassy—described by Angora as *chez les Bolshéviks*—the Gazi was in mischievous mood and began to tease the ambassador. Looking around at the rich carpets and the laden table, above which the portraits of Karl Marx and Lenin struck a bleak and unfamiliar note, Kemal, after some glasses of vodka, turned to his host and said, "I don't see among us any of the men who prepared this feast. Will you not invite them to join us?"

Aralov looked embarrassed but after a moment's hesitation sent for the cook and the other servants, who crowded in to join the guests at what the Gazi now described as a "classless" table. Warming to the theme with more vodka, he delivered a homily on the principles of equality which underlay the Russian Revolution. "Off duty," he said, "men are equal with each other. . . . Your Revolution does not acknowledge differences of class. It is the same in Islam, where rich and poor are equal." He turned to a porter who sat drinking by himself.

"*Tovarich!*" he exclaimed. "You can't drink alone. Come, let's all fill our glasses and drink together. They have a Turkish saying, 'Some drink, and some only watch, and the result of this is Doomsday.'" Toasts were drunk and then all the company danced. "What do you think of that?" Kemal remarked to his friends as they left. "They talk of equality but as soon as it comes to eating and drinking, class differences begin."

An important delegation from the orbit of the Soviets was that of the Ukraine, under General Frunze, who promised substantial shipments of munitions but went too far in offering to draft a plan of campaign against the Greeks, in which Red Army officers might participate. Kemal had not been best pleased when Aralov, on a visit to the front, delivered harangues to the troops on the glories of Bolshevik Russia and the brotherly generosity of its aid to Turkey; nor by the flood of congratulations from the Red Army which followed each stage in the subsequent campaign.

In Constantinople on the other hand, isolated from realities behind the double iron curtain of Anatolia and Russia, it was widely assumed that Kemal in his financial and military embarrassment would call in the Red Army to his aid. General Frunze's mission was interpreted as an attempt "by Bolos and Enverists" to get control; Sir Horace Rumbold himself had an idea, which he mentioned to Curzon, that it might be the intention of the Bolsheviks to instal Enver as their "Viceroy at Angora."

Enver, while the war was going badly for the Nationalists, had indeed organized revolutionary groups among the Turkish-speaking Moslems, and had planned to raise a Caucasian force which would march into Anatolia and overthrow Kemal's regime by a *coup d'état*. He tried through an agent to form a battalion in Trebizond, ostensibly in support of Kemal but in fact for this purpose. He received some support from dissident deputies in the Assembly, mostly former members of the Union and Progress party.

But Kemal's success at the Sakarya put an end to such dreams and conspiracies. Enver had been disappointed in his contacts with the Russians, who had not been inclined to trust him or take him too seriously. Thus, still in pursuit of Pan-Turanian visions, he turned eastwards. Collecting a few followers, he proceeded to Turkestan, where he helped to launch a war against the Bolsheviks with irregular forces of Turkish race. For a while he reigned as Emir of Bokhara. But the Russians sent strong forces against him and one morning in the summer of 1922 he died fighting them, hit by a salvo of machine-gun fire.

Meanwhile Jemal Pasha, who had similarly fallen out with the Russians, sent an officer to Angora with a letter to Kemal, requesting permission to return to Turkey. Kemal refused; and soon afterwards Jemal was assassinated in Tiflis. Thus Trans-Caucasia became a graveyard for the Young Turk leaders.

In the new diplomatic circles of Angora the Indian Moslems created around them a sterner atmosphere than that of the Slavs. At the Friday receptions of the ambassador of Afghanistan there was an abundance of turbans, flowing robes, pelisses trimmed with fur. He was struck, as were the other visitors from the East, by the order, the discipline, the upright bearing of Angora, where even the ill-dressed crowds had a martial air. Pan-Islamic in sympathy, he said to Madame Georges-Gaulis: "Islam is a large body of which Turkey is the head, Azerbaijan the neck, Persia the chest, Afghanistan the heart, India the abdomen. Egypt and Palestine, Irak and Turkestan are its arms and legs. When you deliver rough blows at the head, how can the rest of the body not feel it? England has hit our head too hard, and we have protested."

The East, with its dawning nationalist movements, had indeed begun to look to Nationalist Turkey for example and leadership. Here was the first oriental country to make a stand against Western imperialism and fight to throw off its yoke. The name of Mustafa Kemal spread throughout Asia, as that of Garibaldi had once spread throughout Europe, firing the imagination of all those peoples in whom the First World War had kindled a spark of national consciousness and awakened the desire for freedom. The news of his struggle had its repercussions throughout Syria and Egypt, as far as Persia, India, and even China. Here surely was the prototype, for others to emulate, of the Eastern nationalist revolution.[1]

Kemal was far from aspiring to Asiatic leadership. His eyes were steadfastly fixed on the West. But at this time, with half Europe still ranged against him, he had need of the moral and material support of the East. Watching him at work at Chankaya, Madame Georges-Gaulis observed "this constant communication with two poles; Asia, Europe; this facility of assimilating, without ever allowing himself to be submerged, of turning the helm sometimes to the right, sometimes to the left, to maintain equilibrium; of rallying to himself all the reasonable and conscious elements of the Islamic world." Publicly in his speeches he built up the idea of Anatolia as a "kind of fortress against all the aggressions directed to the East." The struggle was not that of Turkey alone. "It is the cause of the East. And until this purpose is achieved, Turkey is sure that all the nations of the East will stand by her."

Materially, his strongest support came from the Indians, who saw Nationalist Turkey as the only independent Moslem nation. The Khilafat Committee in Bombay started a fund to help the Turkish Nationalist struggle, establishing contact with a representative of Kemal in Constantinople who received constant letters of encouragement:

Mustafa Kemal Pasha has done wonders and you have no idea how people in India adore his name. The honour of the Turkish nation has been once again vindicated. We are all waiting to know the terms on which Angora offers peace to the Greeks. . . .

The Musulmans of India—particularly the poor and middle classes—are doing their very best in subscribing to the Angora fund. . . . May the Great Allah grant victory to the Armies of Gazi Mustafa Kemal and save Turkey from her enemies and the enemies of Islam.

Part of the Indian fund, which eventually amounted to some £125,000, was used to pay the army. But most of it was husbanded and later devoted to the construction of a new Parliament building in Angora and the foundation of the first Nationalist bank.

[1] Early in 1920 two emissaries from Syria had reached a tentative agreement with the Kemalists in Istanbul for Turco-Syrian co-operation against the Western Powers. This envisaged a unified command and ultimately a close treaty relationship between an independent Turkey and Syria on the lines of the former Austro-Hungarian Empire. But it was rejected by Feisal, King of Syria. Zeine N. Zeine, *The Struggle for Arab Independence.*

Roubles meanwhile were now coming from Russia, not indeed to the extent that the Russians had promised but in sufficient instalments to make up for the deficiencies in the promised supply of Russian arms. Much of the money was used for their purchase elsewhere, mainly in Italy, which had become, like France, a steady source of supply through the Mediterranean ports of southern Turkey. For Italy too was now an ally. She had withdrawn her troops from Anatolia and not long afterwards signed an agreement with Angora, comparable to that of the French, promising to support Nationalist claims at the Peace Conference and asking for no economic benefits in return.

Thus the Gazi was in a strong position. He had allies, he had arms, he had a recognized government and an army which was growing in strength from day to day. But he was in no hurry to resume operations. Time was on his side. His troops were defending their own homeland and their morale was high. Those of the Greeks were in a strange land, drawn into an escapade for which they had no great enthusiasm, and their morale was slowly deteriorating. Kemal would strike at them when his forces were entirely ready, when he felt certain of victory—but not a moment before.

Before he did so a last effort was made by the Allies for peace. The resources of the Greek treasury were dwindling. Monsieur Gounaris, the Greek Premier, having tried without success to raise either arms or a loan in London, warned Lord Curzon that the Greek command might be obliged to withdraw its forces from Anatolia. Curzon immediately proposed a meeting of the powers in Paris, with a view to securing an armistice, followed by a Greek evacuation on equitable terms for both sides. In anticipation of it, the Gazi sent his Foreign Minister, Yusuf Kemal, to Constantinople, en route for London. As the first Nationalist minister to visit the capital, he found himself an object of some curiosity, being greeted with marked affability by the French and with polite reserve by the British.

The Constantinople government was now little more than a shadow of a Cabinet, with a puppet Sultan at its head. Nevertheless it was now, as before, to send its own representative to Europe in uneasy harness with Kemal's. Though Rumbold had long since recognized that no settlement could be reached without Kemal, he was still working for some kind of fusion between the two governments, but with the emphasis rather on Constantinople than on Angora. He favoured the policy of strengthening the Sultan by offering him a reasonable treaty. The Sultan's delegate was Izzet Pasha, with whom Yusuf Kemal was instructed by Angora to make common cause. Both, however, left separately for London and were received separately, at Yusuf's insistence, by Curzon. Both stood firm in their interviews on the principles of the National Pact. Both were disappointed by Curzon's insistence that the Greeks should retain eastern Thrace, with Adrianople. He told them that he would try, in Paris, to secure an evacuation of Anatolia by the Greeks, but as a condition the Turks must accept an armistice first.

Curzon led the conference in Paris, wrestling with Poincaré throughout four exhausting days. To Austen Chamberlain he wrote: "I shall come back with a plan which I think it quite likely the Turks may ultimately refuse, but which will approve itself to the public opinion of the world as a just and generous solution." It was put to the Turks and the Greeks in two successive notes. The first proposed an immediate armistice. The armies were to stand on their present lines, with a neutral zone of six miles between them. The second proposed a basis for the discussion of peace terms of which the first provision would be a Greek evacuation of Anatolia. The Greeks accepted the armistice and expressed no views on the peace terms. The Turks accepted the armistice, but only on condition that the Greek withdrawal should follow it immediately, regardless of peace discussions. The Allies rejected this condition.

Passing through Paris on his way home to Angora, Yusuf Kemal explained to Poincaré that if a single Greek soldier remained on Turkish soil the Gazi risked being hanged before the Assembly's doors—at which Poincaré seemed suitably impressed. On Yusuf's arrival in Angora, Kemal remarked to him, "So you'll have what you wanted." As on his return from Russia, a year earlier, his report on the negotiations was in effect to give Kemal the all-clear for an offensive.

In reaching this decision, he was prompted by the conviction that it would be fatal to accept anything short of the National Pact. He had little faith in the British, far less in Lloyd George, hence no guarantee that the evacuation would in fact take place. As to the proposed peace terms, they were still linked, if in a greatly modified form, to the Treaty of Sèvres, the total rejection of whose very name was a fundamental article of the Nationalist faith.

Thus the four months that might have been devoted to the evacuation were in fact devoted to a further period of watching and waiting by the two armies, while the snows melted in the mountains, the crops sprouted on the plateau, and the sun hardened the ground to a point at which a successful advance of the Nationalists became a practicable venture.

38 ► *Preparations for battle*

Kemal, during these months, had been faced with the task of stiffening his own home front. His intransigence in face of the peace offer had not been wholly popular.

In Angora there was an element ready enough to accept peace at any reasonable price, even if it fell short of the National Pact. There was a disposition to trust the Allies, to contend that a settlement was possible without further bloodshed. Let the army stand on its present line and seek the national aims by negotiation.

Kemal was mainly concerned with the effects of such an attitude on the army itself. He thus toured the front to boost morale and found some of his fears confirmed. On announcing to one of his army corps commanders that he had rejected the armistice proposals, he received the reply, "How could you do that? To refuse such proposals was wrong." In the course of his tour he encountered the view that, since the Allies had clearly abandoned the Treaty of Sèvres, there was no reason to endure new and questionable sacrifices.

The deputies, in their ignorance of military matters, adopted a variety of attitudes. On the one hand there were the hotheads who called for an

immediate if only partial attack. On the other there were those who believed that the army was incapable of attacking at all and that Kemal
was merely exploiting his continued position as commander-in-chief to
strengthen his personal hold over the nation. Kemal's problem was that
he could not, for security reasons, disclose the actual strength of the army
or the extent of the arms which were coming in, mainly from secret
sources.

In a secret session of the Assembly he tried patiently to explain to them
that a half-prepared attack would be worse than no attack at all. He
taunted deputies for their defeatism. There were, he stressed, two fronts:
the outward and the inward, the foreign and the home. The outward
front was that of the army, opposing the enemy directly. The inward
front was formed by the whole nation. Neither could be shaken unless
the Assembly encouraged the enemy and discouraged the army by pessimistic orations.

The Gazi's powers as commander-in-chief had been renewed, with
many grumbles, for two further periods of three months. But in May its
renewal for a third term had been rejected by the Assembly, taking advantage of his absence through illness. The army was thus left without
a leader. The Cabinet proposed to resign. But the Gazi rose from his
bed and went down to the Assembly to answer his critics. After lecturing
it on the way in which such bodies normally conducted their affairs
in wartime, he declared that he had no intention of abandoning the army,
which had been for two days without a commander-in-chief. The debate
became heated, and there was a moment when both Kemal and one of
his more irresponsible enemies, Ziya Hurshid, were seen to have hands
on their revolvers. But when the question was put to the vote he was
confirmed in the command.

Nonetheless, many of Kemal's own friends remained uneasy. They
feared a drift from parliamentary government to a form of personal rule
by a strong man, comparable to that which was developing in the South
American republics. With this in mind they now worked on another tack
to redress the balance of power. At present Kemal was not merely President of the Assembly—hence in effect head of state—but Prime Minister
as well, controlling a Cabinet of ministers who were in practice his own
nominees. Though in theory the Assembly elected the ministers, in fact
it accepted those candidates whom it was the President's privilege to put
forward: Kemal could thus effectively impose his will on both the Assembly and the Cabinet. The Opposition now sought to divide his responsibility. They secured the passage of an act providing for the effec-

tive election by secret ballot not merely of the ministers but of the Prime Minister himself. This meant that Kemal not merely ceased to be his own Prime Minister but had to accept in his government ministers who might be opposed to his views. The move had been initiated largely by Rauf who, since he had not actively joined the Opposition, now became the obvious choice for Prime Minister.

At first, despite Kemal's efforts at persuasion, he was reluctant to accept the post. Asked why, he replied frankly, "If I do, you will continue to interfere in my conduct of affairs. I shall be unable to accept this and find myself forced to resign. I firmly believe that you are the one person who, at the head of the armies, can save the country, and I will not be placed in a position of having to disagree with you."

Kemal replied sincerely, "I give you my word of honour. Agree to become head of the government. Form a Cabinet, and I shall not interfere in any of your decisions."

It was a promise which Kemal faithfully kept, henceforward accepting the principle that he did not attend Cabinet meetings unless specifically invited. In fact he was invited when any major issue came up for discussion. But the Cabinet retained its separate and corporate identity.

Kemal, however, was still head of the group for the Defence of Rights, which formed the majority in the Assembly. Here too he compromised. He brought Ali Fuad back from Moscow, where an ambassador of his status was no longer needed, and made him its active president, while himself remaining its supposedly neutral patron. The differences between them had never been personal, and now Fuad stayed with him at Chankaya, where the two old friends sat up together at nights over the raki, talking of the problems that had developed at home in Fuad's absence and particularly of the growing divisions in the Assembly. The rift, as Fuad saw it, seemed likely to grow into an eventual struggle between republicans and constitutional monarchists. Kemal recognized this but stressed the need to postpone the issue until the war was won. The problem was, as he put it, to reconcile this phase of the political struggle with the need for authority and discipline for the final military struggle. In reply to Fuad's contention that Kemal should elevate himself to a neutral position, mediating from above the political arena, Kemal expressed serious misgivings as to the threat from the forces of religious reaction and doubted whether any such neutrality were possible. Meanwhile he counted on Fuad to do all he could to maintain unity on the home front.

The time now approached when it would be necessary to review Ke-

mal's powers as commander-in-chief yet again. This would perhaps be
the last term of renewal. For it was clear that the final offensive was
near. A Turkish success seemed assured. But to make it doubly sure, it
was essential, in the eyes of Rauf and Ali Fuad, that the commander-in-
chief law should this time pass the Assembly without such opposition as
might suggest Turkish disunity and revive the flagging hopes of the
Greeks. At the same time, wholehearted in their support for Kemal until
victory was won, they were becoming concerned as to what might happen afterwards. The Gazi must be given his powers. But it must be ensured that he did not retain and exploit them once peace had been
achieved. The new Turkey must be a democratic Turkey. For the future
their ambitious and victorious friend must be curbed in his dictatorial
designs.

They went to consult Refet, who had been living in virtual seclusion
in his house at Kechiören, a suburb of Angora, since the dispute with
Kemal which had led to his retirement from the Ministry of Defence.
He echoed their views, and Rauf proposed that the three friends should
put them frankly before Kemal. Refet agreed to invite the Gazi to a dinner at his house, which would also serve as a gesture of reconciliation.
The dinner was arranged for the eve of the relevant debate in the Assembly.

The house had a welcoming atmosphere, for Refet appreciated the
refinements of life and knew well how to make himself comfortable.
The four founders of the Revolution sat down on a hot July evening to
an ample meal in a hall where a fountain played. The drink flowed. The
atmosphere soon became relaxed. The conversation was free. They reminisced of old times and speculated on times to come.

Kemal spoke critically of the Opposition group. "I know well how to
carry on a fight," he said, "but this is neither the time nor place for it.
And later no fight should be necessary."

The others stressed that the majority, though they might oppose him
in Parliament, trusted him personally and believed in his success. They
were only concerned with one question. After the cause had been won,
what line did he mean to pursue? His future intentions were the subject
of rumour. Even his supporters feared some *fait accompli* in terms of
his personal power. Doubts on this score created divisions in the Assembly. They hoped that he would resolve them, restoring confidence and
a spirit of unity.

Kemal fenced with his friends, answering their outspoken criticisms
with reserve and circumspection. Touching on the new arrangements

for a Cabinet with an elected Prime Minister, he repeated his assurances that he would respect Rauf's position as such. But on the question of his own ultimate powers he was not to be drawn.

They talked and drank until daybreak, only Rauf, who was a moderate drinker, abstaining. Unfortunately Refet, as the drink took effect, went too far. Never able, in his disrespectful way, to resist scolding and needling and teasing Kemal, he pricked at his pride with home truths about his unpopularity, dragging up faults from the past, gibing at his personal life in the present. Angora—or so Refet declared—was ringing with scandals about his "debauches" at the Azerbaijan Embassy; his reputed affair with a diplomat's wife; the seduction, with Arif's connivance, of an innocent nurse at the front; the installation at Chankaya of a barber's boy, picked up during a visit to Izmit. Kemal stiffened as he drank. His eyes gleamed pale with resentment.

Rauf and Ali Fuad tried to soothe him, to laugh off Refet's indiscreet charges. But on the issue of the future they had no intention of sparing him. They urged that, when the war was over and his main duty done, he should retire from the fray and accept an elevated presidential status, acting as an arbiter and consultant and letting others run the country on democratic lines. Good-humouredly enough, they promised that they would obtain for him a handsome grant from the Assembly, and even produced for him the design of a projected medal, which they would have cast for himself alone as a reward for his salvation of the country.

Kemal brushed this lightly aside but reassured them: "Don't worry. I shall consider your advice. I shall make a statement to calm all this fuss about myself and the country's future."

His friends expressed satisfaction. Kemal drank to their health. "Friends," he said, "it is morning. I think I've pleased all of you. Now let's go home and rest for a while before we get down to business."

Refet showed them to the door. Dropping Rauf at his house, Kemal and Ali Fuad drove up to Chankaya. Fuad slept for a few hours. Kemal took a hot bath, shaved, and dressed. Then he sat down to work on his speech. Fuad appeared in time for luncheon, to find the Gazi, in full field marshal's uniform, standing in a habitual pose, erect with one hand behind his back. His hair was sprucely combed, his eyes were clear, and he showed no trace of fatigue after his sleepless night. They ate briefly and after a quick cup of coffee went down to the Assembly, where Kemal mounted the rostrum.

The Gazi, who normally appeared in civilian clothes, cut an impressive figure in his uniform. He spoke of the commander-in-chief law:

no Parliament in the world would grant such authority to a single person, except on two conditions—that the situation was exceptional and that the person was above all suspicion. The Assembly had shown great trust in him, for which he expressed gratitude. But the time had now come when it was no longer necessary to maintain these extraordinary powers. The moral and material forces of the army had reached such a degree of perfection that the national effort could be realized without them. He continued:

"Then I, like the rest of you, will only be an individual in the nation, and, of course, this will be, for me, the greatest happiness. When that day comes, gentlemen, I shall have two kinds of happiness. The second will be that I shall then be able to withdraw to my former post—the post I had three years ago before we began our sacred fight. [*Cheers.*] Indeed, there is no happiness comparable to that of being a free individual in the bosom of the nation. For those who realize this truth, and for those who have moral and sacred joys within their souls and their conscience, rank, however high, has no value whatsoever."

Disarmed by his tactics, dissolved by his rhetoric, the deputies forgot their misgivings. Had the Gazi not offered to renounce his privileges? Had he not made it clear that, when victory was won, he would become once more a private citizen, dependent on the nation's will? What greatness, what nobility of character! They reinvested him with the powers of commander-in-chief. But this time they imposed no time limit. He was to retain them, subject only to the Assembly's right to withdraw them, until the national aims had been finally achieved. Kemal stepped down from the rostrum well satisfied with his night's vigil and his afternoon's work.

The Turkish offensive could not now be long delayed. It was in fact hastened by a last desperate gamble on the part of the Greeks. Foiled in their designs on Angora, Gounaris and Constantine now switched their attention to Constantinople. They swiftly removed two divisions from Asia Minor and transferred them across the Sea of Marmara to reinforce their troops in Thrace. With a strong force thus threatening the lines of Chatalja, they demanded the permission of the Allies to enter Constantinople.

By this threat the Greeks sought to put pressure on the Allies, who were once again contemplating peace discussions—this time at Venice —to resolve the conflict in their favour, or at least to save their faces. Constantinople was now so lightly held that the Allied troops had been compared to the "jam in a sandwich," of which the Greeks on the one side and the Turks on the other represented thick slices of bread. An entry into the city would be a simple enough operation. It would restore the prestige in Greece of Constantine's regime, revive the confidence of his army, and provide him with a valuable bargaining asset.

"It is quite possible," as Churchill afterwards analyzed the move, "that under cover of a temporary Greek occupation of Constantinople with Allied approval, the escape of the Greek armies from Asia Minor might have been honourably and comparatively painlessly merged in negotiations for peace. . . . At least it could be argued against the Allies that if they would not help the Greeks in their military operations they ought not to hamper them; and if on general grounds they felt compelled to hamper, they ought at least loyally and actively to help them to their ships."

Thus once again, as in the Balkan War ten years before, all eyes in Constantinople were turned anxiously towards the Chatalja Lines. Harington entrusted their defence to a French general, with French and British troops which at once started to entrench. He issued a statement, on his own responsibility, that the troops of both powers would combine to resist any attack on the occupation forces. Rumbold returned hurriedly from leave and an Allied meeting at the British Embassy confirmed Harington's stand. British warships made a demonstration in the Marmara. The Greeks withdrew a short distance but continued to land troops. Lloyd George upheld the Allied decision and the Greeks agreed to advance no further without their approval. The British warships turned to the more peaceable pastime of holding their annual regatta. The Greeks had lost their last chance. Moreover in taking it they had weakened their defences on the Anatolian front.

Lloyd George, however, in his incorrigible philhellenism, elected to give them a final gleam of hope. "In the dying hours," as *The Times* put it, "of a weary session of the House of Commons," he made a speech which could only be interpreted by both sides as an encouragement to the Greeks still to seek a decision by force. The Prime Minister permitted himself a eulogy on the gallant Greek Army in their "daring and reckless military enterprise." They had been compelled to "march through impenetrable defiles hundreds of miles into the country." They had established their military superiority in every pitched battle. They had been beaten only by the conformation of the country and by the long lines of communication "which no other army in Europe would ever have dreamed of taking the risk of allowing."

Then he said, with apparent significance, "Peace the Kemalists will not accept, because they say we will not give them satisfactory armistice terms; but we are not allowing the Greeks to wage the war with their full strength. We cannot allow that sort of thing to go on indefinitely in the hope that the Kemalists entertain that they will at last exhaust this little country, whose men have been in arms for ten or twelve years with one war after another, and which has not indefinite resources."

The speech was received with enthusiasm throughout Greece. The newspapers headlined its more laudatory passages. Extracts from it were published in an Order of the Day to the Greek forces, who became filled with a new hope that the British would, at this eleventh hour, help them to defeat the enemy. The stratagem of the threat to Constantinople had surely achieved its object. There was no more talk of peace.

All these events favoured Kemal's plans. As soon as he got wind of the Greek troop movements he decided to put forward the date of his offensive. For the transfer to Thrace would equalize the Turkish and Greek forces in Anatolia. Now was the moment to strike. He had sent Fethi, his Minister of the Interior, to Rome, Paris, and London, on the off chance of a peace still in terms of a Greek evacuation; otherwise as an emissary for the peace which must follow a victory. Then he left for the headquarters of the western front at Akshehir.

39 ► *Final victory*

While the Allied High Commissioners in Constantinople were discussing the Greek threat to the city, Kemal and his General Staff were watching a football match at Akshehir. This was the security cover he had chosen for a secret staff conference, to settle the date and the final arrangements for the Turkish offensive against Smyrna. The plan of campaign had been drawn up in secrecy nine months before, among Kemal, Fevzi, and Ismet. Fevzi now explained it on a map. Then Kemal asked his generals for their opinion. Several were critical, less of the plan itself than of the timing of its execution. Ismet, irresolute as ever, was not convinced that it could lead at this moment to a decisive victory. He favoured a sound policy of defence, with the object of wearing down the Greeks. If there were to be an attack, then he wanted more time to complete preparations.

The defensive psychology had become deeply ingrained. Others echoed Ismet's doubts. Now that there was an army in being, they shrank from the risk of losing it. It was not, they maintained, really ready. The Second Army commander, who had been one of Kemal's instructors at the War School, protested that the country's very existence would be jeopardized by this risking of a force which was all it possessed. Kemal, enquiring of Fevzi whether it was in fact all, and receiving a positive reply, turned to him and said, "All right, my dear instructor. We are not playing the war game at Harbiye now. We shall throw *all* into the effort of securing a definite result for the country."

Though he had gone through the motions of consulting the generals, Kemal's mind was already made up. With that extra dimension, which his lesser commanders lacked, of decisiveness, flair, political judgment, and psychological knowledge of his enemy, he was as confident of victory as it was prudent to be. He ordered the armies to be ready for the offensive by the middle of August. Ismet rose to his feet, stood at attention and, speaking as the commander of the front on behalf of the rest, said, "You wanted to know our opinion. We expressed it freely. But if what you have told us is an order, we shall obey it."

Kemal returned to Angora, where he had the Cabinet—to say nothing of the Opposition—to deal with. He informed the ministers of his decision and of his belief in success. Fevzi considered that there was an eighty per cent chance of it—allowing twenty per cent for the hazards of war. The two Opposition ministers became less pessimistic. The Cabinet agreed to the attack. There remained the Opposition itself, whose propaganda implied that the troops were demoralized and incapable of action. This, as Kemal admitted to Ali Fuad, had its advantages, since it put the enemy off the scent as to the imminence of an attack. But he took steps to reassure those whose influence counted.

As a modern security-minded officer, Kemal fully appreciated the need for secrecy concerning the date of the attack. For the success of his strategical plan depended essentially on surprise. Only a few people knew of his departure for the front, and they were instructed to talk and behave as though he were still in Angora. Ali Fuad was to pretend to the deputies that they had dined together that night. Rumours were assiduously spread among the agents of the foreigners that the army was not yet ready for an offensive. At Chankaya the sentries were instructed to admit no one: the Gazi was busy. When he was already at his headquarters in the field, it was announced in the press that he was giving a reception next day at Chankaya.

Taking leave of his mother, he said as he kissed her hand that he was going to a tea party. She looked at his field dress and boots and said, "This uniform is not for a tea party." He soothed her and left. Later she rang the area commander to ask where he was and was again told, "He has gone to a tea party."

"No," she replied. "I know. He has gone to the war." She sent him a note:

My Son, I waited for you. You did not come back. You told me that you were going to a tea party. But I know that you have gone to the front. Know that I pray for you, and do not come back before the war is won.[1]

That night he supped with a few of his henchmen in a suburb of Angora, drinking freely in anticipation of the relative abstinence which was his rule at the front. As he said good-bye, with his hands around their shoulders, he remarked, "I'm going straight away to the front, to start the offensive."

Taken aback, one of them asked him, "Pasha'm, what if you don't succeed?"

"What do you mean? Within fourteen days of the start I shall have destroyed the Greeks and thrown them into the sea."

Instead of taking the train he drove by car through the night across the salt desert to Konya. There he took over the telegraph office so that his arrival should not be announced. Fethi had telegraphed from London that Lord Curzon had refused to see him. The moment had come for the offensive. Kemal moved from Konya to Akshehir, where he was soon giving final orders to his two army commanders.

The Greek front stretched over some three hundred miles from the Sea of Marmara to the Menderes Valley. Its strong points were at Eskishehir in the north and at Afyon in the south. The forces on either side were roughly equal, with a slight Greek advantage in arms and a slight Turkish advantage in cavalry. The Greeks expected the attack to come against Eskishehir, in the north, where the Turks had large concentrations, and where intelligence sources—which included the British employees of the licorice industry—reported lively activity. Kemal encouraged them in this expectation but in fact planned to attack in the south, against Afyon, since it commanded the direct supply line by the railway to Smyrna. This was the stronger defensive position, moreover so fortified that British engineers judged it impregnable and likely to prove "the Turkish Verdun." But to Kemal it had the greater strategic importance. He thus laid plans for its reduction.

The keynote of his plan was surprise, first strategical then tactical. Profiting by the methods of his enemy, Allenby, in the Palestine campaign, Kemal withdrew the necessary forces from north to south over a period of a month and with the greatest possible secrecy. All troop

[1] Perihan Naci Eldeniz, in *Beleten*, LXXX, October 1956.

movements were made at night, while the men rested by day in the villages and under the shade of trees, invisible to air reconnaissance. Where roads had to be made they were made also in the inessential areas, to mislead the enemy further. Meanwhile, though only a small force remained before Eskishehir, campfires were lit at night to suggest a concentration of several divisions, and dust was raised on the roads by day to suggest troops moving north to reinforce them. Thus Kemal sought to achieve strategical surprise.

His objective was to turn the Greek right flank, which was concentrated over a front of some fifty miles, around the town of Afyon Karahisar and the supporting region of Dumlupinar, facing in two directions, east and south. To the south it was defended by an irregular range of mountains, rising dramatically to a height of two thousand feet from the plain. It was this bastion of nature that Kemal, in pursuit of tactical surprise, proposed to attack with his First Army, its main force of infantry and artillery supporting a secondary thrust from the east. His cavalry would then sweep westwards to cut the retreat of the Greek armies with a swift enveloping movement, such as Allenby had employed against the Turkish armies in Palestine.

To confuse the enemy Kemal ordered a northward feint attack towards Brusa on his right flank and a southward cavalry move towards Aydin, in the Menderes Valley, farther to the rear. He anticipated a quick success. To a cavalry commander suggesting postponement because of a lack of fodder for his horses, he remarked, "In two days' time you will have food in plenty for men and horses alike." He had calculated the date for the attack on the basis that the grain in the Greek fields would be ripe but not yet harvested; moreover the beds of the streams would be dry, thus facilitating swiftness of movement.

On the evening of August 25 Kemal gave orders to cut all communications between Anatolia and the outside world. He had moved his headquarters up from the plain into the mountain region next to the village of Shuhud, then to a camp behind the crest of Koja Tepe. His troops had marched up by night into position on the slopes, often as close to the enemy as a few hundred yards, taking cover and camouflaging themselves against air observation by day. As zero hour approached Kemal issued a battle order to the troops which had been drafted by Ismet. It read: "Soldiers, your goal is the Mediterranean." The first major offensive of a nation committed, for twelve years past, to defence was about to begin.[2]

[2] See maps following page 587.

In the hour before dawn on August 26 the Gazi rode slowly up the dark rounded hill of Koja Tepe, from which he was to direct the battle. A file of soldiers with lanterns lit the way, as they were lighting it for the horses and pack animals on the slopes around. He was silent and evidently wrapped in thought. Continually he looked eastwards towards the horizon, where presently a slight red glow announced the rising of the sun above the Anatolian plateau. Then with a thunderous roar the artillery barrage began—and the Greeks woke up. Many of them had been out at a dance in Afyon until an hour or so earlier.

Kemal had ordered that all generals should direct their troops from the front line. Now, with Fevzi and Ismet, he surveyed from his hilltop the first line of the general attack which was developing a mile or so off. A broad irregular amphitheatre of other hilltops, steeper and rockier, straggled in echelon across the horizon before them. Each was fortified by the Greeks. Each was the objective of a Turkish division, to be stormed in an uphill attack until the summit was reached. The fighting was bloody but brief. All but two of these objectives were in Turkish hands by nine-thirty in the morning. For the surprise was complete. The Greeks had no inkling of the presence of those forces which had crept up on them overnight under cover of the opposite slopes. Air reconnaissance had shown a mere three Turkish divisions, easy enough to contain. Instead here was a force that overwhelmed them by a local superiority of three to one.

Some time, moreover, elapsed before they grasped that this was the main attack. Expecting it to come from the east, they kept a strong force in the plain to meet what proved only to be a holding attack. By the time their mistake became clear the battle was already as good as lost. For in the meantime the Turkish cavalry had swept round to the Greeks' rear, harrying them from the west and cutting the railway to Smyrna at a point to be known henceforward by the name of Yildirim Kemal—appropriately enough, since this was indeed at last a "lightning" offensive.

At two key points only, one on the left flank and the other on the right, did the Turks meet with an effective resistance and thus fail at first to take their objectives. At Chigil Tepe, on the left, the young officer in command committed suicide on account of his failure to do so. Kemal, ruthless in the heat of the battle, cursed him for dying in vain. The unit had in fact done what Kemal had expected of it, and the position was captured later in the day. It was not until the evening that he relented so far as to remark, "What a pity for this child!"

On the right was an equally formidable strong point, a precipitous slope on which the Greeks, fighting fiercely, repulsed several Turkish assaults. Then Kemal, with the army corps commander Kemal-ed-Din Sami—a man nicknamed in the army "the Lightning Conductor" from his propensity to draw the enemy's fire—appeared on the scene. "I'd sooner see the sky fall than the Greeks win," Kemal said. He harangued the front-line troops. He called for volunteers, but only for men who wanted to die. Every man came forward. Then, knowing as he did the psychology of the Turkish soldier, he taunted and cursed them for their cowardice. They were unworthy of their wives, who should have the right to divorce them.

Bewildered and furious, they asked why. Had they not volunteered to die? Having thus summoned up their blood to boiling point, Kemal ordered them over the barbed wire and up the slope. The Greek fire mowed them down. Soon there were pyramids of Turkish dead before the wire and the earth was red with blood, lying in pools on the hard ground. But more came on, clambering over the bodies of their comrades. Kemal-ed-Din Sami looked away, overwhelmed by the spectacle of slaughter and bloodshed. Then he heard an imam chanting from the top of the rock and knew that the position was captured.

Thus the first line of defence of the Greeks was no more, its hillsides crisscrossed with abandoned fortifications like a huddle of giant deserted ant heaps. They had barely time to man their second and third lines of defence beyond the hills, which fell as quickly to the Turks. During the next two days the main Turkish forces soon reached the road through the valley before Dumlupinar, which led down towards Smyrna, while the cavalry and mobile infantry, now covering up to thirty-five miles a day, wheeled round even farther to the west of them in an endeavour to close the line of retreat. The holding force from the east now moved forward to aid in the pursuit, capturing Afyon itself, which the Greeks had been forced to evacuate with barely a shot fired.

Here in the municipal building beneath Afyon's "Karahisar," the black fortress perched on its towering rock, Kemal now installed his head-quarters, resuming telegraphic contact once more with the whole of his force and the rest of the country. Here Halide Edib—whom with a touch of superstition he had summoned back to his side as a kind of female mascot—first saw him gesticulating and pouring over a map with Fevzi by the light of two lamps. As he came to greet her he had, to her eyes, so exalted and radiant a look that he seemed to be "blinking at a hundred suns all rising over his head. The ring of his voice and the shake of the hand made you feel his excitement—the man with the will power which is like a self-fed machine of perpetual motion." To her congratulations he responded with a mighty chuckle, like the purr of a royal tiger. "Yes, we are doing it at last."

Fevzi was patting his own right shoulder in a moment of satisfaction and sucking his teeth. Ismet was himself. There was an excess of cordiality. Halide, recalling the hard times, was touched by Kemal's exuberant joy and said: "After you take Smyrna, Pasha, you will rest, you have struggled so hard."

"Rest? What rest? After the Greeks, we will fight each other, we will eat each other."

"Why should we?" she said. "There will be an enormous amount to do in the way of reconstruction."

"What about the men who have opposed me?"

"Well, it was natural in a National Assembly."

He spoke in a bantering tone, making fun of her feminine squeamishness; but there was a revengeful look in his eye as he mentioned two of his political enemies. "I will have those lynched by the people. No, we will not rest, we will kill each other. . . . When the struggle ends it will be dull; we must find some other excitement, Hanum Effendi."

On the morning of August 30 he moved his headquarters forward to the region of Dumlupinar. Here the bulk of the Greek forces, endeavouring to retreat, were contained in a wide oval basin by a ridge of scrubby hills whence the Second Army was converging to join the First; by the broad mountain of Murad Dağ, to the west, which no force could surmount; and by the troops of the First Army closing in from the east and south, to draw the noose tighter around them. But for a single escape route down the road to the west, through the long narrow valley of Kiziljidere, the Greeks were surrounded.

That day, four days after the initial attack, half their army was annihilated or taken prisoner, with the loss of all its war material. A large column of troops, including the Greek army corps commander, General Tricoupis, and his staff, found itself trapped in the valley between two Turkish divisions at its entrance and a third which had moved swiftly ahead to block its exit. The scene of the consequent slaughter looked to Halide afterwards "like a disordered dream. . . . Forsaken batteries glistened in the sun; rifles and ammunition in huge piles, endless material of all descriptions lay huddled in a great mass all over the valley. And amidst it all corpses—of men and animals—lay as they had fallen."

The other half of the Greek Army was in headlong flight to the coast, out of range of its pursuers, a fighting force no longer, burning villages and crops, slaughtering men, women, and children as it fled. For this, according to the Greek soldiers' orders, was a "war of extermination."

Such was the victory which, lest the credit for it be disputed between Kemal and Nur-ed-Din Pasha, his ambitious First Army commander, was dubbed by Ismet "The Battle of the Generalissimo."[3] It was the fruit of meticulous planning and a masterly concept of strategical and tactical surprise. The "Verdun" of the Greeks had crumbled before an overwhelming force, directed unexpectedly at a single point and to a swift exploitation of its undefended flank.

In a ruined village by the battlefield Kemal's tent was pitched on the roof of a stable. The peasant women gathered around, staring at him, begging him to avenge the sufferings which they had endured at the hands of the Greeks. His exuberance turned to a mood of depression. He came down to sit silently on a chair by the roadside, watching the droves of Greek prisoners as they filed back, dusty and ragged and blood-stained. The scene of devastation shocked him, inured though he was to the carnage of war. To an A.D.C. he confessed his hatred of it, philoso-phizing on the failings of mankind—and those of the Greeks in particu-lar. Then, seeing a Greek flag lying on the ground, he ordered the A.D.C. to pick it up and drape it over one of the Greek guns.

Among the prisoners brought before him Kemal recognized an officer he had known in Salonika. The prisoner, puzzled to see no badge on his shoulder, asked him his rank. Was he now major, colonel, general, what? Kemal replied that he was marshal, commander-in-chief. The Greek exclaimed in Turkish, "Whoever heard of a commander-in-chief being near the front line of a battle?" Kemal said jovially. "We are soon going to take back Salonika and create an autonomous Macedonia. I shall make you a commander there."

In fact the Turkish victory owed much to deficient Greek generalship. The commander-in-chief, General Hajianestis, who had been appointed for political reasons, directed the battle from a yacht in the harbour of Smyrna, lying in bed or frequenting the coffee shops ashore, alternately terrorizing his commanders and confusing them with irresponsible or unconfirmed orders. He developed signs of insanity, believing sometimes that he was dead, sometimes that his body was made of glass and that, if he rose to his feet, his legs would break. General Tricoupis had received a general order, in the event of a Turkish attack on Afyon, to move southeastwards on the village of Chobanlar, with a view to outflanking and thus checking the enemy. But when the attack came he feared, in

[3] Later Nur-ed-Din had visiting cards printed with the title "Conqueror of Smyrna."

the absence of specific confirmation of the order, to do so. Instead he held on until forced to retreat. He tried to mount a counterattack but his men would not follow him. Hence his capture in the fatal valley by a Turkish cavalry squadron. Only afterwards did he learn that Hajianestis had been dismissed and that he had been appointed commander-in-chief.

A day or so later, with General Dionis, a fellow army corps commander, General Tricoupis was brought to Kemal's headquarters, which had been moved forward by this time to Ushak. Here Kemal received them, standing between Fevzi and Ismet. Halide Edib describes how he did so:

As a soldier one recognized at once in [Kemal] the supreme artist and the supreme sportsman. He kept the rules of his game with dignity, with tact, and with exactitude. He thought neither of the appearance nor of the misdeeds of the Greek generals. Tricoupis, especially, was the man with whom he had played a real game. Now that his military opponent was on the ground, he showed that military art and military courtesy he possessed to his fingers' ends. He gripped General Tricoupis's hand heartily and held it imperceptibly longer than for an ordinary handshake.
"Sit down, General," he said, "you must be tired." Then he offered his cigarette case and ordered coffee.

Tricoupis was looking at him with surprise. "I did not know you were such a young man, General," he said.

They sat down around the table, Kemal fixing his erstwhile opponent with a pale steely gaze. He was eager to talk about the battle. The conversation began, through an interpreter, in Greek but continued in halting French. Kemal asked Tricoupis, as one soldier to another, why he had not foreseen that the attack was likely to take the course it did. Tricoupis confessed that he had been taken by surprise. He was impressed to hear that Kemal had conducted the campaign from the front line itself. He pointed out his own difficulties to Kemal, sounding to Halide's ears "like an amateur speaking to a professional": his absentee commander-in-chief, who knew little of the situation; the refusal of his commanders to obey him; the break in the Greek communications, thanks to the Turkish cavalry, who cut the telephone lines and destroyed the transport; the political squabbles between Venizelists and Constantinists, destroying cohesion and discipline.

They talked of tactics. Why, Kemal asked, had he not done this or that? Tricoupis spoke of his proposed move on Chobanlar, in defence of Afyon. Kemal explained just how he would have countered it. He had allowed in his calculations for every potential move of his enemy. The two Greek generals started to dispute with each other. The Turks looked a trifle contemptuous at this lack of decorum, this contrast between highly strung Greek volubility and Turkish restraint. Finally Kemal asked Tricoupis if there was anything he could do for him. The general asked that his wife, who was on the island of Prinkipo off Constantinople, be told of his capture.

Kemal gave the promise, gripped and held Tricoupis' hand, and said sincerely but with a twinkle in his cold blue eyes, "War is a game of chance, General. The very best is sometimes worsted. You have done your best as a soldier and as an honourable man; the responsibility rests with chance. Do not be distressed."

But Tricoupis made a theatrical gesture. "Oh, General," he exclaimed, "I have not done the last thing I ought to have done." He had not had the courage to commit suicide. At this emotional outburst Kemal narrowed his eyes and gave him a cynical look. "That," he said tersely, "is a thing which concerns you personally."

Two months later Hajianestis was impeached and executed, together with Gounaris and four of his Cabinet ministers, by a Greek revolutionary tribunal. Many years later Tricoupis confessed to the view that the campaign in Anatolia, where the Greeks had no real interests of their own as distinct from those of the European powers, had been a disastrous mistake for his country.

In Angora and Constantinople little was known of the progress of the battle until it was virtually won. Kemal, still intent on security, issued only brief daily communiqués, which announced a series of forward movements without revealing their scale. "Our object," he explained, "was to conceal the situation as much as possible from the eyes of the world." And indeed, ten days from the start of the battle, Rauf had to seek instructions from Kemal on an Allied note, carrying a stage further the old negotiations for an armistice. Kemal was able to reply that the question of evacuation of Anatolia no longer arose, and that he was prepared to discuss an armistice only in relation to that of Thrace.

Angora, closer to the situation than Constantinople, did indeed get some inkling from the communiqués as to the true nature of the advance. When it was realized that operations had started, anxious crowds moved to and fro between the Ministry of War and the Assembly, seeking news and speculating on the laconic reports which were read out to the deputies in secret session. On the second day, when the battle had been virtually won, there was no communiqué. Then, belatedly, came the news of the capture of Afyon. It drew great crowds into the streets, demonstrating for the Gazi and the army and the Turkish people, firing joyful salvoes into the air. From then onwards Angora felt that all would be well. When the news of the triumphant capture of Smyrna was sure, the black flag was removed from the rostrum of the Grand National Assembly. (Brusa itself, for which it was a token of mourning, was to be liberated on the same day as Smyrna.) But Kemal still had his enemies, one of whom grumbled, "Why all this fuss? The Allies would have given us Smyrna anyhow."

Constantinople was less confident of the outcome. Talk was still of an armistice, of a conference in Venice. Eyes were still on the Greek troops threatening the city from the lines of Chatalja. There was a general atmosphere of doubt and defeatism. To many the Anatolian offensive seemed a foolhardy enterprise. News of it came only from the Greek communiqués, which belittled the Turkish successes and hinted at a Turkish retreat. In the clubs of the city the Greeks drank champagne to the destruction of Mustafa Kemal. A rumour got around that he had been taken prisoner. There were long Turkish faces in the streets and on the boats taking the commuters each evening to their homes across the water.

When the first authentic news of the Turkish successes came through the newspapers printed it guardedly for fear they would not be believed. Then the day came when it was evident that the truth far exceeded their most optimistic reports. It was not Kemal but the Greek general who had been captured. The Greek armies were defeated and in full retreat. Falih Rifki, the journalist, was laughing that night on the boat back to Prinkipo, sharing with a friend the good news which could not be released till the morning. Used to his anxious expression, the Greeks looked at him oddly and with an evident twinge of foreboding. "Let's pretend we are defeated," Falih's friend said, "and that the Gazi is a prisoner in Ushak." But their smiles could not be disguised. Next day, when the news was printed in triumphant headlines, the crowd before the newspaper offices was such that it blocked the doors and the papers had to be thrown from the windows.

In Smyrna, right up to the last moment, the Levantines clung to the belief that a conference would solve the problem, that the Allied warships, reassuringly anchored in the gulf, would prevent the Turks from entering the city. And even if they came, surely business would carry on as it had done before they went, with all Anatolia opened up to trade. The export season was approaching; the warehouses were filling up with raisins and figs; the sacks were being sewn up, the packing cases closed;

the merchant ships from Italy, Germany, Holland were standing by to take on board their autumn cargoes.

It took much to shake this mood of false optimism. But doubts began to creep in. The radio bulletins from the Allied warships, pinned on the board of the Cercle Européen, brought increasingly ominous news. A Greek hospital ship cast anchor in the harbour. The wounded and the refugees began to trickle into the city with lurid tales of bloodshed. The merchants in the coffee shops exchanged rumours from the interior, debated anxiously whether they could meet their commitments, whether the Turks, if they arrived, would requisition all stocks. Then suddenly the Bourse was at a standstill. No more wagonloads of raisins and figs came from the interior. The merchant ships sailed hurriedly away with empty holds. Distractions continued. There were *diners dansants* in the moonlight, on the terrace of the Hotel Naim; at the Sporting Club an Italian opera troupe played *Traviata* and *Rigoletto;* the guitarists sang in the cafés until curfew, while the waiters brought *sorbets* and re-plenished the *narghiles* with charcoal. But beneath it all was a sense of deep foreboding.

The retreat lasted a week. The Turkish forces hurried on towards the city, striving to overtake the Greeks before they could decimate all western Anatolia "by fire and sword." The cavalry followed close on the enemy's heels; the infantry, geared over the two hundred miles of wind-ing roads between the plateau and the sea to the pace of its oxcarts and mule trains, moved more slowly. In three days its main body contrived to march a hundred miles. But it still failed to catch up with the enemy. Already most of the towns in its path were in ruins. One third of Ushak no longer existed. Alashehir was no more than a dark scorched cavity, defacing the hillside. Village after village had been reduced to an ash heap. Out of the eighteen thousand buildings in the historic holy city of Manisa, only five hundred remained.

Everywhere the Greek troops, especially those from Anatolia, revenging themselves in desperation and in obedience to orders for generations of Ottoman oppression and persecution, carried off Christian families that their quarters too might be burned and not a roof left for the ad-vancing Turks. They tore up the railway between Smyrna and Aydin. They pillaged and destroyed and raped and butchered. "They went to pieces altogether," as Rumbold recounted to Curzon on the basis of re-ports from his consul in Smyrna. It was "a sickening record of besti-ality and barbarity." There was little, Rumbold added, to choose between the two races, Greek and Turk. Permeating the atmosphere, as the Turks advanced down the valleys, was the stench of unburied bodies, of charred human and animal flesh.

Kemal moved his headquarters swiftly forward in the wake of his army—from Ushak to Salihli, to Nif, on the hills above Smyrna. At Salihli he made his military dispositions in case of a final Greek stand before the city itself. But a personal telegram arrived from the Allied Powers, relayed through the French cruiser *Edgar Quinet* in the harbour of Smyrna. They had instructed their consuls to negotiate with a view to handing over the city to the Turkish Army, and asked Kemal to fix a time and place for a meeting. They added a hope that he would protect the Christian population.

Kemal thumped on the table. "Whose city are they giving to whom?" he enquired. But he now knew that the fight was over, the victory won. He knew also that, from now onwards, the Allies would have to deal with him in person. He replied that he would be ready to receive them at Nif on September 9. Someone brought and read him extracts from an English newspaper. "Poor Lloyd George!" he exclaimed. "What's going to happen to him tomorrow? He'll be destroyed." Already the Greek women, borne away from their villages, were crying prophetic maledictions: "Bad times for George!"

Punctually Kemal arrived at Nif. His car was at once surrounded by peasants. He took off his goggles and lit a cigarette. As he did so a man walked slowly towards him, looked him in the eye, took a crumpled photograph from his pocket, scrutinized it, and looked at him again. "It's you!" he exclaimed. He turned to the crowd and said: "This is the Gazi, Mustafa Kemal."

Kemal entered the headquarters prepared for him, contemptuously ignoring a portrait of Venizelos which still hung on the wall. There was no sign of the foreign consuls, for his message, relayed through Angora and Constantinople, had not reached them in time. Already the advance guard was entering Smyrna. The Turkish Army had fulfilled his orders and had reached the Mediterranean.

Next day Kemal would follow his army into the city. That evening at Nif—soon to be renamed Kemalpasha—he was relaxed and gay.

"What's this?" he exclaimed. "We've taken Smyrna today. Are we going to be so quiet? At least let us sing."

A drink was brought to him but he refused it. Drink and duty, he declared, did not go together. He had not had a drink since the attack began and would not have another till the goal was reached. Stimulated only by coffee, he and his officers sang together around the table, beneath the portrait of Venizelos, to celebrate their victory.

He had won it in fifteen days. When he eventually returned to Angora he apologized to his friends. "Forgive me. One can sometimes make mathematical errors. I was one day out in my estimate."

40 ► *The burning of Smyrna*

The first Turkish soldier to reach the Mediterranean was a young cavalry lieutenant. On the deserted quay at Smyrna he was greeted by a French admiral, who delivered a long speech, advising him to see to the protection of the Christians. The lieutenant advised him, for his own protection, to keep clear of the quay—and as he spoke a Christian bomb fell from a window and a Christian rifle fired, wounding the lieutenant.

The last of the Greek troops, but for a few stragglers, had left the day before—forty thousand of them in a convoy of Greek warships, together with all the Greek civil servants and police. They left behind them fifty thousand prisoners in the hands of the Turks. Filling the vacuum until the Turkish troops should arrive, the Allied warships landed armed patrols to keep order, prevent arson and looting, and calm the fears of the population.

In command of a detachment of British marines and bluejackets—who formed the bulk of the force, since the French and Italians contributed little—was Captain Bertram Thesiger of H.M.S. *King George V*.[1] Guards had been posted at the consulate and at the gasworks and were now

[1] Now Admiral Sir Bertram Thesiger, K.B.E., C.B., C.M.G.

needed at the stores of the railway station, where the captain could see, as he later recalled, "about three thousand Greeks, some armed, cheerfully looting everything. At this moment there was a general scream and a rush. Shots were being fired, and there were yells of 'the Turks are coming.' " They came in his direction—a unit of Turkish cavalry, advancing in extended formation across open ground. They galloped towards the captain with drawn swords and a swashbuckling air.

Foreseeing unnecessary bloodshed, he determined to halt them. He got between Greeks and Turks and held up his hand, looking, as a British eyewitness put it, "for all the world like a London policeman," feeling none too confident since his white uniform was like that of a Greek naval officer. The Turkish commander, however, halted his men and dismounted. Captain Thesiger went up to him. In awkward French he explained that the Allies had landed troops to keep order and that if the Turks would refrain from firing there was little danger of trouble. The Turkish officer, who bore the rank of colonel, replied that he did not intend to fire but wished to enter the city. He suggested doing so by a side street but the captain advised him to follow the sea front. He agreed to do this, and also to place a cavalry guard on the gasworks and station.

Captain Thesiger was struck by the discipline of the Turkish forces. Nevertheless soldiers were demanding money from the Greeks and he saw one of them shoot a Greek dead, presumably because he had refused to comply. Presently the listless hordes of refugees, squatting on the pavements, saw the Turkish cavalry general make his entry into the city, riding the white horse of General Tricoupis, and soon long outlandish files of baggage camels were lumbering slowly along the sea front.

Next day Mustafa Kemal, still unadorned by badges of rank, drove down into Smyrna at the head of a procession of open cars decked with olive branches. It was September 10—three years, almost to a day, since the proclamation of the National Pact at the Sivas Congress. At the entrance to the city the procession was met by a division of cavalry which was to act as escort. The soldiers had been in the saddle, fighting almost without respite, in and behind the Greek lines, for nine days past. When Kemal promised his cavalry food in plenty, once the advance had begun, he had not reckoned with the enemy's scorched-earth tactics.

At this moment of triumph, witnessed by Halide Edib, "men and horses looked spectral. Not one ounce of flesh was visible on either; dresses and gears were worn out, faces and heads of both men and beasts burned by some devastating fever; the eyes of men glistened strangely in emaciated and haggard faces." At the order to march, "in a single lightning flash two long lines of horsemen drew their swords, and the sun gleamed on their steel as they galloped past us on either side. The clash of steel and the beat of the iron hooves became deafening as we crossed the closed bazaars. . . . Along the smooth marble pavement reeled the moving walls of men and steel, horses sliding and rising, and the steel curving like swift flashes of lightning in the sombre air of the arches. Behind the cavalry one saw thousands of mouths as though transformed into an eternal shout—roaring and shouting applause." So Mustafa Kemal reached the Mediterranean.

He drove to the *konak,* the government building on the quay, which had been the Greek headquarters. A large Greek flag had been spread like a carpet on the steps of it, as a Turkish flag—so it was said—had been spread for the reception of King Constantine. Kemal refused to walk on it and ordered its removal. "That is the symbol," he protested, "of a country's independence." From the balcony he looked down on the cheering crowds, on the Allied warships lying at anchor opposite. Three years earlier, in Constantinople, he had looked across at these warships, speculating as to what the Allies would do. Now the initiative had shifted. Their crews looked across at him, speculating as to what he would do.

He was presented with a car by the people of Smyrna. They were preparing to slaughter and sacrifice an ox in his honour. Wincing at such Islamic barbarities, he sent orders to stop the ceremony. But he was too late; the beast was already roasting. He withdrew from the balcony, passed inside through the mirrored hall where dusty khaki-clad figures sat silently awaiting him, and retired to a smaller room, where he sat down with Nur-ed-Din, the commander of his occupying troops. Order had still to be established. Street fighting continued. There was work to be done.

Later Kemal strolled into the lounge of a hotel which the foreigners frequented. The merchants sat over their drinks, discussing the news, wondering anxiously what was to happen. Despite his compelling appearance, they did not at first recognize the young Turkish officer. Nor did the waiter, who regretted that no table was free. Then a customer identified him and he sat down among them, begging them to be at their ease. The Greeks gazed at him curiously as, faithful to last night's promise, he raised his glass to his friends and downed his first victory drink. He turned to the Greeks and asked, "Did King Constantine ever come here to drink a glass of raki?" On receiving a negative reply, he asked, "Why did he bother to take Smyrna then?" That evening he moved his headquarters to the district of Karshiyaka, where two houses had been prepared for him and two elderly Turkish ladies treated him with motherly hospitality.

The situation in Smyrna was tense. Some thousands of refugees had embarked with the Greek forces but more were still pouring in, standing all along the footplates and swarming on the roofs of the trains, passing their dead out at the stations over the heads of the living. They camped in the streets, hungry and hopeless and often sick, with their possessions in bundles around them. Thanks to the burning of the crops there was danger of starvation. With no Greek troops left to protect them, the people of the city, their minds still dwelling on an Ottoman past, had become obsessed with fears of a massacre of Christians. Reprisals were feared for this devastation of the countryside and for the maltreatment of Turks by Greeks on the occupation of the city three years before. The foreign consuls were anxious for the safety of their nationals. Thus one of Kemal's first actions was to issue a proclamation, sentencing to death any Turkish soldier who molested noncombatants.

The British representatives in Smyrna had been instructed from London not to call on Kemal in person, as the French had done. Kemal's own first instinct was to ask the British warships to leave within a stated time. Then he chanced to meet Sir Harry Lamb, the British consul general, in the street, and had an unofficial talk with him. Kemal asked Lamb what his functions were since the change of government in Turkey. The consul said that he represented the British High Commissioner in Constantinople. Kemal retorted that his government did not recognize any such authority. "Technically," he said, "Turkey is still at war with Britain. I should be justified in interning all British subjects in Smyrna. But I do not intend to do so." He added, "Are you not the people who landed the Greek Army in Anatolia? We are the people who defeated the Greek Army and threw them out of our territory. In such a situation it is for you to decide what to do, not us."

This attitude created a flurry on board the *Iron Duke*, the British flagship. Already Turkish sentries had prevented Admiral Brock,[2] the British commander-in-chief, from coming ashore, and the Turks observed that his guns were trained on the city. Later, however, he called upon Nur-ed-Din, who apologized for the incident and, in response to the admiral's assurances of British neutrality in terms of the armistice, declared that no state of war existed.

The admiral sent a note to Kemal asking for official confirmation of

---

[2] Later Admiral of the Fleet Sir Osmond de Beauvoir Brock, G.C.B., K.C.M.G., K.C.V.O.

this contradictory statement and instructed Commander Barry Domvile to be prepared to go ashore and call on the Gazi for an answer. A question arose as to the appropriate dress for the interview. Should the commander, for example, wear a sword? The captain disposed of the problem in summary fashion: "A sword for that fellow? I should think not. I should carry a walking stick."

Kemal had spoken in heat. He replied, confirming Nur-ed-Din's statement. His own remark had been made unofficially and not as the representative of the Grand National Assembly. There was no state of war. On the other hand, diplomatic relations between the two countries did not exist. Formalities would be necessary before these were established. Unofficially he suggested that this should be done, and for the purpose telegraphed to Angora for his Minister of Foreign Affairs.

Thus the incident was closed. But Kemal remarked humourously to Halide, "In the name of all common sense tell me how, Hanum Effendi, could the Greeks have landed in Smyrna without the strong help and desire of the British government? Could anything have happened in the Near East without their express desire? Of course we were at war with them, not with the Greeks—a thousand times so." Meanwhile the British authorities were taking no chances. On instructions from London, Lamb arranged for the evacuation of all remaining British subjects who wished to go. Already a party had left of their own accord some days before.

With the French and especially the Italian representatives Kemal was more cordial. He raised no such question of official recognition. In an interview, conducted in French, with Admiral Dumesnil, at which Ismet was present, he gave assurances as to the protection of the Christian population.[3] The gendarmerie was on its way and would restore order within twenty-four or at the most forty-eight hours. Serious measures were being taken, in liaison with Constantinople, to feed the refugees.

The admiral then referred to the arrest and internment by the Turks of all the able-bodied male Christian population and their threatened deportation to the interior as indicated by Nur-ed-Din. This had caused panic throughout the Greek and Armenian communities, and would create a bad impression abroad, as recent deportations from the Samsun area had done. Kemal replied in a conciliatory spirit. Nur-ed-Din had spoken in military terms, at the moment of victory, concerned to prevent the passage of potential Greek recruits to continue the war in Thrace. In fact the Turkish intentions were not so drastic, and he undertook to

[3] Benoist-Méchin, *Mustapha Kemal.*

reassure the population accordingly. Nonetheless deportations continued.

As events turned out it was not massacre but fire that made a tragedy of the Turkish reoccupation of Smyrna. The excesses committed by the Turkish soldiery against the local Greeks were brutal indeed, but of a sporadic and individual kind. There was no repetition of the organized massacres which had occurred elsewhere and which the Christians feared. An official American observer, contradicting lurid reports in the American press, afterwards estimated the total deaths, from various causes, at about two thousand.

Nevertheless feeling ran high between the Turks and Armenians, and for several nights there was bloodshed, with knives and bayonets, in the streets of the Armenian quarter, where the Turkish troops were ostensibly rounding up suspected traitors and confiscating arms. Typical of such skirmishes was one described, with true British understatement, in the diary of a midshipman on board the *King George V*: "Looking out of the window I saw an Armenian throw a bomb at some Turks. They chased him and he jumped into the sea. They got a boat and chased the Armenian and brought him on shore. He then died unpleasantly."

This internecine violence led, more or less by accident, to the outbreak of a catastrophic fire. Its origins were never satisfactorily explained. Kemal maintained to Admiral Dumesnil that it had been deliberately planned by an Armenian incendiary organization, and that before the arrival of the Turks speeches had been made in the churches, calling for the burning of the city as a sacred duty. Fuel for the purpose had been found in the houses of Armenian women, and several incendiaries had been arrested. Others accused the Turks themselves of deliberately starting the fire under the orders or at least with the connivance of Nur-ed-Din Pasha, who had a reputation for fanaticism and cruelty.

More probably it started when the Turks, rounding up the Armenians to confiscate their arms, besieged a band of them in a building in which they had taken refuge. Deciding to burn them out, they set it alight with petrol, placing a cordon of sentries around to arrest or shoot them as they escaped. Meanwhile the Armenians started other fires nearby to divert the Turks from their main objective. The quarter was on the outskirts of the city. But a strong wind, for which they had not allowed, quickly carried the flames towards the city. By the early evening several other quarters were on fire, and a thousand houses, built flimsily of lath and plaster, had been reduced to ashes. The flames were being spread by looters, and doubtless also by Turkish soldiers, paying off scores. The fire brigade was powerless to cope with such a conflagration, and at Ismet's headquarters the Turks alleged that its hose pipes had been deliberately severed. Ismet himself chose to declare that the Greeks had planned to burn the city.

By nightfall all of it was ablaze, and the flames were spreading down to the waterfront, driving the inhabitants and the refugees towards the sea, until tens of thousands were huddled there in bemused and helpless swarms. The sick and the aged were brought down from the hospitals on improvised stretchers. After midnight almost the whole line of houses along the front caught fire simultaneously. There was, as Captain Thesiger described it, "the most awful scream one could ever imagine." The crowds surged away from the houses towards the sea, and many jumped or were pushed into the water. Had they stayed still, the danger would not have been great, since the houses burned out quickly; but panic took hold of them. Had they moved along the quay away from the fire, they would have been safe; but a false rumour circulated that pickets of Turkish machine gunners were blocking it at either end. Instead they ran around aimlessly, clutching bundles which were often already on fire.

The roar of the flames was deafening, but the wail of the crowds could be heard above it. Soon the fire along the front was some two miles long. "The surface of the sea," wrote Ward Price, a correspondent on board the British flagship, "shone like burning copper. . . . Twenty distinct volcanoes of raging flame were throwing up jagged, writhing tongues to a height of a hundred feet. The towers of the Greek churches, the domes of the mosques, the flat roofs of the houses, were silhouetted against a curtain of flame." The commanders of the warships were concerned largely to save their own nationals and, as neutrals, refused at first to take refugees on board. But women threw their children into boats to save them; men plunged into the water and swam out to the ships; families crowded into caïques, which capsized, so that many were drowned.

On the crowds squatting ashore a paralysis descended. "Starving, dazed and exhausted, they had lost even the capacity for panic," said an eyewitness. "They sat herded together, often in the way of the flames, and if ordered to move, obeyed almost with an animal docility, their eyes only expressing their despair and fatigue." Within their hearing, faithful to service routine at this hour, the naval band of the British flagship played while Smyrna burned, adding the strains of light music to the roar of the flames and the shouts and cries of the victims.

In the early hours of the morning the British admiral reversed his orders and sent all his boats ashore, to save as many foreign civilians as possible, regardless of nationality. The foreign warships did the same. The scene changed instantly. On the quay there was an orderly blowing of Allied whistles, a shouting of orders, a tramping of booted feet. The refugees stampeded towards the fleet of small boats, a torrent of terrified humanity pouring over their bows, disregarding the officers' shouts of "Women and children only!" until the crews had to fight back the men with their fists and with sticks. Some two thousand of them were taken on board the *Iron Duke* alone.

In the morning the wind changed and the fire gradually died down. But it smouldered for several days more, punctuated by explosions as the Greek hoards of explosives went up. The European city of Smyrna was no more, and tens of thousands of homeless citizens now shared the plight of the refugees. Whose fault was it? To the question "Who started the fire?" an American observer returned the pertinent query: "Who started the San Francisco earthquake?"

Kemal, hardened to the disasters of war and its inevitable bloodshed, was not unduly perturbed by the fire—in which, after all, though the loss of property had been vast, the loss of human life had been comparatively small. To Admiral Dumesnil he described it as a "disagreeable incident," and when rebuked for his understatement insisted that, compared to other questions, it was an episode of secondary importance.

For the Nationalists indeed, callous as such an attitude was, it had a certain symbolic justice. For Smyrna was a foreign city, and as such represented all that they had been fighting against. The Smyrna that rose from its ashes would be a Western city—but it would be wholly Turkish. Much of the destruction wrought by Turks, both in the First World War and after it, had arisen from no mere wanton impulse but from that sense of inferiority which sought to eliminate the visible signs of European occupation. Thus, whether or not the Turks had a major hand in the burning of Smyrna, it represented in their hearts a fitting culmination to the Nationalist victory.

Throughout the fire Kemal had remained at his headquarters, his harsh sun-tanned face lit up by the glow of it. A party of Turkish journalists had arrived by boat from Constantinople, not knowing whether Smyrna had yet fallen until they saw the Turkish flag flying proudly from the citadel. Falih Rifki found the Gazi with two British naval officers standing at attention beside him—a sign of respect, he reflected with pleasure, which he had never witnessed in Constantinople. Kemal greeted him jovially: "You don't know what things we have seen. We have become history." He asked for news of Constantinople and added drily, "Do they really believe we are now victorious?"

As the flames came closer his A.D.C.s and friends grew worried and begged him to move. Taking his own time, he did so in his open car, a lorry preceding him to force a way through the crowds. Slowly and imperturbably he drove between thousands of suffering Greeks and Armenians, who exclaimed with fear and wailed, "Oh! . . . Oh! . . . Oh! . . ." at the sight of the conqueror.

Kemal had now moved to the fashionable suburb of Bornova, which the Turks called Göztepe. Soon after his arrival in Smyrna a young woman had come to his headquarters and asked to see him. Impatiently he refused, telling the orderly to send her away. But as he was doing so she walked into his office. Taking a look at her, he dismissed the orderly and asked her to sit down. This was no peasant woman but a lady of evident breeding, unveiled and wearing, with her Turkish headdress, sober but elegant clothes. She was short, round-faced, and stocky in figure, with a fair olive skin, large dark eyes that showed intelligence, and a tight-drawn mouth that showed character. She combined the liveliness of youth with the self-assurance of maturity.

Kemal was intrigued by her forwardness, her frank way of talking, her directness of gaze. Her name was Latife; her father a well-to-do Smyrniot, Ushakizade Muammer, who had interests in commerce and shipping and connections abroad. She had studied law in Europe and spoke French like a Frenchwoman. Her parents were spending the summer in Biarritz, but she had insisted on returning to Smyrna on her own when the offensive seemed imminent, determined to work for the Kemalist cause. She had made a hero of Kemal and sought him out as soon as he entered Smyrna with his liberating army. As she now revealed to him, she wore round her neck a locket with his picture inside. "Do you mind?" she asked him.

"Why should I mind?" he replied with a chuckle, recounting the interview later, with schoolboyish delight, to Halide Edib. Already, Halide guessed, he was imagining her in love with him—though in fact she must be one of thousands of Turkish women who wore his picture in a locket. Nothing better, she thought, could have happened. Latife would have "a humanizing effect on him and keep him out of mischief."

She now invited him to move with his staff to her parents' house, which lay outside the city, away from its confusion and noise and smouldering fires, calm amid the luxuriant gardens of Bornova, where the wealthier Levantines had made their homes. It was large, it was comfortable, it was well staffed with servants. She would look after him and help him in any way he required. She offered him in effect the stimulus of a new feminine attachment in a relaxed Western atmosphere. He accepted the offer. Here surely was the appropriate setting for the conquering hero. From here he issued a highly coloured report to the "great and noble Turkish nation" on the victorious liberation of Smyrna and Brusa by armies which sprang from its "national conscience."

One hot summer evening the Gazi gave a party at the Bornova villa for the journalists from Constantinople and others. Latife, "a very little lady in black" with a black scarf over her head, received the guests with a pleasing dignity at the top of the steps of a verandah festooned at this season with wistaria, jasmine, and a casual profusion of roses. Kemal stood beside her, slim and elegant in a white belted shirt of Caucasian style, his fair hair neatly brushed backwards, his fair eyebrows bristling upwards, his eyes responding with a glint of good humour to the glow of dawning adoration in those of Latife. Introducing her to Halide, he said, "We are celebrating Smyrna—you must drink with us."

Halide refused to touch raki and asked for champagne, raising her glass to wish him happiness. Kemal stuck to raki and remarked that it was the first time he had dared to drink it in Halide's stern presence. He seemed ruffled when Latife too chose champagne, reminding her that she had drunk raki on previous occasions. She at least, he implied, was no puritan.

Throughout the evening he talked, going over the past and the present, restraining for Latife's benefit his usual ironical comments, conceding an unfamiliar measure of praise to his friends in the Nationalist movement, impressing the journalists with conversational talents at once eloquent, gay, and profound. Later there was music. He broke into the Rumeli folk songs he cherished, with a hint of nostalgia in his soft resonant voice, conjuring up in the guests poignant visions of the lost Macedonian mountains. Then he swept them into the *zeybek,* the vigorous masculine dance of the reclaimed Aegean coastlands, in the performance of which his Caucasian shirt became him well.

Ismet, through round eyes, beamed upon the company. He approved of Latife, as Rauf on his arrival was also to approve of her. Himself a marrying man, Ismet saw marriage as the proper state for others, and now especially for Kemal. A good wife at this moment was just what he needed, to soften his hard edges, curb his excesses, present to the nation an image of respectable marital stability. It was time for him to settle down—and with whom better than Latife, clearly an intelligent woman, moreover of Turkish race but Western background?

He took Halide aside and asked, "What do you think of Latife Hanum?"

"She is very charming," Halide replied. She was thinking of Fikriye, of the suffering that awaited her on hearing of Kemal's new attachment.

Latife became in effect Kemal's secretary; she soon emerged from the background which she had at first tactfully chosen, to help him in all kinds of practical ways. In her forceful style she looked after his health and domestic comfort. But she gave him something more besides. With her knowledge of English and French she became an efficient translator of his diplomatic correspondence. She stimulated his mind with her fluent talk, her arguments, her advice, her ideas born of a wide European culture. Here was a woman to whom he could talk as to few of the men around him. It was a relationship he had tasted before, never with Fikriye, but with such European women as Corinne Lütfü and Berthe Georges-Gaulis. But Latife was of his own race and stirred his blood as the others had done only perfunctorily. With a lively masculine mind she combined a desirable feminine body. She excited him physically. Used to women who were "available," who yielded easily, he made vigorous advances.

But she firmly resisted him. She might become his wife but she would not become his mistress. She was an emancipated modern woman. Such were her principles and they conflicted with his. He was a soldier; he had work to do; he could not and would not marry until this work was completed. The oriental male thus met his match in the Western female. For the first time Kemal could not have the woman he wanted. There was deadlock between them. It was still unbroken when he left Smyrna for Angora at the end of the month.

41 ► Crisis at Chanak

The Western Powers waited, with some concern, to see what the victorious Kemal would do next. "It was," wrote Vansittart, "as if a boxer, after being counted out, had risen from the ring, stunned his opponent, knocked the referee through the ropes and levanted with the purse." Churchill put it more sonorously:

The catastrophe which Greek recklessness and Allied procrastination, division and intrigue had long prepared now broke upon Europe. The signatories of the Treaty of Sèvres had only been preserved in their world of illusion by the shield of Greece. That shield was now shattered. Nothing but a dozen battalions of disunited British, French and Italian troops stood between the returning war and Europe. . . . The re-entry of the Turks into Europe, as conquerors untrammelled and untamed, reeking with the blood of helpless Christian populations must, after all that had happened in the war, signalise the worst humiliation of the Allies. Nowhere had their victory been more complete than over Turkey; nowhere had the conqueror's power been flaunted more arrogantly than in Turkey; and now, in the end, all the fruits of successful war, all the laurels for which so many thousands had died on the Gallipoli Peninsula, in the deserts of Palestine and Mesopotamia, in the marshes of the Salonika front, in the ships which fed these vast expeditions; all the divisions of allied resources in men, in arms, in treasure which they had re-quired; all was to end in shame.

What was to be done? Kemal had no intention of halting his opera-tions in Smyrna. His objectives were Constantinople and Adrianople, in eastern Thrace—no more but no less than the frontiers of the National Pact. In a series of press interviews in Smyrna he made it clear that he was ready to seek them by immediate negotiation. To an American journalist he chose to declare that he would be in Constantinople within eight days and would thence proceed to occupy eastern Thrace. He claimed also Mosul but renounced any designs on Mesopotamia. His quarrel, he declared, was not with Britain but only with Greece. He had his peace plans as well as his war plans, and they included guarantees for the security of the Straits. But if the Allies would not accept them he was ready to pursue the Greeks into Europe.

Meanwhile he was moving his troops up the coast towards Chanak, on the Asiatic shores of the Dardanelles. Here was the frontier of the Neutral Zone, the Allied ring around Constantinople which extended from the lines of Chatalja in the west to the Izmit Peninsula in the east, from the Black Sea in the north to the Dardanelles in the south, which the Sultan's government was committed to respect and the Allies to de-fend. When the Greeks had threatened the zone two months before, at Chatalja, the French and the Italians had joined the British in its de-fence. Would they do so again, now that the Kemalists were threatening it at Chanak?

The choice confronting the Allies lay between resisting Kemal or placating him. Before his entry into Smyrna Lloyd George's Cabinet, in-sisting upon the control of the waters of the Straits as a cardinal British interest, had decided that any attempt by the Turks to cross over to the European shore should be resisted by force. London had few illusions as to the probable reaction of Paris and Rome, where public opinion re-joiced at the defeat of the Greeks and mistrusted any intervention which might lead to war. The Cabinet hoped for French and Italian support in defending at least this European shore. Without them, however, the British would defend it alone. But the Asiatic shore was less essential to the control of the Straits, hence should not be defended without such support. Since the French and the Italians seemed unlikely to provide this, General Harington was authorized to withdraw his troops from Chanak.

The general, however, was a man of determined spirit. At a meeting of the High Commission in Constantinople he succeeded in obtaining a promise of support from his French and Italian colleagues. They would join with the British in "showing the flag" by the despatch of token contingents to Chanak and the Izmit Peninsula. Their respective governments agreed and General Harington did not withdraw. Instead Kemal's representative in the city was warned that the three Allies were united in opposition to any attempt to violate the Neutral Zone. The French and Italian troops arrived, to be given a cheerful welcome by a British military band. Three flags flew at Chanak—for the moment at least.

Co-operation among the Allies persisted in the High Commission, where it was appreciated, at a meeting on September 15, that Kemal might soon force the issue, probably by transporting troops across the Straits. To forestall him they urged the calling of a peace conference without delay. London shared these views. On the same day the Cabinet held a meeting at which, acting still on the assumption of French and Italian support, they agreed to send a division to reinforce Harington, and moreover drafted an appeal to the Dominions and to the Balkan states for aid, if need be, in resisting a Kemalist advance. It was hoped thus to show that the British Empire was in earnest, to stiffen the French, and to sober Kemal until arrangements could be made for a conference in Venice or Paris.

The decision was much influenced by Churchill, smouldering as he was with shame at his country's humiliation. For three years he had championed the Turks against Lloyd George's championship of the Greeks. But now that this policy had failed he threw his weight onto the side of Lloyd George in resisting the consequences. An invasion of the Straits, Constantinople, and Thrace by the Turks was a danger to Europe and to the Christian population of Turkey—moreover an affront not to be borne. "Defeat is a nauseating draught; and that the victors in the greatest of all wars should gulp it down, was not readily to be accepted." Kemal must be stopped. "The Press might howl, the Allies might bolt. We intended to force the Turk to a negotiated peace before he should set foot in Europe." Lloyd George's secretary, Miss Stevenson, overhearing a discussion on this Cabinet decision between her master and Churchill, was horrified, seeing in it the prospect of another Great War. She was tempted to send in a note of her fears to the Cabinet meeting but forbore from doing so. These fears were soon to be shared by others.

Harington now prepared, in Constantinople, to put pressure on the French to reinforce in their turn. At this juncture, however, the French High Commissioner, General Pelle, suddenly left Constantinople in a warship for Smyrna, without informing his Allied colleagues. He hoped to extricate France from her predicament by persuading Kemal to respect the Neutral Zone, in return for implied French support at a conference. But the Gazi could afford to take a belligerent line. Playing the victorious general at the expense of the wise statesman, he protested that he and his government recognized no such Neutral Zone. The purpose of military action, he instructed the general, was to follow an enemy rapidly and defeat him. In pursuit of this aim it would be impossible to hold back his troops until they had liberated eastern Thrace. They were already on the move and were preparing to march on Constantinople. He was ready to come to a conference but refused meanwhile to halt his operations, which must be finished by the winter.

Meanwhile Churchill, obtaining Lloyd George's approval but omitting to consult the Foreign Office, issued a communiqué which Curzon, who was spending the weekend in the country and read it for the first time in the Sunday newspapers, angrily condemned as a "flamboyant manifesto." It confirmed, for public consumption and in provocative tones, the decision of the Cabinet, in concert with the Dominions, to resist any Turkish encroachment by force. As Kemal uttered his threats to Pelle, this defiant pronouncement rang around the world. It evoked grumbles about "colonial rule" from the Dominions, whose ministers read it in the press before they had seen Curzon's official telegrams. They gave qualified promises of military support. It awoke Britain to the gravity of the crisis and aroused fears of an imminent war against the Turks, with the *Daily Mail* thundering: STOP THIS NEW WAR. In France it enraged Poincaré and precipitated the change in French policy towards which he had been moving. The French government ordered their forces to withdraw from Chanak and the Izmit Peninsula. The Italians, who had already made promises of neutrality to Kemal, followed their example. Only one flag now flew at Chanak. There could no longer be any question of a British withdrawal from Chanak, whose retention had thus acquired a moral significance greater than that of Constantinople itself. Harington indeed received authorization from the War Office to withdraw from the capital if he thought fit but he was instructed at all costs to hold Chanak.

Curzon hurried over to Paris to confront and reproach Poincaré. After a long and acrimonious dispute at the Quai d'Orsay it was finally agreed to send a joint invitation to Kemal—or a representative of the Grand National Assembly—to attend a meeting at Mudanya, on the Sea of Marmara, to discuss with the Allied military chiefs lines of demarcation beyond which the Turks would not advance. This was to precede a con-

ference, at Venice or elsewhere, to decide upon conditions of peace between the Allies and Turkey and Greece.

Kemal did not at once reply to this invitation. While Curzon, back in
London, was graciously acknowledging the plaudits of his Cabinet colleagues, a revolution took place in Greece. King Constantine was deposed
and hurried into exile. A military government was installed, and Venizelos hurried to London as its ambassador. The hopes of the pro-Greek
party in the Cabinet revived. Lloyd George and Venizelos between them
might once again throw the Greeks into the field or at least press for a
settlement in their favour.[1]

Kemal, sensing this danger—or at least the advantage to be gained
from exploiting it—and encouraged by the defection of France and Italy,
at once intensified his pressure against Britain. On September 23, disregarding a warning from Harington that the British proposed to defend the Neutral Zone, he sent a detachment of cavalry across its frontier
to Ezine, southeast of Chanak.

The Turkish patrols, advancing through rough hilly country, encountered those of the 3rd Hussars, under the command of Captain J. C.
Petherick. The British officers had orders not to fire unless fired upon. It
soon became evident from their tentative attitude that the Turks had
received similar orders. There followed a strange mock skirmish, consisting, as Captain Petherick described it, of "tactics in reverse." Each
side sought to reveal rather than to conceal its forces, stationing them
prominently on the crests of the hills instead of taking cover behind
them. The British squadron—which the Turks thus took to be a regiment of cavalry—withdrew, in this way, to a series of positions around
the battlefield of Troy, while the perimeter of Chanak itself was entrenched within barbed-wire defences.

Soon the Turks were facing the British through the wire, often with
no more than twenty yards between them. Many of them marched in
with rifles reversed, as a disclaimer of hostile intentions. Good humour
and restraint prevailed on both sides. The British officers were happy to
confirm that, as they had always suspected, the Turkish officer was also a
gentleman. The opposing troops fraternized with the exchange of pots
and pans and camp equipment.

[1] Lloyd George was still reluctant to believe in their total defeat and, when Kemal
was advancing on Smyrna, had strongly advised them—without consulting the Foreign Office—not to sue for an armistice, as the Germans had mistakenly done in 1918,
but to hold the Turkish advance before the city, with a view to obtaining better
terms.

One day an agitated Turkish infantry officer asked the British detachment confronting him for a loan of barbed wire. A general was coming to inspect his defences, which were not yet wired. He would faithfully return it after the general had gone. He started to put up the wire, but with little success, so the British troops did it for him.

All this time Harington and Kemal were exchanging polite but firm telegrams. Kemal was warned, through the British admiral at Smyrna, that sooner or later Harington would be obliged to drive his troops out. Kemal reiterated that he did not recognize the Neutral Zone and that his troops were in pursuit of the Greek Army. Later he insisted to the French in Smyrna that he could not withdraw them, but confirmed that he had ordered them not to attack the British. It was shadowboxing, a game of bluff on both sides, and Harington was convinced that a conference could be reached without the loss of a single life. It had to be admitted that a stray shot or a misunderstood order might at any moment cause an involuntary explosion. But among the men on the spot there was little anxiety. It was in London that the danger seemed to lie. As a French officer had remarked to Captain Petherick, Lloyd George was *"peu stable."*

It was evident that Kemal's show of force was building up to substantial proportions, and this was duly reported to London. Five days after the initial incursion Harington estimated that a force of 40,000 now threatened Chanak, while another 50,000 threatened Izmit. This took no account of a general reserve of 40,000 in Constantinople and 20,000 more troops in eastern Thrace.

London, on receiving these reports, became thoroughly alarmed. This must not continue. On September 29 the Cabinet took note of the fact that Kemal had not replied to the Allied invitation to a conference. They drew up an ultimatum for delivery by Harington to the Turkish commander, threatening war unless the Kemalists withdrew.

The moment for this was oddly chosen. British reinforcements were now arriving in Chanak from Aldershot, Gibraltar, Malta, Egypt. The British were in a well-entrenched, well-wired position, with air supremacy and strong artillery support from Gallipoli. From this only a major operation could now dislodge them. It was hardly likely that Kemal, having refrained from attacking them when they were weak, would elect to do so now that they were strong. It would have been in a sense the Gallipoli campaign all over again, but in reverse, with the British and their fleet defending Constantinople and the Turks attacking it. On the other hand Kemal could not afford to lose face by a withdrawal in response to such a threat as the ultimatum implied.

The ultimatum had its opponents in the Cabinet, notably Curzon, who had always judged the danger to be exaggerated and was now more than ever convinced that a solution could be found by diplomacy rather than force. He sought to delay for twenty-four hours and cast around for contact with the Kemalists. Learning that Fethi, whom he had refused to receive as their representative a month before, had left Paris for Rome, he sent urgently for Fethi's deputy, Dr. Nihad Reshad, who hurried over from Vichy and was immediately shown into his presence. Curzon urged him to impress upon Kemal the danger of the situation. The atmosphere at Chanak, he said, was explosive and might well give rise to an incident. But if a Turkish soldier opened fire, this would still not be regarded as a *casus belli* unless an order to do so had been given by Kemal himself.

The Cabinet was divided between those, like himself, who still counselled patience and those who thought that its limit had been reached and that any idea of a conference at Mudanya must now be abandoned. There were even some ministers who, as a day passed without a reply from Harington, wished to send the ultimatum to Angora at once, without waiting. Theirs was the mentality that still saw Kemal as a blustering bandit chief, ready to collapse at the first serious threat. They remained obstinately blind to his emergence as the responsible and calculating founder of a nation, a soldier of genius, with an army behind him strong enough to involve Britain in a major war.[2]

The French meanwhile sent an "unofficial" emissary to Smyrna in the shape of Franklin-Bouillon, who urged restraint on Kemal. In fact he needed no such injunction. He had assessed the position shrewdly enough. There were hotheads in his entourage who urged him to exploit the victory by advancing, regardless of the Allies, not only into eastern but into western Thrace, and thence into Macedonia. Thus a great part of Rumeli could be regained. To one of them he said sharply, "Certainly not. The cry would go up again, 'The Turks are coming!' and every state in the Balkans would be appealing to the powers for assistance against us." Another, dreaming of a reconquest of Salonika, earned the rebuke: "Do you want to make sure that Lloyd George stays in power?" Calling a conference of his generals and his ministers from Angora, he had

[2] Criticizing this attitude, and that of the government in general, Lord Derby had written to Sir Austen Chamberlain: "It is all very well to call Mustafa Kemal a rebel; but transpose England and Turkey; such a man would not have been looked upon as a rebel, but as a true patriot fighting for his country and determined not to see it divided up and given to that wretched Greek nation which is incapable of fighting for or of administrating a great Empire." Randolph Churchill, *Lord Derby.*

found the majority in favour of such an advance. But he overruled them, insisting that Turkey, for the sake of her future international reputation, must on no account go a step beyond the initial demands of the National Pact.

The promise of eastern Thrace, with Adrianople, was his already without a shot being fired. The conflict between the Allies, which he had been quick to exploit from the start, had at the end solved his problems. There was nothing to be gained by attacking the British, who were now committed to retaliation, and for whose power, if they chose to demonstrate it as Churchill had done through his call to the Dominions, he had in any case too much respect. He knew Harington, initially from his conciliatory approach to Angora the year before, and in the last few days from their exchange of telegrams and from intercepts of others, as a man who was not anti-Turkish and who was working for peace. This was one of those occasions, not unusual in history, when the generals were the peacemongers and the politicians the warmongers.

Interviewed in Smyrna by Clare Sheridan, a war correspondent and cousin of Churchill, Kemal said of her compatriots, "I am acting with such patience, in order to give them every chance of retiring with dignity from the attitude they have adopted." It was his policy to tighten his pressure on Chanak and strengthen his forces around Constantinople until the last possible moment, thus gaining the maximum advantage from the conference which would follow. Only such an ultimatum as the British Cabinet had drafted could cause him to revise this policy and fight.

Fortunately the ultimatum was not to be delivered. Harington, who in Churchill's words "knew how to combine a cool and tactful diplomacy with military firmness," had the courage and patience to delay its delivery, to ignore his instructions and gain just the time needed, at this eleventh hour, for peace. He was supported by Admiral Brock and above all by Rumbold, convinced of "the absolute necessity of avoiding any action which might lead to war." Thus national pride on both sides was to be satisfied without it.

Kemal was now drafting his acceptance, in the name of the Grand National Assembly, of the Allied invitation to a peace conference. In agreeing to the conference he insisted on the immediate restoration of eastern Thrace. The preliminary meeting at Mudanya was announced for October 3. Kemal appointed Ismet as his delegate, then left Smyrna for Angora to receive a conqueror's welcome. From the station a group of his more devout subjects bore him off to give thanks at the Haji Bayram Mosque but he adroitly turned aside into the Parliament building and gave thanks from one of its balconies to no dead saint but to the Turkish soldier himself.

In the Chamber a grateful delegation of both groups received him. In a stirring oration he expressed the hope that "the sweet sun of peace will not delay in shining on the horizon of our country . . . watered with the blood of her children." He presided over a great military parade and accepted the freedom of the city. Then he settled down to follow the proceedings of the conference in continuous contact, by telegraph and telephone, with Ismet, and in attendance at all Cabinet meetings with Rauf and his ministers.

Mudanya was a shabby mosquito-ridden port, with cobbled streets and timbered houses, serving Brusa and the interior from the southern shore of the Marmara. The conference, which opened in teeming rain and a boisterous wind from across its waters, was held in the former Russian Consulate, a small house whose shabbiness was hurriedly screened by the hanging of carpets on the whitewashed walls. Since space was limited, only the heads of the four delegations—British, French, Italian, and Turkish—sat down at a table to confer, with interpreters between them. Among the "observers," Franklin-Bouillon—"Boiling Frankie" to the General Staff, "that Prince of Levantines" to Rumbold—was ubiquitous. The British saw him as the archenemy of the Allied cause, and Harington curtly refused his offer of help and advice.

The success of the conference was by no means assured. After two days of discussions some twenty-eight points, mostly of detail, were still not agreed. Ismet, negotiating stubbornly with the evident encouragement of the French, was insisting on an immediate take-over from the Greeks in eastern Thrace, the departure of all Allied missions, and the right to recruit an unlimited gendarmerie.

Eventually a protocol was drafted, covering the essential points, and Harington informed Ismet that this was his government's last word. He was returning in the *Iron Duke* that evening to Constantinople and would come back next day for a final reply. In Constantinople he reported to Rumbold that the situation seemed grave. He made military dispositions for the defence of the city. Seeing that only a restoration of Allied unity could save the situation, Lord Curzon hurried over to Paris once more. He persuaded Poincaré to agree to a compromise by which an Allied detachment would occupy eastern Thrace for a limited period;

the gendarmerie would be unlimited; and the Turks would respect the Neutral Zone. This decision was telegraphed to Constantinople and conveyed to Mudanya in a British destroyer.

Two anxious days followed, while Ismet sought instruction by telegram and telephone from Angora, first on the concessions, then on a draft convention agreed by the Allies. Just before the conference reassembled Harington was handed a telegram from his government, followed later by another, authorizing him, in the event of rejection, to issue an ultimatum to the Turks and, if necessary, to start operations. He put them both in his pocket. But he authorized his army commander at Chanak to open fire at a fixed hour unless otherwise instructed.

The atmosphere, however, was now noticeably different. Only six points remained to be settled, and Ismet's manner seemed friendlier. Agreement was reached on the first four points. On the fifth Harington was obliged to insist on the retention of certain areas in the Neutral Zone from which the Turks must withdraw. As he afterwards described it, "Ismet Pasha said that he could not agree, and that there was a deadlock. . . . The scene is before me now—that awful room—only an oil lamp. I can see Ismet's Chief of Staff—he never took his eyes off me. I paced up one side of the room saying that I must have that area and would agree to nothing less. Ismet paced up the other side saying he would not agree. Then quite suddenly he said, '*J'accepte!*' I was never so surprised in my life!"

The sixth point was easily settled, and Harington realized that agreement had been reached. But he trusted no Turk and was taking no chances. Thus, despite French and Italian remonstrances, he insisted on signature that very night. The conference sat for fifteen more hours, while the agreement—with the aid of inexperienced typists—was recorded in five different languages. The Turkish military band played periodic tunes to keep everyone awake. Finally it was completed and signed.

In the cold blue light of the morning the text was handed to the press. General Harington made a brief nervous speech: "We met as strangers, but we part as friends." The compliment escaped Ismet, deaf as he was, but he replied that this day would be among his happiest memories. To Franklin-Bouillon, who had been in touch with Kemal from the outset, he remarked, "It is your day of triumph, my friend." At last peace was assured.

The Kemalists were now free to occupy eastern Thrace. Here the Greek population was trekking westwards across the plains, whole families tramping, laden with trunks, beside ox-drawn wagons piled with household goods, while their flocks trooped before them and at night their campfires dotted the earth like stars in the sky. It was a spectacle which recalled to Ward Price the migrations of the Thirty Years' War. Such was the culmination of Lloyd George's attempt to create a new Greek Empire; such, in a few days' time, the valediction to his political career.

For some months past the Conservatives had been fretting uneasily at his policies and at the constrictions of the Coalition government. Now at Chanak he and Churchill had brought the country—or so they saw it— to the brink of war. As one of them remarked: "We cannot afford to keep him any longer. It is too expensive." They sought a return to Conservative party rule and found a leader in Bonar Law, who wrote in a historic letter to *The Times* that Britain could no longer maintain other than her own direct interests without Allied support. "We cannot act alone," he wrote, "as the policeman of the world."

The reply of his Conservative opponents in the Cabinet was a decision, confirmed at a dinner in Churchill's house, to dissolve Parliament and go to the country as a Coalition. This meant continued support of Lloyd George. He followed up his apparent victory with a speech, in his birthplace of Manchester, in the course of which he chose to launch a last diatribe against the barbarous Turks and "the scenes of intolerable horror" which they had been perpetrating in Asia Minor over the past years. But five days later, at a meeting at the Carlton Club, Bonar Law, with the last-minute support of Lord Curzon, inspired a majority of Conservative M.P.s to break with the Coalition and go to the country on a party basis.

Thus Lloyd George resigned, remarking to his secretaries as he bade them farewell that he would not be returning "unless I come back as head of a deputation to see Mr. Bonar Law (and Lord Curzon) to ask for a grant for Welsh education." [3] Bonar Law became Prime Minister. Kemal had won his battle. After three years of fighting, the despised Turkish rebel had helped to bring down a British government and a renowned Prime Minister. The romantic had fallen to the realist. The Macedonian had defeated the Celt.

[3] Frank Owen, *Tempestuous Journey.*

42 ▶ *End of the Sultanate*

What meanwhile was to become of Constantinople? Here the position, pending the peace conference, was anomalous. The Allies still occupied the capital. Tevfik Pasha's government still exercised nominal authority. Above all, the Sultan-Caliph still sat on his throne. As Caliph he kept his spiritual powers. All that was now left of his temporal Empire, however, was the city itself. The rest of the country was controlled by the government of the Grand National Assembly, whose leaders he had proscribed as rebels, excommunicated, and condemned to death. But in Constantinople this government still had no status.

Both in Smyrna and afterwards, back in Angora, Kemal had discussed at length with his ministers and friends how the problem of the Sultanate and its government should be solved. He had long ago made up his mind to abolish the Sultanate when the moment was ripe. The Assembly shrewdly suspected that this was his intention and grew agitated at the prospect. To discuss the next step, Kemal, Rauf, Ali Fuad, and Refet, the four founders of the Revolution, met once again for an all-night session around the drink table. Kemal cautiously invited his three friends in turn to express their views on the question.

Rauf replied that he was bound by conscience, sentiment, and tradition to the Sultanate and the Caliphate. He made it clear, however, that he held no brief for Vahid-ed-Din in person, who had played the traitor and must be replaced by another. Refet considered that the Sultanate should become a constitutional monarchy, under which the monarch would merely confirm ministerial appointments, made by a Prime Minister responsible to Parliament. This view was shared by Rauf with his respect for British institutions, and by others in the country. The Angora government, it was being suggested, should move to Constantinople, where the Sultan would be its nominal head, serving as an element of national stability. But effective power would be in the hands of Kemal, as Prime Minister—on the analogy of Mussolini in Italy. Ali Fuad, when asked for his opinion, hedged with the reply that, having only lately returned from Moscow, he had not yet had time to study public sentiment and so to form a concrete view.

Kemal saw that he could not yet force this issue and told his friends that for the present the question of the Sultanate did not arise. He made a statement to this effect in the Assembly, thus reassuring the deputies. The Nationalists, nonetheless, must be represented in Constantinople. Kemal thus decided to appoint a military governor of eastern Thrace, with his headquarters provisionally in the capital, and chose Refet for the post.

Meanwhile, a chief delegate must be chosen for the peace conference which was to be held at Lausanne. Kemal favoured Ismet. Feeling in the lobbies of the Assembly, however, preferred Rauf. Ismet, the deputies argued, was a mere soldier, who knew little of politics and would be worsted by the cunning foreign diplomats. Let him go, by all means, but as deputy and military adviser to Rauf. Kemal in reply championed Ismet's intelligence, foresight, and other qualities which, owing to his long absence in the field, were not properly appreciated in Angora. "Take this table at which I am sitting," he said in illustration. "If I ask any of you to knock it down, you will be able to knock it down in two ways, or in three ways, or at the most in four ways. But Ismet Pasha is so clever that he could knock it down in eight, nine, or even ten different ways." He sidetracked a claim for Kiazim Karabekir on the pretext that he was not on good terms with the Russians, who were expected to be present. Finally the question of protocol was raised. Rauf was Prime Minister. The other powers would be represented by their Foreign Ministers and Turkey, it was argued, should conform to their choice.

This argument suited Kemal, who judged that Rauf, with his independent spirit, his experience of Europe, and his conciliatory way, might not prove easy to handle. He knew how to control Ismet. His will thus prevailed and Ismet was chosen, Yusuf Kemal agreeing to relinquish the Foreign Ministry in his favour. Ismet was thus faced with a *fait accompli.* He was dismayed and reluctant to accept the post, for he saw himself, as the deputies saw him, as a military man, not a diplomat. He had little aptitude for negotiation and had found even the Mudanya conference a strain. But he had no choice. When he hesitated Kemal, once more the commander instructing his chief of staff, made it clear that his proposal was an order.

Soon afterwards Kemal left for Brusa, the holy Ottoman city on the slopes of Mount Olympus whose loss to the Greeks had caused such mourning and recrimination among the delegates to the Grand National Assembly. Alone among the burned towns and villages around, it had chanced to escape destruction. Its inhabitants now hoped that, among other celebrations, Kemal would pay suitable tributes of thanksgiving at the tombs of his Ottoman predecessors. However, he was more concerned to regroup his forces, which now amounted to some 140,000 men, encircling the Neutral Zone. This he did, leaving one group south of Chanak, from which its advance guard had now retired, and another opposite the Izmit Peninsula, while the reserve was concentrated at Brusa itself, ready to reinforce either wing in the event of a breakdown in the peace negotiations.

Ismet and Fevzi were already in Brusa; Kiazim Karabekir, now Minister of War, and Refet arrived with Kemal. Thus he had his commanders around him. The liberated citizens gazed upon the victorious pashas with rapt admiration. There was an air of suppressed excitement. The cars of the generals, the carriages of staff officers thronged the streets, which had been hurriedly decked with triumphal arches. Military bands played. Kemal, spruce in his kalpak, held the centre of the stage.

At a victory dinner he announced Ismet's appointment to Lausanne. Ismet remained silent. He did not smile, as was his habit, but had a sombre, distracted look in his eyes. In a rhetorical discourse, rich with high-flown sentiment, Kemal spoke of him as "the best, the most perfect among us all—the surest counsellor, the most faithful support, the best of comrades, the most ardent of patriots, revered not only by all Turks but by all Moslem peoples, as the defender of their honour, virtue, and probity." Now he carried the nation's mandate to Europe: "Her treatment of him will be for us the touchstone of her feelings towards us."

The nation sought peace, but if forced would know how to make war right to the end.

Kemal did not forget to give Kiazim Karabekir his share of praise, mentioning his intelligence, his hardihood, his powers of organization, his military valour. Kiazim, while many still hesitated, had created an army, with which he had secured and stabilized the eastern frontiers, giving the Nationalist government its first proof of strength. Kemal recapitulated the past—the early struggles, the comrades who had come to him at the start, asking for nothing and hoping for nothing, conscious of the folly of their sacrifice; the three long years that had led to the liberation of Anatolia and the emergence of the Turkish nation, aware of itself, its rights, and its strength. Now the most difficult task of all remained—that of using victory to the full.

How he intended to use it was implied one evening at a large victory rally in a cinema. War orphans in uniform represented the generation of the future; schoolteachers, the generation of the present. The pashas were ranged on the platform, posed against an outsize Turkish flag. All were in uniform with the exception of Kemal himself, who wore with his usual elegance the civilian costume of Angora, with an astrakhan kalpak.

To the women, who outnumbered the men, he declaimed, "Win for us the battle of education and you will do yet more for your country than we have been able to do. It is to you that I appeal." To the men he said: "If henceforward the women do not share in the social life of the nation, we shall never attain to our full development. We shall remain irremediably backward, incapable of treating on equal terms with the civilizations of the West." To all, with a sweeping gesture, he concluded, "And all that will still be nothing if you refuse to enter resolutely into modern life, if you reject the obligations which it imposes. You will be lepers, pariahs, alone in your obstinacy, with your customs of another age. Remain yourselves, but learn how to take from the West what is indispensable to an evolved people. Admit science and new ideas into your lives. If you do not, they will devour you."

There was prolonged applause. The women were in tears. It was a foretaste of the future, that future of which Kemal had remarked to Falih Rifki as they looked down over the smouldering embers of Smyrna, "They think that this is the end, that I have reached my goal. But it is only after this that we shall really begin to do something. It is only now that our real work is beginning."

··

Kemal had brought Fikriye with him from Angora to Brusa. On the road outside the city Halide Edib chanced to meet them as they arrived. Getting out of the car, Kemal explained that he was sending Fikriye to a sanatorium in Munich. Her consumptive condition had gradually worsened and the doctors in Angora had been urging treatment by specialists. There were thus good medical reasons for her departure—though Kemal had other reasons in mind.

It was an appropriate moment to end the affair. Fikriye had become wearisome to him. He was impatient of illness in others. She clung to him in an irritating fashion, the oriental mistress who had distracted him and suited his needs for a while. But no woman could hold his affections for long, and Fikriye now represented a period of his life that was over. For the life that lay ahead she had nothing to offer him. To Halide, though she could not but approve the decision, "coming as it did immediately after Smyrna, it looked as if she were being hurriedly put out of the way."

Halide asked to say good-bye to her and Kemal opened the door of Fikriye's car. Of their meeting she wrote:

She stretched out her hand and caught mine rather convulsively, and I was struck by its resemblance to another hand. Though emaciated to an extraordinary degree, the form was exactly like that of the plump hand of the plump girl from Smyrna—broad palms of a man, thick finger-tips and square small nails. . . . She looked extraordinarily fragile. The pretty little chin was a sharp blade-edge, the small nose almost transparent in its thinness and squeezed, tortured air. . . . But the thing that hurt most was the eyes—out of this devastated mask of pain they looked, the lower and the upper lashes curled and intermingled more than ever; tears falling through their webby edges on the sunken and drawn cheeks. . . . The grave and rather disturbing contralto voice spoke with composure in spite of the tears but there was some anxiety hidden in the tones.

She had not wanted to go, "but Pasha insisted." She was going first to Constantinople. She said, "I will stay a few days in Paris and get myself some beautiful clothes." Scrutinizing Halide's face, she tried to read belief "not so much in her recovery as in her return, decked in beautiful clothes and once more restored to love."

Halide kissed her tenderly and said, "You will be well and you will come back, my dear."

"*Insh'allah,*" Fikriye said fervently, clinging to the other woman and kissing her.

Fikriye was entrusted to the care of Refet and was thus ironically to witness, sick and in despair as she was, the celebration of Kemal's final triumph in Constantinople. Refet's own instructions were left purposely vague; in theory his jurisdiction was to extend over eastern Thrace alone. The evening before he left he sought out Kemal in the hope of obtaining a more explicit directive as to how he should proceed in Constantinople. But all he could extract, as he sat drinking with some press correspondents in Brusa, was a convivial greeting, followed by the airy assurance, "My old friend, you have been with us from the start. We both think alike."

Refet's reception was tumultuous. As his steamer approached the Golden Horn, thousands of small boats sailed out from either bank to greet her, all decked with flags—red and white for Turkey, green for Islam—and with fluttering streamers. The Galata Bridge itself was festooned with garlands. The Turkish flag flew from each roof, each dome, each minaret. Each house was draped with Turkish carpets. Triumphal arches bridged the streets, crowned with portraits of Kemal and his generals, and with inscriptions lauding the heroes of the War of Independence and the power and the glory of the Turkish people. The people themselves, in tens of thousands, expectantly thronged the streets. On the big square by the bridge hundreds of Turkish women, many of them unveiled, stood massed in groups in the Moslem style. Spectators clustered on the roofs of the houses, on the domes and the minarets of the mosques, even on the masts of the boats in the harbour.

As Refet's ship drew alongside the air was rent by a deafening chorus of sirens from every ship at anchor in the Bosporus and the Golden Horn, and a full-throated roar from every man, woman, and child on shore. The A.D.C. of Abdul Mejid, the heir apparent, came on board to welcome Refet, expressing his master's satisfaction at the happy victory and conviction that his arrival would bring justice, security, and welfare to Thrace. In expressing his thanks Refet referred to the fact that Abdul Mejid was heir to the Caliphate, whose preservation was one of the Nationalist government's objectives. When he was received on shore by a deputation including an A.D.C. of the Sultan himself, welcoming him in His Majesty's name, he made a significant reply, expressing his sentiments of religious devotion to the "high office of the Caliphate" but making no mention of the Sultanate or of His Majesty in person. There were knowing looks from those present, and the A.D.C. turned a trifle pale.

Refet's attitude to the rest of the delegation was similar. In accepting a message of welcome from Tevfik Pasha, the Grand Vizier, he made it clear that he did so only from personal respect, but that Anatolia did not acknowledge this government's existence. Later, replying to a speech delivered in the name of the Minister of the Interior, he expressed his cordial thanks but added that he recognized no such minister.

When Refet passed through the barrier the crowds broke the police cordon and mobbed him, carrying him shoulder-high to his car. Along the route of his procession they waved flags and brandished portraits of the Gazi, framed in laurel and pine. Standing up in his car, a small dapper figure at the salute, he was visibly moved by the passionate plaudits of the crowd. He drove straight to the tomb of Sultan Fatih Mehmed I, the Ottoman conqueror. Here, after performing his devotions, he made a brief speech to a group of students, assuring them that only youth, through the sacrifice of its fathers, had made the victory possible. To a large popular concourse he lauded the occupant of the tomb. This great Turkish commander had given them the city, and no Turk would allow it to be torn from them.

The pent-up emotions of three years were released as the various Nationalist organizations, which had hitherto languished underground, came out into the open to rejoice and proclaim their loyalty to the cause. The festivities continued for several days, culminating in the Friday prayer in Santa Sophia, when Refet addressed a huge concourse from the preacher's pulpit, reducing many to tears. Dashing, energetic, loquacious, ubiquitous, he was well cast for his role of popular hero. As the people jostled around him to kiss his garments and abstract objects from his person as souvenirs, he exclaimed, "They will kill me, they will break me, they love me so much!"

A detachment of Nationalist gendarmerie arrived en route for Thrace and were cheered as they marched through the streets. The foreigners, the Levantines, kept out of sight, comforting themselves with the hope that all this Nationalist bravado was no more than a flash in the pan which would subside, leaving things much as they were before. The Sultan meanwhile seemed forgotten, save by a band of students who shouted, "Down with the rascal in Yildiz!" He was said, however, to have voiced some alarm at Refet's continual references to the sovereignty of the people.

Refet swiftly established relations with the Allied authorities. With Harington he was soon on easy terms over a whisky and soda. He was quick to sense the reluctance of the British, now that the Mudanya Convention was signed, to maintain their former firm control over the city. Taking full advantage of this attitude, he spared no effort to make the power of the Nationalists felt. Fencing with the occupation forces, he made courteous demands of the Allied authorities which were for the most part courteously met. When he grew more truculent the demeanour of the British was passive; their protests were mild; their officers were instructed to avoid trouble. Slowly the machinery of the once powerful occupation was being whittled away.

In the administration, Nationalists asserted themselves above the heads of the Sultan's supporters. Vengeance was taken upon traitors to the Nationalist cause. Ali Kemal, a hostile journalist, who as Minister of the Interior had outlawed Mustafa Kemal, and who had since campaigned for the Allies and against the resistance, was singled out as a victim. One evening, in a barber's shop in Pera, he was arrested "in the name of the Grand National Assembly" by members of the Nationalist secret police. They gagged him and took him on board a motorboat, with its lights dimmed to avoid the British patrols, to Izmit, which the Nationalist troops had now entered. Here at dawn he was taken to the *konak* for interrogation by the Turkish army commander. But at midday, as he was being escorted back to the jail, a large crowd set upon him, overpowered his escort, and brutally stoned him to death.

His end caused serious alarm in the Yildiz Palace. Since the fall of Smyrna the Sultan had been wavering irresolutely between one course of action and another. With the fate of Abdul Hamid forever in mind, he planned at one moment to withdraw from Constantinople, at the next to make a show of clemency to the Nationalists. Now his staff began to desert him, and he appealed to General Harington to reinforce his guard.

Thus protected, still hoping to cling to his throne, he received Refet in audience. Refet saw before him a demoralized old man in a frock coat, without decorations, attended by a single A.D.C.—the last symbol of a fallen Empire. Refet, the young general of the new age, stood before him, brisk in his uniform, with a revolver at his hip. He took the initiative. "Sir," he said without further protocol, "the present situation cannot be prolonged much longer. We cannot have in Turkey two governments, one in Constantinople and the other in Angora. I come to beg you to bow before the force of events and to put an end to this dualism, which is contrary to the interests of the nation, by demanding the resignation of your government."

Vahid-ed-Din played for time. He replied that he was ready to consider a fusion between the two governments and demanded to know the intentions of Angora. Refet, now talking on his own responsibility, put forward the view, which he had already expressed to Kemal, that the Sultan should be a constitutional monarch, appointing the ministers approved by his Assembly, with the right to confirm but not to veto legislation. Meanwhile, however, he must dismiss his present ministers, men of a past age who no longer represented the nation.

The Sultan prevaricated. Concerning the dismissal of the ministers he objected that, as a constitutional monarch already, he was obliged to consult them first. Refet replied that the decision must be reached then or never. If the Sultan would agree to his proposal he would put it before the Angora government and try to gain their consent. But Vahid-ed-Din would not admit himself beaten. Still clinging to the hope that something would happen to save him and his throne, he put an end to the audience. Refet telegraphed to Kemal that the Sultan was "far from our way of thinking."

At this juncture the Allies took a maladroit step which gave Kemal just the chance he had been waiting for. Still adhering to protocol and invoking the precedent of past conferences, the Allies sent invitations to Lausanne both to the government of the Sublime Porte and to that of the Grand National Assembly.

At this the deputies exploded in wrath. Sixteen orators in succession denounced the action as a manoeuvre of the Sultan to divide the country in the eyes of the foreigner. They rehearsed at length the crimes of his government. The despatch of its delegates to Lausanne would be regarded as an act of high treason. Ismet, speaking for the first time as Minister of Foreign Affairs, contended that the double invitation was a breach of the Mudanya Convention.

The psychological moment for the abolition of the Sultanate had arrived. Kemal, faithful to his pragmatic methods, decided on an immediate compromise. The Sultanate would be separated from the Caliphate. The former, representing temporal power, would be abolished; the latter, representing spiritual power, would remain. It would be transferred to a prince whose office would be religious but in no way political. A motion was drafted, recording the breakdown of the Ottoman Empire and the birth of the new Turkish state, whose sovereign rights belonged constitutionally to the people.

It was hoped by this compromise to dispose of the Sultan while at the same time placating the religious elements in Parliament. But these, reinforced by Kemal's personal enemies, were strong and vociferous. Kemal tackled the Opposition on their own ground. Briefing himself well, with the aid of his Minister of Justice, on the history and laws of Islam, he pointed out that the Sultanate and the Caliphate had been separated in the past and could very well be separated again. His speech created turmoil in the Chamber, which rang with alternate shouts of "Vahid-ed-Din! Vahid-ed-Din!" and "God damn him!" followed by cheers. The various motions were then discussed in committee, with a learned *hoja* in the chair and Kemal in a corner listening patiently to a flow of hair-splitting arguments. The Opposition sought to prove that the two institutions were inseparable. "They relied," Kemal said later, "on the well-known fallacies and absurdities."

A breath of realism was needed. The problem, from Kemal's point of view, was to find a formula linking the power of the Caliphate with that of the Assembly. When he saw that his own supporters were hesitant he asked the chairman for permission to speak. Standing on a bench in front of the chairman, he said loudly:

"Gentlemen, sovereignty and Sultanate are not given to anyone by anyone because scholarship proves that they should be; or through discussion and debate. Sovereignty and Sultanate are taken by strength, by power and by force. It was by force that the sons of Osman seized the sovereignty and Sultanate of the Turkish nation; they have maintained this usurpation for six centuries. Now the Turkish nation has rebelled and has put a stop to these usurpers, and has effectively taken sovereignty and Sultanate into its own hands. This is an accomplished fact. . . . The question is merely how to give expression to it. . . . If those gathered here, the Assembly, and everyone else could look at this question in a natural way, I think they would agree. Even if they do not, the truth will soon find expression, but some heads may roll in the process."

This implied threat of force, which was followed by a theological disquisition, brought forth, from one of the *hojas* from Angora, the admission, "I beg your pardon, sir, we were looking at the matter from another point of view. We have been enlightened by your explanation."

Thus, by a combination of persuasion and menace characteristic of his political tactics, Kemal achieved a settlement in committee. The draft law now submitted to the Assembly was composed of two articles. The first declared that the form of the government in Constantinople, resting on the sovereignty of an individual, had ceased on March 16, 1920—the date of the Allied occupation of the city. The second declared that, though the Caliphate belonged to the Ottoman Empire, it rested on the Turkish state, and that the Assembly would choose as Caliph "that member of the Ottoman house who was in learning and character most worthy and fitting."

On a proposal for a nominal vote Kemal rose and said, "There is no need for this. I believe that the Assembly will unanimously adopt the principles which will forever preserve the independence of the country and the nation." The chairman, putting the law to the vote, announced its acceptance by acclamation. One opposing voice only was heard to exclaim, "I am against it." But it was drowned by cries of "Silence!" The session ended with prayers, recited no longer in Arabic but in Turkish.

"In this way, gentlemen," Kemal was to record, "the final obsequies of the decline and fall of the Ottoman Sultanate were completed!"

As soon as the news of the Assembly's decision reached Constantinople, Refet informed the Allied High Commissioners that he had taken over the government of the Sublime Porte in the name of the Grand National Assembly. On November 4, 1922, Tevfik delivered up to the Sultan at the Yildiz Palace the seals of office of the last government of the Ottoman Empire. The Allies declared their neutrality in the internal affairs of Turkey. The city authorities called on Refet and placed themselves under the orders of Angora, accepting a regime which was provisionally described as a "national monarchy." Constantinople gave itself over once more to celebrations, with cries of "Long live the monarchy of the nation! Long live Parliament!"

The Sultan meanwhile stayed where he was, now deserted by most of his entourage. Kemal, reluctant to risk the popular resentment which would follow his deposition by force, preferred to await events. Presently the Sultan summoned Rumbold to an audience which was painful and long. He sought reassurance but in vain. Rumbold informed him that the British could now deal only with the Angora government. Otherwise Rumbold confined himself to a promise of personal protection in case the Sultan found himself in imminent danger and felt obliged either to abdicate or to leave without doing so. Soon afterwards Rumbold left for Lausanne, making Harington responsible for the life of the Sultan, who, if his situation became serious, would communicate with Harington through his bandmaster, a man on whose loyalty he could count until the end.

Still searching for some means to escape his fate, Vahid-ed-Din sent his chamberlain to Refet with a message that he was anxious to contact the Gazi. He was ready to receive an emissary from Angora and would openly telegraph or write to Kemal. Kemal and Rauf requested him to write but no letter materialized, and Refet suspected that the Sultan would soon try to leave. He thus enlisted the Sultan's naval A.D.C. to spy on his movements, promising the A.D.C. future employment if he was discovered and dismissed.

At midday on November 10 the Sultan, as though nothing unusual was afoot, proceeded to the ceremony of the *selamlik*—the Friday prayer. He emerged from the palace sunk back in his carriage, arrayed only in the ordinary uniform of a Turkish officer, without decorations and with a kalpak on his head. His features were ravaged, his face so pale as to suggest the mere ghost of a monarch. Behind him were his black eunuchs and a few A.D.C.s, but no one else—no dignitaries, no generals, no ministers, since his Cabinet no longer existed. He drove in a funereal silence. When the meagre cortège reached the mosque the muezzin recited the call to prayer, no longer in the name of the great and victorious Padishah and of the illustrious imperial family, but simply in that of Commander of the Faithful and Caliph. Dull and lifeless as an automaton, the last of the Sultans stepped down from his carriage and entered the mosque for his last *selamlik*.

Within a few days, the bandmaster called upon General Harington to say that the Sultan believed himself in imminent danger and requested the British to remove him at once. Reluctant to act without a direct request, Harington secured it from the Sultan in writing. He was now faced with the problem, as he put it, of getting "the last Sultan of Turkey out of his palace alive." Since the palace was well guarded and the spies of the Nationalists were active, this was no easy task. Confiding only in a few of his officers, he devised a plan for the purpose.

On instructions, the Sultan announced to his staff his intention of spending the night in the kiosk of Merasim, at the far end of the garden, conveniently adjoining the Malta Gate, which led to the British barrack square. This aroused no suspicion. In the kiosk he was joined by his son and by those who were to accompany them: his First Chamberlain, the bandmaster, his doctor, two confidential secretaries, a valet, a barber, and two eunuchs—a suite of nine in all. Throughout the night, with revolvers lying on the ormolu tables, he supervised the packing in trunks of his jewels, precious stones, and other valuables, including a small gold table which had belonged to Sultan Selim.

At six o'clock in the morning the little group left the kiosk. The gate was opened by a eunuch. Two British ambulances with Red Cross markings had been parked outside, while a Guards detachment drilled on the parade ground beyond. Steps were let down to enable the party to enter the ambulances. The rain was pouring down in torrents and the

Sultan's umbrella got caught in the door. But finally they were off, un-observed.

Harington, looking out at the rain from his house at Therapia over an early breakfast of eggs and bacon, reflected that his troops must think their officers mad to hold a parade on such a morning. As he drove to the naval dockyard at Tophane, where he was to meet the Sultan, he saw the officers he had placed at various posts strolling with a forced look of casualness in the rain. On the quay he found Nevile Henderson, chargé d'affaires at the embassy since Rumbold's departure. The second ambulance soon arrived but not the first, though it had started ten minutes earlier. Both looked anxiously at their watches. Had there been a hitch in the operation?

It was only a small hitch. The ambulance containing the Sultan developed a puncture, and the wheel had hurriedly to be changed. But it duly arrived. The general and Henderson greeted the Sultan and escorted him with his party aboard a naval launch which conveyed them across the water to the British battleship H.M.S. *Malaya*. General Harington half hoped that the Sultan would present him with his cigarette case as a souvenir of this historic occasion. Instead Vahid-ed-Din confided to him the care of his five wives, with a request that they be sent after him. Then he walked up the ladder onto the deck of the warship.

On board Henderson told the Sultan that he was now safe on British territory and asked him where he wished to go. He expressed no preference and agreed to the proposed destination of Malta. He dictated a message to his doctor for his wives and daughters, to be delivered by one of the eunuchs. The flustered doctor made a mistake in the draft. Only then did the Sultan, for a moment, lose his equanimity. He turned angrily on the doctor and reproached his suite for losing their heads at a moment when he might have been justified in losing his own.

Formal farewells were exchanged and H.M.S. *Malaya* steamed away around the point of the Seraglio, the old palace of the Ottoman Sultans, into the Sea of Marmara. Henderson, on his return to the embassy, scribbled a postscript to a letter he had written to Rumbold: "All is well. H.I.M. was on board *Malaya* by 8.45 and all proceedings went without a hitch. I am glad he is off."

The operation had been effectively concluded without the interference and apparently without the knowledge of the Turks. Refet had sensed that the Sultan's departure was imminent. Lying in bed in the Sublime Porte, awaiting a report from his agent, the naval A.D.C., he could not sleep. After dawn had broken, the A.D.C. burst into Refet's room, distraught and dishevelled in carpet slippers. The Sultan, he revealed, had left. From a window in the kiosk he had seen Vahid-ed-Din step into an ambulance, escorted by a detachment of British soldiers. There had been no previous warning. Such was the measure of the success of the Sultan's stratagem in moving to the kiosk and thus warding off suspicion.

In a fever of guilt and anxiety the A.D.C. had dashed out of the palace, run for more than a mile in his slippers before finding a carriage, then driven as fast as the mud and the rain would allow over the two and a half remaining miles to the Sublime Porte. Now what was to become of him? He had failed in his duty. He flung himself hysterically on Refet's mercy.

Refet reassured him with a pat on the back. "Go to bed and get some sleep. I am going to do the same." Before doing so he telegraphed Kemal to announce the Sultan's departure. When he awoke an hour or so later he was handed a reply, enquiring who was responsible for letting the Sultan go. Refet would have liked to reply, "I was." Instead he replied in effect, "No one." It was a happy solution. The Nationalists had avoided the odium of the Sultan's arrest and exile. He had fled of his own accord with the aid of the infidel and, far from becoming a martyr, would surely incur the contempt of the Moslem world.

Refet now called, on instructions, on Prince Abdul Mejid, the Sultan's cousin and heir apparent, and invited him to accept the position of Caliph on conditions to be laid down by the Grand National Assembly. A robust upstanding man of fifty-four, Abdul Mejid had been excluded from politics by Abdul Hamid because of his enlightened liberal views, and had devoted his leisure to the arts, designing and embellishing the gardens of his palace, becoming learned in music, dabbling in painting to the extent (after Abdul Hamid's death) of having a picture exhibited in the Salon in Paris.[1] A devout Moslem, he was nonetheless modern in outlook and had shown sympathy with the Nationalists. He now accepted the Caliphate, signing a document which bound him to abide by the Assembly's decisions.

The deputies met next day in secret session. Rauf recalled the various treacheries of Vahid-ed-Din to the Moslem world and called upon the deputies to elect a new representative on earth of the Prophet. A high Islamic dignitary supported him. First the Sultan, who had chosen not

[1] He also painted a portrait of Refet, which he presented to the Turkish commander.

to abdicate, was formally deposed. Then the candidacy of Abdul Mejid was proposed for the Caliphate.

There was excitement among the *hojas,* who poured forth views in wearisome detail as to the character and powers of the Caliph's office. Kemal allowed them to wrangle on for a while, then pulled them up sharply. The matter, he explained to them, was really quite simple. It was no concern of the Moslem world, as certain speakers had insisted, but only of the Turkish nation, which was now in full possession of its sovereignty. In this the Caliphate could have no part. All that was required was the deposition of the fugitive Caliph and the election of a new religious head in his place. Thus finally, by a majority vote, the appointment of Abdul Mejid was agreed.

He was to be bound by the terms of a manifesto which the government must approve before its publication to the Moslem world. This was to be strictly non-political in character. It was to record his satisfaction at the Assembly's choice of him and condemn the conduct of Vahid-ed-Din.

His formal installation took place on a Friday in a ceremony carefully curtailed by the Nationalists. In place of the traditional cloak and turban as worn by Fatih the Conqueror, he wore frock coat and fez. At the Old Seraglio he was received by a delegation from the Grand National Assembly, who handed him a document in which the terms of his office were suitably inscribed on parchment. After appropriate speeches he took over the custody of the sacred relics of the Prophet. But the sword, symbolizing the temporal power, was withheld from him.

Finally the new Caliph drove, accompanied by Refet and followed by a procession of carriages so long and so reminiscent of a Sultan's parade that it displeased the more radical deputies, to the Fatih Mosque, where he celebrated his first *selamlik*. First a band played the new Independence Anthem. Then the Friday prayer was recited—in Turkish. Finally a telegram of thanks was sent by the Caliph to the Grand National Assembly. On the insistence of the more conservative deputies, the house rose to its feet to receive it.

The ex-Sultan was soon on his way from Malta to San Remo, where he settled down in a villa of moderate size. The British Embassy, after Rumbold's last audience with him, had arranged the transfer abroad of his cash and securities. He thus had enough money to live on. A month or so after his departure one of his eunuchs came to Constantinople to arrange for the transfer of the ex-Sultan's wives and family. The news of this brought a telegram to the British Embassy from a certain American impresario. It read: "Hippodrome New York could use wives of ex-Sultan kindly put me in touch with party who could procure them." When this message was shown to King George V he was greatly amused.

Such was the last act in the decline and fall of the Ottoman Empire.

43 ► *Negotiations at Lausanne*

Ismet left for Lausanne with a sense of deep misgiving. A new and grave responsibility lay unsought on his shoulders, involving not merely his own career but his country's future. He was venturing, reluctantly and with an acute sense of his unfitness for the task which Kemal, always his master, had imposed on him, into territory unfamiliar and in all probability unfriendly. He knew how to contend with a military adversary but he knew nothing of the field of European diplomacy, with its artful commanders and its armory of unknown and insidious weapons. He had never before set foot in Europe, except for a few weeks in Austria and Germany for the sake of his health. Ismet was all too well aware that he had big guns against him. Lloyd George had been deposed but Lord Curzon still ruled—with a determination, moreover, to restore at all costs, and at the expense of the Turks, the prestige of his country in the Near Eastern world.

Here was a conflict of psychology. The Allies saw the Turks as a vanquished people; the Turks saw themselves as victors. Turkey was the first of the defeated Central Powers to be in a position to negotiate peace. But she was to negotiate at a disadvantage. For the Allies aspired to impose a treaty upon her, as the Treaty of Versailles had been imposed on the rest. Ismet came to Lausanne hoping to gain for his country respect as an equal. Instead he found himself treated as a suppliant.

Curzon dominated the conference. It was, as Ismet remarked to Madame Georges-Gaulis, who had come to report on it, "always the English voice, and the English fist banging on the table." The English he could accept as his enemies but the French disillusioned him bitterly. With Franklin-Bouillon in mind, he had counted upon them to support the Turkish cause. But Curzon, on his way through Paris, had succeeded with Poincaré in re-establishing the Entente Cordiale, and Ismet found himself faced with a united front consisting of Britain, France, and Italy. If Curzon seemed to look upon him as "one of his subjects in India," Bompard, the French representative, behaved to him, so he said, with the haughtiness of a Grand Vizier of some early Ottoman Sultan. Small wonder that Ismet was touchy, quick to suspect affronts to his country's dignity and threats to her sovereignty, hence the more assertive in manner and obstructive in tactics.

Unable to compete with his adversaries in the thrust and parry of extempore debate, he soon evolved his own methods of fighting. He dug himself in. He contested every point, however small; he pleaded deafness, consulted interminably with his colleagues; he read out long prepared statements. He would demand time to consult Angora and defer his replies until subsequent sittings. He would make a concession and withdraw it the next day. At first he exasperated Curzon and the rest, but as time went on his doggedness, his restraint, his straightforwardness, his evident sincerity, began to earn him some respect. Perhaps after all his war of attrition would succeed in wearing them down, or even in winning them round.

Slowly it dawned upon some of the Allied delegates that they were dealing with a new type of Turk. As Sir William Tyrrell, one of Rumbold's deputies, expressed it to Madame Georges-Gaulis, "We used to know two sorts of Turk: the Old Turk, he is dead: the Young Turk, he exists no longer. We see today the third, quite different from the other two: Ismet Pasha. For us he is the incarnation of the Third Turk. His personality, his attitude have strongly impressed the conference, of which he is today the great figure. Well, it's with that Turk we want to make peace."

Rumbold himself, though one of the old school and still secretly hankering to give these pigheaded people "a real good blow on the head," was familiar enough with the Angora psychology, as reflected by the

Turkish delegation. "I do not see," he wrote to London, "how they can abandon any demand included in the National Pact without exposing themselves to disapproval or even a trial by court-martial." On the other hand, it seemed clear that they wanted an agreement with Britain. "I am inclined to think," he wrote to Henderson in Constantinople, "that if they could absolutely count on Britain being the friend of Turkey after the peace, they would not make such bones about getting out of the Russian friendship." These were shrewd enough assessments. The Angora-Moscow axis had been a measure of expediency, arising out of British hostility. Kemal now sought British friendship. But there was much stony ground to be covered. There was the problem of the Straits, the problem of Mosul, the problem of the Capitulations.

The question of the Straits was discussed early in December, after the arrival of Chicherin. Ismet, gaining time to sound the views of the conference, at first deferred to him as protagonist of the Turkish case. Chicherin, in his high-pitched rasping voice, stated it with an air of protective patronage, basing it on the principles laid down in the Turco-Soviet Treaty and the National Pact. These were essentially defensive. Both countries sought to keep all warships, apart from those of Turkey, out of the Straits, which the Turks should have the right to defend. The view of the Allies, on the other hand, was that the Straits should be internationalized and open to the warships of all powers.

While listening to the Russian delegate's discourse, Curzon "thought M. Chicherin must have mistaken his role and assumed the kalpak of Ismet Pasha." He pressed Ismet to say whether the views of the Turks were identical with those of the Russians. Ismet replied that he was willing to consider alternative Allied proposals, at which Chicherin looked startled. Eventually Ismet agreed, with a few modifications, to an Allied Straits Convention, which Chicherin shrilly declared to be "primarily directed against Russia." He refused to sign it and the rift between Russians and Turks seemed complete.

The convention allowed for an international commission to protect the Straits, with freedom of passage for the ships of all nations. The Turks sought a joint guarantee against aggression from the Lausanne powers but were obligated instead to accept a guarantee in terms of the Covenant of the League of Nations—an institution repugnant to Soviet Russia. This afforded Turkey a more nebulous degree of security and was to call for a revision at Montreux thirteen years later, before the Second World War. Its acceptance now was a measure of Kemal's realistic statesmanship and of his desire for Turkey's admission, on a basis of mutual trust, into the Western community of nations.

This spirit was further displayed when the time came to discuss the Christian minorities, mainly the Greeks and Armenians in Turkey. The Allies demanded measures for their adequate protection, once more under an international commission, and Ismet insisted that they be subject to the Turkish courts, which exemplified the new liberal laws of his country. Curzon rejected this plea with some sarcasm. But he offered Ismet a loophole in the form of a suggestion that Turkey should join the League of Nations, accepting its provisions for minorities as the European member states had done. To this Ismet, to his surprise and relief, agreed. Thus over two issues the future international position of Turkey was strengthened, through the need of the Allies to maintain a balance of power against the Soviet Union.

It was strengthened once again over the issue which had caused all the trouble—that of relations between Turkey and Greece. Venizelos, though he had strayed with Lloyd George into romanticist paths, was a realist at heart. Kemal was a realist too. Venizelos knew that his policy had failed; Kemal knew that his had succeeded. But both knew that Turkey and Greece must live together as neighbours, hence must quickly forget their mutual grievances. The conference was thus treated to the spectacle of the two main protagonists settling their differences in relative harmony.

The frontiers of eastern Thrace and of Adrianople were agreed in a manner consistent with the National Pact. Over the other main problem, that of the large Greek minorities in Turkey and Turkish minorities in Greece, the League was invoked once again. It was to supervise a compulsory exchange of populations between the two countries. Thus within a few years, apart from a Turkish minority in western Thrace and a Greek minority in eastern Thrace, virtually no Greeks remained in Turkey and no Turks in Greece. Such, ethnologically, was the final end to that fusion of races which had symbolized the Byzantine and Ottoman Empires.

Much as the Grand National Assembly might grumble, the Turks had reason, so far, to be satisfied with the progress of the Lausanne Conference. But more formidable problems still lay ahead, notably that of the province of Mosul. Here lay a fundamental conflict between the respective interests of Turkey and Britain. The British had occupied Mosul "as a point of strategical importance" some days after the cease-fire, hence in violation of the terms of the armistice, in 1918. Its occupation had aroused strong protests from Kemal, then in command of the neighbouring army in Syria, to Izzet Pasha, then Grand Vizier.

Strategically it was important to the British for the defence of the frontiers of Irak[1] and the route to India. Economically it was important to them on account of its oil fields, to which France had abandoned her claims in favour of Britain. To the Turks it was important, or so they claimed, for the defence of their frontiers, and as an integral part of Anatolia, whose ports provided the province with its natural outlet to the sea. Ethnologically, however, its inclusion within the frontiers of the National Pact was debatable, for it contained a large population not only of Turks but of Arabs and Kurds, with a mind to their own independence.

The Grand National Assembly felt strongly on the subject of Mosul. The House of Commons, as it happened, felt less strongly. Bonar Law, committed as he was to a policy of peace, was anxious to clear out of Irak "bag and baggage." To Curzon he expressed two convictions: "The first is that we should not go to war for the sake of Mosul; and secondly that, if the French, as we know to be the case, will not join us, we shall not by ourselves fight the Turks to impose what is left of the Treaty of Sèvres." The Prime Minister's views were echoed by the popular press. "Mosul," wrote Lord Beaverbrook's *Daily Express,* "is not worth the bones of one single British soldier." "Mespot" was merely a wastepot, a miserable wilderness of swamp and desert: its proposed evacuation became indeed a paramount issue in the 1922 election.

Curzon, however, was determined to assert British interests in Mosul to the utmost limit—short of war. He had the advantage of knowing more about Mosul than Ismet, who delivered, in support of the Turkish claim, a long, monotonous, and often inaccurate lecture of a historical and statistical kind. Curzon made havoc of his facts. The Turkish population of the province, he asserted, was a mere one twelfth of the whole. Moreover a majority of it had voted, in a plebiscite, for inclusion in the Kingdom of Irak. As for Mosul itself, it was a wholly Arab city, built and inhabited by Arabs. When it came to the Kurdish areas, Curzon replied with some sarcasm to Ismet: "It was reserved for the Turkish delegation to discover for the first time in history that the Kurds were Turks. Nobody has ever found it out before." He concluded with the proposal that the entire question of the frontier should be referred to the League of Nations.

[1] Mesopotamia.

Ismet hedged for a while, his eye cocked nervously on the Grand National Assembly, his voice, as Curzon put it irritably, reiterating "the same old tune. . . . Sovereignty, sovereignty, sovereignty." Ismet proposed first a plebiscite in the area, then independent negotiations outside the conference between Britain and Turkey. But he had in the end to agree that, if these were to fail, the question, like that of the minorities, should be submitted to the League of Nations.

Now that there seemed no danger of a break over Mosul, Curzon impatiently resolved, after many delays, to force the conference to a swift conclusion. Calling for the French and Italian delegates, he proposed that a draft treaty should be presented to the Turks for signature in six days' time. If they could not agree to it within the following four days the conference would be dissolved. He himself proposed to leave Lausanne for London on February 4, 1923.

While Curzon had confined himself to the territorial problems now approaching solution, he had left to the French and the Italians the thornier problems of finance, economics, and the status of foreigners, which concerned their interests more directly than those of Britain. In his preoccupation with a political settlement he had underrated the obstacles likely to arise in these fields. They were, as the French had found, formidable.

To the patriotic Turk, the expulsion of the foreigner from his doorstep availed little without his expulsion from within his house. The Capitulations, those privileges which had in effect created a series of foreign states within his state, rankled with him more directly, and more personally, than any foreign encroachments on his farthermost frontiers. The banks, the railways, the mines, the forests, the public utilities—all were controlled by foreigners. They were exempt from taxes and customs dues and were subject only to the laws of their own courts. It was largely to put an end to all this that the Turks had been fighting so obstinately.

In the negotiations the Allies, and especially the French, insisted on their maximum safeguards; the Turks on their independence from all restrictions. In the domain of justice the Allies proposed foreign legal advisers, or observers, to replace the foreign judges. The Turks rejected all such proposals. The domain of finance, economics, and commerce embraced such thorny problems as reparations and indemnities, the distribution of the Ottoman debt, Turkish property rights abroad and Allied property rights in Turkey, communications, taxation of foreigners, company law, insurance policies, contracts and concessions. In general the

French accepted the replacement of former privileges by agreements on equal terms between foreigners and Turks. The discussions, however, raised intricate problems in which questions of detail, which did not appear important, involved issues of principle, which were. Time and patience were needed, as Ismet insisted, to resolve their complexity.

But Lord Curzon was in a hurry. Moreover, by looking as though he were in a hurry, he judged that he would the better achieve his ends. Still thinking, unlike some of his colleagues, in terms of the old Ottoman Turk, he believed that Ismet was holding out until the last possible moment, bargaining like a carpet merchant to get the best deal he could, but would yield in the end. In his dealings with orientals Curzon was used to the old and often corrupt regimes whose interests overrode principles and the flexibility of personal rule made for compromise.

But here, as he failed to realize, was something new: a patriotic Nationalist movement, unprecedented in an oriental country, in which principles were paramount. Curzon allowed too little for the national pride of the new Turk, for the fact that he had laid down a programme from which his ruler could little afford to deviate. He underrated the Assembly and the power of its extremists; he misjudged the psychology of Ismet himself, who was no bargainer by training and moreover unsure of his position at home.

"What are they going to say in Angora?" was Ismet's eternal refrain to his friends. On the Capitulations he declared to Madame Georges-Gaulis, "On this point we will never yield. If we did our personal power at home would not be worth more than a straw." Thus the danger of a breakdown loomed ahead.

On January 31 the draft treaty was presented to Ismet as planned. He asked for eight days' grace in which to formulate the Turkish reply. Curzon, despite the entreaties of the French and the Italians, refused the request. The Turks were informed that he would leave Lausanne on the evening of February 4 as arranged.

On February 3 Ismet was presented by the Allies with a few last-minute concessions. Early that afternoon he delivered to them his own last counterproposals, in which he accepted eighty per cent of the terms. They reflected, in his view, "sufficient unanimity on fundamental points" for the signature of a treaty of peace. Let it therefore be signed on this basis, and let the remaining terms, reflecting only "small differences" on certain judicial and economic matters, be held over for later negotiation. Lord Curzon rejected this proposal. In the evening he summoned Ismet to a meeting in his room at the Beau Rivage Hotel and informed him that the treaty as it now stood "must be signed here and now." Bompard, the French delegate, supported Curzon. But Ismet remained obdurate. He had gone as far as he could towards judicial guarantees, with a promise to accept foreign assistance in general; he had accepted a number of economic clauses; but the acceptance of those which remained would place Turkey in a position of "economic servitude." Bombarded by the Allied delegates with appeals and menaces, he could only murmur wretchedly, *"Je ne peux pas."*

The meeting broke up and Curzon prepared for his departure. The hall of the hotel was crowded with delegates confidently expecting to assist at the signature of the treaty. Ismet came down the main stairs, took off his bowler hat, bowed right and left to the crowd, forced a smile, and walked out of the hotel, closely followed by the French and Italian delegates. It became known that the treaty had not been signed.

The American observers, in a last-minute bid for a compromise, called upon Curzon but found him pacing up and down in his room "like an angry bull," wringing his hands and declaring that there was nothing to be done. Leaving him, they went across to Ismet's hotel. Ismet, wrote one of them, Admiral Bristol,[2] "was evidently greatly perturbed and several times rubbed his face in a truly Turkish manner, and used a Turkish expression which means, 'My heart is being squeezed. . . . I am wrung with anguish!' " He agreed confidentially to concede a point on the Capitulations, but it must be contingent on Allied concessions on the economic clauses, which he could not accept as they stood. For one thing, he was not entirely sure what they meant. How could he sign unless he knew what he was signing? The Americans hurried to the station to propose a compromise on these lines but Curzon's train had gone. Next day the world learnt that the Lausanne Conference had broken up without agreement being reached.

Ismet returned in trepidation to Angora, faced with the ordeal of a vote of confidence to be debated by the Grand National Assembly.

Kemal's victory against the powers of Europe had not made this obstreperous body any easier to handle. The reverse was the case, for victory had relaxed some of the pressure towards national unity. The Opposition continued in devious forms their moves against him. In December 1922 they had proposed a change in the law for the election of deputies, confining candidature to those born or five years domiciled within the present frontiers of Turkey. This was aimed at the exclusion of Kemal, who had been

[2] Admiral Mark L. Bristol was the American high commissioner from 1919 to 1927.

born in Salonika and thanks to his military duties had not since lived continuously in any electoral district.

Had he done so, he drily reminded the Assembly, he could not have fought the invader and "the country of these gentlemen who have given their signatures would likewise be outside the frontiers, which may God prevent." He continued, "I believed and still believe that our enemies would perhaps have even tried to deprive me of the possibility of serving my country by an attempt on my life. But not for a single moment could I have imagined that there were people, be it only two or three, in the High Assembly who shared the same mode of thinking."

Now, on the occasion of the breakdown at Lausanne, the Opposition deputies chose to vent against Ismet in particular and the government in general their growing mistrust of the Gazi himself. Day after day, in a series of stormy secret sessions, they poured forth their grievances. A victory had been won by the bayonet of Mehmedjik, the Turkish soldier. But now, through the ineptitude of Ismet's diplomacy, the fruits were being sacrificed to the tricks and intrigues of Lord Curzon. The Turkish delegation was a toy in the hands of the British. Procedure was disregarded while deputies interrupted the debates, leaping up from their seats to fire protests at random. "Why do you cheer instead of weeping?" one cried, while another reiterated at intervals, "There won't be any peace." Kemal and Rauf sat through these unseemly proceedings with patience, Kemal intervening with authority at well-chosen moments.

Though the conference had broken down on the economic clauses, these were beyond the comprehension of most of the deputies—including Ismet himself—and were soon referred to committees under the Ministry of Finance, for an expert analysis and report. It was chiefly the prospect of a direct threat to Turkish territory, to the sacred principles of the National Pact, that inflamed them. "They are selling Mosul to the enemy!" was the loudest cry. The Opposition called for war rather than a peace which ceded an inch of its precious soil to the enemy.

Rauf admitted the importance of Mosul and confirmed that it lay within the National Pact frontiers. But at Lausanne the delegates were trying to liquidate a past of six centuries. The problems were complex and must be seriously and responsibly weighed. People must ask themselves, would the resumption of war be to the country's advantage? How long might it last? What might be its results?

At this a member interjected, "Only God can know that!"

Rauf replied, "No doubt. But God has given us a mind that we should think with it. Thus we have thought. . . . We want to negotiate further on the economic problems. We are ready to fight if necessary. But meanwhile we shall do all we can to secure peace."

Kemal followed Rauf, calling for a cool logical approach to these problems. If they insisted now on the retention of Mosul the result would be war, with not only Britain but the whole world against them. If they postponed the issue for a year Mosul might be secured by diplomacy. If not, the country would be in a stronger position to fight. The warmongers, however, were not easily silenced. Their nucleus was a small but vociferous group of Kemal's personal enemies, who had backing from a section of the press. Their ringleader was one Ali Shükrü, the member for Trebizond, a man of fanatical temperament who had long waged a feud against Kemal and was now systematically stirring up trouble.

After a week of these polemics Kemal determined to bring the debate to a close. He reaffirmed the government's peaceful intentions and called upon the Assembly to sanction a new general directive to the Cabinet for the resumption of the Lausanne talks. These would not, he explained, cover the position of Mosul, which had already been dealt with. They would mainly concern the country's right to administrative, political, economic, and financial freedom. Ali Shükrü's repeated objections brought an outburst from Kemal: "You have been speaking for a whole week in a way harmful to the country. What is your purpose?" Ali Shükrü protested, "You have no right to accuse anyone." Another deputy shouted, "Is there no security in the Parliament?"

This created a turmoil. Ali Fuad, who was presiding, tried to restore order but the deputies were uncontrollable. Members of the two groups stood face to face before the rostrum, hurling accusations and threats at each other, with Kemal in the midst of them. At any moment revolvers or other weapons might be drawn. Ali Fuad, in a moment of inspiration, flung the presidential bell between the opposing groups and the clangour was followed by a momentary silence. Of this he took immediate advantage to adjourn the session.

After an interval the members returned to their places and the vote of confidence was taken. It showed less than a two-to-one majority for Kemal, while a large number of abstentions showed the great gulf which now existed between Parliament and government. It was virtually a vote of no confidence.

The Lausanne debate touched off a crisis in Angora which was to shake Kemal's position. Ali Shükrü, the principal troublemaker, continued to rail against Kemal, not only in the Assembly but in the cafés and streets of the town, denouncing Kemal's drinking habits and declaring that he was plotting to make himself Sultan. One day Ali Shükrü disappeared in mysterious circumstances. After two days of wild gossip and worried enquiries from his family, the question of his whereabouts was raised in the Assembly.

The deputies at once assumed that Ali Shükrü had been murdered. How otherwise could a man vanish without trace, in a place hardly bigger than a village, for two whole days? Insinuations were made against the government and against Kemal's own entourage. No country was civilized in which certain men chose to place themselves above the law! Let them be damned a thousand times! Let those treacherous hidden heads be broken! The government must take instant steps to solve the mystery and punish the guilty men.

After some days Rauf was able to report to the Assembly that the corpse of Ali Shükrü had been found. Suspicion had fallen on Topal Osman the Laz, the leader of Kemal's Black Sea bodyguard. Investigations now proved his complicity. Ali Shükrü had last been seen alive walking away from a café in the market place, arm in arm with a captain in Osman's guard. Later screams and other strange noises were heard from Osman's house. Osman reassured the scared neighbours with the explanation that he had merely been beating up two of his insubordinate soldiers. But early next morning a car arrived at the house and drove away with a load of "furniture." The police grew suspicious. Osman disappeared. Not long afterwards a mound of fresh earth was discovered outside the city, with flies swarming over it. The police dug—and only a few feet down found the body of Ali Shükrü, wrapped in sailcloth.

Osman, it later emerged, had in his fierce protective loyalty to his master convinced himself that Ali Shükrü was plotting to kill Kemal. He had thus had him strangled by two of the guard. It was an awkward situation for Kemal, which his enemies readily turned to his discredit. Taking immediate action, he sent emissaries to Osman to give him a chance to confess his guilt, which Osman forcibly denied. He must thus be disposed of.

Fearing for his own security, Kemal moved down secretly after dark from Chankaya to his former office, near the railway station. Feeling himself once more trapped and surrounded by enemies, he was in a highly nervous state. Meanwhile orders were given to round up Osman's force in the morning. The Laz refused to surrender, preferring to fight to the death. From the station below Kemal could hear the sounds of the shots on the hill. A number of deputies went up to watch the engagement, which ended in the capture of Osman, mortally wounded. He died while being carried away on a stretcher. A dozen of his men had died fighting.

In the Assembly, when Rauf made his statement, the opposition made the most of the incident. A deputy who had inspected his friend's "sacred remains" called for curses, which were willingly voiced, against "these brutes, these monsters" who had crushed him and cut him to pieces. Ali Shükrü was a martyr to the freedom of the nation, to the supremacy of the people. But Ali Shükrü was not dead, for there is life in every death. "His soul is with us." The Assembly adjourned for five minutes that the members might pray for his soul. Two of them were granted leave of absence to carry the body to Trebizond. That of Osman meanwhile was hanged and exhibited at the gates of the Parliament.

44 ► *Signature of the treaty*

Clearly, Kemal realized, the moment had come to dissolve his recalcitrant Parliament. This first Grand National Assembly, elected for the conduct of the war, had outlived its purpose. To achieve peace, to vote the sweeping internal reforms which Kemal had in mind for the future, a new Assembly was needed, a body more adult than the old, more moderate, more responsible—and more manageable.

Kemal called upon Rauf to summon an extraordinary meeting of the Cabinet. It took place in Rauf's house and continued all night. It was agreed to dissolve Parliament and to hold elections. The first Grand National Assembly met for the last time on April 16, 1923. As a final precaution before the elections it passed, despite some opposition, a new law extending the penalty for high treason, already covering the misuse of religion for political purposes, to the refusal to recognize Parliament and the abolition of the Sultanate. The country then entered upon new elections with party candidates carefully vetted and chosen by Kemal, and Opposition candidates effectively discouraged.

Already, earlier in the year, Kemal had taken two steps towards this end. As his chief need was for a reliable political instrument, he announced to the press his intention to form a new party, named at first the People's party, to replace his parliamentary group, and called upon the educated men of the country to help him in drafting its programme. In due course the party published a manifesto. Its programme, which was studiously vague, confined itself to a restatement of the principles on which the new state had been founded, together with limited proposals for reform. Kemal, with his empirical approach, did not care in this election to come out into the open with more specific principles, or with any hint of the more fundamental reforms which the new party would be called upon to sponsor.

Next Kemal needed to establish close touch with the people themselves, both to indoctrinate them with his views and to ascertain their own. Thus he went to the country in person, covering, in a month's tour of western Anatolia, much of the ground over which the armies had fought.

Until now, primarily engaged in the business of fighting, he had made few speeches to the general public. But in the course of this month he treated them to thirty-four major orations—some of them lasting as long as six or seven hours—of a patriotic and instructive kind. This was the first of many tours whose routine recalled, in its meetings with officials and notables, his early progress through the country to Sivas and Erzurum. But now all was in the open, with personal appearances before crowds thronging around to hear and to question him. Never before had a Turkish head of state left his capital to address his subjects directly. Thus the Gazi was breaking with precedent to forge a new and personal bond between ruler and ruled.[1]

From now onwards the Turks were to be encouraged to believe that they had a practical say in the government of their country, that its sovereignty did indeed lie in the hands of the people. His was to be, at least in appearance, a "grass-roots" regime, built not from the top but from the bottom. His task was in its way harder than either the military campaign he had just won or the diplomatic campaign he was waging at Lausanne. It involved the preparation of a conservative and obstinate people for a fundamental revolution in their habits and thought, at a mo-

---

[1] Confusion as to his identity persisted, however, for years to come. Inspecting some soldiers in Anatolia, Kemal once asked, "Who is God and where does He live?" The soldier, anxious to please, replied, "God is Mustafa Kemal Pasha. He lives in Angora." "And where is Angora?" Kemal asked. "Angora is in Istanbul," was the reply. Farther down the line he asked another soldier, "Who is Mustafa Kemal?" The reply was "Our Sultan." Irfan Orga, *Phoenix Ascendant.*

ment, moreover, when they were tired and inclined to relapse, now that the threat from the enemy was removed, into their traditional apathy.

The chief obstacle that Kemal had to face lay in the forces of religion. To counteract its more reactionary influences became his main concern, as he now talked his way around the country. At the same time he must still pose as the champion of Islam. From the pulpit of a mosque in the bigoted centre of Balikesir, he declared that Islam was the last and greatest of all religious revelations and, moreover, one which conformed with logic and reason. After complimenting his audience for their piety and heroism, he instructed them that henceforward the Friday sermon should not be in Arabic but in Turkish, so that all might understand it. Pointing out to them that the Prophet himself had set the precedent of discussing public affairs in the House of God, he then preached not only of the Caliphate but of the negotiations at Lausanne and the principles of the new People's party—"a school to give our people political training."

In Smyrna, a more advanced centre, he took a different line, speaking more openly of the way in which the Caliphate had deprived the people of their rightful sovereignty, of the religious propaganda which had incited them to fight for the Caliph's Army. It was thanks to a belief in "selfish and ignorant people like these that the Turkish people had for centuries lived in huts made out of mud and rushes, with their bare feet exposed to the merciless attacks of snow and rain." It was now necessary for them to renounce such fanaticism and regain a proper perspective.

This was where the People's party came in. It would work for the common welfare of all, regardless of any one class. It would teach them modern methods and so augment the fruits of their labours. Help would be given to farmers and producers, and a forthcoming economic congress in Smyrna would show the world that the new Turkish state was to be formed not with bayonets but with the tools of industry. In a later tour he showed his respect for the peasant as the backbone of the country, declaiming in a speech to the farmers of Tarsus:

"In the past you were allowed all the work and suffering but none of the rewards. And the reason for this? There were few who thought about you. When they thought, it was for one of two reasons: either there was a war in process and they needed you to fight in the army, or the Treasury was empty and your money was needed. All this will be different in the future. We shall be better farmers, better soldiers."

It was a far cry from such places as Tarsus and Balikesir to Lausanne,

but Kemal found in such small Anatolian towns a public opinion responsive to news of the peace negotiations—the fruits of the war he had inspired them to fight. At Lausanne, as he later put it,

centuries-old accounts were being regulated. It was surely neither a simple nor
convenient task to find our way through such a mass of old, confused and
rubbishy accounts. . . . The Ottoman Empire, whose heirs we were, had no
value, no merit. . . . But we were not guilty of the neglect and sins of the
past and, in reality, it was not ourselves from whom they ought to have demanded the settlement of accounts that had accumulated during past centuries.
It was, however, our duty to bear the responsibility for them before the world.
. . . What we demanded from the conference was nothing more than the confirmation in a proper manner of what we had already gained. . . . Our greatest
strength and our surest point of support was the fact that we had realized our
material sovereignty, had actually placed it in the hands of the nation and had
proved by the facts that we were capable of maintaining it.

Such was the general theme. At Smyrna, where the press had come
from Constantinople to listen to him, he spoke more specifically. He
stressed the sincere desire of the Turkish people for peace but, if the powers at Lausanne failed to appreciate this and allowed the talks to break
down once again, Turkey would not hesitate to resume the struggle for
the recognition of her claims. The Allies must not mistake her desire
for peace as a sign of weakness. Suiting actions to words, he called up
new classes for military training and recalled others already demobilized.
He declared Eskishehir a military zone and let it be known that important troop movements were afoot.

Before starting on his tour Kemal had received news of the death of
his mother at Smyrna, where she had gone for the sake of her failing
health. On arrival he made a speech over her grave:
"We are leaving my poor mother in the sacred earth of Smyrna. She
has been a victim of a period of tyranny and oppression. . . . While I
was in Anatolia, I sent a close friend to see her. When she saw him alone,
she thought I had been executed. She had a stroke. In three years she
wept every night. She almost lost her eyesight. After the war, when I
rejoined her, she was barely alive any longer. I suffer a lot at her death.
One thing gives me comfort—the fact that the country has been saved from
the rule which destroyed it and dragged it to calamity. I swear on my
mother's grave and in the presence of God that, in order to protect the
supremacy of the people, for which so much blood has been shed, I shall
not hesitate to join her in this grave."
Zübeyde, in Smyrna, had met and approved of Latife, with whom Ke-

mal had been corresponding since his return to Angora. It was an exchange of letters which revealed both Latife's love for him and her concern with his affairs. He readily responded. He had loved Fikriye after
his fashion and had enjoyed her companionship but she could never
have been more than a mistress. What he now needed as head of a Western state was a wife—a woman capable of fulfilling, in the eyes of the
people, the image of educated and emancipated womanhood to which
he now sought to convert them.

Latife, he saw, could fulfil this role. A few days after the death of
his mother, whom Latife had visited during her illness, he insisted that
they marry at once, without ceremony or publicity. She asked for a few
hours' delay. Next day—not a Thursday, the day normally consecrated
to Islamic marriages, but a Monday—Kemal went with her to find a
kadi and asked him to marry them at once. Mastering his surprise and
confusion, the *kadi* agreed. The ceremony took place in the European
style, at Latife's father's house. In defiance of the Islamic tradition that
bride and bridegroom should not see one another until after the ceremony, they took their vows sitting together at a table, with Kiazim Karabekir as Kemal's witness.

After she had had time to settle down in Angora, Kemal took Latife on
a "honeymoon tour," this time covering the main cities of southern Anatolia. He showed her off without the veil as a living symbol of those
social reforms which he now intended to introduce, with her help,
throughout the country. The women of Turkey henceforward were to
be free of this encumbrance and of the state of servitude to the male
which it symbolized. They were to have a status of their own, comple-
mentary to that of the male. They were to be respected in modern civilized terms, as his own wife was respected. Symbolically she stood at his
side, wearing breeches as he did, her white face defiantly revealed
beneath a tight black headkerchief. At a parade she would sit astride on
horseback beside him, as though, he remarked with satisfaction, she
were one of his A.D.C.s.

Kemal at once made it clear how he expected his wife to be treated. At
Adana a group of ladies invited Latife to stay in their house but Kemal
firmly refused, insisting, "My wife has to stay with me." There was to
be an end to the harem, to the separation of women from men. He took
pleasure in showing her off as an educated woman, persuading her to
read aloud a poem by Byron which none understood, then another by
Victor Hugo, of which a few got the gist. When she interpreted for
him with a group of Greek prisoners of war, Kemal looked proudly

around as though to say, "You see what an accomplished wife I have."

Everywhere he was at pains to emphasize the democratic nature of his tour. There was to be an end to those formal ceremonial functions, with exchanges of gifts and elaborate compliments, so beloved of oriental officials. He wanted to mix with the people, to seem approachable to all. At Mersin he lost his temper with the mayor, who at a dinner insisted on waiting upon him in person, doing so, moreover, ineptly and provoking Kemal to the irritated comment, "For God's sake, sit down! Are you a waiter or the mayor of this city?" Later at a fireworks display he refused to sit with Latife in the golden thrones provided, and called for a pair of ordinary chairs, on which they sat with the rest of the crowd.

But his overt display of Latife was not wholly popular. It was shock tactics for a traditionalist country, where segregation between the sexes died hard. Sometimes the shock was effective; more often it provided fuel for propaganda against him, the reactionaries assiduously circulating press photographs of the pair to show how "he exhibits his wife all décolletée."

For all their outward marital harmony, there was soon some friction between Kemal and Latife. This arose over his drinking. As the tour went on he drank more, to relieve the strain of it, and Latife planned subterfuges to prevent him from doing so. On their last evening at Konya a news agency correspondent came to check a report of a speech. Kemal approved of it, boasted of the excellence of the speech, then, turning to Latife, said, "Ask them to bring a glass of raki for this child." The correspondent realized that Kemal wanted a drink too. But Latife replied that all the bottles had been sent to the train with their baggage. Kemal became furious and shouted at her: "This is our guest and you don't even offer him a glass of raki!" Latife gave in and ordered the drinks to be brought.

With the Assembly now safely dissolved, the time had come for "little Ismet" to return to Lausanne. The scale and composition of the conference had changed. Here gathered around the table was no majestic assembly of international statesmen. Curzon had disappeared, handing over to Rumbold; the French too were represented by their man on the spot, General Pelle. The conference, deprived of its great figures, was, as Rumbold described it, a "deflated Zeppelin." In fact its composition was dictated by the nature of its outstanding problems. The political clauses had been settled and there remained only those which involved economic, financial, and judicial matters. These, intricate and crucial in their bearing on the Capitulations, required the attention of technical experts rather than statesmen.

This time "the backwoodsmen from Angora" had come to the conference table better prepared than before. The Assembly had got through their work quicker than Rumbold expected, and Ismet arrived with a counterproposal in businesslike form, covering the whole system of foreign controls. These concerned chiefly the vested interests of the French, who were thus intransigent from the start, bargaining tenaciously for reparations, for the payment in gold of the interest on the Ottoman public debt, for the ratification of concessions obtained before the war from the Ottoman government.

Their attitude was hardened by a fresh incursion into the economic field—that of the Americans, with whom, on the principle of the "Open Door," Angora was now starting to do business on favourable terms. With the encouragement of Rauf the Grand National Assembly had granted a concession to the American Chester Group, for railway and harbour construction and other development projects, and its representatives were firmly entrenched in Angora, to the acute suspicion of their European rivals.

Ismet, in standing firm against the French, thus had the encouragement of Ambassador Grew, the American observer, who relieved Ismet's fears that the Allies would go to war on these issues. He recorded a seven-hour meeting at which Ismet, until two o'clock in the morning, received treatment at their hands "which would make the third degree in a Harlem police station seem like a club dinner." Ismet, as Rumbold wrote to Constantinople, was "between hammer and anvil." His experience at the hands of the Grand National Assembly had unnerved him. He was always aware of the Opposition deputies at home, temporarily silenced by the elections but still lying in wait to discredit him; and now, to crown all, of Rauf, goading and flustering him with an impatient bombardment of telegrams.

Loyal as Rauf had been in his defense of Ismet before the Assembly, he had no great belief in the latter's powers of diplomacy, and now Ismet's reports from Lausanne to the Cabinet suggested a spirit of compromise so disquieting as to prompt a move for his recall. Rauf himself in his sailorly way would have handled things differently. "Take it or leave it" was the line to adopt with the Allies. The Cabinet had briefed Ismet with specific proposals. Let him now insist upon them as a whole and refuse to be drawn into piecemeal concessions. Ismet complained that Angora allowed him too little latitude, dictating not merely the matter of the negotiations but the manner of carrying them out. His deputy compared Rauf's instructions to a series of commands from the quarterdeck of the old *Hamidiye*.

Ismet in his growing mistrust gained the impression that they did not reflect Kemal's own views, and thus appealed to the Gazi over Rauf's head for an assurance that he would follow the negotiations in person. This Kemal now did, attending meetings of the Cabinet as, out of deference to Rauf, he had not in principle been doing, and sometimes drafting its decisions in person. He became the arbiter between the partisans of Ismet and Rauf by (as he expressed it) "agreeing with one party and imposing silence on the other."

The conference dragged on week after week. Nerves grew strained. Once Rumbold lost patience so far as to exclaim in French that the attitude of the Turkish delegation *"m'écoeure,"* at which Ismet broke into smiles, taking the word to mean its opposite, "hearten." He confessed that he had "never been so tired in his life." He took to drinking green chartreuse and developed into the bargain "a dreadful cough." His irritation with Rauf flared up periodically, goading him to compare Angora's interference with that of the palace in its direction of the fatal campaign against the Russians in 1877. Once he demanded that Rauf himself should come to the conference in his place, and thus earned a sharp rebuke from Kemal.

Since neither Allies nor Turks wanted war, the issue over each clause was that of finding a formula, and in the end, thanks largely to British conciliatory efforts, formulas were found which saved all faces. The question of the debt was reserved for subsequent settlement. Reparations were waived. Economic concessions became subject to negotiation under Turkish law, according to the merits of each. A few foreign legal advisers were accepted for a limited period. Kemal could with justice claim, of the treaty now ready for signature, that "Capitulations of any description are completely and forever abolished."

Rumbold, writing to King George V, described it as "not a glorious instrument but the least unsatisfactory terms possible." *The Times* described it as "a model of generosity and justice" and remarked, in a tribute to the conduct of the Turks at the conference, "Has Turkey become, by some miracle, a civilised power?" The treaty was signed, in a brightly caparisoned hall of the University of Lausanne, on July 24, 1923, by Rumbold, who alone wore a grey top hat to the ceremony—"as if," commented the *Daily Express,* "it were Ascot."

Kemal telegraphed his congratulations to Ismet: "You have thus crowned with a historic success a life which consists of a series of eminent services rendered to your country." Rauf's congratulations, delayed for a day longer, had a more reluctant ring. He had toned down the draft prepared for him with the remark that it gave too much credit to Ismet: "Have we done nothing here?"

Together Rauf and Ali Fuad brought the news of the signature to Kemal at Chankaya. The Gazi, who had just risen, received his two friends in an Arab burnous, worn as a dressing gown. He gazed at the historic telegram with evident signs of emotion. Pulling himself together, he admitted, "In these last days I have been hoping that peace would be signed, but I have had constant doubts and hesitations. I always had the fear that these people would change their minds at the last moment. You have given me great joy. I thank you."

Rauf made an emotional little speech, attributing the success of the day firstly to Kemal himself, then to Kiazim Karabekir, Ali Fuad, and Refet. He was happy to have worked in their midst. Ever since Amasya, he confessed, "I have felt like kissing your hand. But I could never reveal this desire. Now let me express this feeling, which has always been with me, by kissing your hand."

Kemal brushed the gesture aside as unnecessary. "Your services to the country," he said, "are no less than ours."

All were in an emotional mood. They drank coffee to steady themselves. They were entertained to dinner by Latife. Kemal remarked that Ismet had left Lausanne for Angora. Rauf, to his surprise, said, "Yes, he has. And with your permission I too intend to leave." He announced his intention, now that peace was signed, to relinquish the premiership, before the second Assembly met, and pay a visit to his former constituency, Sivas. He was overtired and having trouble with his stomach. But he made his real reason clear—Ismet's attitude at Lausanne, not only to himself but to the rest of the Cabinet. "I personally do not wish ever again to come face to face with Ismet Pasha. It is impossible for me to continue to work with him. Since he has signed the peace treaty it seems to me that he should carry out its promises."

Kemal asked, "You mean that you won't even greet him when he comes?"

Rauf replied, "No. Please forgive me. But after so many unjust attacks I do not wish to see Ismet Pasha again."

Kemal tried to soothe him but Rauf adhered to his resolve to resign. There was more behind it than his disagreement with Ismet. There were his fears for the future. He remembered that evening at Refet's house, before the final offensive, when Kemal had undertaken to re-linquish his extraordinary powers once peace was signed. It was now signed; but he showed no disposition to do so. On the contrary, he planned to reinforce these powers by becoming head of the new People's party, and thus, in Rauf's view, prejudicing from the outset the demo-cratic development of the new Turkish state. In his usual frank manner he spoke to Kemal of these misgivings, saying that he envisaged the Gazi's position as that of an impartial arbiter, a head of state above all parties and individuals. But now he was involving himself in day-to-day politics.

Ali Fuad shared these views, which he had voiced at the time of the party's conception, arguing that Kemal's association with it would pre-vent the free growth of political parties in a country committed to popu-lar sovereignty. So indeed it was to prove in the elections, when Kemal intervened actively, using his commanding position as both head of the party and commander-in-chief of the army to preclude the emergence of any Opposition group.

This was to be the dominating issue in the new political phase which now followed the peace. It was the struggle for power between the Gazi in person and the forces of democracy as seen by Rauf and others. Kemal was not at this stage to be drawn into discussing it. He ex-pressed his regret to Rauf at his resignation, to which the latter replied, "Do not be sorry, Pasha. You can govern this country with twelve honest men." He left for Sivas, seen off by his fellow ministers and a large concourse of friends. Kemal appointed Fethi Prime Minister. Asked why he had not chosen Ismet, he replied, "I'm keeping him for later."

Ali Fuad consented to remain for the present Vice-President of the Assembly. But three months later he too resigned, to resume his mili-tary career, consistent in his mistrust of Kemal's one-party rule. To Kemal he had said, "Who are now your 'Apostles'? May we know?" To this he received the airy reply: "I have no Apostles. Those who serve the country and the nation and show merit and ability for service, those are Apostles."

Some days after Rauf's departure Ismet reached Angora with his fellow delegates, to be granted an official ovation. Kemal gave a party in his honour at Chankaya. As the conference was being discussed before din-ner, Ismet could not in his bitterness forbear from referring to the ob-structions he had endured from Rauf and the Cabinet. To Kemal he said, "You—*you* settled all my difficulties. You saved me by coming to my help. Without you my coffin would have come back from Lausanne. My coffin!"

Fethi reminded him with some irritation, "I too was a member of the Cabinet you criticize." Ismet gave him a curt answer and both men rose to their feet in anger. The ladies grew alarmed but the gentlemen restrained the combatants. Kemal ordered dinner to be served but throughout the meal he talked little. A cloud had descended on the guests. It was an awkward homecoming.

In submitting the treaty to the new Assembly for ratification, the government stressed that no territory within the bounds of the National Pact had been sacrificed and that there was no thought of conquering or reconquering lands beyond them. Ismet described the treaty as "the product of the struggles of a whole epoch." Turkey was no longer an empire, as she had been to her loss for half a century past; she was a sovereign state, like any other in the international field, conscious of her strength and jealous of her independence.

Assessing the treaty years later, in historical perspective, he described it as an instrument of durable peace, because "both sides were thoroughly tired of fighting, and the sacrifices were confined within bearable and justifiable limits." It was indeed the only peace settlement signed after the First World War in which one of the Central Powers was able to demand her own terms from the Allies, and the only one to survive the Second World War as an instrument of peace for the future. For it was a treaty based not on artificial theories but on existing facts. It did credit at once to Kemal's restraint, in renouncing any form of expansion, and to Ismet's obstinacy in pursuing his limited objective. Both had proved adroit in exploiting differences between the Allied Powers, both patient in reserving for negotiations such questions as Mosul and the Straits which, as they understood, raised complex international issues, hence could not at once be solved.

Ten weeks after the signature the Allied forces evacuated Constantinople. It was a great day for Harington, whom the Turkish crowds could not help cheering as he drove along the Bosporus with a colour party of guardsmen, none under six feet one inch tall, as an escort. At the quay guards of honour of the other Allied and Turkish forces met the general, with a huge crowd of Turks pressing behind. When he saluted the Turkish flag the crowd broke and "before I knew where I was there were 15,000 Turks between me and my wife." He embarked in the

Arabic, which blew all her sirens. The *Marlborough* escorted her out, playing "Auld Lang Syne." Such was the end of an occupation which had lasted longer than the whole of the First World War.

Not long afterwards the Gazi decided that Turkey should seal the integrity of her territory by fixing her capital in Angora instead of Constantinople, and a draft bill for the purpose was introduced into the Assembly. There was strong opposition from the press and the die-hards of Constantinople, who urged that their city, the seat of the Caliphate, should remain also the capital, as it had been for four hundred and seventy years past—to say nothing of the eleven hundred years of Byzantium before that.

Angora, they argued, was inappropriate on account of its remoteness, its harsh climate, its primitive character, its lack of water and the other amenities of a civilized city. Against this was set its geographic and strategic position, secure against the inroads of the foreigner, and above all the fact that, as the symbol of the Nationalist struggle, it had acquired a mystique of its own. Moreover, Kemal himself had a deep mistrust of Constantinople, with its age-old corruption, its insidious traditions and habits of intrigue. Had he not in his youth dated the doom of the Ottoman Empire from the day the House of Osman moved to the Bosporus from the austere spaces of the Anatolian plateau?

Since the bulk of his deputies were Anatolians, Kemal had little difficulty in passing the bill through the Assembly. "The Seat of the Turkish State," it read, "is the town of Angora." Constantinople would remain the home of the Caliphate; Angora the home of the Parliament, hence the capital of Turkey. It was to become known to the rest of the world as Ankara, while Constantinople as such was no longer to exist. There was to be left to it none among its various names but Istanbul.

III

The rise of
the Turkish Republic

45 ► *Proclamation of the Republic*

"The war is over," it was said in Angora after Lausanne. "Long live the war." Mustafa Kemal the Macedonian had reached his first objective. He had saved and revived Turkey; he had transformed a crumbling, straggling empire, beset by enemies, into a compact homogeneous state, recognized by potential friends. Urgency of purpose, tempered by deliberation of method and galvanized by the flame of a fierce vitality, had achieved this. A realist in an unrealistic age, he had seen what was possible and had pursued it, with singleness of aim, against friends who doubted him and enemies pursuing what was not possible. The task had called for a high degree of foresight; a patience which conflicted with his temperament and could be attained only by a rigid self-discipline; an intuitive sense of essentials and an understanding of the psychology of people, friend and enemy alike; an urge to grasp responsibility and use it decisively. Thanks to these qualities, the power which Kemal had passionately craved since his youth was now his. He had boasted, "I'm going to be somebody"—and now, after years of frustration, he was, at the age of forty-two, somebody.

Basically the work he had done was, for all its political overtones, that of a soldier, of a man skilled in planning, in organization, in improvisation, in action. What he had to do now called for something more—for the talents of a reformer, a prophet, a statesman. Having saved his country, his next objective was to create a new country. His ambition was nothing less than to transform Turkish society—to sweep away a medieval social system, based for centuries on Islam, and replace it by a new one based on modern Western civilization.

It was still in the spirit of the soldier that he now faced the new task. There was to be no resting on laurels; no relaxing before the new campaign, with the Gazi still in command, was launched. This time it was to be a war with moral not material armaments. But its dynamic and its tactics would be similar. As before, it was to be achieved by gradual stages. But the momentum, now that the initiative was his, would be swifter. Farsighted in planning but pragmatic in execution, Kemal had decided as far back as 1920 that "the great capacity for evolution that he sensed in the conscience and future of the nation should be kept as a national secret in his conscience and when the time came should be applied to the whole of society." The time had now come. Turkey was to enter a new phase of her development.

But she was still, as Falih Rifki put it, like a ship which had left harbour for the open sea, and of which only the captain knew the course. What course was he to take? Kemal had made up his mind. Throughout his patient voyage towards victory from Samsun to Erzurum, Sivas, Angora, Smyrna, and now Lausanne, his objective had been clear to him. Turkey, he was resolved, must become a Republic.

He was now in a strong position to achieve his design. Victory and an honourable treaty had sealed his prestige. A new Parliament, packed by himself, and a new party, of which he was the founder and leader, had opened up new channels of power. The launching of this drastic reform was now only a matter of timing and tactical handling.

The idea of the Republic had taken concrete shape in his mind during the summer, while the Lausanne Conference still sat. Devising a draft formula for its Constitution, he sent it confidentially to Seyyid, the Minister of Justice, who had advised him on the abolition of the Sultanate and previous constitutional matters. Seyyid approved the principle of the draft, from the legal standpoint, and returned it with a few proposed changes of detail. It was then laid aside until peace should be signed.

Kemal now began to try out the idea on his closer associates. At a dinner at Chankaya, at which Falih Rifki and a few trusted journalists were present, he remarked that he had been reading the history of the

French Revolution and had made a few notes on the word "Republic" and its equivalent in Turkish—*Cumhuriyet*. A dictionary was sent for and the translation found to be *chose publique*. A discussion was held on the exact meaning. Kemal then divulged his plan, which was still incomplete and on which further work remained to be done. His friends must discuss it among themselves, and in good time it would be put to the party. Someone asked him, "Will you still remain president of the party after you become President of the Republic?" Kemal replied, with a twinkle, "Between ourselves, yes." But he protested curtly when another, referring to the duration of the presidential term, suggested, "For the rest of your life?"

The news spread. For the local press it was still "off the record," but Kemal, flying a kite, revealed his intentions to the world in an interview to the *Neue Freie Presse*, a Viennese newspaper. He took the line that the Turkish state was a Republic already, in all but name. The first article of the law which defined it declared that its sovereignty belonged to the people; the second that the sole representative of the people was the Grand National Assembly.

The two phrases [he continued] may be summarized in a single word: *Republic*. . . . Within a short period of time the form which Turkey has now actually assumed will be confirmed by law. . . . Just as, basically, there is no difference between all the Republics of Europe and America . . . so also Turkey's difference from these Republics is merely a matter of form.

The interview electrified Ankara. The concept of a Republic was one wholly at odds with that of the traditional Moslem state, and this was the first time the ugly word had been uttered in a Turkish context. The threat of the change caused commotion, both in the press of Istanbul and in the lobbies of Parliament, where no serious republican movement had yet existed. Kemal realized that a debate on it might be fatal. The Republic must be forced through by other means before the Opposition had time to unite.

Hitherto the new Assembly had proved responsive enough to his assiduous direction. In its crucial early weeks he seldom missed a sitting, expounding measures before they were debated, making his own views clear, for or against acceptance. Once when the ayes had it, he said, "Please, will you put down your hands. I see I have failed to explain this point to you." He did so, making it clear that he wanted rejection— and on the next vote the noes had it. All the time he was patiently instructing the deputies on the nature of a modern Western state. Once a *hoja,* in the course of an oration, asked angrily, "What does this word 'modern' mean?"; to which the Gazi replied, "It means being a human being, *hoja*. It means being a human being."

For all this it was a soberer body than the first Parliament, younger, more levelheaded, and aspiring to live up to Kemal's definition of it as an "Assembly of Intellectuals." The wilder backwoodsmen were no longer in their places, to bedevil serious discussion, and the balance had been redressed by a group of writers, journalists, and professional men, maturer in mind and with some comprehension of Western ideas.

The Republic was nevertheless such an issue as to stir strong currents of opposition from both right and left. The die-hards, opposed to any radical changes, sought at all costs to preserve the power of the Caliphate, and some argued that if there were to be a Republic, then the Caliph should be its President. The progressives sought to preserve a balance of power. Some played with the idea of a constitutional monarchy, with the Caliph as sovereign; others favoured the Republic, provided it were a real democratic republic on the Western model—that of France, for example, or America. But they feared lest, in the hands of Kemal, it should become in effect a dictatorship, like the republics of South America or the Soviet Union. Such were the views of Rauf and Ali Fuad—at heart constitutional monarchists both—whose disappearance at this moment from the parliamentary scene thus suited Kemal's designs. In either case there was resentment at his apparent intention to spring the Republic on Parliament as a *fait accompli*.

This was in fact what he planned. As a pretext he engineered a ministerial crisis. The Assembly was still responsible for the election of ministers, a privilege which impaired its cohesion by encouraging factional and personal manoeuvres for power. A faction within the party, which Kemal proscribed as a "secret Opposition," now put forward two candidates for vacant posts in the government—one of them Rauf, for the vice-presidency of the Assembly, which Ali Fuad had vacated. Kemal objected to these nominations. Deciding to call the Opposition's bluff, he instructed Fethi and the other ministers to resign, and to refuse posts in a new Cabinet if chosen. The Opposition was then left to draw up its own list of ministers.

This was a challenge to Parliament to come out into the open and fight him—which he knew very well it would be unable to do. He let it be rumoured that, in the event of a showdown, he was prepared to fight back, with his Presidential Guard, confident of the support of the army and of his prestige with the people. The Opposition groups, in the absence of Rauf, tried to compose their differences and produce a list of ministers acceptable to all—but in vain. This created a situation in Parliament which Kemal chose to interpret as anarchy. After the country had been without a government for two days he took action. He invited a few friends, including Ismet and Fethi, to dinner at Chankaya. During the meal he announced, "Tomorrow we shall proclaim the Republic." There was no disagreement. He briefed Fethi and his colleagues on the tactics to be followed, and the party broke up.

Kemal was then left alone with Ismet. Together they completed the draft of the Republic, in the form of changes in the existing constitutional law. To this the sentence was added, "The form of the government of the Turkish state is a Republic." Its President would be head of state and would be elected by the Grand National Assembly. He would appoint the Prime Minister, who would then appoint the other ministers, with the approval but no longer on the initiative of the Assembly. This assured to Kemal the power he needed.

Next day the new provisions were put before the People's party caucus, the body that now counted in terms of political power. By prior arrangement with Fethi, Kemal was called in to "arbitrate." He spoke briefly, if only for the fortuitous reason that he had had a new set of dentures fitted that day, which shifted insecurely and gave a whistling sound to his voice. But he spoke coherently. The present form of government was based on a radical fault. It required each member of the Assembly to participate in the choice and by implication control of each minister. The disadvantages of this system had now been proved. They must be resolved in the way he had decided. The draft of the amended constitutional law was then read out by Ismet. It aroused murmurs of dismay among members of the party, who resented so sudden a move to change the Constitution. But Kemal's ally, the Minister of Justice, argued that its formula involved no innovation but sought only to clarify the existing law.

Despite a number of protests the meeting could do little but accept the new Constitution. Its acceptance by the Assembly itself, that evening, was hardly more than a formality. The *hojas* were stunned into silence, while the poet Mehmed Emin ventured to compare the Ankara Republic to the government founded by the Prophet in Mecca, fourteen hundred years before. Kemal was elected its President by 158 unanimous votes. But there were more than a hundred abstentions. The session was closed with prayers for the Republic's future welfare. The news of the proclamation was celebrated throughout the country with a salute of a hundred and one guns. The date of it was October 29, 1923.

Thanking his "comrades" for their support on this "historic occasion," Kemal, his eye always on the West (and his dentures now secured), stressed the effect of it abroad: "Thanks to the new title of its government, our nation will better succeed in manifesting before the eyes of the civilized world the qualities and merits with which it is endowed. The Turkish Republic will know how to demonstrate by deeds that it is worthy of the position it occupies among the nations."

He made Ismet his Prime Minister, knowing he could count on his friend to carry out his intentions in Parliament, as he had done in the field. Of Fethi, with his more liberal outlook, Kemal felt less sure. One evening at Chankaya, when Fethi was announced in the midst of some talk of a "revolutionary" kind, Kemal had silenced the guests with the words "Hush, children, the government is coming." He made Fethi President of the Assembly. By a masterly technique of timing, surprise tactics, and veiled intimidation, Kemal had assumed paramount power over the country. He was a President in triplicate—head of the state, effective head of the Cabinet and of Parliament, head of the only party. When Tevfik Rüstü, his admiring comrade of the Salonika days, compared him to the Holy Trinity itself, "Father, Son, and Holy Ghost," Kemal admitted with a glint in his eye, "It is true. But don't tell anyone."

Rauf, in Istanbul, was awakened by the sound of the hundred and one guns. So the Republic, he concluded, was a fact. Its abrupt proclamation, without reference to himself, Ali Fuad, or Refet, was to widen the rift between Kemal and his old associates to the point of overt opposition. It aroused outspoken criticism from the Istanbul press, which was freer than that of Ankara—its master's voice. Even an article under the heading "Long Live the Republic!" defined the manner of its introduction as "putting a pistol to the head of the nation." The powers granted to the Gazi, it was written, were such as had never been granted even to a Sultan. How different from the example of George Washington, who had retired to his farm while his Parliament, before electing him President, spent six years working out a Constitution!

These views reflected in principle those of Rauf and his adherents. In view of the failure of the attempt at constitutional monarchy, Rauf now favoured a Republic. But its Constitution should have been carefully studied and debated in the Assembly before it was proclaimed. As to the new method of choosing the Cabinet, which had been rejected by the previous Assembly, he said, "You speak of having a strong government. What I understand by a strong government is an experienced Cabinet which knows its duties and its rights and which is based on the supremacy of the people. I was astonished to hear that some people see a strong government as one which rules the country with the fist." Rauf's words to the press were wilfully misinterpreted in Ankara. Kemal, seeing Rauf and his group as a potential Opposition, sought to discredit him, and for the purpose used the smear of reaction. Rauf had paid a courtesy visit to the Caliph and from this it was easy to impute to him a plot to have the Caliphate now play a political role.

Such was the atmosphere in which Rauf left for Ankara, seen off by Ali Fuad, Refet, Kiazim Karabekir, an A.D.C. of the Caliph, and a crowd of followers who included naval personnel and medical students. Kiazim Karabekir had supported Rauf and the rest with a statement: "I am in favour of the Republic. But I am against personal rule." Thus the four other fathers of the Revolution were now ranged openly against Kemal.

At this juncture Kemal, while walking in his garden, collapsed with a heart attack. It proved to be slight, but he was unconscious for long enough to feel, as he put it to Ali Fuad, that he had visited the other world for a while. Now his doctors had cut him down to two or three cigarettes a day and prescribed a diet which Latife was imposing with strictness. Fuad urged him to take care of his health from now onwards. At his age he had after all completed only half of his natural span. Kemal reassured Fuad. The doctors had forbidden him raki but allowed him an occasional glass of whisky—as they had allowed it to Abdul Hamid when he too was forbidden raki.

On account of his condition, Rauf had only a brief talk with Kemal at Chankaya, in which he forbore from raising political issues. He found himself cold-shouldered in the Assembly. He was summoned to appear before a meeting of the party, to justify his statements to the press. These, it was alleged, were calculated to weaken the Republic, and implied his intention to form a party in opposition to it. Ismet, who presided over the meeting, took an uncompromising line. In disciplinarian tones, drawing parallels from wartime events, he stressed the need for unity of opinion at this second vital stage in the national struggle. Rauf, by these statements of his, was threatening the country with anarchy. Ismet implied support by Rauf of the Caliph, declaiming, "If at any time the Caliph takes it into his head to interfere with the destiny of this country, we shall not fail to execute him!" Finally he enquired whether Rauf meant to withdraw his hostile statements and remain within the party, or adhere to them and leave it to form a party on his own.

Rauf replied with frankness and dignity, reiterating his belief in the sovereignty of the people and insisting (as indeed he had done to the press) that there was no conflict between himself and the government. His statement had been made from the conviction that the only honest policy was to express freely his own ideas and opinions. He had no intention of forming an Opposition party. But if his fellow members chose to dismiss him from the People's party he would accept their verdict. To allow them to decide freely, he left the meeting, uttering the words, "Personalities are not eternal. Ideas are eternal."

His speech was greeted with cheers, and Ismet, sensing the feeling of the meeting in his favour, did not press his demands. Next day it was stated in a communiqué that Rauf had made it clear that he was in favour of the Republic and against the monarchy. He would remain in the party, which was satisfied that a false interpretation had been placed on his statement to the press.

Ali Fuad, before leaving to take up an army inspectorship at Konya, tried to reassure Kemal as to Rauf's views. He was in favour of the Republic, "provided it does not sacrifice the principles of popular supremacy and you yourself remain above the whole organization." Knowing of Rauf's predilection for British institutions, Kemal commented sceptically, "The Kingdom of England is based on the supremacy of the people. But the head of it is a King." It did not yet suit him to quarrel openly with Rauf and Ali Fuad. But later, seeking to discredit Rauf's motives, he declared that the decision in his favour "gave to Rauf Bey and his friends the opportunity of still working for some time in the party to accomplish its overthrow."

46 ▶ *Abolition of the Caliphate*

Kemal's second and more radical move followed a few months later. Like a general following up an advantage, with a secure base behind him, he proceeded swiftly towards his next planned objective. This was nothing less than the complete disestablishment of Islam, the final separation between the spiritual and the temporal power.

Always careful, until the military victory was won, to imply in public the orthodoxy of his religious views, Kemal had over the past years been speaking more freely and critically on the subject of religion. He still professed himself a believer, but a rational believer for whom Islam was a "natural religion," in harmony with reason, science, knowledge, and logic. He was strongly opposed to fanaticism, "a poisonous dagger which is directed at the heart of my people." He took to task those who pretended that a modern outlook was against the Moslem religion. The Friday sermons in the mosques should be in harmony with the truths of science and knowledge; the preachers should follow closely the political and social conditions of the civilized world. That the people might understand them, the sermons in future must be delivered in Turkish, not in an ancient dead language.

For centuries the Turks had "always walked from the East in the direction of the West." They would continue to do so, but this meant that the "moral treasure" of the Caliphate must finally go. Was it not both a symbol and a rallying point for those dark forces of "religious reaction"? Here, as at certain previous stages in his campaign, Kemal's task was made easier by an ill-judged foreign intervention. The Aga Khan and Ameer Ali, another distinguished Moslem leader, wrote a letter to Ismet, pointing out that the separation of the Caliphate from the Sultanate had increased its significance for Moslems in general, begging the Turkish government to place it "on a basis which would command the confidence and esteem of the Moslem natives, and thus impart to the Turkish state unique strength and dignity." This letter was published by three Istanbul newspapers before it reached Ankara. It led to the summoning of a secret session of Parliament, where it caused a tumult of indignation. In Kemal's adroit hands its contention that the Caliphate was a link with the past and with Islam was alone sufficient to ensure its immediate end.

The way thus became clear for him to go ahead and "cut out this tumour of the Middle Ages"—the Caliphate. The news of the abolition of the Caliphate was foreshadowed, as that of the foundation of the republic had been, by a foreign periodical, this time the *Revue des Deux Mondes*. Here in an interview (given in fact some months before) Kemal, playing on two meanings of the word, declared that inherently Caliphate meant no more than administration or government. With the existence of another administration and government it became, he implied, redundant. The Caliphate had never enjoyed universal jurisdiction over the Moslem world, as had the papacy over the Catholic world. The office was an Arab institution adopted by a former Turkish Sultan, whom millions of Moslems had never acknowledged as their spiritual ruler. The new Turkey was not irreligious but needed a religion stripped of artificiality, which implied nothing contrary to reason or hostile to progress. The Turkish press was carefully briefed on similar lines.

Kemal chose the fourth anniversary of the Grand National Assembly as an appropriate occasion on which to introduce his proposal. He did so with the words: "It has now become a plainly evident truth that it is necessary to liberate and to elevate the Islamic religion . . . from its position of being a tool of politics, in the way that has been traditional for centuries." He then put forward three main points: the Republic must be protected from every attack; the principle of unity in instruction and education must be applied to it; and "in order to secure the revival [sic] of the Islamic faith" religion must cease to be a political instrument. According to a routine which had now become common practice, these points were discussed at a meeting of the party, which drafted the necessary laws. Thus, as Falih Rifki expressed it, were "the bridges attaching Turkey to the Middle Ages to be blown up." The resulting scenes in the Assembly itself were so fiery as to recall to him etchings of the French Revolution. At one moment, during a brief suspension of the debate, orators were climbing onto chairs and tables in the lobbies, and shouting themselves hoarse for the expulsion of the Ottoman family; at another, turbaned *hojas* were running in and out of the Gazi's room, declaring themselves ready to abolish the sacred Book itself rather than listen to the terrible pleas being made in the Chamber for the abolition of that religious instruction on which their power depended. But in this relatively sober new body the debate was easily enough managed by Kemal and Ismet, with the aid once more of the Minister of Justice.

The Caliph was deposed and his office abolished; the members of his dynasty were forever forbidden to reside within the frontiers of the Turkish Republic; the Ministry of Religious Affairs was disbanded, the historic office of Sheikh of Islam ceased to exist, the revenues of the Pious Foundations were confiscated; and all religious schools were transferred to the secular arm. By a further decree a month later the religious courts of the sheriat, which still administered the laws relating to such matters of family and personal status as marriage, divorce, and inheritance, were closed, and a Civil Code based on that of the Swiss was planned to prevail over all.[1]

On the night of the Assembly's decision the Caliph, Abdul Mejid, was awoken in the Dolma Bahche Palace by the chief of police and a party of officials, who instructed him to leave Turkey at five o'clock in the morning. He was overcome with emotion but soon recovered his dignity so far as to request that he be allowed to pack some personal possessions and that provision be made for the women of his seraglio. With indecent haste—since the government was taking no chances with public opinion —he was hurried off by car to Chatalja, whence he took the train in the evening to Switzerland. Here he was held up at the frontier on the grounds that polygamists were not allowed into the country. But after a delay he was provisionally admitted, pending a later enquiry into his marital situation.

[1] A last-minute attempt to rescue the Caliphate was made through an emissary, claiming to represent Indian and Egyptian Moslems, who suggested to Kemal that he himself should become Caliph. He refused, pointing out realistically that the various Moslem sovereigns would be unlikely to execute his orders as Caliph, hence the role would be illusory.

In Istanbul the superstitious noted that this last head of the Ottoman family had left Turkey on a Tuesday, the same day of the week as his forebears had chosen to enter Constantinople. On the following Friday the prayer at Santa Sophia contained for the first time no mention of the Caliph. It read: "O God, grant Thy protecting aid to our republican government and the Moslem nation. Make eternal the glory of the Moslems and raise the flag of Islam, which rests upon the Republic of Turkey, above all other flags and make them live by the spiritual Prophet!"

In a few hours Kemal had swept away an epoch of history. He had done so through an unsurpassed faculty for imposing his ideas upon others—Parliament, party, or the press—and an uncanny sense of the psychological moment at which to impose them. He was proved right in anticipating that the abolition of the Caliphate would cause little disturbance, whether at home or abroad. With the abolition of the Sultanate, achieved on a wave of popular indignation against the actions of the Sultan in person, the Caliphate had become little more than a vestigial survival. In the Moslem world its abolition created a certain initial dismay, especially in India where the Turkish Revolution had been seen as a fight by a Moslem state for its freedom, with Kemal as the "Sword of Islam." But this soon subsided as the truth became clear. The Caliphate, deprived of its temporal and hence its political power, no longer had any reality. A prominent Turkish journalist might well enquire, "What is that which has been abolished?"

For a century past Turkish secular reformers had been waging a slow battle against religious conservatism. Kemal, abruptly accelerating it and bringing it to its logical end, became the first ruler openly to assault and to vanquish the entrenched forces of an orthodox Moslem state. But though he might, by a single act of his Grand National Assembly, abolish the political power of the Islamic religion, he could not neutralize its spiritual and social influences, and indeed did not pretend to interfere with freedom of religious conscience. Islam was more than a code of belief; it was a system of living. God still ruled over the minds and the souls and directed the lives of the bulk of the Turkish people, and would continue to do so. The Caliphate itself might be forgotten. The replacement of religious by secular schools, with a scientific positivist curriculum, was to have profound effects on the spiritual and intellectual development of future Turkish generations. But this in its turn was to have its counterpart in the survival of an "underground" Moslem force, widespread in its influence, which was often to erupt to the surface, facing Kemal with a recurrent and radical problem during the years of reform which lay ahead.

47 ► The Progressive party

Ankara, the capital of the Republic, grew slowly. The new deputies to the second Grand National Assembly, many of them used to the civilization of Istanbul and other Westernized cities, the civil servants who came in their hundreds now that Istanbul was no longer the seat of government, were disconcerted by its primitive character. Furniture and other household utensils were unobtainable, since the Armenians who once manufactured and sold them had fled, leaving Ankara without shopkeepers or artisans. There was little or no electric light. "Rooms to let with electricity" was an infrequent advertisement.

Men still slept ten or twelve to a room. Women were scarce, fearing to brave such discomforts and leaving their husbands grass widowers. A deputy, seen one day with his wife unveiled in the street, caused unfavourable gossip in Parliament. The local inhabitants, loyal as they were to the cause, tended to hold aloof from the intruders. They spoke a different dialect, making it hard to negotiate for the purchase of building land, of which they were too ignorant to appreciate the value.

In the summer the land was a dust bowl, at other seasons a muddy morass. The mayor wrung his hands. "You clamour for roads to be built, but at the same time you don't want dust." The landscape, once green with vineyards and forests, had succumbed through the centuries to neglect and erosion. A single pine tree grew before the Parliament building, and deputies reassured one another, "Look, it is growing quite well." In the winter the snows were such that dinner guests might have to stay for two or three nights. Rooms were heated by primitive stoves, which often had to be moved out to make room for the guests. As one of them drily remarked, "There can be no civilization with a temperature below zero." [1]

There were a few rough eating houses, but since prohibition still reigned it was hard to get a drink, and a drink in this atmosphere was needed. It was served only in one of them, in discreet doses, with the connivance of a henchman of the Director of Public Security. Some members were lucky enough to possess vineyards, where they distilled their own liquor illegally and were even known to drink it before it had cooled. But up at Chankaya the drink flowed without interruption.

An innovation now on these evenings around the table was the presence of Latife. Not a wife to remain in the background, she made her personality felt. From the start of the marriage Kemal had drawn from her companionship a stimulus such as no woman had yet given him, as well as practical help and advice in his work, for she still acted to some extent as his "secretary." She was intelligent and well educated; she was self-confident, with ideas of her own; they could hold serious discussions together. Here, as he saw it, was a relationship between man and wife on equal terms, such as prevailed in the West. He discussed with her especially his plans for the emancipation of women.

At home Latife, as their living embodiment, did him credit enough at his table. But she was not always tactful. She tended to run the house as her own and showed ominous signs of trying to run Kemal as well. She behaved rather like the wife of any army officer, seeing it as her role to tame and civilize the confirmed bachelor she had married, to cure his rough ways, to introduce order and refinement into a home which, in her eyes, derived too much from casual garrison habits. She sought to model it rather on that of her own family in Izmir (as Smyrna was now to be

---

[1] In the wintry weather there were often rumours of wolves roaming the town. Once after an official reception at Ismet's house no cars could drive away on account of a heavy fall of snow. The British ambassador (by then Sir George Clerk), as he set off lightheartedly to walk, threw out the macabre observation, "If we are torn to pieces, it will at least be the first time that tail coats and opera hats have been left behind by wolves."

called), with its more correct—and, as she was inclined to imply, more civilized—social standards.

She tried to order his dinner parties, demanding to know in advance just how many guests were expected and objecting to those she disliked; she insisted that wives should be invited with their husbands as in respectable Westernized households. For a while she even introduced evening dress, causing many to decline the invitation who, in this backwoods "capital," did not possess it. One evening the guests, arriving in dinner jackets, were disconcerted to find a palm court orchestra playing in the hall, and amused to see Kemal coming downstairs to greet them, likewise dressed, with a shrug of the shoulders and a mock-martyred smile on his face. Kemal disliked all social pretensions and this was not the way he cared to entertain his friends, unless on a formal occasion. He was a natural host, polite in his manner and assiduous in his attention to guests, but he liked to do things in his own easy way.

Latife was omnipresent, a short stocky figure sitting at the head of the table, even on a bachelor evening when he drank with his cronies. She would try to lead the conversation, for, as the favourite spoiled child of her father, she liked to be listened to—and Kemal did not take easily to the listener's role. Receiving foreign visitors, she would presume to speak for Kemal. To Ward Price of the *Daily Mail* she said in excellent English, "If I tell you anything you may consider it just as authoritative as if you had it from the Gazi himself." She passed on to Kemal information which was not always reliable and sometimes made mischief.

But where Latife most erred in her psychology was in seeking too obviously to moderate his drinking habits. She tried to cut down the drink at the table. She would come into the room and exclaim before his friends, "What's this, Kemal, drinking again?" She would move to break up the party at a reasonable hour. She was even known to bang on the floor above, as a hint that it was time for him to come up to bed. A clash of strong wills, of high-strung temperaments loomed ahead of them.

Kemal found a frequent refuge on the model farm which he was developing on the slopes around his former headquarters at the Agricultural School—an easy ride from Chankaya. Since his boyhood there had grown in him a feeling for nature. Partly it was the love for growing things of a man who had spent much of his life in harsh barren places. He liked to see and with his creative spirit to make the desert bloom. The sight of a pine tree gave him a sense of almost pagan veneration. Once, while

riding with Ismet, then his chief of staff, near Diyarbekir, he had exclaimed, "Find me a new religion." "Let it be a religion," Ismet answered,
"whose form of worship is to plant trees." He admired the old trees of
Istanbul but liked better to see a tree growing day by day before his eyes.

He planned and supervised in person the planting of the orchards at
his farm. But the older trees must not be sacrificed. Once, while driving
through it, he stopped his car and exclaimed, "There was a gum tree
there. What has become of it?" Nobody knew, but he remembered it as
the one living green thing in the days of the war, when the farm was
still almost a desert. "It was a puny old tree," he said, "but it was alive.
It smelled good in the spring." He gave orders for the preservation of all
old trees in future.

The farm was eventually to become an experimental station for the
nation's forestry and agriculture, but at first it was his own personal play-
ground, where his mood was always relaxed. Here he smiled at the world
and at himself, at the fact that this "estate" of his would never pay its
way. Tapping new sources of water, he created two pools amid the trees,
one small and shaped like the Sea of Marmara, one large and shaped like
the Black Sea. In one he installed a fountain, which his manager turned
on one evening after fitting fairy lights around it. At the sight of the
coloured water, Kemal joked in a peasant idiom, "Oh you, Kemal, did
you ever study agriculture? No. Are you a farmer? No. Was your father?
No. There is reason for even the waters to mock you for poking your
nose into things you know nothing about."

Kemal still thought of Fikriye. He had corresponded with her intermittently during her spell in a sanatorium in Munich, and later, when
her health had improved, in Paris. There she had heard the news of his
marriage. Pining away from her love for him and now tormented by
jealousy, she returned to Turkey and wrote to him from Istanbul to announce her arrival. Kemal, whose affection for Fikriye survived, although he did not reciprocate her love, hoped in some way to reconcile
her with Latife. But she came to Ankara and appeared at Chankaya one
day without warning. Here she was told that the Gazi was still asleep.
She said she would wait, and retired to the lavatory.

She stayed there so long that the two aides who had received her grew
worried, for they had noticed her distraught appearance. One of them
tried the door and, receiving no response, broke it open. He saw Fikriye
putting a revolver into her bag. He pretended not to notice, but for
Kemal's safety explained to her that the Gazi could not see her just now,
and asked her to leave. He escorted her to her carriage and she drove to

a neighbouring house, where a cousin was staying. But he was not at home. She then took the revolver from her bag and shot herself dead, there in the carriage. In her desperation she had perhaps come to shoot Kemal, or Latife, or both of them—or to shoot herself before him, as a reproach for his treatment of her. More probably she had no clear idea of what she meant to do.

Kemal was troubled by her death and remained taciturn and morose for some time afterwards. It would not occur to him to feel guilty—no more than he felt guilty for the thousands of men he had sent to their deaths in battle. But Fikriye was the woman for whom his affection had come nearest to love.

Kemal liked, in his vanity, to be loved, and throughout his life chose women who took the initiative in showing their feelings. But he could not endure to be loved too much, to become tied by a woman's emotions, whatever form they might take. Each of these two women in his life was possessive. Fikriye's fault lay in clinging to Kemal, her misfortune in becoming sick and unable to disguise her dependence upon him. Latife's fault lay in seeking to lead him. Kemal would not marry Fikriye because he wanted a wife who would stand beside, not behind him. On the other hand, the last thing he wanted was a wife who, like Latife, might seek to stand before him.

The issue between Kemal and his old friends had now to be joined. Bent as he was on full powers, in the operations for reform as in the field of battle, it had become clear, after the proclamation of the Republic, that his four co-founders of the Revolution—Rauf, Refet, Ali Fuad, and Kiazim Karabekir—were to be denied a fair share in its fruits. The latent differences between them, kept under control before victory was won, now erupted to the surface. With the possible exception of Ali Fuad, they were not personally his kind, nor he theirs. Socially, they had roots which he lacked. Morally, they were imbued with a loftier spirit of idealism. Kemal's own ideals were tempered by expediency and above all by his ruthless sense of realities. His head ruled his heart. He had a colder, more penetrating intelligence than they.

Their differences now proved fundamental. Kemal was embarking on a social revolution. Rauf and his friends, at this stage, preferred social evolution. What need was there for hurry, for sudden and radical change? Give the people time to settle down after their ten-year upheaval. Give them security from brigandage and aid in recultivating their lands. Let social reforms come gradually in response to their needs and demands.

Sovereignty was theirs. Let them exercise it through their own representative institutions, as it was exercised in the democratic countries of Europe. They had an honourable peace. Let them now have two or three years of good government and after that decide, through a referendum, what kind of regime they would prefer. Thus spoke the voice of the liberal Turkish gentleman.

Kemal's mind worked in a more practical way. To bring his country into line with the West he had set up a democratic system in which, on a long-term view, he believed. He stood by his occidental Assembly. But it needed, on the short-term view, a President exercising some degree of autocracy—a power which, though he would not himself have admitted it, was in character oriental.

Kemal knew his people too well to have any illusions as to their political maturity. They were still an oriental people culturally backward and temperamentally unfitted for the literal application of Western democracy. They could not yet rule; they required to be ruled. The strong religious authority of the Sultan-Caliph needed to be replaced by an equally strong secular authority; and this for the present only Kemal himself, by his personal manipulation of Parliament, could provide. Rauf and the rest, by the integrity of their principles and the moderation of their outlook, threatened to undermine it and thus to prejudice that process of reform which no one else but he, as he saw it, had the foresight to plan and the capacity to execute. Here was a struggle for power, with his friends as with his enemies, which, in alliance with Ismet and Fevzi—the two latecomers to the Revolution—and his less scrupulous henchmen, must soon be fought out. It was a struggle between the forces of a liberal democracy, literally interpreted, and those of a democratic structure conditioned by one-party government and personal rule.

It brought out the oriental in Kemal. An atmosphere of intrigue now permeated the anterooms of Chankaya and the lobbies of the Assembly. Schemers and informers flourished, feeding him with mischievous gossip. He grew cold, sly, suspicious of the motives of all who might stand in his way. He launched whispering campaigns to make mischief against Refet and Rauf, minimizing their services to the country and insinuating that they favoured reaction. A useful instrument to him in his various stratagems was Rejep Peker, his Minister of the Interior, a petty despot of ruthless character and Germanic aspect, who issued a press statement in Istanbul that activities aimed against reform would be punished by the same methods as in the War of Independence.

In this atmosphere Rauf, Ali Fuad, and Kiazim Karabekir met together in Rauf's house in Shishli in the autumn of 1924, to decide on a course of action. They agreed on support for Kemal's reforms but insisted that these should benefit national, not sectional interests; they would strive to prevent the Republic from becoming an instrument for the rule of any one person or group; they would take their seats in the Assembly and work through its machinery to these ends, with other friends who might share their opinions.

While they conferred, Kemal was on tour with Latife. He returned to Ankara in time for the reassembly of Parliament. A few days before it opened Kiazim Karabekir, according to a plan prearranged with the rest, resigned his army inspectorship on the grounds that his recommendations were ignored by the War Ministry and that he wished to resume his functions as a deputy. Ali Fuad meanwhile had come to Ankara. He did not see Kemal, who claimed that he had asked him to dinner at Chankaya on his arrival but could not locate him—a claim which Fuad attributed to deliberate ill will on the part of Kemal's entourage. Next day he handed his own resignation to Fevzi, the chief of the General Staff, who showed some dismay.

The two resignations touched off a crisis, which Kemal chose to see as a "great plot" by the generals, in concert with Rauf to overthrow him in the Assembly with military backing. Reviving, for different motives, the argument he had used fifteen years earlier against Enver, he decreed that the army must at all costs be eliminated from politics. For the sake of consistency he obtained the resignation of Fevzi from Parliament, then requested those of his six army corps commanders stationed in different parts of the country. Only two of them refused, preferring to retain their seats and thus lose their commands.

Rauf publicly reaffirmed his support of the Republic and ridiculed the implication that he and his friends were planning a military coup. He had been one of the first to deplore any interference of the army in politics. Was it likely that, at his time of life, having done his duty to his country, he would retire into the mountains like a Chinese general to form a government of his own? All he sought was to prevent any one group from monopolizing the power that rightly belonged to the Assembly.

It was on this ground that the Opposition planned to force an issue. The occasion for the crucial debate was what Rauf described as the "tremendous scandal" of the resettlement of the Turkish immigrants from Greece, under the Lausanne Treaty, of whom an alarming percentage had died from neglect and maltreatment. The Opposition criticism was outspoken.

The debate was stormy, with many bitter exchanges between Rauf, who pressed for a commission of enquiry, and Rejep, who accused him of treachery against the Republic. At one moment Rauf was interrupted with the taunt that he should "go back to the country from which your father and your ancestors came"—a reference to his Caucasian origins. Ismet, however, evaded a division on the issue by turning it into a vote of confidence in the government, which he easily won.

This was more than Rauf and his fellow critics could stomach. Feeling unable to remain in the People's party, they resigned from it in a body and came out into open opposition by forming a party of their own. Rauf in his letter of resignation protested that the form of the debate had destroyed all chance of unity and that he preferred to work independently. Thus Kemal's new Republic was to taste for a spell the methods of Western two-party democracy.

The new party thus founded in November 1924 was at first named the Progressive party. When its rival became the People's Republican party, it stressed its own republicanism by becoming the Progressive Republican party. From the start it aspired not to oust Kemal and to form an alternative government but merely—as Rauf defined its aims to an American journalist—to curb and limit his authority. It was to be in a sense a permanent minority pressure group, standing up for the rights of free speech and discussion and criticism, and hoping thus to influence the government from within. The party contained some thirty members, all of whom had resigned from the People's party. Kiazim Karabekir was its president, thus giving it high prestige, for hitherto he had kept relatively clear of politics, confining himself to his military duties and refusing all government appointments. The party did not intend at first to go to the country and put up its own candidates for vacant seats in the Assembly; it intended simply to support independent candidates. But it set up party organizations in Istanbul and three other provincial centres, with a view to intervention at a later stage. Had it chosen to admit the more conservative deputies to membership, it might have obtained on occasion a majority. But it did not, despite the accusations of its enemies, care to be linked with reactionary forces or to create a serious split in the Assembly.

It claimed to be Turkey's first political party conceived on Western lines. In the past the Turkish "parties," including that of Union and Progress, had been little more than personal power groups of no consistent political colour. The People's party itself was based on no specific programme, but only on a series of general principles, such as all might accept. The Progressives, on the other hand, drew up a full programme and a party constitution of their own. This they submitted to the Minister of the Interior for official recognition, which was formally granted.

In its declaration it stressed that its function was to maintain equilibrium and guard against autocracy within the constitutional framework. It stood for national unity and individual liberty, free from oligarchic or personal pressure. It affirmed its respect for religious opinions and beliefs, thus following a formula used in the West to stress the dissociation of religion from politics, but here in the East laying itself open, as it proved, to the reverse interpretation.

The various points in its programme differed from the principles of the People's party in several important respects. The President of the Republic must remain above party, obliged on election to resign his seat in the Assembly. There must be no modification of the Constitution without a mandate from the electorate. There should be first-degree in place of second-degree elections, bringing democracy closer to the people through direct representation in smaller and more local constituencies. Further, the law alone should reign, nor should judges be removed or transferred without their consent; and administration should be decentralized, with the election in place of the appointment of mayors and the granting of more powers to local authorities, especially in the field of education. The party produced also an economic programme, which differed from that of the government in giving more scope to free enterprise and encouraging foreign capital investment. The press was to be free, and so was discussion within the party itself. Its meetings were to be open, like those of the parties in Europe, whereas those of the People's party were secret.

Initially the attitude of the People's party to its Progressive renegades was to treat them as suspects, endangering the security of the Republic. But within two months Kemal found it expedient to appease the new Opposition by removing their main enemy, Ismet, from the premiership, on the grounds of illness, and replacing him with Fethi, with his more liberal views. For a time the Progressives nourished a hope that this change of personalities might lead to a change of mentality. The extremists in the People's party, seeking power for themselves by encouraging the arbitrary power of Kemal, tried but failed at a party meeting to induce Fethi to hold aloof from the Opposition. Thus the position of the moderates was strengthened.

For the next few months the Progressives played an active and not wholly ineffective part in the Assembly. They had constructive contributions to make in the budget debates, on such issues as economic policy and administrative reform. On defence policy they strongly opposed—but without success—a manoeuvre of Kemal further to strengthen his power through a Supreme Military Council, with a chief of the General Staff independent of ministerial and thus of parliamentary control. But Fethi, steering a course between the two parties, was often, for all his good intentions, in a quandary. Under pressure, he found it necessary to close down an Opposition newspaper for likening the People's party to a parasite, and thus provoked fierce attacks from the Progressives.

The atmosphere was not improved by a brawl in Parliament in which an Opposition supporter, Halid Pasha, was fatally injured. Halid had unearthed the story of a corrupt deal by which a group of Kemal's henchmen—including Arif, his old comrade-in-arms—were drawing money from a state industrial enterprise to finance a secret political campaign against Kemal's opponents. He taxed them with this in the lobby of the Assembly, and a violent dispute followed, in which revolvers were drawn. Halid, a man of hot temper, flung an adversary to the ground and might have killed him but for the restraint of his friends. Emerging from the Chamber to see the fight, another deputy, with the apparent encouragement of those who stood by, then drew his revolver and shot Halid in the back.

He died five days later. Despite strong protests in the Assembly, no action was taken against the culprit, who was declared to have acted in self-defence. The incident, however, could not easily be hushed up and caused general disquiet. But now a disturbance of graver and more national import occurred. An insurrection flared up among the Kurds, in the remote highlands of southeastern Turkey.

48 ► *The Kurdish revolt*

The Kurds, a feudal people of separate race and language from the Turks, were a dissident minority of combative temperament and extreme religious beliefs, who had given periodic trouble to a succession of Ottoman governments. After the war their aspirations to freedom were encouraged by the Allied move, at the Peace Conference, to create an independent Kurdistan, and they were now adroitly playing off the British, in the region of Mosul and beyond the frontiers of Irak, against the Turkish central government.

The leader of the revolt, which broke out in the Dersim region of the upper Euphrates, was one Sheikh Said of Palu, the rich hereditary chieftain or "abbot" of the local Nakshibendi dervishes. He was a picturesque and illiterate overlord who lived on—and largely for—the vast herds of sheep which he bred and grazed on the pastures of his tribesmen and increased at their expense by the exploitation of his religious prestige and authority. His influence extended, through a series of judicious dynastic marriages, over the powerful sheep-owning families of the neighbouring mountains. These feudal powers seemed now to be threatened by the new "Turkified" government of Ankara.

Bent on their retention in an autonomous Kurdistan, the sheikh now stirred up his tribesmen against the abolition of the Caliphate and the godless policy of the Kemalist government. On February 13, 1925, "charged by God" after some weeks of assiduous propaganda, he proclaimed the revolt. Riding beneath the green Islamic banner, in the name of the restoration of the holy law, his forces roamed through the country, seized government offices, imprisoned gendarmes, and marched on the important cities of Elaziğ and Diyarbekir.

At first Parliament made little of the affair, treating it as a local outbreak of brigandage. The situation, so Fethi maintained, could be brought under control by martial law in the region, and a plan of military action was prepared by Fevzi. The success of his operations could not be seriously in doubt, with the army still mobilized and only a few bands of wild Kurdish irregulars to contend with.

But the People's party extremists took an opposite view. They preferred to see the rebellion as an attempt at a counterrevolution, which could spread from Kurdistan to other parts of Turkey in an attempt to overthrow the regime. Martial law should thus be declared not only locally but throughout the country, including Istanbul. Fethi rejected the proposal. His opponents then turned their fire against the Progressive party, claiming that it was they who, by inflammatory religious propaganda, had helped to stimulate the revolt. Fethi became worried and summoned Kiazim Karabekir, Rauf, and Ali Fuad—who sent Dr. Adnan in his place. Fethi asked them, in order to avoid bloodshed, to dissolve their organization and collaborate with the People's party.

Kiazim Karabekir protested with vigour. His party had a legal right to exist, and no government was entitled to dissolve it.

Fethi said, "You know I am always against the use of force. But I fear that I may be in a minority."

Kiazim compromised. He and his friends realized the dangers of the revolt and were unanimously resolved on its suppression. They would not dissolve their party but they would support the government, wholeheartedly, over this particular issue. Fethi thanked them and added that the operations were going according to plan. There should be no need for new measures, since peace and calm reigned everywhere outside the area of the rebellion. Next day in the Assembly, after Kiazim had denounced the rebels and promised support to the government, a law was passed, pronouncing as guilty of high treason those who used religion as an instrument to destroy the public order of the country.

But this moderate policy was not to prevail for long. At the news of the revolt, Ismet had hurried back to Ankara from the island in the Marmara where he had been recovering from an indisposition. He was soon in touch with the Gazi, who summoned a Cabinet meeting. Kemal's reaction to the revolt was twofold. Firstly he saw it in terms of his chronic dread of religious reaction. "If we can manage to keep the right wing under control," he once said, "we do not need to fear the left. . . . One should not wait before crushing a reactionary movement. . . . One should act at once." Such, during the War of Independence, had been his response to the widespread rebellion of the Caliph's Army. Such now was his response to this localized revolt, in which he chose to detect once more the hidden hand of his enemies in Istanbul. Secondly, he saw in it a useful pretext for silencing the Progressives in Parliament. He thus supported Ismet's view of the emergency and rejected that of Fethi, who agreed to accept the arbitration of the People's party.

A party caucus was convoked, in which Ismet and Rejep condemned the government's handling of the revolt and demanded the adoption of more radical measures throughout the country. They put forward a bill to provide for Independence Tribunals, censorship of the press, and other stringent regulations directed against sedition. Fethi, backed by a majority of his ministers, opposed the bill. He persisted in his view that action should be taken only against those who had caused the trouble. When the extremists struck at the moderates by flinging their religious beliefs in their faces, he replied that Islam, after all, was constitutionally the religion of the Turkish Republic. "Is there a single one among you who feels no respect for religious beliefs?"

In the furore which followed the question, a party member drew his revolver but was deprived of it before he could shoot. The moment had come for Kemal's well-rehearsed formula. A member rose to remind the meeting, "Gentlemen, this party has a leader. Let us listen to him." And Kemal was called in from the President's room, where he had been awaiting the summons. Arbitrating in favour of the extremists, he made a long speech in which he reached the conclusion: "It is necessary to take the nation by the hand. Those who started the Revolution will complete it." A motion of no confidence in the government was put to the vote and carried—though only by a one-third majority. Rather than appeal to the Assembly over the head of the party, Fethi chose the line of least resistance and announced to the deputies the resignation of his government. Thus Ismet became once more Prime Minister, this time with Rejep as his Minister of Defence.

··

Meanwhile Sheikh Said and his followers swept through the Kurdish highlands "on the road to God," waving green flags and clutching Korans to their breasts, raiding banks and plundering shops and houses, calling in the name of the Almighty for all Turks to surrender. The preachers inflamed them with promises of heavenly rewards. Leaflets were distributed and scattered from the air, declaring that the Caliph demanded their sacrifice, that Islam was not Islam without a Caliphate. Let them restore the holy law, let them destroy this government, which taught atheism in its schools and allowed its women to go about naked.

The rebels hoped by a swift campaign to gain control of the region before reinforcements from Ankara could arrive. Gathering the support of the tribes as they marched, they drove back the scanty government militia. They occupied village after village. They captured Elaziğ and surrounded Diyarbekir. They mustered a large force outside the walls of the city and, with the aid of a fifth column within, succeeded in reaching the Kurdish quarter by means of trenches dug for sewers. But support from the inhabitants failed to materialize, and the government forces drove them out after twenty-four hours of street fighting, in which Kurds shot at Turks from the minarets. The militia refrained meanwhile from pursuit of the rebels, for Fevzi, after consultation with Kemal and Ismet, had ordered the local militia to avoid major engagements until the regular forces arrived.

It was planned gradually to surround the whole area, then to close in on the rebels in a large-scale offensive, with an army on a war footing of eight divisions, plus air force support. This would take time, since Kurdistan was a country without roads and so mountainous that, in the words of Von Moltke, there was nothing flat in it but the roofs of the houses. At this season it was lashed by blizzards and its passes often blocked with snowdrifts. The reinforcements must march hundreds of miles to reach the front. But the French gave permission for the use of the Baghdad Railway through northern Syria, on the understanding that the operations were not to be aimed against the British in Irak.

While the army completed its preparations Ismet clinched his hold over the country with the introduction into the Assembly of a drastic Law for the Maintenance of Public Order. This was to give the government wide dictatorial powers. For a period of two years (in the event to be extended for a further such period) the Cabinet was accorded the right to forbid and suppress any organization, any attempt, or any publication which might encourage "reaction and rebellion." The law was to be enforced through Independence Tribunals. Most of these would be in the region of the military operations, where they would replace the courts-martial and have the power to carry out death sentences instantly, without seeking the Assembly's approval. There was to be one additional tribunal in Ankara, with jurisdiction over the rest of the country to suppress reactionary propaganda and punish actions threatening to disturb the peace, but requiring the Assembly's approval for death sentences.

The law aroused fierce opposition from the Progressives, who condemned it as unconstitutional, destructive of all liberties, and contrary to the rights of man. But Ismet remained adamant. "National rostrums," he declared, "where every member of the Opposition is allowed to express his opinion are rare in the world." Ignoring shouts of dissent, he defended the law in terms of the overriding need to maintain order and security. Only on such a basis could the national reforms be carried out. He won his two motions by a large majority, and the judges and prosecutors of the Independence Tribunals were appointed by the Assembly from among members unlikely to prove too tolerant of a Progressive Opposition. In a presidential statement, Kemal explained that these extraordinary measures had "given to all government officials the task of preventing an incident before it happens rather than repressing it after it has happened." The state must have the power to suppress speedily "the aggressive actions of drunkards in the streets, bandits in the mountains, rebels who dare oppose the armed forces of the Republic, and those who create confusion in the innocent mind of the nation."

By the end of March 1925 the necessary troop movements were completed and the whole area of the rebellion was quietly encircled. Sheikh Said was blockaded within his own territory, and all routes of escape across the frontiers of Persia, Syria, and the province of Mosul were stopped. It now only remained to close in and exterminate the rebel forces, who were devoid of artillery and moreover known to be averse to bayonet fighting. Sheikh Said had not been wholly successful in rallying his neighbouring tribes, since he had chosen to emphasize the issue of religion above that of Kurdish independence, and they were disinclined to accept the spiritual authority of a Nakshibendi dervish. He had moreover failed to capture Diyarbekir, the obvious capital for any Kurdish state.

The victory of the government was thus mathematically certain. Its progress, however, must inevitably be slow, since the Kurds scattered into their mountains in small mobile groups, incapable of serious resistance, but harassing the enemy by ambushes, fusillades from the hilltops, and surprise attacks from his rear. One by one these forces were rounded up and their strongholds captured. Finally, in the middle of April, Sheikh Said himself was surrounded, with a number of chiefs and a small force of followers. He accepted defeat and surrendered freely. Incriminating documents were found on him, and a large sum of money in gold. His rebellion had lasted just two months.

Sheikh Said's arrival in Diyarbekir, with a cavalcade of some thirty other rebels preceded and followed by detachments of government infantry and cavalry, attracted the attention of the whole population. Tall, slim, and sunburned, he rode with a swagger. Aircraft flew overhead, showering fireworks on the crowd. The authorities received him with studious politeness. Had his journey been tiresome? All campaigns, he replied, were tiresome. He had been ill. How was his health now? It was better, but he still could not eat. He was promised good treatment. The doctors would look after him. Amid a whirring of cameras he was taken away.

A month later he and his various confederates were tried by an Independence Tribunal. Apart from the Public Prosecutor, it was composed of members of the Assembly, who sat ostentatiously beneath a large red Turkish flag, in emphatic and symbolic protest against the green Moslem flag of the Kurds.

Sheikh Said at his trial behaved calmly and even joked with the judges. But he objected as a Moslem to the film cameras in court, pursing his lips and mumbling prayers against them. He declared that he had rebelled because religion was losing its hold on the people. He refused to admit that he had been wrong in drawing his sword against other Moslems, arguing that they had ceased to be faithful to their religion. Had he succeeded, he would have reopened the religious schools, restored the Holy Law, and reimposed the traditional law, cutting off the tongue of the liar and the hand of the thief. Thus Kurdistan would have been once more as happy as in the days of the Prophet.

On these grounds he and his fellow accused pleaded not guilty. They were nonetheless condemned to death as traitors. Sheikh Said and some forty others, of whom nine were sheikhs, were hanged before the big mosque in Diyarbekir. They died for the most part courageously. The sheikh kept up his panache to the end. Before mounting the scaffold he remarked with a smile to the president of the tribunal, "I like you well, but we shall settle our accounts at the Last Judgment." Teasing the military commander, he said, "Come, General, say good-bye to your enemy."

He stood quietly while the shirt was put over his head, and without another word was hanged.

Thus ended the rebellion of the Kurds. The public reaction to it throughout the new Turkey had been hostile. There had been little or no sign, despite the expressed fears of the government, of a sympathetic reaction in other parts of the country. In the neighbouring provinces and elsewhere the peasants had organized their own defence. In Istanbul the students and the porters—the intelligentsia and the proletariat—had come out strongly against these manifestations of religious reaction. As Ismet himself admitted to Parliament, the "children of the Republic" had responded willingly to the order for mobilization. They were angry at this attempt to disrupt the peace which had just been so hardly won and they resented this use of religion for political motives. In this first crisis since the War of Independence the Gazi's new national front had come reassuringly to the fore.

But Kemal was taking no chances. It was not at present his intention to guide it into the channels of too liberal a system of government. The power of his Opposition in Parliament and the press must now be vanquished as the rebels had been. During the revolt, at a moment when victory had become certain, Ismet had remarked to Ali Fuad that an Opposition was unnecessary. To Admiral Bristol, the American representative, he expressed his view even more frankly with the words, "Opposition in this country means revolution."

In this spirit the forces of the government, with its newly won powers, were first turned upon the press. Immediately after the passage of the law five leading newspapers in Istanbul were suppressed. Within a few weeks a mere half dozen of the fourteen newspapers in the city survived, and their circulation dropped low, since they no longer had the power to publish accurate news or to criticize. Hussein Jahid's influential *Tanin* remained circumspect and thus survived until the government turned its forces against the Progressive party by raiding its premises in Istanbul. Jahid was then apprehended for using the word "raid" in his report. With three of his subeditors he was called before the Independence Tribunal in Ankara and sentenced to "perpetual exile" in Chorum, where he remained for some years.

The police found no evidence to incriminate the party as a whole, and the tribunal had to content itself with prosecuting two party members on a charge of exploiting religion for political purposes. It chose to regard their conviction as a pretext for closing down the party. This "nest of reaction" was thus eliminated. Its suppression was followed by the arrest and trial, on various pretexts, of certain members of the Opposition in the previous Assembly.

It led also to further arrests of journalists, some of whom, to their alarm, were transported as far afield as Elaziğ and Diyarbekir for their trials. But the government, well versed in the arts of propaganda, was careful to treat them well. They were formally and politely received by the local authorities; they were given comfortable accommodation; they had long and informative interviews with the governors; they were free to talk to the local inhabitants, to see the sights, to send souvenirs home to their families. This treatment impressed the city-bred journalists, most of whom were setting foot for the first time in the Anatolian wastes. It served to emphasize, by shock of contrast, the general backwardness of the country and the diversity of its social conditions, and to rub in the need for a united effort to cope with its problems. The tribunal dismissed the case against them, and they returned to Istanbul, chastened and potentially converted to the policy of Mustafa Kemal.

This policy of suppression was championed by the Ankara press with the reiteration of such words as Law, Order, Unity, and above all Strength. It was illustrated in terms which were often macabre. One night, staying in the ramshackle inn on the main square which was still Ankara's sole apology for a hotel, the Bulgarian Minister, Simeon Radev, was awakened from sleep by a commotion outside. Going to the window, he saw three sides of the square lined with scaffolds, eleven in number. Lighted up by the flares of torches and the first streaks of dawn, several men were already hanging from them, while others were about to be hanged, crying and protesting their innocence, as soldiers ran hither and thither and officers shouted their orders.

A secretary of the American Embassy, Howland Shaw, came upon the scene at eight o'clock in the morning and thus described it:

> Each man was hung down from a tripod and had on a sort of white smock with a placard pinned to him on which was scrawled his name and some account of his crime. There were groups of spectators in front of each tripod and others, intent I suppose upon a more careful inspection, were seated on the steps of nearby houses. Children were scurrying about and nobody seemed particularly concerned. It was a sight like any other.

Such was the reign of the Independence Tribunal in Ankara, now sitting in the hall of the Turkish Hearth organization, where concerts of Turkish music and other such functions had helped to disseminate Turkish culture throughout the previous winter. Its judges were respected citizens, whose departure to enact similar scenes in other parts of the country were attended at the station by ceremonious official farewells. Thanks to their labours, the new Turkish Republic was able, within eighteen months of its proclamation, to boast that it had effectively silenced all political opposition.

49 ▶ *The Mosul settlement*

The Kurdish revolt had been well enough timed. It coincided with the examination by the League of Nations of the Mosul dispute, and with the peregrinations in the area of a League commission of enquiry, whose members the rebel sheikhs hoped in vain to impress. The question of Mosul, outstanding from Lausanne, still remained to be settled. For the past year it had seriously occupied the attention of Kemal and his ministers in Ankara, in periodic conference with the diplomatic representatives of Britain.

When Ankara became officially the capital of Turkey, the foreign diplomats had begun to trickle into the city from Istanbul. But it was not yet equipped to provide a full diplomatic corps with such amenities as befitted its station. King George V, for one, roundly refused to inflict such a place of residence on any ambassador of his, while the other Western powers took a similar line. It was thus several years before the principal embassies moved to the capital. This was not an arrangement which altogether pleased the Gazi. Once, meeting a junior British secretary and learning that his ambassador was in Istanbul, he commented with some acerbity, "Istanbul is such a pretty place!" But in the absence of accommodation in Ankara there was still no alternative.

The Mosul negotiations were to be handled by Sir Ronald Lindsay, Rumbold's successor as British ambassador. When he came for a day or so from Istanbul to present his credentials to the Gazi, Sir Ronald was obliged to live in a railway coach, shunted onto a siding near the station. In common with his foreign colleagues he left behind him in Ankara a Second Secretary. This was Knox Helm,[1] who thus became the effective representative of his country with the Turkish Republic—a pillar of the young and informal diplomatic corps which came to animate Ankara in these early days, mixing well enough with the young entourage of Kemal.

On behalf of the British government Helm took steps to acquire a piece of land as near as possible to Chankaya—the property, indeed the perquisite, of one of the Gazi's principal aides. Here a few sheds were erected as a provisional chancery, pending the construction of a permanent British Embassy. The French had their embassy in the station and gave their receptions in a former warehouse of the Ottoman Bank, while the Americans had to be content with a very small flat. Only the Russians, well established with their satellites since the early days of the Revolution, yet possessed a full-grown embassy, well furnished and fitted with electric light, where they maintained a complete diplomatic staff.

Here they continued to entertain hospitably, concerned at this stage to further their commercial relations with Turkey. Kemal enjoyed their entertainments, as did his officials and friends. A complaint reached him from a disapproving source that some of them had been seen rolling insecurely down the stairs at the end of a Russian party. But one of the Gazi's aides protested in their defence that this was due, not to an excess of vodka, but to the fact that they were used only to narrow stairs and that these were so wide as to cause them to lose their balance.

Such parties were nonetheless infrequent in Ankara, where the main relaxation in the evening was cards. The favourite resort for this pastime, as for occasional dances, was the Anatolian Club, which Kemal visited often. The British representative was well placed, up at Chankaya, to know when the Gazi was embarking on one of these late night excursions, and thus to follow him if he felt in the mood. For the presidential guard would turn out within earshot to line the road for Kemal's descent —and remain lining it until his return, often in daylight.[2] The club

[1] Later Sir Knox Helm, G.B.E., K.C.M.G., British ambassador to Turkey 1951-54.
[2] Kemal liked to joke, in a rough Turkish way, with his sentries. Going out early one morning, he asked one of them what he was doing. "Watching over the President," was his reply. "You fool!" Kemal exclaimed. "It's I who am watching over *you!*"

was small and hence enabled its few foreign habitués to meet at close quarters, if not always on intimate terms.

The members fell into two groups—the more sedate gathering around Ismet, who played bridge (the game he had learned while on duty in the wilds of the Yemen), usually with a minister or two, at one end of the cardroom; the more convivial at the other end around Kemal, who played only poker, maintaining that bridge was a game with too many rules. He enjoyed the excitement of poker but never took the game seriously, liking to win, but often, to the annoyance of others who had done so, sweeping the chips together and cancelling all debts at the end of the session. The young diplomats, in furtherance of such informal contacts, were ready to stay up playing at the club all night but were often outstayed by Kemal, who continued to play until the sun was well up in the sky.

Kemal adhered strictly enough to protocol in his relations with diplomats. Officially, as head of state, he received them only in the presence of his Foreign Secretary, who now and for some years to come was Dr. Tevfik Rüştü. Tevfik was the old adherent whom Kemal had prophetically designated for the post over the café tables of Salonika in his youth. He was at home in Europe; he spoke several languages; he had a supple enough mind and above all knew that of his master; he was convivial in his habits, with an affable garrulity which endeared him to the foreigners, though it disinclined them to take him too seriously. They saw him often, finding him always communicative if not always consistent, though sometimes fatigued by an all-night session of politics, poker, and drinking with his master. "Poor man," an American ambassador remarked after keeping an appointment with him at 4:30 P.M., "how he must have hated me for breaking into his night's rest!" Tevfik's staff was well trained in preparing elaborate briefs for Kemal on the various countries, so that when he received a foreign ambassador he would surprise and often disconcert him with a barrage of well-informed questions.

Kemal in his lighter moments enjoyed making a buffoon of Tevfik Rüştü, who responded happily enough to the treatment. One evening at Chankaya the President had to receive a foreign ambassador after dinner. The interview was important, and as Kemal's mood was already festive his friends employed various stratagems to dissuade him from drinking further. Seeing through them, he looked crossly around him and said, "Look here, I don't see why you're making such a fuss. If you're thinking of my interview after dinner, you don't need to worry. Whatever my condition is, however drunk I may be, I can never commit blunders as dreadful as those committed by Tevfik Rüştü when he is as sober as a judge."

In the post-Lausanne atmosphere of Ankara, Britons and Turks were soon on amicable terms. Kemal's entourage took to dropping in on its British neighbours at Chankaya for a drink or a game of bridge—so often that their master at the club one evening remarked to Helm, with an expression of mock severity, "You are taking my friends away from me." Helm asked whether this did not meet with the Gazi's approval, and received the reply that it did.

Kemal had always respected the moral and political qualities of Britain. The very fact that she had been his enemy intensified his resolve that she should now become his friend. "Once an enemy, always an enemy" had been the principle, typical of the oriental mentality, which had for centuries underlain and bedevilled the foreign policy of the Ottoman Empire. Under the Republic there was to be an end to such hereditary grudges and feuds. Already Kemal had shown this spirit by his swift reconciliation at Lausanne with the Greeks, and by his patient attitude to the demands of the British, then and at Chanak beforehand. To maintain it was now especially important, in view of the need to solve the problem of Mosul.

At Lausanne it had been agreed to refer the question first to direct negotiations between Turkey and Britain and subsequently, in the event of their failure, to the League. The point at issue was the delimitation of the frontier between Turkey and the new British-mandated territory of Irak. It led first, in May 1924, to an Anglo-Turkish conference in Istanbul, at which Turkey was represented by Fethi and Britain by Sir Percy Cox, the High Commissioner in Irak.

The atmosphere of the conference was studiously friendly but it soon became clear that a wide gulf divided the two parties. Fethi insisted on the restoration of the prewar frontiers of the Mosul province, which the British now occupied, using the ethnical argument that the majority of its inhabitants were Turks and Kurds, two "sister nations" which had "united their destinies in perpetuity." Sir Percy, on the other hand, saw them as two separate races and so argued that the Turks were in fact in a minority and that the Kurdish majority were satisfied with the local autonomy which the British had given them in Irak.

The British, however, were no longer content with the former Mosul frontier. They were now claiming a line farther north, drawn to include the Christian Assyrian minority, who sought their protection. They maintained that this was a "no man's land" without effective Turkish authority. The Turks refused to accept this line and the negotiations broke down. The dispute was then referred to the League Council, which agreed on a provisional line, corresponding roughly with the original boundary. A League commission was thus enabled to tour the area in reasonable security, interviewing representatives of the different inhabitants.

The commission presented its report to the League Council in September 1925. The report held that a plebiscite was impracticable. It found on balance a feeling among the population in favour of Irak rather than Turkey, influenced largely by considerations of security and economic advantage. It proposed union with Irak of the former Mosul province, now excluding the "no man's land" to the north of it, subject to a twenty-five-year mandate of the League, and guarantees for Kurdish rights. The British had undertaken to accept in advance any decision by the League Council. The Turks now refused to do so and on December 16, 1925, they withdrew their delegation from Geneva, leaving the Council to grant a mandate to Britain without their consent.

Kemal countered this diplomatic reverse by producing, the very next day, a non-aggression pact with Soviet Russia. As soon as it became clear that the League decision would go against Turkey, Tevfik Rüştü, who had been handling the negotiations at Geneva, proceeded on instructions to Paris. Here he intercepted Chicherin, then en route from the south of France to Berlin, who proved ready enough to retrieve the setback to his diplomacy at Lausanne. They spent four hours together, in the course of which, without the aid of relevant documents, they drafted and signed a three-year treaty. It disregarded for the moment the economic problems which were at the time the main bone of contention between Russia and Turkey, and confined itself to a reaffirmation of their political harmony, each agreeing to refrain from aggression and participation in alliances against the other. With this document in his pocket, Tevfik returned to Ankara.

The signature of the pact helped to mitigate the storm of indignation which greeted the League award. The press were foreshadowing war. The British became once more the treacherous hereditary foe, continuing in a new guise the policy of the Treaty of Sèvres and the occupation of Smyrna. This time Mosul was their breach in the wall of Turkish national security, while Irak was a spearhead directed straight at the Turkish heart. Their headquarters for this sinister operation was the League of Nations, "the plaything of the imperialist powers."

Kemal did nothing for the moment to discourage such polemics, which provided a serviceable safety valve. If a show of warmongering could scare public opinion in Britain and thus hamper the task of her negotiators, well and good; and in fact the British opposition to the Mosul award both by the Labour party and by the popular press was vociferous enough, if more subdued than in 1922, when the question first arose. Neither Mosul nor Mespot was worth a war, and the *Manchester Guardian* suggested that the next six months might be profitably employed in negotiation with the Turk, "who is by no means so terrible a fellow as he is sometimes regarded."

This reflected Kemal's own attitude. He had no intention either of becoming entangled in a Russian embrace or of fighting the British. Friendship with Britain remained the cornerstone of his foreign policy, and the British themselves, following the decision of the League, showed every disposition to help him out of his difficulty. Sir Ronald Lindsay, the British ambassador, went on instructions to Ankara where he negotiated with tact and ability, his task made easier by a threat from Mussolini to land troops at Adalia (now Antalya) if Kemal marched against Irak. The Turkish press calmed down and the Turkish public was reassured as to Britain's pacific intentions.

The Gazi, in a bantering mood, coached Tevfik Rüştü for the negotiations, bidding him rehearse his words to the British. Tevfik put on his smoothest and most conciliatory manner. "Not strong enough," interrupted Kemal, "no conviction." Tevfik tried a belligerent attitude, thumping the table and implying a threat to attack. Kemal mocked, "What are you going to attack with?" The strong line was no good either. What mattered was to bury the hatchet with Britain. The province of Mosul, unlike those of Adana and Alexandretta (Cilicia and Hatay), contained, quite apart from its Kurdish population, a strong Arab element. Thus its inclusion within the National Pact could be regarded as a borderline case. Kemal the soldier had voiced his indignation in 1918 at the British occupation of Mosul. Kemal the statesman was not one, at this late stage, to prejudice the entry of his country into the Western comity of nations for the sake of any part-Arab *terra irredenta* of the Ottoman Empire. Tevfik Rüştü must obtain the best terms he could from the British.

The terms he was offered involved in effect Turkish acceptance of the British claim to the Mosul province, together with arrangements between Turks and Irakis for co-operation in keeping the peace on their mutual frontier. The Gazi, before agreeing to them, had to contend with stormy opposition from the People's party, whose members at a five-hour meeting argued the pros and cons of war. Some favoured it now, since it was bound to come eventually from the threatening presence of British forces in Irak. But when it came to a vote the members resignedly agreed that Mosul must go the way of other lost provinces of the Ottoman Empire. With the second Assembly well under his thumb, Kemal was now strong enough to climb down, as he could not have done while the first Assembly yapped away at his heels. Thus on June 5, 1926, the treaty was signed at Ankara between Turkey, Great Britain, and Irak. It was followed six years later by Turkey's admission to membership in the League of Nations.[3]

[3] Curiously enough the question of oil, which underlay the dispute, scarcely rose to the surface of the Mosul negotiations. The British government was zealous to keep its record unsullied by the taint of oil politics. The Turkish government thought in territorial rather than economic terms, and seemed unaware of the full relevance of oil to the future welfare of the country. In the treaty Turkey not only ceded the territory but waived her claims to the oil, in return for a ten per cent payment on royalties which she later compounded for a lump sum of a mere £500,000.

The Kurdish revolt helped Kemal not merely to stifle his Opposition but to push through the rest of his religious reforms. The Caliphate, the religious schools, the holy law had been swept away. Now, since the revolt had been inspired by a dervish order of fanatical traditions, the Nakshibendis, it was a good moment to sweep away all the dervish orders, regardless of complexion.

These brotherhoods had played an important part in the religious life of the Turks and had, with some exceptions, prevented them from becoming as fanatical as some of their Moslem neighbours. They represented a breakaway, still within the framework of Islam, from the aloof orthodox hierarchy. It was in the brotherhoods that the ordinary people of the country found the warm human outlet they sought for their intuitive faith.

In so far as they were political the brotherhoods were traditionally opposed to the central authority. The Ottoman state had countered this by adroitly playing them off one against the other. The most enlightened of them, the Bektashis, had given support to the Nationalists following the Sultan's *fetva* against Kemal. Such elements among them might well

have continued to act in his interests, as a solvent: diluting religious
extremism, furthering a policy of a reformation of Islam and its conversion into a constructive social force from within. But this was not Kemal's policy. No Moslem himself, he saw the brotherhoods less as a help
than as a danger. Independent in spirit and used to opposition, they
could as likely oppose his own government as that of the Sultan—
doubly so since it was a secular regime. Moreover they had power over
the masses, and it was the masses that Kemal, having disarmed the formal
religious hierarchy, now feared. To him the brotherhoods were "secret
societies," such as he had learnt to mistrust since his early days in Salonika.[1] Thus they must go.

In August 1925 he pronounced their doom in a speech at Kastamonu.
The Turkish Republic was to be "a state of society entirely modern and
completely civilized in spirit and form." Hence all superstitions must be
crushed:

"To seek help from the dead is a disgrace to a civilized community.
. . . I flatly refuse to believe that today, in the luminous presence of science, knowledge, and civilization in all its aspects, there exist, in the
civilized community of Turkey, men so primitive as to seek their material and moral well-being from the guidance of one or another sheikh.
Gentlemen, you and the whole nation must know, and know well, that
the Republic of Turkey cannot be the land of sheikhs, dervishes, disciples,
and lay brothers. . . . The heads of the brotherhoods will . . . at once
close their monasteries and accept the fact that their disciples have at last
come of age."

A series of decrees clinched the decision. Henceforth Turkey, at least
in theory, was to be free not only from sheikhs and dervishes but from
"fortunetellers, magicians, witch doctors, writers of amulets for the recovery of lost property or the fulfilment of wishes, as well as the services,
dues, and costumes pertaining to these titles and qualities."

At the same time all sacred tombs were closed as places of worship
and religious resort. When this closure aroused opposition in the Assembly—for some of whose members they involved vested interests in the
form of their own defunct ancestors—a friend of Kemal[2] who had been
speaking against it was taken aside by him and enjoined in an undertone,
"Don't oppose the motion. In ten years' time you'll be able to open them
all up again." For all his agnosticism it was not Kemal's policy to attempt the eradication of religion. What he sought, as he once put it, was

[1] In his youth nevertheless he had himself attended Bektashi gatherings in Salonika.
[2] Hamdullah Suphi Tangiöver.

"to disengage it from the condition of being a political instrument, which it has been for centuries of habit." His policy was to break this habit by depriving the people, through a series of abrupt shocks, of such influences as might rival that of the centralized state, and especially of their outward and visible symbols. Today the dead in their tombs were such a symbol, exploited as a living and menacing force to be crushed without scruple. But in ten years' time they might truly be dead and could be resurrected without danger.

On his journey through the region of Kastamonu Kemal struck at another such outward and visible symbol. Its disappearance was to uproot a habit deeply ingrained in every male individual in Turkey. For it involved what he wore each day of his life on his head. This was the fez.

Costume, in the Islamic religion, had a deep symbolic significance. The fez itself, as it happened, was a mere century old as a form of Moslem headgear. Ironically it was a Greek Christian fashion, prevalent in the islands and initially derived from the Barbary corsairs. Manufactured for the Ottoman market in Austria, its introduction was the climax of a sartorial revolution aimed, early in the nineteenth century, at the ultra-conservative turban, and had led to riots in many parts of the Empire. But the fez in its turn soon became a symbol of Ottoman and Islamic orthodoxy as the turban had been, and as such was fiercely defended and as fiercely attacked.

Kemal's plan to replace this symbol with that of the hat was thus a daring revolutionary gesture. It was one which had been quietly simmering in his mind since the days of his youth, when he had been humiliated abroad by the stigma of inferiority conferred by his national headgear. At Chankaya in the evenings he had been discussing the change with his friends, consulting those who had travelled abroad as to which form of hat was most suitable.

In his own costume he had been making experiments. He was photographed on a tractor on his model farm wearing a panama—without a black ribbon. An old friend came upon him one day in a train wearing a cloth cap with his brown tweed suit. "Does this become me?" Kemal asked, as though seeking assurance. He revealed that in recent months he had three times dreamed of the fez. "And whenever I did so Ismet knocked at my door in the morning to report a reactionary movement somewhere in the country." The idea of a reform was unobtrusively canvassed in the press, but still no newspaper dared use the ugly word *shapka,* or hat. The press preferred such euphemisms as "civilized head-gear," "protector from sunshine," or "head cover with a brim."

Kemal deliberately chose, for the disclosure of these various religious reforms, a province known for its reactionary sentiments. Boldly he was striking at the enemy at a strong point where, if his shock tactics succeeded, their impact would be twice as effective as elsewhere. Shrewdly calculating the effect of his public image, he explained to Falih Rifki that in such a city as Izmir, where he was already known, the people would look not at him but at the hat. In Kastamonu they would be seeing him for the first time and would see him "as a whole, hat and all." Kastamonu, moreover, for all its backwardness, was in a sense a symbol of the Revolution itself. Bestriding as it did the direct line of the army supply route from Istanbul, through Inebolu, the Black Sea port, to Ankara, it had played a loyal part in the War of Independence, and its loyalty should survive the jolts which it was now to receive.

Nevertheless Kemal, in that distaste for the darker forces of religion which had haunted him since youth, approached his tour with unusual nervousness, asking for water when he first spoke and finding that his hands, as he raised it to his lips, were trembling. He had left Ankara bareheaded, in an open car. The people, swarming down to the main road from their mountain villages, hardly knew what to expect from this first sight of their national hero. In one village an artist had drawn on a wall an imaginative portrait of the Gazi, the slayer of infidels, as a formidable warrior with sweeping moustaches and a sword seven feet long. The villagers had spread carpets on the streets for him to walk on. One of them, a young student, recalled the scene years later: "When the President walked slowly down the street, greeting the crowds, there was not a sound. The clean-shaven Gazi was wearing a white, European-style summer suit, a sports shirt open at the neck, and a panama hat. The few officials applauded frantically, urging on those near them, but a flutter of hand-clapping was all they would muster, so great had been the shock." [3] For the conqueror was wearing the costume of the infidel.

But the shock was slowly absorbed. Outside Kastamonu itself the Gazi got out of his car and walked into the town ahead of his entourage, first carrying the hat in his hand, then putting it on his head. His aides did the same. Had they done so a generation earlier, they might well have been stoned or manhandled by the crowd. But now they were greeted merely with silent curiosity. Throughout his tour Kemal's interest in

[3] Quoted by Frederick P. Latimer, *The Political Philosophy of Mustapha Kemal Atatürk.*

costume and especially in headgear was made evident to all. Sometimes he remained hatless, in which case a few people out of politeness removed their own fezes. Inspecting a military detachment, he took off the cap of each soldier and examined it with attention. A few months earlier a narrow peak had been added to it, ostensibly for the protection of the soldier's eyes against the sun. For had not the Prophet enjoined his followers always to fight with their faces towards it?

His approach to the sartorial question was practical. At one meeting he turned to a tailor in the audience and asked him, pointing to a man in baggy Turkish trousers and a robe, which was the cheaper—this outfit or the modern, international type of suit. The tailor replied, "The international kind." Pointing the moral, Kemal said to the audience, "There, you see? Out of every costume such as this man is wearing you could make an extra suit."

All this was a mere foretaste of what was to come—an open declaration of national policy in which civilization was equated with costume. For this he chose the port of Inebolu itself. To symbolize their part in the War of Independence, its townspeople had decorated and placed in the square a boat and an oxcart of the type that had carried the munitions. Kemal was pelted with flowers as he drove into the town, which was bedecked with flags and branches. Later, wearing his panama, he walked through the streets while the people crowded around to kiss his hands and his garments. He conversed with all sections of the population, questioning them personally on their problems and enlightening them on his plans for their future.

For two days he took part in organized festivities. Sheep were sacrificed in his honour in barbarous fashion, but out of his sight at his request—a scruple which they ascribed to his deep devotion to animals. Bushels of apples were heaped upon him, products of the annual harvest. School children processed before him, singing the march he had sung on the road from Samsun and crying, "Long live our Father!" Boatmen organized a regatta for his entertainment, danced their traditional dances and sang their traditional songs. All these compliments he returned with appropriate speeches of praise to the inhabitants for the richness of their province and the enlightenment of its people.

The climax was reached on the third day, when he delivered a long oration to a dazed and respectful audience, variously clad, in the clubroom of the Turkish Hearth.

"Gentlemen," he said, "the Turkish people, who founded the Turkish Republic, are civilized; they are civilized in history and reality. But I tell you . . . that the people of the Turkish Republic, who claim to be civilized, must prove that they are civilized, by their ideas and their mentality, by their family life and their way of living. . . . They must prove in fact that they are civilized and advanced persons in their outward aspect also. . . . I shall put my explanation to you in the form of a question.

"Is our dress national?" Cries of "No!"

"Is it civilized and international?" Cries of "No, no!"

"I agree with you. This grotesque mixture of styles is neither national nor international. . . . A civilized, international dress is worthy and appropriate for our nation, and we will wear it. Boots or shoes on our feet, trousers on our legs, shirt and tie, jacket and waistcoat—and of course, to complete these, a cover with a brim on our heads. I want to make this clear. This head covering is called 'hat.' "

The word was out. There was to be an end to all euphemisms. This and his other pronouncements were relayed by the news agencies to all parts of Turkey. In Kastamonu not a murmur was raised at the heresies they contained. He had brought off a daring operation by the shock of his ideas, which at first dazed his hearers, by the rough intimacy of his approach, which then won their confidence, by the commanding impact of his personality, which inspired the reverence of a people given to the worship of heroes but hitherto denied any contact with the remote being who ruled them. Now he had materialized, and they readily submitted their wills to his, as formerly to the will of the Padishah.

On his return to Ankara the Gazi was received, outside the city, by a group of hatted officials and friends. He liked the look of the model worn by Yunus Nadi and exchanged his own for it before proceeding on his way. Thereafter the change in fashion among the upper crust was swift. It must now be extended by legal means to the people as a whole. First a decree banned the wearing of religious vestments or insignia by all not holding a recognized office, and imposed instead the costume "common to the civilized nations of the world"—in other words, the Western suit and hat. At first it was confined to officials only. But the deputies, most of the professional classes, and many students adopted it.

Towards the end of November 1925, when Kemal judged that public opinion was ripe, a new bill was passed by the Assembly which obliged all men to wear hats and made the wearing of the fez a criminal offence. For the present there were not enough hats to go round, and thousands went hatless or crowned with an odd diversity of headgear dumped on the market by the hatters of Europe. It was not until local hat factories came into full production that all were appropriately hatted. For the masses there were produced cloth caps with a peak designed to prevent the wearers from touching the ground with their heads as they prayed, but easily reversible and often reversed.[4]

The hat law, however, caused widespread riots in the East. They were inflamed by placards in the name of religion on the walls of public buildings, which led to mass demonstrations beneath the green flag of Islam. The riots had been anticipated by the government, who sent Tribunals of Independence in advance to the danger spots. They were suppressed by ruthless means.

Of the abolition of the fez Kemal remarked later:

"We did it while the Law for the Maintenance of Order was still in force. Had it not been, we could have done it all the same, but it certainly is true that the existence of the law made it much easier for us. Indeed the existence of the Law for the Maintenance of Order prevented the large-scale poisoning of the nation by certain reactionaries."[5]

By these various reforms the Gazi translated into action those plans which, in the days of the Young Turk intellectuals, had been confined to the realm of ideas. Abdullah Jevdet, an early influence on Kemal and his friends, had written in 1912 that there could be no civilization but Western civilization. His periodical *Ichtihad* published at that time a vision of the future Westernization of Turkey entitled "A Very Wakeful Sleep." It envisaged, among other changes, the replacement of the fez by a new form of headgear; the limitation of the turban and cloak to professional men of religion; the closing of the religious schools and brotherhoods and the use of their funds to assist a modern educational programme; the suppression of vows and offerings to the saints and of the activities of witch doctors and exorcists; and a reform of the whole legal system.

The dream, then considered a fantasy, had now become a reality. It only remained for the Gazi to fulfil its prophecies regarding the freedom of women. According to Abdullah Jevdet, they were to be free to dress as they pleased, to choose their own husbands, without family dictation.

---

[4] In a village near Izmir men wore women's feathered hats from the shop of a deported Armenian. Articles appeared in the newspapers on "How to Wear the Hat." Officials were instructed to greet their superiors no longer with a salute but with a slight inclination of the head and a bow from the waist. But the habit of saluting died hard, and men would knock off their hats in attempting to do so.

[5] The Moslem world as a whole took the reform quietly. When Kemal sent a delegate to an Islamic congress at Mecca, wearing a hat and a lounge suit, the other robed and turbaned delegates treated his gesture with normal politeness.

Here Kemal had to tread circumspectly. It was one thing in Turkey to clap a hat on the head of a man. It was quite another to tear the veil off a woman. No Law for the Maintenance of Order, no Independence Tribunals would enforce such a metamorphosis. He had begun, nonetheless, in the course of his tour to Kastamonu, to prepare the way for its gradual enforcement.

The woman's position in Turkey had changed relatively little since the days of the Prophet. Despite growing discussion of her predicament, both before and after the reign of Abdul Hamid, she still lived subject to the letter of the laws of Islam, in a seclusion which amounted at its worst to personal slavery and at its best to convental segregation from a predatory world.

The average Ottoman Turk, in his masculine pride and possessiveness, chose still to see woman as an inferior species, a female animal deficient in morality and self-respect, who required protection by the male against her own weaker instincts. It had become a collective as well as a personal duty to supervise her behaviour. Not merely the husband and father and brother but the whole street, the whole neighbourhood, was concerned to watch over her, to see that her limbs were totally and decently covered, to catch her out if she seemed to stray for an instant from the narrow path which society laid down for her.

In Constantinople no woman might be seen walking in the street or driving in a carriage with a man, even if he were her husband. If they went out together he was obliged to walk ahead, disregarding her. Never did she appear with him at social gatherings; thus there was in effect no mixed Moslem society. On trams and boats there was a curtain to divide women from men. In girls' schools, when feminine education was introduced, the only male teachers were eunuchs. In the theatre the female parts were played by men, as in Elizabethan England, or by Christian women. When women were eventually allowed into the audience it was on certain "ladies' days" set aside for them. Only in parts of Anatolia, among the peasantry, were women freer, and indeed often unveiled before all but strangers. For (thanks sometimes to the influence of the brotherhoods) the peasants were often less orthodox in their customs and, moreover, their women had, for economic reasons, to work in the fields and perform other outdoor tasks for the family living.

Such taboos prevailed right into the twentieth century. The Young Turks were unable to make much headway against the prevailing prejudice, reinforced as it was by the clerical interest. But they were persistent in their efforts and zealous in their championship of women's rights. It was too soon to talk openly of abolishing the veil, but a pamphlet was secretly distributed, insisting that it had nothing to do with religion but was a more primitive pagan survival.

The Young Turks, however, made progress with the education of women, opening the middle and secondary schools and finally the universities to girl students, and thus preparing the way for their entry into the professions. During the war they replaced men in certain jobs, in factories, offices, and public services, and were even recruited into a labour battalion, of a paramilitary kind, in which they cleaned the streets of Constantinople. Here the veil became an obvious encumbrance and, though it survived in theory, it tended to develop into the long *charshaf,* a headkerchief which did not cover the face unless drawn across it. Towards the end of the war a family law was passed, introducing a form of secular marriage which gave women monogamous rights. It was the principles of this law that Kemal had just made general, with the abolition of the religious courts and the preparation of the new legal code based on the Swiss.

The road had thus been prepared. Kemal was now to carry it towards its final destination—but more tentatively than the other religious reforms. He was quick to remind the public of the part played by women in the War of Independence, declaring once that no other country in the world could show a heroism comparable to that of "these sublime, these self-sacrificing, these divine women of Anatolia." But there was still much ground to be covered. Early in 1923 an uproar arose in the Assembly over the suggestion of a deputy that women should be included in the census for representation under the new electoral law. Nor did it abate when the deputy hastily explained that this would not involve giving them the right to vote. The mere mention of such a possibility caused him to be howled down and prevented him from finishing his speech.

Kemal, however, was already sowing the seeds of a new outlook, deliberately choosing reactionary soil for the purpose. At a congress of teachers in Ankara both sexes were represented; but the women sat apart, separated from the men by several rows of seats. On hearing of the meeting a shocked deputation of *hojas* called upon the Gazi to protest. Kemal sent for the president of the Teachers' Association and loudly berated him: "What have you done in the teachers' meeting? How dare you do it? This is a shame!" The *hojas* looked jubilant. But Kemal continued, "You called the women teachers to the meeting. But why did you make them sit apart from the men? Don't you trust yourselves, or have you no faith in the virtue of these ladies? Let me never hear again of this segregation of women." The deputation stood paralyzed, then slunk out of the room, too astonished to speak.

From now onwards Kemal in his speeches referred frequently to the topic of women. Women must have the same education as men—indeed a better education, for were they not destined to be the mothers of men? "We need men who have better minds, more perfect men. And the mothers of the future will know how to bring up such men!" He could not at this stage go so far as to suggest that women should abandon the veil. Let them continue to be veiled, but only slightly—so slightly as no longer to give the impression that they were blindfolded and embarrassed in their movements.

In Kastamonu he had spoken out plainly. A social body consisted of "two kinds of human beings, called men and women." It could not advance without both.

"Is it possible that, while one half of a community stays chained to the ground, the other half can rise to the skies? There is no question—the steps of progress must be taken . . . by the two sexes together, as friends, and together they must accomplish the various stages of the journey into the land of progress and renovation. If this is done, our Revolution will be successful."

Recounting what he had observed on his tour, he continued: "In some places I have seen women who put a piece of cloth or a towel or something like it over their heads to hide their faces, and who turn their backs or huddle themselves on the ground when a man passes by. What is the meaning and sense of this behaviour? Gentlemen, can the mothers and daughters of a civilized nation adopt this strange manner, this barbarous posture? It is a spectacle that makes the nation an object of ridicule. It must be remedied at once."

It was remedied gradually over the next decade. The women of the towns were to set the example; but many years were to pass before it percolated down to the more bigoted villages.

Soon after his visit to Kastamonu in 1925 Kemal proceeded to the more sophisticated city of Izmin (Smyrna). Here he presided over an entertainment which was in effect the first Turkish ball. Only Moslems and their ladies were invited. An orchestra played Western music, and they were expected to dance together—an ordeal which they faced with reluctance, even after the Gazi himself had opened the ball by performing a correct fox trot with the governor's daughter. Never until this moment had a Turkish woman, in her own country, danced with a man in public.

In Istanbul the habit soon caught on. Elsewhere Kemal had to use all his talents of persuasion to make dances accepted social functions. At first there was little mixing, the ladies remaining in one corner, the men in the other, reluctant to introduce their wives to their friends. On one typical occasion, in the clubroom of the Turkish Hearth in Ankara, Kemal noticed a few bold ladies who stood awkwardly in the middle of the room, imprisoned by masculine eyes. Kemal rallied the men like children at a party. "Go and talk to the ladies standing up. Offer them things. Be nice to them. Let's make the sitting ones jealous. If so they will get up one by one." And so in the end it was to prove.

In Ankara he gave a ball in honour of the foundation of the Republic. It went well enough but late in the evening the Gazi noticed a group of young officers, none of whom was dancing. They explained that the ladies had refused their requests for a dance. Kemal immediately addressed them for all the guests to hear: "My friends, I cannot conceive that any woman in the world can refuse to dance with a Turk wearing an officer's uniform. I now give you an order. Disperse through the ballroom. Quick march! Dance!" Sensitive to the taunt, the ladies rose at the approach of the officers, and soon all were fox-trotting stiffly away. Club dances on Fridays became a habit in Ankara and the main provincial centres, and a new profession, that of the dancing master, began to flourish.

The social ice slowly melted of its own accord as women were admitted to the various professions and finally to politics. Kemal did not hurry this process. But within five years women were given the vote at the municipal level; within ten they were permitted to vote in parliamentary elections; and in 1935, with Kemal's support, seventeen women were elected deputies to the Grand National Assembly.

Ironically Latife, the spearhead of his social campaign, his own outward and visible symbol of emancipated Turkish womanhood, was not with him to witness these manifestations. Asked once why he had married, in the teeth of his often-quoted Turkish proverb, "To be a bachelor is to be a Sultan," he had answered in terms of this very reform. How could he persuade the people to unveil their wives if he himself had no wife to unveil? He had married indeed as much for sociological as for personal reasons. Through a paradox in his nature, that clash between mind and temperament which caused him to think like an occidental and act like an oriental, his marriage had turned out badly.

In Latife too there existed this conflict between East and West. By upbringing and education she was an occidental. She held serious views on such subjects as education and the position of women in a modern society. She could hold her own in discussion with any man, Kemal included. She saw marriage, as he claimed in his speeches to see it, as an institution in which the two sexes should progress together "as friends," each helping and influencing the other.

But in practice Kemal did not want to be influenced or helped, least of all by any woman. His house, his habits of life were his own, and he did not want them changed, as she tried to change them. For all his advanced theories, the conception of the equality of the sexes was in practice against his nature. Women, apart from their physical charms, interested him little as such. Their role was to serve man, as in the harem. What drew him to Latife was not the feminine side of her character but the masculine side of her mind. Here they had something to share. Otherwise he must always be master—and Latife, as befitted a Western wife, would not be mastered. Nor had she the feminine tact with which to dissemble, to manage him without seeming to do so, as he, with his more subtle approach, had always been able to manage others. Intelligent though she was, she lacked the gift for handling human beings. Thus increasingly there were frontal clashes between them.

They alternated nonetheless with periods of harmony. Kemal was for a while faithful to Latife. Fikriye was dead; no other woman especially interested him; and he had too much finesse to introduce loose women into the nuptial home. Often he found himself living what was in effect a family life. The family was hers, not his: her father and mother, her sisters and brothers, who made long stays at Chankaya. They were to become in the end an encumbrance. But Kemal meanwhile treated them with patient politeness and developed in particular an affection for one of her young cousins, a sensitive youth in his teens.

Latife nevertheless was frustrated. Her early hero-worship had developed into passionate love. But Kemal's feeling for her was not rooted in passion, and his initial desires cooled as time went by. She grew jealous; and here the oriental side of her nature emerged, for at times she was unable, like any woman of the harem, to conceal or control her jealousy. She was jealous of any woman to whom he might pay a compliment; jealous of his friends and of their influence upon him; jealous even of his dog and the attention he paid to it. One evening she made a scene when, in a gesture of congratulation, he patted the head of her young cousin as he was playing the piano.

Such outbursts grew more frequent. She nagged at him and criticized him when others were present. She taunted him with his social inferiority and the superior position and wealth of her own family. He drank more, he became angry and brutal, humiliating her in front of his friends, some of whom were only too ready to fan his feelings against her.

The situation came to a head during a visit to Erzinjan in the eastern provinces, where there had been a serious earthquake, and then to Erzurum. Here a luncheon was given to which, at the Gazi's request, officers and officials were bidden with their wives. It was the first time men and women had sat down at table together in this conservative city —hence a social occasion of a symbolic and somewhat stilted kind. Few of the guests were at their ease, and Kemal, breaking the ice, chose to rally his hostess, the handsome wife of the military commander, with expressions of gallantry and admiring glances across the table. Latife showed her displeasure, then lost control and exclaimed, "Be careful of your feet, Kemal. They are reaching as far as me."

Kemal went rigid with anger. The guests became silent with embarrassment. The social experiment had ended in disaster. After it Kemal refused to speak to Latife. Instead he telegraphed instructions to the Cabinet, in Ankara, to arrange on his behalf for an immediate divorce. Latife was sent off by train next day, with two officers for escort. Kemal did not bid her farewell; nor did the wife of the commander with whom they were staying.

From Erzinjan, the scene of the earthquake, she wrote a letter to Kemal at Erzurum, admitting herself to have been at fault and begging that her mistakes might be buried amid the ruins of Erzinjan. She sent it through Kiliç Ali. But Kemal refused to look at it. Kiliç Ali put it in his pocket, awaiting a more favourable moment. Later he remarked to Kemal that the commander's wife had refused to say good-bye to Latife, on the grounds that she was now divorced. Kemal, as he had foreseen, was indignant at this clumsy slight. He asked for the letter and read it. Appreciating its wit, he announced his forgiveness and joined Latife in Erzinjan. They returned to Ankara together.

But the reconciliation could hardly endure. The same quarrels arose once more. One night at Chankaya she again lost her temper, turned on the friends with whom he had been drinking, and tore their characters to pieces before him, one by one. This was more than Kemal could tolerate. The end had come. He declared Latife divorced, and instructed his Cabinet accordingly. Latife's mother came from Izmir to fetch her away. Kemal did not see her before her departure. His ministers saw her off at the station—Ismet urging her to remain, for he saw her presence as a last restraining influence on Kemal. It was given out that she was leaving for Izmir for the sake of her health. The official news of the divorce was announced when she had gone. Both behaved with dignity afterwards— Latife leading a strictly private life and refraining from demands and reproaches; Kemal treating her family with open politeness whenever they came his way.

If there was an irony in the failure of the marriage—the failure of two headstrong oriental natures to come to terms with the give-and-take problems of a Western relationship—there was an irony too in the manner of its end. On marrying her Kemal had been at pains to break with Moslem tradition, adapting the ceremony to Western principles; in divorcing her he reverted to the letter of the Moslem law, which allowed a man to repudiate his wife without question. All he had to say was, "Leave the house" or "I do not want to see you any more." This was in effect what he did, seeking however to soften the harshness of his decision with an announcement that it had been reached in agreement between them.

A few months later his action would not have been possible. For the new Civil Code, which lay at the root of his major reforms, framed on the lines of the Swiss legal code, was then finally passed by the Assembly. Repudiation of a wife by a husband was abolished, with polygamy, and was replaced by civil marriage and divorce, with equal rights for both parties. Henceforward women enjoyed, at least in the eyes of the law, a new freedom and dignity.

In terms of this series of legal reforms, all citizens of the foreign minorities in Turkey became subject to the law of the land, thus finally putting into practice the agreements which had been agreed at Lausanne. Meanwhile a law school had been established in Ankara, to train new lawyers. It was opened by the Gazi with the words: "The greatest and at the same time the most insidious enemies of the revolutionaries are rotten laws and their decrepit upholders. . . . It is our purpose to create completely new laws and thus to tear up the very foundations of the old legal system."

It was indeed one of Kemal's most significant achievements that he gave his country, for the first time, an independent judiciary.

52 ▶ Trials for treason

Kemal was now alone at Chankaya with his drinking companions, his casual women, his court of journalist intellectuals, his amenable ministers —and Ismet. Since his assumption of dictatorial powers and his smothering of the Opposition, his old friends appeared seldom at the table. This was not a healthy seclusion. It made him a prey to suspicions and to the influence of those who sought, by encouraging them, to strengthen their own positions against those of their personal enemies. It left him out of touch with the feeling of the country, where the Independence Tribunals spread fear and resentment. It drove the Opposition underground and led to the exploitation of its more reputable leaders by unscrupulous adventurers. It created an atmosphere in which plots must inevitably thrive.

The initial plotters were men of scant account—small fry with personal grudges against Kemal. One of their ringleaders was Ziya Hurshid, a swashbuckling adventurer from Trebizond, who sought vengeance for the murder of his friend Ali Shükrü by the leader of Kemal's bodyguard. He had led the attack on the government, with strong innuendoes against Kemal himself, during the debate in the Assembly which followed the murder. This was the culmination of a feud of long standing. When, on Kemal's return to Ankara as the conquering hero of the Sakarya, the deputies crowded onto the terrace of the Assembly to applaud him, Ziya Hurshid alone had remained inside, where he wrote on a blackboard: "The nation creates its own idol and then worships it."

His hatred and jealousy had grown by the end of 1925 into a determination to kill Kemal. Mobilizing a pair of desperadoes, a Laz and a Georgian from the Black Sea mountains, he started to explore means of doing so. He reconnoitred the Parliament building and speculated as to the chance of throwing a bomb from the strangers' gallery across to the President's box. He opened a hole in the roof from which to shoot at him. He contemplated a raid on a Cabinet meeting but found the security measures too strict. He considered an ambush outside the Anatolian Club, and chose for the purpose a neighbouring cemetery where the assassins could hide among the trees and the tombstones. But the chief brigand pointed out that the trees at this season were leafless and afforded no cover, and when they lay in wait there one night the Gazi inconsiderately failed to emerge before daybreak.

Among Ziya's confederates was Colonel Arif, the boon companion of Kemal throughout the War of Independence, whom he had afterwards made deputy for Eskishehir. Arif had since grown disgruntled through his failure to make good in politics and through an instance of corruption which had turned the Gazi against him. Another conspirator was Abdulkadir, a former governor of Ankara. But the most influential was another Shükrü, a former minister of the Union and Progress party, who had been notorious for his *komitaji* methods and his association with a secret terrorist committee during the Young Turk period. Shükrü had quarrelled openly with Kemal, whose henchmen had been treating him roughly. In a brawl in a restaurant one evening they threw plates at Shükrü, thus provoking him the more as, by their behaviour in the lobbies of Parliament, they were provoking other opponents of their master. Shükrü was in league with dissident elements in Istanbul, notably with a former Union and Progress party boss, Kara Kemal. Here, where the party still survived "underground" and the press had outspoken habits, Kemal had many old enemies, and the arbitrary acts of his Independence Tribunals had brought him renewed unpopularity. Shükrü hoped also, as a member of their party, to get support from the more disgruntled Progressives.

One evening in Ankara when the execution of the plot was imminent Shükrü, under the influence of drink, dropped hints about it to a third person, a Progressive party deputy, who at once told Rauf. Rauf obtained indignant denials of the story from Ziya Hurshid and Shükrü, who protested, "How can you take seriously the words of that foolish drunken man?" Rauf advised his original informant that if he really believed in the plot he should, as a responsible deputy, tell the government. Meanwhile Arif had hurriedly called off the Laz hired assassin.

Rauf, Ali Fuad, and Refet were inclined to underrate the incident, seeing it as a reversion to the atmosphere of intrigue and conspiracy which they knew all too well from the Young Turk period. But they agreed that if ever again such a rumour arose the government must instantly be warned, however unlikely it seemed. What chiefly concerned them was the risk that the Progressive party might be used as cover for any such future conspiracy. They took steps accordingly, warning their members to be discreet in their contacts, to remain on the alert and report any suspect, and tightening up security precautions within their own premises.

Hence the attempt was postponed for six months. But it was not abandoned. The conspirators transferred their operations from Ankara to Izmir, which Kemal was due to visit in June 1926 at the end of two long tours through Anatolia. A group travelled by boat from Istanbul, supplied with funds by Shükrü and with weapons concealed in valises exempted from police inspection by his deputy's visiting card on the labels. Thus the gang assembled in Izmir.

Here the scene for the crime was chosen at a point between the station and the hotel where three narrow streets met and where the Gazi's procession would thus be forced to drive slowly. The two hired assassins, the Laz and the Georgian, were reinforced by a third, named "Pockmarked" Hilmi. All three, followed if necessary by Ziya, were to fire at Kemal with revolvers and throw hand grenades hidden in bouquets of flowers. Having killed him, they were to escape through the crowd, jump into a waiting car, and drive to the harbour, where a new confederate, a Cretan, would be ready with a motorboat to take them to one of the offshore islands. When the plan was complete two of the conspirators, prudently seeking an alibi, returned to Istanbul.

Their abrupt departure, however, led the Cretan confederate to suspect that the government had learnt of the plot. The date of Kemal's arrival was postponed for twenty-four hours and this seemed to confirm his suspicions. To save his own skin—and perhaps also his conscience—he went to a police inspector and divulged the whole story. The governor acted at once. Ziya Hurshid was arrested at midnight in his hotel, the Georgian and the Laz in a hotel nearby, and the pock-marked assassin

at his house. Ziya made no attempt to evade arrest, nonchalantly handing to the police a revolver from beneath his pillow and two bombs from
beneath his bed.

Kemal himself reached Izmir next day and behaved as though nothing had happened. He had delayed his arrival from Balikesir—and thus
perhaps saved his life—for no reason other than an instinct which may
well have been a presentiment. For suspicions of some such plot were
forever in his mind, reinforced by the reports of his secret police, who had
been shadowing Ziya Hurshid for some time past. Kemal was received
enthusiastically by the people of Izmir, who had read of the plot and the
arrests from an official communiqué and were crying for the blood of
the miscreants. Crowds surged around his hotel, where he deplored to
the journalists that this should occur in the proud city of Izmir, of all
places, which he had delivered from the enemy. But such ignoble
attempts could not extinguish the fire of the Revolution.

The Gazi then summoned Ziya Hurshid under guard to the hotel and
there, coldly polite, reminded him of their collaboration in the revolutionary struggle and asked why he had now been involved in this plot. Ziya
admitted his guilt as the ringleader of the plot, and next day made a
fuller confession. He pleaded for mercy but Kemal replied that the law
must take its course without interference from him.

Kemal summoned also one of Ziya's hired assassins, who was brought
before him unaware of his questioner's identity. The man admitted that
he had intended to kill Mustafa Kemal. He had been paid to do so; he
had been told that Kemal was a bad man who did harm to the country;
the assassin did not know him personally. "But how," asked Kemal,
"could you kill a person you had never seen? You might have picked
the wrong man." The assassin explained that Kemal was to be pointed
out to him before he fired. Kemal then drew his revolver and handed it
over to the other, saying, "Well, I am Mustafa Kemal. Come on, take this
revolver and shoot me now." The man looked at him in amazement,
then sank to his knees and sobbed.

It was clear that the plot had been the work of some dozen conspirators,
led by Shükrü and including Ziya and Arif—who declared afterwards
that he had not seriously believed it would materialize. It was largely
personal in character and could easily have been handled by an ordinary
criminal prosecution. The culprits were, after all, men of the familiar
komitaji type, against several of whom there had been previous charges.
None showed any clear idea as to their political intentions once they
had disposed of their enemy, while the ringleaders were politicians of no

reputable standing. Their sentence should have been enough to uphold public security and act as a deterrent to any future attempts on the Gazi's person.

But Kemal preferred to treat the affair as a major political conspiracy. The chance which it offered of implicating and eliminating at one stroke all his opponents was, in his current mood of suspicion and impatience for complete power, too good to be missed. The Independence Tribunal was at once summoned by special train from Ankara to Izmir. Its president, as in the Kurdish trials, was "Bald" Ali, a "hanging judge" concealing a merciless disposition beneath a kindly and even distinguished exterior which Sir Ronald Lindsay—a Scotsman—had likened to that of an elder of the kirk. Bald Ali's chief confederate was his namesake, Kiliç or "Sword" Ali, Kemal's own most ruthless henchman, a man who disarmed by his bonhomie, knew his master's mind, and stopped at nothing to do his bidding.

Between them they began to order arrests which, in the next few days, mounted up to a formidable total. Those accused of complicity in the attempt consisted not merely of the obvious conspirators, including Shükrü and Arif, but, regardless of parliamentary immunity, some twenty-five deputies. There were, as might have been expected, such former associates of the Union and Progress party as Javid, the financier, and Dr. Nazim, against whom Kemal had long-standing grudges; also Abdulkadir, who was caught at the frontier trying to escape in an ox-cart, and Kara Kemal, who evaded arrest for a while but when the police tracked him down ran away into a hen coop and shot himself. But the accused included also the leading members of the essentially moderate Progressive party, among them Kiazim Karabekir, Refet, Ali Fuad, and two other generals, as well as Rauf and Dr. Adnan, who were in Europe and thus had to be charged *in absentia*.

Kiazim Karabekir was arrested in Ankara on the tribunal's instructions. But Ismet objected and on his own responsibility ordered his friend's release. He insisted, moreover, that none of the generals could have played a part in the conspiracy. This meant an open clash between the government and the tribunal, which thereupon threatened to arrest Ismet himself. Acting as it claimed to do in the name of the Assembly, its members insisted that the government had no authority over it and no right to interfere with its decision. Kiazim's rearrest was ordered and Kemal at once summoned Ismet to Izmir. He arrived and, after attending a session of the tribunal, withdrew his objections, thus according it the government's blessing and leaving the field clear to the two Alis.

For the people of Izmir he wept crocodile tears: "My heart is full of sorrow and I shudder with horror. I had hoped that most of those friends of mine in Parliament, with whom I take pleasure in exchanging ideas, would be incapable of seizing power by means of conspiracy."

After individual interrogation the accused were all conveyed to the Alhambra Cinema, which had been transformed into a courtroom. There, seated in two rows of chairs with an armed guard beside them, amid a subdued hum of voices from the boxes around, they awaited the members of the tribunal who, in a sudden silence from the audience, marched solemnly onto the stage.

From their indictment and from a statement to the press by Ali, the line of the prosecution became evident: the Progressives were to be nailed with the responsibility for the plot. The Unionists, in the persons of Shükrü, Javid, and Kara Kemal, had linked up with them to pursue their counterrevolutionary aims—to assassinate the Gazi and bring a government of their own to power. The Progressives, in a "sleep of ignorance," had allowed their party to be exploited as a cloak for these secret terrorist activities. Had their generals seen what was really happening, they would hardly now be in this plight. As it was they had shown no foresight, they had turned a blind eye to the conspiracy, they had failed to report it to the government, hence they were guilty of the crime of sowing anarchy and disorder in the country.

For this they were to be tried by a tribunal which placed itself above the law of the country and above such constitutional trifles as the privilege of members of the Assembly, to which it was in theory responsible. They had neither counsel for defence nor the right of appeal. They were assumed guilty unless they proved themselves innocent. They were at the mercy of flimsy and arbitrary evidence, obtained by methods akin to those of Abdul Hamid and the Young Turk *komitajis* which Kemal had always so outspokenly deplored. Witnesses were largely dispensed with, and the accused were treated simply to an interrogation and an arraignment by the judge. Faced with this mockery of justice, the generals and other Progressive leaders took the only course consistent with their honour. They refused to plead. Asked if they had anything to say in their defence, they replied, "No."

Interrogation of the real culprits, Ziya Hurshid and Shükrü and their gang, failed to provide any evidence against the generals. Ziya admitted that "of course" his attempt had had a political purpose. But neither Rauf nor Ali Fuad nor any of the Progressives had any knowledge of it. They were "all timorous people." Knowing that they could never defeat the People's party, he and Abdulkadir, who shared Ziya's contempt for them, had formed a group of their own, unconnected with any party, to achieve a coup d'état. Throughout his interrogation Ziya, knowing his inevitable fate, admitted his guilt with a sang-froid amounting to insolence.

The Izmir trials lasted for three weeks. After they had started the Gazi retired to a villa in the neighbouring seaside resort of Cheshme. Here he was able to preserve an appearance of impartiality, pretending that justice must be allowed to run its course and that its outcome was not his concern, but receiving members of the tribunal and other influential persons. The verdicts were thus such as to meet with his approval. Ziya Hurshid, Shükrü, Arif, Abdulkadir (still at large), and eleven others were condemned to death; Rauf and seven others to various periods of imprisonment and exile. Javid, Dr. Nazim, and the group of Unionists were committed for subsequent trial at Ankara. But Kiazim Karabekir, Ali Fuad, Refet, the two remaining generals, and ten others, mostly of a Progressive persuasion, were acquitted. The arrest of the generals, heroes of the Revolution all, had been unpopular with the crowd, and open sympathy had been shown to them from the well of the court. Though Kemal may well have intended rather to teach his former associates a lesson than to hang them, their acquittal was ascribed to the influence of Ismet.[1]

Most of those sentenced to death were hanged that night in various parts of Izmir. Kemal signed their death warrants, including that of Arif, automatically, smoking as he did so and displaying no sign of emotion on his grey mask of a face. For him this was war—against the enemy from within. It was Arif who had taunted him at the Sakarya, "You will always find enough men in Turkey to send to their death, with or without reason." Arif was sure until the last minute that his old friend would reprieve him. After being sentenced he wrote Kemal a letter, recalling their long-standing friendship and pleading for a pardon. On reaching the scaffold he asked whether the pasha had answered his note. "He surely will," he insisted. "Can't we wait for five more minutes?" But no answer came.

Ziya Hurshid prepared himself for the scaffold in dandyish fashion, dressing slowly and with care, sprinkling eau de cologne over his person, and arranging a silk handkerchief tidily in his breast pocket. Learning the names of the ten others to be hanged, he remarked, "There must be

---

[1] Kemal himself later declared to Ali Fuad that he had been spared as a friend and the rest for his sake.

a mistake somewhere. Some of those, I think, do not deserve hanging."
(One of them was in fact a government informer who pleaded without
success that his services as such should be taken into consideration.) Ziya
then gave the money in his wallet to the governor of the prison for his
brother, as the price of a decent grave. "If you don't carry out this wish
of mine," he jested, "I shan't let you alone in the next world. I shall try
to murder you there and this time I shall certainly succeed."

The scaffold had been erected on the spot where Ziya had planned to
shoot Kemal. "What a wonderful contrivance it is!" he remarked. "It
reminds me of a cradle. And it is high, too. All of you will remain
down here and I shall be looking at you from on high." He insisted on
passing the cord around his own neck. It was the hangman who seemed
nervous, insisting, "Hurry up, sir, time is passing!" Ziya laughed: "What
is your hurry? I am the one to die. So don't get worried. . . . In a few
minutes I'll be in the other world. Tell me, can I do anything for you?
Can I give any message to your kith and kin over there?" So he died,
still with a smile on his lips. Next day the crowd saw eleven corpses
hanging, each with a paper attached to its shirt with the verdict inscribed on it.

Ali Fuad and his companions were not immediately released on acquittal. They were taken to a store beneath the cinema where they waited
in apprehension as a night and a day and a second night dragged by.
Still unable to believe in their release, they asked each other anxiously
what this added humiliation, this continued implication of guilt, might
mean. Fuad and Kiazim Karabekir tried to reassure their comrades.
Among them were those sentenced to terms of imprisonment. Two of
them, deputies respectively for Istanbul and Sivas, bewailed the injustice
of their sentences, in tones of indignant despair. They began to clamour
for a retrial. Ali Fuad, who knew them both well, urged them to do
nothing rashly. Such political condemnations were often revised with time.
But the deputies would not listen. They could not live under this stigma.
They must appeal. A warden came to the door and announced, "Those
who want to appeal, come this way." Both rushed to the door, which
closed behind them. The hours went by and they did not return. Later
that night they were seen handcuffed, being led to the general prison.
Their sentences were changed, and that night, together with Rüştü, one
of the generals, they were hanged.

In the morning the acquitted prisoners were finally released. The
generals were mobbed by the crowd outside crying "Thank God, who
has returned our pashas to us!" Concerned at the demonstration, the

governor sent an official car to take them wherever they wanted to go. At first they refused, preferring to walk, but since this became impossible the crowd led them to the car, many clambering in beside them and insisting that it drive slowly that the rest might follow. The prisoners' release thus became a triumphal progress.

The Izmir trials had liquidated all criminal conspirators and silenced the Progressive opposition to Kemal—for the generals and their friends would henceforward be effectively excluded from political life. The Ankara trials, which followed a fortnight later, were intended to dispose, once and for all, of his remaining enemies, the members of the former Union and Progress party. Some fifty were accused, of whom the most prominent were Javid and Dr. Nazim. Here the indictment concerned not a criminal attempt on Kemal's life but a political attempt to overthrow his regime. It was the final culmination of that feud between Unionists and Nationalists, between the followers of Enver and those of Kemal, which had divided the Turkish revolutionary movement. Kemal judged the remnants of the Union and Progress group partly in personal terms, through his own obsessive memories of past rivalries, slights, and intrigues, but partly also in political terms, as the survivors of a regime bounded by individual interests with no radical national programme. What remained of the party, armed as it still was with funds and animated by leaders well versed in underground political intrigue, must thus inevitably be the enemy of his own. Until the Unionists were finally eliminated Kemal could enjoy no sense of security.

The tribunal dragged up the association of the Unionist leaders with Enver, after his flight and during his subsequent attempt to return to Anatolia. It accused them of manoeuvres to change the government during the period of the first Grand National Assembly; of agitations during the elections for the second; of the formation of an Opposition through the Progressive party; of secret meetings for such purposes in the house of Javid and the office of Kara Kemal; and of the inspiration of press articles which supported an anti-government programme.

As at Izmir the accused were assumed guilty unless able to prove themselves innocent, and the negative fact that they did not support the government became, in the eyes of the judges, sufficient proof of their guilt. The absence of any damning revelations against them led to a general public belief that there would be no capital sentences. But Kemal's personal hatred and suspicion of the Unionist leaders was now reinforced by disquiet at reports of economic unrest in the interior, and a show of strength seemed desirable—more especially as the release of the generals might have been interpreted in some circles as weakness. Moreover, continuous pressure for Javid's acquittal had come from Jewish and other organizations abroad, and these sinister implications of the hidden foreign hand did little to weaken Kemal's resolve to be rid of him. The last-minute evidence of Abdulkadir, sentenced to death for his complicity in the plot but only now apprehended, proved sufficient to turn the scale against him.

The announcement was thus made that thirty-seven of the accused were acquitted—including Hussein Jahid, the editor of *Tanin,* whose earlier sentence of exile was, however, still in force; six of them, besides Rauf, were sentenced to ten years' exile; and Javid, Nazim, and two other former Unionist leaders were sentenced to death. Thus the old scores were paid off, the old words translated into deeds. Of both Javid and Nazim Kemal had exclaimed in the early days of the war, "A man like that deserves to be hanged"—Javid for turning down his deal for supplies from Bulgaria, Nazim for blocking his promotion with Enver; and lately Nazim had been taunting him openly as "Gazöz Pasha," [2] the "little Napoleon" who built himself up by imprisoning his friends. Ismet too had his grudges against both Javid and Jahid, for their obstruction of his policy at Lausanne—though, in response to pressure from the press, he had achieved the release of the latter.

The executions took place that night in the centre of Ankara. Javid approached the ordeal with a nonchalant dignity. Reaching the foot of the gallows, he requested the prison doctor to convey his felicitations to Jahid on his release, to embrace his wife and child on his behalf, to transmit his greetings to the Gazi and the tribunal judges with the comment that his condemnation was against all the principles of justice. He recited two lines concerning the punishment of tyrants, from the Turkish poet, Ziya Pasha. Then he turned to the executioner and said, "Do your duty." He climbed nimbly onto the platform and asked what he should do, where he should stand, apologizing for the fact that he had no practice in such a procedure. He assisted the executioner by leaning forward to place his head in the noose. And thus, gallantly, he died. Kemal, when told afterwards that Javid's widow had, in a vindictive moment, threatened to strangle him, commented quietly, "She could hardly do otherwise."

The Gazi was not at Chankaya on the night of the executions. He had spent the day out of reach, on his farm, celebrating its usual

2 *Gazöz:* fizzy lemonade.

anniversary at midday with draughts of *avran* (the sour milk of the peasant) and in the evening with an informal dinner to some of his ministers, members of the tribunal, and friends in the kiosk which he had built by his "Sea of Marmara." In the course of the evening the trials were not discussed.

Among those not present was Tevfik Rüştü, his Foreign Minister, the brother-in-law and lifelong boon companion of Nazim, who had preferred to decline the invitation. A day or so later Kemal went to lunch with him alone. The Gazi expressed sympathy and explained the reason for the trials, which Tevfik had missed through his absence abroad. The point had been reached at which one or other of the two groups in Parliament must go. The matter had been placed in the hands of the tribunal, hence was not on his conscience. But, as he had confessed to Kiliç Ali with a gesture of distaste as he read its reports, the whole affair had been "very disagreeable."

Its instrument was not to survive for long. The power of the Independence Tribunal, thus misused for political purposes, had become such that it threatened to create a dual authority within the state—its judges on the one hand, Kemal's ministers on the other. This so irked and impeded Ismet in the business of government that he persuaded Kemal after a while that the moment had come to disband it. One evening at a party at Chankaya the Gazi remarked casually to Bald Ali, "I have decided to abolish your tribunal. It is no longer required."

Ali replied that he would study the question and furnish his master with a report.

"Report!" Kemal exclaimed. "Report! I have studied the question myself and from tomorrow your tribunal will no longer exist."

Its abolition was confirmed next day by the party caucus. The members of the tribunal, who for two years had tasted irresponsible power, reverted to the status of ordinary deputies. The "reign of terror" was no longer necessary. Kemal's dirty work was done.

53 ▶ *Return to Istanbul*

"It was the people that I was afraid of." Thus did Kemal, in a remark to a friend, seek to justify afterwards the liquidation of his opponents and his assumption of supreme dictatorial powers. It was the people, he was forever telling them, who had saved Turkey. Yet ironically it was for fear of them that he now pursued a policy contrary to all his professed democratic principles. In fact his prestige with the people had never been higher than in the first years of the Republic. They were more securely under his control than they had been under that of any Sultan. Moreover, theirs was now a personal loyalty, based on the fact that he had led them personally in war, saving their lands from the enemy, making his capital in their midst, and as no Sultan had done moving continuously among them as though he were one of them. His hold over the army was unchallenged. Communications, to say nothing of secret service techniques, were now so developed that no centralized administration need fear serious local unrest. Kemal knew better than most the congenital inertia of the Turkish people, whom he alone, at Gallipoli and later in the War of Independence, had known how to galvanize into action; and now, throughout Anatolia, there was no other potential national leader able to do so and thus to threaten his power.

Paradoxically Kemal had become a dictator not in order to obtain power but after he had done so already. In the early days he had had to work democratically—if only because his prestige was not yet sufficiently established to enable him to do otherwise. As a result he had won a resounding victory against the foreigner and had secured an honourable peace, which for the first time admitted Turkey into the family of respected Western nations; he had eliminated the old concept of Sultanate and Caliphate with their well-entrenched political power, and had swept away the institutions of an obsolete medieval society. The main foundations of a new Turkey were now complete—and their last stages had been completed against scant opposition.

This might well have been the moment for an experiment in some kind of liberal democracy, whose principles were after all inherent in the new Turkish Republic. This would have been a fitting culmination to that movement of reform which had been born in the Ottoman Empire a century earlier. The Young Turks, giving it a new brief lease of life, had lapsed from parliamentary democracy into a dictatorial triumvirate at a time of crisis when the foreigner was threatening the empire from every side, and when a parliamentary Opposition had shown signs of endangering the unity of the country. But Kemal had surmounted these very obstacles; he had no need for a dictatorship—for the duumvirate which, with Ismet as his reliable factotum, he had now set up. Extraordinary measures might have been necessary to deal with such local outbursts as the Kurdish rebellion and the subsequent hat riots. But there was no need to extend these over the whole country, and above all no need to use them for the suppression of a parliamentary Opposition of an essentially moderate kind.

But he had decided otherwise. His decision was firstly a matter of temperament. By nature and training a soldier, he might delegate his authority but he could not tolerate the idea of any threat to it; he might plan his campaigns in co-operation with others but he must have sole control of their execution. And what was the transformation of Turkish society but another campaign in which, as he saw it, a rapid decision must be reached?

For his former associates, the Progressives, the problem had a remoter and more complex perspective. Turkish society for them was a deep-rooted organism which could be transformed only by slow and patient stages, and by a process of co-operation, both in planning and execution, with which all must be involved from the bottom upwards. Nevertheless, once Kemal's reforms were decreed, they were prepared to back their implementation in principle, reserving the right only to criticize their administration in detail. They sought not to rival his authority but merely to counterbalance it. They could have served for him as a window on the country, widening the perspective and range of his government's view. They could have furnished him with much-needed governing material, the lack of which was to retard the growth of the state. Where they erred, somewhat naïvely, was in allowing their prestige and their party organization to be exploited by malcontents as cover for subversive purposes of which they wholly disapproved. This was the error used to justify the fatal "purge."

Psychologically, Kemal's emergence as a "hanging dictator" was rooted in two other factors. The first was an obsessive suspicion of all who had spurned and obstructed him. The iron had been entering deeper into his soul from his fatherless lone-wolf childhood onwards. His cold-shouldering by the members of the Committee of Union and Progress, as a young man who knew that he knew better than they; the obstruction of his military career by rivals jealous of his worth and success—all these rebuffs had built up in his imagination a host of powerful enemies who still aspired to drag him down from his pinnacle. Such was the legacy of a past fraught with frustration and nourishing restless revengeful hates; such the reason, in particular, for the execution of Javid, which not only antagonized Western opinion but deprived Turkey of a shrewd financial counsellor.

The second impulse behind his drastic actions was a fear of what he did not understand—the forces of religion. Agnosticism was born in him early and grew in him with time: through reaction against his mother's devoutness; through his secular education and his reading of the rationalist philosophers; through his horror, as a young man, at the Arab fanaticism of Damascus and his growing awareness of its hold, in a different degree, on his country as a whole; finally through his open proscription and condemnation to death by the powers of Islam, followed by a "holy war" against him which he all but lost.

In his rationalism he understood little of the spiritual concept of Islam, which represented an inner need for the mass of his people and which a mere social philosophy, however enlightened, could not easily replace. He saw it as mere superstition of a dark and primitive kind. But he did not underrate its force. It was a secret weapon liable to be used against him by the peasants and the "priests" who controlled them, a "hidden hand" wider in its reach and stronger in its grip than that of any mere rival political party. He understood little, whatever he might say in his speeches, of the social and political principles of Islam as the Prophet had seen them, and as the liberal reformers of the past century had been striving to regenerate them. For Kemal Islam and civilization were a contradiction in terms. "If only," he once said of the Turks, with a flash of cynical insight, "we could make them Christians!" His was not to be the reformed Islamic state for which the faithful were waiting: it was to be a strictly lay state, with a centralized government as strong as the Sultan's, backed by the army and run by his own intellectual bureaucracy.

On a short-term view, this attitude seemed at first justified by results. With the dirty work done, there could now be an end to the policy of force and repression. The period that followed was one of stability and peace in which life and personal liberties were reasonably secure. It was a time of respite from fifteen years of war and revolution, a time of gestation in which the social reforms imposed during the past three years might have a chance to mature in the minds of the Turkish people.

There was a rest from political activity. The press was controlled. But there was reasonable freedom of speech among the people in general. Kemal was no ideologist; he was pragmatic in his ideas and did not attempt to impose on them a rigid conformity. To a group of school-teachers who asked him whether, as certain European writers maintained, he was really a dictator, he returned the soft answer, "If I were, you would not be allowed to ask me that question." As Bernard Lewis defines it, Kemal's was "a dictatorship without the uneasy over-the-shoulder glance, the terror of the door-bell, the dark menace of the concentration camp,"[1] so soon to arise in the West. Admitting once that he was a dictator, he qualified the admission: "But I have not had pyramids built in my honour like the Pharaohs of Egypt. I did not make people work for my sake, threatening them with whips when I wanted an idea to be accepted by the country. I first called a congress, I debated the situation with the people, I carried out my plans only after taking authority from the people. The congresses of Erzurum and Sivas and the Grand National Assembly are living proofs of this."

His was a dictatorship based on democratic forms, within a legal and constitutional framework which he scrupulously observed. For he was building, as his fellow dictators of the period were not, for his own disappearance, trying to lay down a system of government which could

[1] *The Emergence of Modern Turkey.*

survive his time. Into this the true spirit of democracy, which it lacked for the present, could be infused when the time became ripe. It could perhaps have been encouraged to ripen more quickly. But as Ismet, a generation later, explained the delay,[2] "At that time we were on fire."

With his enemies safely out of the way and his capital securely established at Ankara, the time had now come for the Gazi to revisit Istanbul, where he had not set foot since his departure for Anatolia eight years before. His sister Makbule and a group of ladies prepared accomodation for him in the Dolma Bahche Palace—now proclaimed, with the other palaces, the property, no longer of the shadow of God, but of the Turkish people. The Gazi, arriving there in his yacht, received a rapturous welcome, the steamers blowing their sirens while thousands of small boats, dangerously overloaded with passengers, sped out across the Bosporus to cluster around the yacht and escort her ashore. Many had paid as much as a month's salary for the hire of a motorboat. At night illuminations blazed and a torchlight procession paraded through the streets to gather before the palace, where the Gazi, amid frantic cheers, came out onto a marble balcony to salute the crowds. To the people of Istanbul his arrival, after all these years, was a glorious reconciliation. They had been sulking at his neglect, but now they sulked no longer.

The Dolma Bahche Palace, with its ornate nineteenth-century halls of marble and crystal and ormulu, was an incongruous setting for Kemal, who felt caged by its restrictions. But at least, unlike Abdul Hamid's Yildiz behind its high walls, it looked out on the world. The broad terraces spreading along its encrusted façade confronted the Bosporus, and here he could sit drinking and watching the life on its waters—the small boats scurrying across them and the big ships sailing past from the Golden Horn to seas and worlds beyond. When he grew restless he would take a boat and cruise on the waters himself; or he would go up to Pera and pace the streets on foot, revisiting familiar haunts, dropping into some *patisserie* at the tea hour amid unabashed looks of admiration from its feminine clientele.

But it was to Ankara, the cradle of his Revolution and the seat of his government, that his heart and as time went on the hearts of the Turkish people belonged. A serious start was now made with the replanning and rebuilding of the capital. A German and an Austrian town planner were called in to furnish designs. Here, on virgin land, almost devoid of buildings, it should be possible to create the world's most up-to-date

[2] In an interview with the author in 1960.

city. The plan envisaged wide radiating boulevards in the European manner, with a central *étoile* to be graced by an equestrian statue of the Gazi, and handsome public buildings disposed on a variety of well-chosen sites. Thousands of trees were to be planted across the bare arid plateau, leading up to Kemal's official residence at Chankaya and around it. The marsh beneath the citadel was to be drained and transformed into a People's Park. Already Ankara boasted a new Parliament building and, conveniently opposite, a modern luxury hotel. These had been designed in an oriental manner; but the predominant style of the city's architecture was to be, rather, Germanic in character. A high priority was given to the construction of an opera house, such as had impressed Kemal, the young military attaché, above all the civilized Western blessings of Sofia. In time a city was to arise, provincial perhaps in its atmosphere but Western in character and amenity, which did credit enough to the new Turkish Republic.

The Gazi was due back in Ankara in the autumn for the opening of the third Grand National Assembly. In Istanbul he had been working on the speech which was in effect to be his own documented history of the War of Independence and of the Revolution to date. One of the longest speeches in history—just as the Sakarya had been one of its longest battles—it took him three months to write and six days to deliver. He dictated it in advance, sometimes for more than twenty-four hours at a stretch, to his secretaries, who for months past had been collating the necessary documents. One by one he reduced them to exhaustion, so that they had to be reinforced at their desks like soldiers on a battlefield. After dictating all day he would take a bath, then try out what he had written on his friends, then retire with the intention of sleeping but, such was the throbbing energy of his brain, he often resumed dictation and continued right through until morning. Delivered to the Congress of the People's party, it was essentially a political speech, hence often tendentious—notably in its attempts to discredit Rauf and the rest. But it remains the classic account of the Kemalist Revolution.[3]

The opening of the third Assembly in 1927 signalized the end of the "foundation period." The deputies were housed for the first time in the new building, purged of the stormy associations of the first and second Assemblies. Comprising only a single well-disciplined party, it relieved Kemal of all parliamentary worries, and indeed of the necessity to concern himself any longer with the details of politics. He likened his Parliament this time to an "Assembly of Philosophers," as Napoleon's Five

[3] Comparable, it has been suggested, to Julius Caesar's *De Bello Gallico*.

Hundred had been. For a new phase lay before the Republic. Political independence had been won; cultural independence must now be achieved —with the Gazi's "philosophers" as its automatic instrument, and a growing generation of Republican Turks as its fervent adherents.

54 ▶ Reform of the alphabet

The first act of the third Grand National Assembly was to round off the religious reforms by deleting from the Constitution the formula that "the religion of the Turkish State is Islam." Turkey thus became, legally and constitutionally, a secular state, in line with those of the West. Religious belief became a matter of individual conscience. There remained, however, one tie with the East and Islam—the Arabic script, in which Turkish had been written. It thus became the first task of the new Assembly to reform the Turkish alphabet.

The simplification of the script had been discussed at intervals, against strong opposition from the Islamic authorities, for a hundred years past. The alphabet was that of Islam, as used by the Arabs and Persians, and was originally adopted by the Turks for religious reasons, despite the fact that it did not fit the sounds of their language. With its complexity of characters and accents, its paucity of vowels, and its ambiguity of sounds in differing contexts, it was hard for an ordinary person to read, and even the educated Ottoman Turk would often make mistakes in its spelling. This led to the growth of two separate languages, that of the Ottoman mandarin class, which was written but largely unspoken, and that of the people, which was unwritten but spoken. This excluded the bulk of the population from most written literature. How could popular sovereignty thrive without an alphabet which all the people could learn and read?

At the time of the triumvirate, Enver had made a halfhearted attempt at a change in the offices of his War Ministry, by separating the Arabic letters instead of running them together into the normal script, but this was abandoned on the outbreak of war. For fear of religious opposition he had not dared introduce the Latin script. Nor did Kemal, until the people had grown used to his other more radical religious reforms. In 1926 however, at a congress in Baku, the Latin alphabet was adopted for all the Turco-Tartar republics in the Soviet Union. This meant that two large groups of Turkish people would no longer be able to read one another's language, and it provided an argument for a change. In the following year the Latin script was used on a new issue of Turkish postage stamps.[1]

Ismet was at first strongly opposed to a general change. With his methodical staff officer's mind he was dismayed at the prospect of the consequent confusion in government offices, in the army, in the universities and the schools, and in the press, while the people learnt the new letters.

Kemal, though he was determined on the reform and had been discussing it with intellectuals for some years past, did not intend to implement it without unanimous backing. Thus it was not until 1928 that, after a few preliminary fanfares, he launched his campaign. He appointed an Alphabet Commission to prepare a new script. Knowing that, left to itself, the commission might take years to accomplish its task, he attended its meetings in person and gave it the benefit of his forceful views. Early in the proceedings he asked Falih Rifki, his own principal nominee on the commission, how long the change was likely to take. The consensus, said Falih Rifki, was five years. This allowed for a period in which both scripts would be taught in the schools and printed side by side in the newspapers. Kemal protested that in this case people would continue to read the old script, disregarding the new, and decreed, "The change will happen in three months or it will not happen at all."

Thus within six weeks the new alphabet was ready. Kemal was always

---

[1] The Americans were first in the field with Latin number plates on their diplomatic cars, but when they wrote out a customs declaration in Latin characters it was politely returned to them with a request that they resubmit it in Turkish.

shrewd in his choice of an audience. For his introduction of the hat he had chosen a reactionary part of the country. For the introduction of the new letters he chose the more advanced centre of Istanbul. Moreover, he picked on a popular audience, assembled one August evening in the Sarayburnu Park, below the Sultan's Old Seraglia, for a People's party fete. It was in this park that, in defiance of Moslem taboos against the portrayal of the human figure, a statue of the Gazi had been unveiled two years earlier. Kemal took his place on a platform amid plaudits from the crowd, many of whom had not set eyes on their hero before. On a rival platform a modern jazz band played, and alternately a troupe of Egyptian entertainers sang in a mournful Arabic wail. After listening to this impatiently for a while, Kemal called for a notebook and started to scribble in it. As he did so he tore out the sheets and passed them over to Falih Rifki, remarking, "Take a look at this." Falih Rifki saw and approved it as the draft of a speech, written in the Latin script.

Then the Gazi rose to his feet, said a few introductory words, brandished the papers in his hand, and called for someone who could read Turkish to come up to the platform and recite their contents. A youth ran up but on seeing that they were in Latin script was silent. Kemal explained: "This young man is puzzled because he does not know the true Turkish alphabet. I will therefore have one of my comrades read it to you." He handed it to Falih Rifki, who read it aloud:

" 'Our rich and harmonious language will now be able to display itself with new Turkish letters. We must free ourselves from these incomprehensible signs that for centuries have held our minds in an iron vise. You must learn the new Turkish letters quickly. Teach them to your compatriots, to women and to men, to porters and to boatmen. Regard it as a patriotic and national duty . . . and when you perform that duty, bear in mind that for a nation to consist of ten or twenty per cent of literates and eighty or ninety per cent of illiterates is shameful. . . . We shall repair these errors, and in doing so I want the participation of all our compatriots. . . . Our nation will show, with its script and with its mind, that its place is with the civilized world.' "

A pandemonium of applause followed his words. The jazz band and the Arabic singers were silenced. Here was a far more unusual entertainment, with the Gazi himself as its star, a fascinating new game which all, whether or not they could yet read, must now learn, to please their hero. Kemal rose to his feet to drink a toast to the crowd with—to Ismet's consternation—a glass of raki in his hand. Raising it to his lips, he said, "Sultans drank this. Kings have drunk it. I want to drink it with my people." His people showed no signs of disapproval. On his way out of the park he noticed an attractive woman, wearing a *charshaf,* with her husband. He asked her to lift it and reveal her beautiful face. She did so eagerly and gave him an embrace. From that August evening onwards the populace of Istanbul were at his feet.

With the literate classes he knew that he had a harder task before him. A few days later he summoned to the Dolma Bahche Palace a conference of scholars, men of letters, journalists, deputies, and others to discuss the reform. Determined to have his way but expecting certain members of his audience to be critical, he encouraged them to express their views from the platform but conveyed to them privately a hint that their criticism, if too strongly worded, would not be welcome.

Opposition thus effectively stifled, he announced that passages in the new alphabet would be inserted from now onwards in the newspapers, and that within three months it would entirely supersede the old. He ordered that, from the autumn onwards, all teaching in the schools should be done with the new alphabet—an order which caused consternation among schoolmasters, who did not themselves know it. They had neither the necessary textbooks nor the means of having them printed. The presses had no Latin characters until they could be procured by air from abroad, and no compositors to set the type until they themselves could learn them.

Kemal then instructed all the deputies to proceed to their constituencies, to organize the teaching of the new alphabet and to put out propaganda in its favour. Ismet himself was sent for this purpose to his own constituency of Malatya. Expounding the new alphabet as the means of raising Turkey to the level of the literate nations of the West, he remarked to his constituents, "Today the whole country has been transformed into a classroom, and the headmaster in that classroom is the Gazi himself. The Turkish people are going to work hard until they pass the exam of that school."

This was a role that suited Kemal nicely. He had once declared that, after winning his victory, he would like to become Minister of Education and really educate the people of Turkey. Now he had achieved this ambition. Blackboards were disposed around the Dolma Bahche Palace, an article of furniture to which its marble halls had not before been accustomed, and Kemal as he moved through the rooms gave lessons to visitors who came for an audience, to officials, to friends, to guests, to his personal servants. The blackboard became the symbol of the new Turkish Republic.

He became so carried away by these educational activities that he even composed an "Alphabet March" for the people to sing and so master their letters more quickly. He recited the march to the leader of the presidential band with instructions that it should be orchestrated and played back to him early next morning. The musicians worked on it the whole night through. But when they played it he listened morosely and said, "Children, though I composed this march I don't like it a bit." Thus the "Alphabet March" was abandoned.

In November 1928 the new script became law. Introducing it into the Assembly as the "key which would enable the people of Turkey to read and write easily," the Gazi artfully referred to it not as the Latin but as the Turkish script, thus pointing up its distinction from the Arabic, whose use was prohibited from the end of the year onwards. For the first time his speech was broadcast over the rudimentary Turkish radio. As "a token of the gratitude of the Turkish people," the Assembly presented him with a golden board on which the letters of the new alphabet were carved in relief. That evening the alphabet was displayed, in coloured lights, on the main buildings in Ankara.

A few days later civil servants throughout the country sat for an examination in the script, and a "School of the Nation" was founded, whose "chief instructor" was to be "His Excellency the President of the Republic, Gazi Mustafa Kemal." Its object was to create a literate population—from those who could not read and write at all to those who could do so only in the old characters. Within a year more than a million citizens had received its diploma. Inevitably the children and the illiterates, their minds unencumbered with knowledge of a previous alphabet, learnt most quickly, and they were soon giving lessons to their parents and grandparents. For the older generation some effort and strain was involved in the change, and many continued in private to use the old script. But for the younger generation it was the reform above all which appealed to their imagination and aroused their patriotic enthusiasm. It liberated them effectively from the Ottoman past and made them feel that they had a stake in the new Turkey of the Republic.

For the youth of Turkey henceforward, as one dramatic change followed another with the promise of new and expanding horizons, this was an exciting time to be alive.

55 ► Experiment in democracy

While the Gazi busied himself with his country's cultural future, its present economic situation was growing acute. Kemal was no economist. Money and all that it involved was never a matter to preoccupy his thoughts. His attitude towards it was careless. He would laugh at his ineptitude for business, telling against himself a story of how it had led him to lose his war savings to an unscrupulous Smyrna merchant. Personally uncorrupt, he tended to be casual in his attitude to corruption in his friends, provided it did not go too far.[1]

For his country he had, from his early days in Anatolia, scorned the

[1] He seldom carried money on his person. One day, walking on the hills around Chankaya with a rich friend, he fell into conversation with a poor young peasant. After interrogating him on various subjects he asked the boy whether he had any money. The boy shyly said no. Kemal, finding that he had none with him, said, "Do you see this man with me? He is stinking rich. Knock him down and take his money." Hesitantly the boy, obeying orders, began to wrestle with the man in Turkish fashion, threw him, and took his wallet. But it contained only fifty-two liras. Kemal then ordered the boy to take his friend's watch. At this the man protested. Kemal then said to him, "Very well. Take this child's address, send him a hundred liras, and he will send the watch back to you." To the boy he said, "Keep the watch until you get the money. You can't trust these stinking rich people."

notion that lack of funds could make the War of Independence impossible. Not indeed God but circumstance would provide—and so it proved. The war was won by improvisation. The new state was founded on less capital than any small business corporation. Kemal arrived at Ankara to find the equivalent of a mere few shillings in the Treasury. When he sent Yunus Nadi to collect five hundred Turkish liras (£100) to start a newspaper, the Treasurer replied cheerfully, "The safe is open. Help yourself!" for it was empty.

Kemal had to depend largely on local levies and on gifts which, ironically, came oftener than not from the "clergy." The first hard funds of the Executive Committee were three hundred Turkish liras (£60) which a man of religion had collected from his flock and brought to Kemal wrapped in a handkerchief. The day-to-day expenses of the first Grand National Assembly were covered largely by the conversion of public buildings into dormitories and canteens, where the deputies paid for their board and lodging—though the arrears in their parliamentary salaries often prevented them from doing so. After the break with Istanbul Kemal, taking over the civil administration, could draw on the revenues of Anatolia. But the financial situation of the Nationalists and their armies was always precarious.

When victory was won—a victory which followed ten years of continuous warfare—many economic problems had to be faced. Devastation was widespread. Houses and farms were in ruins. Livestock was decimated, fields had become wildernesses, food and clothing and money were scarce. Turkey had emerged from the war much reduced in size but uncomfortably large in relation to her population and means. She needed capital to develop her natural resources but feared to borrow it abroad lest she fall once more into the foreigner's grip, while the foreigner himself was chary of investing until he felt more confidence in the new regime. Trade, which the foreigner had previously handled, was paralyzed. The country lacked not only artisans but bankers and businessmen.[2] For it was largely the Greeks and other foreigners who had fulfilled these roles, and they had departed. Turkey thus found herself in an economic vacuum at a time when it was necessary to raise the standard of living and replace the gospel of religious reaction with that of material progress.

With a view to filling the vacuum Kemal had called an economic

[2] It was a moment at which Javid, one of the few Turks with an international status in the world of finance, might have been helpful, had Kemal chosen to admit him to the fold instead of executing him. Javid had offered his services to the Nationalists at the time of the Sivas Congress but Kemal had rejected them.

congress at Izmir in 1923. Here he voiced once more the doctrine that the masters of the nation were the people, this time carrying it from the political into the economic field. In his opening speech he sought to shake the Anatolian peasantry out of their submission, in the name of Islamic fatalism, to live at a bare subsistence level. The people's era, in his opinion, could be called the era of economic ideals, "the sort of era in which we say, 'Let our country be prosperous! Let our people live in plenty! Let them be rich!' And on this point let me remind you of a philosophical saying: 'Being satisfied [with what you have] is an indestructible treasure.' I say, let this era of economic ideals put an end to the idea that being satisfied is an indestructible treasure and that poverty is a virtue! . . . If what we call our land had been made up of bone-dry mountains, of stones, swamps and naked plains . . . there could have been absolutely no difference between it and a prison. . . . But this country of ours is one that is not only fit but most suitable to be made into a paradise for our children and grandchildren. . . . The arm that wields the sword grows weary and in the end puts it back in the scabbard, when perhaps it is doomed to rust and moulder; but the arm that holds the plough grows daily stronger, and in growing stronger becomes yet more the master and owner of the soil."

There must, in brief, be economic self-reliance. In pursuit of this, agriculture must be mechanized, industries developed, communications improved. To achieve this all classes of Turks—farmers, artisans, merchants, workers—must unite, for each needed the other. Such principles were enshrined, at the end of the conference, in an economic counterpart of the National Pact, allowing for control by the state from the point at which private enterprise ended.

During the next few years certain measures were taken to translate them into practice. The burden of the tithe, by which the peasant had been virtually enslaved, was abolished. State monopolies, in such basic commodities as sugar, salt, matches, tobacco, alcohol, petrol, and shipping, were established, transferring the fiscal burden to the landlords and townspeople who were their principal customers. The monopolies covered so many products that a facetious deputy enquired, "When are we going to have a monopoly of *kebab?*" A start was made with land reform, by changes in the system of tenure and by redistribution of parts of the big estates to landless peasants and immigrants—a policy leading in the former Greek districts to the emergence of a new class of small Turkish landowner. The People's party aspired to take over the role of the former magnates through its own local organizations, "advising" the peasantry. For the country, if it was to feed itself and leave an exportable surplus with which to buy other necessities from abroad, must cultivate more land and grow more produce.

Nevertheless the peasantry and their production languished throughout these years, owing to the preference given to industrial over agricultural development. The economic argument for this was that Turkey could not now afford to buy all the manufactured goods she needed, hence must make them. But there was a political and psychological argument too. Turkey, bent on coming into line with the West, did not wish to be regarded as a nation of peasants. Western countries were industrialized; therefore Turkey must be industrialized. Hence the expenditure of capital, not on the improvement of the soil, but on the creation of factories, blast furnaces, steelworks, mines.

The capital was provided at this stage predominantly by the state, but with a leavening of private enterprise. Four state banks were established. Kemal handed the money subscribed by the Moslems of India for the national struggle to Mahmud Jelal (Celal Bayar), one of his few associates who knew anything of such matters, and told him to open a bank with it—the first Turkish bank. In a derelict shop in the old town of Ankara Jelal did so. It became the Iş Bank (Work Bank) and was followed by three others: The Sumer (Sumerian) Bank, the Central Bank, and later the Eti (Hittite) Bank. The state banks and industries would help to create a new Turkish middle class, filling the gap left by the foreigner. Private enterprise too had its chance, with the granting of lesser industrial concessions to individuals—mainly prominent members of the party and of Kemal's own entourage. Ismet, beyond favouring a rigid system of state control, concerned himself little with economic policy as such. His mind ran primarily on politics and on military strategy. Throughout the war and the Revolution he had been brooding on the lack of communications. Thus his main concern was the construction of railways.

Despite these various measures, the country's economy hung fire during the first six years of the Republic, and with the crash on the New York Stock Exchange in October 1929 and the consequent world depression it slowed down to the point of stagnation. The depression aggravated a general feeling of discontent which had been growing for some years past. Harvests had lately been bad, partly from droughts, partly from the lack of seed to plant, and there were cases of famine. Dislike of Westernization was thus reinforced by fear of starvation. God was not providing, and this was seen as a punishment for godlessness, for the breakaway from religion, so that in the Ramadan fast people flocked back to the mosques to make amends.

There was too little incentive for the peasants themselves to provide, and reassurances that conditions would improve were disbelieved. Government officials were underpaid and thus subject to corruption. Banditry again became rife in the Black Sea mountains, where troops had to be mobilized to round up the gangs. There was a more serious disturbance, once again, in Kurdistan. All these operations cost money. There was resentment at the high prices and other hardships arising from the state monopolies, at the funds spent on the building of railways while the peasants lacked roads to take their produce to market. Ismet's policy was generally disparaged, and from the early months of 1930 it was openly attacked in a new newspaper named *Yarin* (*Tomorrow*). This was the first time in five years that any organ of the press had dared thus freely to criticize the government. Moreover, it was clear that the Gazi condoned the criticism, and Ismet was goaded into promising a new economic programme.

But Kemal's intentions went further than this. Late in the summer he announced the formation of a new party, in opposition to his own government. The economic crisis was at last bringing home to him the disadvantages of one-party rule. It brought him unpopularity, since the mistakes of the government were blamed on him personally; it left him in the dark as to trends of public opinion, and created an explosive situation by blocking the normal channels of public discontent. His censored press told him little; he could not always be in the Assembly to feel its pulse; the ministers revealed to him only the rosiest of pictures and he was thus hampered in assessing the effects of his government's policy and in guiding it effectively. Some form of parliamentary criticism, he had begun to see, was desirable.

Speaking of such matters, he drew a parallel between himself and the enlightened Augustus, the first Caesar, who under the Roman Republic was endowed by the Senate with absolute powers, with the result that at the time of his death the Republic was forgotten and his successors crowned emperors thereafter. This must not happen here. Kemal still disapproved of dictatorship in theory, and it was his genuine desire to create a system which would outlast him and evolve, to the benefit of his country, into a replica of a Western-style democracy.

Foreign opinion, moreover, meant much to him. Abroad, in the democratic countries, Turkey's one-party system was seen as a sign of her inferiority to the West. He had been stung by the criticism of European writers that the Turkish system, though Western in form, was Eastern in practice. He now saw a chance of countering such criticism, of furthering his ultimate aim, and of providing a safety valve for the present discontents in a more democratic form, but still without prejudice to his own authority.

The Progressive party he had suppressed because of its "unwelcome spontaneity" (as a foreign diplomat put it), because of his mistrust of the popularity of Rauf and the generals. Instead he would form a new Opposition party, not independent, as Rauf's had been, but under his own indirect control. He would ride two party horses at once, gaining credit for the successes and evading blame for the failures of either. As the rival leader to Ismet he picked upon Fethi, who since his resignation from the premiership, five years before, had been ambassador in Paris, and whom Kemal knew he could manage and trust. The new party would be called the Free Republican as opposed to the People's Republican party.

The proposition was discussed at the table throughout the summer of 1930, and in effect agreed before Fethi's return on leave from Paris towards the end of July. A few days after his arrival in Istanbul Kemal called upon him and invited him to lead the new party. The burden of his thesis was, "I do not want to die without bringing the regime of personal rule in Turkey to a close. I want to create a liberal Republic." He alluded to Fethi's well-known sympathy for the British parliamentary system and suggested that here was a chance to put it into practice at home. Fethi had also, in recent years, become familiar with the workings of French parliamentary institutions. What better man than he thus to complete the democratization of his own country?

Fethi hesitated, largely because of the personal conflicts in which the venture was sure to involve him. On the other hand he was a convinced liberal. Sitting day after day in the gallery of the Chambre des Deputés, he had pondered regretfully on the limitations of his own country's one-party Assembly. Above all he had from his youth made a serious study of economics: during his exile in Malta he had translated into Turkish a work by Maynard Keynes. He believed profoundly in the principles of a free economy, disapproved of Ismet's rigid statist methods, and had strong views of his own as to the causes of the present economic crisis. Largely on these grounds he responded to pressure not only from Kemal but from Ismet himself, and agreed, on reflection, to accept the proposal.

Discussions followed at Yalova, a watering place on the Marmara which Kemal had created, and where he was now spending much of his time, free from the constrictions of the Dolma Bahche Palace. He made it clear that, though Fethi was to be the leader of the party, he himself would take a hand in its management, as in that of the People's party. He promised Fethi some seventy or eighty seats in the Assembly, at the next election, and asked him to submit a list of candidates. Meanwhile members of the People's party would be encouraged to transfer their allegiance.

Having chosen the leader of his Opposition, it now remained for Kemal to choose its other chief members. But the deputies proved reluctant to join. After five years of one-party rule, the idea of opposition had grown so unfamiliar that prospective members needed reassurance from Kemal that they would not be victimized for opposing him. He gave it emphatically, declaring that he looked forward to watching the fight. However heated it became, both sides would be invited to his table, where they would be expected to speak freely and give him the chance to judge between their respective views. For a start, to help establish confidence, he instructed Nuri Conker, his closest aide and friend, to act as secretary-general of the party. He enrolled also his sister Makbule, a woman who shared his obstinacy and his high-strung temperament, but little of his intelligence and none of his education. Quarrelsome and frank in her speech, she was now, as member of the Free party, to have a chance to deprecate him in public, which she used to the full. Thus did the Turkish Republic embark on its second experiment in democracy.

After a mere three months it was to end in failure. Trouble very soon arose when Fethi visited Izmir, to inaugurate a new branch of the Free party. He did so against the advice of his wiser counsellors, who urged that the party should move slowly and not yet seek electoral representation, but in response to promptings from Kemal, who took the opposite view. It was nonetheless arranged that Fethi's arrival in Izmir should be as unobtrusive as possible. The police feared disturbances against him. In fact the exact reverse happened. Despite these precautions a huge crowd swarmed down to the harbour to greet him as a popular hero. Fethi did his best to calm his overenthusiastic admirers. But so open a demonstration against the government thoroughly alarmed the local authorities, who requested him in the interests of law and order to postpone the party meeting he had planned to address.

Meanwhile the People's party hurriedly organized a rally of their own. They found difficulty in mobilizing sufficient supporters, and their speakers were howled down by a crowd calling for Fethi. The crowd swarmed through the streets to demonstrate before his hotel and before the People's party headquarters and newspaper office. Here windows were broken and the police opened fire, killing a boy of fourteen. A detachment of troops was called in to restore order. When Fethi, on telegraphed instructions from the Gazi, finally made his speech, he did so flanked by police, in a voice growing hoarse and in any case insufficiently powerful to reach the large crowd which had assembled.

He revealed the somewhat nebulous programme of the Free party and praised the Gazi, "the spiritual guide of the people," who had welcomed its formation. He argued against Ismet in favour of a liberal system, giving scope to private enterprise while leaving certain spheres to the state. He was greeted with tumultuous enthusiasm, except by a member of the crowd who withdrew on learning that he had failed to promise the restoration of the fez and the Arabic script.

Fethi then left for Manisa and Balikesir, where he was treated to similar ovations. Everywhere the peasantry seized the chance to ventilate their wrongs. In one place, when he unwisely raised his hat, the crowd removed their own and flung them to the ground with cheers; in another he was greeted with Islamic banners as the defender of the faith against the godless Republic.

"The new party," as Grew, the American ambassador, expressed it, "had become a clinical thermometer for taking the political temperature of the country and there could be no doubt of the fever which it registered." The press of the People's party raised it further in articles against Fethi; in Ankara the alarmed party bosses brought pressure to bear on Kemal. As a result he went back on his policy of benevolent neutrality and affirmed, in a press statement, his "historical" allegiance to the People's party, disclaiming any intention to sever his ties with it. He then tilted the scales against the Free party by deploring the attack on the People's party offices at Izmir and the insults directed against the government by "a few irresponsible persons." These various acts of aggression would be punished by the laws of the Republic.

It was thus a distinctly aggrieved Fethi who now returned to Ankara. Here the two-party struggle was continued within the walls of the Assembly. Kemal, in opening the debate, encouraged both sides by reiterating that he favoured neither at the expense of the other. As Ambassador Grew, quoting the report of his commercial attaché, recorded the scene:

The Gazi sat in his private box watching the tilting between the Government and the Opposition from the tribune—beaming when a telling point was scored, frowning when a point was awkwardly handled. Gillespie says it reminded him of nothing so much as a proud father watching his sons competing in two opposing debating teams. . . . The whole outlook of the Assembly has changed and whereas formerly the measures of the Government were accepted and voted in an automatic and apathetic fashion, now everyone is full of zest, important points are freely debated, and constructive criticism formulated and a real Parliamentary atmosphere prevails.

But this first glow of enthusiasm was soon to fade. Neither of the two parties showed notable signs of leadership or of a new and positive policy. Tension between them mounted to a climax during the municipal elections—a dress rehearsal, as it were, for the general election to come—which were held under police supervision, with ruthless discrimination against the Free party.

On November 15 Fethi launched a forcible attack in the Assembly on the Ministry of the Interior for these fraudulent practices. The debate grew so heated that it began to recall, in its atmosphere of personal abuse, those of the first Grand National Assembly. The Gazi in his President's box listened in silence throughout, with a look of some depression on his face. Were his people, after ten years of his tuition, still ignorant of the decencies of democratic debate? He displayed, however, a clear determination not to become involved in the discomfiture he had brought upon his friend; and at the end of the session the government received a vote of confidence by 225 votes to 10.

Fethi thus decided to dissolve the Free party. With Nuri, his secretary-general, he proceeded to Chankaya with a draft of the terms of its dissolution. It reiterated that the party had been sponsored by the Gazi and that this had ruled out any possibility of opposing him in person. But now that the prospect of doing so arose, its existence must be brought to an end.

Its failure was due partly to mismanagement. Fethi was not the ideal choice for the role which Kemal thrust upon him. Convinced democrat though he was, he lacked the gift of effective political leadership. He was neither a forceful speaker nor an astute debater. He had too few supporters of standing and could make little headway in the Assembly against the well-trained, well-entrenched professional legions of the People's party. For five years he had been out of the country and thus out of touch with the political and personal currents which underlay this Assembly, and with public opinion in general. His tactics, moreover, had been faulty. He would have had a better chance of success had he built up his party more gradually, trying it out tentatively as a small pressure group in the Assembly to act as a corrective to the party in power, as Rauf had at first done with the Progressives, instead of springing it suddenly on the country as a whole. His local organizations had been hastily and casually planned, becoming rallying points for a mixed collection of extremists and malcontents, and thus endangering public security.

But the main fault was in essence Kemal's. Unlike his previous adventures, that of a licensed Opposition had been inadequately thought out and prepared in advance. Instead of being allowed to grow organically, as the Republic itself had done—or had been made to seem to do—it had been abruptly, even capriciously launched upon an unsuspecting country. Such shock tactics as had served well enough for the abolition of the fez were inappropriate to so radical an operation as the introduction of parliamentary democracy, so soon after its deliberate suppression. Kemal had rejected the two-party system five years before, at a time when the momentum of the Revolution and the calibre of his Opposition leaders might have carried it through. He had tried to reimpose it when the momentum waned, at a time, not of military and political victory, but of social and economic depression. Only two factors could have given substance to the democratic form which he had thus failed to achieve: his own willingness to subscribe to it wholeheartedly and his readiness to relinquish some degree of his own power; and the capacity of the Turkish people, retarded as they had been by centuries of autocratic rule, to adapt themselves to so adult and responsible a system. Neither of these factors existed.

The debacle, however, had one good result. It showed that Ankara knew all too little of what was happening in the rest of Turkey. This, at least, could now be remedied. Immediately after the valedictory debate the Gazi set off on a three-month tour of the country, to find things out for himself.

He took with him a large personal staff, including officials from the various ministries. They made a detailed study of social and economic conditions, while Kemal himself conferred with local officials, inspected institutions of all kinds, questioned the people and encouraged them to talk to him of their problems in person. His objective was to translate the letter of reform into its spirit, to probe beneath such superficial symbols as changes in headgear and script to the fundamental mentality of his people.

Always the teacher, he examined quantities of pupils in the schools. He would stride into a classroom, often petrifying the teacher into silence by his presence, and wander around the class, questioning the students and scrutinizing their textbooks. In one of these, written by a young official of the Ministry of Education on his staff, Hassan Ali (Yücel), he detected some Arabic words and summoned the writer to dinner for a discussion on the reform of the language. He fired at his guest a number of questions on mathematics which, as the young man was careful to explain, was only incidentally his subject.

"What is a point? What is a line?" the Gazi asked him. Then, "What is zero?"

Hassan Ali, with his wits about him, replied, "It may best be defined, Pasha, as 'myself in your presence.'"

"But zero," Kemal insisted, "is important."

"So must I be, Pasha, if I am here in your presence."

Kemal filled Hassan Ali's glass with raki, and said aloud before the rest of the table, "You have passed your exam." He was later to be rewarded by many years' service as Minister of Education.

The Gazi made speeches in which he endeavoured to explain to the people the meaning of that incomprehensible word "democracy" and the responsibilities attached to it. In Izmir he said, "When a citizen says 'I want this, I want that,' it should mean 'I must do this or do that.'" Everywhere he took direct action on the spot, changing government and party officials, dismissing the executive committee of the People's party at Samsun, ordering seed for the farmers of Havza, calling for increased sugar production at Ushak, opening banks in various places.

His enquiries had revealed widespread discontent with living conditions in general—moreover, a discontent no longer accepted with the fatalism of the past. On the return of Kemal and his staff to Istanbul a report was prepared, summarizing their conclusions and recommending improvements in various fields. This helped to point the moral that any political reform, such as the Free party had embodied, must first be rooted in a policy of basic reforms in the social and economic lives of the people.

Another moral was pointed, six weeks after the dissolution of the Free party, by an ugly religious disturbance at Menemen, in the region of Ismir. It was staged, as the Kurdish revolt had been, by the fanatical Nakshibendi sect. A group of its extremists, led by a dervish chief, arrived in the town on a pilgrimage from Manisa. Exalted by a preparatory period of religious exercises and fasting, on a diminishing diet of figs and water—but with the occasional stimulus of drugs—they held forth as they marched to the peasantry, urging them to join their ranks and provide them with arms. The extremists gathered in the main square of the town where, in frenzied rhetorical tones, their leaders preached open sedition, demanding the return of the holy law, the veil, the fez, the Arabic script, prophesying the overthrow of the godless Republic by the militant forces of Islam, calling for an army of the faithful to march upon Ankara and thereafter to conquer the world.

The temper of the crowd, which soon massed around the marchers, was uncertain. Some were apathetic, some curious. The dormant fanaticism of others was roused by the words of the speakers. A young officer happened to pass through the square with a small group of soldiers. In an attempt to disperse the rioters, he ordered his men to fire a few rounds of blank ammunition. But when no one was wounded a *hoja* cried out, "You see, they have not been hit. They are saints." The officer then rashly tried to parley with the ringleader, Mehmed the Dervish. The dervish instantly shot the officer; then, as he lay bleeding to death on the ground, sent for a saw with which to cut off his head. This was tied to a flagpole and carried bleeding through the streets, while Mehmed's followers ran wild with fanatical invocations.

The gendarmerie, unable to handle the mob, called in the military. When they arrived the soldiers stood by, reluctant to fire on the holy men. But the officers, without any such scruples, turned their machine guns on the crowd. Several dervishes fell, and the outbreak was quelled without further serious trouble. Martial law was at once introduced, and arrests were made over a wide area, including the city of Izmir. More than a hundred persons were tried for inciting the population to sedition in an attempt to "alter the Constitution by force." Some were sentenced to death and some to spells of imprisonment.

The incident was given wide and lurid publicity in the newspapers. They found it convenient to imply that it was the fault of the Free party, which had in fact been disbanded six weeks before. They made a martyr of the murdered officer, extolling his heroism as an inspiration to Turkish youth and reporting demonstrations in his honour.

The riot showed that the brotherhoods, which had for centuries underlain not merely the religious but the social and political life of the country, had not been eliminated by a mere stroke of the Assembly's pen. Because the people needed them, they still survived beneath the surface, ready to erupt at the least provocation. For Kemal's religious reforms had not been allowed to grow organically, as new habits of life; they were ideas imposed artificially, from the top downwards. A generation or more must elapse before the people could be awakened to the true meaning of the Revolution which had been achieved in their name.

Meanwhile, if the Revolution was to be saved, there must be no further talk of democracy. Instead there must be a strengthening but at the same time a broadening of one-party rule. The "strong man" of the People's party henceforward was to be Rejep Peker, now appointed secretary-general. A ruthless but intelligent autocrat, his political philosophy envisaged a policy of change by "force and coercion," contrasting with Kemal's earlier "step by step" approach.

At the same time the party, which as Ismet publicly admitted had lost touch with the people, was reorganized to become a more flexible instrument, with an extension of responsible leadership at the top and a wider delegation of control lower down. A means of achieving closer touch was devised through the adaptation to a new form of the old Turkish Hearth. Once a cultural institution, it was now converted into a network of People's Houses, which soon proliferated throughout the country, serving also political purposes and helping to fulfil the role, imposed upon the party by Kemal, of "tutor to the nation."

The ideological message now preached to it was symbolized by the "Six Arrows" of what came to be called Kemalism, with the addition in 1931 of Statism and Revolutionism (or Reformism) to the four previous principles of Nationalism, Secularism, Republicanism, and Populism. Each was interlocked with the other—statism insuring through populism against exploitation; populism guaranteed against exploitation by secularism; all protected by nationalism against foreign aggression, and kept alive by the revolutionary dynamic.

Kemal had consistently opposed ideologies as limiting freedom of action. But, with the complexity of the problems which now lay ahead, defined doctrines were needed. With Fascism arising on one front and Communism on the other, it was important for the Turks to show the world that they wanted neither of them. Hence the more flexible ideology of Kemalism, whose principles at least had the merit of being forged not from preconceived theories but from the hard school of ten years' practical experience.

In terms of statism the government now embarked on a Five Year Plan for the increased development of state-financed industries. This was inspired by the precedent of Soviet Russia and aided by Russian machinery and an interest-free loan. But Kemal was zealous to point out that statism was based on no socialist theory. Communism, he maintained, had failed to achieve its aims and promises. Liberalism too was dead.

Turkish statism was to be something different from either, leavening state control with a certain element of personal enterprise.

Whether it achieved the best or the worst of both worlds, it at least gave the country useful industrial enterprises. Where it still failed was in its persistent neglect of agriculture, the country's most valuable natural asset. It was not until a Second World War began to cloud the horizon that the urgent need was expressed for an agricultural policy "based on serious studies," and within the grasp of all peasants, none of whom must now be left without land.

The new economic policy brought to the fore a new political figure. He was Celal (Bayar),[3] a former Unionist with a crafty mind, who had become a respectful adherent of Kemal. Once a bank clerk in Smyrna, he had been employed by the Gazi to organize the banking system of the Republic. "I gave him a bag of gold," Kemal would say of him, "and he gave me a bank." Celal was now to become Kemal's Minister of Economy. Henceforward Kemal left economic policy, in which he had never been seriously interested, to Bayar. It was to foreign policy that he now devoted his principal personal attention.

[3] Mahmud Jelal.

56 ► *Turkey's place in the world*

Frustrated in his hope of presenting to the Western world a new Turkey shaped in its own democratic image, Kemal was nonetheless determined on her acceptance within it as a free and responsible sovereign power. There must be concrete proofs of his own international statesmanship. The conception of the one-party dictatorship was nothing new to the Europe of the 1930s. What was new, and what Turkey must now manifest to her neighbours, was the existence in the world of a one-party "dictatorship" which, unlike those of Hitler and Mussolini and Stalin, was essentially pacific, nourishing no territorial or political ambitions at any other country's expense.

Peaceful co-existence, "Peace at home and peace abroad," were Kemal's watchwords. The Turks were the friends of all civilized nations. The hatchets of the past, with its lust for conquest, were buried. The Turkish mind harboured no thoughts of reconquest or revision of frontiers.[1] As

[1] Once, to a Hungarian diplomat bemoaning the fate of his former empire, Kemal showed marked lack of sympathy. "But *you* have no children," the Hungarian protested. "All the Turkish people are my children," Kemal replied. Then he said, "Listen to me." "Yes, sir." "I am a Macedonian. But I make no territorial claims."

Kemal's Foreign Minister defined his country's policy, "Turkey does not desire an inch of foreign territory, but will not give up an inch of what she holds." [2]

Of all the dictatorial regimes, that of Turkey had been alone in basing itself on a policy not of expansion but of retraction. As far back as 1921 Kemal had been saying, "Let us recognize our own limits." By keeping Turkey small he would make her great. The Turkish Republic desired only its territorial integrity and freedom. As long as the West respected this, Turkey in return would offer the West a zone of peace in an explosive corner of the East. The new sovereign Republic, geographically poised between East and West, was to be a stabilizing element.

Thus there were to be pacts both with Russia and her neighbours and with the European powers, both with the Arab and with the Balkan worlds, the former provinces of the Ottoman Empire. Above all there was to be loyal and unquestioning co-operation with the League of Nations. As a revolutionary power, Turkey would be doubly scrupulous in honouring her engagements, seeking a name for giving never less but sometimes more than she promised. Reconciliation with Britain had been achieved with the Mosul agreement. It now remained to complete the reconciliation with Greece.

The surgical operation of the exchange of populations agreed between Turkey and Greece at Lausanne led to a pact of friendship between the two countries, which settled their outstanding problems in a common-sense fashion. It was followed, in October 1930, by an official visit by Venizelos to Turkey on board a Greek warship. His welcome in Ankara was well organized, with Greek flags flying and inscribed Greek banners stretched across the street. But it was not quite spontaneous enough for the exuberant Greek Premier, who could not help remarking to Ismet that a Turkish athletic team had been more warmly received in Athens. To this Ismet replied amicably that the Greeks were the more effervescent people. Moreover, their territory had not been invaded, like that of the Turks.

There was a grand ball at the Ankara Palace Hotel, to celebrate the happy coincidence of Venizelos' visit with the anniversary of the Turkish Republic, a banquet at the Ministry of Foreign Affairs at which the Gazi showed evident enjoyment, and a military parade which they attended together. In their political talks, official and otherwise, Kemal and Venizelos understood one another, and Venizelos went so far as to throw out the imaginative idea of some kind of union between the two coun-

[2] J. Walter Collins, *Contemporary Review*, XIV (London, 1933).

tries, which was discussed at some length. It was not long afterwards that Kemal, burying religious with political hatchets, authorized the conversion of Santa Sophia, which had been a mosque for five hundred years, not indeed back into a church, hung again with bells as the Greeks had for long hoped, but into a museum and a symbol of cultural affinity between Turkey and Europe.

The Turco-Greek pact had been preceded by a Turco-Italian pact which, as the thirties wore on and the imperialist aims of Mussolini became clearer, acquired the character of a defensive alignment against him. The Gazi, who had discarded military uniform to become a civilian dictator, had no great respect for the Duce, whom he saw as a civilian strutting about in uniform like an actor pretending to be a soldier. Mussolini, he judged, would sooner or later be unable to resist playing the role of a conquering Caesar. To a friend Kemal predicted, "He will be hanged by his people, one of these days." Once at Chankaya, where Mussolini's ambassador was pressing the renewed claims of his country to the Antalya (Adalia) region, Kemal listened in silence, then excused himself for a few minutes and left the room. He returned wearing, for the first time since the proclamation of the Republic, full-dress field marshal's uniform. Without comment he sat down and said, "Now go ahead, please." But this time it was the ambassador who was silent. Rejep Peker, on the other hand, Kemal's party boss, submitted a report to him after a visit to Italy, in which he praised the Fascist system and proposed, in some detail, a similar form of government for Turkey. Kemal glanced at the report and handed it back with the remark, "You'll do all that after I die."

As for the Hitler regime, Kemal approved the dictum of an anti-Nazi German friend that, whereas his own dictatorship had freed an enslaved people, Hitler's had enslaved a free people. Kemal described the German dictator as a tin peddler, and after reading *Mein Kampf* expressed horror at "the meanness of his language and the madness of his thoughts." Thus the Germans got no political change out of a long-term financial credit and the supply of railway materials under the Turkish Five Year Plan.

But of Stalin, the supreme realist, Kemal declared that in a hundred years' time, "when the fame of all other dictators will have vanished," history would single him out as the most important international statesman of the twentieth century. This respect for Stalin made him the more vigilant in his relations with Soviet Russia—signing agreements which were essentially commercial, resisting all Russian blandishments of a political kind, maintaining a polite friendship but refusing to be weaned away from his closer relations with the West.

The rise of Mussolini and Hitler drew Turkey closer not merely to Greece but to the other Balkan countries. Already she had agreements with Yugoslavia, Hungary, and Bulgaria. What she now sought was a Balkan Entente, as a counterweight to Italian and German imperialism. With this object meetings were held between Turkey and the five Balkan states in their various capitals, until a Balkan Pact was signed early in 1934. It was an incomplete and precarious combination, affording its member states guarantees rather within their own ranks than against the aggression of a great power. But it helped to give Turkey a reputation for international leadership. The Comte de Chambrun, the French ambassador, when the Gazi talked to him of his plans for thus uniting his neighbours, remarked, "You talk just as Monsieur Briand does."

"That's because I think as Monsieur Briand does," was Kemal's reply. What he was trying to do was to set up, as it were, his own regional "League of Nations."

One evening, after dining officially at a Western embassy for the first time as the guest of the British, in honour of Princess Alice and Lord Athlone, Kemal gathered around him a circle of foreign representatives and lectured them on the need for peace between nations. Of the Russian, the Rumanian, and the Czech he demanded, "Why can't you gentlemen settle your differences amicably instead of always quarrelling about territorial and other questions?" There was an embarrassed silence, which was broken after a moment by Lord Athlone. "Your Excellency," he suggested, "the trouble is that nations still distrust each other." At this observation the Gazi exclaimed, "Bravo! Bravo!" The party then proceeded to the poker table.

King Alexander of Yugoslavia, in the course of an informal visit to Istanbul, developed a hero-worship for the Gazi and expressed readiness as a soldier to obey him in the event of a war. After dining with him Alexander voiced an ardent desire for his friendship, and confided that, had he believed the promises of certain European countries, it would have been the Yugoslavs instead of the Greeks who landed in Anatolia. To this the Gazi replied, "Then you had a narrow escape, Your Majesty. Instead of the Greeks it would have been the Yugoslav Army which would have been thrown back into the Mediterranean." Kemal despatched a decorative symbol of good will to the Balkans in the shape of his adopted daughter Sabiha, who had graduated as the first woman pilot in Turkey, and who flew a new American bomber on a Balkan tour.

The former enemies of Turkey in the Balkan Wars were now, ostensibly, her friends. Her Western frontiers were reasonably secure. So were her frontiers with Russia. It now remained to secure those other eastern frontiers, with Russia's neighbours and with the former Arab provinces of the Ottoman Empire. The Balkan Pact must be supplemented by an Eastern Pact. A start had been made ten years before, with the aid of Soviet diplomacy, by a treaty with Afghanistan. A treaty with Persia proved harder to negotiate, on account of frontier disagreements in the Kurdish areas and religious hostility in Persia to the abolition of the Caliphate. These differences, however, were now forgotten and a treaty of friendship with Persia was followed, in 1934, by an official visit of the Shah to Turkey.

Riza Shah had a personal admiration for Kemal, as a soldier and states-man, which overrode their marked differences of temperament. He shared Kemal's views as to the vital need for a good-neighbour policy between their two countries. The negotiations for the settlement of the Turco-Persian frontier, along the foot of Mount Ararat, had threatened to break down over a small but vital hill, which each side claimed was essential to its own strategic security. But the good will of the two rulers broke the deadlock. Tevfik Rüştü, negotiating in Tehran, bewildered the Persians by calling, on the Gazi's instructions, for the arbitration of the Shah himself. A senior staff officer brought maps to the Shah and spread them out before him, to put the Persian case. Presently, however, he real-ized that his master was not paying attention and was looking not at the maps but at himself. The Shah interrupted the officer, saying, "There is only one thing I am interested in. That is friendly relations with Turkey." The result was a face-saving agreement, to the advantage of the Turks, which drew the frontier along the ridge of the hill.

In his personality the Shah was the antithesis of the Gazi—a strait-laced, taciturn man. But he was familiar with the Turkish dialect of Azerbaijan, where he had served as a soldier, and brushed it up to talk the better with his host. He greeted the Gazi as "My Brother." His first evening at Chankaya ran true to Kemal's late habits. The guests did not sit down to dinner till nine-thirty. At ten o'clock precisely, after finishing only his first course, the Shah, liking to retire and to rise early, took his leave. Kemal escorted him back to the house where he was staying, then re-joined the guests, whose dinner had cooled in the meantime. The eve-ning soon took on a more convivial air.

The Shah preferred poker to polite conversation. One evening he played a game at the Persian Embassy with the Gazi and Sir Percy Lo-raine, the new British ambassador, to whom Kemal had taken a strong fancy. He and Sir Percy had played together before. On that occasion, when the game finished in the small hours, they had talked together frankly and intimately until long after dawn, about all outstanding Turco-British and Mediterranean problems, thus establishing a personal relationship which was greatly to benefit the two countries and indeed their allies as well.

Now Kemal, after taking a hand, left the poker table to wander around the room, but returned to stand behind the Shah and to give him advice as to how to bid against Sir Percy, while guests stood around, surveying the scene with some curiosity. They took especial notice when the Gazi remarked to Loraine, with a twinkle, upon the blessings of such close international co-operation. "We are good adversaries," he said. "How much better shall we be as allies!"

During his visit the Shah made a tour of western Anatolia with the Gazi, visiting the air base at Eskishehir and the battlefields and forts of the Dardanelles. As soldiers the two found much in common. In other respects their differing habits led to some awkward moments. On the presidential train Kemal drank freely. When they reached Ushak, on the line to Izmir, a large crowd swarmed around the train, kissing the hands of the two heads of state. Among them was a *hoja,* in turban and robes. On seeing him the Gazi started to growl insults at Islam.[3] The *hoja* deftly removed his turban, dived into the crowd, and escaped. But Kemal, before proceeding, ordered the imprisonment of the local governor and instructed that the town of Ushak be bombarded and razed to the ground the next day. Next day, when the order was submitted to him for confirmation, he shamefacedly cancelled it.

Before the Shah left for Persia the Gazi, taking him on a farewell visit to the army, paid his guest a compliment. "If ever," he said, "I cease to be head of the Turkish state, I trust that Your Majesty will permit me to serve, with these other officers, as a member of your staff."

The remaining link still to be forged in the chain of Eastern defence was with Irak. Britain granted the country self-government in 1930, and soon afterwards King Feisal paid a visit to Ankara, in which Turco-Arab differences were settled, with the benediction of the British, in a round of diplomatic entertainments. During a talk at a reception in

[3] The Gazi, in such moods, was inclined to "see red" when confronted with a fez or a turban. At a reception in Ankara one evening his eye lighted on the fez of the Egyptian ambassador. The Gazi sent a waiter with a salver for the fez, remarking, "Tell your King I don't like his uniform." To avoid an incident the ambassador removed the fez and took his leave. When the news of the episode reached Cairo, King Fuad was furious, and a break in relations with Turkey was only avoided by tactful diplomacy on both sides.

which the King lowered his voice lest others should hear, Kemal interrupted him and said with an amicable nod towards the British ambassador, "There is no need to whisper. The ambassador will know it all in any case tomorrow."

When similar relations had been achieved between Irak and Persia, Kemal at last had his Saadabad Pact in the East to balance his Balkan Pact in the West. Neither pact was to amount in effect to much more than a pious expression of good will. But both at least advertised, to the rest of the world, the change from aggressive to pacific intentions inherent in the demise of the Ottoman Empire and the rise of the Turkish Republic.

Kemal, surveying the world around him with his perceptive international vision, saw clearly the way it was heading. With General Douglas MacArthur, who visited him in 1934, he had several conversations in which he prophesied its course with uncanny insight. The period in which they were living, he believed, was no more than an armistice. For the Allies had made a conqueror's peace, without regard for the root causes of the war or the characteristics and problems of the nations defeated; the Americans had withdrawn from Europe, abandoning the Wilson policy and so preventing the armistice from becoming a peace; the Germans thus held the fate of Europe in their hands, as before. "The moment these seventy million people," Kemal said, "who are industrious and disciplined and have extraordinary dynamism, get caught by a new political element which will stir up their nationalist ambitions, they will have recourse to the liquidation of the Versailles Treaty."

The war, he predicted, would break out between 1940 and 1945. The French no longer had the qualities which made for a strong army, and the British would be unable to rely on them for the defence of their island. The Italians, if they kept out of the war, could play an important part in the peace which followed it. But Mussolini's ambitions would prevent them from doing so. Thus the Germans would occupy all Europe except Russia and Britain. The Americans would be unable to remain neutral, and their intervention would cause Germany's defeat. But the real victors would be the Bolsheviks, with their use of new political methods unknown to the Europeans and Americans, and their capacity for taking advantage of the slightest mistakes made by their rivals:

We turks, as Russia's close neighbour and the nation which has fought more wars against her than any other country, are following closely the course of events there, and see the danger stripped of all camouflage. The Bolsheviks are exploiting with marvellous skill the minds of the awakening nations of the East, and know how to caress and to flatter their nationalistic ambitions and to stir up their masses. The Bolsheviks have now reached a point at which they constitute the greatest threat not only to Europe but to all Asia.[4]

Kemal was a nationalist; but there was nothing parochial in his nationalism. He saw that the day of empires was done and that the day of nations had arrived. But with his global sense he saw beyond this conception towards that of a federation of nations, an amalgamation of sovereignties such as Wells envisaged in his United States of the World. Although he was attracted by the idea that a number of individual federations might precede something of the kind, he was too much of a realist to believe that such an apotheosis could readily be achieved. But he saw that Russia would seek to achieve it in terms of the Communist ideology, and that the principle of internationalism would animate the second half of the twentieth century as that of nationalism was animating its first half. Meanwhile the welfare of nations was interdependent:

We must think of the whole of mankind as being a single body and of each nation as constituting a part of that body. . . . We must not say, "If there is sickness in a certain place in the world, what does that matter to me?" . . . If there is such sickness, we must be just as much concerned with it as though it happened right in our midst.

[4] Washington correspondent of Ankara *Cumhuriyet*, November 8, 1951.

57 ▶ *A new language and history*

When the Balkan powers first conferred in Ankara to seek a basis of unity among themselves, the Gazi assured the delegates, in an opening discourse, that their various ancestors derived from Central Asia: "Coming by routes to the north and to the south of the Black Sea, following one after the other, like the waves of the ocean, for thousands of years, these streams of humanity which settled in the Balkans—in spite of the fact that their groups carried quite different names—are in reality kindred peoples who come from a common cradle and in whose veins circulates the same blood."

This idea was but one manifestation of the new theories which were obtaining a strong hold over Kemal's mind—if not always to the exclusion, then sometimes to the distortion, of other and more important problems. His reform of the Turkish alphabet was leading, logically enough, to a reform of the Turkish language, in terms of the elimination of Persian and Arabic forms. Less logically, this was accompanied by researches designed to discover a new version of Turkish history. For these two purposes Kemal founded two learned bodies, the Turkish Linguistic Society and the Turkish Historical Society.

Kemal's own cultural background was scrappy. He had studied subjects *ad hoc,* in periodic bursts of concentration—skimming through them, on occasion, to rationalize some intuitive preconceived notion. But he had never acquired the habit of systematic reading. He knew much of the military and a little of the political sciences. The science of linguistics, to which he now turned his restless attention, was distinctly beyond his range. But with his quick impatient mind he was adept at picking the brains of others, and this he now did voraciously. Summoning around him all the linguistic specialists he could muster, he soon had forcible views to express on a reform of the Turkish language designed to bring out its "genuine beauty and richness" and "elevate it to the high rank it deserves among world languages." [1]

The views of these experts reflected two schools of thought. There were those who favoured merely the simplification of the language, as mooted twenty years earlier—the elimination only of those Persian and Arabic words for which a Turkish equivalent could be found. There were those, on the other hand, who favoured purification—the elimination of all Persian and Arabic words and the coining of new Turkish words to replace them. Kemal himself was a purifier.

The seat of the annual deliberations of the Linguistic Society was the ornate throne room of the Dolma Bahche Palace. Those present at the inaugural meeting numbered a thousand, the hall was wired for radio, and Kemal's speech was broadcast through loudspeakers to the public squares of all the main towns in the country. The delegates ranged from lexicographers of international reputation to a village schoolteacher who had prepared a dictionary of a remote Anatolian dialect, and an Armenian from Sofia whose articles on language had caught the Gazi's attention.

From now onwards Kemal spent much of his time surrounded by piles of dictionaries, old and new, searching for "pure Turkish words" or trying to trace some philological link between Turkish and foreign words. In pursuit of purification the whole public was invited to co-operate in the suggestion of Turkish equivalents for lists of words published daily in the press. The Gazi would try out in his speeches new and incomprehensible words, to the bewilderment of his audience, while Falih Rifki, hero-worshipper though he was, would "writhe with fury" at the sound of them and "helplessly ask myself how he could possibly bring himself to perpetrate so heinous a crime." Those anxious to gain favour found themselves avoiding in his presence the use of essential everyday terms

[1] The object, as Dr. Adnan defined it, was to free the Turkish language from the "linguistic capitulations of Arabic and Persian."

simply because their origin was Arabic or Persian, while others tried to please him by learning new words and dragging them into the conversation.

At one moment Kemal was seduced by the theory of the "Sun Language," thrown out by a Viennese philologist. According to this, primitive man uttered his first sounds, which evolved into words, in response to the awe induced in him by the sun. Attempts to link them to Aryan and Semitic roots had failed. But now the link was discernible in the Turkish language, which might thus be the "mother of all languages." Kemal at once ordered the Sun Language theory to be taught in the new Faculty of Letters in Ankara, and sponsored the publication of a quantity of literature on the subject. It had the obvious advantage, for the linguistic reformers, that all Arabic, Persian, Latin, and other words in the Turkish language could now be ascribed to a Turkish source, hence might continue to be used with impunity. But the theory came in for sharp criticism from more serious scholars and was eventually dropped, to the discredit in Kemal's eyes of those experts whom he had encouraged to develop it.

In time he realized that his linguistic operations were leading the Turkish language into a blind alley. It threatened to become a mandarin language as artificial and incomprehensible to the ordinary Turk as that of the old Ottoman ruling class. A halt was finally called when he was presented with the draft of a speech for his delivery at the annual opening of the Grand National Assembly, and realized that it would seem to the deputies to be couched in a foreign tongue. Thus the policy of purification was abandoned and the principle adopted that words need no longer be sacrificed simply because their origins appeared to be foreign. Henceforward, if no Turkish equivalent for a foreign word could be found it was "naturalized" and permitted to remain in the language. The Turks thus found themselves with a reformed language which closed the gap between the written and the spoken word and was comprehensible to any Turk who had learnt his ABCs. This, more perhaps than any of Kemal's other reforms, made them conscious of their "Turkishness."[2]

[2] On the other hand, a number of new European words were clumsily and often unnecessarily inflicted upon the language, so that today the Information Bureau at the Izmir International Fair becomes the Enternasyonal Fuari Enformasyon Bürosu, while the Turkish betting man goes to a *konkuripik* in the hope of becoming a *ganyan*. The phraseology, however, was so simplified that the republican civil servant will now write, "I have been thinking about your suggestion," where his imperial predecessor would have written, "Your slave has been engaged in the exer-

··

These researches ran parallel with those designed to investigate the history of Turkey and the Turks. One morning the Gazi's private secretary, Hassan Riza, returned to Chankaya from Istanbul, expecting to find his master still asleep, for he knew his employer's habits—late to bed and late to rise. Usually when Kemal awoke, sitting cross-legged in his nightshirt in the oriental posture, drinking a cup of black Turkish coffee and smoking his first cigarette, he would send for his secretary and discuss with him the business of the day, confirming or more often countermanding the orders he had given the night before. For he subscribed to the Sultan's old adage, "A *firman* issued while drinking must never be executed in sobriety." Then he would be shaved by his barber, who lived on the premises, take his bath and perhaps a massage, dress fastidiously, and sit down to work, at which he seldom followed a regular routine.

But this morning was different. The secretary was told that the Gazi had not been to bed at all for two nights. For forty hours at a stretch he had been reading, drinking only black coffee and taking hot baths at intervals. Hassan Riza found him in his library, wearing a dressing gown over the habitual nightshirt, as he pored over a book. He was wide awake, he insisted. But his eyes looked tired, and he was dabbing them at intervals with strips of fine linen. The book he was reading was H. G. Wells's *Outline of History*.

It was to become for him a book of revelation. As soon as he had finished it he gave orders for its translation into Turkish, and its publication by the Turkish government a year or so later was followed by that of an *Outline of Turkish History,* on similar lines. Wells became Kemal's principal hero, and the Gazi was soon quoting long passages from his work at the table. He was a great historian and prophet; he was Britain's "master thinker." He opened Kemal's eyes to a new view of history.

What Kemal was seeking to do, in making a nation of Turkey, was to wean his people away from their old sense of identity with the supranational "fatherland" of Islam and to create for them a new allegiance to their own national fatherland. One of his problems was to link this in their minds with a past which fitted the history of Turkey into that of the world as a whole, thus eliminating the conflict, which forever possessed him, between East and West, and to lead them towards that

---

cise of cogitation in respect of the proposals vouchsafed by your exalted person." G. L. Lewis, *Turkey*.

"civilization" to which in his own mind only the West belonged. Wells, with his theories of the common origins of mankind, showed him the way, and it remained to fit the history of the Turkish race into some such universal context.

Thus in 1932 he convened, under the auspices of his society, a Turkish Historical Congress in Ankara, attended by professors and teachers of history from all parts of Turkey, and by scholars and other delegates from abroad. Its task was to carry out research with a view to "proving" the theory that the Turks were a white Aryan race, originating in Central Asia, the cradle of human civilization. As their lands progressively dried up they moved westwards, migrating in waves to various parts of Asia and Africa and carrying their civilization with them. Anatolia had thus been a Turkish land since remote antiquity. By teaching the Turks this Kemal hoped to give them that sense of unity between land and race which creates a spirit of patriotism in the Western sense.

Such was his objective political aim. But there was behind it also a subjective personal impulse. As he grew older and his work neared its end, Kemal needed a mystique of his own. One side of him was the man of action, the saviour and reformer of his country—a concrete image, visible and comprehensible to all. But there was another, inner side of him, that of the solitary, turning from action to speculation as he rode over the hills of Chankaya or strode through the groves of his farm before sundown, his dog following behind him, his shoulders stooping and his hands in his pockets. This was the more nebulous image of a man alone with his thoughts. There were times when the frontiers of Anatolia and the confines of his daily life, now so inactive, seemed to imprison his spirit. As food for his imagination he needed something more than the mundane tasks of government; the brutish nature of his people, bound to their arid somnolent steppes; the limited company of his own entourage—the yes-men who were his slaves, the so-called intellectuals who nonetheless heeded no one but him.

A man without human ties, he found love only in an atavistic feeling for the land that had nourished him. A man without spiritual beliefs, he nevertheless felt the need to identify himself with something outside and beyond himself. Who was he and whence did he come? The answer was perhaps to be found in the history, stretching back to an age before man was troubled by religions, of a race—*his* race—spreading its various branches from the homeland of humanity itself over all parts of the world.

Turks, as depicted by Kemal to the American Ambassador Sherrill, "early gained the qualities of the eagle—far of vision, swift of flight and strong of body to house that spirit. Restless within any restricting environment, whether of things physical or mental, it revolted against the isolation of that high central birthplace." It caused them to speed over the earth, creating conflict and crisis, fighting and mingling with other racial groups—all from the same root—but forever bestowing upon them the benefits of the Turks' own special civilization. They were, in short, the fathers of the civilized world.[3]

Such paradoxically were the daydreams of a mind hitherto remarkable in its attention to objective truth, whether it was assessing the facts of a military or of a political situation; a mind highly sceptical of such unrealistic concepts as racial expansion and the wishful-thinking emotions which prompted them. Turning as it now did from action to speculation, in fields unfamiliar to it, governed by an obstinate need to believe what it wanted to believe, Kemal's mind began to lose itself in a labyrinth of those truths tangled with errors and half-truths which beset the untrained intellect. More and more did he now surround himself with a court of experts, so-called experts, charlatans, and cranks in the sciences of history, archaeology, anthropology, phrenology, etymology, and philology, all propounding their pet theories and trotting out their pet works for his edification.

The table at Chankaya now became a seminar, a "brains trust" for the study and discussion of these problems of language and history—with occasional excursions into music and poetry. On the more formal occasions, when women were present, a European orchestra often played. For this spelled progress, civilization. Kemal had banned from Ankara Radio the "whining and wailing" of Turkish music, which he personally preferred. On less formal evenings there would be a Turkish orchestra and often Kemal sang to it himself in an undertone, with an adequate grasp of the quarter-tone scale of those Rumeli folk tunes of his childhood. When a foreign gramophone company presented him with a recording machine for his speeches, he often sang into it, listening afterwards with pleasure to the sound of his voice and expecting his friends to do the same.[4]

[3] Ambassador Grew was once asked whether there did not exist some book showing the influence of Turkish civilization on the American Indians. A British diplomat was startled by Kemal's statement that Kent was a Turkish name, and its existence in the country a proof that the Turks had conquered Britain, while an Irish colleague was dubbed a Turk on the grounds that all words with the prefix "ir" were of Turkish origin.
[4] The cleavage in his musical tastes emerged in Istanbul, where he once had two orchestras, one Turkish and one European, brought to the Park Hotel. He listened

When an evening was devoted to poetry, some famous poet like Yahya Kemal would read his poems aloud—with perhaps those of Victor Hugo thrown in for good measure. The Gazi liked to supplement these recitals himself with remembered quotations from the nineteenth-century Turkish poets. His respect for poets survived even a scene one evening when one of the moderns, Nazim Hikmet, on being asked to recite, replied rebelliously, "I am not a cabaret singer," and left the table. At this Kemal expressed a regret without rancour, since he had genuinely wanted to talk to the young man of his art.

Whatever the company, there was a certain ritual about these evenings at Chankaya. Meticulous in his habits, the Gazi liked the table to be properly set, and would often adjust cloth or cutlery before sitting down. The guests sat where they chose, only the most important being allotted their places. When they were seated the drink began to circulate. It was usually raki, with a roughage of nuts to help digest the alcohol, and appetizers of chick-peas, olives, and white sheep's cheese. Unless the occasion was formal the drinking often continued for an hour or so before any solid food was served; and even then the host, if he were not yet hungry, might send it away, so that when it came back reheated, perhaps around midnight, it had lost much of its savour. Kemal took no interest in food, eating what came, with a preference for such plain peasant dishes as dried beans and pilav, to which he had grown used in his campaigns but which disagreed with his stomach. He ate little during the day but liked eggs at all times. All he needed of life, he liked to say, was "a piece of bread and to be able to eat and drink with friends." With these friends, old and new, most evenings were now devoted to serious debate. The proverbial blackboard, with its chalk and its mop, stood permanently at the end of the room and was in frequent use, both by the Gazi himself, never wearying, and by guests trying hard to disguise their weariness as the night wore on.

Kemal, the dictator turned educator, treated his guests like a class, interrogating them one after the other around the table—and learning from them as much as he taught them. All were expected to express their views, which some did with more circumspection than others. He dis-

---

with constant interruptions, commanding one to stop and the other to play in turn. Finally, as the raki took effect, he lost patience and rose to leave the restaurant, saying, "Now if you like you can both play together." Another evening, incensed by the sound of the muezzin from a mosque opposite, which clashed with the dance band, he ordered its minaret to be felled—one of those orders which was countermanded next morning.

liked blind agreement and preferred guests who argued with him, if only for the satisfaction of battling with them and battering them into submission. He enjoyed dialectic, however tedious and pedantic it might become, and would persevere until dawn, despite the entreaties of an aide to spare himself the trouble, to convince by his powers of logic an obstinate if negligible adversary. Nor, if the talk got out of hand and Kemal out of temper, would he bear a grudge against a man who disagreed with him at table. He was too confident in his own superiority to mind the lapses of lesser creatures.

One of his methods was to set a guest an essay at dinner and make him read it aloud the following week. A historian was once interrupted in the midst of his recital and afterwards kept back when the "class" was dispersed. Kemal took the man to his study and dictated the essay as he wanted it to be. At the next session the guest read it out, to receive praise from the Gazi and applause from the rest of the company.

Kemal's gift was for synthesis. Looking around his table with those cold appraising eyes that saw two ways at once, he could listen, even when talking, to several conversations, suddenly intervening to pounce on some point he had overheard. He plucked at ideas, pieced them together, and summed them up to propound a thesis which all must accept. But now, leaving the field of politics for the deeper waters of scholarship, he found the synthesis less easy to achieve. In the historical domain it was eventually to be achieved by others, providing the Turks with a history which at once fed their natural pride and approximated, so far as it could be known, to the truth.

Of his feminist reforms the personal symbol had been Latife. For his cultural reforms he found a new personal symbol. What the country needed above all at this time was teachers. It was thus to their recruitment and training that, in his tours throughout the country, he devoted his main efforts of persuasion. On one such visit to Izmir he met a young woman named Afet, who had completed her schooling and now aspired to graduate as a teacher. She was fresh-looking, with a pleasing expression, and Kemal took a fancy to her responsive ways and her nicely rounded feminine form. She had no parents to look after her, so he offered to adopt her, accepting responsibility for the completion of her education and her subsequent professional career. The offer was gratefully accepted.

For Kemal there was nothing unusual in such a step. Once or twice before he had adopted children—usually war orphans encountered on his campaigns, who were handed over to his mother to bring up and educate. Two small girls, named respectively Zehra and Rukiye, already lived in his house at Chankaya, adopted one from an orphanage and the other from an impoverished family, at the time of his childless marriage to Latife. A third was the aforementioned Sabiha, a fair, lively, and intelligent child. These three were now joined by Afet and a little later by a fifth, Nebile, a slim dark girl with blue-green eyes who had once been a maid in his house.

Adolescents attracted and interested him, and when the girls reached the age at which they sat regularly at table he began to take notice of both their charms and their talents. None of them was exceptionally pretty; nor had they the graces of women of the world. But they provided him with the ideal "harem." They were in his power, thanks to their youth and their dependence on him. He could groom them and mould them and guide them in the direction he wanted them to follow. He could use them as he chose—and, when he no longer chose, could "wean" them and launch them into marriage or into a career. For the girls themselves, so ambivalent a father-lover-schoolmaster relationship might create certain psychological stresses. But for Kemal it provided the family background he needed, one from which irksome ties of blood were missing, and in which wife and children became in effect one.[5]

The position of Afet, who was to become a professor of history, was different from that of the rest. She was no longer a child when Kemal first "adopted" her, but a girl on the threshold of maturity. Gradually, from then onwards, she became what a wife might have been to him. She was homely, good-natured, undemanding, serious-minded. She kept house for him. She sat at the head of his table. She appeared with him in public, causing problems of protocol to foreign ambassadors. As "Her Master's Voice" she assiduously recorded his ideas, taking pains to interpret them in the counsels of the Turkish Historical Society and of the various organizations for social reform. Above all she gave him restful companionship.[6] Thus the domestic hiatus which had prevailed at Chankaya since Latife's departure was closed, and Kemal entered on his fifties still a bachelor, but not wholly deprived of a private life.

[5] On several occasions he adopted young boys, paying for their education and installing them in jobs. But they did not live with him at Chankaya, as the girls did. Rukiye and Nebile married respectively an officer and a diplomat, with Kemal's blessing. Zehra was unhappily killed, falling from a train in France, while studying abroad.
[6] She remained with him till his death, not herself marrying until afterwards, and is known today as Dr. Afetinan. (See Bibliography.)

Early in 1935, while economic problems multiplied at home and the
threat of Axis aggression darkened the horizon abroad, Kemal introduced two last measures of Westernization. Already the old Turkish
calendar, based on Christian months and an Islamic year, had given place
to the complete Gregorian calendar of the Christian Era. From this it
was a natural step to the abolition of the Moslem Friday and its replacement as a day of rest by the Christian Sunday. Thus the Western weekend, regardless of its infidel implications, became an integral feature of
the life of the ordinary Turk.[1]

More important, he was now instructed by law to follow Western practice by adopting a surname. Hitherto the Turks, like the Arabs and
other Moslems, had not used family names. A man was known by his
birth name and perhaps that of his father—Ahmed son of Mehmed,
for example, was a normal designation, despite the confusion caused
everywhere by its multiplication. But from now onwards all must have

[1] This measure was combined with the adoption of the twenty-four-hour international clock.

family names, and Kemal amused himself at the table by conferring suitable patronymics on his friends. Ismet became Inönü, after the site of his victory; Tevfik Rüştü added Aras, the name of the river defining the frontier which he had negotiated between Turkey and Persia; Celal (Mahmud Jelal), the Minister of Economics, was dubbed Bayar, or "Sublime." Fethi had chosen a name in consultation with his family but was obliged by Kemal to abandon it for Okyar, a "spiritual companion." Sabiha, the air pilot, was given the name Gökçen—"of the skies." At the same time the old titles of Pasha, Effendi, Bey, and Hanum (Lady), following the name, were officially abolished and replaced by plain Bay and Bayan (Mr. and Mrs.) preceding it. The President of the Republic himself renounced the titles of Gazi and Pasha,[2] and chose a name, as no ruler of his race had done before him, which displayed pride in his Turkish origins. He became Atatürk, or Father Turk, dropping the Arab name of Mustafa and signing himself Kemal Atatürk.

Atatürk was indeed the father of the Turks. The Turkey which now existed on the map, a compact whole salvaged from the wide-strewn fragments of the Ottoman Empire, was his creation. But for him it might have been reduced to a mere fragment itself, enclosed by the empires of others and perhaps eventually absorbed as a satellite by one of them. He had made of it a nation, reviving its patriotism and restoring its self-respect. He had given it a durable political system. From among its people he was moulding a new type of Turk, fitting him by education and example to rank with the peoples of Europe, releasing him from a dead past to seek a place for his country in contemporary civilization.

Atatürk had above all created a legend. In a land needing heroes his mystique was such that a child, blessed by his handshake, would for weeks leave his hand unwashed, lest the virtue depart from it; an old peasant woman, once asked what her age was, replied, "Seventeen," for her life had begun only when she first saw him with her eyes during the War of Independence. For the youth of his country his words were to become a gospel and his deeds a mythology, destined to point and illuminate the national ideal for perhaps generations to come. Meanwhile both words and deeds inspired youth with the sense of a new, challenging life in the present and new foundations on which to build for the future. All this, within little more than a decade, had this modern "Cromwell of

[2] The title of Pasha, however, died hard. One evening Atatürk rounded on a minister and scolded him for using it: "You will please not call me Pasha any more. Is that clear?" To which the minister replied, "I promise not to do it again, Pasha."

the Near East" (as an English writer[3] was to describe him) achieved—through a fanatical personal ambition directed into patriotic channels, phenomenal energy and will power; and a rare combination within him of an Eastern temperament with a Western mind.

But was it enough? It was Atatürk's task, as he once put it, to form men, much as a gardener cultivates plants. He had thus formed a new elite, with new values. But it must take longer to form a new Turkish people; the mass of the Anatolian Turks still remained as of old. To succeed in his Revolution, as he had seen from the start, he must first conquer the people. For a while he had conquered them—their inertia, their fatalism, their conservative prejudice. He had followed up his conquest by suppressing at least the outward symbols of their more backward traditions.

But in so doing he had in a sense left a vacuum; and it was a vacuum which only time could fill. Many more decades were needed before his work would be complete, and inevitably he would not himself be there to complete it. Atatürk was like a successful commander forced to leave the field of battle before he knows the final result. For a man so used to the swift tempo of war it was hard to accept the slower tempo of peaceful evolution, to admit to himself that there was little more he could now do to assist the growth of the people he had fathered; hard to bequeath to his successors the task of transforming his country into a civilized Western state.

A rationalist without a rationalist philosophy, he fell into moods of disillusion and despondency. A man of action with no actions left to perform, he fell back on the familiar substitute, alcohol; and this began to undermine his physical and mental condition. Atatürk saw no reason to fuss about his health. Ever since his heart attack in 1923, repeated in a mild form a few years later, he had assumed this to be the danger to which he was prone. If his heart was all right, as it had been since, then nothing need trouble him. His principal doctor, a heart specialist, had encouraged him accordingly. Hence, oblivious of the fact that he might be taxing not his heart but other organs in his body, he continued to drink; and his doctors did all too little to discourage him.

His friends, however, noticed with growing concern that Kemal Atatürk was not the man Mustafa Kemal had been. His mind was deteriorating. Losing himself in the maze of linguistics and historiography, he would say one thing one moment, another the next. His memory was

[3] *The Times,* November 11, 1938.

failing. Talking of everyday affairs, he would forget altogether what he had said the day before. His nerves were no longer under control. He lost his temper more easily, the tiger now forever caged, snarling abruptly at friends and enemies alike.

As a rule he had vented his rages only on adversaries tough enough to take the assault. But now no man was safe. Spoiling for trouble one evening at the club, he picked on a harmless professor of history. In his usual schoolmasterly style Atatürk examined a group of young people around him on their historical knowledge. Dissatisfied with their answers, he rounded on the professor, who was the author of one of their textbooks, and treated him to a long and contemptuous diatribe on his methods of training the young. The professor, too paralyzed with alarm to answer back, sought to mollify him by eulogies and rose to drink his health. Disgusted at such lack of spirit, Atatürk shouted, in tones audible to all: "You are an ass. Go and dance"—and the professor slunk hurriedly away.

Such scenes caused general gossip. Often, however, as his adherents knew well, Atatürk's bark was worse than his bite, and his explosions amounted to mere horseplay. One evening, in the Dolma Bahche Palace, he took exception to an attack made by one Reshid Galib on the Minister of Education, and ordered him to leave the table. But Galib refused on the grounds that it was the People's Table, not the President's, and that in a republic any citizen had the right to criticize another. In reply Atatürk said, "Very well, we'll leave you with the people," and himself left the table, taking his other guests with him. A few months later he had his revenge on Reshid Galib. One evening Reshid was invited to Chankaya. He took his place with some apprehension, fearing a scene. He had hardly done so when Atatürk called in a pair of sentries and ordered them, "Lift that gentleman from his seat and take him away." Reshid was removed and Atatürk said with a grin, "That's how we get rid of people in this Republic." Afterwards Reshid Galib was appointed Minister of Education in place of the man he had criticized.

Atatürk's moods were capricious. How would he be tonight? his friends would ask one another. Sometimes he was Satan personified; at other times a matador, restlessly seeking a bull. More and more often at Chankaya, when there were women at the table, he would send them home early and sit drinking without restraint until dawn with his masculine cronies. Once, still sitting there at five o'clock in the morning, he felt like going for a ride. His two aides, to discourage so rash an enterprise, told him that his horse was lame. Next day he learnt that this was a lie, and in the evening instructed Hassan Riza, his secretary, to terminate the appointments of the two officers. The secretary, as usual, took no action, but next morning submitted the note to his master, who smiled sheepishly and instructed him, "Forget it."

Restlessness gnawed and devoured him, especially at nights. Often he would disappear all of a sudden, leaving his ministers in the dark as to where he had gone. Sending for Ismet one night, he learnt that his friend was on the way from Istanbul by the night express. On a sudden impulse Atatürk ordered a special train, so that he might go to meet Ismet. Only a shunting engine was available, but a train was made up and he set off. When the two trains met early in the morning Atatürk was asleep. Ismet, rather than wake him, ordered the presidential train to be shunted into a siding, so that the express might proceed. The President woke up later in the morning, asking his entourage where he was. He did not get back to Ankara until the evening. The press meanwhile had announced that he had left on a visit to Eskishehir.

Reluctant to sleep, he would call on friends or even strangers in the middle of the night, often dragging them from their beds to receive him. One evening at the table he was told that a certain rich merchant had compared his aloofness with that of the Sultan. No one, the merchant said, ever saw either of them. The remark nagged at Atatürk and he continually reverted to it: "Did he really say that?" Finally, around three o'clock in the morning, he rose from the table and said, "Come on, we'll go and ask him." To the alarm of his companions, he strode into the man's house unannounced. To their relief he embraced the man, had his children brought from their beds that he might embrace them too, spread his charm all around, and won a lasting adherent.

Atatürk in his mid-fifties was a man alone—without wife, family, or loves. Afet was at hand to look after him and give him some comfort, but otherwise his home life remained essentially the mess life of the bachelor officer. When his guests left him at night he was lonely and often self-pitying. Marriage, apart from the brief episode with Latife, he had renounced; it was a state for which neither his career nor his temperament fitted him. But the subject of marriage was often on his mind, if only for others. As "father of his people" he enjoyed playing the matchmaker's role. Frequently young persons, prevented by their parents from marrying, would come to him for advice and assistance and he would send for the father and secure agreement to the marriage. He discouraged divorce and would mischievously invite divorced couples to his table together. When his friends married he liked to visit their houses, often unannounced, and to inspect each room with an appraising eye, criticizing the arrangement of the furniture here, straightening a curtain there, and paying special attention to bedroom furnishings and sanitary arrangements.

As Atatürk grew older he became fonder of children and liked to collect them around him. He did not regret his own lack of a son, remarking once that the sons of great men were too often degenerate. A son, moreover, might have been inconvenient politically, since Atatürk abhorred all dynastic conceptions. But he took an interest in the children of others, playing games with them and singing Rumeli songs to them. Once, at a children's party at Izmit, a small boy, after gazing at Atatürk for a while with rapt adoration, suddenly rushed upon him and started to kiss him. The other children instantly broke away from their teachers and were soon clinging to him and showering him with kisses. Atatürk turned to a group of grownups and said, "You see, these children are of my own generation."

But it was when children reached school age that they interested him most. He would seat a child by his side at the table and examine him. He had a series of stock questions, of which his favourite was, "What is the difference in French between revolution, rebellion, reform, revolt, insurrection?" Some were subjected to a more searching examination. The intelligent student daughter of one of his ambassadors was interrogated at the dinner table for several hours on historical subjects, principally that of Napoleon. She remarked that he had been in love with Josephine. Atatürk became angry. It was impossible for such a man to fall in love, with all he had to do. "You're boring me," he said to the girl. He changed the subject to that of Caesar. Was he greater than Napoleon? She replied that he was because Caesar did not need to take a title, since his name became one. Napoleon had to make himself Emperor.

Atatürk commended her and summed up: "Napoleon started with his country and ended with himself." For Napoleon as a general he had great admiration, though he was not flattered at the comparison of his own victory at the Sakarya to that of Austerlitz. But Napoleon was a man, he maintained, without a sound political idea, more concerned with his ambition for world conquest than with the national interest of France. Atatürk liked to compare Napoleon's advance to Moscow with the Ottoman advance to Vienna, at the expense of the country's internal welfare. Napoleon, asked what was his programme, had once replied, "I just go ahead and my progress is the result of my movements." Atatürk commented: "Those who 'just go ahead' finally knock their heads against the rock of St. Helena." Napoleon, he believed, had been carried away by events which he thought he could control. Thus "democracy was delayed for sixty years."

Another hero of history to whom Kemal used to give qualified praise was his fellow Macedonian, Alexander the Great. Once, comparing Alexander unfavourably with himself, he remarked, "He forgot about his country and went far away." It was a mistake he himself never made.

As Atatürk aged the myth which had been woven around him by the foreign communities of Ankara and Istanbul assumed a yet more fanciful shape. They had for long magnified him, in their imagination, into a debauchee of Roman proportions, ruthless and insatiable in his appetite for women, with whom he was said to indulge up at Chankaya in licentious and disreputable "orgies." It was a picture of him, deriving initially from the gossip of his political enemies in Istanbul and from the strictures of his more puritanical Moslem supporters in Ankara, which shocked agreeably the conventional susceptibilities of the *corps diplomatique*.

By its standards Atatürk was indeed a loose-liver. Like many an army officer, he had used women fitfully and casually, taking them when he wanted them and throwing them aside when he did not. He had made no more secret of these proclivities than he had of his drinking habits, preaching frankness as a virtue, liking to outrage the bourgeoisie and the men of religion and, moreover, judging that a reputation for virility in a ruler was not distasteful to the mass of his people. Such was the image of himself that he liked to encourage. In fact it reflected a side of his life which meant relatively little to him. Just as work, when he was young, left him no time for marriage, so as he grew older did drink cool his lusts. In his youth and in the prime of his manhood he had enjoyed women freely when opportunity allowed. But from his mid-forties onwards his desires and with them his powers declined; and now the less potent he became the more he chose to advertise his potency.

Thus the dining rooms of the embassies and the clubs and the Ankara Palace Hotel hummed with the latest gossip about Atatürk's public behaviour. No woman was held to be safe at his hands. Turkish mothers might indeed thrust their daughters at him (and Turkish husbands their wives), but diplomatic mothers would hurry their daughters away from a party for fear he would invite them to his table. When he did so he would often merely subject them to a *viva voce* exam. Taking a fancy to a young Polish girl at an embassy party, he was heard asking her for proof of the existence of God. With a married woman the interrogation might be on the more intimate subject of her relations with her husband. He had always sensed just how far to go with women and was a good judge of husbands, never flirting with the wife of one likely to be jealous, and continually warning his less discerning friends against blunders of this kind. Occasionally, however, a scandal arose when the wife of some diplomat allowed herself to become emotionally too much involved with the President, and once Ankara was diverted by tales of an American lady who, in pursuit of him, lay down across the road by which he drove through his farm and was invited to stay for some days at Chankaya.

But for all his vagaries and the scandal concerning him, Atatürk was still seriously respected by the diplomatic corps for his unimpaired faculties in the field of foreign affairs. On such matters as history and language his mind might wander; on the problems of the actual world, now increasingly threatened by the European dictators, it remained as acute as ever. Ambassadors to whom he talked beyond the bounds of protocol might be subjected, however late the hour and convivial the atmosphere, to examinations as searching as those to which he had accustomed his countrymen. "Sometimes," wrote Sir Percy Loraine, "it was a drumfire of questions: at others a long statement of his own views: then an interrogative pause, marked by a piercing look from those ice-blue eyes from beneath contracted eyebrows. One came to be able to translate that look. It meant, don't shilly-shally: we speak as man to man. You are right: you are on the mat a bit: but I detest yes-men and I want to hear what *you* think. Maybe you've got something. Let's get at it."

His main attention was now given to those questions remaining to be settled between Turkey and the West before the Second World War, which he had confidently predicted, began. In the preparatory war of nerves it was Mussolini who first threatened Turkey. In a speech in the spring of 1934 he defined his historical objectives as Asia and Africa—a clear threat of war and annexation. The Turks retorted with ostentatious manoeuvres on the coasts of the Aegean. When Mussolini began to fortify the island of Leros, off the Turkish coast—in fact as a prelude to the invasion of Abyssinia—Atatürk chose his own method of making his attitude clear.

Dining one evening with a party at the Ankara Palace Hotel, he observed the Italian ambassador at an adjoining table. The Albanian envoy was also present. As it happened, Atatürk was sober. But it suited him to pretend that he was not. Leaning towards the Albanian, he said, "Asaf Bey, I see lots of funny pictures in the newspapers. What's going on in

Albania? Are you performing an operetta?" He was alluding to the photographs of King Zog, with his gaudy uniforms. "Anyway," he continued, "what was wrong with the Republic? Why did you think it necessary to have a King? And, what is more, you are following a dangerous policy. The Italians will use you in order to infiltrate into the Balkans."

The Italian ambassador tried to intervene. Turning to address him through an interpreter, who repeated his remarks loudly for all to hear, Atatürk protested at the fact that in Rome Italian students had been demonstrating in front of the Turkish Embassy with demands for Antalya (Adalia). "Antalya," Atatürk explained, "is not in the pocket of our ambassador in Italy. It is right here. Why don't you try to come and get it? I have a proposition to make to His Excellency the Duce. We'll allow him to land Italian soldiers in Antalya. When the landing is completed, we'll have a battle, and the side which wins will have Antalya."

The ambassador asked, "Is this a declaration of war, Your Excellency?"

"No," replied Atatürk. "I am speaking here as a mere citizen. Only the Grand National Assembly can declare war in the name of Turkey. But try to remember that, when the time comes, the Grand National Assembly will take into consideration the feelings of mere citizens like myself."

Atatürk, satisfied with the effects of his calculated indiscretion, then left the hotel. When the war broke out Turkey voted, as a member of the League, in favour of sanctions against Italy, thus emphasizing Atatürk's policy of co-operation with the community of nations. It was emphasized more strongly in the spring of 1936, by an official request from Turkey for a revision of the regime for the Straits as laid down by the Lausanne Treaty. This no longer emphasized the issue of their freedom, as at Lausanne, but the issue of their security, invoking an article in the League Covenant which allowed for joint consultation in the event of a threat to the Straits.

Both the manner and the timing of Atatürk's request were faultless. They owed much to his close relations with Sir Percy Loraine, whom he had once described over the poker table as the holder of the only ace in the Mediterranean, and who had emphasized to him the necessity of avoiding any hint of an ultimatum or of a threat to march troops into the zone. The request came at a moment when Britain was greatly concerned as to the security of the Straits. It had been feared at Geneva, following the German occupation of the Rhineland and the Italian invasion of Abyssinia, that the Turks might march into their demilitarized zones and so present the world with another *fait accompli*. Atatürk's choice of the correct juridical approach to the issue thus favourably impressed the Western powers, and the British—fearing rapprochement between the Turks and the Germans as in 1914—were ready to make important concessions for the sake of an Anglo-Turkish understanding.

The resulting conference was held at Montreux. It was boycotted by the Italians, and the matter was speedily settled. Turkey obtained all she needed. She was allowed to remilitarize the Straits; the former International Commission was abolished; she regained absolute control over the waterway, such as the Ottoman Empire had enjoyed in the past; she now had the right to control the passage of warships in time of war and, if she believed herself threatened by war, in time of peace as well. Thus at midnight on July 20 thirty thousand Turkish troops marched into the demilitarized zone of the Straits, where the whole of the Turkish fleet, led appropriately by the *Yavuz*—the *Goeben* in Turkish guise—awaited them. Here was a triumphant reversal of the historical precedent of 1914, against which Atatürk had protested so strongly but with so little effect.

Neither Italy nor Germany was pleased at this outcome. But they could afford less than ever to quarrel with Turkey. Early in 1937, at a meeting in Milan, Count Ciano tried to bargain with Tevfik Rüştü with the offer of a trade agreement and to draw Turkey into some form of alignment with the Rome-Berlin Axis. But her government publicly clarified its allegiance "only to the *bloc* of peace and to no other *bloc*." To the Germans a veiled snub was administered by the granting of the contract for the refortification of the Straits not to Krupp's, with whom Turkey was in commercial relations, but to Vickers, who had offered less favourable terms. When the Germans objected to certain clauses of the Montreux Convention they received from the Turks the sharp reply that this matter, since Germany was neither a signatory of Montreux nor a Mediterranean power, was no concern of theirs.

Russia too was displeased by the Convention. It had given her advantages but not all she had hoped for—in essence the closing of the Straits to foreign warships in time of war. Since it was a cardinal point of Atatürk's foreign policy to remain on good terms with the nearest great sea power, Britain, and with the nearest great land power, Soviet Russia, he sent Tevfik Rüştü with a delegation to Moscow, to reassure the Russians both on the Montreux Convention and on the Saadabad Pact.

A chance publicly to display his friendship with Britain arose in September 1936, when King Edward VIII paid an informal visit to Turkey in the course of a Mediterranean cruise in the *Nahlin*. Sir Percy Loraine had encouraged the visit as a gesture of good will at a time when Britain was competing in the economic war against Germany for a loan to the Turks. It was the first visit in history by a British sovereign to Turkey, and the first by a European sovereign since the Kaiser's reception by Abdul Hamid forty years earlier. Thus Sir Percy urged that the visit should be official and that the King should come to pay his respects to the President in Ankara. But the King, being on a holiday cruise, preferred to treat it as unofficial. Atatürk, momentarily disconcerted but no servant to protocol, thus proceeded to Istanbul to meet Edward.

The King's yacht anchored off the Dolma Bahche Palace. With Atatürk he drove to the British Embassy, through the streets of Istanbul, in an open car. This, Sir Percy explained, was a compliment from a head of state used to traversing the streets in a bulletproof limousine. Thousands had spent the night by the banks of the Bosporus to await the King's arrival. The Union Jack and the Star and Crescent flew from the rooftops, and after dark floodlights shone from the minarets, with streamers inscribed, "Welcome Eduarde Rex." The entertainments provided for the King and his party—of which Mrs. Simpson was an honoured member—included a "Venetian night," in which Turkish warships took part, on the moonlit waters of the Bosporus, and a regatta on the Sea of Marmara. At one of several dinners a waiter dropped a large dish of food on the floor, prompting an apology by Atatürk to his guest: "I could teach everything to this nation but I couldn't teach them to be good lackeys."

In the course of their talks, which were conducted in German, the King and the President established friendly relations. The visit was indeed, on King Edward's part, an exercise in cordial diplomacy to rank with the foreign excursions of his grandfather, King Edward VII. Psychologically it transformed the attitude of the Turkish people towards Britain, to whom they had grown used, from the outbreak of the First World War, as an enemy. King Edward VIII helped to create a new climate of Turkish public opinion. For many years afterwards the walls of coffeehouses in Istanbul and throughout Anatolia were adorned with bright coloured pictures of the two rulers, seated together beneath their respective national flags, a symbol, not to be forgotten, of the Anglo-Turkish Entente Cordiale.

It still remained for the Turks to establish a similar entente with the French. The question of the sanjak of Alexandretta, or Hatay, outstanding from the Franco-Turkish agreement with Franklin-Bouillon, remained to be settled. It concerned the future of a province which marched with Syria, which contained—or so it was claimed—a majority of Turkish inhabitants, and which in Iskenderun (Alexandretta) provided Turkey at that time with her only effective Mediterranean port. The matter had been amicably shelved by the creation, under French mandate, of a special regime for the province which safeguarded Turkish interests. But now, in the summer of 1936, France proposed to grant independence to Syria and to include Hatay within its new frontiers. The question was put before the Council of the League of Nations, which debated a Turkish request for the withdrawal from the province of French troops and their replacement by a detachment of neutral gendarmerie. But the League at this stage would agree only to the despatch of three neutral observers to report, pending further discussion.

Atatürk now took a personal hand in the dispute. Backed by a party meeting which protested against the slowness of the proceedings, he decided on a show of force against the French. Shrewdly timing his movements to coincide with the return of their ambassador, Monsieur Ponsot, from Paris, he proceeded by special train to Konya, the headquarters of his Southern Command, with the apparent intention of moving troops towards the frontier. The cautious Ismet dissuaded him from going beyond the Taurus. But Atatürk's action served its purpose. The French grew alarmed by a rumour that Turkish troops were concentrating on the borders of Hatay, and by subsequent clashes, between Turks and Arabs, within the province itself. Negotiations followed between Paris and Ankara in an atmosphere favourable to the Turks.

When a settlement was ultimately reached it was largely through Atatürk's favourite methods of ballroom diplomacy. Its foundations were laid at a ball at the Ankara Palace Hotel. To the table in the alcove where he normally sat, and where he was now sitting with Sir Percy Loraine and a few others, Atatürk summoned Ambassador Ponsot and his wife. After they had conversed for a while he ordered the music and dancing to stop, and broached the subject of Hatay. Stressing his fervent desire for Franco-Turkish friendship, he assured the ambassador that, nonetheless, he had promised the Grand National Assembly to take back the province and could not break this promise. Hatay was for him a personal issue.

On this basis he now discussed the problem with Ponsot, calling in a French-speaking lady from among the guests to interpret, and instructing her, lest any mistake should be made, to write down his own words in Turkish before translating them into French. Sir Percy Loraine, who had promised Atatürk his help with the French when the time for it should come, was brought into the discussions. They conversed on the problem until the light of dawn filtered in through the mock-oriental windows of the Ankara Palace Hotel and Atatürk, in a moment of inspiration, suggested the lines of a feasible solution.[4]

Ponsot himself was ready enough for a compromise. Hatay, he had to admit, was not essentially Arab; moreover, Iskenderun, wide open to the Cilician plain, was a natural harbour for Turkey and would be hard for the Syrians to defend. But the Quai d'Orsay was slow to accept such a "dismemberment" of Syria, involving as it would the stigma of a military withdrawal. Atatürk, for his part, realized that a country which had refused to fight for the Rhineland was unlikely to fight for Hatay, but he realized also the need to safeguard French amour-propre. Hence, while keeping up the pressure on the spot, he acted with patience at the conference table.

Finally the intricate quadrangular negotiations between Paris, Geneva, Ankara, and Syria led, early in 1937, to a settlement by which Hatay became a separate political entity, enjoying full independence in its internal affairs but linked by a customs and monetary union with the state of Syria, which would be responsible for the conduct of its foreign affairs. Both Turkish and Arabic were to rank as its official languages. It only remained to be seen how this arrangement would work out in practice.

[4] On another informal occasion, at the Russian restaurant of Karpich, Atatürk applied a more eccentric form of pressure. Seeing the French ambassador, he called upon the ladies at his table to raise their hands and shout, "We want Hatay!" One of his adopted daughters chanced to have a toy revolver in her bag and he made her fire it off. The explosion took Monsieur Ponsot aback and Atatürk playfully sent for the police and had her arrested for the illegal use of firearms. He then informed Ismet that the women of Turkey must have Hatay and instructed him to make representations on their behalf to the French.

59 ► *A serious illness*

Throughout that summer in Istanbul Atatürk was increasingly restless. He fretted with impatience at the "prison" restrictions of the Sultan's vast gloomy palace which so incongruously housed him. He was always plotting to escape from it and played with the idea of building himself a kiosk on the hillside above it, close to a popular café. Occasionally he succeeded in escaping without being observed. One evening, like a schoolboy playing truant, he rose from the table on the pretext of going to bed early, eluded his guards by a ruse, slipped out of the palace, and disappeared into the night. He was found eventually in a Greek fishermen's *taverna* on the shores of the Bosporus, drinking and dancing a Greek dance with his arms around the fishermen's shoulders, to the music of a lute player from Trebizond.

On another such night a group of military cadets were amazed to see a taxi draw up beside them, with Atatürk seated alone in it. He sat down with them by the roadside and talked of military matters. Soon the noise of cars and motor bicycles was heard in the distance, and he exclaimed, "Oh, I am done for. They're coming after me." The cars drew up and a worried group of officials led the President of the Republic away.

He liked, in these long summer days and nights, to sail up and down the Bosporus, across the Marmara, and around the islands in his motor yacht the *Ertuğrul,* which became a familiar sight to the people. One night, when the boat reached the last station on the Bosporus, he suddenly ordered the captain to turn into the Black Sea and head for the mining port of Zonguldak. Then he retired to his cabin and slept. His guests were worried. The *Ertuğrul* was a long slim boat, not equipped to face the storms which could suddenly sweep down on these treacherous waters. She reached Zonguldak safely, however, and Atatürk spent the morning ashore inspecting mines and factories. But on the way back the ship ran into a sudden storm and began to roll in a dangerous fashion, so that the crew had to rip the auxiliary sails with their knives. Atatürk only laughed at their anxiety and, in boyish high spirits, put a *zeybek* record on the gramophone, to which he insisted on dancing until the *Ertuğrul* sailed back into the calmer waters of the Bosporus.

To escape from the palace Atatürk spent many of his days, not only at Yalova, which had now developed into a large thermal resort, but at Florya, a place which he had revived as a bathing resort, with a presidential villa built right on the beach. Here he liked to mix with the people, rowing boats and teaching himself to swim. His constant companion was a young child, the last of his adopted daughters, whom he had named Ülkü, the Ideal. She was a lively little girl with Tartar features and slanting Mongol eyes and he became much attached to her and used to say that, of all his entourage, she was the only person upon whom he could count always to tell him the truth.

In the entourage, undertones of conflict were now rumbling uncomfortably beneath the surface. The theme of them was Ismet, now Inönü. Atatürk's friends had never been Ismet's friends. Ismet, the respectable family man, had little in common with those dissolute and often unscrupulous henchmen at Chankaya and in the Dolma Bahche Palace. These men sought two things, power and money, and Ismet was an obstacle to the acquisition of both. He was hardly likely to further their ambitions for influential posts. Nor indeed was Atatürk himself. He knew his friends well enough to keep them in their places and would never appoint to a responsible place a man who lacked the capacity to fill it. To quieten them, he gave them latitude in business dealings, allowing them pickings from the industrial enterprises and refraining, unless public scandal threatened, from too close an enquiry into their methods of seeking their fortunes. But this outlet too was often obstructed by the scrupulous Ismet.

At "court" there was thus a perennial atmosphere of personal intrigue, of which the principal motif was mischief against Inönü. Atatürk managed this situation astutely enough by division and rule, now pitting the contestants against one another, now forcing them in his presence to make up their differences. He liked to bring his enemies to his table and confront them with the remarks they had made against one another, and this treatment was applied alike to the friends and the enemies of Ismet. Sometimes he would get an aide to criticize the Cabinet in Ismet's presence; once in Ismet's absence he banged the table and exclaimed of him, "I can take a man and raise him up. But if he can't understand this and thinks he has risen by his own worth, I can fling him away, like a rag."

This now was his prevalent mood. As Atatürk's health deteriorated, so did the mutual irritation which arose from their basic differences of temperament grow. The pinpricks on both sides multiplied and festered. Ismet resented Atatürk's caprices, his criticisms of the ministers, his habit of giving orders to them over the Cabinet's head. As time went on Ismet found it harder to bear the taunts and outbursts, and in unguarded moments expressed his annoyance to others, who repeated his words to Atatürk. For years Atatürk had taken in his stride Ismet's fussiness, his pedantry, his slowness in reaching decisions. But now these shortcomings, combined with a growing presumptuousness, got on his nerves.

The restrictive trend of Ismet Inönü's economic policy had ranged many opponents against him. But it was over foreign policy that his relations with Atatürk became especially strained. When Italian submarines, masquerading as Spanish, started to sink merchant shipping in the Mediterranean, Turkey, on Atatürk's instructions, co-operated fully in the international patrol set up by a League Committee conference at Nyon to counter these piratical acts. But Ismet showed timidity over the agreement, fearing war with the Italians and favouring a submarine patrol in which each country remained in its own territorial waters. Atatürk, resenting this, took more and more to by-passing Ismet and dealing direct with Tevfik Rüştü. He resented also Ismet's restraining hand over Hatay. Telephoning from Istanbul, he overrode in strong terms a Cabinet proposal not to press for the use of Turkish as the official language of the province.

The tension between them came to a head one evening at Chankaya, ironically enough on a minor issue—a matter of economic policy concerning a beer factory. Ismet lost his temper and blurted out, "How much longer is this country going to be governed from a drunkard's table?" Atatürk coldly replied, "You seem to forget that it was a drunkard who appointed you to your post," and the conversation jolted awkwardly on to less explosive topics. After Ismet had left, Atatürk gave way to his anger and threatened to denounce him in Parliament. He was dissuaded from this. But clearly the moment had come for him to change his Prime Minister. He broke the news to Ismet next day, summoning him to his private compartment on the presidential train, in which he was starting on an official tour. He proposed that Ismet should officially take a few weeks' "sick leave," during which a deputy Prime Minister would serve in his place.

Ismet Inönü, for whom this had simply been one among a number of recent disagreements, was dismayed, after fourteen years in the office, at so abrupt a dismissal. Throughout the journey he wrote notes of contrition to Atatürk, imploring him to reconsider his verdict. But they remained unanswered; Atatürk's mind was made up.

As Ismet Inönü's successor he chose Celal Bayar, whose power had been growing and whose economic ideas were less rigidly statist than Ismet's. Bayar initiated his premiership with an economic programme which involved more equitable taxation and a second Five Year Plan. But Bayar was not the competent "chief of staff" that Ismet had been, and Atatürk was soon missing his old Prime Minister. He could not delegate to Bayar as confidently. To a woman friend who remarked on his look of fatigue after Bayar had been a few weeks in office, he complained, "With my new Prime Minister I can no longer sleep calmly at nights." He remained on friendly personal terms with Ismet, who continued on occasion to dine at Chankaya.

During that winter of 1937 it became evident that Atatürk was seriously unwell. His mind, preoccupied with the coming war, still showed flashes of insight. He expressed a low opinion of General Gamelin, saying, "As long as such men are at the head of things in France, France is doomed to be destroyed." He compared the Maginot Line to the tomb of Nasreddin Hoja, the Turkish storyteller: it had a single façade, with a huge lock, but the rest of it was open so that anyone could go round the edge of it. Of the customary reception for the anniversary of the Republic, at the end of October, Sir Percy Loraine, after sitting at his side for hours, could still write: "It was a first-class opportunity for observing Atatürk's fantastic power of concentration. He had something to say to, or learn from each newcomer to the circle; everything he said was leading somewhere, and one could sense the unflickering purpose and the tireless spirit of inquiry that lay behind it. An inquest, as you will; but not an inquisition."

Nevertheless, for a year or so past he had shown signs of fatigue, in both body and mind. He had headaches and suffered from the cold, as he had not done before. He had aged in appearance; the skin had grown pale, the lines in the face had deepened, the hair was thinning, he had developed a paunch. He was becoming listless in his movements. His energy declined and he slept until late in the afternoon, with the aid of sedatives. Still tired on waking, he began to drink earlier than before, but by the end of dinner his vitality had waned once more. He walked seldom and had a lift installed for him in the Dolma Bahche Palace. He was always seeking a pretext to sit down, sometimes cross-legged on the floor. He had two bouts of influenza, and feared pneumonia. His doctor one day warned him to be careful and to drink less.

Early in 1938 he went from Ankara to Yalova, where he was examined by the doctor of the spa. He complained of itching on his legs and thought that the baths would do him good. The doctor told him that his liver was enlarged and hardened, and that the itching was due to his diet and especially to alcohol. His own doctor now made the same diagnosis. The remedy was to rest, take care what he ate, drink only in moderation. Raki, with its aniseed flavour, was especially bad for his complaint. For a while he drank a little less. After ten days the itching had stopped and he went, as he had previously planned, to Bursa (as Brusa was now spelt).

Ali Fuad went with him. Of the old friends whom Atatürk had tried for their lives, Fuad alone, more easygoing than the rest, had returned to the fold. Atatürk had been reconciled with Refet but their former relations were never resumed. A reconciliation with Rauf had been prevented, after his return from exile, by the People's party bosses. Kiazim Karabekir had come, on Atatürk's invitation, to a meeting of the Historical Congress in Istanbul. But, owing to a misunderstanding, the two did not meet. Thus, of these friends of his youth, only Ali Fuad was now at his side.

At Bursa Atatürk delivered an exhortation to the youth of the country which was to become a text for a generation or more to come. In effect it appointed them guardians of the future. If ever the Revolution were in danger,

the young man of Turkey is not going to say, "There is a police force in this country . . . there is a gendarmerie . . . there is an army . . . there is the machinery of justice in this country." The young man of Turkey is going to intervene himself, to protect his work. The police will come, and instead of catching the real guilty man, will arrest the young man. The young man will say, "This means that the police is not yet the police of the Revolution and the Republic!" A tribunal will sentence the young man. Again he will think, "This means that the justice of the country has still to be adapted to the regime." He will be thrown into prison. He will defend himself legally. But he will not try to get out of prison by begging for mercy or by asking for special treatment. The young man will say, "I have acted according to my convictions and beliefs. I am right to intervene and act thus. Since it was unjust that I should be put into prison, it is my duty to correct the reasons and motives which caused this injustice." This, according to my ideas [concluded Atatürk], is how a Turkish young man and the youth of Turkey should behave.

These injunctions echoed the even more prophetic peroration of his Six-Day Speech, in which he put forward the hypothesis

that those who hold the power of the government within the country have fallen into error, that they are fools and traitors, yes, even that these leading persons identify their personal interests with the enemy's political goals, it might happen that the nation came into complete privation, into the most extreme distress; that it found itself in a condition of ruin and complete exhaustion. Even under those circumstances, O Turkish child of future generations, it is your duty to save the independence of the Turkish Republic. The strength that you will need for this is mighty in the noble blood which flows in your veins.[1]

On leaving Mudanya for Istanbul by boat after his visit to Bursa, Atatürk became suddenly unwell during dinner. He was pale and in pain. Ali Fuad persuaded him to retire. He did so on condition that the party continue with Fuad as host, but no one was now in the mood for a party. Soon after midnight Atatürk called Ali Fuad into his cabin. The doctor had given him drugs and the pain had decreased. Atatürk hoped that he would now be able to sleep. But it looked, he added, as though his illness might take a long time. "And if I have to stay in bed, I shall be terribly bored. I shall be able to bear it only with the help of friends like yourself."

When the boat arrived at Dolma Bahche early in the morning Atatürk looked better. In the evening he went with Kiliç Ali to dinner at the Park Hotel. They stayed there until four o'clock in the morning, sitting at a table in the window where they began to feel the cold. Next day Atatürk had a high fever and developed a touch of pneumonia.

---

[1] The words of both these exhortations were widely quoted in 1960, as an inspiration to the youth of the country which had been largely responsible for the overthrow of the Democrat government of Celal Bayar and Menderes, and its replacement by a provisional military regime.

He was in bed for more than a week. Before he had fully recovered he insisted on leaving for Ankara, and his friends there were shocked at his appearance. He looked exhausted, he could stand only with difficulty, he complained of eruptions on his legs and stomach. At a dinner in honour of the Yugoslav and Greek Premiers he arrived late, owing to a hemorrhage from the nose which he had been unable to stop. If this arose from his liver condition, it was an ominous symptom.

The Turkish doctors examined him and recommended an outside opinion. Atatürk was reluctant to call in any foreign specialist. The news of his illness would thus become known abroad and might prejudice the solution of the Hatay problem, where a hitch had arisen. But finally Celal Bayar persuaded him to summon Dr. Fissinger, a specialist from France, who came to Ankara and at once diagnosed cirrhosis of the liver. It was a disease of which the Turks say of its victims, "He has swallowed a monster." This, his friends now realized, was the monster that had been gnawing away at him all these months.

If he listened to his doctors the illness could still pass. Fissinger was reasonably optimistic. "I am going to cure you," he said to Atatürk, "but you will have to cure yourself first. You may be a great commander who has won great victories. But now I am your commander, and you have to help me." The simile appealed to Atatürk and he promised to do what he was told. Hitherto he had been truculent with his doctors, refusing a blood test, lying as to the number of cigarettes he smoked a day. (If he said fifty, they would cut him down to ten, so he said two hundred.) But now, aware of the gravity of his condition, he was ready to compromise. He must lie down for three months, rising only for an hour each day. After that he must lead a restful life for a year. He must follow a special diet and drink no alcohol. If this were only for three months, he replied, he could endure it.

A special chaise longue was brought from England in which he could lie at full length, and in this he was able to read and write and deal with state papers. But the prone position irked him, and he would often rise and sit cross-legged, which was bad for the circulation in his liver. Most evenings he would dine in his chair, with a few friends around him, and retire to bed reasonably early. After a month or so of this treatment he looked better and seemed less tired. He had regained some appetite; his energy and spirits were slowly returning. Overconfident in his strength, he became restless for action once more.

For his mind was never at rest. As in his youth he had lain awake at nights, grappling with problems of military and afterwards political science, so now, in the spring of 1938, he lay awake grappling with the problems of a world on the brink of war, and with the need to round off his own life's work against its outbreak. The incorporation of Hatay within the frontiers of Turkey had still to be finally clinched.

60 ▶ *Death of Atatürk*

Turkey had secured the autonomy of Hatay. But elections had still to be held to decide who should control it. The International Commission sent by the League to organize the elections devised a system of registration which revealed the Turks to be in a slight minority, with the Arabs and Armenians in the majority. A Turkish mass meeting was staged in Antakya (Antioch), which led to the suspension of the registers. If the Turks were to get their way, direct pressure must be turned once more on the French. As before, there must be a show of force, and in this Atatürk, despite his illness, insisted on taking a personal hand.

He rose from his invalid chair and, after a tiring day at a youth festival in the stadium at Ankara, took the train with his doctor to Mersin, the Turkish port near the frontier of Hatay. As the train moved south the heat grew oppressive and Atatürk confessed to a friend, "This illness is something different, something I have never known before." Looking down at his stomach, he remarked, "I am putting on weight. My trousers are getting too small. I shall have to have them let out."

At Mersin he faced an exhausting programme. For forty minutes he stood in the damp torrid heat, taking the salute at a military parade. He had difficulty in standing, and Kiliç Ali and Salih, his aide, standing behind him, murmured, "Lean on us." But he proudly refused, only giving the order "Quick march!" that the troops should move less slowly. There followed visits to railway yards and to the classical sites nearby. Finally, in the relative cool of the evening, he had a few hours' relaxation in a motorboat out in the harbour. Next day he was able to rest. He played Turkish music on the gramophone, listening absently as though lost in thought, and sometimes quoting with philosophic melancholy some line from the song. On the third day he stood through another and longer parade, at Tarsus. He proceeded to Adana, to help celebrate the anniversary of its liberation from the French. Then he took the night train back to Ankara, fretting in the heat amid the ritual of unending good-byes, devouring a basket of fresh oranges, and sighing with relief as he lay down in his bunk for a feverish sleep.

After two days in the dry heat of Ankara he left for Istanbul. Normally, at Haydar Pasha station, he walked down the strip of red carpet from the train to the motorboat. This morning he knew he would have difficulty in walking, so to shorten the distance his car was hitched to the front of the train. But he refused help and even stood by the boat with an outward attempt at gaiety to watch the transfer of his baggage. He could not, however, hide his true condition, which was noticed by the crowd with concern.

That day he spent in the relative coolness of Florya. Driving back to the palace in the evening, he had a sudden acute pain at the heart. The car was stopped and Salih gave him his heart medicine.[1] Back at the palace the doctor explained that this was no ordinary heart trouble but a symptom of the liver complaint.

Atatürk knew by now that his disease was cirrhosis. He had looked it up in a French medical dictionary and remarked, "It looks as though my days are numbered." The Yalova doctor examined him again and diagnosed that he had reached the secondary stage of the disease, when the liver, having previously expanded, contracts. His increase in weight was due to an accumulation of water and gas in the abdomen, with a consequent dropsical condition. He must go to bed and lie prone, moving as little as possible. Fissinger was called in again, without Atatürk's

---

[1] Salih (Bozok), unwilling to live without his master, was to shoot himself through the heart on the day of Atatürk's death.

knowledge, from Paris, and confirmed the diagnosis. He found his patient's condition worse than he expected. Atatürk had risen too soon and
his trip to Mersin had neutralized the effects of the period of rest.

Fatal as it might prove to him personally, his journey, coinciding with
Tevfik Rüştü's strong protests at French interference in Hatay, was to
have the political effect he had hoped for. For it had helped to create an
impression in Paris, as his similar tactics over the Straits had done in
Geneva, that Atatürk was preparing an *Anschluss* in the familiar style
of the other dictators. His own diagnosis of the international situation
was proved correct. The French were far too preoccupied with Hitler's
activities in Europe to bother themselves about a portion of a Syrian state
which would in any case cease, sooner or later, to be theirs. Nor was
this the moment to quarrel with a friendly Turkey, which controlled
the Straits and could thus, if she chose, bar French access to Soviet Russia, a potential ally in the forthcoming struggle.

The French government opened talks with the Turkish ambassador in
Paris. They led to an agreement by which a Turkish military mission
was admitted to Hatay, to keep order in the elections. Early in July a
treaty of friendship was agreed between the two nations, which allowed
for the policing of Hatay by French and Turkish forces, and amounted
to their effective control in the form of a joint Franco-Turkish guarantee
of its autonomy.

Impatiently Atatürk, as he lay on his sickbed in Istanbul, sent a telephone message to Tevfik Rüştü in Ankara, demanding immediate implementation of the treaty. The preliminary detachment of Turkish
troops must march into the territory the following Wednesday, at the
latest. Tevfik Rüştü realized the reason for his impatience—the fear that
there might be further delays and that he would not live to see Hatay
within the frontiers of his National Pact. But it was now Saturday, and
the final details of the take-over had yet to be settled. Tevfik explained
the urgency of the matter to Ponsot who, respecting Atatürk as he did,
showed his sympathy but explained that Paris must first agree, and that
the Quai d'Orsay did not function over the weekend. He promised, however, to do his best.

Tevfik Rüştü, with the aid of his son-in-law, a Foreign Office official
named Zorlu, typed out in person a draft agreement, completing the
treaty, and despatched it to Paris for signature. The Turkish ambassador
contacted the Foreign Minister, who was away in the country. To carry
out such a formality on a Sunday was unprecedented. It involved disturbing the weekend rest of several responsible officials. But when Atatürk's

condition was explained, the minister came up to Paris and in the evening the treaty was formally signed. The Turkish troops marched into
Hatay on the day appointed. Conveniently the electoral register, published
in the following month, showed a majority of Turks, who occupied
twenty-two out of the forty seats in the subsequent Assembly. Its deliberations were to open the way, a year later, to the complete incorporation
of Hatay within the Turkish Republic. Thus Atatürk's last work for
his country was done.

The year before he had ordered a seagoing yacht named the *Savarona*
which had been built for an American millionairess. Hitler had made an
offer for her but withdrawn it when he learned that the Turks had been
first in the field. She chanced to arrive just at this moment when Atatürk's last illness began. He remarked ironically, "I waited for this yacht
like a child expecting a toy. Is she then to become my grave?" In the
stifling heat of Istanbul he was moved from the palace to the *Savarona*,
which at least caught the breezes, and which became in effect his hospital ship.

Fissinger now seldom left his bedside. Atatürk treated their daily con-
sultations like staff conferences for a battle, whose issue was now his own
life, with himself no longer in command but a mere private soldier submitting to orders. Hearing that Ismet too was ill and unable to come to
Istanbul to see him, he asked Fissinger to visit and examine him in Ankara. Reluctant to leave his patient for long, Fissinger went to Ankara
for only twenty-four hours, and on his return told Atatürk that Ismet
had diabetes but that he had advised against an operation. Finally Fissinger had to return to Paris. When Atatürk urged him to stay the doctor
remarked to an aide, "If I stayed one day longer I should find myself
obeying *him,* his will is so strong."

Atatürk in his chaise longue settled down to the monotonous routine
of the invalid. In the morning the sign that he was awake was the sound
of the gramophone in his cabin. Then Ülkü, the little girl, would go in
to him, keeping him amused, as she did for most of the day, with her
games and her prattle. Usually on emerging on deck he remained in his
nightshirt, sitting thus among his friends—Kiliç Ali and Ismail Hakki,
the former captain of his bodyguard, his two or three aides, and often
Afet or Sabiha, his other "daughters." But when official visitors came he
would dress carefully, donning a white yachting cap with a blazer and
perhaps a flower in his buttonhole. While they discussed state business,
Ülkü would sit on his lap and he would fondle her affectionately.

One of his more illustrious visitors was King Carol of Rumania. The visit, however, was not a success. The King said to him, "The Sudeten affair is of primary importance in Europe today. The President of the Czechoslovakian Republic, Dr. Beneš, is complicating the situation by his obstinacy, and the result is that there may be a war in Europe." Atatürk stiffened in his armchair and with a flash of the old fire turned to Tevfik Rüştü, saying, "Ask His Majesty this. What sort of attitude does he expect from a President of the Republic who is the person mainly responsible for the independence of his country?" The King went pale and switched to the safer subject of Rumania's adherence to the Balkan Pact.

Presently Atatürk began to find even the *Savarona*, with the low ceilings of her cabins and saloons, unendurably hot. Blocks of ice were placed around his cabin to cool it. But Atatürk, in his pain and fever, complained, "My belly is swimming in water. Can such a man go on living?"

Once or twice he sailed down into the Marmara and back, seeking fresh air. One day, in a motorboat, he paid a visit to Florya—his last. The people on the beaches, seeing him thus, well dressed as always in the yachting cap which so suited him, went wild with enthusiasm and broke into cheers. He rose awkwardly to his feet, walked to the prow of the boat, and waved back to them. Reluctant to return to the *Savarona*, he cruised up the Bosporus. From the streets and from the houses by the shore the people cheered him.

Back on board the yacht, he had a high temperature which lasted for several days. One night, distraught by his fever and the pain of the water in his belly, he cried out, "I'm being strangled," and staggered out on deck, flinging himself on the chaise longue. His friends begged him to go in, out of the damp heat, but he said with resignation, "Whatever is destined to happen will happen." He had difficulty in walking back to his cabin. There he sank into an armchair and said to Kiliç Ali, "Telephone your mother and ask if she has not some household remedy for this temperature and pain." Kiliç Ali did so, and his mother sent over a bottle of rose vinegar which she had treasured for years. Cloths were dipped in it and placed on Atatürk's forehead and wrists, giving him a certain relief.

As the fever mounted it was decided to transfer him back to the palace, where it might be cooler. The move was made at midnight with the lights on the quay extinguished so that no one might see. The doctor ordered that he should be carried ashore on a stretcher, since it was dangerous for him to walk, but he refused angrily. Instead an armchair was brought, and in this he was carried ashore and into the lift of the palace. On reaching the first floor he pushed his helpers aside and, despite their protests, walked to his bedroom.

It was a high room with a carved walnut bed and other furniture in a Frenchified style. The three windows were elaborately draped with brocade curtains. The floor was of parquet, and the room was illuminated by a crystal chandelier. Atatürk sank down with relief on the bed, which was draped with a mosquito net, and exclaimed, "How wonderful! This place really *is* cooler than the yacht." But the rooms of the palace proved almost as hot, and every day firemen came to spray water on the outside walls of his bedroom. He looked often with a sigh towards a picture on the wall, portraying a cool Alpine scene with fruit blossom in the foreground and forest trees above. With the pressure of the fluid and the gas his pains grew worse. His belly continued to swell, he found it hard to lie down and to breathe. He was ivory pale, and his eyes seemed to have grown larger. He begged his doctors to draw off the fluid, but they wished to postpone the operation for as long as possible.

Realizing its dangers, Atatürk sent for Hassan Riza, his secretary, to make his will. At first they talked of the world situation. Hassan Riza read him the news summary, to which he listened with interest. It confirmed his own opinion. There would be no war this year. Neither the Germans nor the Italians were ready for it. It would break out either in 1939 or in 1940. Showing some signs of emotion, he then stretched out a hand to Hassan Riza and with his aid sat up cross-legged in bed. Looking out through the long windows at the Asiatic shore of the Bosporus, he instructed his secretary to make a list of all he possessed. A typewritten draft of the will was prepared, and Atatürk transcribed it in his own handwriting, making a few changes of detail and phrase.

A notary was summoned. To receive him, Atatürk rose from his bed, had himself shaved, and changed his nightshirt for a pair of silk pajamas and a red brocade dressing gown, with a red silk scarf around his neck. They sat by the window overlooking the Bosporus, drinking coffee and discussing the new law which governed the duties of notaries. Then Atatürk handed him the will. By its provisions, signed and dated September 5, 1938, he left all his estate, including Chankaya and its contents, to the People's party, to be administered as hitherto by the Iş Bank. The income was to go, in specified sums, to his sister Makbule and his five adopted daughters. Sabiha Gökçen was to receive in addition money sufficient to buy herself a house, while Makbule was to retain her house at Chankaya for her lifetime. Funds were to be set aside for the higher education of the children of Ismet Inönü.[1] The residue of the income was to be divided equally between the Linguistic and Historical Societies.

Fissinger returned from France and examined his patient carefully. He could hardly sit up in bed, and the time had come for a puncture to draw off some fluid. To Kiliç Ali, Atatürk murmured afterwards, "Did you see the water they took out? How could one bear it if so much water were put in a container and laid on one's belly?" He seemed to his friend to have suddenly become very thin, as though he were shrinking in bed from hour to hour. He was weak, but still signed documents, read the newspapers or had them read to him by Afet, listened to the gramophone and radio.

He saw few visitors, partly because the doctors discouraged them, partly because it suited the entourage to keep away those they mistrusted. Ali Fuad, after several unsuccessful attempts, finally succeeded in gaining admission. Atatürk pulled up the coverlet on his bed to conceal his swollen belly. He complained of his difficulty in breathing. Then, frowning and fixing his steel-blue eyes on Fuad, he took a long breath and launched into a discussion of the future. The present situation was far more critical than any they had faced together at the time of the armistice. A pair of adventurers was trying to conquer and rule the world by force, and there were no statesmen strong enough to stand up to them. Soviet Russia would know how to profit from the errors of both sides, and the whole international balance would change.

"If we commit the slightest mistake," he said, "we may possibly be faced with a catastrophe. . . . I *have* to be well enough to take the state in hand at that time. You know that here, in this country, one can never control anything from one's bed. I've *got* to be at the head of affairs." He talked of his illness, and Ali Fuad spoke words of reassurance. But Atatürk said, "Fuad Pasha, you're trying to soothe me in vain. One has to see the truth exactly as it is." They embraced and said good-bye. Despite further attempts, Ali Fuad was not admitted to see him again.

The fifteenth anniversary of the Republic was approaching—October 29, 1938. Some weeks before the celebration Atatürk called Kiliç Ali and Salih. Pointing to the bandages and the long woollen socks on his bedside table, he said, "Which shall I put on when I go to Ankara?"

1 Ismet himself had adequate means to support and educate his family. But Atatürk believed him, at this time, to be more ill than he was, and was providing for his possible early death.

Humouring him, Salih said, "Pasha, I have some stockings at home made for varicose veins. They will support your legs better." When they came, Atatürk said, "I will put these on my feet and a scarf round my neck. We can leave the train at the Gazi station and go straight to Chankaya. We must do this quickly."

But a few days after the puncture he fell into a coma which lasted for more than forty-eight hours. The doctors moved him into a narrower bed. Occasionally he opened his eyes, which were lifeless and dull. Intermittently he muttered, "Ah no, Effendim. No, no!" This might, it was feared, be the end. But he regained consciousness. By his bedside he found Celal Bayar, summoned from Ankara. "What happened to me?" he asked.

"You have slept deeply," Bayar replied. "A few hours longer than usual." Lest he suspect, Ülkü was told to tell him that he had slept for twelve hours. Instead she said, "You have slept a long time." As usual, he had the truth from her. He asked why his bed had been changed, and was told, "This one was cleaner." "Well," was his comment, "let me not ask too many questions." He started to talk once more of going to Ankara. His speech must be prepared for the Assembly. Let the various ministers provide notes, let Bayar prepare a draft which he could then write, in his own style, in Ankara. If he felt too tired he could shorten it. For the ceremonies a special lift was installed in the stadium, to take him up to his box; a special rostrum was constructed in the Assembly, in which he could lean back, half sitting but apparently standing.

But the doctors pronounced the journey impossible. The vibration of the train alone might be fatal. Rebelliously he insisted, "Let us go to Ankara. Whatever is going to happen to me, let it happen there." But, realistic to the last, he accepted their verdict. "All right," he concluded, "there is no sense in my going." He must at least be able to walk from the train to his car and from the car into the Assembly, and this he now knew he was too weak to do.

The speech must be read to the Assembly by Bayar. Atatürk received his Prime Minister in a dressing gown and insisted on hearing the whole of it. His mind was as lucid as ever, and to occupy it with politics, far from tiring him, seemed to give him renewed life. He made Bayar repeat paragraphs, corrected errors, redrafted with him the beginning and the end. To this he added the words, "I wish the Grand National Assembly success in all the business they undertake." These were the last of his words to be spoken in public.

The day of the fifteenth anniversary of the republic arrived. A group of cadets from the Kuleli Military School passed in a ferryboat before the Dolma Bahche Palace, shouting in unison, "We want to see Atatürk!" He heard them and insisted, despite efforts to restrain him, on going to the window. He was helped to a chair and looked out on the cadets. When they saw him they broke into a roar of welcome. Some of them jumped into the water in their uniforms and swam towards the palace to see him more closely. That night there were illuminations in the Sarayburnu Park. Celal Bayar returned from Ankara and gave Atatürk a detailed account of the parade there, and the people's enthusiasm.

There now remained only one problem to decide—that of the succession. Atatürk wanted Inönü to succeed him as President of the Republic and had sent an emissary to Ankara to ask his old friend to come to his bedside. He was told that Ismet was too ill to travel. He suspected, however, that Ismet's enemies among his entourage might be keeping him away. At one moment he even had the delusion that Ismet was dead and that the news was being kept from him. He thus secretly sent a second emissary in the shape of his dentist, Dr. Gunzberg, to report to him on the position.

In Ankara, the city of rumour, there were indeed some who believed that Celal Bayar and his friends were plotting to seize power on Atatürk's death. Inönü was thus strongly advised by responsible persons not to go to Istanbul, lest he be assassinated. These fears proved groundless. Bayar, much as he may have hoped for the succession, realized that the weight of opinion was in favour of Inönü. Fevzi (now Çakmak), the only other possible candidate, renounced his claims. Fethi (Okyar) went to Istanbul to clinch the matter of Ismet's succession with Bayar. When the end seemed near both Ismet and Fevzi were summoned to a Cabinet meeting in Ankara, at which one of Atatürk's doctors reported on his condition and the transference of the presidency was settled.

On November 6, Atatürk got up for the last time. Afet and his attendants helped him to his feet. His shoulders were thin and bony. Only his hands had not lost their shapeliness. He held out a hand to them and one by one they kissed it, sure that they would never do so again. Next day the doctors gave him another puncture, drawing off a large quantity of fluid. Afterwards he had a craving for an artichoke. They were out of season, and a consignment of them had been ordered from Hatay. But when the artichoke came he could not eat it. Not long afterwards, after a painful paroxysm, he murmured, "Good-bye." He fell into his last coma, still and apparently peaceful.

Next day towards midnight the climax approached. It became clear that he was dying. One of the doctors was weeping. The two others were massaging his feet. Hassan Riza, Kiliç Ali, and Ismail Hakki stood at attention by the bedside, like soldiers. Hassan said to Kiliç Ali, "Look. A piece of history is passing away."

Atatürk's face was drained of all colour. Soon after nine o'clock on the morning of November 10, 1938, he opened his eyes, which for a moment gleamed blue as ever, without recognition, at those around him. Then he closed them. His head fell back on the pillow. Kemal Atatürk was dead.

Istanbul was stunned into a poignant silence. Children tore ribbons and bows from their heads; women wept and muttered prayers in the streets before his photographs, now swathed in crepe. His embalmed body lay in state beneath the painted dome of the throne room, its chandeliers extinguished, in the Dolma Bahche Palace. The Turkish flag covered the ebony coffin. Six torches illuminated it; four officers of the land, sea, and air forces, with drawn swords, watched over the catafalque in shifts. For three days and nights he lay thus, while the people of Istanbul in their hundreds of thousands filed endlessly, reverently past him, bowing silently, whispering prayers, intoning softly, *"Ata, ata,"* for their father who was dead.

On the last night they stayed out in the streets until morning. They thronged the pavements, perched in the branches of the trees, clambered onto the domes and minarets of the mosques to see the long funeral cortège pass by. After a few brief prayers (on which his sister Makbule had insisted) the coffin was borne on a gun carriage, drawn by soldiers, in a slow procession to the quay below the Old Seraglio. Behind it an officer marched, carrying on a velvet cushion a solitary medal, that of the War of Independence. The procession crossed the Galata Bridge to the strains, unfamiliar to Turks, of Chopin's "Funeral March." The coffin was conveyed to a torpedo boat, then out to the *Yavuz,* which lay off Seraglio Point. Flanking her were the ships of all the nations so soon to be at war, among them H.M.S. *Malaya,* which had carried the last of the Sultans into exile. After salutes had been fired they slowly escorted the *Yavuz* out of the Bosporus and into the Marmara, where they bade her farewell.

At Izmit, in the evening, the coffin was placed in Atatürk's private saloon on the white presidential train, for burial in Ankara. The six torches surrounded it, the four officers carrying naked swords kept watch.

As the darkened train steamed off into the night, his compartment alone formed a rectangle of light, moving slowly over the infinite Anatolian landscape. Peasants in their thousands crowded down to the track to await the train and see the last of their "father." They waved torches and poured their scant rations of petrol on the ground, setting alight to it to blaze his way back into that homeland which he had made into a new Turkish nation.

► *Epilogue*

Kemal Atatürk had created a new Turkey. He had left it in the hands of an experienced leader, an efficient administration, and a flexible parliamentary system, capable of evolution in more liberal terms when the time became ripe.[1] He had transported his country from the Middle Ages to the threshold of the modern era and a stage beyond. It was now the task of his successors, covering new ground and filling in ground behind him, to carry it on a stage further.

The progress had been rapid—too rapid for some. In a mere half generation Atatürk had sought to build a new Turkish society. He had abruptly uprooted the traditions of centuries but had not yet evolved a new culture in place of them. This had caused some dislocation in the mind and the life of the ordinary Turk, whom a leader more sympathetic to Islam might well have weaned more gradually from one civilization to the other. As it was, some twenty years after Atatürk's death, a

---

[1] This happened in 1950, when free elections returned an Opposition party, that of the Democrats, to power, with Celal Bayar as President of the Republic.

successor was to imperil his Revolution by reviving and exploiting dormant forces of religion for political purposes.[2]

Socially, before Turkey could consolidate the unity which Atatürk had given her, a gap remained to be closed between the "two nations" of her illiterate peasantry and her literate bourgeoisie. It was this class, essentially urban in character, which was for the present the true beneficiary of the Turkish Revolution. Formed by Atatürk as a Westernized elite for the support and direction of a centralized government, it still needed to achieve close touch with the mass of the rural population, to whom the full benefits had not yet been able to percolate. Only the spread of education could close this gap, together with an effective grasp of economic problems which the generation of Atatürk lacked. Twenty-five years after his death his successors were engaged in a fresh national struggle to establish the country as a whole on a productive economic basis.

These, however, are hardly more than the growing pains of any new country. What Atatürk left to the Turkey he had freed was strong foundations and a clear objective for her future growth. He gave her not merely durable institutions but a national ideal, rooted in patriotism, nourished by a new self-respect, and promising fruitful rewards for new energies. He created, by his deeds and his words, a personal myth, to feed the imagination of a people given to the worship of heroes. He infused them with a belief in the values of Western democracy, which they learnt sincerely to respect, differing only as to the means of achieving it. All that he gave them survives as a living force in the Turk of today.

The logical outcome has been the emergence of the Turkish Republic as a reliable ally of the West. The soldier in Atatürk saved his country, confounding, as no other man at that time could have done, the designs of the European powers against it, and thus changing the face of its history. The statesman in him then won their acceptance of his country on equal terms, and ultimately its incorporation into the Atlantic Alliance, as a bulwark against Russia—its hereditary enemy—and an element of stability in the shifting Middle Eastern world.

Such was the life's achievement of Mustafa Kemal, "Father of the Turks."

LONDON-ISTANBUL-ANKARA-LONDON,

1960-1964

2 This was Adnan Menderes, the Democrat Prime Minister. His autocratic tendencies, suffused with an aura of "divine right," provoked, in 1960, a bloodless revolution which overthrew his regime and, after an interval of military government, established a new Constitution.

Appendix

► *The National Pact*

Close translation from the Turkish, made independently of the French version, of the text of the National Pact, as printed in the Proceedings of the Turkish Chamber of Deputies *of February 17, 1920.*

The Members of the Ottoman Chamber of Deputies recognise and affirm that the independence of the State and the future of the Nation can be assured by complete respect for the following principles, which represent the maximum of sacrifice which can be undertaken in order to achieve a just and lasting peace, and that the continued existence of a stable Ottoman Sultanate and society is impossible outside of the said principles:

First Article—Inasmuch as it is necessary that the destinies of the portions of the Turkish Empire which are populated exclusively by an Arab majority, and which on the conclusion of the armistice of the 30th October 1918 were in the occupation of enemy forces, should be determined in accordance with the votes which shall be freely given by the inhabitants, the whole of those parts whether within or outside the said armistice line which are inhabited by an Ottoman Moslem majority, united in religion, in race and in aim, imbued with sentiments of mutual respect for each other and of sacrifice, and wholly respectful of each other's racial and social rights and surrounding conditions, form a whole which does not admit of division for any reason in truth or in ordinance.

Second Article—We accept that, in the case of the three Sanjaks which united themselves by a general vote to the mother country when they first were free, recourse should again be had, if necessary, to a free popular vote.

Third Article—The determination of the juridical status of Western Thrace also, which has been made dependent on the Turkish peace, must be effected in accordance with the votes which shall be given by the inhabitants in complete freedom.

Fourth Article—The security of the city of Constantinople, which is the seat of the Caliphate of Islam, the capital of the Sultanate, and the headquarters of the Ottoman Government, and of the Sea of Marmora must be protected from every danger. Provided this principle is maintained, whatever decision may be arrived at jointly by us and all other Governments concerned, regarding the opening of the Bosphorus to the commerce and traffic of the world, is valid.

Fifth Article—The rights of minorities as defined in the treaties concluded between the Entente Powers and their enemies and certain of their associates shall be confirmed and assured by us—in reliance on the belief that the Moslem minorities in neighbouring countries also will have the benefit of the same rights.

Sixth Article—It is a fundamental condition of our life and continued existence that we, like every country, should enjoy complete independence and liberty in the matter of assuring the means of our development, in order that our national and economic development should be rendered possible and that it should be possible to conduct affairs in the form of a more up-to-date regular administration.

For this reason we are opposed to restrictions inimical to our development in political, judicial, financial, and other matters.

The conditions of settlement of our proved debts shall likewise not be contrary to these principles.

From *The Western Question in Greece and Turkey*
by Arnold J. Toynbee

► Chronology

1876 August 31. Abdul Hamid II proclaimed Sultan of Turkey.
      December 22. Abdul Hamid proclaims parliamentary Constitution.

1877 April 24. Russia invades Turkey.
      May. Abdul Hamid suspends Constitution and dissolves Parliament.

1878 January 31. Turkey sues for an armistice.
      March 3. Treaty of San Stefano.
      June 13-July 13. Congress and Treaty of Berlin.

1881 Birth of Mustafa to Ali Riza and Zübeyde at Salonika.

1883 German military mission established in Turkey.

1893 Mustafa enters Military Secondary School at Salonika, where he is given the
      additional name of Kemal.

1895 Mustafa Kemal enters Military Training School at Monastir.

1896 Revolt by students of Military Medical School in Constantinople suppressed.

1897 April 17. Turkey declares war on Greece, following a Greek threat to annex
      Crete. Peace settlement by intervention of the European powers.

1898 State visit of Kaiser Wilhelm II to Turkey.

1899 March 13. Kemal enters War College in Constantinople.

1902 Kemal graduates as lieutenant to Staff College in Constantinople.

1905 January 11. Kemal passes out of Staff College with rank of staff captain and is afterwards posted to Fifth Army in Damascus.

1906 October. Kemal helps to found Fatherland (*Vatan*) Society in Damascus.

1907 June 20. Kemal promoted to adjutant major.
September. Kemal posted to Third Army at Salonika.

1908 July 24. Young Turk Revolution in Salonika. Committee of Union and Progress forces Abdul Hamid to restore Constitution of 1876 and recall Parliament.
October 5. Bulgaria proclaims independence.
October 7. Austria-Hungary annexes Bosnia and Herzegovina.
October 12. Crete votes for union with Greece.
Kemal sent to Tripoli on mission for Committee of Union and Progress.

1909 April 13. Counterrevolution in Constantinople. Union and Progress striking force, with Kemal as divisional chief of staff, marches on the city from Salonika.
April 27. Deposition and exile of Abdul Hamid. Succession of Mehmed V as Sultan.
Kemal attends Congress of Union and Progress party in Salonika.
September 6. Kemal appointed commander of Third Army training course and later commander of 38th Infantry Regiment.

1910 Kemal serves as chief of staff in suppression of revolt in Albania.
Kemal sent to Paris with military mission to attend French Army manoeuvres.

1911 September 13. Kemal posted to General Staff in Constantinople.
October 5. Italian invasion of Tripoli.
Kemal with Turkish forces at Tobruk and Derna.
November 27. Kemal promoted to major.

1912 October 8–December 3. First Balkan War. Montenegro, Serbia, Bulgaria, and Greece invade Turkey. Severe Turkish defeats. Loss of Salonika. Armistice agreed before Constantinople. Kemal returns home.
Coup d'état against government by Union and Progress officers.
November 25. Kemal appointed director of operations for relief of Adrianople.
Fall of Adrianople.

1913 May 30. Treaty of London between Turkey and Balkan states.
June 30–July 20. Second Balkan War. Bulgaria attacks Greece, Serbia, and Rumania. Turkey recovers Adrianople.
September 17. Treaty of Bucharest restores territory to Turkey.
October 27. Kemal appointed military attaché in Sofia.

1914 March 14. Kemal promoted to lieutenant colonel.
June 28. Assassination of Archduke Franz Ferdinand at Sarajevo.
July 16. Kemal sends despatch to War Minister from Sofia, urging a policy of Turkish neutrality in the event of war, with a view to possible later intervention against Bulgaria and Central Powers.
July 28. Austria declares war on Serbia, with support of Germany.
August 2. Turkey signs secret alliance with Germany.

August 11. Turkey purchases German warships *Goeben* and *Breslau* on arrival in the Bosporus.

October 28. Turkey shells Russian Black Sea ports.

November 3. Russia declares war on Turkey.

November 5. Britain and France declare war on Turkey.

1915 February 2. Kemal appointed to reorganize and command 19th Division, in Thrace.

February 19. Unsuccessful Allied naval attack on Dardanelles.

February 25. Kemal establishes headquarters of 19th Division at Maidos, on Gallipoli Peninsula.

April 25. Allied military landings at Ariburnu (Anzac). Advance checked by Kemal, with 19th Division.

June 1. Kemal promoted to colonel.

August 8/9. Kemal appointed to command of Sixteenth Army Corps. Checks second Allied advance.

1916 January 9. Allied evacuation of Gallipoli Peninsula.

January 14. Kemal posted to Adrianople in command of Sixteenth Army Corps. Transfer to Caucasus front.

April 1. Kemal promoted to general and pasha.

June 27. Sherif of Mecca proclaims independence of Arabia.

August 6/7. Kemal recaptures Bitlis and Mush from Russians.

1917 March 5. Kemal appointed second-in-command—effective commander—of Second Army.

March 11. British forces capture Baghdad.

July 5. Kemal appointed commander of Seventh Army in Syria.

September 20. Kemal sends report to government on the poor state of the army and the country and relinquishes his command.

October. Kemal returns to Constantinople.

December 11. British forces capture Jerusalem.

December 15–January 5, 1918. Kemal visits Germany with Crown Prince Vahid-ed-Din.

1918 July 3. Death of Sultan Mehmed V. Vahid-ed-Din succeeds him as Mehmed VI.

August 7. Kemal reappointed commander of Seventh Army, in Palestine.

September 19–30. British forces under General Allenby drive Turkish forces out of Palestine and Syria. Kemal defends frontier north of Aleppo.

October 30. Armistice signed between Turkey and Britain at Mudros.

October 31. Kemal takes over command of army group at Adana.

November 7. Dissolution of army group.

November 13. Kemal returns to Constantinople. Allied fleets enter Constantinople.

November 21. Dissolution of Parliament.

1919 January 18. Opening of Peace Conference at Versailles.

April 30. Kemal appointed inspector general of Ninth (later Third) Army in Anatolia.

May 15. Greek forces land in Smyrna, with Allied approval.

May 19. Kemal lands in Samsun.

June 21. Kemal issues "Declaration of Independence" at Amasya. Summons Nationalist Congress at Sivas.

June 23. Kemal ordered by government to return to Constantinople.

July 8. Kemal resigns from the army and is dismissed by government.

July 23–August 6. Nationalist Congress at Erzurum, under presidency of Kemal. Issue of National Pact.

September 4–September 13. Nationalist Congress at Sivas under presidency of Kemal. Confirmation of National Pact. Establishment of Representative Committee.

October 5. Resignation of government.

November 7. New Parliament elected in Constantinople, with Nationalist representation.

December 27. Kemal establishes headquarters at Angora, with Representative Committee.

1920 January 28. National Pact adopted by Constantinople Parliament.

February 9. Evacuation of French garrison from Marash and start of general withdrawal from Cilicia.

March 16. Military occupation of Constantinople by Allies.

April 11. Dissolution of Constantinople Parliament.

April 23. First Grand National Assembly meets at Angora.

May 11. Kemal condemned to death by Sultan's government.

June 10. Treaty of Sèvres presented by Allies to Sultan's government.

June 22–July 9. Greek Army advances into Anatolia and captures Brusa.

August 10. Treaty of Sèvres signed by Sultan's government.

August 24. Draft treaty initialled in Moscow between Soviet Union and Nationalist government.

September 28–November 2. Nationalist forces invade Armenia and capture Kars.

December 2. Soviet Union establishes Armenian Republic at Erivan.

December 3. Treaty of Gümrü settles Turco-Armenian frontiers.

1921 January 6–10. Greek advance checked at first battle of Inönü.

January 20. Grand National Assembly at Angora adopts Constitution Act, based on popular sovereignty.

February 23–March 12. London Conference fails to reach agreement with Nationalists on modifications to Treaty of Sèvres.

March 16. Treaty of Moscow between Nationalist government and Soviet Union.

March 23–April 1. Greeks resume offensive in Anatolia and are checked at second battle of Inönü.

July 10. Greeks resume offensive and capture Eskishehir.

August 5. Kemal given full powers as commander-in-chief by Grand National Assembly.

August 23–September 13. Battle of the Sakarya. Turks check Greek advance before Angora.

September 19. Kemal given title of Gazi and rank of marshal by Grand National Assembly.

October 13. Treaty of Kars between Nationalist government and Transcaucasian Soviet Republics.

October 20. Treaty of Angora between Nationalist government and France.

1922 August 26–September 9. Nationalist forces defeat Greeks in counteroffensive and capture Smyrna, which is destroyed by fire.

September 23. Nationalist forces enter Neutral Zone at Chanak, threatening Constantinople.

October 3–11. Conference at Mudanya agrees on armistice between Allies and National government.

October 19. Resignation of Lloyd George and his government.

November 1. Kemal proclaims abolition of Sultanate.

November 17. Flight of Sultan Mehmed VI from Constantinople.

November 20. Opening of Peace Conference at Lausanne.

1923 January 14. Death of Zübeyde, Kemal's mother, in Smyrna.

January 29. Kemal marries Latife in Smyrna.

February 4. Breakdown of Lausanne Conference.

February 17. Kemal opens Economic Congress in Smyrna.

April 23. Resumption of Lausanne Conference.

July 24. Treaty of Lausanne.

August 9. Foundation of People's party.

August 11. Second Grand National Assembly.

October 2. Turkish forces occupy Constantinople, following Allied evacuation.

October 9. Angora (Ankara) becomes capital of Turkey.

October 29. Proclamation of the Turkish Republic, with Kemal as President.

1924 March 3. Abolition of the Caliphate, Ministry of Religious Affairs, and religious schools.

April 8. Abolition of religious courts.

November 17. Foundation of Progressive party.

1925 February 11–April 12. Revolt in Kurdistan.

March 4. Law for the Maintenance of Public Order gives government exceptional powers.

June 3. Suppression of Progressive party.

August 5. Kemal divorces Latife.

August 30–September 2. Kemal tours Kastamonu Province, announcing abolition of fez, suppression of religious brotherhoods, and closing of sacred tombs as places of worship.

1926 February 17. Adoption of new Civil Code.

June 5. Agreement on Mosul. Treaty of Angora between Turkey, Britain, and Irak.

June 15–July 13. Plot against life of Kemal in Izmir (Smyrna). Trial and execution of ringleaders.

August 1–26. Trial and execution of "Young Turk" leaders and others in Ankara.

1927 July 1. Kemal revisits Istanbul (Constantinople).
October 15–20. Kemal makes historic speech to Congress of People's party.
November 1. Third Grand National Assembly. Kemal re-elected President of the Republic.

1928 November 3. Introduction of Latin alphabet.

1930 August 12. Foundation of Free party.
November 17. Dissolution of Free party.
December 23. Religious riot at Menemen. Trials and executions.

1931 April 15. Foundation of Turkish Historical Society.
May 4. Fourth Grand National Assembly. Kemal re-elected President of the Republic.

1932 July 12. Foundation of Turkish Language Society.
August 12. Turkey becomes member of League of Nations.

1934 January 9. First Five Year Plan for industrial development.
February 9. Balkan Pact concluded between Turkey, Greece, Rumania, and Yugoslavia.
November 29. Kemal takes name of Atatürk, in terms of new law requiring Turks to adopt surnames.
December 8. Women made eligible to vote in parliamentary elections and to become members of Parliament.

1935 March 1. Fifth Grand National Assembly. Atatürk re-elected President of the Republic.

1936 May 29. Dispute regarding future status of Hatay (Alexandretta) referred to the League of Nations. Autonomy agreed between Turkey, France, and Syria.
July 20. Montreux Convention signed, regulating future Turkish regime for the Straits.
September 4. Visit of King Edward VIII to Atatürk in Istanbul.

1937 January 27. Autonomy of Hatay agreed between Turkey, France, and Syria.
July 9. Saadabad Pact signed between Turkey, Irak, Persia, and Afghanistan.

1938 March 11. Illness of Atatürk officially announced.
July 3. Franco-Turkish agreement to send French and Turkish troops into Hatay, to supervise elections.
September 2. Grand National Assembly votes nominal Republic of Hatay, with Turks in effective control.
September 18. Second Five Year Plan for industrial development.
November 10. Death of Atatürk.
November 11. Succession of Ismet Inönü as President of the Republic.

► Selected bibliography

UNPUBLISHED SOURCES

Presidential Archives, Çankaya, Ankara.
Papers on the History of the Revolution. Ankara University.
National Archives. Washington.
Papers of Admiral Bristol. Library of Congress, Washington.
Papers of Louis E. Browne. Stanford University, California.
Papers of Ambassador Joseph C. Grew. Harvard University.
Frederick P. Latimer. *The Political Philosophy of Mustapha Kemal Atatürk.* Doctoral Dissertation. Princeton: 1960.
Papers of Sir Horace Rumbold. Private.
Naval Memoirs of Admiral Sir Bertram Thesiger, 1875–94. Private.
Walter F. Weiker. *The Free Party of 1930 in Turkey.* Doctoral Dissertation. Princeton: 1962.

BOOKS: TURKISH

Dr. Afetinan. *Atatürk Hakkinda Hatiralar ve Belgeler* (Memoirs and Documents on Atatürk). Ankara: 1959.
Samet Ağaoğlu. *Babamin Arkadaşlari* (My Father's Friends). Istanbul: n.d.

Kiliç Ali. *Atatürk'ün Hususiyetleri* (The Characteristics of Atatürk). Istanbul: 1955.
———. *Hatiralarini Anlatiyor* (Recollections). Istanbul: 1955.
———. *Istiklal Mahkemesi Hatiralari* (Recollections of the Independence Tribunals). Istanbul: 1955.
———. *Son Günleri* (The Last Days). Istanbul: 1955.
Asim Arar. *Son Günlerinde Atatürk* (Atatürk in His Last Days). Istanbul: 1958.
Mehmet Arif. *Anadolu Inkilabi* (The Anatolian Revolution). Istanbul: 1924.
Kemal Atatürk. Edited by Uluğ Iğdemir. *Anafartalar Hatiralari* (Recollections of Gallipoli). Istanbul: 1955.
———. Edited by Enver Ziya Karal. *Atatürk'ün Söylev ve Demeçleri* (The Speeches and Statements of Atatürk). 3 vols. Istanbul: 1945; Ankara: 1954–59.
———. *Atatürk'den Düsünceler* (Thoughts from Atatürk). Ankara: 1956.
Falih Rifki Atay. *Mustafa Kemal'in Mütareke Defteri* (Atatürk's Armistice Notebook). Istanbul: 1955.
———. *Babamiz Atatürk* (Our Father Atatürk). Istanbul: 1955.
———. *Atatürk'ün Bana Anlattiklari* (What Atatürk Told Me). Istanbul: 1955.
———. *Çankaya.* Istanbul: 1958.
Sevket Süreyya Aydemir. *Suyu Arayan Adam* (The Man Who Searched for Water). Ankara: 1959.
Niyazi Ahmet Banoğlu. *Fikra, Nükte ve Çizgilerle Atatürk* (Anecdotes concerning Atatürk). 3 vols. Istanbul: 1954–55.
Ahmet Hamdi Başar. *Atatürk'le Üc Ay* (Three Months with Atatürk). Istanbul: 1945.
Celal Bayar. *Atatürk'ten Hatiralar* (Recollections of Atatürk). Istanbul: 1955.
Mustafa Baydar. *Atatürk ile Konuşmalar* (Interviews of Atatürk with Journalists). Istanbul: 1960.
Mevlut Baysal. *Çankaya'da Gazinin Hizmetinde* (At Çankaya: In the Service of Atatürk). Istanbul: 1954.
Tevfik Biyiklioğlu. *Atatürk Anadolu'da* (Atatürk in Anatolia). Ankara: 1959.
Behçet Kemal Cağlar. *Dolmabahçe'den Anit-Kabir'e* (From Dolma Bahche to the Mausoleum). Istanbul: 1955.
Ali Fuad Cebesoy. *Milli Mücadele Hatiralari* (Recollections of the National Struggle). Istanbul: 1953.
———. *Moskova Hatiralari* (Moscow Recollections). Istanbul: 1955.
———. *Siyasi Hatiralar* (Political Recollections). 2 vols. Istanbul: 1957–60.
Behcet Cemal. *Seyh Sait Isyani* (The Sheikh Saïd Rebellion). Istanbul: 1955.
Cevat Dursunoğlu. *Milli Mücadelede Erzurum* (Erzurum during the National Struggle). Ankara: 1946.
Ahmet Cevat Emre. *Iki Neslin Tarihi: Mustafa Kemal* (History of Two Generations: Mustafa Kemal). Istanbul: 1960.
Tayyip Gökbilgin. *Milli Mücadele Başlarken* (The Beginning of the National Struggle). Ankara: 1959.
Mustafa Selim Imece. *Atatürk'ün Şapka Devriminde Kastamonu ve Inebolu Seyahatleri* (Atatürk's Journeys to Kastamonu and Inebolu during the Hat Reform). Ankara: 1959.

Mahmut Kemal Inal. *Osmanli Devrinde Son Sadriazamlar* (Last Grand Viziers of the Ottoman Empire). Istanbul: 1940–53.

Feridun Kandemir. *Siyasi Darginliklar* (Political Quarrels). Istanbul: 1955.

———. *Izmir Suikastinin Ic Yüzü* (The Inside Story of the Izmir Conspiracy). Istanbul: 1955.

———. *Serbest Firka Nasil Kuruldu Nasil Kapatildi* (How the Free Party Was Formed and Suppressed). Istanbul: 1955.

Kiazim Karabekir. *Istiklal Harbimiz* (Our War of Independence). Istanbul: 1960.

Yakup Kadri Karaosmanoğlu. *Atatürk*. Istanbul: 1946.

Macide Vildan Kunter. *Atatürk'ün Hayati ve Basarilari* (The Life and Achievement of Atatürk). Istanbul: 1953.

Yunus Nadi. *Ali Galip Hadisesi* (The Ali Galib Incident). Istanbul: 1955.

———. *Mustafa Kemal Paşa Samsun'da* (Mustafa Kemal in Samsun). Istanbul: 1955.

———. *Ankara'nin Ilk Günleri* (Early Days in Ankara). Istanbul: 1955.

———. *Birinci Büyük Millet Meclisi Açilisi ve Isyanlar* (The First Grand National Assembly and the Insurrections). Istanbul: 1955.

———. *Çerkes Etem*. Istanbul: 1955.

E. Behnan Şapolyo. *Kemal Atatürk ve Milli Mücadele Tarihi* (Kemal Atatürk and the History of the National Struggle). Istanbul: 1958.

Ismail Habib Sevük. *Atatürk Için* (For Atatürk). Istanbul: 1939.

Feridun Fazil Tülbentci. *Cumhuriyet Nasil Kuruldu?* (How the Republic Was Founded.) Istanbul: 1955.

Ali Fuat Türkgeldi. *Görüp Isittiklerim* (What I Saw and Heard). Istanbul: 1949.

Ruşen Eşref Ünaydin. *Anafartalar Kumandani Mustafa Kemal ile Mülakat* (Interview with the Commander of Gallipoli). Istanbul: 1954.

———. *Atatürk'ü Özleyiş* (Longing for Atatürk). Ankara: 1957.

———. *Atatürk ve Milli Tesanüt* (Atatürk and National Solidarity). Istanbul: 1954.

———. *Türk Dili Tetkik Cemiyeti Kuruldüğundan Ilk Kurultaya Kadar Hatiralar* (Recollections of the Turkish Language Society). Ankara: 1933.

———. *Tarih ve Dil Kurumlari Hatiralari* (Recollections of the Language and Historical Societies). Ankara: 1959.

———. *Atatürk'ün Hastaliği* (Atatürk's Illness). Istanbul: 1959.

Atatürk'e Ait Hatiralar (Recollections of Atatürk). Istanbul: 1949.

30 Agustos Hatiralari (Recollections of the Victory of August 30). Istanbul: 1955.

Atatürk'un Yakinlarindan Hatiralar (Recollections of Atatürk by His Friends). Istanbul: 1955.

Atatürk'ün Nöbet Defteri 1931–1938 (Atatürk's Appointments Book). Ankara: 1955.

Minutes of the Grand National Assembly. 1920–23.

PERIODICALS AND NEWSPAPERS: TURKISH

Makbule Atadan. "Recollections of Her Brother, Atatürk," *Milliyet*, Istanbul: November 1955.

Kemal Atatürk. "Letters to Corinne Lütfu," *Milliyet,* Istanbul: November 1955.

Ömer Sami Coşar. "The Change in the Alphabet," *Milliyet,* Istanbul: November 1960.

Necmeddin Deliorman. "Recollections of Atatürk in Sofia," *Her Gün,* Istanbul: September, October 1955.

Perihan Naci Eldeniz. "Recollection of Atatürk," *Belleten* LXXX, Ankara: October 1956.

Çerkes Etem. "Recollections," *Dünya,* Istanbul: May-June 1962.

Ismet Inönü. "Recollections," *Akis,* Istanbul: January-September 1959.

Rauf Orbay. "Recollections," *Yakin Tarikhimiz,* Istanbul: March 1962–January 1963.

Military History Commission, Turkish General Staff. *Askeri Mecmua* (Military Journal), Istanbul: 1939.

BOOKS: OTHER LANGUAGES

W. E. D. Allen and Paul Muratoff. *Caucasian Battlefields.* Cambridge: 1953.

Tekin Alp. *Le Kémalisme.* Paris: 1937.

Brigadier General C. F. Aspinall-Oglander. *Military Operations: Gallipoli.* 2 vols. London: 1929–32.

Harold Armstrong. *Turkey in Travail.* London: 1925.

Kemal Atatürk. *A Speech.* Delivered at Angora, October 15–20, 1927. English translation. Leipzig: 1929.

Oliver Baldwin. *Six Prisons and Two Revolutions.* London: 1925.

C. E. W. Bean. *The Story of Anzac.* 2 vols. Sydney: 1921, 1924.

Lord Beaverbrook. *Politicians and the Press.* London: 1935.

———. *The Decline and Fall of Lloyd George.* London: 1963.

Ernest N. Bennett. *With the Turks in Tripoli.* London: 1912.

J. G. Bennett. *Witness.* London: 1962.

Benoist-Méchin. *Mustapha Kemal, où la mort d'un empire.* Paris: 1954.

Norbert de Bischoff. *La Turquie dans le monde.* Paris: 1936.

E. Brémond. *La Cilicie en 1919–1920.* Paris: 1921.

C. Roden Buxton. *Turkey in Revolution.* London: 1909.

Major General Sir C. E. Callwell. *Field Marshal Sir Henry Wilson: His Life and Diaries.* London: 1927.

Richard Washburn Child. *A Diplomat Looks at Europe.* New York: 1925.

Randolph Churchill. *Lord Derby.* London: 1959.

Winston Churchill. *The World Crisis: The Aftermath.* London: 1929.

Roderic H. Davison. *Turkish Diplomacy from Mudros to Lausanne* (in *The Diplomats 1919–1939*). Princeton: 1953.

Jean Deny. *Souvenirs du Gazi Moustafa Kemal Pasha.* Paris: 1927.

Halide Edib. *Memoirs.* London: 1926.

———. *The Turkish Ordeal.* London: 1926.

C. J. Edmonds. *Turks and Arabs.* Oxford: 1957.

Grace Ellison. *An Englishwoman in Angora.* London: 1924.

———. *Turkey To-day.* London: 1928.

E. E. Evans-Pritchard. *The Sanusi of Cyrenaica.* Oxford: 1949.

Lord Eversley. *The Turkish Empire*. London: 1917.

Louis Fischer. *The Soviets in World Affairs*. Vol. 1. London: 1930.

Paul Gentizon. *Mustapha Kemal, où l'orient en marche*. Paris: 1929.

Berthe Georges-Gaulis. *Angora, Constantinople, Londres*. Paris: 1922.

——. *Le Nationalisme Turque*. Paris: 1921.

——. *La Nouvelle Turquie*. Paris: 1924.

Sir Philip Gibbs. *Adventures in Journalism*. London: 1923.

Philip P. Graves. *Briton and Turk*. London: 1941.

Sir R. W. Graves. *Storm Centres in the Near East*. London: 1933.

Joseph Clark Grew. *Turbulent Era*. Boston: 1952.

General Sir Ian Hamilton. *Gallipoli Diary*. London: 1920.

General Sir Charles Harington. *Tim Harington Looks Back*. London: 1940.

Joan Haslip. *The Sultan*. London: 1958.

Alaeddine Haidar. *A Angora auprès de Mustapha Kemal*. Paris: 1921.

Ernest Hemingway. *The Snows of Kilimanjaro*. London: 1963.

Sir Nevile Henderson. *Water under the Bridges*. London: 1945.

Aubrey Herbert. *Ben Kendim*. London: 1924.

Uriel Heyd. *Foundations of Turkish Nationalism. The Life and Teachings of Ziya Gökalp*. London: 1950.

——. *Language Reform in Modern Turkey*. Jerusalem: 1954.

E. R. Vere Hodge. *Turkish Foreign Policy. 1918–1948*. Geneva: 1950.

E. M. House and C. Seymour. *What Really Happened at Paris*. London: 1921.

Harry N. Howard. *Partition of Turkey*. Oklahoma: 1931.

Ismet Inönü. *Negotiation and National Interest*. (In *Perspectives on Peace, 1910–60*.) New York: 1960.

Islamic Encyclopaedia (Islam Ansiklopedisi). *The Life of Atatürk*. English translation. Ankara: 1961.

Ernest Jäckh. *The Rising Crescent*. New York: 1944.

Gotthard Jäschke (with Erich Pritsch). *Die Turkei seit dem Weltkriege*. Berlin: 1929.

——. *Mustafa Kemals Sendung nach Anatolien* (in *Aus der Geschichte des Islamischen Orients*). Tübingen: 1949.

Ahmed Jemal. *Memoirs of a Turkish Statesman*. London: 1922.

Hans Kannengiesser. *The Campaign in Gallipoli*. London: 1928.

Kemal H. Karpat. *Turkey's Politics: The Transition to a Multi-Party System*. Princeton: 1959.

Ismail Kemal Bey. *Memoirs*. London: 1920.

E. F. Knight. *The Awakening of Turkey*. London: 1909.

Commandant M. Larcher. *La Guerre turque dans la guerre mondiale*. Paris: 1926.

T. E. Lawrence. *Seven Pillars of Wisdom*. London: 1935.

Bernard Lewis. *The Emergence of Modern Turkey*. London: 1961.

G. L. Lewis. *Turkey*. London: 1955.

D. Lloyd George. *The Truth about the Peace Treaties*. London: 1938.

Pierre Loti. *Disenchanted*. London: 1906.

E. G. Mears. *Modern Turkey*. New York: 1924.

Dagobert von Mikusch. *Mustapha Kemal*. London: 1931.

Alan Moorehead. *Gallipoli*. London: 1956.

H. Morgenthau. *Secrets of the Bosporus*. London: 1918.
Harold Nicolson. *Sweet Waters*. London: 1928.
———. *Lord Carnock*. London: 1930.
———. *Peacemaking 1919*. London: 1933.
———. *Curzon. The Last Phase*. London: 1934.
Irfan Orga. *Phoenix Ascendant*. London: 1958.
Irfan and Margarete Orga. *Atatürk*. London: 1962.
L. Ostrorog. *The Angora Reform*. London: 1927.
Frank Owen. *Tempestuous Journey: Lloyd George, His Life and Times*. London: 1955.
Michel Paillarès. *Le Kémalisme devant les Alliés*. Paris: 1922.
A. A. Pallis. *Greece's Anatolian Venture—and After*. London: 1937.
Franz von Papen. *Memoirs*. London: 1953.
Sir Edwin Pears. *Forty Years in Constantinople*. London: 1916.
Sultane Petroff. *Trente Ans à la cour de Bulgarie*. Paris: 1927.
John Presland. *Deedes Bey*. London: 1942.
G. Ward Price. *Extra-Special Correspondent*. London: 1957.
E. E. Ramsaur. *The Young Turks*. Princeton: 1957.
A. Rawlinson. *Adventures in the Near East*. London: 1923.
Richard D. Robinson. *The First Turkish Republic*. Harvard: 1963.
Earl of Ronaldshay. *Life of Lord Curzon*. 3 vols. London: 1928.
Sir Andrew Ryan. *The Last of the Dragomans*. London: 1951.
Liman von Sanders. *Five Years in Turkey*. London: 1927.
Leon Sciaky. *Farewell to Salonika*. London: 1946.
Count Carlo Sforza. *Makers of Modern Europe*. London: 1930.
———. *European Dictatorships*. London: 1932.
Clare Sheridan. *Nuda Veritas*. London: 1927.
———. *Papers Relating to the Foreign Relations of the United States, 1919*. Washington: 1934.
———. *Lausanne Conference on Near Eastern Affairs 1922–1923*. H.M.S.O., London: 1923.
C. H. Sherrill. *A Year's Embassy to Mustafa Kemal*. New York: 1934.
Elaine Diana Smith. *Turkey: Origins of the Kemalist Movement and the Government of the Grand National Assembly. 1919–1923*. Washington: 1959.
Ivan Spector. *The Soviet Union and the Moslem World*. Washington: 1956.
Willy Sperco. *Mustapha Kemal Atatürk*. Paris: 1950.
H. M. V. Temperley. *A History of the Peace Conference of Paris*. Vol. 6. London: 1924.
Major General Sir Charles Townshend. *My Mesopotamian Campaign*. London: 1920.
Arnold J. Toynbee. *The Western Question in Greece and Turkey*. London: 1922.
Sir Robert Vansittart. *The Mist Procession*. London: 1958.
Sir Telford Waugh. *Turkey: Yesterday, To-day and To-morrow*. London: 1930.
A. P. Wavell. *The Palestine Campaigns*. London: 1929.
———. *Allenby, Soldier and Statesman*. London: 1946.
Donald Everett Webster. *The Turkey of Atatürk*. Philadelphia: 1939.
The Duke of Windsor. *A King's Story*. London: 1951.
Ahmed Emin Yalman. *Turkey in the World War*. Yale: 1930.

————. *Turkey in My Time.* University of Oklahoma: 1956.

Francis Yeats-Brown. *Golden Horn.* London: 1932.

Zeine N. Zeine, *The Struggle for Arab Independence.* Beirut: 1960.

Survey of International Affairs. 1925, Vol. I; 1936; 1938, Vol. I. Oxford: 1927, 1931, 1941.

NEWSPAPERS, PERIODICALS, ETC.: OTHER LANGUAGES

A. Adnan, "Ten Years of Republic in Turkey," *Political Quarterly,* VI, London: 1935.

J. Walter Collins, article in *Contemporary Review,* XIV, London: 1933.

Sister Ethel Curry (Mrs. McLeod Smith). "A Prisoner in Aleppo," *Nurses' League Journal,* VII, Kensington, London: December 1919.

"Turkish Facts and Fantasies," *Foreign Affairs,* III, New York: July 1925.

Major General James Harbord. "American Military Mission to Armenia," International Conciliation, CLI, New York: June 1920.

————. "Investigating Turkey and Trans-Caucasia," and "Mustapha Kemal Pasha and His Party," *World's Work,* XL, New York: May, June 1920.

Enver Ziya Karal. "History-writing in Turkey," *Middle Eastern Affairs,* New York: October 1959.

"King-Crane Report," *Editor and Publisher,* New York: December 1922.

Sir Percy Loraine. *Kemal Atatürk: An Appreciation.* Reprint from broadcast delivered November 10, 1948, B.B.C., London.

Clair Price. "Kemal Pasha: Creator of a New Turkey," *Current History,* XVI, New York: 1922.

Dankwart A. Rustow. "The Army and the Founding of the Turkish Republic," *World Politics,* XI, New Haven, Conn.: 1959.

————. "Foreign Policy of the Turkish Republic," in *Foreign Policy in World Politics.* Englewood Cliffs, N.J.: 1958.

Talat Pasha. "Posthumous Memoirs," *Current History,* XV, New York: 1921.

Daily Express.

Daily Mail.

Chicago *Daily News.*

Manchester Guardian.

The Times.

ORAL SOURCES

As listed in Acknowledgments.

Maps

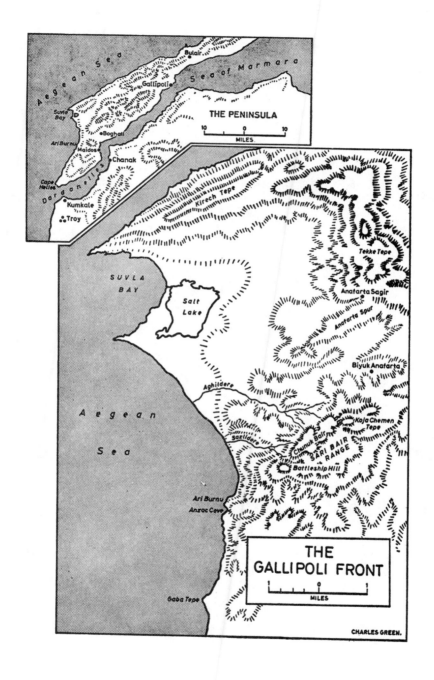

THE PENINSULA

Aegean Sea

Bulair

Sea of Marmara

Gallipoli

Suvla Bay

Boghali

Ari Burnu

Maidos

Chanak

Dardanelles

Cape Helles

Kumkale

Troy

MILES

10   0   10

THE GALLIPOLI FRONT

Kirech Tepe

Tekke Tepe

SUVLA BAY

Salt Lake

Anafarta Sagir

Anafarta Spur

Biyuk Anafarta

Aghildere

Aegean Sea

Sazlidere

Koja Chemen Tepe

Chunuk Bair

SARI BAIR RANGE

Battleship Hill

Ari Burnu

Anzac Cove

Gaba Tepe

MILES

0

CHARLES GREEN.

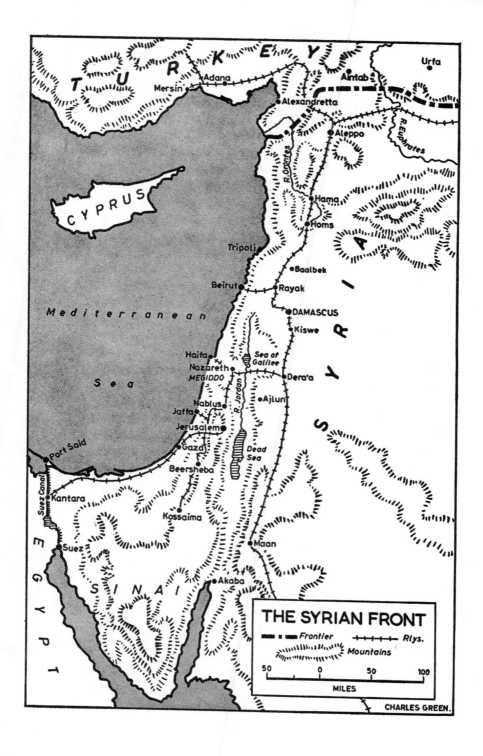

THE SYRIAN FRONT

Frontier — · — · —   Rlys. +++++++

Mountains

50   0   50   100

MILES

CHARLES GREEN.

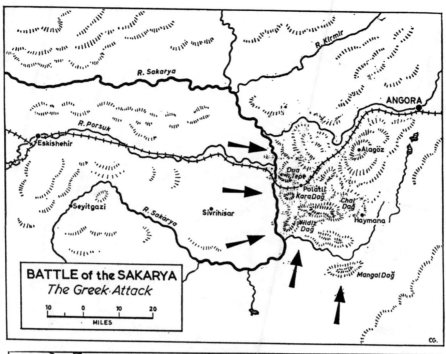

BATTLE of the SAKARYA
The Greek Attack

R. Kïrmïr

R. Sakarya

ANGORA

R. Porsuk

Eskishehir

Alagöz

Dua Tepe

Polatlï

KaraDağ

Chal Dağ

Seyitgazi

R. Sakarya

Sivrihisar

Hïldïr Dağ

Haymana

Mangal Dağ

```
10    0    10    20
        MILES
```

CG.

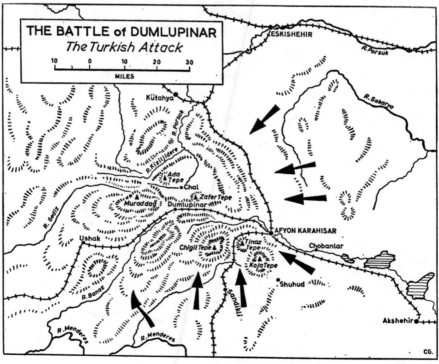

THE BATTLE of DUMLUPINAR
The Turkish Attack

```
10    0    10    20    30
        MILES
```

ESKISHEHIR

R. Porsuk

R. Sakarya

Kütahya

W. R. Porsuk

R. Kizil Idere

Ada Tepe

Chal

Zafer Tepe

Muraddağ

Dumlupinar

R. Gediz

AFYON KARAHISAR

Ushak

Chigil Tepe

Tïnaz Tepe

Chobanlar

KojaTepe

Sandïklï

Shuhud

R. Banaz

R. Menderes

Akshehir

R. Menderes

CG.

THE OTTOMAN EMPIRE
at the time
of its greatest extent

100   0   100   200   300
MILES

RUSSIA
R. Don
R. Volga
R. Dnieper
R. Dniester
Caspian Sea
YEDISAN
Odessa
CRIMEA
Novorossisk
Sebastopol
Black Sea
GEORGIA
Tiflis
AZERBAIJAN
Batum
Trebizond
Kars
R. Arpa Chai
ARMENIA
R. Aras
R. Çoruh
CONSTANTINOPLE
Samsun
Mt. Ararat
Erzurum
Adrianople
Sivas
Lake Van
KURDISTAN
Angora
Brusa
Diyarbekir
AZERBAIJAN
PERSIA
Eskishehir
ANATOLIA
Kayseri
Smyrna
Konya
Adana
Mosul
MESOPOTAMIA
Alexandretta
Aleppo
R. Tigris
Adalia
RHODES
SYRIA
R. Euphrates
Baghdad
CYPRUS
CRETE
Damascus
Beirut
HAURAN
R. Jordan
Sea
Basra
Jaffa
Jerusalem
Gaza
Beersheba
ARABIA
Suez
Akaba
Cairo
HEJAZ
R. Nile
EGYPT
Red Sea
Medina
Mecca
ASIR

Black
BULGARIA
EASTERN THRACE
Edirne
(Adrianople)
R. Maritza
Chatalja
Bosporus
Üsküdar
ISTANBUL
Sea of Marmara
Gallipoli
Chanak
Dardanelles
Tenedos
Ezine
Bandirma
Mudanya
Yalova
Izmit
Adapazari
Bolu
Eregli
Zonguldak
Inebolu
Sinop
Kastamonu
Chorum
Bursa
Mt Olympus
Bilejik
R. Sakarya
R. Kizilirmak
Inönü
R. Porsuk
Eskishehir
ANKARA
(Angora)
Polatli
Haymana
Yozgat
Kirshehir
Balikesir
Ayvalik
Mitilene
Kütahya
Murat Dag
Dumlupinar
Menemen
Manisa
R. Gediz
Izmir
Cheshme
Salihli
Ushak
Afyon Karahisar
Shuhud
Koja Tepe
Akshehir
Lake Tuz
Aydin
R. Menderes
Denizli
Isparta
Konya
Ulukishla
Antalya (Adalia)
R. Göksu
Tarsus
Mersin
DODECANESE
RHODES
CYPRUS
Mediterranean Sea

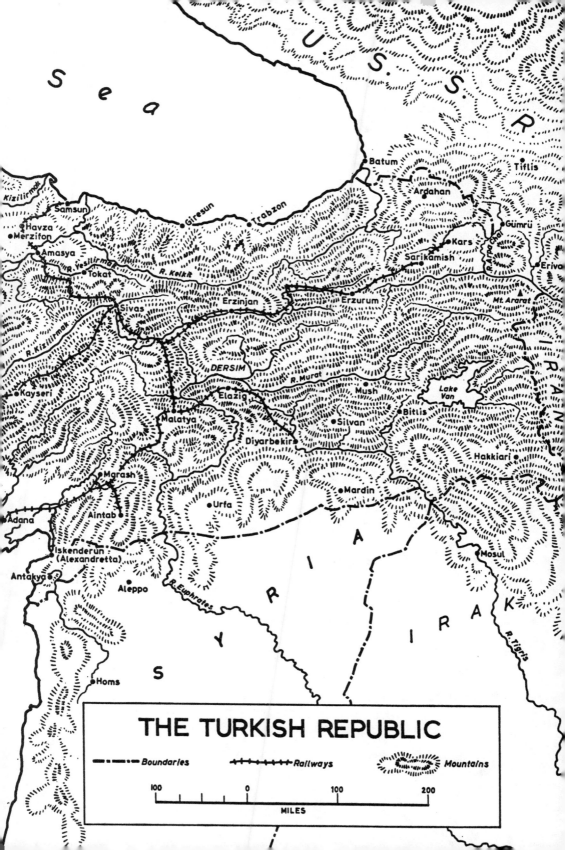

THE TURKISH REPUBLIC

— ·· — ·· — *Boundaries*	+++++ *Railways*	*Mountains*

100   0   100   200

MILES

Index

Coming Home

Coming Home

by
Katharine O'Flynn

Seraphim
EDITIONS

The publisher gratefully acknowledges the financial assistance of the Canada Council for the Arts and the Ontario Arts Council.

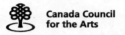

ONTARIO ARTS COUNCIL
CONSEIL DES ARTS DE L'ONTARIO
an Ontario government agency
un organisme du gouvernement de l'Ontario

Library and Arhives Canada Cataloguing in Publication

O'Flynn Katharine, 1940-, author
    Coming home / by Katharine O'Flynn.

ISBN 978-1-927079-42-3 (paperback)

    I. Title.

PS8629.F59C64 2016   C813'.6   C2016-904202-2

Editor: Bernadette Rule
Front cover photo courtesy Creston & District Museum & Archives, Creston BC.
Design and Typography: Julie McNeill, McNeill Design Arts

Published in 2016 by
Seraphim Editions
4456 Park Street
Niagara Falls, ON
Canada L2E 2P6

Printed and bound in Canada

To Libby and John

Acknowledgements

I would first like to offer my sincere thanks to editor Bernadette Rule, publisher Maureen Whyte and designer Julie McNeill for their very kind help and encouragement in bringing this book to completion. Their commitment to and enthusiasm for the project kept me going. Thank you.

Thanks also to the staff of Creston Museum for their help in providing access to their excellent archival collection.

I would also like to express my thanks to the late Huw Evans for information about the Evans family in Australia. And finally, of course, thanks and fond remembrance to Olwen, my mother, who even in old age never forgot Creston and loved to talk about her childhood there.

The following chapters first appeared in slightly different form in these publications:

For King and Country in *Engraved, Canadian Stories of World War One*, 2014

Love Calls me by my Name (under the title Leaving Saskatchewan) in *CommuterLit Selections Arrivals and Departures*, 2014

Leaving the Empire in *Canadian Stories*, Vol. 16, No. 92, 2013

Grace Paley once said that any story told twice becomes fiction. The stories of *Coming Home* have been told at least twice, and probably several times more. In my re-telling of these family stories, I have changed some names, occasionally altered the sequence of events, and imagined people's thoughts and conversations and the settings for these, but, as far as I know, the events and the characters of the stories are true.

Table of Contents

Chapter 1

*W*estward the Star of Empire Takes its Way

My Gran, Mildred Young, had one blue eye and one brown. This was not a matter of subtle shading; one eye was distinctly pale Viking blue and the other a deep, dark Celtic brown. This anomaly gave her a strange, somewhat disturbing appearance like a Picasso portrait. She herself was not at all embarrassed by the peculiarity. Indeed, she considered it a distinction. "To have eyes of different colours is a sign of great beauty," she claimed.

Even as her hair turned grey and her blue eye and her brown dimmed, she continued to think of herself as an exceptionally attractive woman and felt it was only right that she should adorn herself in a manner appropriate to such beauty. She could not limit herself to only one piece of jewellery at a time. Rows of colourful brooches flashed across her ample bosom like military medals, and ropes of artificial pearls and glass beads clattered among them. She favoured garments of silk and velvet in rich colours: peacock blue, crimson, or purple. And she would never dream of leaving the house without topping off the ensemble with a magnificent hat, laden with artificial flowers or fruit, ribbons, veiling and feathers. As she was not tall – barely five feet – and stoutly built around a narrow waist in a pouter pigeon sort of shape, it required confidence to carry off the look. Gran believed in her beauty.

"How nice you look, Gran!" always brought a regal smile in acknowledgement of the obvious.

"But how I wish you could have seen me when I was young," she might say then with a sigh, "when my complexion was unblemished, and my hair was golden and hung to my waist. Then it was that my beauty caught admiring attention on all sides."

She liked to tell the story of how as a young girl, she had once hurried through the streets of London, late, late at night. "My sister Lucy was ill with fever; my father was away; my mother could not leave Lucy's side. I was the only one who could go to fetch the doctor, so I went. I ran through the dark and dangerous streets of London, a beautiful and defenseless girl with long blond hair rippling loose. I was only sixteen years of age, and all alone in the midnight city. The wonder was I wasn't captured for the white slave trade or kidnapped, or worse. How I ran with my golden hair streaming behind me! I fetched the doctor." She loved that image of her beauty shining through a dark and dangerous landscape, and so did all who heard her story.

But my story of Mildred begins later in her life, in 1907, when she was forty-seven and proprietor of a boarding house for professional gentlemen in the Hammersmith district of London. In her years of youth and beauty she had never imagined that her life would bring her to earning her own living, but so it had turned out.

She had been born into a family of writers, not the great writers of the Victorian era, but competent essayists and writers of popular sketches. She had had no formal education but she had acquired the arts and graces considered appropriate for young ladies of the time. She could paint pretty scenes in watercolours, though in truth she preferred to sketch dresses and hats. She excelled in needlework both plain and fancy. She learned to carry herself with dignity, to sit with a ramrod straight back, to converse politely in society. Because her family was not so very well off, she also learned to keep a sharp eye on the servants and the tradespeople's bills, and when necessary, she could pitch in and help with household chores. Proud of her family's connection with the literary world, she was well read, attended the theatre and opera regularly, and spoke like a lady in a Jane Austen novel.

At seventeen, she married James Young, a clerk in the Office of Public Works, charged with monitoring the expenses of the royal household. He also held the post of external examiner in mathematics for Cambridge University. Mildred and James had five children. Whether or not theirs was a happy marriage is not known. One suspects it was not, for James had a reputation as a martinet with a fierce temper. Examination candidates, though grown men, were said to quake before him and his children were terrified of him.

At the early age of forty, James died of a heart attack, a victim perhaps of his own choleric temperament. He collapsed in a railway carriage on the way to an examination and was dead on arrival in Cambridge. (One likes to imagine the astonished relief of the examination candidate on hearing the sad news!)

Mildred was left in the classic sad story situation of the penniless widow with growing children to care for cast suddenly adrift in the harsh world. Fortunately, she was not the kind of woman to sink down spinelessly into genteel poverty. Instead, she turned the family home into a boarding house for single gentlemen: clerks in government offices, most of them. She learned to make substantial and tasty meals with cheap cuts of meat, lots of potatoes, and large, sweet, filling puddings. She became a careful shopper, finding the best prices among the local greengrocers and fishmongers. She supervised her two servant girls strictly and she stood for no nonsense from her gentlemen boarders. She managed well.

Mildred's children grew to adulthood. Her two sons found employment, her eldest daughter a suitable husband. Now there were only the two youngest daughters, Sarah and Charlotte, at home. Mildred had more rooms to let. The boarding house business was going well.

At that time a new boarder moved in, Tom Evans, a young Welshman working as a clerk in the post office. Mildred liked him at once for he was an aspiring poet, a literary scholar, and a professed admirer of the works of her no longer illustrious grandfather and father. Tom was handsome in a romantic, gypsy-like way, with wild, thick black hair and a swarthy complexion, and he had the Welsh gift for poetry and song and lively talk. Evenings, when he wasn't out singing or poeticizing with his Welsh friends or drinking with the Bohemians at the Café Royale, he would get up entertainments in Mildred's parlour: play readings, musical programmes, hymn sings, recitations. These cultural evenings brought Mildred to relive the happy days of her childhood when literary lions gathered for talk and readings in her grandfather's parlour.

All the residents of the house enjoyed the performances and were eager to participate. Mildred recited Tennyson, Tom read from the work of the new poets Stephens, Middleton or Davies, and the girls gave comic performances of Belloc's newly published *Cautionary Tales for Children*. Some evenings there were play readings: Mildred was Lady Macbeth, the girls were giggling witches and Tom was Macbeth. Mildred was Lady Bracknell and Sarah was Gwendolyn Fairfax. Some evenings Tom pounded out hymns on the cottage piano and everyone sang; or Sarah played while Tom and Charlotte sang a duet; Sarah and Tom sat side by side at the piano and played a duet and Charlotte danced. Once in a while the company might persuade Tom to read from his own work. His poems were in Welsh so none but the Welsh cousin who shared his room could understand a word, but Mildred said it sounded very nice anyway and Sarah and Charlotte agreed. "That is because Welsh is the language of Heaven itself," the cousin told them with a serious satisfaction.

One evening, after Tom had been living in the boarding house for a few months, he sat beside Mildred on the settee. They had just finished a reading of selections from *A Midsummer Night's Dream*. "May I have a word with you, in private?" Tom asked.

"Certainly." Mildred's heart began to beat quickly. He would ask then. She had thought he might, though she was, to be sure, more than ten years older than he, but still, you might say, in the prime of her beauty. She touched her hair, its rippling gold fading perhaps just a little. She willed the others to drink up their tea quickly and go. The boarders went off, one by one. There were only Sarah and Charlotte and Mildred and Tom left.

"Run along to bed now, girls; it's late. Tom and I have a business matter to discuss," Mildred said. Since the arts entertainments had begun, all the occupants of the house were on first name terms, a familiarity Mildred had never before allowed her boarders.

Charlotte wanted to linger to pester Tom with questions about a reading list he was preparing for her, but Sarah, the dear girl, dragged her off.

"Now?" Mildred turned towards Tom.

"Sarah," Tom said without any introduction. "I love her. Have I your permission to court her?"

The tea cup in Mildred's hand trembled in its saucer. She set it down on the small table beside her. "Sarah?" she said. And again, "Sarah." Through her mind rushed a stream of images: Sarah sitting close to Tom on the piano bench, their hands crossing and recrossing each other playfully along the keyboard; Sarah playing an adoring Juliet to Tom's Romeo; Sarah brushing against Tom as she reached to take his tea cup or pass him another slice of cake. Mildred should have paid closer attention, read the message in these signs. "Sarah is very young," she managed to say.

The stream of images went on: Sarah trying to pronounce the words of some Welsh poem and Tom's hands moulding her cheeks to the desirable shape for the double 'll' sound; Sarah beside Tom when they all went walking on Hampstead Heath one fine afternoon – Sarah, who was no longer a child, but a nineteen-year-old beauty with ash blond hair and pale blue eyes. "She is too young."

Tom was twenty-five, Mildred knew. That made him, when reckoned more carefully than she'd been inclined to do, twenty years younger than she was, not ten. In his view she would be an old lady, a game old girl reciting poems from the last century, a mother of grown children, and far too old for him. She saw it now with perfect, painful clarity. What could she have been thinking of? Well, she hadn't thought; that was the problem. She had only felt and let her foolish feelings run riot over her common sense. Now it was quite clear: Sarah was the obvious magnet for Tom's affection. Charlotte was too young. She, Mildred, was too old. Tom had chosen wisely and well.

"Sarah is nineteen," Tom was saying, as if Mildred didn't know. "Old enough, surely. So beautiful." He blushed, and added, "In character, as well as in her person. I love her dearly and thanks to the promotion I have had, I am now in a position to support a wife."

Mildred took a deep breath. "And Sarah? Have you made your feelings known to her? Do you have reason to think that she reciprocates your affection?"

"I believe I can safely say she would be willing to be courted," Tom said with a knowing smile. "With your permission, Mildred."

"Then I grant you my permission," Mildred said with a self–control that cost her dearly.

She should have seen how it was. She should never have allowed herself those fanciful dreams of running her hands through Tom's thick black hair, of drowning in his deep dark eyes. She could only be thankful that those dreams had remained unspoken and, she was fairly certain, unsuspected by Tom or anyone else.

She might have wept a little in the privacy of her own bedroom that night, but by next morning she showed no signs of any disappointment she might have suffered. She had never spoken of the feelings she had cherished, she never would, nor would she allow herself even to think of them ever again. She would rejoice in her Sarah's happiness, and Tom's.

Fearing that Charlotte might also find Tom's choice disappointing, Mildred woke her youngest with a cup of tea and the bad news. As she had suspected it might, the revelation threw Charlotte into a torrent of bewilderment, anger, jealousy, disappointment. "I thought he loved me too," she wept. "He does love me too."

"He does, indeed, but not in the way he loves Sarah," Mildred said. "Some day, when you are older, you too will experience the feelings those two have for each other. It is quite different from the affection you feel for him and he for you." It was hard on the poor girl. "Try to be happy for your sister," she urged. "It is her time now. Your turn will come when you find your own love."

"I have found my love," Charlotte wailed. "And he has chosen Sarah!"

"I think not, not yet, my dear," Mildred said, but Charlotte would not be comforted. Though the sisters had always been close, Charlotte now avoided Sarah as much as she could. She would no longer join in the musical evenings or the readings. She pretended to suffer from headaches and spent a lot of time in her room.

Mildred behaved correctly. She sewed wedding clothes and hemmed sheets and pillowcases and smiled at the happy couple whispering together on the sofa, stealing kisses when they thought she wasn't looking. She was happy for Sarah, although sometimes a look from Tom, or the way he laid a hand on her arm as he made a point in his impassioned talk of poetry, made her want to be as sulky and cross as Charlotte. She did not yield to the impulse. Self-discipline was one of the great Victorian virtues she was imbued with.

Mildred encouraged the young lovers to marry as soon as they liked. Both she and Charlotte would be much better off without Tom's presence in the house tempting their thoughts to stray where they should not go. Sarah and Tom married early in 1907.

And then Mildred announced her plan to emigrate to Canada.

She discussed with no one the reasons for the sudden departure. In truth, it wasn't just the marriage of Sarah and Tom that had brought her to the decision. Years ago her parents, her brother Percy, and younger sister Mae had gone to Canada. She had envied them the adventure. But she was a wife and mother by then, and travel to distant lands was out of the question for her. In her family's letters she had read accounts of vast forests where deer and bear and wolves still roamed, of lakes as wide as seas, towering mountains, vast plains, busy new towns and cities, and a railroad that crossed the whole huge country. She had longed to go to Canada and see this new world for herself. And now she was free. Now she could go. In the streets of London she saw posters and red wagons advertising the new Dominion with pictures of bright maple leaves and fields of wheat. The slogan on the posters, "Westward the Star of Empire takes its way", appealed to her. She made her way to the Canadian Emigration Offices on Charing Cross Road and booked passage for herself and Charlotte to Canada.

"Why?" her astonished family asked. With her business running smoothly and only one child left in her care, Mildred could sit back and enjoy her later years in comfort and security, they thought. Why ever would she want to strike out for a new country now?

She wanted to go because now with her children, all but one, married, independent and established in their own households, she could follow an old dream of her own and at the same time escape the pangs of a more recent dream that had failed. She didn't care to discuss all this with her children. "I think it best," she said.

"Why Canada?" Sarah asked.

"It is a land of cold winters and deep forests. I fear you will miss the cultural amenities of our London," Tom said.

That is not what she would miss. "I have always wanted to go to Canada. We have family connections there." Though her parents had returned to England, her brother and sister had remained in Canada and still sent reports of life on the frontier there, and another brother, blind from birth, was completing his education at a special school in Brantford. She would visit them and see the country for herself.

"But the rest of your family, your children, and a grandchild now as well, are here in England," her son Took pointed out.

"Charlotte will travel with me."

"I don't want to go to Canada," Charlotte protested at once. Charlotte was the delicate flower of the family, beautiful as Mildred herself had been, with the same golden hair, though both her eyes were blue, a dreamy grey-blue the colour of an early summer dusk. Charlotte had been singled out by a rich aunt to receive a convent education in Belgium. She could speak French, and sing prettily and dance and paint charming watercolours and Tom had recently awakened her interest in the theatre arts, in which she showed considerable talent. She did not wish to waste these talents on lumberjacks and cowboys and red Indians in some remote colony.

Mildred did not care to argue with her children. "I am sure you will like Canada very much. And so shall I. We leave in a fortnight."

Charlotte continued to protest. She had hardly spent any time in London at all. She did not want to be separated again from her dear brothers and sisters. She did not want to leave her friends here. Tom was getting up a play and she was to have the starring role in it.

Charlotte was too young to know what was good for her. "There is a great deal to be done and time is short," Mildred told her. She had bought the tickets and given notice to her boarders and recommended other boarding houses and residential hotels to them. She had written letters to the Canadians of the family, advising them of her impending visits. Now she had to divide up her furniture among her married children. She had to run up smart travelling costumes with matching hats and a couple of light summer dresses as well for wear in the Canadian summer, which was said to be very warm. Charlotte could help with the sewing. She took some slight interest in this, which Mildred took to be a good sign.

All was settled: the leasehold sold, the lodgers gone, the furniture disposed of, the tickets in hand.

Tom accompanied the ladies to Euston Station to see them on to the boat train. He embraced first Charlotte, who wept and clung to his coat shamelessly, and then Mildred, who herself had to fight back tears as she received a first and last chaste kiss from the lips of her handsome, beguiling, and all too dangerous son-in-law.

Mildred would not allow herself to pine for what was past. On board ship she dressed in her most elegant new costumes. She enjoyed the delicious and ample dinners served in the dining saloon. She joined whist parties and gambled small sums of money and occasionally won. Charlotte, despite continued lamentations at her hard fate as an exile from all she held dear, did sometimes appear to find a few moments of pleasure in the evening dances and entertainments and occasionally she condescended to promenade the desk with some suitable young man.

But on the train journey that followed the sea crossing, Charlotte's complaints grew more bitter, with, Mildred had to admit, some justification. Hour after hour for a day and a night and another day the ladies sat in a swaying drafty coach, passing by woods and fields and very few towns, waiting to arrive at their first destination, Brantford Ontario and its School for the Blind. There were no entertainments to pass the time on the train as there had been on the boat. Charlotte was bored and cross, and even Mildred found the journey wearying.

At last they reached Brantford and the school, and found Bob waiting for them in a reception room. Tall and thin with a mop of bright red hair, he looked more like a growing boy than a man in his thirties. "Caaaaan it reaaally be you, Miiiiiildred?" he greeted his sister and reached to touch her face to make sure. His voice was a screeching, high-pitched drone.

"It is I, and here is Charlotte with me."

"Chaaaarloooootte!" Bob searched the young woman's face with his fingers. "Beauuuuutiful, like her moooother."

Poor Bob, Mildred thought. How would he ever know such a thing? But it was gallant of him to say so. "You look well yourself, not a day older than when you left England," she told him.

"Aaaaand you as weellll," Bob assured her.

Mildred was pleased to see how Bob had profited from his stay at Brantford. He was able to show his visitors around the school and grounds. He walked confidently through rooms and corridors, avoiding furniture and obstacles, opened and closed doors, pointed out trees he was especially fond of on the lawn, and introduced the ladies to teachers and pupils they met on their tour.

In a private interview with Mildred, the director praised Bob's skills: he had learned braille quickly and had become an avid reader. He had achieved a high level of independence in getting about and in looking after himself. Unfortunately he was not so apt a pupil in learning the trades taught at the school: chair caning, hammock weaving and piano tuning. He was clumsy with his hands and had no ear for tonal distinctions. There had been some hope that he might become a teacher of braille, but his manner of speech would be a torment to pupils in the classroom, the director feared. Unfortunately, there was no other work available for Bob. He must resign himself to living on his family's charity.

It would be hard for Bob to know himself excluded from useful employment despite all that he had learned, Mildred knew, but it could not be helped. Apparently he could not learn to speak with normal pace and intonation. Mildred's other brother in Canada, the Reverend Percival Young, had offered to take Bob into his home in Edmonton. Perhaps there he would find some useful tasks he could perform and some pleasures he could enjoy. Mildred and Charlotte would accompany Bob on the journey to Edmonton, and would look about with a view to settling in that city.

"Diiiiistances in Caaanaada are considerable," Bob informed the ladies when they boarded the westbound train. They were appalled to learn that they would be on this train for two days and two nights. Bob didn't seem to mind. He ate his way contentedly through large meals in the dining car, or sat looking out the window at endless dark forests and snow-covered plains he could not see, while Mildred and Charlotte found the scenery dull and the coach drafty and dirty and wondered again and again if the next station mightn't be Edmonton.

Eventually they arrived, in the middle of a snow storm. "Snow! In April! Mildred exclaimed. "Dear me!" She took an instant dislike to Edmonton. The northern frontier had sounded exciting in letters and stories, but in actual experience Mildred found it cold and bleak and uncomfortable. She soon knew she could never live here. She was sorry to leave Bob in such a place, but there was nothing else for it. He seemed to have settled in easily. In two weeks, Mildred and Charlotte were ready to move on. "Westward the Star of Empire takes its way."

This time the journey was one of only a few hours, and more south than west to Pincher Creek in southern Alberta where Mildred's sister Mae lived. Mae had, since her emigration to Canada, married a Swedish settler by the name of Helmer. It was a delight for Mildred to see her dear sister again, but she hardly knew what to make of her taciturn brother-in-law. She couldn't help but think he was angry at the presence of two extra females in his household, although Mae assured her that Helmer was always rather silent, and a little shy because his English was not quite fluent. Mildred and Charlotte could stay as long as they wished. Mae was very glad of their company, and so was Helmer, even if he didn't say so.

But they did not wish to stay long. Pincher Creek was even worse than Edmonton in Mildred's estimation. Here the snow had yielded to a sticky, cold mud. The houses were small and mean and far apart and hardly anyone in town spoke English. People were mostly all as silent as Mae's husband. Even Mae herself seemed to have lost the knack of lively conversation. The talkative and gay young woman Mildred remembered from earlier years had become a stout matron, slow of speech and seldom brought to laughter. Perhaps living in this hard new country made people harder, sterner, shaped them like the landscape itself. Mildred confided this theory to Charlotte as the two women prepared for bed in the cold, cramped bedroom they shared.

"No surprise there," Charlotte agreed at once. "You'd be feeling quite grim too if you had to face a lifetime in this country. When are we going home?"

"We are not going home," Mildred answered. "We have emigrated."

Charlotte brushed her hair with short, angry strokes. "We should never have come," she said. "Never. We were quite happy enough at home in England."

They were not quite happy in England, Mildred knew. In any case, she would neither argue nor put up with defeatism. "We shall stay here with Mae for at least a week or two," she said. "Mae is my sister and we have much to talk about.

She suggested a distraction that might amuse Charlotte. "Why don't you try some sketching of the scenery?"

"Paint scenes of brown mud? I don't think!" Charlotte flung herself into the bed and pulled the blankets over her head. She hadn't wanted to come to Canada; she didn't like the country, and she was not going to hide her displeasure at having been made to come. But Charlotte was young, she would adapt and come to love this strange new country, Mildred told herself as she unpinned her long, thick hair that had once been her crowning glory. Now it flashed with silver amid the gold in the pale glow of the oil lamp on the dresser. Yes, Charlotte would soon feel at home in Canada, but would Mildred herself? Change and adaptation do not come as easily to the old. For the first time, doubts about the wisdom of the venture crept into Mildred's mind. Thus far she had been almost as disappointed in Canada as Charlotte was, though she would never admit that aloud. This country was too large, too raw, too close to the emptiness of the sky. One could be lonely here, as she guessed Mae was lonely among the silent Swedes and the vast fields and the endless railway. Her parents had not loved the country enough to remain long. Percy had stayed, but he had his vocation to spread the gospel that kept him here, and Mae had her silent, but kind, husband. What was there here for a middle-aged widow and a pretty, talented, eighteen-year-old girl who had hopes and dreams of love and a beautiful and happy life?

Mildred did not allow herself to think such discouraging thoughts for long. Perhaps, she told herself, their next place of call would have more appeal. They were to move on to Creston in southeastern British Columbia. There they were to stay with Mae's daughter from her first marriage, Olive. Olive had married an English army officer after the Boer War and emigrated with him to this small town in the Kootenay

Mountains, close to the American border, and she seemed to be very happy there.

If they found nothing to hold them in Creston, Mildred didn't quite know what she'd do. Move on to Victoria at the very outside edge of Canada? Return to England and set up another boarding house? In truth, she feared she hardly had enough money left for either of those schemes. She was disappointed and a little frightened as well. But she was not going to admit it. "I am sure we will both like Creston very much." Mildred climbed into the cold bed and blew out the oil lamp.

For the next week Mildred and Mae talked and talked about a past that didn't much interest Charlotte, who stared out the window and sighed. When Helmer wasn't at work, he sat silent in a corner smoking his pipe, and slowly reading a newspaper, pointing to each word. He was doing this to improve his English, Mae explained. On Saturday evening everyone got dressed up and neighbours arrived by foot and in wagons to meet the visitors from England. It was a subdued gathering. Hardly anyone knew enough English for a conversation and those who did hardly knew what to say. They ate cake and drank coffee. One red-faced young man engaged Charlotte in a brief conversation about the weather and then blurted out a marriage proposal. "No thank you," Charlotte answered politely and turned away. So did the young man. He hadn't really expected an acceptance. Charlotte didn't even know his name. She almost felt sorry for him. He probably didn't like being stuck in this forlorn place either.

Sunday morning they attended a church service in a hall above the general store in town. At least they heard English spoken there.

And then at last it was time to move on to Creston.

Helmer helped the ladies into the coach and stowed their bags on the luggage rack. As Mildred hardly felt on kissing terms with this brother-in-law, she shook his hand in farewell, but Charlotte offered her cheek for a kiss, either out of her naturally affectionate nature, or out of joy at the departure. Then Helmer hurried out to stand beside his wife on the platform. Mildred waved vigorously. "Do wave to

Mae," she urged Charlotte. "She'll miss you, you know. She says you remind her of her Olive."

Mildred watched the two silent figures growing smaller on the bare platform. Only when they and the station had disappeared did she turn away. It was too sad to think that her sister lived in such a place with such a man, however kind he was inside his silence.

Charlotte removed her hat and gloves and settled back in her seat. "Another train journey," she sighed.

"This one won't be so very long," Mildred answered.

"That's what you said when we left Saint John. That's what you said when we left Brantford. This country goes on and on. Forests and fields. Forest and fields. It never ends. We shall fetch up in China eventually, I expect."

"Nonsense. I've spoken to the conductor. We arrive tomorrow morning, he says." In the distance they could see a range of mountains on the skyline.

"Creston is situated in those mountains," Mildred said. "I think we shall like it very well there."

"Hmmm," was all that Charlotte replied to that. But when the train puffed its way in among the mountains, she sat up and looked at the scenery with some interest. As they were carried deeper into the mountains, her admiration for the scenery increased. She and Mildred marvelled at the snow-covered peaks, the steepness of the wooded valleys, and the wild torrents of cascading streams as the train wound its hair-raising way over high trestle bridges, puffed up grades and ground down them, clung to ledges that dropped away into chasms far below. It was magnificent. "I do wish I had my sketchbook to hand."

It was the first positive thing she'd said about Canada so far, and Mildred was pleased to hear it. "We'll unpack your painting things the minute we arrive," she said. "I expect we shall enjoy this visit very much. Olive writes that Creston is a delightful place. I believe you will find Olive a most congenial companion as well. She is a cheerful soul and close to your own age. Mae says you are very much alike in manner."

"I suppose Aunt Mae said Pincher Creek was delightful too," Charlotte said, reverting to her poor opinion of Canada again. Yet only a moment later she was admiring the intense blue of the sky against the bright green of new-leafing trees.

In due time the conductor called out, "Creston! Creston is the next station stop." Mildred and Charlotte adjusted their hats and straightened their wrinkled and soot-smudged travelling costumes. The conductor pulled their ticket stubs from the clip above the window and swung down their cases from the luggage rack. "This way out, ladies!"

On the station platform a tall man with a great deal of blond whiskers about his face strode towards the travellers and swept them up in hearty hug. "You must be Aunt Mildred. And Cousin Charlotte. How do you do? Welcome. Welcome." This was Olive's husband whose name was Robert George Lester William Sinclair Smith. People in Creston, Mildred soon learned, called him Alphabetical. He let go of Mildred and waved to the conductor. "Hello Rodney. How's tricks?" Without waiting for an answer, he turned back to the ladies. "How was the journey? Terrible? But you've stood up to it well, I see. Olive is looking forward mightily to your visit. It's because of her condition she isn't here at the station, don't you know? That'll be your box?" He gestured towards a leather trunk being unloaded from the baggage car. "Hi there, Ed," he called to a young man in a smart checked suit and a brown bowler. "Give a hand here."

Ed and Alphabetical heaved the trunk into a high-wheeled wagon that stood beside the station, then Alphabetical linked his hands to form a step. "Up you go, ladies." When they were settled, he pulled himself up and shook the reins over the team of well-matched blacks. "Walk on, lads!"

They drove along a muddy thoroughfare, lined with wooden storefronts, picking their way through tree stumps, throngs of people afoot and on horseback, and the occasional pig or cow. At least there wasn't any snow on the ground.

"We'll have those stumps out by next winter," Alphabetical said. "And sidewalks put in. You wait and see. This is a go-ahead kind of place." He certainly was not afflicted with the silence of this country, Mildred had noticed straight away. He pointed out the sights, asked questions about the journey and didn't wait for answers. Mildred and Charlotte had only to sit and gaze around them.

Creston was built on the lowest slope of Goat Mountain, set between ranges of mountains that rose to the east and to the west, purple-blue masses in the hazy blue-white sky. Below, the Kootenay River wound its way through a widening valley where grass rippled like a green sea.

"Beautiful!" Mildred said. "The mountains. The valley. So very beautiful."

"Yes, yes, the scenery is grand," Alphabetical agreed. "And just wait 'til we get this town going. Creston is going to be the centre of a vast fruit-growing region. We've got the soil for it. We've got the railway. We're working on the roads. We're seeing about getting telephone lines. We'll upgrade the hotels." He frowned as a couple of drunken men lurched out of the open door of a shabby wooden shack bearing a sign saying "Hotel and Bar" over its door. "We've got new businesses coming in. New settlers. New fruit ranches. We're a go-ahead place here, growing every season. It's a grand place, Creston."

"Indeed," Mildred murmured politely.

Olive, hugely pregnant, was waiting at the open front door of a white-washed frame house to welcome her visitors. "Here you are. Come in. Come in. How lovely to see you! I'll wet the tea while you wash up. Let me show you your room."

She bounded up a steep narrow staircase while Mildred tried to protest, "We'll find our own way. You must rest. In your condition..."

"Nonsense. I don't know why women make such a fuss of confinements. I've never felt better. Bring up that trunk, Bob," Olive shouted down to her husband.

Mildred was hoping for a bit of a rest, but Olive said, as she left them, "Hurry along now. I want to hear all about home before the party starts. I've told people to come at two."

"There is no need for a reception. You must not tire yourself," Mildred called after her. "In your condition..."

"Oh, baby will wait a day or two more, I expect," Olive shouted back. "Why miss a chance for a party?" Olive, it seemed, was as much of a go-getter as her husband.

Mildred had barely time to brush off her skirt and dab cold water on her face and hands before Olive was calling up, "Tea's ready! Do come. I'm dying to hear all your news."

The ladies enjoyed a cup of tea and thick roast beef sandwiches and Mildred was just starting in on an account of their journey when there was a rap on the door and without waiting for an answer to the knock, the first of the visitors walked in. "Mind you enjoy yourselves, you two!" Olive advised Mildred and Charlotte in a stage whisper as they hurried from the kitchen to the front room to greet the visitor. "You'll have your choice of beaux. Men outnumber women about ten to one here. The bachelors are all dying to look you both over."

Charlotte giggled and wondered if she would receive another sudden proposal such as she had had at Pincher Creek. Mildred tutted at the silliness of the very idea.

Olive introduced the first arrival, an eager young man by the name of Andy Talbot. He immediately took up a position beside Charlotte and started a conversation, but before long a half dozen more men were crowding in on him. Older men bowed politely to Mildred and asked her how she did, and how she was liking Creston so far. There were a few couples as well. Mildred shook hands with Mr. and Mrs. Mallandaine and remembered she'd seen him at the station. She met the Rogers and the Frenches and then she began to forget names. The new postmaster, and the pastors of the Anglican and the Methodist Churches were there, and the shy schoolteacher who had not long ago arrived from Spokane Washington, and a courtly gentleman from Tennessee who was "considering prospects," and the bank manager who was so excited when he had a chance to talk with the beautiful Charlotte that he spilled his tea and retired in confusion. Mildred answered questions about the state of "the old country" and nodded at invitations. "Come out and see our orchard." "Let me drive you down to the flats." "Do you play cards? You must come round for a game one evening soon." "We must get up a picnic to the falls." She guessed Charlotte was receiving as many invitations, probably more, and no doubt more sincerely intended. Some of the young men were close to elbowing each other aside in their eagerness to secure positions close to the young lady, or to urge tea or lemonade and cake upon her.

"Well, Mrs. Young, what do you think of our little town so far?" The question was delivered by an older man. Fred Little was his name, Mildred remembered. He sat in the most comfortable of the overstuffed chairs and Mildred had noticed that he was treated with great deference by all. Now the hubbub of general conversation quietened and everyone listened as Mildred answered politely that she found the town was most scenically situated and seemed to be a centre of great activity. She could not bring herself to say "a get up and go sort of place".

Little seemed satisfied with her answer as a launch for his story of the town's founding, a story he'd most certainly told before, and enjoyed telling again. "I staked the first claim in this township," he began, "back in 1892 that was. I looked at this valley, saw the good soil and knew at once what a great place this could be. The railroad was a-building then, and I knew it was through this valley it would have to come. I could see a town here – houses, schools, stores, churches and people. I could see wheat growing on the flatlands and orchards on the benchlands. I could see market gardens, dairy farms. All we needed was that railroad to bring in supplies and settlers, and to ship out the fruit and grain we'd grow and the lumber we'd cut and the ore we'd dig out of these mountains.

"Well, in '98 the CPR survey team came through, just as I knew it must do, and I welcomed those boys with open arms, by golly, I did. Ed here can tell you all about that."

He waved to Ed Mallandaine who took up the story seamlessly. "Yes I brought the survey team in. Fred told me his idea and I could see he was right. I liked the potential. I liked it so much that when I'd done the survey, I bought land and stayed on."

"And here we are in the best town in the best province in the best country in the world," the patriarch Little cut in. "Isn't that so?" As a Londoner Mildred took a sceptical view of that assessment, but she nodded and said, "Indeed!" as if she agreed.

At five the guests began taking their leave. "So nice to have met you. Do come and see us soon," they said in farewell. They shook hands and the young men held Charlotte's as long as they dared.

On the following morning, having satisfied herself that Olive was unlikely to give birth within the next few hours, Mildred set off with Charlotte to explore the "best town in the best province in the best country".

Though the streets were muddy, and the buildings of unpainted wood seemed to be set here and there at haphazard among stump grounds and piles of lumber, still Creston was beautiful. It was May. Through the settlement and the surrounding benchlands apple trees were coming into full bloom. Masses of palest pink petals glowed like bridal bouquets. Their sweet scent mingled with the raw, tangy smell of fresh cut pine and fir, the gunpowder smell of stumping powder, and the smoke of burning slash on land being cleared. Farther off the mountains ranged like battlemented walls to east and west, guarding the valley and the lush green plain below. The air seemed filled with the tension of new agricultural development mixing with the old west of forest, Indians, trappers and prospectors. On Canyon Street a bearded old-timer loaded up his packhorse with a grubstake getting ready to head up out into the wilderness. Lumberjacks and miners caroused their pay away in one of the many noisy bars. A Siwash brave, with buckskin leggins and a store-bought shirt, his long black braids hanging down his back, engaged in horse trading on the corner by a hotel while his wife offered hand-made rush baskets for sale. Two ladies in long silk dresses, carrying dainty parasols, studied the window display at the general store. Mildred didn't recognize them from the party of the evening before. Were they ladies, she had to wonder, or those dance hall girls she'd heard about? A Chinese laundry man, his eyes downcast, scurried by with a heavy bundle of sheets from one of the hotels. Andy Talbot, the first visitor at the previous evening's gathering, dashed out of the livery stable and, uninvited, took up the post of guide and escort. The gentleman from Tennessee emerged from Hatfield's barber shop and pool hall, smoking a cigar, his soft leather riding boots polished to a perfect shine. He bowed and wished the ladies a pleasant morning and attached himself to the tour. At the blacksmith's a Mr. Compton joined them and then a Mr. Murdoch. Had the town been a large one they would soon have formed a parade, Mildred reflected. From this public spectacle Mrs. Rogers saved them by calling from her neatly fenced front garden to "come in, all of you and have a cup of coffee." Mr. Murdoch, Mr. Compton and the gentleman from Tennessee whose name no one seemed to know, regretfully cried off, having business to attend to. But Andy Talbot stayed with the ladies and before they finished their coffee Mildred and Charlotte had agreed to a drive out to Alice Siding to see the Talbot orchard on Friday afternoon and, at Mrs. Rogers' urging, to attend a whist party at the Mercantile Hall that same evening. "And a fortnight hence, there'll be the blossom ball," Andy said. "Everyone comes to that."

"I shall look forward to it," Charlotte answered with her prettiest smile.

After their coffee, nothing would do but that Mr. Talbot accompany the ladies back to the Sinclair Smith residence, choosing a most indirect way, Mildred noted, that involved walking down the hill and back up again when surely they could have simply followed Canyon

Street straight along. Charlotte seemed not to notice the detour. Along their way, they met other acquaintances from the evening before, who enquired after their health and urged them to drop in for a visit any time.

"Well, what do you think of Creston now?" Mr. Talbot wound up the tour at the Sinclair Smith door.

"I think it the prettiest town, in the prettiest province in all of Canada," Mildred answered with a slight smile. "And the inhabitants are very friendly." Mr. Talbot seemed pleased with her answer and bade the ladies farewell.

In the front room Olive was resting in the big armchair. Mildred saw the signs and at once took charge. She first helped Olive up to bed, then sent Charlotte to run back to Speers store for arrowroot and Bovril, tied on an apron, built up the kitchen fire and set to work making custards, beef tea, and arrowroot broth, as well as a more substantial dinner for Alphabetical himself when he should return from his business concerns in town.

Early the next morning Doc Henderson was sent for, and by that evening Olive was delivered of a fine healthy boy. The doctor said it was about the quickest and easiest first confinement he'd ever attended.

"My wife knows how to go about these things," the proud new father boasted. "She's a go-getter."

Nevertheless, Mildred insisted Olive take at the very least ten days' bed rest, and Olive was content to lie back against the pillows and admire her son, while Mildred ran the household.

Charlotte was excited about the new baby, but not so excited that she forgot the drive Mr. Andy Talbot had promised her and Mildred, and she reminded Mildred of the engagement on Friday morning while she cleared up the breakfast things. "We'll have to postpone it. I can't possibly leave Olive alone," was Mildred's response.

"It's only for an hour or two. Olive will be all right. She's fine. She says she is. And baby sleeps all the time anyway."

But Mildred was a conscientious nurse, and she was in charge. "Next week, perhaps," she told Charlotte, who was already dressed for the outing in primrose yellow muslin with pale blue trim, hidden now under one of Olive's large aprons.

Charlotte said they couldn't let Mr. Talbot down at such short notice. "He'll be on his way here by now. Or," she suggested with an innocent air, "perhaps he and I could go without you."

"Unchaperoned! Never!"

Charlotte sulked and must have told Olive about her disappointment because, when Mildred brought up her lunch tray, Olive said young ladies in Creston were not so closely chaperoned as in London. "There's no need for it, really. Everybody here knows what everybody else is up to. If Andy should so much as lay a finger on Charlotte – which he would never do; he's a good fellow – he'd be run out of town in ten minutes and never dare show his face again. Charlotte will be perfectly safe with him."

"That may very well be, but there is indiscreet talk as well as indiscreet action. Your vigilant citizens can hardly monitor conversation, I believe." Mildred took baby Sonny from Olive's arms and rocked him gently.

Olive reached for the lunch tray. "Andy's a gentleman. You can trust to that. But if it will make you feel better, I daresay Mrs. Hunt would enjoy a run out to Alice Siding. Tell Charlotte to run over and ask her.

"Now, don't you think I could go ahead with a bit of cherry pie or something a little more substantial than custard for dessert?"

"You need the milk in it," Mildred said, but she allowed Charlotte to go off in Mr. Talbot's buggy with Mrs. Hunt as chaperone.

Over the next two weeks Mildred ran the Sinclair Smith household with the efficiency she'd learned in her Hammersmith boarding house. She saw to the laundry and cooked substantial meals. She soon realized that it was best to provide extra at each meal as Alphabetical was likely to bring home a new settler or a prospective businessman. Often the two kingpins of the town, Fred Little and Mr. Mallandaine would drop by to discuss some new business plan and stay for dinner or tea.

The cleaning up Mildred left to Charlotte who did it in a slap-dash sort of way, but no one complained. Cleaning had never been Mildred's forte; she found she couldn't take the same interest in it as she took in cooking or sewing. It didn't matter. Olive was so besotted with the baby and its care that she didn't notice the odd dust bunny or stained tea cup, and Alphabetical, like most men, paid no attention to the state of the household as long as meals were served regularly and his wife and child and guests were happy.

Charlotte practised dance steps as she swept or mopped, sang as she washed dishes and always found time to go out walking or for a carriage drive or a sketching party with the young people of town, properly chaperoned if the party consisted of only one young man and herself. As Mildred had predicted, Charlotte and Olive became good friends. Charlotte doted over the new baby almost as much as Olive herself. Olive teased endlessly about the conquests Charlotte was making among the young bachelors in town, and Charlotte blushed and protested and giggled and got Olive to tell her all the gossip about each of them. Not once since they'd arrived in Creston had Charlotte asked when they would be going home to England. Mildred noted all this and was pleased.

By the time of the blossom ball, Olive was ready to step out into Creston society again. She consulted with Mildred about a dress to wear. She held a blue silk gown in front of herself at the bedroom mirror. "Do you think you could let this out enough so that I could fit into it?"

"Surely you're not thinking of going to that dance!" Mildred said, but she took the gown Olive was holding and began to examine the seams.

"Everybody goes to the blossom ball. I couldn't miss it."

Mildred thought it inadvisable, but she could see that Olive was as bent on going as Charlotte was. "I suppose I could get you three good inches at the waist." She sat by the window and set to work picking out stitches. "My velvet opera cloak would go very well with this. You must wear it."

"You'll wear it yourself surely," Olive said.

"I shall not. I shall be right here watching over little Sonny," Mildred said.

"Nonsense. Everybody goes to the Blossom Ball. We'll take Sonny in the picnic basket."

"An infant barely two weeks old ...You can't..." Mildred began, then stopped herself. People did things differently here. As a visitor, it was not her place to give orders. Sonny would be comfortable enough in the picnic basket, she supposed. And if she went too, she could keep a sharp eye on him. "Very well," she said.

Mildred anticipated a decorous and dull evening during which she would sit on the sidelines, sipping fruit punch and watching Sonny in his basket. Nevertheless she took care to dress suitably for the occasion in her best yellow satin with the black lace overskirt. She wore her amethyst necklace on a modest décolletage and pinned three of her favourite brooches to the bodice. She borrowed a black lace shawl from Olive in exchange for the fur-trimmed opera cloak which she insisted the young woman wear because of her still delicate condition.

She and Olive had barely found a safe, warm place in the hall for Sonny and his basket when, to her surprise, Fred Little approached, bowed and asked her for the honour of a dance. She discovered that although she might be an old woman in some men's eyes, she was not at all too old to enjoy the glide and whirl of a waltz. Alphabetical claimed her for the next dance, and then Mr. Speers. Even that brash young man Andy Talbot asked her to dance. He held her firmly and led with such mastery that she felt herself able to swirl ever more quickly and gracefully. For a moment she remembered her son-in-law Tom and wondered what it would have been like to dance with him. But he was Welsh and the music he loved was too sad for dancing.

When the dance was over, Andy saw her back to her place and swept Charlotte away into a lively polka.

Sonny slept peacefully in his picnic basket.

Olive was dancing too many dances and too vigorously in Mildred's opinion, but then she herself was being asked to dance far more often than any middle-aged woman had a right to expect, and she was enjoying it too.

Charlotte of course danced every dance. Mildred watched her laughing with her new friends, flirting with the bachelors, graciously allowing herself to be trotted around the floor by some of the old-timers, helping to serve the sandwiches and cakes, speaking to people whose names and likes and dislikes she seemed to be familiar with already. In only a few short weeks she had found her place in this small town society, and appeared to be happy in it. She was on the way to forgetting her English past, and looking forward to the future, like a true go-ahead Crestonite. It was a quick transformation. Only the other day, there had come a letter from Tom, and Charlotte had glanced through it quickly before dashing off to help decorate the hall for tonight's dance. Mildred read the letter more slowly and more carefully, but she too was happier now. She'd had some few moments of doubt since leaving England, but now she knew she had done the right thing. She and Charlotte would do very well in Creston, she was sure.

Chapter 2

$\mathcal{R}$osebank

Blossoms fell and spring turned to summer. The weather was hot and fine. Olive's home was a hub of activity. Visitors came and went, some to discuss business with Alphabetical, some to admire the baby and gossip with Olive, some to chat with the ladies from England. Mildred served tea and scones at all hours of the day. Evenings there were often card parties or musical soirees in different homes or entertainments in the hall above the Mercantile.

The strawberry crop ripened. Mildred made strawberry short-cake and strawberry trifle and strawberry jam. Then the raspberries came in, and the apricots. Mildred had never tasted such sweet, fine fruit as grew in Creston. When she told that to Fred Little, he quoted her all through the town.

Telephone lines were run along Canyon Street. An office was set up in the Sinclair Smith front room and Olive was the operator. There were six subscribers. "Central here," Olive would answer in a business-like voice when the ring sounded. "I will connect you, sir." Then she would return to the kitchen to tell Mildred and Alphabetical, "That was Fred Little calling Ed Mallandaine. They'll be talking about this new Board of Trade they want to set up."

The Board of Trade was set up, and Mallandaine was its first president.

A Knights of Pythias lodge was organized and Mallandaine was its first Grand Master.

The new Goat Mountain Waterworks was established to pipe fresh water from the river into town. Mallandaine was the president of that project.

Mallandaine was a man who'd always had a knack for being in on any important doings. If you look at the famous photograph of the driving of the last spike at Craigellachie on the Canadian Pacific Railway, you will see a very young man in a round felt hat standing right behind Donald Smith, watching the proceedings. That's Ed Mallandaine, in on the action even then.

Fred Little had founded Creston. Ed Mallandaine was getting it running. He was making it into a go-ahead kind of place. Alphabetical, who thought of himself as ex-army officer more than business man, confined himself to helping in an advisory capacity for every go-ahead project.

When the harvest for the early apples and plums started, Charlotte appeared at the breakfast table one morning in her plainest cotton dress. She was going to work as a picker at the Mason's ranch that day, she said.

"A daughter of mine, working as a farm labourer! I think not!" Mildred set her cup down decisively and tea washed over into the saucer.

"Oh, everyone works at the harvest," Olive said, as if Charlotte's doing so was nothing unusual. "I'd go picking myself if I weren't needed here for the telephone."

"For wages?" Mildred was appalled. "Like a factory girl?"

"Of course for wages. You couldn't expect a person to work all day in the hot sun for your profit and not her own, now could you?" Olive asked the question of Sonny who sat on her lap and gazed at Mildred incredulously.

"Women as well as men?" Mildred couldn't quite take it in. She poured the slopped tea back into the cup.

"You worked at the boarding house to make money," Charlotte reminded her.

"Not for daily wages," Mildred said.

"But for money all the same. Have some more tea, Ma. That will be cold." Charlotte gestured with the teapot and Mildred passed her cup.

To Mildred it seemed obvious that arranging rooms and preparing meals for a dining room full of guests and being handed a discreet envelope at the beginning of each month was a far more respectable way of obtaining money than laboring in a field, keeping a tally of bags or baskets and lining up for a pay packet at the end of a day or a week, however pickers might be paid. She remembered rowdy bands of hop pickers filling the trains out of London to Kent: gypsies and vagabonds and poor folk getting up to who knew what in the hop fields. She turned to Alphabetical who, as an ex-army man, was more conscious of social distinctions than was his wife. "What kind of people are these fruit pickers?"

"Townspeople. The same people you meet on Canyon Street, in the Mercantile, at the whist parties, at church." Alphabetical was no more concerned than Olive about the idea of Charlotte's working as a field labourer. "Everyone works at the harvest. You need have no fears."

"You need have no fears." Mildred remembered that slogan from the posters advertising emigration that she had read back in London. "You need have no fears." Canada was a safe country. Things were done differently here, that was all. Here women could work for wages in the fields alongside men. Mildred drank her tea and Charlotte went off to work in the new and flourishing orchards wearing a gingham dress, a plain white pinafore, a broad-brimmed straw hat and no gloves because, Olive said and Alphabetical confirmed, "You can't pick with gloves on."

The girl would ruin her beautiful soft hands.

Mildred herself donned hat and gloves and sometimes carried a parasol as well whenever she ventured out in the summer sun. This she did most days, now that Olive was up and about. Mildred's favourite walk took her down the Fourth Street hill to the place where she could see the flat valley of the Kootenay widening towards the south, protected by the mountain ranges to east and west. She liked the sense of shelter the mountains gave. They stood in magnificent wilderness, but it was wilderness bounded, keeping the benchlands and the valley safe. Here in Creston one "need have no fears".

Mildred liked the way this scene was always stirring, always changing according to the weather and the time of day. On still days the mountains were no more than hazy, pale mauve shapes in the distance. On brisker days they seemed to draw nearer, sharp-etched against an intense blue sky. On the valley floor the grass rippled green or blue or purple, sometimes even black, according to sunlight and cloud.

After enjoying the view for a while, Mildred would turn around at the pretty little cottage with the For Sale sign on the porch and make her way up to Canyon Street. There she was likely to encounter townspeople who would greet her and stop to chat. She knew their names now, and the names of their babies and children and even their pet dogs and cats. Her advice was sought on matters as diverse as fashions in London, remedies for teething and stomach aches, transcontinental travel and millinery fashions.

Mildred liked the Creston people. She admired their generous pioneering spirit. They pitched in wherever they saw help was needed, welcoming newcomers with advice and know-how and the loan of tools or implements to tide them over 'til they got themselves established. The women didn't consider it beneath them to undertake menial jobs like scrubbing floors, washing clothes, digging gardens or picking fruit for some needed cash money. The men were able to turn their hands to any kind of work: they could run a business, administer an organization, read the lesson in church. They knew how to go about clearing land, planting and tending orchards, building roads and houses, breaking a horse, hunting bear, draining swamps, connecting telephones. These were people who got things done.

They liked a good time too. They were never too busy to organize a party, games, a picnic, a drive. They would travel miles through any kind of weather to attend a dance and stay at it with gusto 'til the small hours of the morning. The best dancer of them all was Andy Talbot, and as the summer turned to autumn, Mildred could see he was dancing his way into Charlotte's heart.

It was time to find out more about this young man. Mildred chose a morning when she and Olive were at work in the kitchen peeling and slicing apples for drying. "I can't help but notice that Charlotte seems quite smitten with Andy Talbot," she began. "Who is he? What kind of family does he come from?"

"His family are in Ireland," Olive said. "Andy's a good worker, an honest friend, a churchgoer, and great fun. He's as good a man as any in Creston."

Andy was a pleasant young man but he had not, thus far, struck Mildred as a likely choice for Charlotte, who expected and was expected by all the family to "marry well". "What does he do for a living?" she asked.

"He's taken up land near Alice Siding, wants to go in for fruit ranching. He's already planted apples and plums, and he's putting up a tidy little house on the property, doing the work himself. He clerks at the Mercantile sometimes."

"What is he then? A carpenter? Or an agriculturist? A shop clerk?"

"He's a rancher," Olive answered. "Like most newcomers here. This town's prosperity will be built and sustained by fruit growing. We have the soil and the climate and the railroad. Some see a future for the dairy industry as well. But fruit ranching is a sure thing." She sounded as though she was quoting her husband.

"I see," Mildred said. Andy Talbot was one of those jacks-of-all-trades who were building this pioneering community. Such men were admirable. But however capable he was, Andy was hardly gentleman enough for Charlotte, who was surely destined to wed a man of distinction: a great musician or writer, a Member of Parliament, a barrister, a bishop or even a baronet. And now here she was, apparently infatuated with a penniless backwoodsman who grew apples and clerked in a shop. This was, Mildred had to admit, her fault. It was she who had brought Charlotte to a place where there were no barristers, bishops or baronets to woo and win her.

They should not have stayed here so long. They should have moved on west to Victoria. Victoria, Mildred had heard, was a cultivated little city with a pleasant location on the sea. Living in Victoria, some said, was almost exactly like living in England. There were Members of Parliament in Victoria, and very rich lumber barons and ship owners. And surely also writers, musicians, and men of culture and refinement. Instead they had lingered in Creston, beguiled by its beauty and by the welcome of its people. Mildred had thought too much of their present comfort and pleasure, and not enough about Charlotte's future. But perhaps it was not yet too late to rectify the matter.

She mentioned the idea at dinner one day and shocked the entire Sinclair Smith household. "You're surely not thinking of leaving Creston!" Olive wailed and her astonished cry woke Sonny and set him to howling. Alphabetical's fork was paralysed half way to his plate. "Victoria? Nonsense! You don't know anyone there. You wouldn't like it at all. Creston is the place for you. You're comfortable here, aren't you? You'd say if you weren't. You stay here. Creston is where you want to be."

"It's where I want to be," Charlotte said with such certainty that Mildred felt unable to argue the point further.

Besides, Alphabetical was right. Mildred knew no one in Victoria. She had no idea how she'd go about finding a place to stay there nor what they'd live on if she did find accommodation. Her financial resources were dwindling. It seemed that she and Charlotte were settled in Creston for better or worse. For herself, Mildred was glad of it. She didn't really want to go to Victoria, however charming it might be. She liked Creston. She only wished Charlotte had set her cap for that bank manager, or the schoolteacher, one of the pastors or the nameless gentleman from Tennessee instead of for that dancing Irishman with the winning smile. She liked Andy well enough; he was personable and pleasant, and a popular man in town. But there was no telling what kind of a family he came from. With an accent like his, it could hardly be a good one. She wished he would at least call himself by his real name. She loathed that vulgar diminutive 'y' some people chose to attach to half a name.

Over the next days Mildred watched Andy Talbot more closely. He worked hard on his own property and just as hard and just as cheerfully when he was clerking or carpentering for others for wages. He it was who organized a benefit concert for a new family whose cabin had been destroyed by a brush fire. He'd also got up a committee to see to setting up rules to prevent and contain forest fires which too often threatened the homes and orchards of the town. He was friendly with the native Siwash and spoke on their behalf when there was a dispute about their rights to graze their horses on the flats. He was usually the last to leave a party, one of the few gentlemen who volunteered to help the ladies clean up, although Mildred suspected that was a ruse to give him more time to flirt with Charlotte, who herself had become quite community-minded in offering her help at church and social events. Mildred reflected further. Society was organized differently in this country. Andy was a carpenter and a fruit rancher now, but things moved quickly here. Who knew but what some day he might become a Member of Parliament or mayor of the town or a great landowner? What was certain was that he made Charlotte happy, and Mildred could not help but rejoice in that. The two were the very image of joy when they moved together on the dance floor.

And when one late August evening Charlotte and Andy walked hand in hand up to the porch where Mildred and the Sinclair Smiths were enjoying a soft cooling breeze and said that they would like to marry, when she saw Charlotte looking more beautiful than ever, bronzed from her work in the sunny orchards and radiant with happiness, when she saw the happy hope in Andy's eyes, when she saw Olive and Alphabetical already beaming with delight, what could she say but, "God bless you both. I hope you will be very happy." This was a marriage Mildred never would have imagined for Charlotte, yet she grew more certain as the days went by that it would be a happy one.

The young people wanted to marry soon. Mildred set to work. There was the wedding gown to sew and a bit of a trousseau as well. Charlotte should have a wedding gown fit for a princess. Mildred made the gown, and then she made a pale blue travelling costume for the honeymoon trip to Spokane, and a hat to match. She made two afternoon dresses with matching hats. She made three extra hats because she loved making hats best. She sewed nightgowns and petticoats and hemmed sheets and towels.

In the evenings when the light started to fail she and Olive baked. They made cheese straws and pie dough and shortbread and lemon curd. As the wedding day drew close, they made pies and dainty cakes and cooked a ham. Since the new church was not yet completed, the wedding and the reception were to be held in the Sinclair Smith drawing room. Olive and Mildred filled the windows with banks of flowers and Olive warned all telephone subscribers not to dare to make a call that afternoon.

Charlotte was a dream of a bride in ivory satin with an overdress of white lace. The mother of the bride was resplendent in lilac silk with beaded jet fringe, the outfit topped off with a huge sort of turban in lilac tulle adorned with purple ostrich plumes.

The guests admired the finery. "Did you order your hat from New York?" Mrs. Mallandaine asked.

"No," Mildred said with quiet pride, "I sewed it up myself."

"Too clever of you!" Mrs. Rogers said. "So chic!"

"Thank you." Mildred bowed in acknowledgement of the compliments, and the purple plumes of her hat nodded.

Charlotte had found her life's place in Creston. It was time for Mildred to settle her own life. She had had a letter from Sarah and Tom in England. They were expecting their first child in the New Year. "Will you come home in time to be with me for the confinement?" Sarah wrote. She had never really believed in her mother's departure as emigration.

"No," Mildred wrote back. "I have grown to like Creston very much. I shall make my home here." She felt a little cruel to write that, but even if she had wanted to go back, which she didn't, she couldn't go. She couldn't afford the journey.

Nor could she stay on indefinitely with Olive and Alphabetical even though they were kind enough to say that she was a member of the family now. She mustn't think of leaving, they told her just as they'd said when she mentioned Victoria. They'd never manage without her. But Mildred knew her help was not needed now as it had been in the month or two after Sonny's birth. Olive could manage her household very well without her, and the young family would appreciate having their home to themselves. Mildred needed to find a place of her own.

Money was the problem. Mildred had thought she possessed great riches when she left England, but the expenses of the journey and then the wedding had whittled the fortune down to exactly forty-three dollars and twenty-seven cents. She needed money. The only way she could think of to earn it was by running a boarding house as she had done in Hammersmith. "Do you know of any houses to let?" she asked her advisors, Olive and Alphabetical.

"This isn't London. People here generally don't take a lease on a house; they just buy it," Olive answered.

Mildred could never afford to buy a house. "Or rooms, then?" Perhaps she could work out something with sub-tenants.

"The only rooms to let would be at the hotels, and you certainly don't want to stay there!" Alphabetical said.

Mildred thought of that pretty little cottage on Fourth Street that she passed on her daily walk through town, the one with the For Sale sign in front of it. She did admire that house. She'd noticed lately that the lot around it was becoming more and more overgrown. It needed work done on it soon. Perhaps the owners would be willing to rent it, at least for the time being.

She mentioned the idea. Alphabetical thought. "That little place on Fourth? About half way up the hill? I'll ask about it for you tomorrow."

But in fact he asked about it that very evening over a game of whist with the Mallandaines in the front room.

"Ah yes, that little cottage. Nice enough and on a good lot. If you like it, why not buy it?" Mr. Mallandaine arranged his cards with a satisfied look.

It was all very well for him to talk. He was the richest man in town. Mildred coughed delicately. "My financial situation at this time, I fear, precludes the purchase of property."

"Have you got five dollars cash?" Mallandaine asked in his forth-right Canadian manner.

"Certainly I have that much," Mildred said with a sniff, and took the trick.

"Offer five dollars as a down payment. Pay the rest off as you are able." Mr. Mallandaine re-arranged his cards.

Mildred was confused. Surely five dollars was too little. "Do you think…? The amount seems so small?" she stammered.

"No harm in offering." Mallandaine shrugged. "It's the Langs own it and they probably want rid of it. See what they say." He snapped down a winning card, and another. It was irritating the way he almost always won.

"I'll run you over there first thing in the morning if you like," Alphabetical offered and swept up the cards for the next deal.

And so it was that almost before she knew what was happening, Mildred bought a house in Creston for five dollars down and a mort-gage of two hundred and ten dollars.

"I shall call my house Rosebank," she announced when the deal was done and she was enjoying a celebratory cup of tea with Olive after the signing.

"Rosebank. I don't remember seeing any roses on that property," Olive said.

"No, but there will be," Mildred promised.

Rosebank was small. Mildred paced the rooms and thought about how she would place furniture, if she had furniture. But no matter how she arranged things, there was really only one rentable room, perhaps two if she herself slept in the enclosed porch. Rosebank was too small for a boarding house. Moreover she soon learned that single gentlemen in Creston preferred to stay in a hotel room with a bar on the premises and single ladies stayed with their families, not in boarding houses. Mildred's boarding house idea was a failure before she even moved in.

Still she could not regret her purchase. Her mind churned with plans for the house and even more so with ideas for the garden. She would plant fruit trees on the south facing slope and set out a kitchen garden on the west side of the house and leave a few shade trees in the east corner to form a spinney. There'd be two wide herbaceous borders leading to the front door and climbing roses growing along the fence and over an arbour at the gate and, most important, there'd be a formal rose garden with tea roses of every shade of pink and red. Rosebank would be a beautiful place.

To realize this dream, she needed an income. Since she couldn't run a profitable boarding house, she would have to find a job. If Charlotte could work for wages, so could she. Unfortunately it was too late for fruit picking or packing now, for the harvest season was over, but Alphabetical might know of something, or Mallandaine or Fred Little. She'd ask.

Fred Little knew of something. A cook was wanted out at the Elsie Holme mine. He told Mildred about the position at afternoon tea in Olive's kitchen. "About thirty men to feed, I believe. Pay's good." He buttered a scone and added a dollop of cream and then strawberry jam.

"Oh but Aunt Mildred, you'd be the only woman on the place. You really couldn't..." Olive for once showed some hesitation about the proprieties.

Mildred had no qualms. "I cooked for gentlemen lodgers in Hammersmith."

"Those miners out at the Elsie Holme are a far cry from civil service gentlemen in Hammersmith," Olive said.

"I needn't associate with them, only cook for them," Mildred argued. At the mention of the good pay, she had warmed to the idea of working at the mine. Cooking would be an easy job. There was nothing to it. Men were easily pleased with any kind of food as long as there were plenty of potatoes.

"Shame to waste your fine cuisine on a bunch of rough fellows like that," Alphabetical said and helped himself to another fresh-baked scone.

"The pay is good," Little repeated. "And they like to keep their workers well-fed and in good health. They're not a cheese-paring out-fit. I've enjoyed a dinner or two out there myself. Good wholesome food is what they require, and a cook who won't stand for any non-sense in the eating hall. I expect you could handle the job."

"I believe I could," Mildred said. "I think cooking at the mine would suit me very well, if they would have me,"

"I'll speak to the boss up there," Little promised.

"That would be very kind," Mildred said.

The next day Fred called in on his way home from dinner at the hotel. "Well, Mrs. Young, are you still thinking of taking up that cooking job at the Elsie Home?" He accepted the cup of tea she hand-ed him.

Mildred loved the way people here spoke of employment as something the applicant chose to take on, almost as if only to oblige the employer. It was quite different back home. She remembered from the time when her sons were looking for employment as government clerks how nervous they'd been when they were granted an interview, how honoured they felt when they were at last successful.

"Yes, I thought it appropriate to try for the situation," Mildred answered, trying to sound as though she'd be doing the mine owners a favour by consenting to consider the job.

"Well, that's settled then. I've spoken to Hugh about it." Fred set down his cup, slapped his knees, and stood up.

"But will Mr. Philips not want to interview me?"

"No. He'll take my word on you. When did you say you can start? Next week?"

Why not? "Yes," Mildred said.

Rosebank was hers, but for a time her home would be somewhere on a rail line out in the wilderness. Mildred handed over the keys of Rosebank to Alphabetical who promised to keep an eye on the place in her absence.

Fred Little was to drive Mildred to the station. He arrived in his buggy with a large brown and white spotted dog sitting in the luggage trunk. "This is Tinker," he said.

"Hello Tinker." Mildred patted the dog and his tail thumped loud against the wooden floor.

"Good. He likes you. I thought he would," Fred said. "I got him off a prospector fellow I know raises good dogs.

"He's yours now. Keep him by you all the time up at the mine there. Keep him in the kitchen with you in the day and keep him in your room at night. He'll see you come to no harm."

Mildred lived in a lean-to at the back of the cookhouse, a log building with a huge black range and two long oilcloth-covered tables. She cooked bacon and eggs, steak, beans and flapjacks for breakfast; pot roast and Yorkshire pudding or stews for dinner with berry pies or suet pudding for dessert. Suppers were thick soup with ham and cabbage, or scalloped potatoes with cheese and sausages, or fried

49

potatoes with salt pork. Sometimes there was fresh trout one of the men had caught, or roast venison or bear stew. In the spring there were berries from the ranches of the valley and fresh lettuces and celery and radishes. With all the meals there were gallons of tea stewing in giant blue granite pots on the back of the stove. The miners thought Mildred was a fine cook.

They were polite to her, as she was to them, and they kept their distance. The faithful Tinker stayed at her side, day and night. She never had any trouble at the mine.

And at the end of a year she had saved enough money to buy a few sticks of furniture and move into Rosebank. Now Mildred was ready to create the house and garden she'd dreamed of. But once again she had no money. She would have to find another job and this time she wanted work that would enable her to live in her own home while she earned a livelihood. She made enquiries.

Fred Little helped her out once more. He asked if he might eat his dinners with her instead of at the hotel. Such an arrangement would be convenient for him, as he lived directly across the road from Rosebank. He'd pay the same rate as he was paying at the hotel and as an added bonus he would give Mildred one of the prized Jersey cows he'd had shipped in from Ontario so that she could have fresh cream daily. To that proposal Mildred agreed at once. It was not exactly a boarding house business but something on the way towards it. Perhaps in time she would find other gentlemen requiring dinners but not rooms.

But Olive came up with a better idea. "Why don't you set up a hat making shop, Auntie? You make wonderful hats, and Creston could do with a good milliner."

That was true. The Mercantile carried only a few dowdy, old-fashioned hats that no woman would buy unless she was desperate. And women were desperate for hats, for no lady ever went anywhere, even to the post office, without a hat. And more and more women were coming to Creston; there'd been new families claiming lands all through the summer and many more scheduled to arrive in the spring.

Yes, a millinery establishment might do very well indeed, Mildred reflected. And she loved making hats! She began planning with enthusiasm. She could run the business from Rosebank. The enclosed side porch would be perfect for a showroom. She hired Andy in his role as carpenter to build shelves for the merchandise. She sent away to Montreal for buckram shapes, felts, velvets, straw, ribbons, feathers, flowers. As her clientele would be all female, she might as well carry waists and corsets too. And perhaps things for babies and small children. A fancy goods shop. But the millinery would be the main attraction.

When all was ready, she placed an ad in *The Creston Review*. "Full Line of Millinery," it said. "Showing all the Very Latest Fashions in Ladies' Hats, Trimmings, Flowers, Ribbons."

Customers came. Soon all the ladies in town wanted to have one of Mildred's original hats. Large hats were in vogue in those pre-war years and no one was ashamed of extravagance. More was more, and Mildred loved it, giving free rein to her delight in ribbons and bows, feathers and flowers, and swathing veils. Her hats were much more elegant than any you could get at the Mercantile. Of course, you paid a little more, but you got an original; you wouldn't meet yourself going into church or taking tea after the musical program in the concert hall. And Mildred had a knack for knowing exactly what little extra touches would make the hat perfect for a new dress or costume. Also, it was much more agreeable to look at corsets and undergarments in the discreet and all female ambiance of Mildred's shop than to have to pick out such things with a male clerk hovering near. The business thrived.

One morning not long after the opening of Mrs. Young's Millinery, Charlotte sat at Mildred's kitchen table. She picked up her tea cup and put it down. She rearranged it in its saucer. She retied the bow at the neck of her maternity smock, then made sure her hair was correctly fastened back. Mildred continued to sew artificial pansies on to a wide ribbon. "Who is the hat for?" Charlotte asked. She'd asked the same question a few minutes before.

"Mrs. French," Mildred answered again. Then, because this kind of nervousness was most unusual in Charlotte, she had to ask, "Whatever is wrong, dear girl? Is everything going as it should?" She nodded towards Charlotte's growing girth.

"Yes, yes. Everything's fine. I'm fine."

"And Andy?"

"Andy's fine. He's working at the store this morning."

"Yes. You mentioned that before." Mildred continued sewing and waited.

At last Charlotte managed to say, "It's about you, Ma. People are talking about you and Fred Little. They say he's over here every day."

"He is. He's arranged to take his noon dinner here as a paying guest. I've told you that. The arrangement works well for both of us."

"Just the two of you?"

"Just the two of us, most days," Mildred confirmed. She smiled, remembering how, not so long ago, she had been concerned about chaperoning Charlotte. Now Charlotte seemed to want to chaperone her. "I think we are old enough to behave ourselves."

"Fred was seen last week carrying a bouquet of roses to your door, hot-house roses he must have ordered from Nelson."

Creston people didn't miss much that went on in their little town. "Yes, he was kind enough to give me flowers."

"Well, for heaven's sake, what does it all mean? What's going on? Tell me!"

Mildred set down the flowery ribbon. Charlotte might as well know. If people were talking it would be better to set out the truth sooner rather than later. "Fred asked me to marry him. I refused. Of course." Mildred spoke with the weary self-assurance of a beautiful, single woman who is quite used to receiving marriage proposals that she has no choice but to refuse.

Charlotte was silent for a few moments. Then, "Why do you say 'of course'? You like Mr. Little, don't you? He has a nice house. He's rich. You could have a good life with him."

"I have a good life now." Mildred liked owning her own home, she liked the hats she made, and she liked earning her own livelihood. She liked Fred, but she preferred independence. She had put romance behind her when she came to this country. "I have no wish to marry again," she said. "You might mention that if you hear any more gossip on the subject. And please, say nothing about the roses. I wouldn't like Fred to feel embarrassed."

Charlotte couldn't argue against the certainty in her mother's tone. Whether she squelched the rumour, or whether it simply died away for lack of further evidence, the idea of a romantic liaison between Mildred and Fred Little was soon forgotten in the town.

Mildred's hat shop continued to prosper. Each spring and fall Creston ladies were invited to come to Rosebank to take tea and look over millinery styles for the coming season. These teas were grand events. Ladies arrived dressed as if for a reception at Buckingham Palace. Mildred herself was attired in her best silk ornamented with an impressive array of brooches and necklaces. Sitting ramrod straight at a lace-covered table she poured tea from her silver tea service, a relic from her past when as Mrs. James Young she had served tea in her Hammersmith home, never dreaming that one day she would be a working woman pouring tea for potential customers in her own shop.

She directed a banal conversation about the weather 'til she judged the time was ripe. Then she led the ladies into the side porch where the new hats were displayed on tables and shelves. Some relaxation of decorum was now allowed. Ladies might express their delight in excited little cries, and try on the hats.

Any woman crass enough to mention the word "price" was frozen with disapproving silence. Shows were social events, not sales. The purchase of a hat was a matter to be settled privately.

The business thrived and so too did the garden. Mildred cleared out brush and undergrowth. She planted an apple tree and a cherry tree and an apricot, as well as raspberry canes and currants. She got Andy to renovate an old shed on the property to house the Jersey cow and a flock of chickens, then to build an arbour over the gate for the climbing roses. She dug up ground for herbaceous borders. She studied seed catalogues and drew up plans. Each season the garden grew more and more beautiful. Flowers bloomed according to the season: peonies, iris, day lilies, bachelor buttons, delphiniums, foxgloves, daisies, dahlias, asters – just like the English country gardens pictured in the copies of *Country Life* that her daughters sometimes sent out from England.

This was a working garden too. Vegetables grew aplenty. Fruit trees and canes flourished. The chickens provided eggs and the occasional roast. Tinker kept away marauding deer and foxes.

But the real pride of the garden were the roses: roses of every shade of pink and red, yellow and white, climbing roses, shrub roses and tea roses, hybrids, damasks, and floribundas, blooming all summer long and filling the air with their sweet, nostalgic scent. Mildred tended them almost as if they were children.

Rosebank had become the home that Mildred had dreamed of. "The best home in the best town in the best province in Canada," she boasted, and Fred Little concurred.

Late in 1912 I arrived at Rosebank with my mother, Sarah, and my younger brother, and I met Mildred, my Gran, and began my life in Creston. I was five years old; my brother David was three. How Gran felt about sharing her tiny house with the three of us, I don't know. It made something of a crowd in the cottage intended for one.

But it was only a temporary arrangement. In the spring, when our father arrived, we would move to a place of our own. Perhaps we'd go in for fruit ranching, like Uncle Andy and Aunt Charlotte. Or perhaps our father, who worked in an office in London, would prefer to work in the post office or the bank. Something suitable would be found.

Meanwhile Creston was fun. We loved Gran and Tinker and the Jersey cow. We loved Fred Little who came to dinner every day. We called him Gramps.

Gramps was proud of being Creston's first pioneer. At the dinner table he told stories about the old days in Creston. "When I settled here," he said "there were no roads, only paths through the forest. There was no railway, no stores, no post office. The nearest place where we could get supplies and mail was Port Hill, down at the border. We'd have to tramp down there and tramp back with fifty pound packs on our backs on a rough trail and cross the Goat River on a bridge we made out of downed trees. It was not an easy trip. And what we could get at Port Hill was nothing fit for a cook like your Gran. Our bill of fare, it was always the same: bacon and beans and mush, mush, mush six days of the week. On the Sabbath for a change we had beans and bacon, left out the mush and went hard on the bacon. Summer or winter, that was what we had. You youngsters don't know how good you have it with all the fancy things you can buy uptown nowadays, and your Gran, the best cook in Creston, fixing it for you." He winked at Gran to show his appreciation of the meal he'd done justice to.

He was a pioneer, he said, because he saw not just what was there now but what could be there in the future. "I can see the way the wind is going to blow," he told us. "I have an eye for the future."

Shortly after our arrival, his eye for the future saw the automobile as the coming boon for mankind. He went to Cranbrook and bought one, a beautiful maroon red machine with "Pioneer" printed in gold letters on the wind shield. He was the first car owner in Creston. He didn't drive himself, said he was too old to get the hang of it, but on fine days he'd get Mr. Bevan to take him out for a spin and sometimes he'd take me and Dave and Mum along. Gran refused to enter that 'noisy and dangerous machine'. Pretty soon Mr. Mallandaine bought a car too, and others in town, but Gramps was the first, the Pioneer who saw the way the wind blew into the future.

Once in a while Gramps would go through a spell when "he was not himself" as Gran described it. She would lock the house door then and though Gramps would pound on it and shout, she would not open it. "I am not at home," she would call out the kitchen window, which struck Dave and me as very funny, but neither Gran nor Mum laughed.

By the next day, Gramps would have quieted down. Gran would leave a pot of stew or soup on his doorstep and after that he'd be back at the dinner table, only maybe looking a little pale and not talking so much as usual.

In December the first snow fell. It was beautiful snow, soft and white, not at all like the grey slush we'd called snow in London. In the darker afternoon light it turned blue, then purple, striped with black shadows of the trees in the yard and down the hill. Down the hill! Sledding was our greatest joy in Creston winters. Everyone went sledding, adults and children alike. Well, not Gran; but Mum was a great sledder and an expert steerer. "Lean!" she would shout at just the right moment, and we'd lean and whiz past a tree or a fence. Fourth Street was the best of the sledding hills. We'd start at the station and slide down, way past Rosebank, waving to Gran as we passed.

Gran was not our only family in Creston. The town was full of our cousins and aunts and uncles. There was Uncle Robert, who most people called Alphabetical. He was easy to talk to because he answered all his own questions. He and Aunt Olive lived in a big new house and knew everyone in town. Their boy Sonny was a little older than I and didn't much like playing with girls, though he did sometimes if our mothers told him to. Out at their ranch at Alice Siding lived Aunt Charlotte and Uncle Andy and their three kids. The oldest, half a year younger than me, had the strange name of Noonie. Then there was Andrew and Charles was the baby, but soon he wouldn't be, for a new baby was on its way, Aunt Charlotte told us. Visits to their house at Alice Siding were always fun. The house was small and cramped, but there was room for a large trunk of dress up clothes: costumes from plays Aunt or Uncle had been in, an old top hat, a real cowboy belt with holsters, a wedding veil that was more holes than lace, and fancy bits of trimmings from Gran's hats. Mum and Aunt Charlotte and Uncle Andy would often join in the dress-up games and sometimes even Gran. We'd play out a fairy tale or the grown-ups would teach us a minuet with lots of bowing and curtseying and state-ly strutting. Later Mum and Gran and Aunt Charlotte would get to talking out on the verandah and Andy would lead us kids away to set up some kind of practical joke, like sticking the ladies' tea cups to their saucers or rigging up a pail of water to dump on the head of the first person who opened the door of the outdoor biffy. Gran was not amused, and Mum and Aunt Charlotte would say they weren't either, but they'd laugh all the same. Andy would let us drive his team of horses on the sleigh. He let us climb trees our mothers considered too high, and let us sled down hills they thought were too steep. "They'll come to no harm; they know what they're capable of," he'd say when the mothers scolded him. We were never afraid with Andy there. He'd see that we came to no harm.

In town Mum was making new friends through Aunt Olive and Uncle Robert. She became a member of the group that called them-selves the Ish Kibbidle Club and usually met in Aunt Olive's house, so that she could keep an ear out for any telephone calls coming through. They played cards and had play readings and musical eve-nings. Gramps teased them about their highfalutin' tastes and called them the "codfish aristocracy".

With the aunts and uncles and sometimes with Gran too, Mum went to concerts at the Mercantile hall, to lectures, box socials, mas-querade balls. Uncle Andy was often the emcee for these events, and generally the life of the party as well. He squired all three of "his" ladies – Aunt Charlotte, Mum and Gran – and always declared them the undisputed belles of the ball, though we knew he really meant Aunt Charlotte.

There was always something doing in Creston. We were all happy to be there. But sometimes on a quiet afternoon as I sat inside watch-ing Gran sew on one of her hats, while Dave slept and Mum read a book from the lending library, I would think of my father alone in London and not having any of the fun we were having. I wished he was here too. I knew we were not a proper family without him, not like Aunt Charlotte and Uncle Andy and their kids, or Aunt Olive and Uncle Robert and Sonny. "When is Daddy coming?" I would ask Gran then.

"When he can get away."

"But when?"

"You'll have to ask your mother."

I ran over to Mum's chair. "When is Daddy coming?"

"In the spring, most likely." Mum would turn back to her book to show she wasn't going to answer any more questions on that subject. Then I would stand at the window watching the shadows on the snow and sing softly one of the songs my father and I used to sing together.

Winter ended in a rush. Ice broke up in the river and the water rose and frothed with coffee-coloured foam, flooded the flats, and then ebbed back to its banks, leaving the earth green with new grass. The tamarack by the side porch turned pale, feathery green and in the orchards the tree limbs sprouted green and then blossomed pink and white and beautiful.

Now there were new games to play, and new events to observe: Gran's spring show of hats; the church garden party, which was to be held that year at Rosebank; a travelling show come to town; the Sunday school picnic.

Once school was out we made new friends among the town kids. Creston was small and we were allowed to roam all over the place as long as we promised that the older kids would look after the younger and that we'd all stay off the railway tracks. On Canyon Street we lay on our backs on the ground under the new wooden sidewalks and looked up through the cracks and made naughty comments about the ladies' underwear we saw, or imagined we saw. We sat on Rosebank's front steps and talked with the Siwash when they stopped for the 'muck-a-muck' Gran gave them: tea with lots of condensed milk and sugar and raisin buns or thick slices of bread and butter and jam. We made forts and teepees in the spinney, made dolls out of faded holly-hock blossoms, pestered Gramps with questions about life in the pioneer times, hunted for bear in vacant lots. There was always lots to do.

At harvest time Mum and the aunts worked in the orchards, picking and packing, and Gran made hats and hats and hats because women had to have good hats for all of the goings on around town, and everyday hats for wearing when they went uptown. We kids had little jobs to do around the place to help out; we picked raspberries and currants for Gran, fed the chickens and collected eggs, fetched the paper and the mail when the trains came in.

There was so much going on that I didn't think about my father much anymore. By autumn, when he had still not arrived, I came to realize his non-arrival was a taboo subject, though I didn't know why. He was never mentioned any more, not by Mum or Gran or any of the aunts and uncles. My brother didn't talk about him because he couldn't remember him at all, and my memories of him were faint, though I remembered the songs he and I used to sing. I didn't miss him, not really. We had Uncle Andy and Alphabetical and Gramps to tell us new stories and teach us new songs.

I started school, then the next autumn Dave did. We liked living with Gran. She knew just about everyone in town. She knew all the Anglicans because she was a pillar of Christ Church, especially in the matter of organizing refreshments for ladies' teas and the Sunday School picnic and the annual Garden Party. Through Aunt Olive and Alphabetical she knew the smart set of the Ish Kibbidle Club. She attended every whist drive in town and was known as a high roller who played for stakes as high as twenty-five cents when she was on a winning streak. She knew all the shopkeepers. Being known as a good cook, she was sometimes call on to help out in the kitchen of the hotel when they were short staffed. Because she bought ginger and licorice roots from the Chinaman at the laundry and gathered medicinal roots and weeds like the Siwash woman, she gained a reputation as a healer, though when she was asked for medical advice, her answer was almost invariably, "Take a small glass of port mixed in a pot of clear tea, rest, and if you don't feel better in two days, go and see Doc Henderson." Because of the friendly Tinker, she knew all the town's children and they and Tinker all knew enough to keep their distance from her flowers, especially her prized roses. Most of the kids and adults too called her Gran just as we did. But she was really our Gran and we were proud of her.

When I think now of Gran and Rosebank in those days, it seems in my memory to be always summer. The garden is blooming with roses of every colour and the house is full of marvellous hats, and warm sunshine, and love.

Chapter 3

Ruth's Songs

I loved my Creston aunts and uncles and cousins. We had good times together. But I had had other aunts and uncles in England. Some of them were not as much fun as the Talbot gang, as Mum called them, but some were, especially the ones who talked the way my father talked. I thought about them sometimes. I remembered Uncle Will who found sweets for me in the strangest places and Uncle Llew who also gave me sweets but I had to say a Bible verse first, and Aunt Megan whom Mum used to imitate behind her back. My favourite was Aunt Ruth. She was my aunt, but she wasn't even a grown up; she was just a big girl exactly ten years older than me. She'd come to live in our house right after I was born to help Mum look after me. As I grew, she and I became good friends. She told me about her terrible life before she came to live with us. She'd lived in Wales in an orphanage full of children who had no families to look after them. They had to behave very, very well, those children or they'd get a beating and only bread and water for their dinner. I was glad she'd come to live with us, and so was she. We had good times together, Ruth and I. She played games with me, and showed me how easy it was to remember Bible verses if you sang them to yourself instead of saying them. And she taught me many songs, so that we could always find a tune to suit a Bible verse.

But when we left our house in England, she disappeared. She'd put me to bed one night, and the next morning Mum woke me up and told me were going to Canada. My father took us to the station and settled us into the train, but Ruth wasn't there. Then he got out and stood on the platform, and only when the train started up did I realize that he wasn't coming with us. Mum and David and I were going to Canada, but not my father and not Ruth. Why, I wanted to know.

I couldn't ask my father because he was out on the platform waving and getting left behind, and I couldn't ask Mum because she had covered her face with her scarf and she was crying behind it. So I cried too, and David, who was too young to know what was happening, cried because I was crying and then he fell asleep.

After a while Mum stopped crying. She mopped my face with her handkerchief and said we'd have a nice cup of tea. When the train stopped, she opened the door and a man brought us milky tea in heavy white mugs, and big iced buns. I was so excited about this picnic that I forgot to ask about my father and Aunt Ruth.

When I asked about them later, Mum's answers were short. She sounded as if she was angry. "Daddy is coming to Canada later," she said. "Auntie Ruth can't come. You will meet your Aunt Charlotte and Aunt Olive in Creston. And your cousins too." I would have preferred my father and Aunt Ruth but I knew I wasn't going to get them any time soon.

In fact, I never saw my father again. And it was more than fifty years later and I was an old woman before I tracked down my dear Aunt Ruth. Not that I'd tried to keep in touch through the intervening years. She'd dropped out of my life when I was a child and as a child I simply accepted that that was the way it had to be. It was 1968 when I at last revisited England and thought of looking up Ruth. I was able to get her address from an aunt in Australia. Ruth was living in a small village in the Midlands, I discovered, and would love to see me.

Her husband answered the door to my knock and ushered me in like a butler. "Please step this way, madam." The cottage was dark and low-ceilinged. I stood at the threshold of a room and saw in the dimness a figure seated by the window. All I could distinguish was a mass of white hair and a flash of dark eyes. It was Aunt Ruth and she was waiting for her dramatic moment. She rose. "*Croeso, Olwen fach*! Welcome, my little Olwen!" In a strong, rich contralto she began to sing a Welsh song:

> *Huna blentyn,yn fy mynwes*
> Sleep my baby, sleep in peace,

Somewhere in the storehouse of my memory, a door creaked open, and the words of her song came to me. I began to sing with her.

> *Huna blentyn, nid oes yma*
> *Ddim i roddi iti fraw;*
> Harm nor hurt will never touch you

She danced towards me and I towards her. And there we were: two crazy old women, laughing and crying, dancing and singing an old Welsh lullaby of our childhood, long ago.

After that, we settled in to talk. We talked through the three days of my visit. I told her my life and she told me hers. We drank tea and we talked. Every so often Ruth would call out to her husband, "Make us some more tea, will you? There's a love." She'd roll us a couple of cigarettes and we'd light up and go at the talking again.

"I loved living with you in London," she told me. "It was so good to be free of the orphanage, to be in a real family with my big brother Tom and in the great city of London."

"Why were you in an orphanage anyway?" I interrupted to ask.

Ruth shrugged. "There were ten children. Our mother died. Our Dad couldn't manage. None of the relatives wanted to take me in. That's just the way it was in those days."

She went on with her story. "You were an easy baby to look after. God knows, I'd had lots of practice with the babies in the orphanage. They were training us girls at the orphanage to be domestic servants, you see, nurse-maids or scullery girls. I knew more about how to keep a house and care for a baby than your own mother did, though I say it who shouldn't. I was very fond of you.

"I didn't have to work very hard. I was happy in your house, especially when your father was home. We'd have singing then, and dancing. He showed me how to play the piano, and I practised whenever I could. 'You've got a gift for music,' he told me. Your mother said so too.

"Some evenings Tom would read us his poems or plays. Your mother wasn't so happy then, because she couldn't understand. I don't know why she didn't learn Welsh. She just didn't.

"And many evenings your father wouldn't be home at all. I could see your mother was lonely for him, and then she'd get angry. 'Your place is here at home,' she scolded him when she had him there to listen to her. 'Not always gallivanting off with your Welsh friends.'

"When I was older, Tom occasionally took me to a concert or play if it was in Welsh and your mother didn't want to go. They were wonderful, those theatre evenings. Tom and I would come home late, talking about the play we'd seen, acting out scenes from it. Or if it was a concert we'd been to, the music would still be playing in our heads and we'd have to try it out on the piano, as soon as we got in. Your mother would come down in her nightgown, with her long golden hair in a braid down her back, saying 'Sh! You'll wake the baby.' But Tom could usually jolly her out of her anger and we'd have a midnight concert, the three of us.

"Oh yes. Those were happy days."

"And then your mother decided to go to Canada. I wanted to go with you, but there wasn't enough money. My job as nursemaid was at an end."

Ruth was fifteen. It was time for her to find a proper situation in domestic service. She hated the idea of going into service and opposed it with all her will. "I didn't want to slink in and out of the servants' entrance of some great house; I didn't want to bow and bob and say 'yes, ma'am' and 'no ma'm.' Oh no. Not me.

"What I wanted was to sing and dance. I had ambitions for a music hall career. I had, as your parents had pointed out, a gift for music. And I was, though I say it who shouldn't, quite a beauty. An exotic, foreign sort of beauty, you know: black curly hair, coal-black eyes, an olive complexion."

Her husband set down a tray with fresh tea on the table. "She was beautiful all right," he whispered to me. "Still is, for a girl of her age." Ruth smiled and tossed the dregs from our last cups of tea over her shoulder and poured fresh. Her house looked immaculate, yet I noticed that she tossed tea leaves and scattered cigarette ash wherever she went. I supposed it was her loving husband who cleaned up after her, unobtrusively.

"Your father tried to help me, but nothing came of it. We couldn't find gigs that paid enough for me to live on, and I didn't have the luxury of waiting for a breakthrough to stardom; I had to earn my own living."

In the end, Ruth got a job at a London hospital as a sort of nurse's aide, serving and scrubbing and fetching and looking after people. But at least she wasn't a servant. Not quite.

And she was noticed. With her personality and looks and her habit of singing and dancing through the corridors when matron wasn't around, she could hardly not be noticed. The young doctors were impressed, and soon she was being invited to smart parties where people were having fun, despite the wartime austerity.

"For one of those parties I dressed up as a gypsy. I had a Spanish guitar. My brother Will had won it in a card game and gave it to me. I'd often listened to the gypsies playing in the markets and at fairs, and it was easy to pick up their tunes. So I had my guitar, and I wore all three of my skirts, one over the other, and a paisley shawl and a kerchief over my head and went barefoot. Everyone said I looked the real thing. I sang and danced and played the guitar. I sang in Welsh and said it was gypsy language and no one knew the difference.

"After that, every party I went to, they'd always beg me, 'Bring your guitar, Gypsy-Ruth. Sing for us, and dance.'

"And I did. I sang 'Counting the Goats' and I counted them white and black, blue and orange and pink, pink, pink, and they thought I was singing of wild loves.

"I sang the sad words of Myfawny's love:
Forget now all the words of promise
You made to one who loved you well.
Give me your hand, my sweet beloved,
But one last time to say farewell.

"'Those gypsy songs are real heart-stirrers,' people said."

After the war, Ruth became engaged to one of the young doctors. "He came from up north, around Carlisle. He was very upper class, very rich, but not a snob, not a looking-down-your-nose sort of gentleman at all, I thought. His name was Alan. He took me to parties and to the cinema and to the music halls, or we'd drive out to the country in his car and have a picnic and almost make love but not quite, because I was a good girl, and I knew from my days at the orphanage what happened to girls who didn't wait for marriage, and what happened to their poor little babies too.

"He gave me a ring: a diamond as big as an acorn with little rubies all around it. I was happy as a princess.

"Then one day at the hospital I was carrying a tray of empty cocoa mugs down to the wash-up, when I heard Alan and his mates talking in the stairwell just below. As I got closer, I realized they were talking about me, so I crept over to the stair rail to listen, thinking how I'd tease Alan later about what I'd heard him say about me.

"'You're not seriously going to marry that little chit, are you?' one of the doctors asked.

"'We-e-ellll,' Alan answered in one long drawn-out, indecisive word, and everyone laughed, and my heart's blood froze.

" 'She's a pretty little thing,' one of them said, 'but, do you know, I wouldn't be a bit surprised if she really was a gypsy. Imagine marrying into the travelling people!'

" 'Oh, he's just having a joke,' someone else said. 'I bet he hasn't taken her home to meet the family, have you, you devil?'

"Alan didn't answer and it came to me for the first time how odd that was, since we were engaged and all. I'd introduced him to my brothers.

" 'Just as I thought,' the other fellow jeered. 'Your intentions are not honorable, sir. And thank God for that. You'd ruin your career if you married a little tart like our singing gypsy.'

" 'I suppose. But, oh, I do love that sweet little body of hers,' Alan said and drew pictures of me in the air and the men all laughed again.

"I dropped the tray of cocoa mugs down the stairs so they'd be sure to know I was coming. I walked down towards those men as though I was the Queen of England and they were a gang of convicts I'd just ordered to be executed. I was in a rage, but a calm white rage, not the least bit inclined to cry or shout. That came later.

" 'I believe you dropped this,' I said to Alan and threw the ring he'd given me at his feet and it pinged on further down the stairs. I walked slowly after it.

"When I glanced at it at the bottom of the stairs, I saw that the stone had fallen out. If it was a half decent ring that would never have happened. I think he must have bought the damned thing at Woolworth's."

Alan ran after her and apologized and offered excuses, said he was only joking with the fellows. But Ruth would not forgive him. "You're a cad. A sly, low, lying cad," I told him to his face. "Whatever high class family you come from, however much money you make at your gentleman's job, you don't deserve me," I told him. "I told him straight. And I'm glad I did, though my heart was breaking. What a fool I was, ever to have believed his promises.

"I wasn't as kind as Myfawny's lover. I wouldn't 'take his hand but one last time to say farewell'. I was through with him."

A month later Ruth married Fred Anstruther, a porter in the hospital. Fred was a humble man who had worshipped the ground Ruth walked on from the day he had first held open a ward door for her. He was overwhelmed with happiness at the one marvellous stroke of good fortune in his existence that had made the beautiful Ruth his wife. For the rest of his life he loved her with unquestioning, unswerving devotion, like a pet dog.

Ruth wouldn't work at the hospital any longer. "The General wasn't big enough for me and Alan. 'We shall go to Australia,' I told Fred.

" 'But we don't have the fare, Ruthie dear,' Fred said.

" 'We'll get it,' I told him."

Ruth took her gypsy act to the street, and it was just as much a hit with people in queues in front of the cinemas or theatres, or with the vendors and shoppers in the markets as it had been with the bright young things at the posh parties. Only now, the act had a concluding flourish: Fred passed the hat.

They got to Australia.

There Fred got a job in a hospital in Sidney. "I could probably have found work there too, but I wanted to look around for something different. I was so tired of scrubbing and carrying.

"And then" – Ruth's voice implied a fanfare of trumpets – "and then I met Roland. It was love at first sight. Love that thrilled right through me." Ruth's face lit with remembered joy as she told me about it. "This was a love that pounded through the blood in my veins, throbbed right into my fingertips. This was a love that made me think the feelings I'd had for Alan were nothing but flirtatious silliness.

"This was a love whose force there could be no holding back. I loved the sound of his name and the way he walked and the clothes he wore. The smell of him. His voice. The way his jaw tightened when he was serious, and the way he laughed. I wanted the times with him to go on forever and yet I was almost sick with the force of the joy and excitement of them."

She paused for a moment in her account, and her expression darkened. "But I didn't hope for anything either. Anything beyond one more hour with him. After Alan, I never let myself have hope of lasting love."

Roland was, as he told her straight off in the first days of their relationship, a married man with no intentions of leaving his wife. When Ruth became pregnant with his child, he gave her the money to go back to England with Fred. She went. "I didn't see what else I could do. Since I couldn't have Roland, I didn't care where I went or what I did. It was best to go home, away from the hope of the chance of meeting Roland in the street or in a store or at the cinema.

"But I didn't regret the months I'd had with him. Never."

Back in England there were more hard times and more singing on street corners, for now she and Fred had little Rhys to support as well, and Ruth was determined that Rhys would be well-fed, well-dressed, and well-educated. She wanted the best of everything for him. All the passion of her heart turned to love for her son.

One day she saw an advertisement in the newspaper: 'Wanted for widower with infant son: butler/housekeeper couple for small estate in Midlands countryside. Would accept couple with child. References required.'

"I'd seen my brother Will cook up references. It was easy enough. I wrote one in the name of a parson's wife and gave the address of my sister in Cooma, Australia. Odds were the widower would never take the time to write to Australia and then wait for an answer.

"Fred was scared, of course. 'But, Ruthie dear, I don't know how to be a butler,' he said.

" 'Fred,' I told him, 'you were born to be a butler. Here, take this tray, and we'll practise.'

"He was a natural. He bowed and bobbed and said 'yes, sir,' and 'no, sir' with perfect humility.

"We got the job. After all my years of trying to avoid domestic service, there I was in the end, a servant, and happy to be one. I suppose you could say it was my fate catching up with me.

"This particular situation had one great advantage. I'd seen the possibilities of it in the advertisement. I told the master I could mind his son as well as my little Rhys while I did my work. 'My son could be a companion for your lovely little boy,' I said. I knew that's what the man wanted. Why else would he have said he'd take a couple with a child? 'And you would be spared the expense of a nanny,' I pointed out to him.

"We were good servants, Fred and I. And Rhys grew up with the son of the house, enjoying all the advantages the gentleman's son had: acres of park to play in, and farmland to roam through, a tennis court, an ornamental lake where the boys learned to swim and boat. They had a private tutor for their education. The master thought his son was delicate, and didn't want him to go away to prep school like most of his class do, so we were very lucky there. Rhys learned all the things a gentleman learns: how to ride, how to write in Latin and do algebra sums. He could swim and dance and play cricket and tennis, and his manners were perfect.

"It lasted 'til the master's son went to Eton. Then Rhys was able to get a place at the grammar school in Coventry, and got his A-levels. He couldn't have had a better education. But," she sighed, "it's his heart that's got him into trouble since he's been a grown man, and who am I to blame him for that? The village girls were all in love with him before he even finished grammar school, and older women too, who should have known better. He loved them all, but he'd never settle on one. He went off and joined the navy. I don't see him often now. I miss him. All those lovely girlfriends, and he still hasn't married and settled down. But he may yet. Don't you think so?"

"Sure," I said to please her. "Lots of men don't marry until they're in their late forties and even their fifties."

Ruth concluded her story. "Fred and I worked on at the great house. We were used to it. We liked the master and suited him well. Before he died, he gave us this cottage to live in. He was good to us. So you see, I was fated to live a life in service, and it turned out to be not so bad."

She stood up. "Come along now. I must go to the church to look over the music for tomorrow. I'm the organist now.

"Fred," she called as we left, "you can clear up the tea cups and peel some potatoes for our dinner. There's a love." We walked along the village street, past the half-timbered pub and the one store and post office to where the grey stone church with its squat tower stood looking out over the rolling farmland beyond. We walked through the lych gate flanked by dark yew trees and along the gravel path through an overgrown graveyard. At the church door Ruth paused to take a last drag on her cigarette before butting it out, and then we passed from the bright blue day into the dim amber light of the church and the smell of cold stone, mildewed hymn books, furniture polish, candle wax and dying flowers. It's the smell of Anglican churches everywhere and it hushes you into religious readiness as soon as you catch a whiff of it.

Ruth sat at the organ bench and began to push buttons. "When did you learn to play the organ?" I asked.

"Oh, I don't know about learning. I just knew I could do it. You can play any instrument, I think, if you listen to it a while and let the sound of it into your heart."

Ruth played some hymns and some Bach and Mendelssohn while I sat in the front pew and listened. Then she turned and smiled and launched into the lullaby she'd greeted me with, and once again the tears came, and the shadow of old, old memories of a home and a family and a language I'd been born into and lost in a new world.

71

Chapter 4

$\mathscr{F}$or King and Country

On August 4, 1914, King George V declared war on Germany. In our remote corner of his empire, in Creston, British Columbia, we didn't hear about the declaration until the next day. Then the whole town went wild. People rushed up to Canyon Street to find out what others knew and to share their excitement. When the train came in from Nelson with yesterday's papers, everyone hurried to the station to see what had been reported so far. Nothing much, except that Britain was at war, and so, of course, was Canada.

The news was not unexpected; the politicians had been talking about readiness for the past month. And certainly the news was not unwelcome. Most of Creston's citizens were British born or of British descent, and their loyalty to the British cause was unquestioning. "Canada is loyal to the very core" the editorial in *The Creston Review* declared.

Everywhere people were eager to show their support for the war. The Dominion government sent a million bags of flour to Britain in a gesture of "practical patriotism" and the government of British Columbia followed that up with a carload of tinned salmon.

In Creston, young men dashed around trying to find out where the deuce a fellow went to enlist. The ladies stormed the Mercantile and plundered it of all soldierly brown and green yarns and material available. My mother carried off two yards of beige cotton, and began cutting out and hemming military handkerchiefs for the volunteers. Gran cornered a dozen skeins of brown wool and started knitting.

The Review preached: "It behooves all young men of Creston to join and assist those who have been put in charge and help bear their share in the dissemination of loyalty to our glorious Empire."

Half a dozen men from Creston enlisted straightaway, including our uncle, Alphabetical Smith, who was a soldier already, having served in the Boer War. Others soon followed. These men were feted as conquering heroes before they even got their uniforms.

It came as no surprise to us to learn that Mr. Mallandaine also was already in the army, had been since the North West Rebellion, in some sort of reserve force. Now quite naturally he was ready in place for the important business of organizing recruitment and getting Creston on a wartime footing. We were to call him Captain Mallandaine.

The rector at Christ Church preached on Sunday and on many following Sundays about the glory of war, the wickedness of the Hun, and the righteousness of the British cause. He told us that even those of us who were not going into battle ourselves could help win the war by showing support for our soldiers in every way we could. We took his message to heart.

Gran was knitting socks for the gallant boys, setting herself a goal of a pair a week. She and Mum taught me how to knit too. Young as I was they agreed that I too could do my bit. As soon as I could make a four-inch square, with the rows even and no dropped stitches, I was entrusted with the knitting of a scarf in brown four-ply.

I worried that the war would be over by the time I got it finished.

The volunteers worried that the war would be over before they'd got themselves kitted up and trained and transported to England, and from there to France.

Patriotism swept through the country and through our little town. Union Jacks blossomed everywhere. Advertising got on the bandwagon. There were flags or military insignia or information about the armed services in ads and on packages of just about everything, so the consumer could feel patriotic by drinking Frye's cocoa or using a Gillette safety razor or putting True Blue blueing in the white wash.

Gran bought red white and blue ribbon and tried, in vain, to include the colours in the new autumn models for her hat shop. In the end, aesthetics triumphed over patriotism in the millinery sphere. "If the war is still on in the spring," she reflected, "I could do the red, white and blue in boater styles, but it simply can't be done with felts. I won't have my ladies looking like the chorus in the pantomime."

"The war will be long over by next spring," everyone assured her. "But never mind, you can use the ribbon to decorate the Odd Fellows Hall for the farewell party."

The only two people I knew who were not wildly keen on the war were Uncle Andy, and Dorothy Bacon.

Uncle Andy said the war was nonsense, a fool's game. This upset Mum, but Gran told her to pay no attention to him. "It's the Irish in him," she explained. "He says what he says to lead you into an argument. I'm sure he doesn't really believe it. I would advise you to ignore him."

Dorothy Bacon, who came two afternoons a week to Gran's house and shop, Rosebank, to do the plain sewing for the autumn show, didn't like the war because it would take her fiancé Bill Mason away from her. "I wouldn't mind so much if it was only to Vancouver or Calgary he was going," she told us, "but England is so far away, and France farther. I'll miss him fearful bad."

"Away is away, whether it's two hundred miles or two thousand," Mum said. "You must be very proud that your future husband will be a hero. And don't worry; the war will be over and he'll be back before you know it."

"I suppose," Dorothy said, but there was still doubt in her voice and she got weepy when she tried to teach me songs like "Let me Call you Sweetheart" and "Love's Old Sweet Song" as she sat sewing ribbons.

Among the volunteers, Archie Murdoch was our special friend. During the weeks of preparation for departure he often came round to Rosebank for afternoon tea. Mum and Gran were making him handkerchiefs and socks and gloves. "I'll be the best equipped soldier in the front lines," he said as he tried things on.

Often when he visited he brought his wonderful dog Bobby with him. Bobby was a border collie-spaniel mix, a clever and patient dog, capable of performing a dozen tricks. While the adults had their tea, my brother David and I would get Bobby to do a special show of "Roll over and play dead German," or "Chase the wicked Germans away" for their entertainment.

One afternoon when Mr. Murdoch arrived at Rosebank's gate with Bobby trotting at his heels as usual, he called out, "Olwen! David! Could you keep Bobby from destroying Gran's borders while I talk to your mother for a few minutes?"

Sure we could.

Presently, Mum and Mr. Murdoch walked out to the garden. "Mr. Murdoch has a request for you children," Mum said in a very serious way.

A request? For us? I was puzzled. We were children. Adults told us what to do; they didn't make requests of us.

"What it is, children," Archie said, "is I was wondering if you would look after Bobby for me while I'm away at the war? Your Mother says she thinks you could manage it."

Would we? You bet we would! Gran's old dog Tinker wouldn't be so enthusiastic about the idea as we were, but he would tolerate the newcomer with the calm patience he was known for. Mr. Murdoch shook hands with David and me, as if we'd concluded a serious business arrangement.

I felt immensely grown up and patriotic and happy. Looking after Bobby would be much more fun as war work than knitting that interminable scarf. There was no hope of its being finished in time to present to Mr. Murdoch.

A few days later, the volunteers were ready to leave. Everyone, absolutely everyone, even Uncle Andy, went to the station to see our boys off. David and me and lots of other kids had Union Jacks to wave. The brass band played and there was a holiday mood in the air.

Captain Mallandaine gave a speech and got everyone to stand at attention for "God Save the King" and our soldiers stood self-consciously the straightest and the tallest and the most solemn men there. Then Gramps Little led hoorahs for our gallant boys and the holiday mood returned.

"Give the Kaiser what for!" people shouted. No one had scruples about expressing aggressive hatred of the foe.

The only people who cried at the station that afternoon were Mr. Hastings, the widower, saying goodbye to his only son. Poor old man, it was embarrassing for him, but still, he shouldn't have come to the station if he couldn't keep control over himself, was the general opinion. And Dorothy Bacon clung weeping to her fiancé Bill 'til the very last minute, "making an exhibition of herself," as Gran remarked.

At last the train puffed out of the station with the soldiers leaning out the windows and we ran along the platform as far as we could, waving our flags and shouting wildly until the train was out of sight.

"Those boys will have the war knocked into a cocked hat by Christmas," Mum said with satisfaction as we walked back Fourth Street towards Rosebank.

Through the next months, news came back from our boys. They were at Sam Hughes' great army camp at Valcartier in Quebec, training. They hoped to be sent overseas soon. Alphabetical Smith wrote that there were ten thousand more men than were needed for Canada's first contingent to the war. He feared that married men might be sent home. But in fact he was one of the first of the Creston men to get to France, having been attached to the Strathcona Horse Regiment.

David and I put out a bowl of water for Bobby every morning. We fed him twice a day on leftovers and bones and scraps the butcher gave us. "It's for Archie Murdoch's dog. We're keeping him while Archie's away at the war," Mum explained so the butcher would be sure to give him a good bone, and she'd get something extra for old Tinker too.

"Your master will be home soon," I told Bobby, stroking his thick black and white fur or rubbing under his chin which made him close his eyes in ecstasy. "Just as soon as he gives the Kaiser what for."

My scarf progressed one sweaty row at a time.

In September, the Masons received news that their boy Bill was ill in hospital in Quebec. While they were deciding whether they should travel all that way to see him, a telegram came. He had died of pneumonia.

"And he didn't even get to the war," people exclaimed over and over, knowing what a disappointment that must be to the Masons and to Dorothy, his intended. "Perhaps she had a premonition," my mother speculated. "Remember the way she carried on at the station the day the boys left?"

She was taking the news of his death hard, her family said. "Stayed in her room howling, for hours," they reported.

Gran and Mum and I paid a sympathy call. Dorothy was up in her room and wouldn't come down. "Why don't you go up to her?" Mrs. Bacon asked me. "She's fond of you. Maybe you could cheer her up a bit."

I liked Dorothy, even if she was a bit soppy. She had started to teach me how to crochet, and she was going to teach me how to do lace making. I hoped all this howling wasn't going to put an end to her afternoons with us at Rosebank. I went upstairs.

I found Dorothy sitting on her bed, with piles of clothes and linens around her. She wasn't howling, but she was sniffling. "Is there anything I could do to help?" I asked. Mum had told me to say that.

"Yes. Go to the Mercantile and get me a roll of white tissue paper." Dorothy gave me a dime. "And come straight back."

I ran to the Mercantile and back with the tissue paper. By then Dorothy had a large trunk ready in the middle of the floor. "Everything has to be wrapped in tissue," she told me. "To save it nice."

I cut the tissue into squares and she wrapped each item and packed it neatly into the trunk. There were fine lawn nightgowns with lace work on the collars, and linen sheets with drawn work hems, embroidered pillow cases, appliqued luncheon cloths and napkins, tea towels with smiling tea pots embroidered on them, and hand towels with wide crocheted borders.

"Bill died for King and Country just as much as if he'd been killed in battle," I said. That's what my Mum had said to Bill's mother.

"No, he didn't," Dorothy said. "He died of pneumonia because of sleeping in a damp tent. It was a stupid, stupid waste. He shouldn't have gone at all." And then she began to sob out loud.

I wasn't being much of a comfort about Bill, so I tried another subject. "Where are you sending all these things?" I asked. "To the Belgian refugees?" This didn't seem like the kind of stuff that went into packages for the soldiers.

"I'm not sending them nowhere," Dorothy said. "I'm just keeping them nice."

And she did. She would keep them nice all her life long.

She showed up for work at Gran's again the next week, and she finished teaching me how to crochet, but we never got started on the lace making. There was no more singing, and of course she didn't talk about Bill any more. She didn't talk much at all now, so it was no fun anymore sitting with her while she worked.

Meanwhile our Creston boys had progressed from Valcartier to England. Archie Murdoch wrote from Salisbury Plain. They were closer to the war, but not in it yet. Worse luck. It was cold and wet, and war would be a treat, compared with the endless marching through the mud they were doing just now. He hoped Bobby was well.

In February he wrote again. All the other Creston boys had gone off to France. Only he'd been kept on at Salisbury to do some stupid office job. "Just my rotten luck," he wrote. "How's Bobby?"

On the home front, patriotic fundraising was in full swing. There were teas and dances and concerts for the benefit of the Patriotic Fund. We schoolchildren were recruited to stage a patriotic pageant and sing "Rule Britannia" and "Oh Canada". Of course we'd sing "God Save the King" at the end as well. Every show and concert always finished with "The King". I longed to be chosen as Britannia for the pageant, or failing that, at least Canada. Two pretty blond girls got those roles. I got to be "our native friend". Gran gave me her plaid shawl to wear and several strings of beads and a pair of moccasins from her shop. Mum braided my black hair and tied a ribbon around my head and said the Siwash would greet me as a long-lost cousin. I wondered why a real native child wasn't given the role, but Mum shushed me up and said that wouldn't do at all.

In March the Hastings boy was killed in action. The news sobered all of Creston. He was our first casualty, not counting poor Bill, who was a sort of unfortunate accident.

Everybody went to the memorial service at Christ Church. Crestoners began to realize that war wasn't just flag waving and fine speeches. Men were getting killed, even men we knew.

Christmas was long past and the war hadn't ended, as everyone had predicted it would, and now it looked as though it wasn't going to end for a while yet either.

In August, Creston observed the first anniversary of the war with prayers for victory. Letters from our boys in France came and were passed around, some even printed in *The Review*. One soldier wrote, "Little old Creston on the flats would look like heaven to me now as I sit on a box of ammunition and wish that the bally war was ended. Another complained that he'd like some shirts and socks. "I haven't had a change of socks for three weeks – we generally get a bath and a change of sox and shirt every two weeks – but not always." One said that he and his mates felt they'd done their stint and would like to see some others taking over. He hadn't had his boots off for five days. He was tired of the war and he'd like a rest from it.

Alphabetical sent long letters directly to *The Review*. He too complained of poor organization at the front. They had body belts and bully beef enough to burn, he wrote, but a shortage of socks and tobacco.

I was sent up to the station with two cents every day at train time to buy yesterday's Nelson paper with its wider and more current war news. Gran and Gramps Little and Uncle Andy pored over the news and maps and had long discussions about how the battles were being fought and what the generals were doing wrong and how they could improve. Gramps began to mutter about useless tactics and the waste of lives. "If Britain can't do any better than this, the Hun will win," Andy said when he read about the Somme offensive.

Mum overheard. She would not tolerate criticism of the British army. "Britain will win. She's won every war she ever fought," she said.

Andy grinned. "She didn't do so well in the American Revolution."

"England didn't want the American colonies," Mum said grandly.

She was annoyed too that Andy had not yet volunteered. "My husband is fighting. Alphabetical is fighting, and dozens of your friends. Why aren't you there? You could show them how to do it right, instead of criticizing from afar."

Andy flushed and folded up the newspaper he had been reading at Gran's kitchen table. "I have a wife and four young children dependent on me," he said. "I have a ranch where fruit trees are growing and need tending. I've my duty as fire-warden to protect the forest. I'm a lot more use here than I would be in France getting myself blown into smithereens for the Empire." He would not be goaded into fighting a war on another continent.

All over the country other people in other towns were realizing, like our war experts, that the Germans were a much more formidable enemy than they'd thought. Either that, or the British army wasn't as fine and efficient a fighting force as we'd been led to believe. It was now admitted that this war would be a long one, though Germany's ultimate defeat was inevitable.

Attitudes hardened against the Germans. In England the King changed his German name to the English Windsor, and in Creston Mr. Weissenthal took his mother's maiden name of Jones. Gramps Little, who had had a difference of opinion with Mr. Weissenthal-Jones on a financial transaction, made a point of continuing to address him loudly and at every opportunity as "Herr Weissenthal."

Across the country, thousands of enemy aliens were interned in camps. Patriotic Canadians refused to buy from businesses with German names and wouldn't give work to anyone of German origin. The miners of the Crow's Nest refused to work underground with enemy aliens. It was too dangerous, they claimed. Under threat of boycott, the town of Berlin in Ontario changed its name to Kitchener. German was no longer taught in schools, and some musicians refused to play works by Beethoven or Wagner or other German composers.

My mother had a hard time with this. She didn't mind so much about Wagner but she loved to play Beethoven sonatas on Aunt Olive's piano. Eventually she found the solution in the name Beethoven. Who had ever heard of any Germans named Beethoven, other than Ludwig van himself? Therefore it couldn't be a German name. Even if he had been born in Germany, the family wasn't German. They must have come from Belgium, Mum guessed. So it was all right, it was even patriotic, for her to play Beethoven songs and sonatas and peasant dances at the Ish Kibiddle Club's musical evenings.

Some bad boys threw stones at Mrs. Baker's dachshund. "That's going too far," my mother said. "Poor innocent dog! He's not German. Mind you," she added, "I've always thought those dachshunds are a ridiculous looking breed. I would never have one myself."

The war went on and on because it couldn't stop until one side won. Britain would win in the end, of course, but victory was taking much longer than anyone had imagined.

The knitting and the bandage-rolling continued. There was talk of conscription.

I finished the scarf. Mum helped me wrap it up and we took it to the Red Cross meeting and it was added to the Creston women's parcel for the war effort.

We got something called a field postcard from Archie Murdoch. "Going up to the front now," was scrawled in pencil. "Hurrah! Will write later."

Only a few days later the news reached us through a letter from Alphabetical Smith. Archie had been killed in action on his first day in combat.

Mum cried and wrote a letter of sympathy to his mother in Edinburgh.

"What will we do about Bobby?" I asked.

"We'll keep him," Mum said. "It's what Archie would have wanted."

Poor Bobby. I stroked his thick furry ruff. "Mr. Murdoch died for King and Country," I told him. I wondered if the dog knew his master was dead. Myself, I could hardly remember Mr. Murdoch by now. "Don't worry, Bobby. I'll look after you," I promised.

At the memorial service we sang,

> *We by enemies distrest*
> *They in Paradise at rest;*
> *We the captives – they the freed -*
> *We and they are one indeed.*

I was sad about Mr. Murdoch's getting killed, especially on his very first day fighting. But now Bobby was going to stay with us forever. I couldn't help but be happy about that.

"Stop grinning like a Cheshire cat," Mum hissed to me.

On the way home we stopped at the Mercantile to buy wool for my next scarf. Would this war never end?

The war didn't end. It was costing unheard of amounts of money – four million dollars a day it was reckoned. Prices were going up. The Department of Agriculture urged us to grow fruit and vegetables and raise livestock to help feed Britain. Fundraising was more or less constant now. We collected for the Patriotic Fund, the Red Cross, the Belgian Refugees, the tobacco fund, the machine gun fund. We were urged to "make our dollars fight" by buying Dominion of Canada War Savings Certificates. Soldiers invalided out of the army gave lectures. Admission fifty cents. Proceeds to the Patriotic Fund. A Red Cross tea will be held at the home of Mrs. Mallandaine. Admission ten cents. A garden party to be held at Rosebank, home of Mrs. M. Young. The Creston Band will entertain. Admission twenty-five cents. Proceeds to the Belgian Refugee Fund. Aside from monetary contributions, women were expected to knit socks and scarves and body belts, sew shirts and pajamas for the Red Cross, and provide sandwiches, cakes and squares for the refreshments tables at the fundraising events.

Just about when we thought we couldn't knit another row or wave another flag or sit through one more presentation, it was announced that a forestry service unit was to be raised and trained right here in Creston under the command of none other than Captain Mallandaine, who became Major Mallandaine for the job. Since this was a service unit, men who did not meet the medical requirements for combat service would be accepted. You could be up to forty-eight years old and less than five feet tall, you could be partly deaf, flat-footed or disabled in a variety of other ways and still get in. It was a splendid chance for those who had been disappointed in previous attempts to enlist for fighting service to step in now. Men did step forward. Recruiting was brisk. From January 'til April of 1917, Creston streets were full of marching men, shouted orders, military salutes. And in April we turned out in force to see them off to Ontario from where they would go on to service in France. The band played, the people cheered. The sad news of battles and deaths was forgotten for a while. These men were going out to do a useful job of work they knew how to do well. They would be in no great danger. They would build roads, fell and saw trees for huts and field hospitals and duckboards, all to help the war to its conclusion, which surely must come soon.

In the new spate of enthusiasm I knitted my second scarf to a satisfactory end.

Chapter 5

*F*ear of Falling

Later that year Creston was rocked by a scandal that surpassed even the war news in interest for a few weeks. Mrs. Dixon, a prominent member of Creston society, had run off with Steven Hunt, and – this was said in hushed whispers – she was going to have his child. Most people in town clucked and shook their heads sanctimoniously. They'd always known that clique of socialites, the group Gramps Little called the codfish aristocracy, was a fast bunch. The women smoked and drank. And now their leading figure, Mrs. Dixon was in trouble like a hired girl. That's what came of fast living. Hunt wanted to marry her. At least that much could be said for him. But first she'd have to get divorced.

Divorce was a scandalous business then in Canada, which had one of the lowest divorce rates in the western world. Few were willing to go to the trouble and shame of proving adultery, virtually the only grounds for obtaining a divorce.

In the U.S., however, divorces were easier. So Mrs. Dixon moved across the border to Bonner's Ferry in Idaho to establish residence there, and get her divorce more quickly and easily.

Mrs. Dixon was a good friend of Mum's, and so was Steven Hunt. Perhaps Mum sympathized with their illicit romance. Perhaps she had been unhappy in her own marriage and so was more liberal than her contemporaries on the issue of divorce. Perhaps she was simply fed up with Creston, and the dreary atmosphere of a small town with its good men gone to war, some of them never to come back. Whatever her reasons were, Mum packed us up and we went to Bonner's Ferry to keep Mrs. Dixon company and to try life in the U.S.A.

The U.S. had just entered the war that year, so when we arrived in Bonner's Ferry we found ourselves plunged into the same flurry of flag-waving and patriotic speeches and fundraising that we'd known in Creston for the past three years. Only now the flag was the Stars and Stripes and the music was "Oh say can you see?"

As it happened, most Bonner's Ferry people had been pro-war since the beginning and welcomed the chance to get in on it. The Bonner's Ferry doughboys were one of the first contingents of American soldiers to embark for Europe. Reporters and photographers from all over the nation came to record the send-off. There was even a team of camera men to take a moving picture that would be shown in movie houses all across America. Talk about excitement!

The Bonner's Ferry ladies, like the ladies of Creston, wanted to give their departing heroes some "small token of esteem". They decided on a kit box for each soldier filled with oddments: a little sewing kit, shaving soap, letter paper, cigarettes, chocolate. As part of the ceremonies on send-off day, each soldier was to be presented with his kit by a school girl of the town. I was one of the school girls.

We wore starched white dresses and white stockings and we each had a huge white satin bow tied flat on our heads.

"I know two soldiers who already got killed," I boasted to the girl next to me in line.

"No you don't," she began to argue. "They can't get killed 'til they start to fight in France, stupid."

"These were British soldiers. Lots of them have got killed already. One of them gave me his dog to look after, and now that dog is my dog. I'll show him to you if you don't believe me." The American kids didn't know anything about this war.

"No American soldiers are going to get killed because they're the best," the girl said.

I could never get the better of these kids in argument.

"Girls, stop talking!" A teacher shushed us up. "Listen for the start of your music."

"Some of them will get killed just the same," I whispered the last words of the argument. "Bound to." This knowledge didn't make me any less excited about being part of the grand send-off spectacle.

When the music started I marched proudly forward carrying the little tin box in both hands, like a bouquet of flowers, the way we'd been shown how to do.

The band played. The soldiers stood in a long straight line and we girls marched smartly up to form a line opposite. When the music stopped, each girl handed her kit box to the soldier partner across from her.

"Thanks, sugar," my soldier said. "What a nice present! What's your name, honey?"

"Olwen," I said to his polished boots where the reflection of my white bow bobbed up and down.

"What? I didn't catch the name." He leaned down close to me.

Shutters clicked and the movie camera rolled

"Olwen," I repeated. People never caught my name. What was so complicated about it anyway? But people never got it right. I hated that name.

An officer shouted something, the band began to play again, and my soldier straightened up and marched away. We little girls ran to our proud mothers. But before I could reach my Mum, a very angry lady marched up to me and yanked the white ribbon on my head.

"You bad girl!" she said. "You were supposed to hand over the kit, not strike up a conversation. You've ruined the picture. What do you think you were doing, chattering away to my boy? All the other soldiers were standing straight and tall, the way soldiers should, smiling for the cameras, but my son had to lean down to listen to your nonsense. You ruined the whole thing. You're a very naughty girl."

I tried to tell her I wasn't chattering. "It was him who was talking to me," I tried to say, but she wasn't listening.

"A very naughty girl," she said again and flounced away.

"I didn't talk to him; it was him who talked to me," I wailed when Mum found me.

"What did he say?" she asked.

"He asked me about my stupid name," I said.

"It's not a stupid name," she said with a sigh. This was an old argument. "Never mind. It wasn't your fault. He should have stood straight like a soldier instead of talking about names.

"It's too bad that woman wasn't going off to fight the Germans herself. Wouldn't she give the Kaiser what for!" she added to try to joke me out of my shame, but it was too late. The soldier's mother had convinced me that I'd ruined the ceremony.

When the pictures came out, it was just like the woman said: a row of soldiers, straight as bowling pins, facing the cameras of America, except for only one in the line, bending down to talk to a naughty little girl in a stiff white dress.

When we went to the movies to see the newsreel I had to hide my eyes at that part. I'd ruined the whole thing, and it was all because of my horrible name.

Our family went in for ridiculous names. The funny thing was that most of them had chosen those names. Uncle Took's real name was a perfectly ordinary Henry but he chose to be known instead as Took. Worse still was Aunt Boo, who could have used her real name of Elizabeth. Then there were those who had changed their given names for good reason. My brother's official name was Eifion, a name even worse than mine, but he was sensibly called David. My cousin Hirell Talbot was known as Noonie, though in her case Noonie wasn't much of an improvement, I thought. Only I was left with my original horrible name, that Mum pretended to believe was a beautiful and distinctive name that I should be pleased to have. "Shall I call you Boo instead?" she'd ask when I complained. "Or Anghararadwyllnwll?"

She'd do one of her imitations of what she thought Welsh sounded like and I'd have to laugh. I was stuck with Olwen.

In Bonner's Ferry, the excitement of the doughboys' send-off faded in the months of war that followed. War, the women of Bonner's Ferry were learning, as the women of England and Canada already knew, was more than marching bands, and waving flags, presentations of useful kits and fund-raising socials. Lists of American casualties began to come in. Some of those men who stood straight that festive day of their departure were now fallen.

Then, in 1918, as if war hadn't brought enough of death and suffering, a new scourge devastated the country – the Spanish influenza. There was no cure for the sickness; some pulled through and some didn't. All that could be done was to try to prevent the disease from spreading. People avoided going to public gatherings, and when we did have to go out, we were warned to wear gauze masks. Some said wearing a hot mustard plaster or a hot bread poultice would protect you. Others took hot milk spiced with ginger. Despite these precautions, the flu came to Bonner's Ferry, and deaths. The school was closed. All meetings were cancelled.

My mother was especially worried for me, because she considered me a delicate child. Thinking I'd be safer in a smaller place, she sent me to stay with Gran in Creston.

Although I'd travelled back and forth to Creston several times, this was my first trip alone on the train. I would have preferred to face the danger of catching flu in Bonner's Ferry to that of getting on the wrong train when I had to change at Yahk, and being carried away helpless across the continent.

"You'll manage," Mum insisted. "You're quite capable of undertaking a two-hour train journey on your own. "Everybody in England rides trains all the time," she added. "I used to ride the train to school every day."

"But did you have to change?"

"No," she admitted. "But I daresay I could have done it. Tell you what," she suggested. "I'll write down the names of all the stations, and you can cross out each one as you come to it, so you'll always know where you are."

Not only did she give me the card, but she also introduced me to the conductor, a Mr. Hooper, who promised to keep an eye on me. He did too. He stood right beside me when he called out the stations, and I marked them off on my card. At Yahk he walked across the station platform with me, and told the station master to see that I got on the Creston train.

I completed the journey safely.

One of the first cases of Spanish flu in Creston was Gran. And then I caught it too.

We were both dreadfully ill. Gran's neighbour, Mrs. Spaulding, and Mrs. Mallandaine prepared food for us, brought it to our door, knocked to let Gran know it was there, and left. They could not enter the house for fear of infection.

Gradually Gran got better and, even more gradually, I did.

Then the day cook at the Creston Hotel came down with it. The hotel manager came round to Rosebank. Would Gran consider filling in during the emergency? Certainly she would.

Since there was no school because of the epidemic, I was allowed to go to work with her. We got up early and walked up to the hotel in the cool morning as the sun was lightening the sky behind the Purcell range to a yellowy- greeny-blue, while the Selkirks to the west remained in deep purple darkness.

In the hotel kitchen Gran tied on a long white apron and covered her hair with a white kerchief that made her look like a Duokobor, though she didn't care for the comparison when I made it. She oiled the gas range-top and got the coffee going. "First order of the day!" she called to me.

"Two eggs, sunny side up, bacon, toast and coffee," I read from the menu. I always got to order first and I always ordered the same thing. It was the best possible breakfast, I decided, and when I grew up I would eat exactly that every morning. I ate at the end of the enamelware table where Gran mixed the batter for pancakes in a big yellow bowl, and where she kept her own pot of tea so she could sit and sip a bit and nibble some toast between orders. After I'd eaten, I watched the toaster for Gran and helped the kitchen maid with the dishes and she or the manager usually gave me five cents for my work. I was sorry when the regular cook recovered and returned to work and Gran and I lost our jobs.

One afternoon just when we were beginning to believe life was getting back to normal, Aunt Charlotte's neighbour, Mr. Compton pounded on Gran's door. "Andy's sick bad, and the kids, and Charlotte too," he said. "She says can you come out to the ranch and help them out."

"Of course," Gran said.

"Olwen," she turned to me, "run and ask the doctor to drive out. If he can come before dark, you wait and go with him. If he can't, go to Aunt Olive's for tonight, and walk out to the ranch tomorrow. I'm going to go right now with Mr. Compton."

I ran up Fourth towards Doc Henderson's house. My black pig-tails bobbed up and down as I ran and I thought of Gran's story of her famous run for the doctor through the dark and dangerous streets of London with her beautiful golden hair streaming behind her.

It was only late afternoon, and Creston was not the sort of place where one feared getting kidnapped or captured for the white slave trade. Still it seemed to me that because of the war and because of the flu epidemic, I was running through a world that had grown as dangerous as the dark streets of London had ever been in Gran's beautiful youth.

Doc Henderson was in, and he hitched up and we drove in his buggy to Aunt Charlotte's.

"Gran," I asked that night as I was being tucked up to sleep on the couch in the front room, "You know when you ran through the dark and dangerous streets of London with your golden hair streaming behind you to fetch the doctor for Lucy?"

"Yes?"

"Well, what happened to Lucy?"

"Ah, that's the sad part of the story. She died, poor girl."

Aunt Charlotte and all the children pulled through. It was Andy who died. He died on the tenth of November, 1918, the day before the armistice.

Gran took me aside and told me what had happened. Uncle Andy! Dead! But he was a Dad. He was a man who saw to it that no harm would come to us. Now the worst harm had come to him. It didn't seem possible. Old people died, and soldiers in battle, but not Dads. Aunt Charlotte and the cousins wouldn't be a family without Uncle Andy. Of course, my family didn't have a Dad either, but that was different. He wasn't dead, only away in another country, and we were used to his absence. We'd had Uncle Andy as his substitute. Only now we didn't.

Gran said I must not tell anyone about this. My cousins were not to be told of their father's death. "They, and their mother, are too weak to sustain the shock," Gran explained. "You must carry on as you have been and not say not a word, not even to Noonie." Noonie was the cousin closest to my own age and she and I were involved in an intense love-hate relationship.

It was a hard secret to keep, not so much at first when Aunt Charlotte and the kids were too sick to talk to or play with anyway, but later, when Noonie was well enough to get up and sit in the kitchen by the stove for an hour or two in the afternoons. One day she and I were sitting there, squabbling over a game of checkers. We were both restless and out of sorts.

"I know something you don't know, All-Went," Noonie said.

91

She always called me All-Went when she wanted to make me mad. "You do not," I answered back.

"Do so!"

"Yeah, what then?"

"Your father's dead. That's what. He got killed in the war. Blown up by a bomb."

"Did not!" I said, but somehow I knew what Noonie said was true. I'd noticed certain looks exchanged between adults when the subject of the war came up. I remembered half sentences overheard as I came into a room. Noonie had only told me what I already knew, but hadn't allowed myself to acknowledge. I was filled with rage at her for telling, for making me stop pretending.

"I know something you don't know too!" I cried.

"Do not!" she countered.

"Do too!" I remembered then what Gran had told me. The news of her own father's death could make Noonie sick again and she could die too. I'd promised I wouldn't tell. And besides, she probably already knew, or half knew. That's why she had told me about my father.

"What are you two girls bickering about?" Gran came into the kitchen with an armload of dirty sheets and stuffed them into the huge washing copper on the back of the stove.

"Nothing," I muttered and put on my coat and ran out to the barn. Noonie wasn't allowed outside yet. I sat in the dusty hayloft and cried because, even though I could scarcely remember my father, it was a terrible thing not to have one. And I cried for Uncle Andy, who'd sometimes seemed like a father to me, even if he wasn't, and for Noonie. Now neither of us had a father, neither of us had a real family anymore.

My mother came back to Creston for Uncle Andy's funeral. She told me then that my father was dead, and I cried again, but not very much.

There were many deaths those last months of the war. Hardly a family was not in mourning for a soldier fallen in battle overseas or for a victim of the terrible flu. All the hats Gran made were black.

There were no wild celebrations in Creston to mark the end of the war. People were too tired and too sad to celebrate, and besides, public gatherings were still prohibited on account of the flu.

After the war was over, and the flu epidemic, after Gran at last began making hats in fuchsia and lavender and blue again, there were two more deaths in Creston.

Aunt Charlotte had been much affected by her beloved husband's death. She had always had a goitre problem, and the stress of her grief seemed to exacerbate the condition. She was operated on and died on the operating table. She was twenty-nine years old. My six Talbot cousins were now orphans.

And then there was one more death.

The Spauldings lived on a small farm down the hill from Rosebank. There were four children in the family, of whom Sally, a girl a year younger than me, was my special friend.

The Spauldings kept a dairy herd and supplied most everyone in town with fresh milk. Every morning before school the Spaulding kids would walk through the village with covered pails of milk in a handcart. There were no bottles. You brought out a jug or a lard pail and the Spauldings filled it for you.

Mrs. Spaulding did the milking. The kids delivered the milk and helped with the separating and washing up. Mr. Spaulding kept the accounts.

Mr. Spaulding couldn't do the milking on account of his hands, which had been crippled when he was an infant. He'd been sitting in a high chair by the kitchen fire and the high chair toppled over, straight on to the fire. His hands were burned so badly that they could never be healed, but remained small, stiff, red claws.

The other permanent effect of the traumatic accident on Mr. Spaulding was that for the rest of his life he was terrified of falling. He hated ladders and was in a panic when anyone stood on a chair. He warned all parents of young children to beware of high chairs. He wouldn't have one in his house. He designed and built a small table and chairs for his children to use when they were little to protect them from the fate that had befallen him.

Mr. Spaulding was a gregarious fellow. He liked to walk uptown and have a cup of coffee with the salesmen who were passing through town and staying at the hotel. Then he might go on to hang around the Mercantile for a while and talk to the locals as they came and went. He knew everyone in town and everything that went on. Whenever you were asked about anything going on in town and didn't know the answer, you'd say, "Ask Spaulding!"

One early spring evening, Mrs. Spaulding was in the barn doing the evening milking. Mr. Spaulding had just sent the youngest child, Fred, off to bed. It had been a warm day, and they'd let the fire out in the kitchen range but it would be needed now for heating water to wash the separator and pails after the milking. Mr. Spaulding shook out the ashes, and laid in a twist of newspaper and built kindling in a pyramid. He filled the reservoir with fresh water. He set a match to the kindling and went out to fetch wood. On his way back from the woodpile with an armload of logs, he saw a car chugging up the hill towards town. There were only about a half dozen cars in Creston then, and this wasn't one of them. Spaulding was curious. Who could it be? American tourists come up from Bonner's Ferry? Or had Mr. Dixon gone ahead and got the automobile he'd been talking about buying? Spaulding wanted to walk up to the hotel and find out.

He dumped a couple of logs on the fire. "I'm just stepping up the street for a minute," he called towards the front room as he hurried off. Sally was in the front room, learning her spelling words.

Suddenly she heard a scream from the kitchen. She dashed in to find her youngest brother on fire. Flames were licking up his long flannel nightshirt. He ran towards her and the flames burned brighter.

Sally grabbed the drinking bucket, and dumped it over the boy, but the water seemed to have no effect on the flames.

"Ma! Ma!" She ran screaming to the barn and Fred ran after her, a torch of burning flesh and hair and cloth.

"A blanket!" Mrs. Spaulding shouted when she took in the scene, and ran to push her boy to the ground and smother the flames in the damp grass and her apron. By the time Sally returned with a blanket, the flames were out. "Fetch Doc Henderson," her mother said. "Quick!"

There was little the doctor could do. Fred lived for a day of pain, and died.

Sally was tormented with guilt. "I should have kept an eye on him," she said. "When Ma and Dad are out, it's my job to keep an eye on the little ones."

"It wasn't your fault. Fred was supposed to be in bed," I tried to comfort her.

"I should have kept an eye on him. I should have heard him coming down stairs and playing around in the kitchen. And I was too stupid to think of a blanket for the flames. If I'd thought of the blanket, I could have saved him, and I didn't."

"You can't be sure. I think it was your dad's fault for going out and leaving the matches on the table. And it was Fred's fault for playing with the matches. He was old enough to know better."

But Sally could not be comforted.

My mother took me and my brother to the funeral. As we looked at the small coffin, my mother whispered to me, "Let this be a lesson you never forget. Fire is dangerous."

That was a lesson I already knew. I looked now at the faces around me and learned other, deeper lessons as well. I saw the shocked grief on the face of Mr. Spaulding who feared falling more than he feared fire and thought he had sufficiently safeguarded his family, and I learned that it is not always what we fear that destroys us. Sometimes I saw a look steal across Mrs. Spaulding's face when she looked at her husband that taught me that there are some things that cannot be forgiven, even of those we love. And I saw Sally's guilt and grief and learned that responsibilities can fall upon us without our agreeing to them or even knowing they are there, and they can crush us, even so.

Chapter 6

A Love of Trees

Mum was staying at Rosebank again, having had to give up the house in Bonner's Ferry. My father's pension hadn't come through and she had no money at all. David and I were there too, of course, and Margie, the youngest of the six Talbot orphans. The older Talbot children shuttled back and forth between Rosebank and their uncle's house. Rosebank was overflowing. Some of us were sleeping on feather ticks we rolled out on the shop floor at night. At meals we crowded around the table, two children to a chair. Gran's dream of a little house for herself was long gone.

And then came the news that Uncle Bob was coming for a visit.

Bob was Gran's blind brother. He had been sent to Canada to be educated at Brantford School for the Blind in Ontario, and then he had gone to live with Uncle Percy, a clergyman in Edmonton.

Now Uncle Percy had three almost grown up daughters that he and his wife wanted to see well married. Rightly or wrongly, they felt that the presence of a blind and somewhat eccentric family member in the household was jeopardizing the girls' chances of finding suitable husbands. Their solution was to send Bob on to Gran. "We've done our duty by him; it's time you took a turn," Uncle Percy wrote. "All your daughters are safely married."

When Gran heard of Bob's imminent arrival, she held her hand, palm outward dramatically on her brow, as she liked to do in moments of tension, and wondered how we would all manage to cram into Rosebank. The answer came from Gramps Little, who had a gift for finding generous solutions to problems of all kinds. "He can stay in the shack down by my barn," he offered. "No one's been using it since the hired man joined up."

Gran was grateful. She simply couldn't fit one more body into her little Rosebank. "Thank you, dear Fred. You are always a kind friend to me."

Embarrassed, Gramps busied himself with his pipe. "Well, I've no use for the place. Someone might as well get the use of it before the roof caves in."

Crestonites made a careful distinction between a shack and a house or cottage, though there was often little outward sign of the difference. As far as I could see the main difference was that a shack didn't have curtains on the windows and a house did.

But Gran and Mum hung curtains on the shack that Uncle Bob was to occupy, swept it out, made up the bed and put a clean cloth on the table. Gran even put a vase of spring flowers on the little table by the bed. "Bob is very fond of flowers," she told us, "even if he can't see them."

And so one day in April 1919 Uncle Bob tapped his white cane down the steps of the CPR train westbound from Fort McLeod and into Gran's waiting arms. "Sooo thiiiis is Creeeeston," he said, sniffing the air, turning to face each direction as if to admire the view. He spoke slowly in a high-pitched screech. He was a peculiar looking man, small and thin with bright red hair. Though he'd be close to fifty then, he looked much younger.

"Come along. I'll take you home, Bob." Bob took Gran's arm and easily hefted a battered leather suitcase almost as big as himself, and they set off down the hill to Rosebank and then across the road to the shack that was to be Bob's home for the duration of his visit.

Just as Gran had told us he would be, Bob was very pleased to find the flowers by his bed. He knew immediately that they were daffodils and narcissi. He could identify flowers, trees and all kinds of plants by touch and smell. In a matter of a few days, he could find his way around Rosebank and Creston. He knew the apples trees and the plums and the cherries in the orchards, their scents, and the textures of their bark, and later their blossoms and growing fruits. He especially loved the red cedar by the door of his shack. "Like feathers," he said, stroking the soft needles, "like seaweed." He knew the soft feel of the path through the spinney to the barn and he knew the rows of vegetables in the garden. He knew his way up across the tracks and through town, and down the hill to the flats. He walked with a bouncing step, tapping his cane in front of him, and often humming a dirge-like tune. He soon became a familiar figure in Creston, tap-tapping his way along the wooden sidewalks and the muddy roads.

"Good morning, Bob!"

"Goooood moooorning, Mr. Spaulding."

"Helloooooooo, Louis!"

Once a month he fetched from the post office a parcel of books in braille from the lending library of the Institute for the Blind. He loved to read poetry and could recite reams of it in his terrible, screeching voice: Kipling and Tennyson, Longfellow, Thomas Hood. He loved to read and he loved to be read to. David and I took to reading our schoolbooks aloud to him. When we fell in love with the poems of Robert Service, Uncle Bob fell in love with them too. Soon we were all three able to recite long passages of the swinging *Sourdough Ballads* to each other.

Service's poems infected David and me with gold fever and a desire for the rugged outdoor life. We wanted to travel deep into the wilderness and camp out and have many adventures and in the end find an unknown creek bright with gold nuggets and pan them out and come back to civilization bronzed and hardened by the rugged outdoor life, and immensely rich.

"Don't be silly. You're much too young!" was the response we got from both Mum and Gran when we suggested we take a camping trip in the bush.

"Well, if you came with us…" we suggested.

"No."

"Or Gramps?"

We were too young but Gramps was too old, we were told.

Despite our discouragement, we studied maps and made plans, to be ready just in case an opportunity came along and Mum relented and let us go.

And one day opportunity did come. Packrat Robinson was in town, advertising his guiding services. He was the best guide in B.C. If anyone could lead us to the river of our dreams, he could.

Still Mum wouldn't hear of our going. "We couldn't let you children go off into the woods with only Old Packrat to look after you," she said. "And anyway, we couldn't afford it."

To our astonishment, Uncle Bob piped up, "Perhaaaaps I could go with them, look after them, like."

How Mum thought blind Uncle Bob could protect us in a wilderness emergency, I don't know, but when Bob cinched his argument by saying, "I still have tweeeeeelve dollars from the travel money Percy gave me, so I could paaaay Packrat's fee," Mum gave in and said we could go.

"What for would a blind man want to go walking around in them mountains?" Packrat asked when he came round to discuss terms with us.

"I'm foooond of trees," Uncle Bob replied. "I'd like to live amongst them just once in my life."

"Maybe you won't be so fond of 'em when you walk into them, crack your head on 'em, trip over 'em," Packrat said.

"Oh he can walk real good," I assured Packrat. "Show him, Uncle Bob, how good you can walk." Uncle Bob obliged by walking through the Rosebank garden, neatly avoiding trees, wheelbarrow, flowerbeds and baskets. Of course he knew the layout of that garden as well as he knew his own shack.

But Packrat must have been impressed. Or maybe he was in bad need of clients. There weren't so many sportsmen and tourists in the Kootenays, not like there had been before the war. He tugged at his white beard, pushed his leather hat back to scratch his head for a while and finally said, "Well, if that's what yez want, I guess I could take yez up to Clear Lake."

"Hoorah!" Bob gathered David and me up in one of his bone-crunching hugs.

"This ain't no stroll in the garden," Packrat warned us. "You be ready for some hard walking. And don't pack up no feather beds and parlor organs and such. I ain't got but the one hoss."

"Only the one hooooosss," Uncle Bob repeated.

And I burst into one of my renditions of a Service verse:

> This is the law of the Kootenays and ever she makes it plain:
> Send not your sick and your feeble
> Send me your strong and your sane
> Sane for the battle before them
> Strong for I harry them sore…

"That's a pretty verse," Packrat said in surprise.

"I know more," I said. "I know 'The Shooting of Dan McGrew' and 'The Cremation of Sam McGee' and 'The Man from Eldorado'."

"You'll be an entertainment around the camp fire," Packrat said. "Meet me at Kootenay Landing station from Monday's train." He shook our hands.

Mum and Gran made us up bedrolls, and we borrowed fishing gear and early on a brilliant August day we took the train to the Kootenay Landing station where Packrat and his "hoss" were waiting to take us out into the wilderness.

We walked all day on a forest trail, up a long, steep incline, then down into a cool, damp valley, and then up again. Packrat led the horse, Bess, and we followed. I held Uncle Bob's hand, supposedly to guide him, but after a few hours he was helping me along more than I was helping him.

At noon, on a height of land with nothing but forest all around, we lunched on the tomatoes and hard boiled eggs and jam sandwiches Mum had made for us, and drank water from our canteens. "Faaaar from the maaaadding crowd," Uncle Bob said with satisfaction.

After lunch, we followed a trail only Packrat could see winding down into another valley. Gradually this valley widened and the woods thinned out. There were patches of open meadow now. The land began to slope upward again. Not another ridge to climb! I thought. We were following a small stream which led us up to a lake, little bigger than a pond. After following the lakeshore for a short way, we came to a grassy promontory shaded by a huge old pine tree. The lake water was still, almost black in the late afternoon light. "Here we are, folks. The Kootenay Ritz!" Packrat pointed at a fire ring of blackened stones at our feet.

But he wouldn't let us flop down on the soft grass and enjoy the view. He said, "Matter of fact, I guess maybe this ain't the Ritz 'cause there ain't no dining room staff. We got chores to do."

Tired as we were from our trek, we set about getting the tent up, finding firewood, and unpacking the bedrolls and cooking utensils. Well, you had to be tough to survive in the wilderness, we reminded each other.

"Make a lot of noise while you're working, lads, scare off any of them rattlers or grizzly bears might be hanging around," Packrat warned us with a scary leer. You also had to be brave to live in the wilderness.

Packrat hobbled the horse and walked along the lakeshore to a fishing spot he knew of to catch our supper, while we got the fire going and put a pot of water on a flat stone to heat.

In a surprisingly short time Packrat was back with a mess of bass. He showed us how to lace them on green sticks to grill. We ate them with great chunks of bread off tin plates, using only knives for cutlery.

After we'd eaten, Packrat brewed up a billycan of thick green tea and lit up his pipe. We sat quiet, cradling enamel mugs of the hot tea, and listening to the sounds of the night beyond our campfire: the splash of a fish in the lake just a few feet away, or, more disturbing, a swish of branches as though some animal was moving through the brush. I was glad Packrat was with us.

"Have you ever actually seen a grizzly?" Dave asked, as if he were thinking the same fearful thoughts as I.

"Seen a grizzly! I'll say! I've seen 'em, and I've shot 'em, and one time I recall I was dang near caught by one. Chased me up a tree, he did."

"How did you escape?"

"Well, I'll tell you how. I was a-chewin of tobaccy at the time, do you see. Now when that bear came up the tree after me, I waited 'til he got so close I could feel his breath on my heels, then I looked down, and waited just a tad longer 'til the brute opened his mouth to bite off my feet, than I took my aim, and splat! I sent that tobaccy juice right into his maw. Well didn't he yelp and holler! I sent a couple of squirts more down, hoping to get him in the eye, but I won't swear I did. I couldn't take proper aim, do you see, cause the critter was tossing his head this way and that, and backing out of the tree. When his feet touched the ground, he shambled off, looking for water, I doubt.

"I don't never go out in the woods without my tobaccy ever since. You never know when it might be needed."

Uncle Bob and David and I all began to wonder if maybe we ought to take up tobacco chewing.

The fire was dying down. When Uncle Bob suggested it was time to turn in, none of us argued.

Packrat slept outside by the fire; he got to feeling crowded up in a tent, he said. I was glad he was out there, his mouth full of tobacco, guarding us from the dangers of the night.

The bedrolls were not quite as comfortable as they'd seemed when we tried them out on the floor at Rosebank, but we were so tired we could have slept on the bare ground, or even standing up.

The days that followed were as perfect as our dreams. We woke to the smell of bacon and coffee, and, shivering as we breakfasted close to the fire, we watched the sun burn the mist off the little lake. David and I spent the daylight hours swimming and fishing and panning for gold in the stream that flowed into the lake. While we panned, Packrat sat against a tree and smoked and thought up stupid jokes, like "Poor old Bess. How the deuce is she going carry out all the gold you kids are finding. Heh heh." And "You kids become millionaires on this trip, I'm a-going charge you double rates, I give yez fair warnin'. Heh. Heh."

We didn't mind the teasing. We were finding lots of rocks that looked like they might have gold streaks in them. Anyway, it was fun standing in the cold, clear river water or sitting on the bank, our feet and hands blue with cold while the sun baked our backs and we sifted through likely-looking gravel and sand.

While we worked, Uncle Bob whittled or played his harmonica or walked around touching trees, stroking their bark, feeling their leaves or needles. Sometimes he told his stories or recited poems to Packrat who listened attentively, not minding how long it took Bob to get through a story with his slow voice.

We ate bacon and bannock for breakfast, cold bacon or cold fish and bannock and dried apples for lunch, and grilled fresh-caught fish for supper. Uncle Bob was the best of us at the fishing, because he was patient enough to wait quietly 'til he felt a tug on the rod. Of course he wasn't as good as Packrat though.

After supper we gazed at the fire or up into the night sky where the stars blazed with a brightness we'd never seen before. We listened to Packrat's stories and then Packrat would get us to recite the Service poems over and over. Or we'd sing to Uncle Bob's harmonica: "Clementine," "My Darling Nelly Grey," "John Peel," and the new song from the war, "It's a Long Way to Tipperary". Packrat said it sure was some different from guiding fellows who came out to the woods to drink themselves drunk.

On the morning of the fourth day we folded up the bedrolls, took down the tent and loaded up old Bess, choosing only a few of our very best rocks to carry out, and began the long walk back to the real world.

It was the best holiday of our lives, we all agreed. For me, those few summer days remain etched in my memory as the last perfect days of my childhood. Never again was I so purely, so unthinkingly happy as I was then.

For Uncle Bob, it was the greatest adventure and probably the highlight of his life. He talked about it as long as he lived. "When we were caaaamping at Cleaaaaar Laaake," he would begin.

His "visit" to Creston went on for years and years, almost to the end of his life.

Chapter 7

The Return

It was a cool summer evening and Rosebank was strangely quiet. Little Margie was asleep; the other Talbot children were at their uncle's ranch for the day, and our David with them. Gran and I sat at the kitchen table hulling strawberries for tomorrow's jam making. This was the moment Mum chose for her announcement.

First she filled the blue granite-wear tea pot and set it to steep at the back of the kitchen stove. She set out cups and saucers. "I have come to a decision," she announced. She poured milk into each cup and added a spoonful of sugar to mine. In our household, any momentous news called for a ritual tea drinking.

Gran pushed the basin of strawberries aside. "Yes?"

Not 'til she had poured the tea and taken her place at the table did Mum reply. "I shall return home to England."

"England? Home?" I was astonished. Though to be sure England was always referred to by Mum and Gran as "home", to me it was as unreal a place as "our heavenly home" in church services and prayers. Creston was home.

It seemed that Gran too was baffled. "Home! To England! Do you really mean to go?"

"I do." Mum sipped her tea calmly. "You know I've always intended to return."

Gran clasped her red-stained hands to her aproned bosom. "But this is so sudden. I had thought that you meant to remain in Creston for some time."

Mum smiled. "You can hardly say we haven't had a good long visit! It's going on nine years we've been here. High time to take our leave, I'd say."

In the face of Gran's handwringing and my open-mouthed astonishment, Mum marshalled her reasons. "I want to have my own house at last. All this time I've been crowding in with you – not that I'm not grateful – or renting places. I'd like to settle down for good in a home of my own, and now that the pension money has come through at last, I have the means to do it."

"But not here in Creston?"

"No. England's *home*. I want to go back before it's too late. I want the children to go to proper English schools, to have cultural opportunities they're not getting here. I'd like them to get to know the family, and Tom's family in Wales too. They have no idea of their heritage, growing up here. If it hadn't been for the war, I'd have returned ages ago. Creston's all very well, but, well, it's a backwoods place."

"In any case," she pointed out, "one of us will have to take the Talbot children over to Boo and Took and Walter." It had been arranged that three of the Talbot children were to be given new homes with aunts and uncles in England, while Mum took in the youngest, Margie, and Gran took the oldest two, Andrew and Noonie. "I see," said Gran. She looked sad.

"I can't think why you want to stay here yourself, now that Charlotte's gone. Think of it. Once the children and I are back in England, your whole family will be there: Boo and Took and Walter, and almost all your grandchildren as well."

"Yes," Gran agreed. "But I shall have Noonie and Andrew here. And Uncle Bob. And Olive is close by, and many, many dear friends." She looked over towards Gramps' house. "And Mae and Percy not an unreasonable journey from here should I wish to travel, which I doubt I shall."

"You must do as you think best," Mum said.

"As must you," Gran agreed. Each of the women thought she was doing the right thing; each was disappointed that the other disagreed. The parting would be painful.

We children were excited at the idea of the coming adventure. We talked of nothing else but The Return. Mum showed us on a map the route we would follow all across Canada to Montreal and then across the Atlantic Ocean to Liverpool, England, and then by train to London, the centre of the whole British Empire.

England, we children knew, was a wonderful place where everything was exactly the way it should be. We knew this from years of comments from Mum and Gran. If, for instance, the Creston sun was too hot on a July day, or the train bringing the newspaper from Nelson was late, or there appeared a spelling mistake in that paper, Mum or Gran would remark that such a thing would never happen "back home". If anything broke or wore out too fast – the handle off a tea cup, the kitchen clock, a pair of shoes – then the most likely reason was that the item was of shoddy foreign manufacture. "Canadian quality," Mum would sniff. She always tried to buy products with "Made in England" stamped on them. They were bound to be the best.

David and the Talbots pestered me with questions about this marvellous England that we were to see at last. I pretended that I remembered England, though really it was as much of a fairyland to me as it was to them. I repeated what Mum and Gran had told us and described what I'd seen in the photographs in the *Country Life* magazines Aunt Boo sent us.

"The roses are magnificent. You have different money and it's worth a lot more than Canadian money. The grass is always green. London, which is where we'll be, is the largest city in the world. There are no mountains. It rains a lot. Everyone talks like Mum and Gran. Children are always polite and obedient."

"And I'll be going to a boarding school, and I'll have a cap with my school's crest on it," David put in.

This was a sore point. There was no question about David's getting to go to a boarding school and wear a smart uniform, just because he was a boy, and all nice boys in England went to boarding schools, according to Mum. But girls did too, I reminded her. I had read all about them in the Angela Brazil girls' boarding school stories that my English aunts sent me at Christmas. I longed to go to a school like the ones in those stories. I wanted to wear a gym tunic and a tie and a hat with a rolled brim, and live in a dormitory and have friends with names like Penelope and Daphne. I was going to be furious if I didn't get sent to a boarding school too, I warned.

"We'll see, after we talk to Uncle Will about our financial situation." That was as far as Mum would promise.

After my father's death, his brother Will had taken charge of financial matters for Mum. She had given him power of attorney to facilitate the signing of documents, since he was on the spot in London. There was an insurance payment, and a generous pension from the army. It seemed that Mum would be richer as a widow than she'd ever been as a wife. She was grateful to Will for his help in sorting things out.

She was to have one of the new houses the government was providing for officers and officers' widows. "Houses for Heroes" they were called. Mum applied for the lease of one in Havering, a small town in Essex close to her brother Took's home.

"That will be most convenient for you," Gran said. "You will be not far from Boo and within half a day's journey of Walter as well."

In all the excitement of anticipation, it was not 'til our suitcases were packed up and we were making our round of farewell visits that I realized that going "home" meant leaving home. A sense of loss overwhelmed me. Gran was a second mother to me and Rosebank the only permanent home I knew. Mum had moved me and David to Bonner's Ferry and back and in and out of rented houses from time to time, but Gran and Rosebank had remained the same, always welcoming us "home". I could hardly comprehend what life without Gran close in the background would be. And Uncle Bob. Who would read to him and listen to his slow, screechy recitations? And the Talbot kids. Even if Noonie and I had our spats, we were close as sisters, and now we would be half a world apart. And there was Sally Spaulding down the road: she and I were writing a play together. Now we'd never have a chance to finish it, let alone stage it. Yes, I wanted to go to this wonderful place called England, but I wished we could take everything and everyone with us, or that we could go and take a look, and then come back to Creston. It was sad and frightening to think of a life in which Rosebank and Creston would be far, far away. I wondered if I didn't envy Noonie and Andrew, even though they said they envied me.

And then there were last minute changes in the plans. Uncle Took wrote to say that much as he'd like to take in and provide for one of the Talbot boys, he really couldn't. He and his wife had four children of their own and were barely managing. Then Fred said that if Bob wasn't going to England, he wouldn't go either. He'd run away if they tried to make him. If they put him on the train, he would jump off. If they got him as far as the boat, he would jump off that. He and Bob were sticking together. They'd get jobs. They'd look after themselves. They wouldn't be a trouble to anyone, but they were staying here.

Their protest threw Gran and Mum into a dither. Gran alternately wrung her hands and pushed the news away from her troubled brow with open palm. Mum was thin-lipped with anger at first but soon looked more sad than angry. She and Gran and Aunt Olive, and the rector from the church and others held long conclaves at Gran's kitchen table. I overheard snatches of their deliberations. "The children must stay in the family." "Charlotte and Andy would want their children to be happy above all. Money wouldn't matter to them." "Too much change will not be good." "Those two boys are so close." The upshot of the talks was that Fred and Bob would remain in Creston under Gran's guardianship. Olive and Alphabetical and others in the community would help out. Crestonites would see to it that those four Talbot kids always had a roof over their heads and food to eat. They'd be all right.

That left only two Talbots, Margie and Charles, who would travel with Mum, Dave and me to England. Margie, who was too young to know where she was going, would stay with us, and Charles was to be delivered into his Aunt Boo's keeping. He was a little uncertain about his future in England, as were David and I, but full of excitement about the journey and all the new experiences that lay in store for us.

Any misgivings were forgotten as plans progressed until one day in August, dressed in smart new clothes, we boarded a Pullman coach on the CPR, heading east. We travelled in style. We sat on plush velour seats that at night a porter transformed magically into comfortable bunks with heavy canvas curtains pulled across and net hammocks for holding our clothes. It was like sleeping in a moving tent. You could push up the stiff brown blind and look out on the night sky with clouds scudding by and now and then the lights of a town or a lonely farm winking far away.

During the day we could walk through the swaying coaches to the open observation platform at the back of the train. We travelled through the beautiful and exciting Crow's Nest Pass, the train seeming to be suspended on the edge of precipitous slopes. We would plunge suddenly into the thundering darkness of a tunnel, cross chasms on high trestle tracks, catch sight of the engine as the train turned back on it itself and then lose it again on a straighter stretch. When we passed through towns, we waved to children who stood on station platforms and stared at us enviously.

Three times a day we swayed through more coaches to the dining car with its two rows of tables covered with spotless stiff white damask cloths. The white-coated waiter held Mum's chair for her with an obsequious bow, and flicked out a large starched white napkin for each of us, while Mum decided what we would order.

She insisted on plain food. "I don't want any of you falling sick on me." But even plain food tasted exotic when served with such elegance.

At our last dinner on the journey, as a special treat, Mum let us order whatever dessert we wanted and I chose chocolate cake. I was eating my way slowly through the large piece on my plate, savouring each delicious mouthful, and, as was my custom, saving the best part, the icing, for the last.

Just as I was about to plunge my fork into its sweet, creamy chocolate thickness, a hand reached out and whipped the plate away from me. "Never save the best for the last," a deep voice above me said.

Immobilized and struck dumb by the swiftness and the unexpectedness of the action, I watched a white-haired gentleman in a black suit stride on along the aisle between the tables and disappear behind the swinging door at the end of the coach. I put my empty fork back on the table. David and Charles turned to stare down the aisle after him.

"Did the waiter take that away before you were finished?" Mum asked. She had been spooning the last of an ice cream sundae she was sharing with Margie into the child's eager mouth and hadn't noticed the quick scooping away. "Really! He might have asked."

"It wasn't the waiter who took it away," I answered.

"I imagine it was. They want to hurry us along and get ready for the next service. I'll ask him to bring it back," Mum raised an arm, but I tugged it down.

"It wasn't the waiter. It was just a man. An old man. And I think he passed the plate into the kitchen."

"Well of all the nerve!" Mum was up on her feet, ready to fight for my lost bit of cake.

"Please don't," I urged her.

It wasn't just that I didn't want her to make an embarrassing fuss. It was because I saw in a sudden flash of recognition that the old man was right. It was silly always to save the best for the last. It wouldn't taste any better then. I wouldn't do it again. It was like that poem we learned in school. "Gather ye rosebuds while ye may."

"Eat your icing while ye may." I muttered this aloud. I would make it a rule of my life.

David heard me. "I've already eaten mine," he said.

"Me too," Charles said.

"Too," Margie crowed, and beamed at us. She didn't know what we were talking about.

I was the only hoarder, but I never would be again.

"Sit down, Mum," I said.

And Mum, though she ranted on for a bit about perfect strangers who make bold with other people's dinners, sat down and drank her tea.

I have remembered the strange man's lesson all my life.

Our journey from Montreal to Liverpool on the *SS Metagama* was even more luxurious than the train had been. The *Metagama* was one of the CPR's cabin class steamers, boats designed for the increasing number of middle-class travellers who wanted comfort, but who were a little too modest or too parsimonious to choose the aristocratic first class. All the accommodations in cabin class steamers, the advertisements said, were of first-class standard, at a reasonable rate.

I enjoyed the first few hours of the journey. I ate a grand dinner in the palatial dining room finishing with a *"gateau surprise"* from which I ate the icing first. Then I got seasick. From then on the luxury and delights of the journey were wasted on me. I stayed in our cabin or, at Mum's insistence, out on a deck chair, wrapped in a blanket and benefitting from the sea air. I consumed almost nothing but dry crackers and tea. The boys made me even sicker with reports of the meals the rest of them had just eaten and the great games and entertainments going on. Even little Margie tried to tell me about a wonderful rocking horse she rode on in the playroom. The thought of riding a rocking horse on this rocking boat made my stomach heave over again.

I was furious with myself to think of what I was missing. I wish I could have packaged up the trip to enjoy it on dry and steady land.

We arrived at Liverpool in a heavy rain. A porter found our bags and conducted us through the din of a huge echoing station to the London train and we moved out into an afternoon that was almost as dark as night. We had tea in the dining car, but here the table cloths were not so stiff and white, and the waiter was not so attentive as what we had come to expect on the CPR. I still couldn't eat anyway. Back in the compartment, the boys and I put our faces against the damp windows to see what we could of England but we saw only darkness and rain and sometimes a dim-lit station.

Chapter 8

*O*rphan

Aunt Boo didn't know what to think. Long after Clary had left for work and Percival gone to school, she sat on at the breakfast table in her North Finchley home. For the third time she read the letter that had come in the morning post from her sister Sarah and still she could not quite believe its news. Sarah was proposing that Boo and Clary adopt one of poor Charlotte's orphans. Actually, she wasn't proposing, or suggesting or asking. She was bringing the child to them. They were almost on their way. They would arrive in a month's time. "Charlotte's last thoughts were for her children. She was most anxious that they should remain in the family," Sarah's letter said. "We thought Charles would fit in best with your family as he is almost the same age as your Percy."

Another child would not fit into Boo's family. Her family was complete. She and Clary were not among those people who adore children, dogs and playful kittens indiscriminately. They had the one child – a miniature adult really, was young Percy – and that was quite enough.

Another child, a child they did not know and did not want, would disrupt their life. Boo really didn't see how she could cope.

On the other hand, how could she disregard the dying wishes of poor Charlotte? Grief at her sister's death overcame Boo once again.

How could it be that Charlotte, the youngest and the dearest of the family, would die at such a young age? And her husband before her. And six children left orphaned. Of course the family must care for them now. Of course she would take one of those dear little children and care for him as if he were her own. She must. It was her duty.

But really, it would be so terribly inconvenient for her and Clary and for Percival too. It was too much to ask of them. She'd never be able to cope. She and Clary weren't good with children. Their nerves weren't up to it. Couldn't Sarah take the boy? After all, she too had a boy more or less the same age. Why couldn't Charlotte's boy fit in with her family, instead of with Boo's? Furthermore, Boo didn't like the way Sarah had decided the child's fate without consulting with her. Perhaps she might have preferred to take in one of the girls instead of the boy.

Charles, the boy was called, after his mother, poor Charlotte. Boo wept fresh tears. She folded the letter back into its envelope. She would see what Clary had to say when he came home from work this afternoon.

What Clary had to say was this: "How dare your family foist an unwanted child upon us? 'They've decided this boy is to live with us,' they write. Write back at once and say he can't come. We won't have him."

"I dare say that would be the thing to do," Boo said. It was what Clary wanted. In truth, it was what she herself wanted. It was the most sensible way to deal with the problem. But Boo couldn't make herself write that letter. Every time she thought of doing so, the image of her dear, dead sister came before her, weeping for her little boy. If the roles had been reversed, Charlotte would have taken in her Percival without a moment's hesitation, she knew. But Boo was not so loving and easy-going a person as Charlotte and not so fond of children either. Imagine Charlotte's having had six of them! She really shouldn't have had so many. The mere thought of another child always underfoot gave Boo nervous palpitations. And Clary, she knew, would be at the end of his tether if a noisy little boy should create mischief around their beautiful house, which this boy would no doubt do. Colonial children, Boo believed, were generally an undisciplined lot.

If only she could say a clear "no", they wouldn't have to deal with the problem. Their little family could go on undisturbed in its ways.

But if Boo wrote that "no" letter, her mother would never forgive her for her selfishness, nor Sarah, and worst of all, Boo would never be able to forgive herself.

She didn't know what to do.

Every day she determined to write the letter of refusal, and every day she couldn't bring herself to do it. She needed to think about it more. Perhaps she could come up with an alternate plan that would suit everyone. Was the child too young for the navy, she wondered. She seemed to remember hearing that midshipmen were taken on at a very early age. Or there were live-in apprenticeships with chances for a boy to advance: gardener's boy or under-footman for a ducal establishment. How old was the boy again? Boo calculated. He'd be nine or ten, she thought: too young then for apprenticeship. Boo turned over ideas and thought and fretted and did not write the decisive letter. To make no decision is preferable to making the wrong decision was one of the maxims by which she directed her life. Sometimes, she had found, the problem solved itself; sometimes Clary solved it for her; and sometimes it proved to be not a great problem at all. So perhaps the arrival of Charles would be no problem. Or perhaps Sarah's plan for him would change and he would go elsewhere.

Boo fretted and thought until it was only a week before Sarah and the boy were to arrive and then it was too late to do anything. The problem had not been solved but at least the agony of making a decision was over. Boo broke the news to Clary at breakfast time when he wouldn't have time to rage at her for long because he'd have to leave for work.

Understandably, Clary was furious. "I could not do it," Boo said. "It would have been quite wrong." She took the moral high ground in her defence. "It is my duty – it is our duty – to give my orphaned nephew a home."

Clary folded his newspaper carefully. "I should have written the letter myself. I might have known you wouldn't be up to saying no; you've always been too soft-hearted." He sighed dramatically and stood up from the table. "The die is cast. Let him come, if he must." He picked up the folded newspaper. "I'm taking this to read on the tube." He leaned over to give his wife a cold kiss on the cheek. "Just don't expect me to be pleasant and fatherly to the boy."

"But you are never pleasant to anyone, dear!" Boo smiled. "Except to myself and dear Percy."

"I don't *need* to be pleasant to anyone. I supply the funds for you to be pleasant," Clary fired a final salvo, and left for work.

That was just Clary being cranky, Boo knew. He'd be good to the boy, not overly friendly, but correct and fair. That's what a boy needed really, not a chum who played cricket and built model boats with him. Look how well their Percy had turned out under Clary's parenting. Boo just hoped she could fill the role of surrogate mother as effectively.

While she prepared a bedroom for the new family member, the doorbell rang. It was the telegraph boy with a wire from Sarah. When she had deciphered the cryptic message between the "stops" Boo ascertained that Sarah and her children would be staying for an indefinite time "to help Charles settle in". This was worse and worse.

"Sarah's lot won't stay long, of course," she offered as comfort to Clary when she told him at tea time of the added trial they were to endure.

"How many children does Sarah have?" Clary asked, rolling his eyes.

"Two, I believe. Possibly three." Boo stirred two precious teaspoons of sugar into her tea. "Let us hope that it is the lower number."

"Does that woman think we're running a residential hotel here as well as an orphanage?" Clary asked.

Boo laughed in her peculiar high-pitched sort of whinny, and Clary continued, "Does she know food is still rationed here? Who does she expect to feed and house her and her brood while they're here? Good old Clary, of course! She has an infernal nerve, she does. Traipsing across the Atlantic the way you or I might undertake a trip across London! She should stay in Canada, the silly woman. And all the rest of your family with her."

Clary was working himself into one of his rages. It was so bad for his heart. It was up to Boo to calm him down. "There really is no help for it. We can't, we really can't, put my own sister out on the street, no more than we can refuse to give Charles a home. Besides, you used to quite like Sarah, I remember."

"I may have, but that was before she was in charge of an infant army needing homes."

"I expect Charles is a lovely little boy," Boo said.

"Do you, indeed?" Clary stomped out of the room.

"...and will be a good companion for our Percival," Boo called after him to the closing door.

The day came. The visitors were to arrive on the late train and take a taxi to the house. Boo would wait up for them alone. At nine o'clock, his usual time, she tucked Percy into his bed. "When you wake in the morning you will have a new brother. Won't that be nice?" she asked with false cheerfulness.

Percy considered. "What if he's a naughty boy?"

What indeed? Boo wondered even as she assured Percy that Charles was his own cousin and therefore sure to be a very nice boy. "If he isn't, I shall bite him," Percy decided.

"Oh no, dear. That will hardly be necessary. Good night now." Boo turned off the light and closed the door half way, as Percy liked it.

Clary went to bed at ten, as he always did. As was his custom, he turned off the electricity in the house. "It's too risky to have electricity running into the house when I'm not up and alert," was his belief. "Fire might break out and the house burn to cinders while we slept."

"Tonight I could turn it off before I come up to bed," Boo suggested.

"You wouldn't know how to cope." Clary left her two candles.

Boo waited. There. The sound of a motor on the street. Yes, stopping. A door slamming. Footsteps. Boo took up a candle and hurried to the front door.

"We're here!" Sarah's well-remembered voice called in greeting. A sudden vision of their girlhood came to Boo and she held her sister close for a long, sweet moment. "Sarah, my dear!"

Then she recollected herself. "And the children!"

Sarah put an arm around one of the boys. "This is Charles."

Boo looked at the pale, solemn boy who stared back at her with her dead sister's round grey-blue eyes. She had not expected the boy would look so much like Charlotte. It was almost frightening.

"And this is Margie, Charlotte's youngest, poor little mite." Sarah turned the baby she held in her arms for Boo to admire. Boo glanced at it without interest. All babies looked more or less alike.

"Well now, come in, all of you," she waved them in. "These other children are your own?"

"Yes. You remember your Aunt Boo, don't you, Olwen? And David?" Olwen and David stepped forward to be kissed.

"Well, I expect you'll be tired as that little one." Boo nodded at the baby sleeping on Sarah's shoulder. "You'll want to go to bed straightaway. We'll talk in the morning. Don't come down until I call you." She was too tired to visit tonight. She didn't want to know anything more about Charles or about Charlotte's death or about the rest of the family. She couldn't cope. She wanted only to sleep.

She showed her visitors to the attic room she'd readied for them. Sarah and the girls could share the bed. The boys would sleep on the floor. "Boys don't mind a hard bed," Boo told them. It would not do to make them comfortable here. Lord knows how long they'd stay if she made things too agreeable. She left them a candle and bade them good night.

Four children in the house! Five, counting Percy. Oh dear, oh dear! Boo was tired of the company of them already. She pulled on her nightgown and slipped into bed beside Clary who was snoring in that soft soothing hum he had. She told herself that perhaps the situation would look more normal in the morning, although, really, she didn't believe that it would. She wished that boy didn't look so much like his mother.

In the morning, after Clary had left for work and Percy for school, Boo called the troops from Canada down for breakfast. She gave the three older children slices of bread and dripping and sent them out to play.

"What will we play?" Olwen asked, looking out at the mournful grey street.

"You'll think of something," Sarah said.

Charles immediately set out to climb the tree in next door's garden. "Come down out of that!" Boo shouted, but too late. Her neighbor Mrs. Briggs was already at her door threatening to call a bobby.

"Sorry!" Boo called to appease Mrs. Briggs. This was even worse than she had feared. The child hadn't been out for two minutes and already there was trouble with the neighbours. Mrs. Briggs nodded, offered a brief "good morning," glared at Charles 'til he was off her property and then retreated, slamming her front door behind her.

"Stay on the pavement and don't go past the corner either way." Boo closed her own door against the three unhappy children slouching against her garden fence.

In the sitting room Boo addressed her sister. "Now then. Put that infant somewhere where it can do no harm. You and I must talk."

Sarah's account of Charlotte's death was heart-rending. "She was weakened by her own bout with the flu and with nursing the children, and then Andy's death nearly finished her. If it hadn't been for the children, I think she would have turned her face to the wall and died with him. But for the sake of those children, she fought for her life through the pain. When she knew she might die, she was frantic with worry for them, pleaded for them with her dying voice. We promised her we'd look after them, see that they would be loved and cared for and that they would have the best lives they could have.

"Telling the poor little souls their mother was dead was the hardest thing I've ever had to do. They were in shock for days afterwards.

We've all been trying to do our best for them and I think they're coming along. Charles is a grand boy," Sarah finished. "He'll be good company for Percy."

"I suppose," Boo said. She was moved by Sarah's description. She too wanted to do her best for the little boy. "But I honestly wonder if my nerves are up to the strain of another child. It comes as such a shock to me. I have never been as strong as you, Sarah."

"Nonsense," Sarah replied to that. "You are perfectly well. And two children are no more trouble than one. They amuse each other."

"Percy has never been a trouble," Boo reminded her.

"Nor will Charles be. He's a good boy. Once he's been here with you for a couple of months, you won't know how you ever got along without him, I'm sure."

"You're sure of too much, Sarah. Clary, I tell you straight out, is not at all pleased at the thought of another child in our household."

"Clary will come to love Charles as much as you will."

Boo doubted if that was how it would be. But they would at least do their duty by the boy.

Clary greeted his visitors upon his return from work at tea time.

"Well, well, here's our orphan from Canada," he shook Charles' hand. "Lost both parents. Dear, dear. You know what Oscar Wilde said: 'To lose one parent may be regarded as a misfortune; to lose both looks like carelessness.' Ha!Ha! Ha!"

"Ha! Ha! Ha!" Cousin Percy echoed.

Charles flushed red, balled his fists. "I didn't lose them. They died."

"Yes, dear. Your uncle was joking." Aunt Boo gave him an awkward little hug. Not a very funny joke, Charles thought.

Everyone sat down to tea then, and while the adults talked family, Charles and Percy eyed each other suspiciously over plates of fish paste sandwiches and walnut cake.

"Percy will show you the room we've chosen for you," Aunt Boo said when Charles had refused a third piece of cake to be polite, though he would have taken it if he'd been urged.

Percy led the way. It was a grand house, huge by Creston standards. Charles was impressed as he followed Percy, lugging his case down from the attic bedroom, careful not to bang it against furniture. Percy opened a second-floor door to a room with a neat wooden bedstead and a chest of drawers and a table and chair by the window. It would be the first time Charles had ever had a room to himself.

"How do you like it?" Percy asked.

"Skookum," Charles said, overawed, "real skookum."

Percy snorted. "What on earth does that mean?"

Charles set down his case. "It means 'very nice'."

"Indeed," Percy said with another snort.

Charles had a bad feeling that despite the grandeur, he wasn't going to like his new home. He thought it might be lonely sleeping all alone in a room.

And he didn't much like Percy.

"You'll get used to life in England," Aunt Sarah had said. "Soon, you'll be so busy, you and Percy, that you'll forget about little old Creston and your friends and family there. And you must always be grateful to Aunt Boo and Uncle Clary for taking you in and giving you a home."

Well, he would do his best. He'd already noticed Aunt Boo was going to be pretty fussy about tidiness and wiping his boots when he came in and about exactly where he could play and where he could not. He wasn't used to that. There weren't many rules in their house on the ranch. Mostly he and his brothers and sisters got on with their chores and with whatever games they wanted to and only got yelled at when they did something really stupid or dangerous or mean, and that was only fair. He wondered how he'd get on with Aunt Boo and her rules, and Uncle Clary who made strange jokes and this boy who wore a tie all day long and talked like a grown-up.

As for England, Aunt Sarah had made it out to be the greatest place on earth, but so far he wasn't much impressed. England was grey rain and tiny little fenced gardens with trees you weren't allowed to climb and dirty, crowded streets.

He didn't think much of it. And he'd never forget Creston, no matter what Aunt Sarah said.

Chapter 9

A Hero's Home

Our stay at Aunt Boo's house was not pleasant. Every night when Mum tucked me and Margie, way too early, into our cold bed in the cold bedroom, I'd ask," When are we going to move into our Hero's House?"

"As soon as it's ready," was her reply. "And let us pray that will be very soon," she'd add with a wink.

I envied David who had left for his boarding school the day after we arrived. He wore his new cap and blazer with the school crest on them and he had a tin trunk with his name painted on it. I felt sorry for myself and little Margie because we weren't going anywhere for a while, and even sorrier for my poor cousin Charles who was to stay at Aunt Boo's forever. I wondered if he was wishing he'd made a protest about leaving Creston too. At least he got to go to school during the day though, and I didn't.

After a week or two of boredom, Mum left Margie in the care of Charles and a reluctant Aunt Boo and took me on a trip to Wales to see Uncle Will and my father's family. We broke our journey in Birmingham to see Uncle Wyatt, another of my father's brothers, and his new wife, Oliver.

Oliver? That was a strange name for a woman, and another to be added to my list of strange names in the family. Oliver herself was also strange. She was more than six feet tall and thin as a rake. She wore trousers and high boots and smoked like a man.

They were packing up, Wyatt told us in apology for the disorder of boxes and crates that filled the room where they received us. They were going to emigrate to Australia. "England is finished," Wyatt told Mum. "The war has done for us. You should never have come back."

"I should say Australia is the right place for those two nuts," Mum said when we were back on the train to Wales.

Uncle Will met us at the train station in Caernarfon with a hired car and driver to take us up into the hills to the little village of Llanaelhaearn, where grandfather Evans lived. In contrast to morose Uncle Wyatt, Uncle Will was all smiles and charm, and he was very good looking as well. He embraced Mum and me and gave a tender speech about the sadness of our loss, and how all Tom's family mourned with us and what a wonderful man Tom had been. Then he got us into the car and asking solicitous questions about our health and the rigour of the journey, tucked a rug over our knees and squeezed mine as he did so. He complimented Mum on her hat and me on my beautiful hair. Before we'd gone far, Mum was chatting happily and I was thinking Uncle Will was about the most glamorous uncle a girl could have.

"I'm afraid I had to use some of poor Tom's money," he apologized to Mum when the subject came around to the business affairs he'd handled with power of attorney.

"That's quite all right," Mum replied graciously. "I realize you will have had certain expenses to meet, bills to settle and so on."

"Ah, good. You know how it is then." Will smiled. We drove on into Llanaelhaearn.

Wales was better than England. The weather was just as wet, but there were mountains, although nothing like as high and wild as the Kootenays around Creston. There were no orchards and no forests; only green fields dotted with white sheep and separated by low stone walls. In grandfather's small grey-stone house in the village, a huge crowd of Evanses were always hanging about: aunts and uncles and cousins and half-cousins. Once you got used to the crowded conditions and the lack of light and the din, the cottage was a friendly place. All day long, it seemed, men argued, babies cried, women and children shouted to be heard and sometimes everyone broke into song. There was always washing festooned around the kitchen range, and meals of bread and tea and bacon were served at all hours on the long blackened table that nearly filled the rest of the room. Mum spoke in a loud clear voice and the Evans answered her in lilting sing-song English.

Among themselves and to me they spoke Welsh, and I found I could understand what they said, though I always answered in English. I had forgotten my father, but some memory of his language had remained in my unconscious.

A few days after our arrival, Mum asked Uncle Will to show her Tom's papers, and explain where she stood financially.

I noticed the nervous glances that flew around the room among the Evans' and then Grandfather –Taid as I was to call him – took my hand and said, "Will you walk along to the church with me, Olwen, and I'll teach you how to play the harmonium? Would you like to play some hymns? "

I would.

Taid sat on the high stool in front of the harmonium and, pumping the two wide pedals vigorously, he pounded out "Guide me, o Thou great Jehovah". "There now. You try it," he said after a couple of run-throughs.

I sat and pumped the pedals and laid my hands on the keys. "Which ones do I press on?"

"Why, the ones for the tune," he said. "The tune I just showed you. Sure you know it well yourself."

I did know the hymn. We sang it sometimes in church, but I couldn't understand how that would tell me which keys to press. "Could you show me again, please?"

Taid played the tune another couple of times. "Now then."

I peddled and let my hands move over the keys but all that came out were moaning discords, nothing like the tune.

"You must sing it to yourself so you'll know what to play," Taid advised.

I sang, but still the wrong sounds came out of the instrument. "When my mother plays, she uses a book with the notes written in it," I hinted.

"Ah yes," Taid conceded. "Some play with the books. But there's easier it is just to play what you hear." He was puzzled. "I taught your father thus, and he had no trouble."

Then we went home, both of us disappointed that I had not inherited the Welsh gift for music.

We found Will gone, and my mother fuming. "He spent all the money!" she was raging at poor Nain Jane, who held out a cup of tea to her with one hand and tried to wave her onto a chair with the other. "Every last penny! The cad! Out of the hands of widows and orphans! And for what? Gambling and carrying on, I shouldn't be surprised! The cad!"

She noticed our entry and shouted at Taid, "What sort of a family is this where a man steals from his own dead brother?"

Taid looked down at his feet. "Will is not a reliable man in matters of money, I fear. You did not do well to trust him with Tom's."

"Fine advice *now*," Mum shrieked. "Why didn't you say anything before?"

"It was too late when I heard of it. I am sorry, sorry, Sarah. Will has a weakness for the horse racing, you see. He was not on a winning streak, else he would have the money for you, sure. I'd pay myself if I could, but..." He held up empty hands. It was evident that he and his new family had no money to spare. "When his luck changes, Will will pay you back, I am certain. Sit down now and drink some tea."

"Tea and promises will do me no good," Mum said but she sat down and took the cup that was offered her and drank from it in sharp, little sips.

My mother and I left Wales the next day. And that was the last we heard or saw of the Welsh side of the family for more than forty years. Except for a Christmas card and letter every year from that strange Aunt Oliver and morose Uncle Wyatt.

When we got back to London, we were pleased to hear that our Hero's House was ready. We moved in. Located in the village of Havering in Essex, the house was one in a row of grey stucco cottages with a bare strip of grass in front. There were two rooms downstairs and two up. The plaster felt damp to the touch and the rooms smelled of fresh paint. But there was electric light, and a bathroom with an amazing gas-fired machine called a geyser that produced hot water. There was a big kitchen with a shiny black range for cooking and heating, and a scullery with a sink and tap.

And it was ours. We settled in, Mum and Margie and myself, a small family, I found, being used to the crowd at Rosebank. I missed them all. I missed David and Gran most of all. I began to write letters and watched for the postman's arrival every day. The replies were disappointing. They were mostly addressed to Mum and were never as interesting as I expected them to be. David wrote that he was fine. He was learning Latin and playing cricket. Could Mum send him a cake? Charles wrote that he was fine, the weather was wet, and Aunt Boo was kind to him. I didn't believe that last bit. Noonie wrote that she'd made eight dollars picking apples and was going to buy a new winter coat. Gran wrote that she was preparing for her autumn show and putting up plums and that she missed us, and so did Uncle Bob and Gramps who sent best regards. Uncle Bob particularly missed our poetry readings.

The only people we knew in Havering were Uncle Took and Aunt Georgie and their four children. They lived a half mile down the road towards Romford. The children were all younger than I, babies, almost, and I considered them rather naughty and not much fun. We walked down to visit them most afternoons. While Mum and Georgie talked, I'd be sent out to "play" with the children. I was thirteen years old. I didn't want to play with four-year-olds and infants.

I was too old to make friends of my own age in the village. Girls of thirteen didn't just go out and stare at other girls until they were asked to play, which was the way Margie made friends with the toddlers in our row of Heroes' Houses. There weren't any kids of my age in the row anyway. I sometimes saw girls walking to or from the village school, but they didn't speak to me and I was too shy to speak to them. I needed to get to that school if I was going to have any friends at all in this country. After Will dropped the bombshell about Mum's money being all gone, I'd given up hopes of a boarding school and said good-bye in my heart to my imaginary friends Penelope and Daphne. Now I would settle happily for the village school, but Mum still had higher standards for my education and would not let me go. "Have patience," she told me. "Wait 'til I clear up this financial muddle we're in. It won't be long."

But it was long. The "financial muddle" continued, as did my loneliness.

Some days we'd take the bus to Romford and have tea at a café or in one of the department stores. Mum or Aunt Georgie would ask me to keep an eye on the children on these outings. This was no easy task as the kids were quick at grabbing at things on the counters in the shops, or running off into the crowds, or dipping their fingers into iced cakes in the tea shop. These outings were more like work than pleasure for me.

In compensation Mum would sometimes arrange to leave Margie with Aunt Georgie and organize an excursion into London or a visit to a stately home for the two of us. We visited the Tower of London, Westminster Abbey, Hampton Court, Blenheim Palace. I was awed to see places where history had taken place so long ago. In Creston there was hardly a single building that was any older than I was. Those were wonderful days, with Mum as excited and moved by what we saw as I was. Then England was a wonderful place.

But most days we spent in Havering, where the grass was indeed greener than any we'd see in Creston except maybe in May, and it was already October here; and the roses in the small front gardens were maybe superior to Gran's, though I didn't think so; and there was a village green and an old pub, but we never went in there; and a very old church that we attended every Sunday and I tried to feel the history of it, but really it was very much like the church in Creston and the sermons just as boring; and a school that I was not allowed to go to because we were waiting to get back the money from Uncle Will to send me to one of those schools with gym tunics and girls called Penelope. Havering was boring and I was lonely. I longed to go school. I waited and waited.

"Are you crazy?" Noonie wrote back when I complained to her in my weekly letter. "You are so lucky. No school and all holidays." She didn't know what she was talking about.

Mum bought me a bicycle to cheer me up, so that I'd be able to get out on my own. Where could I go? A bicycle was not what I wanted. I wanted to go to school. I couldn't learn how to ride that bicycle. I've never in all my life known anyone else who was unable to learn to ride, and now, looking back, I think what I was doing was subconsciously refusing to learn to ride. I was never a rebellious child, but this was my protest against the decision my mother had made for me. I would not ride a bicycle that was given to me as a substitute for school.

We began to go into London more often. We called on some of my father's Welsh friends. They talked and talked of publishing a book of his poems, but nothing came of it. Mum couldn't read the poems for herself because they were in Welsh, but she was sure they were worthy of publication and was disappointed to be told that there were too many collections of the work of poets killed in the war and not enough paper to publish them. We called on Aunt Boo and, if Charles was around, he and I would walk up and down the dreary street and have a good commiserating talk about how much we missed Creston and everyone there.

At about this time a terrible thought came to me, so shocking in its disloyalty that I did not dare to say it aloud. The thought was that, so far, I didn't like England. Even if it was the land of hope and glory, the mother of us all, the proud centre of the Empire on which the sun never set, the strongest nation on earth, I didn't like it. Canada was much nicer. Canada was home.

I sensed that Mum too was not enjoying England as much as she had thought she would. Long absence from the country must have made her forget some unpleasant features of London, such as the dirty and crowded streets, trains, and buses; yellow fogs thick with coal dust; and days and days of rain. She had expected to find a happy prosperous country celebrating victory. She had not reckoned on seeing so many people dressed in black and with sad faces. She had not expected to see soldiers, officers even, selling pencils and apples on street corners or struggling by on crutches or in wheel chairs or with empty sleeves. These were men who had served their country and were now, it seemed, unappreciated. It was not right. The reality of England in 1920 had more the atmosphere of defeat than victory.

Everything was much more expensive than Mum remembered it to be, and in short supply too. There wasn't even enough paper to publish a small volume of her late husband's beautiful poems. The pension from the War Office, that had seemed generous back in Canada, was only enough to live on in England. Mum was not as rich as she had expected to be.

Many others were in the same plight. Jobs were scarce and pay was low. There were strikes. People's spirits seemed as grey as the rainy grey skies.

It was the Hun that was to blame for this, Mum and Aunt Georgie agreed. The war had spoiled everything. "To think England should win, and then come to this!" They shook their heads.

Slow months dragged by. In the mornings we went to the shops. Mum talked about the terrible quality of the goods for sale. The bacon was streaky, and the butter was "off" and the leather on my new shoes was thin, cheap stuff. "This bread I got at Johnson's this morning is half stale," she complained as she buttered slices for our supper one evening. "And here's another letter from David came this morning asking for a food package. He says they don't get enough to eat at Amberley. Considering what I'm paying to send him there, I think it's shocking, I really do. I've a mind to write to the head master."

Another day it was the quality of the fruit available at the green grocer that raised her ire. "He's asking a shilling for a half peck of apples and hard, miserable little things they are. In the Kootenays we'd throw fruit like that to the chickens." We left the shop without buying any.

"Do you remember the apples from Gran's tree at Rosebank?" I asked as we walked back to our Hero's House with the shopping basket almost empty.

"Those were the best apples I've ever eaten, bar none," Mum said with regret.

"And the apricots," I reminded her. My mouth was watering.

"And the raspberries and currants." Mum was walking faster and faster. "I've put up no preserves at all here, not a single quart. There is simply no decent fruit to be had in the shops. We've had to do without all winter. Do without. I think that's become England's new motto."

We turned into our Hero's Home. "Well, then," I ventured aloud the idea that had been with me for weeks, "why couldn't we go back to Creston? I think it's nicer there than here."

Mum looked at me sharply but she did not argue against what I'd said. After that, on our visits to Aunt Georgie's, I noticed the two women talking in urgent whispers, sometimes arguing. I suspected something was afoot.

Mum went in to London alone "on business". She came home with steamships tickets. We began packing straightaway. We would be ready to go as soon as David's school term was over.

We left England on a day as dull and wet as the day we arrived. We had been "home" for a year and a half and now we were going back to our real home, Creston. We were all very glad.

Chapter 10

The Black Sheep

Long after we got back to Creston, Mum continued to write letters to solicitors in England trying to get back her widow's money that Uncle Will had made off with. Whenever an answer came to one of her pleas, she'd call in Colonel Mallandaine – he'd been promoted to that rank during the war – to look the letter over and give her his advice. The answers were always the same: it was most unlikely she would ever recover the money. The Colonel agreed with the English solicitors. "I'm sorry, Mrs. Evans, but there it is. And even if, by some fluke, you won your case, you wouldn't get the money because the man would have spent it all by now. There's no use suing a man with empty pockets." The Colonel sipped his tea with a calm Mum must have found annoying.

"He could be made to pay in instalments," she argued. "If those solicitors had any sense of justice, they'd make him."

"Well, they can't find him, for starters. And their advice is it's not worth paying out money to try to locate him, given his record." Mallandaine pointed to the latest letter. "And you did give the man power of attorney."

"I didn't give him the power to rob me!" Mum snapped. She paced back and forth, letting her tea get cold. The Colonel sat back and winked at me as she raged. We both knew that Mum was continuing her argument strictly as a matter of principle; she knew the solicitors and the Colonel were right. Her letters were a waste of time and postage. She just kept on because she hated to give up what was hers by right and she did hate to lose an argument.

For myself I found it hard to believe that the handsome, charming man who'd driven us to Llanaelhaearn, who'd spoken so lovingly of his dear brother, my father, could have done such a wicked thing as rob us, and if he had taken the money, well, perhaps there was some reason we didn't know about that had driven him to it.

Many years later I heard the whole of poor Will's story from a cousin in Australia. According to him, Will had certainly taken the money and gambled it away. He was a blackguard through and through, a con artist you might call him. Even after hearing that condemnation, though, I kept a soft spot of sympathy for Will. He was a man of great charm and many talents, and his life might have been different had he not been afflicted with one unfortunate and embarrassing handicap. He was incontinent.

He'd been a bed-wetter since childhood. No beating from his dad could cure him, nor no medicine his mam bought when the peddler made his rounds in the little village of Llanaelhaearn.

By the time Will was eleven years old – this was in 1899, the year his mam died – he was still wetting himself like a baby, almost always at night and sometimes in the day as well. He wouldn't curb himself. He wouldn't learn sense. Perhaps in self-defence, perhaps because he really didn't care, he took on a defiant attitude to his problem. Who cared about a bit of spilled pee? He didn't.

After their mam's death, aunts and uncles descended upon the bereaved household to take the younger children away and give them new homes. It was the Reverend Uncle Thomas and Aunt Mair from London who chose young Will. Graceful and fine-featured with deep blue eyes and tawny gold hair, he enchanted them with his beauty and his angelic smile.

His dad, our Taid, might have warned the Reverend Thomases about Will's problem, only they'd made him cross the way they'd examined the children and discussed their features as though they were choosing a Christmas goose.

Anyway, the change might be just what Will needed. He'd enjoy the excitement of life in the big city. Living as a gentleman in a grand house and wearing fine clothes would maybe teach him the self-restraint he needed. If it didn't, then maybe the holy preacher could knock some sense into the boy and cure him of his filthy habit.

"If you behave well, you will have a good life and many opportunities," Taid advised his son.

"I'll behave," Will promised. Promises came easily to him.

"Be of use to your Uncle Thomas. Try to earn your keep in his house."

"How could I be of use to a preacher?"

"You must look about you to see what's to do. Run errands. Shine his boots for him. Read him sermons in the evenings.

"And, for God's sake, remember to pee last thing before you go to bed."

"Ah, that's not a problem for me now." Lies also came easily to Will.

He had no sense of shame.

The reverend uncle and aunt had no more success than Taid had had in teaching Will restraint. And, as he grew older, Will picked up new bad habits as well: drinking, gambling, betting on the horses. By the time he was seventeen, the parson and his wife had lost all patience with him and his sinful and disgusting ways, and they sent him home to Wales in disgrace.

In the meantime, Taid had married again and he and his new wife were raising a second family.

Will arrived back in Llanaelhaearn in a fine suit and shiny top hat.

"A gentleman you've become, is it?" Taid greeted him.

"I suppose I have, rather," Will answered in English. He'd forgotten his Welsh, he said. He looked about him as if he'd never seen the cottage of his childhood: the stiff parlour with its lace-curtained window; the steep stairway leading from the front door to the tiny bedrooms above; and the kitchen with its great, blackened fireplace.

He treated his young stepmother with elaborate courtesy. He rose when she entered the room, pulled back her chair for her when she sat down to her tea, offered his arm and carried her shopping basket when she went up street to the shop.

He delighted his little half-brothers by conjuring sweets out of their ears, like a real magician.

And he was not too proud to take his old Dad around to the pub for a drink and to sing the old songs with the men there. His Welsh came back to him better then.

But the little brothers, who shared his bed, were soon complaining to their mam about wet sheets. Will said, "It's themselves who are doing it, only they don't know, the poor loves."

And his stepmother found that though Will was a great one for opening doors and fetching her shawl for her, bowing as though she were the Queen of England, he couldn't seem to understand her at all when she asked him to dig up the potato bed or fetch water from the stand pipe for the washing.

She wrinkled her nose at the smell of his wool trousers. "It's the sea you are smelling, and the sheep," Will insisted, and with his pocketknife he snipped off a wild rose from the hedgerow by the gate and tucked it into her hair. "There's the scent of the flowers of the fields will surround you now this day." He smiled his winning smile and she had to smile back. It was hard to stay angry with Will.

In 1914 when the war came, Taid saw in it a great opportunity for his older sons to better themselves. "Enlist," he told them. "Try for the officers' training. There's gentlemen you could become."

Tommy joined up, and Wyatt. But not Will. "I'll not go and get myself killed for King and Country," he said "That's a mug's game."

Even when conscription came in 1916, Will wouldn't go. He got himself declared unfit for service. " 'It's my kidneys,' I said to the medical blokes," he reported to Taid. " 'I have no control.' Then I pissed all over the floor to prove it. They chucked me out soon enough."

"The army might have cured you, if you'd behaved better," Taid grumbled. "They'd know what to do with a problem like yours.

"And isn't it your duty to serve King and Empire? That's Tom's opinion."

"Oh, piss on duty. Piss on the Empire. Come on down the pub." Will had won on the horses while he was in town at the medical board.

Even if he didn't join the colours like his brothers, Will made a pretty good thing of the war. He got down to London often. There he knew how to find his way into clubs where card games went on 'til late late at night, where a clever fellow could win enough to drink champagne and dance with beautiful women and bet on fast horses and live in hotels where the servants would never dare to remark on the state of the sheets on the beds.

Sometimes he came back to Llanaelhaearn with money for drinks at the pub, sweets for the little ones, a trinket for his stepmother. Just as often he came home with his head in his feathers, as Taid would say, and his pockets empty.

Then Taid would urge him to find a proper job. "There is work at the quarry. I could speak for you to the manager."

"Swinging a sledgehammer, is it? Thanks, but I think not."

"And there are jobs down the pits in the south."

"I have not the strength for the coal mines," Will said.

"Your brother Llewellyn is earning good money at the coal," his stepmother reminded him.

"Llew was always the better man." Will had no false pride.

"Now, Dad, I'm expecting a money order in the post any day. I wonder if you could you see your way to letting me have a few pounds to tide me over?"

Taid lent him a pound, and Will was away.

He was soon back.

"When will I have back that pound I lent you?" Taid asked.

"Well, now," Will said, "didn't I meet a poor, shoeless beggar on the street, and seeing his great need, I gave him the pound. I knew you'd have wanted me to."

"Ah, hush with your storytelling. You gave the money to no beggar."

"All the same," Will grinned, "it went to a man in need. Don't worry. I'll pay you back. Soon."

And after a lucky card game with some soldiers on leave, he did. And then he was off to London again.

In 1918 the war was over. Wyatt was wounded and never the same man again, and poor Tom killed at the very end.

Will looked prosperous though, when he brought Tom's English widow and her daughter home to Wales.

"Will's been kind enough to see about dear Tom's money for me," the widow told Taid. She sat on a stiff chair in the parlour and gestured towards a stack of official-looking papers on the table. "The insurance and the officer's bonus. It's all so very confusing."

"You've been handling her money, Will?" Taid blanched as he turned to his profligate son who stood by the feeble coal fire, twirling a new silver-handled walking stick.

"Yes. Investing it for her, don't you know?" Will said,

Taid turned away. He knew how this would end.

When the widow discovered that it was horse races Will had been investing in, she fell into a fury. "Thief!" she shrieked. "Blackguard! I'll have the law on you for this. Don't think I won't." Her shouts could be heard all up and down the village street. Grandmother Jane hovered over the visitor, offering a cup of tea to try to soothe her. Jane spoke no English and had no idea what had made the English lady so angry, though anyone would know Will had something to do with it.

Will thought it best to slip away that night.

Australia was the place to go. He had family there: his two sisters, Megan and Ruth, had emigrated there. Yes, Australia would be the best bet.

Pity about the money. He wouldn't have put so much on Heart's Folly except he'd had a sure tip on her. Just bad luck all round. The winnings would have been a great thing for Tom's widow and her little family. She was a pretty woman, with lots of spirit to her. He liked her. If he made his fortune in Australia, he'd pay her back, every penny, she could count on that.

Will signed on as a waiter on the *Sophocles*, bound for Sidney. The first day out of port he talked the steward into letting him give tango lessons in the first class salon. He danced with professional grace, and he knew how to charm the rich war widows who were travelling to new and warmer climes to restore their shattered spirits. He danced those lonely, grieving widows across the wide, wide southern ocean, guiding them with seductive steps, exciting them with melodious, whispered flatteries, daring them to let go of their sorrows in the breaking bubbles of bitter-sweet champagne.

He very nearly caught himself one of those widows for a wife through his lessons. He might have done it, too, if his old problem hadn't caught him out once he'd inveigled himself into her bed.

Truth was, he was not entirely disappointed. He was not the marrying type.

In Sydney, he jumped ship.

He was ready to seek his fortune in the new world.

Considering the size of the country, the first thing he'd need was a car. He paid ten pounds cash, and signed a paper agreeing to pay eight pounds per month for many, many months to come. But he needn't worry about that.

The salesman shook his hand to close the deal. "Were you by any chance at Gallipoli?" he asked.

"No, I'm afraid I never got past France."

"I hear it was no picnic there either."

"It was not." Will looked solemn.

"That's the DSO I see you have," the salesman nodded at the row of Tom's medals on Will's jacket.

"Oh yes. Ran into a spot of bother at Cambrai, and some Colonel or other mentioned me in a dispatch." Tom had probably been at Cambrai, Will thought. Or some place near it.

"We owe a lot to you fellows. Don't think we don't appreciate it, those of us who didn't get a chance to serve," the salesman told him.

"Only doing our duty. A man can't do more. Or less." Will let his hand be shaken again. He liked being a war hero.

He liked his new car too.

He drove along to a pub and stopped for a celebratory drink. There he got into a card game and won ten quid. Not bad for his first day in the land of opportunity.

When he was ready to apply for a job, he wrote himself a nice letter of recommendation on a page of War Office stationery he'd pilfered when he'd gone to sign for Tom's insurance. The letter and the medals worked on the first try. He was hired to work in an insurance office, a stuffy old place, as he soon discovered. He wrote dull letters and filled in forms. There was no excitement in it. He couldn't stick it. He left at the end of the month. No hard feelings.

He dropped round to the place where he'd bought the car and made his first payment in cash. A person had to establish an honourable reputation before he could get away with much.

Now that his money was gone, he thought about visiting his sisters.

Will drove up to Megan's place in Cooma in his swell car.

"Do I have the pleasure of addressing Miss Megan Evans?" he asked the woman who answered his knock at the door.

"Miss Megan Evans that was; Mrs. Harry Prentice now," the woman said.

"Ah Megan, my dear, do you not recognize your own brother, Will?"

She did then, though she swore she could have walked past him on the street and never have known. You could knock her over with a feather.

"I knew you right away," he said. "You don't look a day older than when I last saw you."

"I was twelve then, Will. And you did not recognize me." Megan had always been a sour one.

"Well now that I've come all this way, are you going to invite me in for a cup of tea?" he had to ask.

He came in and met Harry. They drank beer and Will told his stories of the widows and the tango lessons. He whirled Megan around the kitchen to demonstrate and told her she could dance rings around any of the first class ladies in their golden slippers.

"Hark at your foolishness!" Megan scolded, but she laughed and blushed and half believed his flattery.

Will talked about his job in insurance, and how he was looking for something better now. Harry was a teacher, and Will wondered if there might be anything for him in that line. He could teach dancing, history, English, singing, card tricks. Whatever was required.

There happened to be a vacancy in the junior school staff.

"But Will, you're never qualified to be a teacher," Megan said.

"Sure I am." He showed her Tom's M.A. diploma. Nobody would ever look at the exact name in all that Latin, and it wasn't doing old Tom any good now, was it?

He got the job. But it didn't last. He was a grand teacher. The children loved him. It was only that there was some trouble with the secretary, and questions about a cash box. He left in a hurry.

Megan gave him Ruth's address in Sydney. They were a matching pair, Will and Ruth, she told Harry. "Lord knows what they'll get up to, the two of them together. And it's she can wash his smelly sheets!"

Ruth and her dull little husband were no use to Will. Fred had some menial job at the hospital, washing floors, or bedpans. He offered to put in a word for Will, but Will thanked him and said no. Catch him scrubbing floors for a living! Not bloody likely!

Ruth was out most days. She said she was looking for work, but Will knew a person didn't get that happy glow on a job search. He'd bet his last penny Ruth was getting something on the side, and enjoying it too.

Well, and more power to her. Will wasn't the man to blow the whistle on someone having a bit of fun.

He took her to the horse races one Saturday afternoon. She told him some tall tale about how she'd learned fortune-telling from the gypsies, and he let her choose the horse to bet on. Damned if the nag didn't win.

He bought her a pint and let her pick for the next race. Another winner.

Maybe there was something in this gypsy claptrap.

"Who'll it be in the third?" he asked.

"Sweet William."

How could Will lose on a horse of that name?

Sweet William lost.

"Damn you! We've lost the wad." Will and Ruth stood by the rail and Will searched through his empty pockets, hoping he might find a forgotten pound note.

Ruth was not going to stand quietly and be shouted at. "Damn you! I didn't say put it ALL on Sweet William. And he would have won if the stupid jockey hadn't run him into the fence."

"You don't know what you're talking about, you daft gypsy." There was not a penny in any of his pockets.

Ruth searched through her handbag and found a shilling. "I know I'd have saved enough cash to buy us another drink."

They drank one last beer at the refreshment stand and quarrelled and laughed all the way home.

Fred cooked beans and toast for their supper and Will found enough change in the pockets of his other trousers to buy more beer.

Through the meal he and Ruth talked about what they would have done with the money if Sweet William had won.

"I'd have bought ten new dresses," Ruth said.

"I'd have bought a decent pair of shoes and spent the rest on drink," Will said.

"Not you. You'd have bet the lot on the next race and lost it."

That set them laughing again. They laughed 'til Will wet himself, and then Fred laughed too. Will left the next morning.

He went to Tenterfield where he got a job selling farm machinery, but the farmers were maddeningly slow to make up their minds whether or not to buy, and when they did buy, they drove a hard bargain. The police caught up to him then about the car and took it away. Piss on it; the clutch was shot anyway.

Without a car he couldn't be a salesman and that was a good thing too. He was getting sick and tired of the job.

He called on Megan again, but she said he'd never get anything in Cooma now, not after the business at the school.

Well, piss on the working life. He could make his money gambling. The Aussies, bless them, would bet on anything.

Sometimes Will won; more often he lost. Occasionally, he worked. He ran a taxi service for a bit. He fell in with a fellow who was studying aboriginal music and they got a programme going on Australian radio. The programme lasted a few months. Will liked the Abos; they didn't take work so bloody seriously either. He liked the Aussies too. Anzac Day he'd put on old Tommy's medals and walk into a pub and everyone would shake his hand and buy him drinks 'til he passed out.

He liked the country with its wide spaces and its hot sun and its friendly people. It was a good life he was having. Better than he'd ever have had in old Llanaelhaearn, with its one narrow street of grey houses and Taid telling him to get a job of work and his stepmother complaining about the smell of him.

·From time to time over the years that followed, Will visited his sisters. Sometimes he arrived with nothing but a swag bag on his back. Then he'd try to touch them for the price of a new suit or a stake to get himself started again.

Other times he'd drive up in a fancy car and peel bills out of a fat wallet, buying everyone drinks.

They never knew when he'd show up or what state he'd be in.

Then, in 1956, Megan saw an article in the newspaper: the body of a man by the name of William Evans, a gold prospector, had been found bludgeoned to death in the shack on his claim near Bloomfield, on the Cape York Peninsula. Theft was the motive suspected. On the evening preceding the slaying, the victim, a man known to the police, had been seen and heard in the Southern Star Tavern boasting about having struck pay dirt.

Megan sent copies of the article to Ruth and home to Wales, but none of the Evans family went to claim the body. They didn't dare.

This was just as well because, about ten years later, didn't Will show up again like the proverbial bad penny?

Hippies discovered him. When they moved into the remote Cedar Bay area, seeking an alternate lifestyle, they found an old fellow called Will Evans already living there in a driftwood shack. Will, they soon learned, could tell them a thing or two about dropping out, hanging loose, finding inner peace, and letting the answers blow in the wind. That's what he'd been doing all his life.

The hippies loved Cedar Bay Bill, as they called him. They made him their guru. When he died in 1972, they gave him a real groovy funeral with flowers and incense and prayers for his soul wafting up in smoke.

To this day people still bring flowers to his grave. Not the Evans family though. They said you'd never know what Will might be trying to pull off this time.

But when I eventually heard the end of Will's story, I promised myself that if I ever got to Australia – though it seemed most unlikely that I ever would – I'd visit that grave and lay a wreath of white lilies on it, for forgiveness. Will was indeed a rogue, but he was not a vicious or mean-spirited man. And, after all, we'd managed without the money that he took.

Chapter 11

$\mathcal{C}$oming Home

Although Charles was living with Aunt Boo and Uncle Clary and cousin Percy, he didn't go to the same school as Percy. This was because Percy's school, as Uncle Clary explained, cost a lot of money. Charles didn't mind a bit. Fancy paying out money to go to a school where you had to wear a pink jacket and knee pants and a stupid little beanie hat! Charles thought that was about the limit. The lads back home wouldn't be seen dead in duds like that.

The state school was not bad, as schools went, although even there, it turned out you had to wear a tie. Charles made some friends, fellows who knew a lot more about fun than cousin Percy. He learned how to play the English games: cricket and football and rounders. The music master told him he had a very good voice and that he should join the church choir. This pleased his aunt who began to talk of Charles' going into holy orders, which made Percy snigger, and Charles too, this time. At choir, he made more friends. He kept busy.

He kept away from his aunt and uncle as much as he could. He thought that would please them best. He had heard Aunt Boo complaining to Clary about her nerves, stretched to the edge with that great boy to take care of.

In this family, he couldn't seem to get it right. If he cleaned his plate at mealtimes, Uncle Clary complained about being eaten out of house and home. If he left something on the plate, Uncle Clary was likely to say something about picky eaters. If he invited Percy to play snakes and ladders or catch or tag or even cricket, Percy complained that he cheated or was too rough or didn't know how to play properly. "And you needn't expect me to coach you, because I won't." If he stayed in his room, Aunt Boo accused him of skulking and not being any company for Percy. It was not easy to be an orphan and to know you were not behaving right in the house you were told was home.

The best thing was to keep busy at school and in the choir and stay out of the way as much as possible.

Despite Aunt Sarah's assurance that he'd get used to England, Charles didn't. Aunt Boo took him to the Tower of London but it was dark and grey and all about history. The changing of the guards was better, but you didn't go to the changing of the guards every day. Mostly you just went back and forth past the same rows of yellow brick houses with their tiny little squares of green grass in front of them.

Every day was the same. The menfolk went out after breakfast and Aunt Boo stayed home and did whatever she did. They had tea at exactly five and went to bed at exactly the same time every night. Aunt Boo and Uncle Clary never went out, never had friends in. Everybody kept themselves separate.

Charles missed his family and the ranch. It was always busy there, people coming and going, work to be done, different things going on every day. In the summer the kids worked alongside their parents in the orchard and afterwards they'd run down for a swim at the creek, all of them together. Saturday afternoons they'd get up a game of base-ball and maybe have ice cream at the drug store for a treat. In the win-ter the small frame house was crowded and snug. After supper they'd play cards or have a singsong, or friends would come calling. Often the friends would stay all night and the kids would get to stay up as late as they wanted and then sleep on the floor. Sometimes his parents went out dancing and the kids would stay at Gran's, and Uncle Bob would recite long, long poems for them, or Gran and Gramps Little would tell stories. Charles missed his family so much he sometimes woke up at night crying for them.

He missed Creston too. He missed the wide river flats, and the woods above the town and the pools along Dead Horse Creek and the baseball diamond by the school. He missed the cold, clear winter days, and the heavy haze of hot summer days.

But he was doing all right. For an orphan, he was doing all right.

He wrote to Gran once a week.

"Dear folks:

How are you?

I am learning how to play cricket.

We went to Kew Gardens and looked at flowers."

It was hard to be an orphan in a strange country. He kept forgetting to do things the way Aunt Boo and Uncle Clary liked. He was supposed to polish his shoes every day, every single day! He was supposed to wear a tie to eat in the dining room. He couldn't see the sense in that. He was not supposed to get dirty, never to get in fights with other boys, not to say "Skookum" or "jake" or "zowie".

Maybe it was hard for them to get used to having him around, too. He could see that they were trying to be nice, or at least Aunt Boo was. She took him and Percy to that Tower place and to watch the guards and to the greenhouses. She came to his school concert and said he'd done his part well. When he did a solo at church, she told him he sang beautifully and asked was he still thinking about going in for holy orders. Uncle Clary didn't have much to do with him, but he left pocket money for him every Monday morning on the breakfast table, same as he did for Percy. Percy was never nice, but then Percy was a drip; he'd known that right from the start.

Charles remembered what Aunt Sarah had told him about being grateful for being given a home, so he tried his best, but he never really felt that this was his home.

Things didn't get better. Through the winter he caught colds and bronchial coughs in the damp, sooty air that smelled of coal fires. He wondered if he would die too, like his Mum and Dad. His aunt complained of the germs he was picking up from the common children at the school and made him wash his hands far too often.

The last straw came when Percy stole his pocket money. For two weeks there was no sixpence at Charles' place. He didn't like to ask about it; perhaps Uncle Clary was running short of the ready. His father often had. Not that Charles or any of the other kids had ever had pocket money at home. Pocket money was one of the advantages Aunt Sarah said he'd have in his new home.

The third Monday he entered the dining room just in time to see Percy pick up and pocket the sixpence at his place. This was too much. "You dirty sneak!" He lunged at Percy, intent on recovering what was his by rights.

Percy wouldn't fight, but crammed his fist into the pocket into which he'd slipped the coin and lay on the floor and howled. Charles tried to drag him to his feet.

Aunt Boo entered the room. "Charles!"

Charles let go of Percy who ran to his mother. "What has he done to you, darling?" she asked.

"Hit me and tried to take my pocket money, but I wouldn't let him," Percy cried.

"That's not true," Charles started to explain.

"Please leave the room at once," Aunt Boo said.

Charles left.

Percy was not hurt, Boo ascertained. She managed to soothe him and send him off to school in time.

Then she sat in her well-ordered drawing room and wept. Her worst fears had been realized. It had come to fighting in her once peaceful home, fisticuffs even. And theft. Boo couldn't bear the way Charles had looked at her when she sent him out of the room. His eyes, Charlotte's eyes, had accused her, even though it was he who was the thief and the brawler.

She'd known all along that there would be trouble. Her peace of mind was shattered; Percy was threatened; and Clary had never taken to the boy at all. His coming had ruined their happy home.

For Charlotte's sake she had tried to love the boy, but she couldn't. He was not at all like her Percy. Whenever he looked at her, she fancied she saw her dead sister looking through his eyes, accusing her of not really wanting him, of not being kind enough to him. In Charles' look she could see that he was not happy here either, and that increased her guilt. They'd been a comfortable family – she and Clary and Percy – 'til Charles had been foisted upon them and spoiled everything. The arrangement wasn't working for anyone, not for her or Clary or Percy, and not for Charles either. He simply didn't fit in.

"Send the boy back to Canada. That's my advice," Clary said when Boo reported the incident to him that evening after Percy had gone to bed. "Young Charles is too much for us. We've given the boy a fair trial, and look where it's got us. Your nerves are shattered. The only solution is to send him back to the place whence he came. He'll be better off there, happier. It's what he's used to and where he belongs. That's my advice."

Clary had his faults, but he was a sensible person. Boo thought over his suggestion. He was probably right. If she'd followed his advice before Sarah arrived with the boy, this would never have happened. She had half a mind to write to Ma and tell her she must take Charles back, for his own good, as well as theirs. The climate here obviously did not agree with him. He'd had some shocking colds this winter. His school work was not up to standard, his teacher had told her. He was not getting along well with Percy, and it was evident that he was still missing his own brothers and sisters. Boo's mind was busy gathering arguments for sending the boy back to Canada.

If only the decision could be made, it would be easy to make the arrangements. Dear Clary helped her; he took care of everything.

"He's to leave on August 11th," he said, "on the *Empress of Scotland*. There's a special third class rate going for boys and men, as they're in need of harvesters to work on the prairies."

"Will he be all right, mixed in with farm labourers?" Boo worried.

"The lad knows how to look after himself," Clary assured her. "I'll see him on to the boat train, and he'll be fine from there on."

The surprise was that Charles didn't seem to mind at all when he heard he was to leave almost immediately. He actually grinned from ear to ear at the news he was to go back to Canada "I'll get my things packed then," was all he said, and bounced away.

"He doesn't realize what's happening. It'll hit him at the station," Clary predicted. "You'd best not come. It'd be too hard on your nerves."

"I've never cared for stations anyway," Boo agreed. "So noisy. I don't want Percy going either. I think he may be coming down with something. He's feeling his cousin's departure."

Following Clary's advice, Boo made a label of strong pasteboard and tied it around Charles' neck on a string. "Charles D. Talbot," it said. "En route Southampton, England, to Creston, B.C. Canada. In event of emergency, please contact Mrs. M. Young, Creston, B.C."

"You look like a parcel," Percy said when Charles stood ready to go.

Charles realized that a parcel was exactly what he felt like. Aunt Boo and Uncle Clary were going to ship him off to Canada like the parcel of old magazines and outgrown clothes that they didn't want any more that Aunt Boo had packed up at Christmas time for the others back in Creston.

Well, he didn't care. However he was going, he was glad to be going. Lord, if he'd known attacking Percy would have this effect, he would have punched him all around the house months ago.

He was so pleased to be saying good-bye to the little drip that he shook his hand and said, "Goodbye, old chap!" That was one of those silly expressions the English boys liked to use.

He walked through the tiny green garden and out through the dinky little iron gate for the last time, careful to latch it behind him as Aunt Boo liked. She and Percy waved from the front door and Charles waved back.

At the station, Uncle Clary looked in at each third class carriage of the boat train until he found a decent-looking family. He addressed the father: "I'd be obliged if you'd keep an eye on this young man for the journey."

"Right you are, govn'r." The man tipped his cap and Clary handed him a pound note which the man stared at in some surprise 'til his wife signalled him to put it in his pocket and help the boy stow his case on the luggage rack. Then the three children shifted over on the bench so that there was a place for Charles to squeeze in.

First he turned to Uncle Clary. "Good bye, sir," he said without a tremor in his voice. A brave little lad, in the end. The stay in England had been good for him. Clary tipped him half a crown, shook his hand, and stepped out on to the platform. A guard slammed the door. Charles was on his way.

The family who were to keep an eye on him were called the Carvers and they were going to Toronto. One of the children, Stephen, was the same age as Charles and the two of them were soon on the way to becoming fast friends. The Carvers had accents that Aunt Boo would call common and Percy would make fun of, but they were jolly people and easy to talk to, as excited as Charles was to be on their way to Canada. When they learned they had fallen in with a real Canadian before they'd even got on the boat, they were delighted. They peppered him with questions about Toronto, refusing to believe he wouldn't know, being a Canadian himself.

"Creston is quite a distance from Toronto actually," Charles explained.

"Still it's in the same country, inn't?"

Charles named all the provinces and their capitals, surprised that he remembered them from Grade Four, when he'd left. He explained Canadian money to them and laughed when they found it more difficult than their own complicated shillings and pence system that he'd had such a hard time with at first.

At tea time Mrs. Carver opened a bag and unpacked thick bacon sandwiches and handed him one just as if he was a member of the family. Charles realized he felt more at home in a couple of hours with the Carvers than he'd ever felt at Aunt Boo and Uncle Clary's.

The train made a stop and the children clamoured to be allowed to get off and run on the platform and the parents reluctantly agreed. "But none of yez goes out of my sight or I'll crown yez all," Mrs. Carver threatened. She included Charles in her admonishing stare.

The children hopped up and down on the platform and then the whistle blew and Mrs. Carver shouted and stormed until everyone was packed in again and she said her nerves was played out, but she must have had a different kind of nerves from Aunt Boo's because her attack included fits of laughing.

When they reached Southhampton, there was great excitement getting off the train and on to the boat and poor Mrs. Carver began to cry and everyone patted her on the back and said, "There now, lovie, it's all for the best," so Charles did too. Then the band began to play and a tremendous whistle sounded somewhere above them and scared them out of their wits, but only for a minute, and Charles flung his cap high in the air and shouted, "Hurrah for Canada! Hip hip hooray!" And the Carvers, and all kinds of other families gathered along the rail, joined in on the "hoorays!"

Gran sat in Creston, sewing yellow straw ricking on to a buckram hat form and worrying about Charles. What could Boo have been thinking of to send an eleven-year-old child to cross an ocean and then a continent alone? He'd be kidnapped, Gran fretted. Such people as there are in the world today! He would be robbed, taken advantage of in ways she couldn't bear to think of.

Boo had never been noted for her good sense, but this latest fool-ishness of hers verged on the criminal, in Gran's opinion. It was no doubt Clary who had put her up to it. If only she had realized what their plans were! "Impossible keep Charles," Boo's telegram had said. "Sending him Creston. Dates follow."

And they sent him off on the first boat available. She thought they'd at least wait until someone from the family was travelling. Or that they would entrust him to the care of an emigrating friend. Someone would be sure to be going sooner or later. If only they'd waited. She would have found the money and gone herself to fetch the boy, if she'd known what they were planning, Gran thought.

If anything happens to that boy, I shall never forgive Boo. Never, Gran vowed to herself, even if she is my own daughter.

She picked up the hat again. While she set tiny stitches into the buckram form, she imagined her grandson boarding that huge ocean liner, all by himself. If he'd managed to reach Southhampton safely, that is. What if he lost his ticket? What if he got on the wrong boat? Set off for India, or China? And if he did reach the boat safely, would he find his way around? Those ocean liners were huge. Would he find the dining saloon? Would he get anything to eat? She imagined him sitting on the third class deck, staring out an empty sea, alone and afraid.

On the *Empress of Scotland*, Charles was having the time of his life. The third class kids played tag and hopscotch and rounders and other games they made up as they played.

He sat with the Carvers in the dining room and they all ate their way happily through the huge meals. Corned beef hash for breakfast and porridge and all the bread and jam you could eat. Fish *and* meat for dinner. A meat tea as well. And a supper of bread and cheese if you could stay awake long enough to eat it.

He shared a cabin with three taciturn farm lads from Somerset, going to the Prairies to work at the harvest. But Charles spent very little time in his cabin and with his roommates. He and Stephen and the Carvers were together all day, eating and playing and talking about Canada. He hadn't had such a good time since before his parents had died.

At last the *Empress* docked in Quebec and they had to part – the Carvers to take the CN line to Toronto, and Charles to board a CPR train bound for Winnipeg, Calgary, Fort McLeod and Creston. The Carvers saw him on to his train and passed on the pound note Uncle Clary had given them to the Somerset boys who would be travelling on the same train as Charles, along with many instructions to see that the lad came to no harm. "And you write to us, the minute you get to your Gran's, you hear?" Mrs. Carver ordered Charles. "You've got that address in your case and don't you lose it!"

"I will," Charles promised. "You write to me too."

The five days on the train were ten times as long as the six days on the boat. There were no other children in the long third class carriage, only babies that howled and stank.

The seats were hard and pulled down into berths that were harder. He and the farm boys were too shy to eat in the dining car. They changed Uncle Clary's pound to Canadian money and bought bread and tinned beans that they cooked on the little stove at the end of the car. They bought cups of tea at the stations. They were afraid of spending too much of their small supply of money too fast. Charles was hungry all the time, and tired, and so were the Somerset boys and many others on the train. They were all orphans here.

At Regina the Somerset boys got off and handed over to Charles the rest of Uncle Clary's money. There was just enough to buy a package of chewing gum and an American comic. Charles was tired but didn't dare to fall asleep, in case he'd miss Fort McLeod, where he had to change for the Crow's Nest Pass Line.

A kindly farmer's wife going to visit her sister took the seat beside him and when she opened her lunch bag, she handed him a tomato sandwich. The thick slices of bread were soggy with the juice from the huge slab of the tomato. Charles realized he hadn't had a tomato like that all the time in England. 'Tom-ah-toes' they called those hard little red fruits they ate there. He devoured the sandwich hungrily.

Seeing his appetite, the woman gave him a handful of sugar cookies too.

She was nice, but a bit of a fusser. "All the way from England you've come! My! My! Aren't your folks worried about you all alone?

"An orphan – ah now that is too bad."

Soon everyone in the coach knew his plight and fed him sandwiches and cookies and candy bars 'til he was well and truly stuffed.

At Fort McLeod they handed him into the care of the station master, who passed him on to the charge of the conductor on the Crow's Nest train. He didn't have to worry about a thing.

Soon after he got on the Crow's Nest train, he could see the mountains with clouds hanging over their peaks. Ah yes. This was the way a country was supposed to look. He hadn't realized how much he'd missed the mountains 'til he saw them now and remembered the way they turned purple as the darkness came down fast on autumn nights; and how they sparkled after a winter's snow; he remembered them pale blue against the pink sky of an early spring morning when he set out for fishing down on the flats.

Yes, and he'd be able to go fishing again, and swimming in the cold clear water of the creek. He could play baseball and pick sweet plums and apples warm off the trees, and slide down the Fourth Street hill in winter and build snow forts. How good it was to be going home.

He'd get to play with his brothers again, and kids from school. He'd even be glad to see his bossy old sister Noonie again. His mother and his father would not be there, not ever again. But Gran would be.

A sudden fear clutched him. Would he feel the same sense of not being welcome at Gran's as he'd felt at Aunt Boo's?

He thought about the Carvers and how they'd made him forget he was an orphan when he was with them. They made room for him

at the table, in their games, in their family conclaves. Aunt Boo and
Uncle Clary and Percy weren't like that; their little circle was so tight,
he reckoned, there was no room for anyone else to fit in, no matter
how good he'd been. Even Little Lord Fauntleroy probably couldn't
have got it right with them. They were like a secret club, all tied up
in the rules and schedules and likes and dislikes they'd made up for
themselves, the only three members.

What would it be like at Gran's, he wondered. He remembered
how it was when he'd stayed there in the past. Gran was always busy,
sewing her hats, pottering around the garden, cooking, baking. She
had no time to fuss. People came and went, staying to visit for an
hour or a day or a week or months: Uncle Bob, Gramps Little, Aunt
Sarah, Olwen and David, he and his parents and brothers and sisters.
Gran just set another place at the table, found another straw tick or
a feather mattress to roll out on the floor at night. Gran was like the
Carvers. She would make room for him. He'd be all right at Gran's.
Surely he'd be all right at Gran's.

Fernie. Cranbrook. Yahk. His excitement grew. Here was a mountain
that looked familiar. Could it be Goat? Yes. Yes. That was surely its
peak. And here was the siding for the mine. Then the trainman came
along the aisle shouting, "Creston! Creston is the next station stop.
Creston next." He took the ticket out of the window blind above
Charles' seat and handed down his case.

They crossed Goat River Canyon and Charles thought he could
hear the river roaring down below. Even in the train he could smell
the raw, hot scent of the forest. Then he could see ordered rows of
orchard trees, and then there were the Flats, and then the first houses,
and the squat white steeple of the church.

The whistle sounded. Charles stood on the open platform
between cars, straining to see around the trainman who blocked the
door. They were slowing down. There. The hotel. The Mercantile.

Now, now there it is. The station! And on the platform a little old lady under a huge hat. Gran!

The train puffed to a standstill, sending out clouds of white steam. The trainman set the nobbled brown stool on the platform, and reached up to give Charles a hand, but the boy was already running along the platform towards outstretched arms. "Gran! Gran!" he was shouting, "I'm home!"

Chapter 12

$\mathcal{S}$aving the Grand Piano

The first my brother Dave and I knew Mum intended to marry Mr. Hooper, the train conductor, was the morning she took us to Christ Church, sat us down in a front pew beside Gran, and handed us a prayer book open at the page headed "Sacrament of Holy Matrimony."

This was back in 1922 when kids were seen and not heard and their opinions never asked for. Anyway, even if we had been consulted, we would most probably have said, "Fine. Go ahead." Mr. Hooper was okay. He was very good-looking, blond, quite a lot like the movie star Douglas Fairbanks. He'd taken Dave and me fishing a couple of times at Kootenay Lake and swimming. We couldn't remember our own father so we weren't able to make unkind comparisons and had no old loyalties to fight. Mum seemed to like him a lot. "Good idea," we'd probably have said if we'd been asked.

None of the Hooper family attended the wedding. This upset Gran. "It's not as though it's an arduous journey from Cranbrook to Creston," she grumbled to Mum while we three "ladies" were "freshening up" in the Creston Hotel washroom before the wedding lunch.

"Rodney says his people don't like travelling," Mum explained. "And there's no afternoon train; they'd have to stay overnight and they don't like doing that."

"I'd say they can't think much of the match if they won't travel a hundred miles to see it solemnized," Gran maintained.

"Oh, no; they're ever so pleased. They've given us over their house for a wedding present. It's a beautiful cottage with four bedrooms, modern kitchen, indoor bathroom, electric light, and right in town, close to the shops. Fancy! A house! So very kind of them."

At the lunch in the dining room, Colonel Mallandaine gave a speech and Mr. Hooper saw that Dave and I got the biggest pieces of the strawberry shortcake. "Call me Rodney," he said. There was no question of our having to call him "father".

The cake was delicious. Rodney was all right.

Mum and Mr. Hooper had a three day honeymoon and then we moved out of Creston to our new home in Cranbrook. Mr. and Mrs. Hooper senior and Rodney's sister and brother-in-law stood on the front porch, waiting to meet us.

Clinging to Rodney's arm, Mum walked towards her new in-laws, a beautiful bride, smiling, ready to like and be liked. She was well turned out, as always, in a new navy blue suit and a hat with one magnificent drooping feather flashing emerald and wine red.

Behind the bridal couple followed the rest of us: myself, a shy, slouching fourteen-year old; David, eleven, with a bouncy step and mischievous eyes alight with interest in these new people and sur-roundings. Gran had advised leaving Margie with her at least tem-porarily, to which Mum had agreed. Two older children would be enough for Rodney to cope with for a start. We did however have our dog Peppie, successor to the beloved Bobby. He barked and bounded about us as we approached our new home, glad to be out of the train. A wagon load of goods, including a cat yowling in a wicker basket, lumbered up the street behind us. This caravan was probably not what the Hoopers would have imagined when they pictured their Rodney bringing home a bride.

Still, they applauded with a show of enthusiastic good will when Rodney picked Mum up and carried her across the threshold of our new house. Dave and I looked away in embarrassment. It was quite mortifying to be attached to a couple so sloppily in love.

Our Peppie became the first target of Hooper disapproval. He left his "calling cards" in the garden, Rodney's sister complained.

"Calling cards!" Mum rolled her eyes, and Dave and I giggled.

Next came the *contretemps* of the curtains. Rodney's mother was aghast when Mum took down the lace curtains in the front room and replaced them with flowered chintz. "They make the house look like a booth at the fair," she said. "What will the neighbors think?"

"It wouldn't be any of their business, would it?" Mum answered pertly. "So why should we worry? I'm fond of the flowered look myself."

"What do you think, Rodney?" Mrs. Hooper appealed to her son, and he – the traitor – said he didn't like those flowery things either.

Mum's face took on a stubborn cast, and the chintz curtains remained in the sitting room, waving defiance at the senior Hoopers, who were well placed to observe all changes taking place in their old home, as they had moved only as far as next door. Rodney's sister lived in the house directly opposite. It was a Hooper family compound. And the Hoopers found many things to complain about in it.

The cat scratched the wallpaper. My posture was terrible; I should be made to wear a brace and take ballet lessons. Mum should put less starch and more blueing in the water when she washed Rodney's shirts. Dave and his friends should not be allowed to play baseball on the lawn. It was only a matter of time 'til they would break every window.

And there was the care of the Chickering grand piano. The Hoopers had been good enough to leave their most prized possession in the big house for the use of Rodney and his new family. It was a wonderful piano. The tone was exquisite. Percy Grainger had played on it once, which made it almost a sacred object.

Now Mrs. Hooper worried that it wasn't being treated properly. She thought she might have heard David banging on the keys one day. Children should not be allowed to touch the piano, much less bang on it, she told Mum. And when she dusted it, Mum should be sure to use lemon oil – not too much – and a clean flannel cloth dipped in milk for the keys. Mrs. Hooper gave a demonstration as she instructed. During the performance, Mum wiped picture frames at the other side of the room and cast only an occasional glance towards the lesson.

Mrs. Hooper left, after bestowing on Mum a bottle of the best brand of lemon oil and a handful of clean flannel cloths. Immediately Mum turned on Rodney, who had been reading the paper throughout the demonstration. "Why didn't you stand up for me?"

"Well, you know," Rodney drawled, "I guess Mama has a good system figured out. She's sure kept that piano looking like new all these years."

"And you think I can't?" Mum demanded. "I too have owned pianos," she sniffed.

"She's only trying to be helpful," Rodney said. "There's no need to get upset."

Rodney's family were all musical. His father had been an organist and choir master until he went deaf as Beethoven, and had to give up his profession. Rodney's mother and sister were talented pianists and singers. So was Rodney. His tenor, everyone said, was every bit as good as John McCormack's. All the Hoopers loved to perform, so on many evenings we had musical gatherings around the Chickering grand.

Occasionally Mum was accorded the honour of playing the accompaniment for one of the singers. She was a good pianist, though not as good as the Hoopers. One evening she began the intro for

"Danny Boy", one of Rodney's favorite solos. She rolled the opening notes.

"Oh you never get that right!" Rodney's sister suddenly exploded. "It's la la la Lah, not la Lah la Lah. Here, let me show you." She plopped down on the bench and pushed Mum aside.

Mum said nothing. She came and sat beside me and Dave on the sofa. She had a dangerous set to her mouth and a steely glitter in her eye.

We listened to Rodney sing "Danny Boy" to his sister's accompaniment. Then they did "The Rose of Tralee".

"'The Ash Grove,'" old Mr. Hooper called out then, no doubt meaning to be kind. "The Ash Grove" was one of Mum's favourites.

Rodney's sister rose to surrender the bench.

This was Mum's moment. "My playing has not been found satisfactory," she declared. "I will not offend you with it again."

No amount of persuasion would move her. She declared she would not play the piano that evening, or ever again.

Later, after the in-laws left, Mum fought it out with Rodney. "She pushed me off the bench like an unwanted cushion, and you let her. You didn't say a word in my defence. You let them insult me and order me around. You never stick up for me."

"I don't know why you're making such a fuss," Rodney said. "Belle was only trying to help. You did have the dynamics wrong." He ran a hand through his beautiful wavy hair. "I tell you, all this bellyaching gives me the pip. It's bad for my nerves."

"Playing the piano in this house is bad for *my* nerves," Mum said.

As the weeks went by, Mum's annoyance increased. She was used to running her own household. She valued independence. She did not take kindly to advice and what she called interference. "I can't make a move in this house without those women noticing and commenting," she complained.

The Hoopers inspected the laundry Mum hung on the line; they saw when the lights went off at night and when they came on in the morning; they watched Mum go downtown to shop and came over when she got back to see what she'd bought and to ask how much she had paid for it. If she went out alone when Rodney was at home, they rushed over to see if he was all right. If Mum and Rodney went out together, the Hooper women had to know where to, and get a full report afterwards.

They knew Mum was pregnant almost before she herself did and rushed over two and three times a day after that with concoctions or advice for the expecting woman and for the coming baby.

Mum hated having such a fuss made. She felt fine and didn't want to be treated like an invalid. "I have borne and raised two children already," she reminded them as they darted about with cushions and footstools and shawls for her. "Neither of my children suffered from colic," she said when they offered recipes for gripe water. "I doubt any kind of remedy will be needed." She accepted more hand-knit bootees and bonnets and matinee jackets than one baby could possibly use. She packed them away in a dresser drawer. "Shall we give these to the church sale?" she asked me with a wink. "Or save them for your babies to wear some day?"

"Can't you get them to leave me alone?" she asked Rodney after they'd brought her some foul-tasting tonic from the drugstore to build her up because she wasn't gaining enough weight. "They're acting as though it's going to be their child, not ours."

"They only mean to be helpful," Rodney explained. "They're excited about the baby. So am I. We wouldn't want anything to go wrong." Mum knew that, but still she found the hovering of the elder Hoopers irksome. "Why don't they stay in their own house and knit more bootees and matinee jackets then?" she asked Rodney. "Can't you tell them I don't want them hanging about in here?"

"I couldn't say that." Rodney was shocked at the idea. "They mean well. It's their way of showing how much they care for you."

"Well then I wish they didn't care for me so much," Mum said. "I don't like their interfering." Then she and Rodney quarrelled about the difference between "caring" and "interfering."

Later they made up with apologies and assurances of undying love on both sides. This was the way of their marriage. It followed a pattern of ups and downs. For a while they'd be happy as honeymooners. They laughed and flirted. Rodney sang, though accompanying himself now, for Mum stuck to her resolve never to play that piano again. They danced. Dave wound the gramophone for them and I would try to copy the steps

Then the in-laws would annoy Mum again, and again she and Rodney would quarrel. You could tell the marital temperature of the household by the music being played. When Rodney and Mum were getting on well, it was dance music on the gramophone and sentimental songs and Rodney's sweet tenor at the piano. When Rodney and Mum were having a disagreement, Rodney would play Bach, hour after hour of quiet fugues intended to demonstrate what a reasonable and restrained man he was. After an all-out fight, the gloomy, dramatic music of Liszt or Gottschalk would thunder through the house, rattling the dishes on the shelves and the pictures on the walls.

"Music is Rodney's greatest solace," his mother told us one afternoon while Rodney pounded the Chickering. We had taken refuge in the kitchen where we were drinking the peppermint tea Mrs. Hooper had recommended, and not liking it very much. "Rodney's nerves have never been strong. It's so bad for him to be subjected to aggravations." Mrs. Hooper looked at Mum.

"Well, I'm sure he has no aggravations from me," Mum bristled. "And my nerves must be considered as well, especially given my condition. It's outrageous the way Rodney hammers that piano for hours on end. I shouldn't be expected to put up with it."

Now Mrs. Hooper was offended. "For my part, I have always enjoyed Rodney's playing. He has a masterful touch."

Mum referred to Rodney's masterful touch as "infernal hammering". After Mrs. Hooper left, Mum marched into the sitting room. "I can't bear that infernal hammering," she shouted at Rodney, who was bent over the keyboard banging out Liszt. "I cahn't bear it." She still spoke with an accent as strong as it had been the day she left England. The accent infuriated the plain-speaking, proudly Canadian Rodney. "La de daaah," he stopped playing to say. "Why don't you talk ordinary?"

"I cahn't help my accent," Mum insisted. "It's the way I was taught to speak." She and Gran were the only people I ever knew who actually pronounced the gh in 'taught.' "Tawgggghhht." It was a long drawn out sound. Rodney went back to Liszt.

Mum shouted again, "I caahnn't bear that racket. It gives me a dreadful headache." Rodney continued playing. Mum found some cotton wool and stuffed her ears full and paraded past the piano. Rodney closed his eyes and went on playing.

Mum, defeated, put on her hat and gloves. "Let's walk downtown," she shouted an invitation to me. "We'll leave himself to the solace of music and we'll solace ourselves with ice cream."

Once in a while we solaced ourselves with a trip back to Creston to see Gran and to keep up with events there, like the dedication of the war memorial, for instance. That monument had been the cause of a little war of its own among the townsfolk of Creston, and Gran had kept us apprised of its progress. Some had wanted a stone and mortar cenotaph like those being built in cities and towns all through the Empire to honour the war dead, while others had argued for using the money that had been collected towards the building of a hospital or clinic with only a bronze plaque to commemorate our heroes. In the end, the "right side" as Gran put it, prevailed, and a granite monument was erected. When it was learned that the Governor General himself, Baron Byng of Vimy and his lady were to make a special trip to Creston for the dedication, differences of opinion on the appropriateness of the monument seemed to vanish. Everyone wanted to be there for ceremony. Mum was certainly not going to miss it.

Canyon Street was decorated with evergreens and a triumphal arch. Colonel Mallandaine and the town councillors were delegated to meet their Excellencies at the station and escort them through the evergreens to the monument. Schoolchildren and veterans marched, Piper Ross played a lament, Baron Byng laid a wreath. Creston's war was over at last.

Back in Cranbrook, domestic battles continued and peace accords were celebrated. Dave and I didn't dare to bring school friends home. There was no telling what might be going on: irate shouts and pounding music, or an amorous idyll. The one state of affairs was as almost as embarrassing as the other.

The first baby was born, an adorable little girl, and a year later there was a boy. They were sweet little creatures with white blond hair and blue eyes. Dave and I loved them, and they adored and hero-worshipped us, but we felt more like aunt and uncle than sister and brother. And who else of our friends had to stay home babysitting on Saturday nights while their parents went to the Gyro's dance?

The quarrels and the romantic idylls alternated in the usual pattern. Sometimes, while a quarrel was raging in the front room, Dave and I would sit at the top of the stairs, eavesdropping, and reminiscing nostalgically about the peaceful old days. We wondered if Mum regretted her decision to marry. "She didn't know what she was getting into," Dave said. "She can't have known Rodney all that well; she married so soon after we got back from England."

"She knew Rodney from before, from way back when we were in Bonner's Ferry. Don't you remember?"

Dave couldn't remember, but I could. Mum used to go down to the station when his train came through. Anyway it wasn't so much Rodney that was the problem. It was his mother and his sister, I thought. "They start most of the arguments and they egg Rodney on. Rodney tries to please everyone and winds up pleasing no one, and then he gets mad because his nerves are bad."

Mum also blamed her in-laws and, after three years of living in the family compound, she took steps to escape. She persuaded Rodney to move away from Cranbrook and take up fruit farming. Rodney could still keep his job with the railway as he was on a schedule of three-day runs to Spokane followed by four days off, which would leave him plenty of time to manage the ranch. Mum would help too of course. Rodney's nerves would benefit from the physical work in the open air, Mum maintained. Her own mental state would improve in direct ratio to distance from the Hoopers. The ranch would be a money-maker. Everyone would be much happier.

They found a beautiful little ranch with a clapboard house and a small barn and thirty acres of fruit trees in the Kootenay Valley, very close to Creston.

A removals wagon was hired to carry all Mum's precious goods: her Axminster carpet, the black walnut dining room suite, dark paintings in gilded frames, Gran's old silver tea service that she'd passed on to Mum. Rodney's Chickering grand was delivered separately in a special conveyance by a firm of piano movers who came all the way from Nelson.

David and I changed from the Cranbrook school back to the Creston school again. By this time I was two grades behind my contemporaries, which was a little embarrassing, but I had learned to be grateful to be at school, whatever grade I was in. And I was in luck with my teacher, a man who loved poetry and recitations. Every day when we entered the classroom, there was a poem written on the blackboard. We copied it out and if we had free time through the day we were to memorize it. I memorized dozens of poems, short and long, and I could recite them all: "A garden is a lovesome thing," "Oh to be in England, now that April's here," "Lochinvar." "The Highwayman" "Shall I compare thee to a summer's day?" I loved them all. I was, for once in my school career, at the top of the class.

Our family settled into life in Creston and at the ranch and we were happy there for a while among the orchards. Another child was born, a boy named Rodney, like his father.

But by and by, troubles returned. Mum and Rodney began to quarrel again. Why had Rodney stayed at his mother's overnight in

Cranbrook instead of coming to his own home where he belonged? Mum might demand.

Why should he come home only to be shouted at? Rodney would answer.

Why wasn't his good suit pressed when he needed it?

How was she to guess when his good suit was next needed since he never kept her informed of his comings and goings?

When Mum was especially angry, she would pack up a suitcase and take us to Gran's. Of course she never admitted that she did this to get away from Rodney. The pretense was that she was in town to shop, or to help Gran with the spring cleaning, or the fall hat show. But Creston was a small town, and everyone knew what was going on.

After a few days at Gran's, Mum's temper would cool off and we'd go back. Or Rodney, grown lonely and penitent, would come to Mum, begging her to return. He could be very persuasive. Besides, there was strong social pressure to keep them together. In those times a woman who left her husband lived under a cloud of disapproval. Rodney might be a man with a temper, but he was never physically violent, he didn't drink, was a steady worker and a good provider. Therefore he was a good husband, and it was Mum's duty to stand by her man. Married was married, for better or worse. So back we'd go to Rodney and the marriage with its ups and downs, sharp and steep as the mountain walls around us.

It was during one of the times we were staying at Gran's that the marriage ended in a dramatic and unexpected way.

Colonel Mallandaine heard the news first, and he hurried to tell Mum. "Rodney had a truck out at the ranch early this morning and he's packed it full of your furniture," he reported. "The postman saw it! You've got to get out there p.d.q. Hurry!"

When Colonel Mallandaine said hurry, people hurried.

Mum tore off her apron, and she and I jumped into the Colonel's Ford.

"Rodney's got the contents of the house and you'll have the deuce of a time getting them back, I'll tell you that straight out," Mallandaine lectured as we drove towards the ranch.

"Possession is nine points of the law," he continued. He was county magistrate and knew about it. "You must take possession of the house or he'll have that too. Get in there and stay. No court in the land will put you out. We'll get the youngsters out there with you. Stay put. And don't let him in."

Rodney had taken everything: the Axminster carpet from the front room and the green and maroon velvet three-piece suite, the chintz curtains from the windows, the dining room set, and the dishes, all but Gran's tea set and a few things from Mum's first marriage. He'd taken the pots and pans out of the kitchen, and even the preserves off the cellar shelves: the raspberries, plums and cherries Mum and I had put up in the hot, steamy kitchen during the past summer, sweating over the kitchen range while Rodney played Chopin in the front room.

"That bastard," Mum said, running her hand along the empty shelves. "The bloody baahstard!" It was the only time I'd ever heard her use profanity. I knew right then that this fight would be worse than any of the others. This had the feeling of permanent rupture.

The one thing Rodney hadn't taken was the Chickering grand. "He'll come back for it," Mum knew. "He wouldn't risk it on an ordinary moving wagon. He'll have booked the piano movers from Nelson to come for it."

Sure enough, Rodney arrived the next day with the "Willis Pianos, Nelson" truck.

Mum was ready for him. She'd discovered he hadn't emptied the barn, and in it she'd found the shotgun used against marauding animals in the orchard.

She stood on the front steps waiting, with the gun cradled in her arm. She looked like one of the women in Rodney's family photos of tough Cranbrook pioneers, hard as nails and loaded for bear.

"I've come for my piano," Rodney said.

"You own no piano here," Mum answered.

"Come on, Sarah. That's my piano. I need it."

"The only piano here belongs to me."

"You know damned well that's my piano. I've got the men here to move it. We're wasting their time." He took a step forward.

Mum lifted the gun. "The only piano in this house is mine. You can't have it."

She spoke with quiet, deliberate fury. "You caahn't have it." Possession is nine points of the law. It was her furniture he'd taken. She pointed the gun at Rodney's chest.

"Put that thing down, woman!"

"Leave my property!"

"It's not your property."

"It is now."

They stared at each other in a long weighing up. Did he dare to walk on up the steps?

Would she fire?

The piano movers stood well back by their van.

Enter Colonel Mallandaine. You could always count on the Colonel. This time he rode on to the scene in an RCMP car. He was out of the car and running towards Rodney before the car came to a stop. "Now then, sir. Now then," he bellowed in his loud military voice. Two officers emerged from the car. The Colonel indicated that one should take charge of Rodney, the other disarm my mother.

"It isn't loaded," Mum told the officer who took the gun gently from her.

Rodney was being treated less politely, but he was making more of a fuss. "My piano," he was shouting. "She's got my piano in there and I need it. I have arranged to have it moved by professionals."

The officer nudged him forward towards the car and Mallandaine, swishing his military walking stick back and forth, made it clear to Rodney that he wasn't going to get his piano that day or any other day to come.

We never saw Rodney again. Mum was left to manage as best she could.

Our standard of living fell with a thud that echoed all through Creston. Mum sold the ranch and moved us into a cheap rented house in town. When the money from the sale was used up, my once proud mother with her stylish hats and her posh English accent had to take day work cleaning for the doctor's wife and the banker's and the dentist's. We ate potatoes and pancakes and the cheapest cuts of meat. We wore mended and re-mended clothes and hand-me-downs from Aunt Boo and Uncle Clary in England. We got by, barely.

I quit school. I was almost nineteen, too old for sitting in a classroom with younger kids memorizing poems and the dates of the reigns of English kings. My teacher had suggested I take senior matriculation and then go to normal school to train as a teacher but I didn't have time for all that education. I needed to learn something fast, something useful that would get me a job so that I could earn some money soon. A secretarial course was the obvious choice. Unfortunately there was no business college in Creston. I would have to go to Nelson, and we could never afford that.

I was in despair until the British War Office came to my rescue. Although Mum had lost her widow's pension when she remarried, she discovered that some funds were available for the education of deceased officers' children. She and I wrote letters and filled in forms and battled through red tape for almost a year and eventually I was granted an allowance to pay for a two-year secretarial course in Nelson.

Those two years should have been happy years for me, giving me a first taste of independence, but they were not. My allowance was adequate but not generous. I stayed in the cheapest boarding house I could find, crammed in a room with two other girls. Pittman shorthand, typing, and basic accounting were not as interesting subjects as poetry and history and geography. I had to study hard, always worried that I might not pass and thus disgrace myself in the eyes of the British government and of my family. Some of the girls in the class were local girls, putting in time before marriage. They wore nice clothes, smoked cigarettes at lunch hour, and talked about movies and boyfriends. The rest of us, easily distinguishable by the dowdier clothes we wore, desperately needed the jobs we were training for. We stuck together, envied the others, worked hard, spent as little money as possible and did not have a good time. Our graduation day ceremony was brief and businesslike. We hurried away to find jobs. We did not promise to keep in touch with our classmates.

These were hard years for Mum too, bringing up three children on her own. Perhaps she wished she had been less feisty, more tolerant of Rodney and his family and more amenable to their way of doing things. If she did have regrets, she never said so. "We're managing," was her invariable response to questions about how she was getting along.

We managed, barely. There were no luxuries – except for the grand piano. No matter how tough things got, Mum held on to the Chickering, even if she never did play it. It filled the small sitting room; it dominated the house.

And every week, no matter if we had to do without meat, or without stockings for school, even if we had to go to church or Sunday School without a nickel for the collection plate, Mum would manage to scrape together fifty cents for the children to have piano lessons from Miss Bailey, graduate of the Royal Conservatory of Music. "A beautiful instrument, this," Miss Bailey could be depended on to say at least once during the lesson and Mum, darning or mending in the cramped corner by the window, would nod in satisfied agreement.

Two of the children had inherited the Hooper gift for music. They played at school concerts, at church and Sunday School and at the Legion. In Kiwanis competitions and talent shows they almost always won for both duets and solos.

Whenever people congratulated her on her talented offspring, Mum had a ready answer. "Of course, my children have an advantage as musicians. They're used to playing on a concert grand, you see. We have a Chickering at home."

Chapter 13

*N*ew Shoes

"Any mail?" Mum called as soon as she opened the door. She was waiting as anxiously as I for replies to my job applications. "No letters," I answered. "Only the parcel from England." I nodded towards the large, brown-papered box on the table.

"The parcel from England!" Mum's tired features brightened. She stamped the snow from her galoshes and, with a puff of relief, sat in the rocker to unclip them. She'd been working at the Mathesons all day, "obliging" as she called it, polishing their silverware or waxing their floors or ironing, to earn half a dollar. "Did you think to call in at Rosebank to tell Gran?" she asked.

"Yes, she'll be along soon. Old Mrs. Hunt was in to get new ribbons for one of those bonnet things she wears."

"There you are then; blessings abounding. We'll wait for her before we open the parcel. Put on the kettle, will you?"

I hooked the round burner plate off the stove to check on the fire. The wood was smouldering again. That load of wood the hobo had chopped for us was too green. I went to the woodbox for newspaper and kindling.

"Gainful Occupation Instead of Relief Is the Aim of Your Government" was the headline on the paper I crumpled and poked in among the charred bits of wood. That was a promise good only for burning, I thought. I laid on a couple of sticks of kindling, banged the burner back and pulled the kettle over it.

Before the water boiled, Gran appeared, wrapped in her old plaid shawl. Her eyes darted to the parcel. "What will it be this time, do you suppose?" she asked. Her look suggested she thought it might be gold bricks.

I rolled my eyes. "Old clothes," I said. "Same as always." Every spring and autumn, Aunt Boo, over in England, went through the closets in her house and sent the things she and her family no longer wanted to us in Creston. For Mum and Gran it was a red-letter day when the box arrived. They treated those clothes as though they came from Worth of Paris. When I was younger, I used to be excited about the parcels too. Now I knew better.

There'd be a frumpy old wool dress in navy blue or grey. A tweed skirt. A silk blouse with a stain down the front or a tear under the sleeve. Maybe a cardigan with darned cuffs or elbows. A scratchy woollen vest. A housedress. Uncle Clary's or cousin Percy's old trousers or plus fours, shiny across the seat and bagging at the knees to be cut down for the boys. At least Aunt Boo wasn't sending any more of those awful grey kneepants English boys wore. For a few years the young John had had to wear them to the Creston school to hoots of derision, and calls of "bare-legged Englishman!" It was a happy day for him when Cousin Percy graduated to long pants.

I sighed. It would be so nice to have something new to wear. Something from Eaton's Catalogue, for instance. Eaton's always had the smartest things. But Eaton's was too expensive for the likes of us who had no regular wage earner in the family. Mum's work brought in only a few dollars a week. My brother David was making his keep and seven-fifty a month at a government work camp. The younger children were still in school. And I was a useless, unemployed weight on the family budget. In our household, we considered it a good month if we got by and a bonanza if we managed to whittle down our bill at the Mercantile a little.

I'd graduated from the Nelson Secretarial College at the end of 1929, just as the Great Depression was getting going, and in two years of job searching since, I had not been able to find work. I was not alone in my predicament. Thousands were unemployed. Thirteen percent of Canada's population was on relief. This depression was worse than any financial crisis there had ever been before.

Compared to many, our family had no great cause for complaint, Mum used to say. We had vegetables from our garden and eggs from our chickens. Fruit could be had free for the picking at Gran's or at some of the orchards around town. Down in the cellar were shelves full of canned tomatoes, beans, pickles, and fruit to help feed us through the winter. Sportsmen, like the Talbot boys, brought us venison in season, and brook trout. So we weren't what you could call "in want". We just didn't have any money.

There were many worse off than us. We saw them on their way through Creston: men riding the freights east, having heard there were jobs in the factories of Ontario and Quebec; men riding the freights west, following rumours of work in the lumber camps and mines of B.C.; men riding the freights because no town would let them stay and they didn't want to go home and be one more mouth to feed. We saw families packed into old cars with chairs and crates and mattresses and washtubs, looking for a new life. We saw pinched men and women waiting outside the relief office, furtive and ashamed. We saw men camping in the Hobo's Nest down in the ravine where the railway crossed Dead Horse Creek.

Sometimes these fellows came into town to beg at back doors for food in exchange for work. They weren't often turned away hungry. Even in homes like ours where there was little to spare, they'd get a bowl of stew or a plate of beans and a cup of tea. We all knew young men who were living like these fellows, and in a kind of faith in a mystic exchange we believed that if we gave to the stranger at our door, somewhere another stranger would be feeding our Jack or Tom or Fred.

We weren't on relief and we had enough to eat; we had much to be grateful for, Mum said, and I supposed that had to include Aunt Boo's old clothes.

Mum untied the string from the parcel and rolled it into a neat coil to put in the sideboard drawer. Gran folded the brown paper. String and paper would always come in useful. Then the two of them shook out each item of clothing, one by one, and examined it with minute attention.

"Feel the quality of this serge," Gran said. "Boo always buys the best."

"Look at the buttons," Mum exclaimed.

"Tweed," Gran crooned. "This will wear forever."

I couldn't see what they were so thrilled about. This batch of clothes was the usual mothball-smelling old lot, as far as I could see.

When they had finished unpacking and admiring, Mum and Gran drank their tea and got down to the serious business of planning which castoffs to allot to whom and how they could best be transformed into garments we could wear without too much shame.

"Two housedresses for you, Sarah, and perhaps I could have the serge skirt to go with my black jacket?" Gran suggested.

"Certainly. You ought to have one of the housedresses, too."

"I'm well enough for this season. Cut it down for Liz or Olwen."

"All right," Mum agreed. "The blue one would be pretty for Liz. And the flannels. I'll take this pair in for David. Do you think I could get two pairs out of these for John?"

Gran examined the old trousers carefully.

"No," she decided. "You'd have seams all over in the wrong places. They'd look terrible. You'd do better to get the one good pair out of them. And here are two shirts. We'll turn the collars and they'll be as good as new."

"But no overcoat this year." Mum sorted through the pile again just to be sure. "That's a pity; I was hoping for something to make into a jacket for John. The one he's wearing is far too small."

178

I pulled out a brown wool jacket she'd overlooked. "What about this?"

"That's a lady's coat," Mum said. "And here's the skirt that goes with it, do you see?"

Gran took the ugly jacket from my hands. "Why, this would be the very thing for you, Olwen, dear!" Her theory was that because I had brown eyes, I looked good in brown. I didn't. My colouring was sallow, and brown made me look drab as potato sacking.

"You see," Gran was saying, "we could take material from the skirt to set into the side seams here to get that new boxy look in the coat you like. A – what is you call it? – a swagger coat?"

I didn't see the possibilities, but Mum did. "Yes! It'll be perfect. Very stylish. Such fine material. You'll be the best dressed secretary in town." "Secetary", she pronounced it. This irritated me since I was not a secretary at all. I was an unemployed graduate of Nelson Secretarial College. My diploma wasn't getting me anywhere.

"With a peach-coloured silk blouse, I think," Gran decided. She was looking at an orangey–pink nightgown thoughtfully.

Oh, surely not. I turned away. "I won't need a suit and a silk blouse to pick strawberries and raspberries at Turner's ranch, which is about the only paid employment I'm ever likely to get," I complained. "If I even get that," I added darkly.

Mum poured me another cup of tea. "You'll get your office job. Just wait. Your ship is bound to come in one day, and it'll be very soon now, I expect."

She'd been saying that for the past two years. I didn't see how she could still believe it. She was putting on a front to keep me from discouragement. I wished she wouldn't bother because, in fact, I was discouraged, and bored and angry and ashamed. I'd applied everywhere. "Dear sir," my letter went. "In the event of a vacancy arising in your office (store) (company,) would you please consider my application for the position?" I'd written to every office, store and company in the Kootenays. But there wasn't a job to be found. Not in Creston. Or Nelson. Or Sirdar. Or Cranbrook. I'd tried them all. No one wanted to hire a typist, no matter how many words per minute she could type. No one wanted a stenographer, no matter how skilled at Pittman's shorthand.

I was almost twenty-four. I wasn't a schoolgirl and I wasn't a housewife and I wasn't a career girl. I was nothing. I was worse than nothing. I was another drain on the all too slender household finances. It was humiliating. It was enraging. I'd worked hard at business college and graduated at the top of my class. And all for nothing.

Mum pretended she needed my help looking after the younger kids, and doing the housework, but I knew they could easily manage without me. Most of the time I hung around the house and tried to make myself useful, cleaning or mending for Mum and Gran, helping Gran with her garden, helping my half-sister Liz with her homework. Sometimes I'd spend an afternoon with blind Uncle Bob. He seemed to be content with a life of unemployment. Perhaps I could learn from him. But reciting poetry had lost its appeal for me at that time. Nor did I care much for joining Bob on his walks around and around the familiar streets of Creston, even though I could see the views that he could not. I was grateful for the public library. I did a lot of reading, and a lot of dreaming of the time when I would have a job and a salary and a useful life.

In the summer, like most folks in the Creston valley, we'd all had a few weeks' work picking fruit, but the ranchers had grumbled that they couldn't afford to pay pickers and shippers, considering the prices the fruit was fetching, and the season ended early. Some were saying they would let the fruit rot on the trees this coming season.

After the harvest, I'd begged Mum to let me go in her place to the day jobs she had in town, but she wouldn't hear of it. "No, no. You're a qualified 'secetary'." She was proud that I had been able to go to business college and that I had acquired career skills; she didn't want me to squander them. "You'll get a job offer one day soon. Your ship will come in."

The bank manager's wife advertised for a nursemaid to look after her two small children. I wanted to apply, but again Mum restrained me. "You don't want people to think of you as a nursemaid, Olwen: you're a trained 'secetary'. You wait 'til you're offered a job suitable to your qualifications."

I would wait my life away. "Did you read the editorial in this week's paper?" I asked. "It said companies aren't hiring new young workers any more. If an opening comes up, it goes to someone who was let go earlier."

"I'm sure the editor is referring to young people with no professional training," Mum answered. "Your 'secetarial' diploma is your open sesame."

You couldn't squelch Mum's optimism.

Gran and Mum set to work straightaway, ripping out the seams of Aunt Boo's brown suit.

"Don't rush," I told them, as I cleared the tea things off the table out of their way.

"Suppose a job offer came for you tomorrow." Mum unpicked stitches with little jabs of the scissors. "You haven't anything suitable to wear. Gran is quite right. This will make up into a lovely outfit for you."

Over the next couple of weeks, working on days when Mum had no "clients" to attend to, Mum and Gran made the "secetary's" suit. Mum did the machine sewing and Gran did the finishing work. They took in the skirt and made a swagger jacket and a blouse of peach silk, and Gran made me a cloche hat of brown felt to match.

Considering that it was brown, and considering what they had to work with, the outfit wasn't bad. I wasn't pleased, really, but I was grateful. I knew that Mum and Gran had done their best for me. But the fact remained that when I tried on the finished ensemble, I looked a lot like the brown velour couch in the sitting room

"You look lovely, dear," Gran said.

"Like a real career girl," Mum added. "You could walk into any office in the country today and not look out of place." She looked down at my shoes. "Except for the shoes. We'll have to get you new shoes."

"Oh, these will do," I protested, looking down at my worn black oxfords. Why waste money on something I wasn't going to wear?

"Prospective employers always pay particular attention to your shoes," Mum said. "Your shoes and your collar. If those items are not spic and span, you have no chance of getting the job. If they are neat and clean, you will most likely get the position."

Mum had some crazy ideas. "What would you know about getting an office job?" I asked her rudely.

"It's what my father always said," Mum replied. "An employer chooses according to your shoes and your collar, he said."

I wished the formula for getting a job really was that easy.

Mum insisted, so we walked up town to buy new shoes to go with the suit. "It's you need the shoes more than I do," I pointed out. Mum's shoes were not just down at heel, like mine, but cracking at the sides as well.

"Oh not me," she laughed. "I won't be swanking off to a job in an office like you. These are quite comfortable for the sort of work I do. They give more room for my bunions."

In his store Mr. Speers showed us some brown kid pumps that had just come in, with cross straps and three neat buttons across the arch.

"They're lovely," Mum sighed, feeling the leather.

I didn't even touch them. I knew what I had to do. "I prefer oxfords," I said. I chose the cheapest pair in the shop: square, clunky things, but only a dollar seventy-five. "Just in case my ship hasn't come in by next summer," I said with heavy sarcasm, "these will do well for apple-picking shoes."

Mum ignored my remark. "Please put these on our bill," she told Mr. Speers with dignity.

Mr. Speers made a big to-do of rifling through the pages of his accounts book so that we'd be sure to notice all the money he was owed. "Absolutely No Credit" said the sign above the till. But that was there for any outsiders who might come in. Speers would give credit to his home-town customers; he pretty well had to. Creston was a small place. How could he refuse to provide tea or flour to the woman who sang in the same church choir as he did? How could he refuse seeds or a handful of nails to the rancher who was his lodge brother?

The one family we knew who were eventually refused credit was one who lived extravagantly. Every week they ordered sirloin roast and leg of lamb from the butcher. At the grocery, they asked for the best teas and coffees and imported biscuits and marmalade. Speers sent them bills and warnings and final notices. They ignored the bills and continued to order the same expensive items they always had until at last he cut them off. The butcher, emboldened, did the same. Finally the bank manager foreclosed on their house and they disappeared from town. "They ate their house!" Mum said of them in shocked disapproval.

Now Speers kept a pretty sharp eye on what people bought. He'd give credit on necessities but we wouldn't dare to ask it for luxuries. I bet he'd have made us pay at the very least half down on those six-dollar brown kid pumps.

He wrapped the oxfords in newspaper and tied the bundle with a bit of string.

"There now. Let's walk on to the post office," Mum said. "Perhaps there'll be a letter for you today."

"Sure," I said. I wished I could have afforded those pumps. I swung the parcel of my new shoes by its string as we walked along Canyon Street. These were the first new shoes I'd had since high school. It would have been nice to have a good pair that I could like.

We walked into the post office. "Letter for you today, Olwen," the postmistress called from behind the brass cage. She handed me an envelope with "Canadian Imperial Bank, Cranbrook" printed on it. I tore it open.

"Dear Miss Evans,

"We are pleased to inform you that a vacancy has arisen..."

Mum had to read the rest for me. The vacancy was for a clerk typist. I was to present myself next Monday for a second interview.

I'd gone for an interview last spring and I thought they'd forgotten all about me.

"A second interview!" Mum exclaimed. "That means they'll almost certainly hire you."

"Provided my shoes and collar pass inspection." I grinned.

"What a good thing we have everything ready: the new suit and the shoes and all," Mum said with satisfaction.

We called in at Gran's to share the good news and drank a cup of tea in celebration. By the weekend we'd managed to scrape up a dollar ten for the train fare to Cranbrook. I went for the interview and I got the job. The pay was to be fifty dollars a month.

I arranged to board with a family called the Somers. They were recommended by Mrs. Speers and they would let me pay the first month's rent in instalments. I started work the following Monday.

The whole world looks and feels different when you're employed, I discovered.

I walked along Baker Street to the bank in the crisp early morning air, glad to have a day of purposeful activity ahead of me. I walked between the imposing white pillars of the entrance into the hushed, high-ceilinged edifice, into the busy smell of ink and paper and brass polish.

I loved the work. In the mornings I typed letters for the manager. One of the first letters I typed was to the millionaire William Astor Drayton who lived nearby and banked with us. I typed his name the way it sounded: William Aster Drayton.

Two days later Mr. Drayton stormed into the bank, waving the letter. "I am not a flower!" he bellowed. I had never heard of the wealthy American Astors, had no idea who this man was and why he was so angry until my mistake was pointed out to me by the manager. I was terrified that I'd be fired for my mistake, but soon everyone, even the manager, was laughing. He admitted that he should have seen the mistake when he signed the letter. "But for heaven's sake, don't make the same mistake again!" he warned.

I told the story at supper that evening to my landlady's family. "I can't imagine anyone making such a fuss about the misspelling of a name," I complained. "Hardly anyone spells *my* name right."

"Well, yours is a tough one, Oliven," Mrs. Somers said. She still hadn't got it right, and never did.

There were three banks in Cranbrook at this time. Our business came mainly from the railway and from some big lumber companies of the area. Substantial accounts were also kept by Camp Skookumchuck in the Rockies, a posh summer camp for wealthy Americans, as well as by a few wealthy individuals like our Mr. Astor Drayton. I was astonished at the vast sums of money that flowed in and out of our establishment every day. I typed letters to our wealthy clients and to the poor ones as well.

These last were often reminders of overdue mortgage payments or threats of foreclosure. I soon came to learn that the manager would never actually fulfil the threats his letters contained. What would the bank do with another property no one could buy? Might as well let the poor folks in the place stay put. They'd pay when they could. Businesses in Cranbrook ran on the same principles as those in Creston.

At lunch time I walked along streets of shingled cottages behind whitewashed picket fences to my boarding house for a hot dinner, then back to work for the afternoon.

I counted up sums on cancelled cheques, clipped them together and passed them to someone else to count again. I added columns of figures the teller had already added, then I added them again and passed them back to him. Female employees always worked in the background. Only men could be trusted to count out money to customers.

My favourite assignment was to accompany a teller in the delivery of the day's clearings, that is cash and cheques for the other two banks in town. In case one of the tellers might be tempted to make away with the loot, the delivery was rotated among them on an irregular schedule, and the teller chosen had to be accompanied by another employee, sometimes me. One of us carried the leather bag with the clearings and the other carried a loaded gun in case we should be hijacked along the way. The fact that none of us knew how to shoot the gun was of no concern to anyone.

My co-workers teased me about liking the clearings job. They pretended to believe I was the mysterious thief who had held up the Creston branch of the Imperial Bank back in 1925. One of the partners in that famous robbery had been caught with half the loot. The other had eluded capture and disappeared with several thousand dollars. "Watch her carefully," my colleagues would warn the teller when he and I would set out with the clearings. "She's waiting for a chance for her next heist."

What I liked about the clearings job was walking through the business district of town, feeling the excitement of its commerce and knowing myself to be a part of it. Here was the business of the day, gathered into a leather bag, and entrusted to me, a working woman of independent means.

At work I wore the brown suit and I had three blouses to go with it. "Sweet blouse," one of the girls, Betty, said to me the day I wore the ex-nightgown orange-y-pink one. Betty became my best friend. She'd been working at the bank for three years. She had some beautiful clothes, and what really astonished me was that she was saving up to buy herself a car. A car! The possibilities of what a salaried worker could buy were dazzling.

At five o'clock, tired after my day's work, and so grateful for it, I walked back to my boarding house, dawdling past the shop windows on Baker Street, planning what I might buy with my first pay cheque at the end of the month. Well, not a car. Not yet.

On late shopping nights Betty and I walked around downtown and looked through Fink's department store and Doran's and Wilson and Haynes. So many things tempted me: a soft blue coat, a green silk crepe dress, a smart navy skirt with narrow pleats. I wanted to buy them all.

I also wanted to send something to help Mum. But she'd told me, "Buy yourself what you need. I've managed this far; I can manage a little longer without your help. You'll need smart clothes for the office. And some spending money for movies and concerts and things. You have yourself a good time." With me gone, too, there'd be one less spoon dipping into the stew pot. She'd manage.

Still, once I'd bought myself a few of the clothes I really needed, I would certainly send home a little each month. Even a couple of dollars would help.

When payday came at last, I had to keep telling myself to be prudent. I would have liked to ask for all the fifty dollars in dimes, so that I could take them home and count them and gloat over them like a miser. But I made myself take a business-like attitude, befitting a bank employee. I took the money in bills and counted them. I had room and board to pay. I owed my landlady for the coming month and half of the past month as well. That would come to thirty-three dollars. And it would be prudent to put something aside for an emergency. Say ten dollars. No, five.

That would leave me twelve dollars to put in my purse. I was rich.

I would go home to Creston for the weekend and show off a bit. I'd go shopping at the Mercantile on Saturday with Mum and Liz. Perhaps I'd go ahead and buy those smart brown pumps. I hadn't seen any nicer in the Cranbrook stores. There'd still be enough left to buy treats for Mum and Gran and the kids. Maybe ice cream, or Saturday evening at the movies. Or both. Oh, it was good to be rich.

Creston looked good. It was April; the cherry trees were coming into blossom, soft pink, like dawn clouds. Below, the flats shimmered hazy blue-grey, like a vast still lake among the dark mountains.

Mum was at the station to meet me. She wore her best housedress, gloves and hat, as she always did when she went up town. As we started for home, I noticed that, though the street was quite dry, she was wearing galoshes. They were tied around the ankles with black grosgrain ribbon but they flapped at every step.

"Why are you wearing galoshes?" I asked.

She answered indirectly. "Do you remember your great uncle Walter – the vegetarian pacifist, you know? Well, another of his theories was that shoes are bad for the feet. Going barefoot is much healthier, he always said. He made all his family go barefoot, everywhere. This was right in the middle of London, too. Just fancy. His eldest daughter was married in bare feet. A lovely wedding gown and bare feet. Imagine that. Anyway, I'm trying it out. I just slip on the galoshes for going uptown."

"Your shoes wore out entirely, did they?" I asked.

"To bits and laces," Mum admitted.

"But," she added as her optimism took hold again, "these galoshes are surprisingly comfortable. The ribbon was Gran's idea. Who knows? I may be setting a new fashion in footwear."

"Stop pretending," I said. "You know they're awful."

We walked along Canyon Street.

"Let's stop at the Mercantile," I said. "There's something I want to look at."

I bought Mum a pair of the best black leather oxfords in the store. They cost three-fifty and I paid cash. She wore them home and said they were the nicest shoes she'd ever had.

Chapter 14

$\mathcal{L}$ove Calls Me by My Name

A thin man on a thinner horse plodding slowly down a long straight road. Dust rises in clouds at each footfall and blows in gritty gusts around them, covers both in its fine grey powder so that they appear to be one substance, one creature. "Black blizzards" they call these dust storms here.

"Whoa!"

The man pulls a clean handkerchief from an inner pocket, takes off his wire-rimmed glasses and polishes them, then peers through them into the dun-coloured gloom.

Sky and land are merged in a featureless haze. Wheat fields lie on either side of the road, he knows well enough, although the grain can hardly be seen. All the fields look the same. There are no landmarks to guide him. He is lost, again.

No matter. The horse will know the way home. He lets the reins hang loose, nudges the ribby sides with his heels. "Ged-up!" The horse plods forward on the long straight road past the monotonous fields.

It is late August. Harvest time. The hymns of the season play through his mind.

Come ye thankful people come,
Raise the song of harvest home
All is safely garnered in ...

But in these fields, there is little to harvest. There has been no rain since May. The topsoil has blown away. What little grain there is stands short and thin and the kernels flat. Another bad harvest. They're saying it's hardly worth the effort of cutting and binding and stooking and drawing in.

"Plough it back into the land, might as well," most of the farmers are saying. "That is, if it ever rains so we could run a plough through the earth."

This is the third straight year of drought in southern Saskatchewan.

The first failure was bad, but farmers knew they had to expect some bad years. Most had some savings put by. They tightened their belts, and said, "Next year's bound to be better."

They needed a good crop of wheat, and they needed a good market to sell it in, like they'd had in the war years. But since 1929 the price of wheat had fallen from a dollar sixty-five a bushel to thirty-some cents a bushel. Prime Minister Bennett couldn't do anything about the weather, but he had promised them the price of wheat would rise again, and the farmers believed him. Bennett was a smart man; he'd started out poor and become a millionaire by his own hard work and good sense. He must know what he was talking about.

But the next year was worse than ever. The crop was bad, and the prices were worse. There was no money now for new machinery, no money for parts to fix the old, no money to buy gas for the cars bought in better times. Farmers took out the motors, hitched horses to the cars and called them Bennett buggies, poking fun at the prime minister's false promises.

That year there was real privation, but they survived.

They even made jokes. "My hired man's working to buy the farm off of me," one of their favourites ran. "When he gets done paying for it, I'll work to buy it off of him. That way we'll both keep gainfully employed."

They still had hope when they planted the third spring. "Third time lucky," they said. "You never get three bad years in a row."

At Sunday services they sang hymns of hope and faith:

We plow the field and scatter
The good seed on the land,
But it is fed and watered
By God's almighty hand.

They prayed for the yearly miracle of growth and harvest. But this year was turning out as bad as the last two.

Now the people had nothing left, not even jokes. Families were packing up and leaving. Most of the young men were already gone. They rode away on the freight trains looking to find work on the west coast or in the big cities back east. If they didn't find anything, at least there'd be one less mouth to feed at home.

To those who remained on the farms around the hamlets of Wyndam, Willow Bend, and Bell's Corners, Reverend Gordon McGuinness had been assigned as Presbyterian minister for a year's mission field service after his ordination last spring. It was his job to conduct Sunday services in the schoolhouses at the three hamlets – the congregations were too poor to afford churches – to minister to his flock's spiritual needs, and to sustain them in their faith.

"What can you preach to these people of faith and hope?" he'd asked his predecessor who had taken him around on his first Sunday to show him the ropes.

"I stick to the psalms," Reverend Halloran said. "There's comfort in the psalms."

So today instead of the harvest hymns that perversely would not leave his mind, they'd sung:

O God our help in ages past
Our hope for years to come,
Be Thou our guard while troubles last,
And our eternal home.

Only eight people had shown up for the eight o'clock service at Willow Bend. Fourteen cents in the collection plate.

More at Bell's Corners, of course. A dozen at the three o'clock at Wyndham.

A total of fifty-six cents for the young minister to buy food and tobacco this week. He'd manage. Not in abundance, but in sufficiency.

The horse stopped.

Ah yes. A pole barn, mud chinked, roofed with sods. Home sweet home.

He dismounted, pushed open a sagging door and led the horse into its stall. There he removed the bridle and bit, fetched a pail of water, scooped out a small measure of oats and tossed the grain and then a forkful of musty hay into the manger. "Good night, Beauty."

He latched the stable door, then walked around to the front of the building and let himself into his home. A beaten earth floor, a west-facing window curtained with yellowed newspaper, a wooden table and chair, a plank bookcase laden with books and papers, a straw mattress laid on an old door propped up on bricks, and a couple of wooden crates serving as kitchen cupboard and wardrobe.

He lit the kerosene lantern.

Supper time.

He wasn't hungry. The McLaughlins had invited him for dinner after the eleven o'clock at Bell's Corners School. They'd had roast chicken and potatoes with gravy and canned peas. A white cake for dessert. The food had nearly choked him for he knew the McLaughlins would be eating nothing but porridge for the next week after putting on a spread like that.

He'd pretended to enjoy it. They'd have been shamed if he had refused their hospitality, or if they hadn't been able to offer a decent meal to the minister when it was the Sunday of their turn.

He brushed the dust off a hard-boiled egg from the supply he'd cooked up in the morning and cracked it open. He ate a lot of eggs. Eggs were cheap.

There was just enough water in the pail to do for a pot of tea. Good. He boiled a kettle on the kerosene stove, and sitting at the table, rolled the first of the evening's cigarettes, a voluptuous pleasure, a self-indulgence he could not bring himself to even try to resist.

Monday morning, after he'd fetched water, and done his few barn and household chores, he began work on his sermon. He usually dedicated mornings to study and sermon writing. Afternoons and evenings were for pastoral visits and meetings.

He worked hard on his sermons, tried to make them interesting and inspirational. What could he tell these people to sustain their faith and their belief in God's goodness and mercy?

He wondered if he himself would be able to keep his own faith if he knew he was to share these people's future. Yes, he shared their hardships now, but he would be rescued at the end of the year, and go to a better parish. He remembered the look of joy and relief on Reverend Halloran's face when he'd climbed aboard the eastbound train last spring. He'd almost literally shaken the dust of this place off his shoes. And next spring, it would be his turn to leave. How then could he dare to talk to these people of keeping the faith, of trusting in the Lord? They had endured two failed harvests and were facing a third. And there was no new posting coming for them.

He had been here only half a year, though it seemed much longer. The winter hadn't started yet. How would he manage in this place through the long cold months? The parishioners were going to put in a wood stove for him, but the cold would come up from the earth, and in through the chinks between boards. There would be days, they said, sometimes weeks, when he'd be snowed in. Would he go mad with cold and loneliness and despair?

No. Surely with God's help and his own willpower he would endure. And he would be sustained by the knowledge that in the spring his trial would be over.

Meanwhile, what message could he preach without sounding smug?

Could he talk of Joseph's seven fat years and the seven lean? No. These people couldn't survive seven lean years. That story would be an incentive to despair. Despair was a pernicious sin.

Stick to the psalms. The psalms are always a comfort. "Why art thou cast down, o my soul? And why art thou disquieted in me? Hope thou in God."

His meditation was interrupted by a knocking on the door. It was the young Forster lad.

"Little Ellie is dying," he announced with no emotion in his voice. "Mum and Dad say can you come?"

"Yes, of course."

"Did you walk over?" he asked the boy.

"Yeah."

That would be a good seven, eight miles. "Sit down. Eat." He gave the boy a drink of water from the dipper and one of his hard-boiled eggs. He had nothing else to offer. "I'll get ready."

He put on his clerical collar, bridled the horse. He had no saddle. He hoisted the boy to sit in front of him. The boy was asleep before they'd gone a mile.

What to say? How do you comfort a bereaved parent? What did he, a young man who had neither wife nor child, know of such sorrow?

Mr. Forster opened the door to him. "She's gone," he whispered.

Reverend McGuiness took the father's hand. "The Lord giveth and the Lord taketh away. Blessed be the name of the Lord."

The mother and two children were sitting at the kitchen table, their hands folded, not knowing what to do.

He walked around the table, touched each of them, sat down on the chair beside the dry-eyed woman. He wished for a moment his church allowed some rituals, like the Catholics. He would like to busy himself with oil and candles, get these people down on their knees counting beads and murmuring comforting, familiar words.

He had only the Bible and his own awkward and diffident pity.

"The Lord is my shepherd," he read, "I shall not want."

When the psalm was finished, they seem satisfied that something fitting had been said, though the words about green pastures and still waters didn't seem right in this landscape.

"Would you like to see her?" the woman asked.

He rose and followed the woman into a curtained-off end of the main room. A child lay tiny and still in the middle of a large bed. Flies buzzed around, busy at the lips and at the corners of the closed eyes.

"She was too good for this world." The mother brushed the flies away.

"Let us pray," the Reverend McGuinness said. He watched the flies settle again as he spoke.

"You'll have a cup of tea?" the woman asked when he was done.

"Thank you."

While the tea steeped, they discussed the few details of the funeral. Then, because there was nothing else to talk about, he asked about their crop. They would harvest what they could, Mr. Forster said. "It'll feed the chickens maybe. Anyways, we might as well work as sit idle."

"Yes," the preacher agreed.

He was relieved when the tea was drunk and he could go.

At the funeral the next day a few neighbours and church people gathered round the grave. The dust blew in, covering the small coffin too soon.

Later that day he made another start on his sermon.

"Today," he began, "I buried a child of this parish." From that bald beginning, he wanted the sermon to soar upward to an affirmation of faith in God's goodness. The sermon refused to soar. Whenever he took it past that first sad sentence, it sank deeper. "And I will bury others before my year among you is over. Death is in your eyes as silent and empty as that small child's body."

Go back to the psalms. Always to the psalms. "Many a time have they afflicted me; yet they have not prevailed against me."

On Friday he stopped in at the general store in Bell's Corners to pick up the few grocery items he needed, and the precious packet of tobacco. "Mail for you," Mrs. Bell handed him two envelopes: one from the Board of Missions, one from home.

In front of the store he tore open the envelope from Ontario, lifted it to his face, and breathed in the smell of home that permeated the pages.

His mother's uneven handwriting spread all over the page. He imagined her writing it last Sunday, after the evening chores, sitting at the kitchen table, newspaper spread over the faded oilcloth, the coal-oil lamp spreading a shadowy light on the white pages of the writing pad.

"My dear son,

"Hope this finds you well. We are all well here.

"The threshers was here this last Wednesday. Many asked after you and send kind regards. The Hughes boys, the McFaddens, and Violet, who was kindly helping me with the kitchen work.

"The crop was good. John says near thirty-five bushels to the acre, we are thankful. The weather has held good.

"John and Dad go tomorrow to the Harrisons if it don't rain, which we hope not.

"This week I will pick and do down the blue plums. Also John is set to plough up the potatoes for me."

Potatoes and plums and a good harvest. Such good fortune seemed marvellous to Gordon now.

If he was back at home what he'd like to do would be to run out to the south pasture and roll in its greenness, like a horse let out in the spring.

Wouldn't that set the folks wondering! He smiled at the thought of it.

"I was sorry to hear how hard times continue for your people out there. They must be fearful disappointed and suffering."

There was not a word about her own hard time. Her bad leg would be swollen up from running around the kitchen with all the extra work of baking and cooking and cleaning up for the threshers. And now she was turning to and making plum preserves, and walking along the fresh-furrowed field stooping and gathering potatoes. It was too much for a woman in her sixties with no other woman to help her.

But maybe she was glad to have work, to have plums and potatoes to gather and food enough to provide good meals for her family. Here the women had the never-ending work of sweeping away dust and grime that settled again in minutes, of cooking meal after meal of porridge and eggs, and often not enough of those.

"Dad and John send their love.

"We think of you every day. Your loving mother."

Only when he was back at his place, unpacking his sack of groceries – another week's supply of rolled oats and eggs and tobacco – did he remember the second letter, the one from the Board of Missions.

"Dear Reverend McGuinness,

"This is to inform you that a change of assignment for your mission field service has become necessary.

"The church of St. Andrew's in Cranbrook, B. C. having fallen vacant due to the sudden death of the incumbent, you are to be transferred there, as soon as the arrangements can be made.

"Whilst it is not our policy to make changes of this sort, we feel that in this particular case, a move is imperative. St. Andrews has a congregation of about sixty families, while you are ministering to only thirty-two families where you are now placed.

"Services in your present charge will be taken by Mr. Lamb, a lay preacher from Yorkton. He will be in touch with you shortly."

Gordon glanced quickly through the rest of the letter, relief and joy pulsing through him. He was to leave, to leave this joyless place.

He would not have to spend a winter here watching the brown dust change to bitter white snow. He would no longer have to try to offer hope where there was no hope. The Lord had blessed him, unworthy as he was.

But why should he be spared? Was it not his duty to stay and suffer with the cold and hungry here? Or would that be pride? Who was he to think he could do a better job of ministering to these people than Mr. Lamb of Yorkton? And no doubt Mr. Lamb was in need of the pitiful stipend the Mission would pay him. Best do as he was bid.

Where was this Cranbrook place anyway?

Cranbrook was in the Kootenay mountains of British Columbia. Though it was the first of October when he arrived and snow covered the peaks round about, the town seemed marvellously green, as beautiful as the Promised Land. Truly, the Lord had delivered him. Ah, the sermons he could preach here of God's goodness!

He walked the first Sunday to the church along streets of shingle houses and tidy lawns and gardens bright with late blooming zinnias and geraniums. All this week he had savoured the luxury of living in a real room with plastered walls and wooden floors and curtains on the window and a real bed. He had enjoyed eating good meals cooked and served to him by a smiling landlady. He had delighted in seeing smiling people in the streets.

This morning the town sparkled in the clear mountain air. No dust, Lord, no dust. People on their way to the four different churches of the town greeted him. They looked content, even prosperous, not like the grim-faced people of Bell's Corners and Wyndham.

Of course he knew there was poverty here too, as there was all through the country. Many would have little more to put in the collection plate than the folks on the prairie. But at least they had enough to eat. They had harvested the fruits of their gardens and orchards. Why had the Lord not done as much for the farmers of Saskatchewan?

He had had no final inspiring message to leave with his congregations there.

> God be with you 'til we meet again,
> Till we me -ee-eet
> Till we me-eet
> Till we meet at Jesus' feet.

When they sang the parting hymn at his last service, the tears had come to his eyes, but not to theirs. He was just one more loss to them, and not a very significant one.

He preached his first sermon to the Presbyterians of Cranbrook and they listened with attention. Then he stood at the door and shook hands with the congregation as they left and many said his sermon was good. He was pleased.

After the evening service there was a reception with tea and cakes in the church basement and a big crowd showed up, even more than had been at the morning service, which was a good sign. People shook his hand and bid him welcome and he tried to remember their names and wondered if he could dare to light up a cigarette.

"Hello. I'm Betty Ferguson," a young woman said. "You've met my father; he's clerk of session."

"How do you do, Miss Ferguson. I'm pleased to meet you."

"And this is my friend Olwen Evans," Betty said.

"Olwen," he said. "What a beautiful name! Welsh, is it?"

For some reason that set the two young women laughing. Reverend McGuinness realized his mistake immediately. He should have said, "How do you do, Miss Evans."

Miss Evans rescued him from embarrassment. "It's because it's the first time anyone's ever said something nice about my name."

"And you pronounced it right first time," Betty said. "Took the rest of us ages."

Reverend McGuinness looked at the laughing girl called Olwen Evans. She was tall and slim, and her face was kind. He felt there was a great deal more he'd like to be the first to tell her. He'd like to make her laugh again, too. She had such a joyful laugh. All those months in Saskatchewan, he'd hardly heard any laughter.

Betty leaned closer to him. "I have to warn you, Olwen is not of the elect. She's an Anglican. You must try to convert her."

Reverend McGuinness smiled and, with a boldness he would never have thought himself capable of, said, "In that case, may I call on you later this week, Olwen Evans?"

"Yes," she said. "Yes, that would be very nice."

Chapter 15

$\mathcal{W}$e Have Done Very Well

I'd been working at the bank in Cranbrook for three years and liking it. Although I'd had two pay cuts instead of raises, that was nothing to complain of in these hard times. I had to consider myself fortunate to have a steady job and regular pay cheques, however small, when so many people had no jobs and no pay.

I was fortunate too in that I liked my work and I liked Cranbrook. It was a bigger town than Creston, and there was more going on. I had friends here now: Betty Ferguson and her fiancé, Jim; Ruby Somers, the daughter of the family where I boarded; her friend Frank; and Gordon, the young minister Betty had introduced me to recently. He and I had been going about together since we met and we'd been having a good time, or as good a time as a Presbyterian preacher was allowed to have. We went for walks, to the movies, to the occasional play or lecture when something came to town. I'd taken to attending evening services at his church, not so much out of piety as for the opportunity to gaze at him without shame for the full thirty minutes of his sermon. Some evenings we sat in the Somers's front room and read aloud to one another, or I did some of my recitations from Robert Service or from *Cautionary Tales for Young Children*. Gordon preferred Shakespeare and Browning to my favourites and I began to see that it was perhaps time for me to enlarge the scope and seriousness of my literary interests. In the secrecy of the Somers's kitchen, we occasionally played euchre with Ruby and her family, but we had to be careful that word didn't get out about that, as some of Gordon's parishioners did not approve of card playing.

We did not go dancing. Gordon said his church disapproved. I suspected this disapproval had as much to do with Gordon's disinclination as with church doctrine, but I didn't argue the point. I wasn't as keen on dancing as Betty and Jim were. They went to just about every dance going in Cranbrook and vicinity. They knew all the latest steps: the Black Bottom, the Turkey Trot, the Fleahop, jitterbugging, all of the crazes.

Betty was an energetic young woman who liked to keep on the go and have a good time, and she liked everyone around her to be having fun as well. She scolded Gordon for his refusal to dance and, when that had no effect, she started in on me. She chose a day when business was slow at the bank. She and I sat idle at our side-by-side desks, talking in low voices, with a stack of papers at hand to turn to should the manager walk in. "I don't know whether I did the right thing in introducing you to that preacher," she began. "I realize we can't expect Gordon to frequent the jazz bars, and frankly I can't see him doing a Charleston, but I don't know why he has to be so stuffy about good clean ballroom dancing. The Gyro's dances are very respectable; it's all fox trots and waltzes. Lots of Presbyterians go. Me, for example. It seems to me Gord could step out on a dance floor once in a while without endangering his immortal soul or shocking the elders to death. Myself, I wouldn't give ten minutes of my time to a man who couldn't dance."

"We can only be thankful that Gordon at least has nothing against movies or card playing, like the Baptists," I reminded her. Out of the corner of my eye I saw the assistant manager heading our way, reached for a form letter and put an end to our conversation.

I was much more concerned about our idle afternoons at the bank than I was about the ethics of dancing. If I lost my job, there'd be no more dancing for me at the Gyro's or anywhere else. The manager had been kind enough to explain to me that the pay reductions I'd had were no reflection on my work, only an unfortunate but necessary step in view of the business slowdown, but I worried that if business slowed down any more, the next unfortunate but necessary step might be my dismissal. It had happened to plenty of others.

Betty, who lived at home with her wealthy family, was not so much affected by the pay cuts. She was able to spend her whole salary on herself. She bought beautiful clothes and recently she'd actually bought a car. Like old Gramps Little in Creston with his Pioneer motorcar, Betty was convinced that the automobile was a necessity of modern life. Everyone should have a car and know how to drive it. She wanted me to try it out.

I'd never be able to manage it, I told her. I was a person who was unable to learn to ride a two-wheeled bicycle and could therefore not even hope to be able to control a four-wheeled vehicle. And anyway, I could never afford to buy a car, so what was the point of trying to drive?

"Because you'll have a car, sooner or later. You'll have to. And then what are you going to do? I can't see you as Lady Dum-Dum sitting in the back seat giving orders to your chauffeur. Do give it a try. It's not at all like riding a bike. It's easy. You'll pick it up in no time."

I knew that there were some people who just instinctively knew how to drive. My brother Dave was one of those. At his work one day the manager asked him to take his car and pick up some documents in Nelson, and David, with typical Young self-confidence got in the car and drove to Nelson and back without mishap and never let on it was the first time he'd ever driven a car. You didn't need a license back then, just the confidence that you could manage. Unfortunately, I didn't have that confidence. Full of doubts and trepidation, I got behind the wheel of Betty's Buick and, at her urging, set the vehicle in motion. I was appalled but not really surprised when I immediately crashed into a nearby fence post.

Betty took the mishap calmly. "This is not a problem; it's just a small dent." She took over the wheel, backed the car out of the fence and drove back into the Somers's laneway where we got out and examined the fender.

Mr. Somers came out of the house to offer his opinion and began the teasing about my driving that I feared might go on for the rest of my life. He also fetched a mallet and banged out some of the crumpling. It did look better after that, but I wanted to have it fixed properly for Betty. Even a small dent, I knew, could cost a lot of money to repair. I hoped I would have enough to cover the cost.

Betty ran her hand along the dent. "Actually," she said, "I kind of like it. It gives the old girl character. We'll leave it as it is." I thought at first she was saying that out of generosity to spare me the expense of the repair. But eventually I came to believe she really did become fond of that dent, the way one can come to love the imperfections in favourite things: the ink stains on a desk, the broken spine of an often-read book, the hollowed place on an old kitchen table worn down from years of use. And Jim said it was a good warning to other drivers to give Betty a wide berth on the road.

But for weeks I flushed with shame every time I looked at Betty's car, and it was twenty years before I dared to get behind a steering wheel again. I did it then only because, just as Betty had predicted, I did need to drive. Eventually I even managed to acquire a driver's license. But I never did like driving.

Betty loved that dented car of hers. She drove it with panache. She tore along the mostly unpaved and precipitous mountain roads around Cranbrook at speeds I found alarming, taking the hairpin curves with verve and often on two wheels. She drove us on wonderful excursions to Moyie Lake or St. Mary's Falls and the surrounding countryside. She drove to go shopping, to go to the movies; she even drove to work sometimes, though it was only a distance of less than a mile.

"I don't know how we ever managed before I got my old flivver," she said one Saturday afternoon when she was driving me home from downtown. She and I had just spent several hours on Baker Street looking at the shops, finishing up with a good look through Fink's department store. I was tired, and a little discouraged. Betty had bought a blouse, a silk scarf, and some very lacy, very expensive underwear. I'd bought a pair of stockings for work. So many beautiful things I'd seen, but I couldn't possibly afford them.

Betty, happily ignorant of the state of my finances, went on reminiscing about the days before she had her car. "We never went anywhere. It must have been so dull. I think we sat at the kitchen table and embroidered, didn't we? Without even a radio to listen to. I actually can't remember, can you Ollie?"

"We had sing songs," I said. "We read books. We went for walks or skated or sledded." I remembered the wonderful sled rides down Creston's Fourth Street hill and walks along the track to Aunt Charlotte and Uncle Andy's ranch and felt a wave of nostalgia for those slower, quieter times when we were satisfied with less. "We played word games, made toast over the fire, recited poetry." I remembered evenings of Robert Service poems with Uncle Bob.

"Gosh, it was awful, wasn't it?"

I wasn't at all sure that she was right.

But as the months went by, I became more involved with the faster-paced Cranbrook life and its excitements, and with my circle of friends there. I hardly ever went home to Creston on the weekends now. Of course it was always good to see Mum and the youngsters and Gran and Uncle Bob, but my brother, Dave, most of my old friends, and some of the Talbot kids had left Creston to find jobs in bigger places. There really was not much going on in Creston.

It was a backward, old-fashioned place, small enough that everyone knew what you were up to. Ladies still had to wear hats and gloves to walk uptown to the Mercantile or the post office, or they risked censure. Mum and Gran were appalled beyond reason the day I tried to go out with a kerchief tied over my head instead of a real hat. They felt it was a disgrace to the family, especially to the family of a respected milliner.

Ladies had to wear correct hats and gloves, and ladies did not smoke, at least not in public, and certainly not at Rosebank. I'd got into the habit of smoking with Gordon, and Mum, I discovered, used to enjoy the odd cigarette back in her Ish Kibbidle Club days. So after the kids were in bed and the streets quiet, she and I would sit out on the back steps and light up, risking discovery by night-prying eyes. That was about the only high living that went on during my Creston visits.

In Creston it was always necessary to be proper, or at least to give the appearance of being proper, even if everyone in town knew the real improper truth. Everyone knew, for instance, that Gramps was on a bender when he "was not himself" as Gran put it. Another pretence that irritated me was that no one was ever to mention the break-up of Mum's second marriage. Mum continued to be known as Mrs. Hooper and she acted as though the separation were a necessary, but temporary, absence, even though we hadn't seen hide nor hair of Rodney for years.

To me, it didn't matter if the neighbours knew that Gramps sometimes got drunk, that Rodney was never coming back, or that Mum and I were smoking on the back porch, but some of the hushing up that went on verged on the crime of aiding and abetting, in my view. There was a rancher who was known for mounting the ladders behind female pickers and thus getting into a good position to grope at them. Everybody knew this, but instead of confronting him, Creston women warned each other to keep an eye out for him and his lecherous habits. "It would be such a shame for his family if accusations were made publically," was the reason for the silence. The rancher's position as a respectable member of the community and an elder in his church was never challenged, and he went on groping any unwary female picker in his orchard.

Crestoners wanted no shame, no public embarrassment. We pretended that we were all model citizens in model families. We ignored any unseemly reality.

It should not therefore have come to me as a surprise that when Aunt Boo and Uncle Clary announced that they were coming to Creston for a visit, Mum and Gran pretended to be delighted, because a person is supposed to be delighted when family members come for a visit, especially when they take the trouble to travel halfway around the world to do so.

The news came on a Friday afternoon in July on a weekend that I happened to be spending in Creston for a change. Mum met me at the station in a state of high excitement, bursting with the good news. On the way down to Gran's to talk over the impending visit and make appropriate plans, we stopped at the bakery to pick up one of the Battenberg cakes Gran was partial to.

"Fancy them coming all this way. Oh my! It will be good to see them again," Mum said as we turned in to Rosebank.

"Isn't this wonderful?" Gran greeted us. "It has been years since I've seen Boo. And dear Clary. Does she say anything about Percival in the letter? Will they bring him too?"

Mum fished the letter out of her handbag. "Not a word about Percy. Though it's hard to imagine Boo would be apart from her dear boy for a whole month." She grinned. "She'll have to write him every day, or even telegraph, I expect."

"They're staying for a whole month!" I exclaimed.

"Yes, they'll be here for August. Won't it be lovely?" Mum set out cups and saucers on the kitchen table. "Boo always writes such good letters, but letters are never the same as a good face-to-face chin wag, especially with Boo. She can be so funny." Mum turned to Gran. "Remember the marvellous imitations she used to do? The suffragette and Lloyd George? With both voices? She could have gone on stage with that one it was so good. And the time she fell off the omnibus into the mud, and blamed the driver for it and had him down on his knees apologizing to her, and all the passengers applauded?"

"And the time she sent her twelve-year-old nephew away across the ocean?" I interrupted the reminiscences.

"Yes. I can't think why she did that. Inexcusable, really. But it did turn out for the best. Charles has done so well for himself." Indeed Charles appeared to have suffered no damage from the adventure of his childhood. He had stayed in Creston, finished school and was now managing the drugstore in town and courting a local girl. "Charles has always been a Creston fellow through and through," Mum declared.

Gran remembered what a help Boo had been to her in the early days of her widowhood and the Hammersmith boarding house. "I don't see how I could have managed without her. I shall be so happy to see her again."

I'd had enough of this hypocrisy. In my opinion the proper answer to Boo's announcement would be a telegram saying. "Do not come. Not welcome." I slammed the lid on to the enamel tea pot and cut savage slices of the pink and white cake. "You don't like Boo and Clary. You were so angry about the way they sent Charles away."

"I can't understand why you would think that." Gran brushed aside the reminder of that incident and changed the subject. "Boo is very fond of scenery. I am sure she will be delighted with the mountain views here."

"She says she is looking forward to seeing your garden." Mum pointed to the letter on the table. "And Clary hopes they will see a grizzly bear. I must tell him not to hope for that."

I could hardly believe this. They didn't seem to be pretending. They seemed to be genuinely pleased that Boo and Clary were coming. Did they really not remember what those two were like?

Soon they were busy with plans. Boo and Clary would stay at Rosebank with Gran. They would have the larger bedroom and Gran would move into the little room off the kitchen. Mum's house was too tiny, and Boo and Clary would not enjoy having the three Hooper children hanging about.

"I'll say!" I agreed with that, remembering our visit at Boo and Clary's in North Finchley and how we children stood for hours outside on the street because we were not welcome in the house. "I think they have a nerve expecting to be put up for a whole month. I don't see how you're going to manage, Gran, I really don't. Perhaps they could board at Mrs. Winter's?"

"I hope I have houseroom for my own daughter and her husband," Gran replied. "There is plenty of space. We shall manage very well."

I thought of the cost of extra food as well. Mum and Gran were always short of the essentials and I knew they'd want to put on the dog a bit for Boo and Clary. It was characteristic of both Mum and Gran not to worry about money. They would manage somehow. The bread and the fishes would extend themselves. To me, the way they kept their households going without any steady income was as much of a miracle as the Bible story. Mum was raising her children on almost nothing and Gran brought up the Talbot children on insurance money barely enough to pay for their needs. And now both women were delighted at the idea of welcoming two demanding people into their homes for a whole month's visit. I would have to keep a sensible eye on expenses for them.

"How very fortunate that your holidays fall in August so that you will be able to enjoy the visit with us, Olwen," Gran said.

"Very fortunate indeed," I muttered. I'd been hoping to spend at least part of my two-week vacation with my Cranbrook friends. Betty had come up with the idea of an automobile trip to Banff. All four of us would go: Betty and Jim, Gordon and I. We would take tents and camp along the way at the new parks that were being set up for tourists. But I might have known that the plan would fall through in the end, I thought to myself. We really weren't vacationing kind of people, Gordon and I. He'd never been on a holiday in his life, and except for the wonderful camping trip to Clear Lake, and the trips back and forth to England, neither had I. Tourist travel was for the likes of Betty and Jim, and, apparently, Boo and Clary.

Once again I would be doomed to spend my annual holidays in Creston. I couldn't leave Mum and Gran to the mercies of their unpleasant visitors. I would be the watchdog. I wouldn't let Clary order Gran around and I wouldn't let Boo make demands and complain that her nerves were shattered. I wouldn't let them be mean to the youngsters. I would watch the spending to see that Mum and Gran didn't go to extravagant lengths to please. I would help with the cooking, I'd try to keep the kids out of the way, and perhaps I'd even get some mornings' work picking in the orchards. Some holiday!

My friends were disappointed when I returned to Cranbrook and told them that the Banff trip was off for me. That meant it was off for them too. Gordon wouldn't go without me, and Betty's parents would never allow her and Jim to go off on a trip on their own. Cranbrook people were modern in their outlook, but not as modern as that.

"Ah, well, we'll make the best of it." Betty was never unhappy for long. "Mountains look the same pretty well anywhere, I guess." Soon she was making alternate plans. "We'll go up to the lake for a day. Maybe take a spin up to the Hot Springs." I envied Betty her freedom.

"Every cloud has a silver lining." She tossed me a careless consolation. "You'll have a good time with your family."

"I doubt it. Not with Boo and Clary in residence."

"Oh gosh! They aren't the ones who shipped your little cousin from England to Canada with a label around his neck, are they?"

"The very ones."

"Oh dear. Well, I hope it won't be too awful."

"What hopes!"

So at the beginning of August I went back to Creston. I wasn't happy about spending my holiday there, but when the train pulled up to the old hip-roofed station, the sight and scent of the place stirred my heart, as it always did. I loved the tang of evergreen forests that wafted down from the mountains and the dry, hot aroma of ripening grass and grain from the flats. Each peak outlined against the sky was like an old friend to me. Betty was quite wrong in saying that mountains are pretty well the same everywhere. The Kootenay mountains of Creston were *my* mountains, different from all others and dearer to me than the equally beautiful mountains around Cranbrook or Banff.

Creston had changed in the years since I'd begun to work in Cranbrook. Thanks to a new diking project, the flats along the river below the town would no longer flood each spring. The old flood plain was now prime agricultural land. There, where once in summer, wild grasses grew lush for anyone to cut and harvest, fields of wheat were now being cultivated. Where the Siwash had once set up their summer teepees and fished the river and grazed their horses, now ploughs and harrows, mowers and binders would clatter through the spring and summer months. The Siwash had drifted away like the smoke from their cooking fires. Only the mountains remained, to east and west, solid and friendly, the beautiful bastions guarding our valley.

There were changes in town too. The depression had made most of us poor, yet still we had luxuries and conveniences we wouldn't have thought of owning twenty years ago. A new dam on the Goat River provided the town with hydroelectric power. Most homes – although not Rosebank – now had electric lights and telephones, radios or gramophones, and even indoor toilets!

Uptown Creston had modernized itself. A new grain elevator stood by the tracks ready to receive the plentiful harvests that would come from the newly reclaimed fields. A new hospital could provide care for a dozen patients. Canyon Street was paved for car traffic. The splintery wooden sidewalks had been replaced. The telephone exchange had long since outgrown Aunt Olive's front room and now had a building of its own. We had a movie theatre where you could see a double bill for fifteen cents, and afterwards you could get an ice cream soda for ten cents at the new soda fountain.

On the benchlands around the town, the orchard trees in neat rows still blossomed and bore fruit plentifully. But somehow Creston had never become the premier fruit-growing region that Alphabetical, Gramps Little, and Mallandaine had envisaged. The Okanagan Valley had won that distinction. It was to that valley that settlers had flocked in larger numbers, bringing new business and prosperity, while Creston had remained just another small town with a few solvent businesses, a population that was getting by, and hopes for the future.

211

Gran, Mum, myself and the kids stood on the station platform lined up like an honour guard waiting for the arrival of the TransCanadian. Boo and Clary stepped off the train, smiling and waving like royalty. There were hugs and kisses all around, though mine were of a restrained nature. Then we all marched down the hill to Rosebank. I made sure that Clary did a fair share of the luggage toting. I was keeping a sharp eye on him.

Boo was enchanted by the mountain scenery, just as Gran had said she would be. It was actually hard to get her into the house for tea. She seemed to want to stand at the gate, exclaiming, "Beautiful! Magnificent!" over and over again, turning this way and that to take it all in.

Inside at last she drank down a great many cups of tea. "Delicious," she said. "The train journey was wonderful – I can't tell you – the scenery! The comfort! The meals in the dining car! Wonderful! But the CPR could not produce a decent cup of tea. A terrible brew they served! And yours is so good!" she passed her empty cup back for more.

"It's the pure mountain water," Gran said as she poured.

"I told her she should have ordered coffee on the train. That's what I did," Clary said. "The coffee was fine. Americans all drink coffee, don't know a thing about tea, I told her."

I bristled to attention. Here was Clary pontificating in his old authoritative manner.

Young Liz, who had no idea that she was contradicting a virtual dictator, indignantly pointed out that the CPR was Canadian, and that this was Canada, not America that Uncle Clary was talking about. I expected Clary to answer that with a scowl and a bad-tempered "Bah!"

Instead he asked in a perfectly pleasant way, "Ah, are there differences, then? In England, you see, we say America and we mean both Canada and the U.S.A." Soon we were all discussing distinctions in language, attitudes, food, commerce, cars. Gran got to air her view that British Columbia was a special case, almost a separate country on its own. The natural barriers of the mountains, she believed, protected us from nefarious influences from outside, both American and Canadian.

I couldn't remember conversations like this ever going on during our unpleasant visit in Finchley all those years ago. I seemed to remember mostly long cold silences there and a strong desire to get the meal over with and leave the table.

We were all still sitting around the table when Cousin Charles dropped in on his way home from work. Boo and Clary greeted him like a long-lost son. No one referred to the circumstances in which they had parted all those years ago. Charles was kind enough to enquire after cousin Percival. Cousin Percival was very well, Clary said. "He would have loved to join us on this journey but his office couldn't consider giving him a month's leave. He is very well thought of at his office, Barking and Sloane, Solicitors."

"Such a pity!" Boo added. "He would have loved the scenery here. All beautiful! The forests that go on for miles and miles. And the Prairies. Miles and miles of wheat. No hedge rows or fences. Just wheat!"

"And dust," my friend Gordon might have informed her. "Thin wheat and lots of dust."

"And most magnificent of all, the mountains," Boo continued. She seemed to have taken up talking in gushing superlatives. I didn't remember that habit from earlier times either.

I kept up a careful watch for signs of the old arrogance and cold-hearted indifference to others that I did remember, but I saw none that day, nor in the days that followed.

Boo and Clary loved Creston. They declared they were very comfortable in their room at Rosebank. They made no complaint about the outdoor biffy.

They loved walking through the town and watching the trains come in. They discovered the soda fountain and its ice cream sodas, and after that they'd round up the three kids and sometimes me and Mum too every afternoon and take us out for sodas. Gran wouldn't come. She believed that ice-cold drinks caused jaundice and warned us against them.

Mornings Clary worked as a fruit picker or accompanied Uncle Bob on his walks through town and listened to the long, screeched story of the caaaaaamping trip to Cleeeeeeear Lake.

One evening Charles took the guests to a baseball game and Clary never missed an in-town game after that. He sat in the stands and called out loud encouragement like a local: "Bring him on home, boys. Bring him home." Occasionally his old authoritarianism took hold of him and he'd shout, "Not to third, you idiot!" or "Hold on to the ball, butterfingers!"

As for Boo, her admiration for the landscape was insatiable. I would sometimes come upon her standing in front of Rosebank, simply gazing at the mountains or down into the valley, muttering, "Splendid! Magnificent!" She was an artist in spirit, if not in fact, she informed us. She took rolls and rolls of film. Charles had them developed at the drugstore but when I brought the photos down to her one morning and she spread them out on Gran's table, she was disappointed. "Without colour the beauty is not apparent. Nor is there any sense of the shimmering light and shadow. Percival will never be able to see in these the beauty I've been writing to him about." She went out again to look at the real thing and gather material for the daily letter to Percy.

I took advantage of the temporary absence of the two guests to gossip about them with Mum and Gran in the kitchen. "I can't believe two people could change so much," I said. "Has age mellowed them? Or is it because they're on holiday here? They're so different."

"Boo is as she always was," Gran said quietly. "I could never understand why you formed such a poor opinion of her. Of course, you were very young when you knew her. As for Clary, he has, I believe a forceful character. That is always an asset in a man and of particular benefit to a man married to Boo, who can, at times, be a little indecisive – I could even go so far as to say irresponsible."

"Like when she sent Charles away."

"Indeed."

Mum said, "You didn't see them at their best, Olwen. Clary and Boo were going through a hard time when we were there in twenty-one. Clary had wanted to enlist in the war, you see, but the government wouldn't allow it because he was needed in his engineering work for the railways. His brother did enlist and was wounded terribly at Mons and spent years in a hospital for hopeless cases before he, blessedly, died in twenty-five. Clary used to visit him two or three times a week and he'd come home from each visit either raging or weeping, Boo told me. It wasn't easy for her either. And then she herself was in shock from Charlotte's death. We were all sad, but Boo had always been especially fond of Charlotte. I should never have left Charles in their care at that time. I thought he might cheer the household up, but of course he couldn't, poor boy, only made things worse. It's a blessing that in the end everything worked as well as it did."

"Things generally do work out for the best, I find." Gran took a dish of scalloped potatoes out of the oven, and I hurried to set the table for dinner.

On the last weekend of my two-week holiday, Dave drove up from Trail where he was now working at a bank. On the Saturday he took Clary and the youngsters up to Kootenay Lake for a day of fishing.

We womenfolk would make use of the quiet day to do down preserves from the fruit Clary had picked. We worked all morning in the stifling kitchen with a good hot jam-making fire crackling in the kitchen range. We peeled and chopped and pitted, boiled and stirred and skimmed "like the witches of Endor" as Mum said until the last sealer was filled, the fire in the range allowed to burn itself out, the canning pots washed, the table wiped down and the beautiful sealers, glowing with their fruit, set to cool on the sink shelf. Then we retired to the porch and sat on the stairs to cool ourselves.

"Dinner," I said after a time. "I'm getting peckish."

"I cannot and I will not cook another morsel today," Gran declared. "With the men and children away, there is no need to exert ourselves.

I suggest a sandwich luncheon." Another of the old-fashioned ideas that prevailed in Creston was that women didn't need to eat proper meals; it wasn't worth bothering cooking for us. Only men and children deserved three proper meals a day.

"Jam sandwiches, I suggest," Mum said, and Boo shrieked her terrible laugh and said she intended never to eat jam again.

"There's a small bit of yesterday's pot roast left, and tomatoes from the garden. That should do us nicely," Gran said. I was just heaving myself to my feet to set about fixing this bit of a scratch meal, when a familiar Buick with a dented left fender pulled up in front of the porch. The driver tooted the horn like a trumpet fanfare, and out climbed Betty, Jim and Gordon.

"Surprise! We've come to drive you back to Cranbrook!" Betty shouted while I and the other women of my family hastily pulled off our jam-spattered aprons and stepped down to meet the visitors. "Thought you might like a bit of a motor trip to finish off your holiday, since the great Banff caper was nixed.

"What a drive!" Betty bounced up the path. "Three flats! Lucky to have two stalwart men along to fix them. Such a pretty town Creston is. We've driven all around it looking for you. And here you are." Betty gave me a hug. "Grand to see you, Ollie. You're looking swell." Then she looked towards Gran, Mum and Boo lined up behind me.

What will my friends be thinking of this family? I worried. Here we are, Gran's house smelling like a jam factory, and the three of us sweating like work horses and probably smelling like them too, my hair all straggly – I was planning to wash it this afternoon – and it's dinner time and what on earth will we offer them to eat? I worried all the time I was going through the introductions. If Betty should ask to use the little girl's room and I had to lead her out to the biffy in the garden, I would die of shame. Why did they have to arrive at dinner time anyway? Had they no sense of tactful timing? Could we get away without offering them anything to eat? Cold tea, perhaps. Gran almost always had a sealer of cold tea in the cellar.

And then, for that matter, what will Mum and Gran be thinking of the ebullient Betty, wearing trousers, and with two men in tow, and talking as usual. If she lights up a cigarette Gran will faint dead away.

Whatever Gran was thinking, she was playing the gracious Duchess. "Do come in. I believe it is a little cooler in the drawing room." The "drawing room" of course was hotter and smellier than the porch. "I am so pleased to meet you. Olwen has spoken of you often. You will have luncheon with us, won't you?"

"Wouldn't say no to that. I'm famished," Jim said.

"Motoring is indeed taxing on the strength." Gran spoke as if she knew.

"'Specially when it's Betty driving," Jim said. Gordon laughed, and Betty pretended to be vexed.

I couldn't laugh. Luncheon! Trust Gran! Betty would be thinking of jellied chicken or ham, perhaps; potato salad, sherbets or ices, and we had nothing but yesterday's pot roast to offer.

After a few minutes of conversation about the journey, Mum and Boo slipped away to the kitchen. While Gran held forth on the delights of Creston, I followed. "What on earth are we going to feed them?" I asked in despair.

Mum was nonchalant. "Don't worry about the food," she said. "We'll manage."

"Leave it to us, my dear." Boo shooed me towards the door.

"But there's only that bit of cold roast we were going to finish off for sandwiches," I worried.

"Stop fretting," Mum said. "We shall do very well off a sausage," and she and Boo went off into peals of laughter. That old family joke again. I could never understand why Mum and her sisters got such a kick out of it.

It concerned an occasion in their girlhood when Mum, Boo and Charlotte were at dinner at an elderly aunt's and she served them one sausage, cut into three. When they'd finished the frugal meal, the aunt said, "There now, girls, you've done very well off your sausage. Very well indeed."

217

Whenever she served a skimpy meal, or a particularly lavish one, Mum would bring out the old punch line and I remembered how it never failed to render her and Aunt Charlotte helpless with giggles. And now Aunt Boo as well.

"Go back to your visitors," Mum gasped. "We'll do our best for you."

And of course they did. They sliced the meat thinly and surrounded it with pickles so that it didn't look so pitifully skimpy. There was plenty of bread and butter and a great platter of tomatoes and for dessert, inevitably, plum preserves.

"Delicious," Betty and Jim said.

"A feast," Gordon said.

"Thank you," Mum said. And then she couldn't resist; she had to say it. "We have done very well off a sausage." And she and Boo went off into hoots of laughter.

"It's a family joke," I explained to my mystified friends.

After lunch, Mum was clever enough to suggest that we walk over to her house so that I could finish packing my suitcase, and so we escaped to a house that had a bathroom at least, not to mention a grand piano.

If we were to drive all the way to Cranbrook, it was time to be off. Mum had conjured up a picnic supper and we loaded it into the car along with jars of preserves for Betty and the Somers. We stopped in at Rosebank to say good-bye. My farewell to Boo was much warmer than my welcome had been. "And do give my love to Clary and tell him I'm sorry I missed saying good-bye to him myself." I wasn't at all worried about the rest of their visit. They were perfect guests. Everything was working out well, just as Mum and Gran said it would. And then we four piled into the car and we were off, with Betty honking farewell, and Gran, Mum and Aunt Boo waving good-bye.

Gordon leaned toward me and took my hand. "You're not sore at us for crashing in on you and your family, I hope. It was my idea actually."

"Not that he had any trouble persuading us," Jim added. "Betty's always up for a drive."

"Why would Olly mind us coming to drive her back to Cranbrook in speed and comfort and style?" Betty asked. "This is better than a dirty old train any day of the week, I'd say."

"We meant it as a consolation prize for having to miss the Banff trip, and for having to spend your whole holiday with your family," Jim said, "though actually I thought your aunt with the crazy name wasn't so bad – a little too ecstatic about scenery, maybe – and your Mum and Gran are very nice."

"Boo is not so bad after all, I discovered," I said. In truth, I hadn't minded spending the holiday at home at all. I'd enjoyed it. Everything had worked out well in the end.

"But I'm awfully glad you came," I said. I was happy to be with my friends again, going back to Cranbrook and my job. I was happy Boo and Clary's visit was going well. I was happy to be sitting beside Gordon with my hand still in his.

We stopped at a clearing beside a mountain stream to eat our picnic supper. Betty and Jim went off to explore upstream. That was when Gordon proposed. And I said, "Yes."

Chapter 16

$\mathcal{L}$eaving the Empire

In Cranbrook, B.C., we had connections with the Prince of Wales. For one thing, he loved the Rockies and the Canadian West. He'd said so. And he'd bought himself a ranch, which happened to be just across the Alberta line, but still very close to us. He'd travelled on our Crow's Nest Pass Railway and admired the scenery.

We even had personal connections. My friend Ruby Somers, my landlady's daughter, had travelled all the way to Revelstoke to stand on the station platform to see the Prince when his train stopped there on its way to Vancouver, and Edward had come out and waved. "He looked straight at me, he did," Ruby claimed. "Handsome? My word! Photos don't do him justice. You have to see him for yourself."

Even more exciting than merely seeing the Prince was having the opportunity to talk to him. And there again we knew someone, or at least knew of someone, who had had that honour. It was the older brother of Ruby's friend, Frank. This brother was a waiter on the CPR and he had once served afternoon tea to the Prince of Wales on the royal train.

Everyone in Cranbrook knew the story. Frank was often called on to tell it. "My brother George was very nervous about the job, see. Course he's used to waiting on big shots, working in the dining car, you know, but royalty, well that's something special. So he was pretty darn scared. Pleased to be chosen, mind you, but nervous. They tell him he's supposed to call the Prince Your Royal Highness. 'Would you care for another cup of tea, Your Royal Highness?' he's supposed to ask.

"But when the moment comes he's so nervous he can't get it out right. 'Would you care for more tea, your Highness?' he starts, and then he sees his mistake and goes back, 'Your Yoyal,' is what he gets out this time, and then he really gets the heebie jeebies.

"The Prince smiles and, nice as you please, he says, 'It's all right. Just call me sir. And yes, I'd like another cup of that delicious tea.'

"'Yes, sir,' George says, and pours the tea. Doesn't spill a drop. That he can do right.

"He wasn't stuck up at all, George says. Just a swell fellow."

Whenever Betty and I heard the story, we would sing,

"I danced with a man,who danced with a girl,

Who danced with the Prince of Wales," just to tease Ruby. She was so stuck on the royal family that I sometimes suspected her attachment to Frank was based largely on his brother's having spoken to the Prince.

Ruby carried it to an extreme, but the fact was that most of us in the Dominions adored our royalty, and especially the Prince of Wales. Probably just about every community in the Empire treasured its own particular anecdote or connection to the popular Prince. He had toured Canada and the U.S. in 1919, and in the next years he visited Australia and New Zealand and India. In 1927 he was back in Canada for the Diamond Jubilee of our Dominion. His travels were recorded in detail by the press, and we read about them with avid interest. Everywhere he went, he had a magic gift for endearing himself to his people. He was our golden Prince, and when in January, 1936 he succeeded to the throne, we knew he would be a glorious king. Edward VIII must have been the most popular British monarch ever.

Until the autumn of 1936, that is.

That was when the rumours started.

Our King had apparently become close friends with a Mrs. Wallis Warfield Simpson, a commoner, an American, and a divorcee. And if the American papers had it right, he intended to marry her!

Loyal subjects were shocked. Bad enough that she was not a princess, not even a duke's daughter, bad enough that she was not British, not even a British subject, bad enough that she was divorced once already, but worst of all, she was still married to Mr. Simpson. The King could therefore not possibly marry her.

Yes, the pictures in the magazines were evidence that the King was going around with her. That seemed to be clear enough, and no doubt they were good friends. But could they really be intending to marry?

At home in Creston at Thanksgiving, I discussed the question with Mum and Gran.

Gran scoffed at the very idea of our King's marrying Mrs. Simpson. "It's gossip from those American magazines everyone is reading," she said. "Edward would never demean himself to marry that woman."

Mention had been made of something called a morganatic marriage. We looked up the meaning of that and didn't think much of it. Mum said she'd read of it in connection with some penny-ha'penny European monarchs, but it would not apply to the British royal family.

Abdication was another solution being offered, but that course of action would be far worse. Look what happened to the Czar of Russia after he abdicated! Such things could never happen, not in Britain, not to our King.

"Stuff and nonsense is all it is," Gran claimed. "Those magazines will print anything to create a sensation."

"He caaaahn't be thinking of marrying that woman," Mum said. "Queen Mary would never allow it."

Back in Cranbrook, as the autumn progressed, there was more difference of opinion on the subject.

My landlady, Mrs. Somers, shared my view. "Even if he is in love with her, he'll see his duty clear, and give her up for the sake of the Empire."

My friends Betty Ferguson and her fiancé, Jim, professed to be shocked by such hardness of heart. "I don't see why he should give her up," Betty said. "Not if they're in love. Why should they have to forfeit their chance of happiness just because of some stuffy old Victorian prejudice against divorcees?"

Ruby and Frank, for whom the King could do no wrong, didn't know what to think.

And my fiancé, Gordon, didn't care. He groaned in boredom and tried to change the subject whenever I or one of the others got going on the subject of the King's marriage. Everyone else in Cranbrook, in Canada, in the whole of the British Empire was concerned. We talked about it endlessly, but not Gordon.

"I don't give a darn whether the nincompoop marries her or not," he said in irritation one evening as we walked up town to meet our friends at the Star Theatre.

"You can't call the King a nincompoop," I hissed, and looked around to see if any one might have overheard. Luckily, Baker Street was almost deserted as the autumn evenings were drawing in, and the air was cold. "Mrs. McBride would have you thrown out of church for a remark like that."

Gordon leaned close to whisper in my ear, "Yes, but I trust you not to tell her." Then he continued in normal tones, "I wish the man would hurry up and decide one way or another so that the country can get back to caring about what really matters. We should be concerning ourselves with unemployment, the drought on the prairies, fascism – not fretting about the love life of two very silly people."

"He's not silly; maybe she is." We closed the argument there, seeing Betty and Jim, Ruby and Frank waiting for us in front of the cashier's box at the Star.

Anyway, Gordon and I had had the argument before, and there was no making a monarchist out of him, I feared. He didn't seem to see the point of it. "Might be all right for the British," he would concede, "but not for us in Canada." He would stand for "God Save the King" in deference to society's view, but he would never sing the words. "It's a disgrace of a national anthem," he claimed. "It doesn't say a word about our nation. It's all about the English king and I can't, in all conscience, pray for preferential treatment for him."

Gordon was not to be spared further discussion of the great controversy that evening, for the News of the World showed Edward and Mrs. Simpson disembarking from the yacht *Nahlin* some place on the Mediterranean.

This was much more interesting than the main feature, and we set to discussing it as soon as we'd all squeezed into a booth at the Zenith Cafe and asked Fran to bring us coffee and pie.

"Oh pshaw. Here we go again," Gordon sighed.

"Eat up your pie and pay no attention to us." Betty slid a plate across the table to Gordon.

"Now then, girls, what do you think they were up to on that big fancy white yacht?" She raised her eyebrows suggestively.

"They looked more like movie stars than royalty, didn't they?" I mused.

"What does he see in her anyways?" Ruby wanted to know. "She's way too skinny to be attractive."

"Definitely. And did you notice the shoes he was wearing?" I asked

"Yeah. Like ballet shoes," Ruby said.

"Not at all the kind of shoes a king should wear," I agreed.

"Exactly what kind of shoes should a king wear?" Betty asked indignantly. "Army boots? On a yacht?"

"And his shirt open," Ruby continued. "I tell you, Queen Mary sees that newsreel, she'll be mad as blazes. It's that Mrs. Simpson that's to blame. You never saw him like that before he met up with her. When I seen him the once at Revelstoke? He was wearing a proper suit then."

"He likes informality," Betty argued. "He's not stuffy like old King George was, eh? Do you know, they say King George wore his army uniform to bed, including the boots and all his medals."

I ignored Betty's facetiousness. "Informal is fine. But going around in public with an open shirt is taking it too far."

"I blame Mrs. Simpson, I do," Ruby said. "She has no idea of what's fitting for royalty and what isn't."

"Lord, I wish he'd send that floozie packing," Frank agreed. "And the sooner the better."

"He will," I said. "Don't worry. He will, and any time soon."

"Don't be so sure. Two bits says he'll marry her." Betty held up a quarter.

"Never," Ruby and I chorused.

"No gambling, if you please," Gordon said in his preacher's voice. But he couldn't get us off the subject.

"A divorced American Queen will do us good," Betty said, being provocative. "She'll shake up the Empire a bit. Maybe it will be one of those – what do you call them? – marriages. Sounds like a kind of horse?" she searched for the word she wanted.

"Morganatic?" I supplied.

"Yeah. Maybe it will be one of those. But they'll marry for sure. Love will find a way."

"No," I insisted. "He'll do the right thing. He'll renounce her."

But he didn't.

He abdicated.

We read it in the paper, but we still couldn't quite believe it. What was this Instrument he was supposed to have signed?

"I, Edward the Eighth, of Great Britain, Ireland and the British Dominions beyond the Seas, King, Emperor of India, do hereby declare My irrevocable determination to renounce the Throne for Myself and for My descendants."

The news broke on December tenth. The King would broadcast a message to his people the next day, they said. We were on tenterhooks, waiting. At the bank, on the streets downtown, in the shops, everyone wondered what the King would say. Was it true? Had he really, truly abdicated?

At Mrs. Somers's boarding house, we gathered round the radio in the kitchen, anxious not to miss a word.

"At long last I am able to say a few words of my own," the King began.

My heart leapt. He was going to tell us it was all a hideous mistake. It had come about because those news reporters didn't know what they were talking about.

But he said it was true. He'd abdicated. He said he'd made the decision himself.

Bitter and angry disappointment surged through me.

He talked about duty. "...you must believe me when I tell you that I have found it impossible to carry on the heavy duties and responsibilities and to discharge my duties as King as I would wish to do without the help and support of the woman I love."

Duty was a hollow word coming from him, I thought. All my life I'd heard of duty to King and Country and Empire. Men had left their loves, their families, their jobs, and gone to die for King and Country and Empire. My father. Dorothy Bacon's Bill. Young Archie Murdoch. Thousands and thousands of others. They gave their lives because of duty. And their families bore the pain of their sacrifice proudly. And this man, our King, wouldn't even give up marriage to a loose-living woman for us and for his Empire?

The shock and disillusionment were terrible.

In his closing words our ex-king tried to rally us to the old passion. "And now we have a new King. I wish him, and you, his people, happiness and prosperity with all my heart. God bless you all. God save the King!"

Ruby burst into tears. "How could he?" she sobbed.

"I'm ashamed of him," Mrs. Somers said when she could speak. "He's shirked his duty, the scrimshanker."

"Oh don't say that!" Ruby wailed. "He spoke so good. I guess Mrs. Simpson put him up to it. Oh what will we do now?"

I tried to imagine what Mum and Gran would have to say about the news. Nothing, I guessed. Would Gran, who mistrusted radios and wouldn't have one in her house, have gone to Mum's to listen to the broadcast? Even if they had listened together, they'd be too ashamed to discuss it, both of them. In the best tradition of the British army, they'd close ranks and ignore the fallen. George VI had stepped into the King's place. Edward VIII was to be obliterated from our minds. The Empire would march on. Ours not to reason why.

"We have passed through the most anxious and astounding day in the history of our empire," the newspaper reported the next day. "Nothing will assuage the universal disappointment that the King was unable to respond to the entreaties not only of Mr. Baldwin (the British Prime Minister), but of all his subjects."

Betty was indignant. "I think it's a shame that the papers aren't sticking up for him. They used to print such nice things about him. Now all they can do is find fault. It's a disgrace that he was forced to abdicate for love. And now he's being hounded out of his own country like a thief in the night. It's just horrid. The poor dear man. I feel so sorry for him."

"So do I. So do we all," I agreed. "But he should never have let himself get into the situation in the first place."

"It's his family that created the situation," was Jim's opinion. "Queen Mary, she's made of solid steel. She wouldn't bend one inch to accommodate anyone."

"It's the Simpson woman," Ruby said. "She's the one to blame."

"He would have been such a good king, if only they'd let him," Betty said.

"Well, you've got another king now. The institution of monarchy will apparently survive." Gordon really couldn't understand what all the fuss was about.

"But it's not the same," we said.

"Do you know what I read in a magazine a while ago?" Ruby asked us. "I think it was *The Post*, but I'm not sure. I didn't say nothing at the time 'cause I didn't believe it, but now I do. It said Edward claims he's five foot seven, but really he's only five four."

"A short little man," I said. "Huh. Maybe that's why he couldn't find a princess to marry. They all towered half a head or more over him, and being a King and Emperor himself he wouldn't tolerate that."

"Funny, he didn't look so short that time I seen him at Revelstoke. I always thought he was a tall man. Tall and handsome," Ruby said.

"Well, he still is handsome," Betty said. "Don't get nasty about the poor guy now. I hope he and Mrs. Simpson will be very happy together."

"They don't deserve to be," Ruby sniffed.

Whatever our reactions, the abdication came as a profound shock to all of us. Whether we felt his act was due to an appalling dereliction of duty, or to a hard-hearted imposition of an outdated code of morality upon a good man and woman, it was an act we had believed could never happen. Yet it did, and because of it, our world changed. As we listened to the fateful words on the radio we could almost feel ourselves slipping forward into a new era.

So many changes! Twenty some years ago, when I had come to British Columbia as a girl, there had been no radios. Now every home had one, and our King could speak to us in our own kitchens.

Back in 1913 Gramps Little's automobile was such a novelty we'd all run out to the street to stare in wonder as it passed. Now the roads were full of cars and even I might learn to drive one someday, but not yet. Airplanes we had thought were strange machines of war, and now the rich rode in them to reach destinations faster than a train could take them, and even ordinary folks could send a letter by airmail across the country or even across the sea.

Everything was changing and no one knew any longer what was right and what was wrong.

Not so long ago Bennett had said he'd get rid of unemployment or perish in the attempt. As soon as he became Prime Minister he said unemployment was not a problem. He said all the country needed was a sound dollar. He said no one needed relief. Poverty, he said, was the greatest asset a young person could have in life.

But through the years of the depression we'd seen many hard-working, honest men, who surely deserved to prosper, lose their jobs. They and their families lived in poverty, while dishonest boot-leggers had made fortunes selling booze to Americans – respectable Americans, too – who were openly breaking the law of their country.

Everything was changing.

In 1935, with an election coming up, Bennett had changed his tune and said the country needed reform and relief programs to get people on their feet again. He lost the election anyway, and we got our old prime minister, Mackenzie King, back, and he said we couldn't afford the relief programs so they were gradually dropped.

Back during the Great War they'd said this was the war that would end all wars. Then they decided the world needed a League of Nations to keep the peace. Now they were saying the League of Nations was no use at all and there was war in Abyssinia and in Spain.

Everything was changing. Our prime minister had lied to us, and our King had betrayed us. Who could you trust?

I'd decided to put my trust in Gordon and in his simple pioneer values. In the spring he and I married and moved east and began our new life together.

I've never regretted the choice I made and my life with Gordon. But still I have only to think of the day of the abdication, and a wave of sorrow comes over me as I remember how Ruby and I sat until late that night in the kitchen and drank tea and cried.

I cried then, not just for a weak-willed king, but for lost certain-ties. I cried for my father's death, and all the deaths and suffering of the war in which he died and the wars that would come. I cried because I was leaving my family, my friends, my beautiful mountains and I knew that even if I came back, they would never be the same. I cried because I was leaving my working girl's independence to start a new life with a man who set no store by kings, a man who believed in duty, yes, but duty to God, to family, to the work one had chosen or the land one tilled. A man who had no truck with an Empire across the sea, or with fine houses and fancy hats, titles, and proper accents and grand pianos. I cried because the King was leaving his Empire, and now, for better or worse, I was leaving mine.

Chapter 17

*T*he Hero on the Wall

I didn't go back to Creston for many years. There was never the opportunity or the money for the trip. In 1944 Mum came to visit me back east, bringing Rodney, the youngest, with her. They stayed all winter. I was beginning to wonder if this was going to turn into a visit like ours to Creston that had started in 1912 and went on for years. But in the spring, the thought of apple blossoms and green mountains drew Mum and Rodney back to the Kootenays. A part of me would have liked to go with them, but my life was in Ontario now with my husband and children.

It wasn't until the summer of 1952 that I finally had a whole month free of responsibilities and money enough on hand to undertake a visit to my old home town.

You don't realize that your home country has its own unique scent until you come back to it after a long absence, and there it is, enveloping you in its old familiar breath. Creston's breath was the smell of pure mountain air and woods and cultivated fields, cold rivers and fresh lumber and ripening fruit, and it hummed faintly with the drone of bees at work in the orchards. It flooded me with the physical sense of home the moment I stepped off the train. In my years away I had come to love the Ontario countryside, its small towns of red brick houses with peaked roofs, its untidily fenced fields of green pasture and grain, the weathered cedar barns, the sombre swamplands and the bright autumn woods. They were beautiful. But this was home. I stood on the station platform and breathed it in. I felt like a girl again.

And then there they were, hurrying along the platform to meet me, Mum in a pale grey dress with matching jacket and a stylish hat in darker grey straw with a purple band, Gran in magenta, dazzling with several glittering brooches and a broad-brimmed hat in electric blue. But she was leaning on a cane. It came to me in a sad rush that she and Mum were old, and I was no longer a girl either. But that didn't matter now; I was home.

We went straight to Mum's new place and got the tea going and set to talking. We talked through dinner and supper and all through the evening. I'd been too long away from talking. Gordon's family, taciturn Scotch Presbyterians, would sit together through a Saturday evening in almost total silence and consider at the end that they'd had a very good visit. Here we were talkers: we talked of the old times and new changes in Creston. I told them all about my Ontario family, even though they knew all the news from my letters, and they told me all the news of my Creston family, even though they'd already told me in the stream of letters that had flowed between us over the years.

My brother David and the three younger children, most of the Talbots and my old school friends had all gone to Vancouver to find work. It was what seemed to happen in small towns.

Mum, who had always liked change, had taken to spending the winter in Vancouver and returning to Creston for the summer. Gran had had to give up her beloved Rosebank. She couldn't manage the wood stove and the garden and the walk up to town any longer. She'd taken up residence in Mrs. Bolton's boarding house for elderly ladies, which she said was quite satisfactory. She was doing very well there, though of course she missed her roses.

And she missed Uncle Bob. He too had become frail with age and it was thought best that he should live in a home for the handicapped. As none was available in Creston, he'd been taken off to Vancouver, acquiescent, as always, to the arrangements made by others for his welfare. "But I shall never forget the sadness in his look as he called out his long 'Goooood byeeeee! God bleeeeesss!' when we saw him onto the train." Gran shook her head and took another sip of tea. "Poor Bob. He died among strangers in Vancouver a few months later."

Gramps Little too was dead, and Colonel Mallandaine, and Alphabetical. Gran was one of the few pioneers left.

We talked all that month long, Mum and Gran and I. We talked of family and gardening and orchards and family and cookery and fashions and family and books and music, and family, family, family, past and present.

Yet in all those family stories, there was one conspicuous silence. I heard again the stories of Grandfather Young and his terrible temper, of eccentric Uncle Walter and his barefoot daughters named after the Greek muses, the sad story of Uncle Bob's brother, blind from birth, like Bob, but sent to languish in an institution, while Bob was educated at the Brantford School for the Blind. I heard about Uncle Roland who had invented new kinds of bombs in the Great War. There were even one or two stories about my father's family: the wicked Uncle Will, and the opera singer, and the connection with the famous poet, Hedd Wynn. But there were never any stories of my father himself. I couldn't remember Mum talking to us about him, ever. There must have been letters from him, but she didn't share them with the family. I remembered helping Mum pack up parcels for the Creston soldiers during the war, but I didn't remember our packing any parcels for my father.

The only time I'd heard from him myself was during the war, at Christmas 1917. I got a Christmas card from him then, a regimental card with a picture of the Welch Fusiliers in furious combat. "Merry Christmas" was the printed message. "*Nadolig llawen*." Underneath he'd written, "Daddy," nothing else.

I never heard from him again. I knew almost nothing about him.

I was five when I saw him for the last time, and had only the vaguest remembrance of him; the scenes I recalled seemed more like memories of memories. I remembered a man in a scratchy black jacket holding me on his knee and singing. I think that was my father. But I'm not sure. Mostly it's the black jacket I remember and the smell of tobacco.

A little clearer is a memory of entering a dark office. My father and I are hand-in-hand, laughing with the pleasure of anticipating a joke we are about to play. A man stands at a high counter, dipping a straight pen into a bottle of ink, and asks, "Name of child?"

"Eifion," my father says and spells it for the clerk, while smiling down at me, his fellow conspirator. We are registering the birth of my brother David as Eifion Evans, so that he will have a real Welsh name, like mine.

My mother was not amused when she heard what we had done. She had decided on the name David, which was quite Welsh enough. She, for one, would call the boy David whatever name was on his birth certificate.

Any other memories of my father faded as completely as our laughter that day of our Welsh joke.

I had two photographs of my father, both given to us by his family during our brief, unhappy visit to them after the war. One is of a woman in black, seated, holding, stiffly, an infant in her arms. The woman is my grandmother, Mary Evans. We aren't sure that the infant actually is my father, Thomas Richard, her first child, but most probably it is. Mary looks thin, tired, worn out. Her large dark eyes appear to be on the verge of tears. If that is indeed my father in her arms, then she, poor woman, is only at the beginning of her weary years of travail. She was to bear nine living children and die at the age of thirty-one, giving birth to the still-born tenth child.

The other photograph was taken on the day of her funeral. It shows grandfather Hugh Evans surrounded by his nine surviving children, all of them dressed in their best funeral black. The death, the funeral service and its poetic reminders of the transience of life must have urged upon my grandfather the desirability of recording the image of the family that remained. Besides, when else would all the children be so clean, dressed up and presentable?

My father, the eldest, stands in the back row. Like the other children he looks solemn and frightened either by the photography studio or by the death that has torn apart their world. At the same time, he appears eager. He leans forward, staring directly at the camera. He seems to be looking towards the unknown future, anxious to get started in a world of his own making. While the other boys wear flat Eton collars, he is dressed in a man's suit and collar. A watch chain stretches importantly across his narrow waistcoat. He is already a working man.

After that photo was taken, the family dispersed. The younger children were sent to different relatives in Wales, America, and Australia. My father went back to London, where he had found employment as a junior clerk in the customs office.

There he worked and studied with energy and ambition. After his work days at the customs office, he took evening classes and wrote poetry.

As his circumstances improved, he moved into the respectable boarding house in Hammersmith run by Mrs. Mildred Young. And there he fell in love with her second-youngest daughter, the beautiful Sarah, my mother. In March, 1907 they married. She was nineteen; he was twenty-five. If there was a wedding photo taken, I've never seen it.

As a child growing up in Creston I had learned not to talk about my father. In later years his role in the family history was eclipsed by Mum's flamboyant second husband.

Yet he was not entirely forgotten. In all the many houses we lived in, a corner of the living room was always organized as a sort of T.R. Evans memorial. There were his two Welsh bardic chairs of oak: one solid and simple and one ornate with rampant lions and twining grape leaves, both uncomfortable and much too historic to be sat on. Behind these throne-like chairs hung the wall display, consisting of his ceremonial sword, a framed photo of him in uniform, and, also framed, the letter of condolence upon his death, signed by

George V himself. These objects made a sort of family shrine, like the sacred heart or the statue of the Virgin in a Catholic household. "He was a Welsh poet." "He died for King and Country." "He made the Supreme Sacrifice." This was what was said about my father whenever a visitor remarked on the display.

Familiar objects are seldom really seen. I never really looked at the face in the sepia photograph. I dusted those chairs for many years and never gave them a thought. They were just there, part of the landscape of home.

When I married, Mum gave me the ornate chair and the framed photograph with the King's letter and I dutifully set up the T.R. Evans corner in my living room down east.

Now, on this family visit, I was an adult with children of my own, and I wanted to learn more about my forgotten father. I determined to pry into the silence that surrounded him. Even if what I learned proved to be one of those shameful secrets that Creston people were so good at keeping quiet about, I wanted to know what it was.

There came at last an evening when Mum and I were alone. We sat on her front verandah watching the purpling of the mountains in the distance. I began my questioning. "What was he like, my father?"

"A brave man. A hero." She trotted out the old, familiar litany. "He died for King and Country."

"What about before the Great War, before he became a hero?"

"He was a poet. He won bardic chairs."

Because the chairs were so large and impressive, we'd always assumed he'd won them at the great National Eisteddfod. I'd managed some time before to find a list of the winners of the chair since the first national Eisteddfod was held in 1880, but my father's name was not on it.

I learned then that there are dozens of 'chair' eisteddfods in towns and cities of Wales every year. These are contests in which prize money and a chair are awarded for the best poem in the classical Welsh form, the *awdl*. The chair symbolizes the welcome given to ancient bards in the great halls of the Welsh kings, and is a sign of the esteem that Welsh society accords its poets.

Mum had no copy of the chair-winning poems, nor did she know where and when the chairs had been won, only that it was after we'd left. The chairs had been stored at Aunt Boo's house until we collected them after the war. Aunt Boo had removed the brass plates that had been on them, giving the date and place of the Eisteddfod because she thought "they made the chairs look as if they'd been stolen from a public hall". Now, it seemed, we'd never know where and when they'd been won, nor the works that won them.

The only evidence of my father's literary career Mum had was a copy of an English magazine called *The Bookman* with a notice of a Welsh play he'd written, and underneath a picture of him still looking young and eager and ambitious. The date on the magazine was 1913. She'd shown it to me before.

"So did you go to the play?"

"Of course not. We were in Canada then."

"Well, did you read it?"

"No. It was in Welsh."

"What was it about?"

"I don't know. But it says in the article it was well received."

And that was all I could find out about my father as a Welsh writer.

The writings having led to a dead end, I asked my mother again, "What kind of a person was my father? What was he really like?"

"I told you. He was brave. He won the DSO." A dedicated member of the Canadian Legion, my mother never, her whole life long, lost her belief in the glory of his hero's death, no matter what the historians said, or what some cowards or shirkers had written in their memoirs. Her faith in the rightness of the British cause and the infamy of the Hun never faltered

I interrupted her patriotic paean. "I mean, what was he like as a person?"

"Oh." She paused to think, and perhaps to censor her memories. "He was a great talker. Talk. Talk. Talk. I'd have his tea ready at six, and he wouldn't get home 'til the last train got in after ten o'clock. 'Where have you been all this time?' I'd ask him.

" 'Talking with some chaps,' he'd say. And he'd start in telling me all the things they'd talked about – politics and the theatre and poetry, 'til my head would be spinning, and I'd be dropping with tiredness."

"Were you happy together?"

"Of course we were. We were married."

"Yes. But." My mother's second marriage, the one all too clear in my memory, was a marriage of love, but also one of strife and monumental rages that eventually turned the love into a passionate hate.

Were there similar elements in the first, forgotten marriage, I wondered.

My mother had come to Canada to visit her mother, bringing my brother and me with her. In later years, during her second marriage, a visit to her mother was always the reason she gave for her temporary separations from her husband.

Of course, there was good reason for Mum to make a trip to Creston. She had always been close to her mother, and must have missed her in the years after Gran left England. She would want her mother to see David and me before we grew up. And from London to British Columbia was half way around the world, not a journey to be undertaken for a two- or three-week visit. But we stayed in Creston until 1920, 'til after my father was dead.

True, the war intervened and travelling was more difficult and dangerous. But people did make the journey. Gran herself went back to England for a visit in 1916.

Why, I wondered, did my mother not travel back with her? I couldn't believe she would be afraid for her own safety. Perhaps it was us, her children, she was concerned for. Perhaps my father had urged her to remain where we were safe. Or had my father talked himself out of her affection? Did she spin out her sojourn in Canada deliberately? Did he encourage her to do so?

"Can't you tell me anything more about him," I pleaded.

Mum sighed. "It was so long ago. I was very young.

"He was an ambitious man and he worked hard for us. At the office all day. Out most evenings at his university classes, or with his literary and theatre friends. I hardly saw him most days.

"He was never mean about money; I'll say that for him. I remember once when you were little, only about three, I took you to the shop for new shoes, and the silly salesman showed us a pair of beautiful patent leather boots, much too expensive for us.

"As soon as you saw them you were bound and determined you'd have them. Kicked and screamed when we tried to fit some other shoes on your feet. I had to take you home in disgrace with no new shoes at all.

"When your father heard about it, he gave me his dinner money for the week. "Buy her the pretty shoes," he told me.

"You loved those shoes. And your father went without dinners for a week so that you could have them.

"Then, when I wanted to go to Canada to see Gran, he came up with the money for our passage. I don't know what he did without to pay. We came to Canada. Then the war came. We wouldn't have seen him much even if we'd been in England. He was at camp, or out on the front. He sent us money every month." She paused. "Most months," she corrected herself.

That was all I could learn about my father from Mum.

So I tried Gran. I chose an afternoon when Mum was busy at the Canadian Legion and Gran and I were having a cup of tea in her room at Mrs. Bolton's. She sat in the rocker by the window. She liked life at Mrs. Bolton's. She enjoyed having a warm room, a comfortable rocker with a view over the garden, and endless cups of tea. I sat with my feet up on the bed. "Tell me about my father," I asked, once we were comfortable.

"What would you like to know?" she asked in turn, giving me some hope.

"Well, for one thing, was he intending to follow us to Creston? Would he have come if war hadn't broken out?"

"No." Gran was certain. "Whatever gave you the idea he would do that? He never had any intention of coming to Canada. He was very much involved with the Welsh community in London, you see. He had ambitions as far as they were concerned, writing for their magazines and such. Perhaps he had political aspirations even."

I'd got the idea from the way we used to talk about his coming that first winter. He was supposed to come in the spring. And then in the fall. And then we didn't talk about it. He was going to come and then he wasn't. No one ever explained why. Now, according to Gran, he had never intended to come at all.

"I know he was a poet and a soldier, but what else do you know about him?" I pressed Gran for more information. "What do you remember about him?"

"He was not a handsome man," Gran began, "but he had a beautiful voice and manner, so that when he spoke, one was quite charmed by him. He turned my quiet boarding house upside down with his play readings and poetry readings and musical evenings. He had us all taking parts, the girls and I and the other gentlemen. I was Lady Macbeth one evening. That was my best role, I believe. Another time your mother was a wonderful Puck in Midsummer Night's Dream. And then there were poetry evenings. Tennyson and Swinburne, we had. Sometimes Tom read his own poems. The girls and I were even learning a little Welsh. Oh, we had quite the literary salon!" Gran smiled at the memories but had no more to say about them. "It was so long ago," she excused herself. "I've forgotten most of that time. It didn't last very long. Your mother and Tom married and set up their own household."

"And then you left for Canada?"

"Yes."

"Why did you come, Gran, you and Aunt Charlotte?"

"I thought it best," Gran said, and offered no other reason. Well, she was right. If she hadn't come, then neither would Aunt Charlotte and Mum and David and I. She had led us all to Creston. It was for the best.

Some years later, in the sixties, I was able to fulfil a dream I'd been cherishing and saving for since my visit to Creston. I took a trip to England and Wales. I visited my Aunt Ruth in her little cottage in the Midlands and listened to her memories of her days as an *au pair* in our young family. She spoke of my father as if he had been some kind of musical saint. She sang me songs he'd sung, but couldn't tell me much about him as a person. "A lovely man," she called him, and that was all.

I visited the village of Llanaelhaearn where various members of the large Evans family were still living in the dark crowded cottage on the main street. They proudly showed me his name on the war memorial, but few of them could remember him. They had no photos. They knew nothing about the bardic chairs.

Finally I visited Uncle Took who still lived in his cottage in Havering near our old Hero's Home. Took was able to tell me more about my father, but only in the context of the war.

"Tommy and I were in it right from the start. Different outfits, though. Tommy wanted to be with the Welch Fusiliers. I was with the Essex regiment, start to finish.

"Say what you like about the Great War, the British infantry put up a good fight, we did. Oh yes, there were blunders – bound to be when you've got a fighting force of that magnitude to deal with – but on the whole I'd say we British were as fine a body of fighting men as the world has ever seen.

"Back then we believed in values like courage, patriotism, pride, keeping a stiff upper lip, the sort of thing everyone makes jokes about now. But we believed in those principles and we fought by them. Those were the values that kept us going. The Hun had to be crushed, and by Jove we did it. We all pitched in. No matter how filthy the conditions were, or how dangerous or distasteful the job was, we got it done. I've never seen in peacetime anything like the spirit of cameraderie, the loyalty, the adventure of that Great War.

"Oh yes, the casualties were terrible, quite terrible. That was the price we had to pay. We were all prepared to pay it.

"Tommy, for instance, could easily have wangled a safe staff posting. Or even something in Whitehall. No one would have blamed a married man with two young children for taking such a job, especially once he'd already done his stint at the Front. But Tommy wouldn't take the safe posting, not he. He stayed on the Line, in active service.

"He was a good soldier.

"I was the last of the family to see poor Tommy alive. It was in September, 1918. We were preparing for the show on the St. Quentin canal. All kinds of units were in on that; the training for it went on for weeks. My battalion was just coming in for training and Tommy's going out. The adjutant came to tell me there was some sort of snafu about our billets; another regiment was already occupying them.

"I set out for the commanding officer's billet, ready to chew his head off for the mix-up. From outside the farmhouse, I heard a familiar voice, talking, talking in that Welsh sing-song. 'Tommy Evans!' I shouted as I burst into the kitchen, 'What the hell are you doing here?'

"Tommy leapt up from the table and bounded over to slap me on the back. 'Took, of all people! You old son! This calls for celebration.' He called to a woman standing by the stove, '*Vin rouge, s'il vous plait.*'

"I wanted to sit down and drink and enjoy the visit, but I had the billets problem on my mind.

"'Muck in with us. Plenty of room. See to it, will you, Mr. Jones?' Tom called to a young lieutenant who saluted smartly and ran off at the double.

"'Now sit down, Took, old chap. Meet your hostess. Madame Mercier.' Madame had just brought in a bottle of wine and glasses. She set them down on the table before us and smiled and bobbed.

" '*Merci beaucoup. Tres bon. Tres bon.*' Tom gave her a warm smile. '*Souper. Soon.*'

"The woman went back to the stove.

" 'Now, what news, Took?' We settled in to talk and wine. Presently madame served us an omelette with fried potatoes and more wine. Tom and I caught up on family news and discussed the progress of the war. Tom was sure it would end by Christmas. We drank to victory and to our families and to our regiments and to madame, who sat on Tom's knee to receive the toast. It was a fine evening we had.

"Tom's regiment fell in about one in the morning to march back up towards their assembly point. I was vaguely aware of him gathering up his things in the room we shared, of orders being shouted in the courtyard, of the tramp of hob-nailed boots on cobblestones, snatches of song. I drifted back into sleep.

"He was killed shortly after the great battle for the St. Quentin canal. At least he had the joy of that success. His outfit covered themselves with glory. He'd have been so pleased.

"He copped it in some counter-attack. I didn't hear about it 'til the war was over. Couldn't believe it. Tommy Evans dead. And the war over.

Some time after the war, Uncle Took went back to France to tour the old battlefields, and to visit my father's grave. He had a picture of the grave to give me, and I added it my pitifully small collection of memorabilia: the photos and the Christmas card.

Took lived to be 102, a firm believer in the British Empire to the end. Until well on into his nineties he never missed an opportunity to don his uniform and medals for a church parade or Armistice Day ceremonies. He would snap to attention for "God Save the Queen" and stand so ramrod straight, he seemed to be in peril of toppling over backwards.

Was my father just as avid a supporter of the empire? Was he too imbued with the heady, idealistic patriotism of the times, offering, like

Rupert Brooke, thanks to God "who has matched us to His hour?" Was he driven by a sense of duty? Or did he go for the adventure of it? What did he feel as, after a leave, he crossed from England to France for another tour of duty in the trenches where the danger and confusion, the mud and cold and misery, the horrible, futile suffering have been so graphically described by men who experienced it?

I returned from Britain with pictures of a war memorial and of a grave and still not knowing much more than before about my father.

Then towards Christmas in 1974 a parcel arrived for me from Auntie Oliver. Auntie Oliver was the wife of my father's brother, Wyatt. Mum, I knew, had disliked Oliver. An "outrageous woman," she called her. Oliver had been a militant suffragette. She dressed like a man, called herself Oliver and finally went off with Wyatt to Australia, and a good thing that was too, in Mum's opinion. But every year at Christmas there came a letter and a card from the outrageous Oliver, giving news of all the Evanses in Australia.

Oliver, an old woman by now, was dying, her letter said. "It's the big C, and the doctor gives me six months. Never mind. I've had a good innings. One thing before I go though, Olwen. I want you to know that your father was the one and only love of my life. After he was killed, I married Wyatt, but it was always Tom I loved.

"I'm sending you the letters he wrote to me from the war and a few of his unpublished lyrics that I managed to get hold of. I've kept them all my life. Now I'd like you to have them."

Here then, after all these years, was the answer to the questions Mum would never answer. My father had not followed us to Canada because he had been in love with another woman! The outrageous Aunt Oliver! No wonder my mother had always disliked her.

I tore open the bundle of letters. By the time I'd read only one or two of them, I was beginning to doubt the great love affair Oliver had written of. These were not love letters. They were letters full of light, friendly chatter. "Hope this finds you as it leaves me, in the pink."

"I'm sure you'll enjoy reading Wells' latest novel." "Thank you for the very nice gloves." These were pleasant letters that could have been written to anyone: an old aunt, a hostess, a friend. There appeared to be no sense of deep attachment to "My Dear Oliver", though I gathered that Oliver might well have been in love with my father. I remembered Gran's words. "We all loved your father. He carried us along with his enthusiasms." But, on this evidence I had to suspect that my father's affection for Oliver was not as strong as hers for him.

The other curious thing about the letters was that they could have been written almost any time; the war was mentioned the way an office job might be referred to. It was just an occupation, sometimes annoying. "The weather is very wet." "My office hut has burnt to the ground." "I am suffering through a wretched cold." There was nothing about suffering through a wretched war, nothing about death or fear of death, nothing about grief or horror or hopelessness, nothing even of the misery of cold, muddy trenches. Perhaps this was the correct way for officers to write about the war. My father, Took had said, had been a good soldier.

I turned to the poems. They were all in Welsh, of course, written in a tiny, neat script on pages now yellow with age. My father had been a clerk before the advent of typewriters, when a fine hand was a requisite for an office job. It touched me though that he hadn't been able to resist adding in last-minute alterations with a blunt lead pencil even though it spoiled the fine copy.

Were these war poems? love poems? With a Welsh dictionary to hand, I tried to read them. Welsh poetry is difficult. As far as I could make out they seemed to be nature pieces about the beauties of the sea, of a mountain stream, of a green valley. One word I did recognize and found recurring several times through the pages was *hiraeth*, an evocative Welsh word which means something like 'longing for something, but at the same time knowing you could never have it'.

I still wonder what it was he longed for, this unknown father of mine, before he was killed, and became a name on a grave in France, a few vague memories in my heart, a bundle of poems, a packet of cherished letters, and a stranger to me. A hero on the wall.

Afterword

Olwen, when she was a young child, imagined England as the most wonderful place on earth. She had come to this belief by listening to her Mum and her Gran reminisce about their native country where, to hear them talk, you'd think everything was just about perfect. When the family moved back to England she discovered that it wasn't so, that really she much preferred British Columbia.

In my turn, I, Olwen's daughter, grew up in Ontario with the conviction that the Kootenay mountains of British Columbia were the Mecca of the west, the Garden of Eden on earth, and Creston was their centre. Certainly it was beyond dispute that the hills of British Columbia were higher than any in Ontario, and the valleys deeper, but it appeared also that gardens were greener there and fruit sweeter, the snow crisper, the sun warmer, the sky bluer. People were friendlier and more colourful. Happy days lasted longer and sorrows were less distressing. All this I gathered from my mother's stories.

I was an adult before I finally got to see Creston with my own eyes. The Creston I saw was and was not the same place as Olwen grew up in. There were the mountains to the east and to the west and the broad flat plain of the Kootenay River between them. The old station was gone and the CPR trains no longer stopped in the centre of

247

town, though the grain elevators of the thirties and forties still stood waiting for them. There were more roads and wider, and a traffic light too, and motels instead of hotels. The buildings of downtown Canyon Street had changed owners and purposes and show windows but still stood, most of them. Orchards were flourishing on the benchlands and now vineyards as well. Gran's Rosebank still stood on Fourth Street, but her roses were gone.

Gran was gone too. She died in 1959 just before her hundredth birthday. The rest of the family – Sarah, Olwen, David, the Hooper kids, the Talbots – were scattered in faraway places.

The Creston I saw was a beautiful mountain town, but it surprised me that I could see no trace of a heavenly aura surrounding it. That's an aura, I've since learned, that lies in the eye of the beholder, and attaches itself only to the landscape of one's childhood. It comes from the conviction that this place is exactly the way a place is supposed to be; it's mother earth's own lap. Whether that landscape is mountain or seaside, busy city street, northern woods, prairie or farmland it imprints itself on one's emergent soul and sets a standard that stays with one for life of what a home place should look like and what makes it beautiful.

To discover then that Creston was after all not quite the heaven that Olwen's stories made of it was not a disillusioning insight for me. It was, rather, a reassuring proof that she had spent a happy childhood and youth there.

At the age of ninety Olwen fell victim to the old lady's nemesis: she fell and broke her hip. She spent some time then in a rehab centre building up her strength to walk again, but even after a good recuperation, it was clear that she would need household help and the services of caregivers if she was going to remain in her own home in Peterborough, which she dearly wanted to do. My sister and I agreed that we would each spend a month with her at her home to help her adjust to her new condition and household arrangements.

I approached my month with some trepidation. I am not the Florence Nightingale type. Administering a whole month of tender loving care might do me in, I feared, and perhaps Mum as well. What could I do to make a month of talking and tea drinking and slow, slow walks around the block more appealing for both of us? That's when the idea about her stories of her life in Creston came to me. She'd often told us those stories, and from time to time we'd urged her to write them down, but Olwen was a talker, not a writer. During our month together, I suggested now, she should tell me her stories, and I would write them down.

It turned out to be a wonderful month for both of us. She told her stories. I listened and took notes and prodded her memory with questions and read back my notes to her. This book is the result of that happy month of storytelling and writing.

Like Gran, Mum died just short of her one-hundredth birthday. I was with her the day she died. She was beyond speech by then, but at one point she looked out the window to a sunlit Ontario May morning and she smiled as though she was seeing out there something amazingly, joyfully beautiful. At the time I thought it was the sunshine and the play of light on the lace curtains that pleased her. But later I got to wondering if it could have been the pearly gates of a Presbyterian heaven she saw out there waiting for her. Or could it have been a last fond vision of the Creston valley of her childhood, and Rosebank and Mum and Gran?